DATE DUE			

OLD DRURY OF PHILADELPHIA

CHESNUT STREET THEATRE

OLD DRURY *of* PHILADELPHIA

A HISTORY OF THE PHILADELPHIA STAGE

1800–1835

Including the Diary or Daily Account Book of
William Burke Wood, Co-Manager with *William Warren*
of the Chesnut Street Theatre, familiarly known as
Old Drury

By

REESE D. JAMES

Assistant Professor of English
University of Pennsylvania

GREENWOOD PRESS, PUBLISHERS
NEW YORK   1968

792.09748
W85o
85·341
Oct 1973

First Greenwood reprinting, 1968

LIBRARY OF CONGRESS catalogue card number: 69-10108

Printed in the United States of America

To
N. D. J.
&
A Certain Gracious Lady

FOREWORD

THIS book, which takes its title from the name given the Chesnut Street Theatre, Philadelphia, in the late Eighteen Twenties, consists of (1) a general introduction covering the history of the Philadelphia stage from 1800 to 1835, (2) the text of the *Diary or Daily Account Book* kept by William Burke Wood, co-manager with William Warren of "Old Drury," (3) prefaces to the record of each of the seventy-one seasons of which the *Account Book* is composed and (4) indexes to the plays and players mentioned in the *Account Book*.

The introduction to Wood's record is self-explanatory.

As for the *Account Book*, it is a record, hitherto unpublished, of the activities of the Chesnut Street company in Philadelphia, Baltimore, Washington and Alexandria. In 1810 Warren & Wood were operating four theatres; and the text of Wood's record will be more intelligible if it is borne in mind that "Philadelphia occupied the entire winter season, say generally from November till late in April," as *Durang* (see below) points out, "Baltimore till . . . the 4th of July" and that the "summer months were spent at Alexandria and Washington city."

In its orderliness, the *Account Book* reflects Wood's capacity for taking infinite pains. Its entries are made according to a simple and logical scheme. The left of the page has been reserved for the date; and there follow the titles of the plays, ballets and olios performed and the amount of the day's receipts. The space to the right of each Saturday's entry has been used for the amount of the week's receipts. Frequently, at the extreme left of the page, are given the names of players receiving benefits, filling engagements, etc.; and, at the lower right of each day's entry, the state of the weather.

The manuscript is in nine volumes.

There are duplicates of the record of seven seasons, namely: The Baltimore Autumn Season of 1810, the Philadelphia Season of 1810–11, the Baltimore Spring Season of 1811, the Philadelphia Season of 1811–12, the Baltimore Spring Season of 1812, the Philadelphia Season of 1812–13 and the Baltimore Spring Season of 1813.

For the printed text, the Volume 1 versions, which are better, have been followed.

It will be observed that the name of the producer precedes the preface to each season and the name of the theatre, whenever necessary, follows it. As for the preface itself, it is a compilation of facts which it has been inadvisable to include in the general introduction or impracticable to include in the editor's notes in the text. (Observe that every date in each preface to which a reference is made in the notes is printed in **bold face** type.)

The notes, as a general rule, identify the rôles in which, according to newspaper advertisements, given players are to appear.

These advertisements are to be found in newspapers whose names have been abbreviated as follows: (Philadelphia,) A for Aurora, ADA for The American Daily Advertiser, DC for The Daily Chronicle, DP for The Democratic Press, TA for The True American and USG for The United States Gazette; (Baltimore,) ACDA for The American and Commercial Daily Advertiser, BP for The Baltimore Patriot, FG for The Federal Gazette and FR for The Federal Republican; (Washington), DNI for The Daily National Intelligencer, NI for The National Intelligencer and WG for The Washington Gazette; and (Alexandria), ADG for The Alexandria Daily Gazette and AH for The Alexandria Herald.

There are a few other abbreviations which it is necessary to explain.

"Durang" refers to a history of the Philadelphia stage which appeared in The Philadelphia Sunday Despatch, beginning with the issue of May 7, 1854. It was published in three parts or series (indicated, throughout the present volume, by the Roman numerals I, II and III). This history has never been published in book form, though it may be found complete, pasted up in bound volumes, in the libraries of the Philadelphia Library Company, of the Historical Society of Pennsylvania and of the University of Pennsylvania, whose copy is extra-illustrated with about three hundred engravings, autograph letters and playbills.

"Recollections" refers to Wood's autobiography, *Personal Recollections of the Stage*, published in 1855.

"Life" refers to the autobiography of Francis C. Wemyss, published in 1847 under the title of *Twenty-Six Years of the Life of an Actor and Manager.*

There is a symbol, printed after titles in the text, which it is also necessary to explain. This is an asterisk (*); and it is used to signify that the plays are being offered for the first time in the city.

The reference to Warren's *Diary*, made frequently throughout the introduction and prefaces, is to be unpublished manuscript of a journal kept, from September 10, 1796 to December 6, 1831, by the partner of William Burke Wood.

FOREWORD

It is a coincidence that the manuscript of Wood's *Account Book* and of Warren's journal have both survived. The former was found, in 1889, by Mr. Joseph Jackson, historian and biographer of Philadelphia, in a pile of miscellaneous books and papers which had been sold by Thomas J. Worrell, Wood's son-in-law, to a second-hand bookdealer. Recognizing its worth, Mr. Jackson bought it and later re-sold it to the University of Pennsylvania, its present owner. Warren's manuscript has had a less checkered career. At his death, it had passed into the hands of his niece, Emma Marble, an actress fairly well known in her time, who attended him during his last illness. Just prior to her death, Miss Marble gave it to her niece's husband, Mr. Channing Pollock, the playwright, its present owner.

Upon its publication, it will supplement Wood's record with a record of fourteen years antedating the first entry in the *Account Book* and with a wealth of background material. Meanwhile Wood's will be the only available record of the activities of the Chesnut Street company during its "halcyon days."

It will remain the most detailed.

What makes it especially valuable is that it furnishes a check against the inaccuracies of newspaper advertisements, which mention haphazardly, if at all, the changes in bills and the postponements occurring in performances. (The errors in Wood's record are usually of the most obvious sort. "June 2," in the year 1812, for example, should be June 1, June "4," June 3, June "6," June 5 and June "7," a Sunday, June 6, as Wood has apportioned May only thirty days. For the same reason the other June dates, certainly June "21" and "28", both Sundays, are incorrect. In the year 1815, April "9," a Sunday, should apparently be April 10, April "16," a Sunday, April 17 and June "25," a Sunday, June 24. In the year 1817, August "24th" should, of course, be August 23; and, in the year 1818, May "3," May 2.)

The author wishes to thank Mr. Jackson for his foresight and Mr. Pollock for permission to quote from the Warren *Diary*. He also wishes to thank the Board of Graduate Education and Research of the University of Pennsylvania for a grant which helped to defray the expenses entailed in securing material for this book and to thank Dr. Arthur Hobson Quinn of the same university for invaluable advice and encouragement.

R. D. J.

[ix]

CONTENTS

CONTENTS

CONTENTS

ILLUSTRATIONS

GENERAL INTRODUCTION

On THE night of Tuesday, December 17, 1799, word reached Philadelphia of the death of General Washington. "While attending to some improvements upon his estate" he had been "exposed to light sleet or rain, which wetted his neck and hair," writes Durang in *The Philadelphia Stage*.[1] "Not conceiving any immediate danger from this exposure, he neglected taking any measures of relief and retired to bed as usual. During the night he was seized with a violent inflammatory affection of the windpipe, accompanied by ague, pain and cough, with suffocating stricture in the throat. Physicians being sent for, they found him beyond hope. All their skill and unremitting exertions proved fruitless; and this great and good man, in the full possession of his intellect, expired without a struggle, on the 14th December, 1799, in the sixty-eighth year of his age."

"All amusements were suspended throughout the country," Durang continues. "Sorrow presided in public halls and private dwellings. The Father of his Country was no more."

It was an inauspicious beginning for the first theatrical season of the new century; and, on the same night that Philadelphia was saddened by the news from Mt. Vernon, "a dreadful fire broke out, in Rickett's circus, corner of Sixth and Chesnut street, which soon communicated to the adjacent buildings.—The Circus (which was built of wood) was soon entirely consumed, as was the large and elegant Hotel, in the tenure of Mr. James O'Ellers, in Chesnut street. The fine row of new buildings in Sixth Street, were very much damaged, and five or six of them nearly destroyed. The wind blowing from the N. West saved the New [Chesnut Street] Theatre and the other opposite buildings."[2]

As Lailson's Circus had collapsed in 1798 and the old Southwark Theatre had outlived its day, the fire that threatened the Chesnut Street Theatre came near to robbing Philadelphia of its only legitimate playhouse.

Wignell & Reinagle, the managers, had opened the season on December 4, 1799, with a company including Warren, Bernard, Wood, Cain, Blissett, Marshall, Francis, Morris, Cromwell, Warrell, Hook, Mitchell,

[1] I, XXXII. See Foreword, p. viii.
[2] See The Gazette of the United States, December 18, 1799.

[1]

Darley, L'Estrange, Radcliffe, Stanley, Master Harris (a pupil of Mr. Francis); Mesdames Merry (the future Mrs. Wignell and Mrs. Warren), Oldmixon, Marshall, Morris, Warrell, Francis, Bernard, Doctor, Stuart, Gillingham, Solomon; and the Misses L'Estrange, Arnold and Solomon.

The company had appeared in the first Philadelphia performances of Dibdin's comedies of *Five Thousand a Year* and *The Jew and the Doctor* and Dibdin's adaptation of Kotzebue's farce entitled *The Horse and the Widow*, when the Chesnut Street Theatre closed, for a short period, out of respect for General Washington.

When it reopened, on December 23, it was with a monody to his memory and the tragedy, appropriately chosen, of *The Roman Father; or, The Deliverer of His Country*. With the pillars of the boxes "encircled with black crape and the chandeliers festooned with the tokens of woe," writes Durang,[3] "the orchestra struck up *Washington's March*, after which several solemn dirges were played, when, the curtain slowly rising, discovered a tomb in the middle of the stage. In the center was a portrait of the sage and hero encircled by oak leaves. Under the likeness were swords, helmets, the colors of the United States and other military trophies. The top of the catafalque was a pyramidal form, surmounted by the figure of an eagle weeping tears of blood." Reinagle, recalling the occasions upon which he had conducted the general to his box, contributed some music of his own and delivered the monody.

The season proceeded to its close, on May 19, without further interruption. There was little or no competition from the Southwark; and Wignell & Reinagle presented, for the first time in Philadelphia, an American musical "entertainment" entitled *The Naval Pillar*, as well as the native translations of Kotzebue's *False Shame* and *The Wild Gooce Chase*; the foreign comedies of *The Secret, Reconciliation* (from Kotzebue, as altered by Dibdin), *The Life of the Day* and *Laugh When You Can*; the farces of *Fortune's Frolic* and *Tony Lumpkin in Town*; the tragedies of *King John* and *Pizarro*; the musical *Zorinski, The Positive Man* and *The Double Disguise*; and *The Count of Burgundy* (from Kotzebue).

Meanwhile, on May 1, 1800, the Southwark had opened with an entertainment called "The Thespian Panorama," consisting of short comedies, "dancing on the wire," music and pantomime.[4] The title was interesting

[3] I, XXXII.
[4] The opening bill, as advertised in The Gazette of the United States, included a "Comedy (in one act) called *The Cob[b]ler at Home; or, The Devil upon Two Sticks*.

but its use offended a group of amateurs known as "The Thespian Society;" and their president, "having observed a performance given out at the Old Theatre, South street, under the title of 'The Thespian Panorama,'" cautioned the public "not to be led there by the name of *Thespian*, as 'tis evident the intention of this STRANGE GANG, in assuming the title, is only to mislead the curious, and thereby gain a crowded house, and consequently *crowded pockets*. The friends of the members are well assured that the object of the Thespian Society was not emolument. It is therefore hoped that the public will not countenance imposters."[5]

The "imposters" replied, over the signatures of "Jno. Durang" and "Jno. B. Rowson," that they were "truly sorry to find that they should, by any means whatever, hurt the feelings of the *Thespian Society*, by assuming, it seems, their title. But this," they added, "we must beg leave to observe to them is a grand mistake, as it was a thought of Mrs. Rowson's own (who is now a member of the [Southwark] society) for her benefit at Mr. Ricket's [*sic*] Circus, in May 1798; and what they mean by cautioning the public against a gang of *imposters*, "the Southwark group replied with asperity, The Thespian Society "are perhaps themselves unable to answer; as it can very easily be proved, that Mr. Durang and Mr. Rowson, as well as the rest of the company, have always conducted themselves with the strictest propriety, both in Mr. Ricket's [*sic*] company and others which they have played in; and why the Thespian Society should wish to be so illiberal as to injure and prevent, in any degree, honest industry from gaining a livelihood, is only to be answered by illiberal *minds*."[6]

The public must have felt the same, for the Southwark enjoyed a season which ran to July 14.

At the end of the month it opened again for two nights, under Hodgkinson and Barrett, with "The Feast of Reason and the Flow of Soul," in which Hodgkinson, "after 5 years' absence," gave an "occasional address" and sang popular songs by Dibdin "never yet heard in America."[7]

Dancing on the Wire, by Mr. Durang. Clown to the Wire, Mr. La Feavre. The much admired Ballad called *Rosina; or, Harvest Home*. Told in Action. With Songs, Dances, &c. To which will be added, a grand Pantomime Entertainment, with music, scenery, machinery, tricks, leaps and decorations, prepared for the piece, called *Harlequin Neptune; or, The Temple of Hymen*."

[5] The Gazette of the United States, April 30, 1800.

[6] See The Gazette of the United States, May 1, 1800.

[7] The Gazette of the United States, July 29, 1800.

In the Spring of 1800 the Chesnut Street Company had left Philadelphia to establish a new theatre in Washington. With the Southwark closed, the dancing academies, the only source of entertainment other than the Chesnut, had served less "to divide [the] attraction" of the theatre, as Bernard suggests, than "to make parties for its support," as the "balls and quadrilles occupied the intervening nights of the, play."[8] As a matter of fact, the dancing master Quesnet and Francis, dancing master as well as comedian (re-established at No. 70 North Fourth Street after having been driven out of O'Ellers by the fire), were aiding Wignell & Reinagle, in helping to develop an intelligent appreciation of the ballets so admirably performed behind the lamps of the Chesnut.

As for the circus, Rickett's attempted to regain its lost prestige at No. 42 South Fifth Street, but in morning and afternoon performances that seem to have been none too lucrative.

It was without a serious competitor, then, that Wignell & Reinagle began the season of 1800–01, on October 6, with a request that "Ladies and Gentlemen . . . send their servants to keep places in the boxes at a quarter past five o'clock" for a performance to commence "at candle light." Eager to be worthy of their monopoly, they had strengthened the company with Usher, skilful in the portrayal of "cruel uncles" and "heavy villains," with the Misses E. and J. Westray (shortly to become the wives of the younger Darley and W. B. Wood), with Mrs. Shaw, admirable in the rôles of "comedy old ladies" and "heavy mothers" and now returned after an absence of four years, and with Prigmore, though the comedian brought to America by Henry in 1792 was a doubtful asset, for the "grimace" and "low buffoonery" with which he played the rôles of "comic old men" was "far from acceptable to the judicious."[9]

There was nothing for the "judicious" to grieve over, however, in the season's budget of plays. Before the closing of the Chesnut, on April 11, 1801, there were presented, for the first time in Philadelphia, the American tragedy of *Edwy and Elgiva*; the foreign comedies of *Management, The Votary of Wealth, The East Indian, Speed the Plough, Liberal Opinions, The Blacksmith of Antwerp* and *The Man of Ten Thousand*; the farce of *A Peep Behind the Curtain*; the tragedies of *The Law of Lombardy, Paris Avenged* and *Cato*; the musical *St. David's, A Trip to Fontainbleau, Netley Abbey, Buxom Joan* and The *Siege of Belgrade*;

[8] *Retrospections of America*, 1797–1811, by John Bernard, p. 189.
[9] *Durang*, I, XVII.

[4]

the pantomime *Aladdin*; and *The Corsicans* and *The Virgin of the Sun* (both from Kotzebue).

On July 4, 1801, the Chesnut Street Theatre opened "in honor of the day;" and it was announced that there would be two more performances "for the purpose of introducing Mr. Fullerton from the Theatre Royal, Liverpool, who [was to] make his first appearance in American as Octavian in *The Mountaineers*."[10]   While improvements were being made on their building, a detachment of the Chesnut Street Company joined with Messrs. Barrett, Placide and Robertson in a season at the Southwark Theatre lasting from August 7 to August 21.   There followed another season at the old theatre, beginning on August 31 and ending on October 2, during which the Chesnut street players were assisted by Robertson, "the Antipodean Whirligig," who performed, as *Durang* reveals, "a wonderful feat by standing on his head and whirling round in that position like a top in its quickest motion."   Somewhat more in keeping with its old tradition, the Southwark, during this season, produced O'Keeffe's comedy of *The London Hermit*.

The Chesnut opened for the season of 1801–02 on October 14 with an occasional musical prelude entitled *The Election; or, The Theatrical Candidates*, the music by Reinagle.   It was without the services of Cooper, who, having adjusted a difference with Dunlap, had gone back to New York; but it had secured the services of Mr. and Mrs. Whitlock and William Greene, all members of Wignell's original company in 1793, and of Miss Arnold, Mr. and Mrs. Jones, newly from England, and of Master Lynch, celebrated for his singing of *The Old Woman of Eighty*.

At the beginning of the season, now that they had improved the theatre and "therefore look[ed] forward with confidence to the patronage of the public to reward their endeavors, and to their support . . . in the maintenance of . . . decorum," Wignell & Reinagle begged the men in the audience to desist from smoking "segars, a custom which two or three winters ago, was almost exploded from the Philadelphia Theatre . . . and in some instances, on the first evening of this."[11]   They also pleaded for public co-operation . . . in abolishing the custom of giving away or disposing of [pass] Checks at the doors of the Theatre, as tending "to encourage a crowd of idle boys and other disorderly persons about [its] avenues" and resulting in the admission of "very improper company."

The "co-operation" was obviously lacking, for, early in February, the

[10] See *Durang*, I, XXXIV.
[11] The Gazette of the United States, October 20, 1801.

[5]

hissing in the Chesnut drove poor Fullerton to suicide, for all the imposing Reinagle could do to quiet the rowdies.

The managers, however, deserved better treatment. Prior to the end of the season, extended a day "By Desire" to April 15, there were produced, for the first time in Philadelphia, the foreign comedies of *The Poor Gentleman*, *Life*, *The Honest Thieves*, *Folly as It Flies*, *Reparation*, *Falstaff's Wedding* and *More Ways Than One*; the farces of *What Would the Man be At?* and *The Review* and the humorous "prelude" of *The Manager in Distress*; the tragedy of *The Distressed Mother*; the musical *The Blind Girl* and *The Enraged Musician*; the pantomimical *Obi* and *Hercules and Omphale*; the "ballet pantomime" of *La Fête des Vendages*; the historical *Deaf and Dumb* and the romantic *Il Bondocani*, *Joanna of Montfaucon* and *Adelmorn the Outlaw*.

On July 7, 1802, after a postponement "on account of inclement weather," a detachment of the Chesnut Street Company, with "the permission of Messrs. Wignell & Reinagle," opened the Southwark Theatre with the new "pantomimical sketch" of *The Federal Oath*, inducing an audience to walk a mile from the center of town, for two nights more, to see the first Philadelphia performance, on July 12, of *The Red Cross Knights*, founded on *The Robbers*, by Schiller.

With the opening of the Chesnut Street season of 1802–03, which began on December 13, the company was weakened by the loss of the Whitlocks, who had gone to New York, and of the Hardinges, who had sailed for London; but Fox, erst-while etcher and engraver and the original singer of *Hail Columbia*! had rejoined it. Moreover, there was Mrs. Barrett to take Mrs. Whitlock's place. Hogg, from the New York theatre, was soon to appear; and Cooper, Fennell and Hodgkinson, whom Durang pronounces the only "stars" of the time, were shortly to play engagements.

The season, however, would have been relatively uneventful, save for the death of a member of the firm and the effect it had upon the policies of the Chesnut. On February 21, 1803, Thomas Wignell, who had married Mrs. Merry during the first week in January, died as a result of an injury sustained from a spring lancet.

"The public [were] respectfully informed that the Entertainments of the Theatre [would] recommence on Monday next, under the direction of Mrs. Wignell and Mr. Reinagle, and with the assistance of Messrs. Warren and Wood, as acting managers." As ran the announcement in The Gazette of the United States of February 23, 1803, "The friends of

[6]

the Drama [might] be assured that every exertion [would] be made to merit a continuance of their patronage and approbation."

Wignell's loss, providentially, was not what it might have been. For "several years previous to his death," Wood reveals "Wignell [had] appeared rarely on the stage;"[12] and Bernard, who had every right to express an opinion, assets that, "in a professional light," Wignell "had but moderate claims." Bernard opines that Wignell had "variety as an actor, but with limited power. He had enjoyed the good-fortune of being the first general comedian who had crossed the Atlantic; and by the side of the stiff humor of his friends, Henry and Hallam, both of whom belonged to the old school of London, he had certainly shone as a spirited actor; but the term of his partnership proved also that of his fame. When, in 1793, he returned from England, to open the first complete theatre America had witnessed, he brought with him a company containing several comedians who were much his superiors, and who at once obtained a fame that put an end to his efforts."[13]

Wignell, for all that, had been a great favorite in his day; and the new acting managers, Warren and Wood, had their predecessor to thank for the training that made it possible for them to take charge of the Philadelphia, Baltimore, Washington and Alexandria playhouses.

Already in actual control of the Chesnut, they carried the season of 1802–03 to a successful conclusion on April 4, helping to produce, for the first time in the city, the comedies of *Notoriety* and *Which Is the Man?*; the farces of *Sancho Turned Governor* and *Rahma Droog*; the tragedies of *Abaellino* and *Alfonso, King of Castile*; the "musical farce" of *The Sixty-Third Letter*; the "comic opera" of *The Doctor and Apothecary*; the "new modelled" pantomime of *The Corsair* and *The Second Part of Henry the Fourth*.

In the spring of 1803, Wood went to England, Durang asserts, "to engage performers and to procure new pieces, &c." He returned with Twaits, who had a reputation as a burletta singer; and the dwarfish, hook-nosed comedian, together with Joseph Jefferson, who joined the company at Baltimore in October, made it, in the words of Durang, "very powerful in comedy," as it already included Blissett, Warren and Wood. Mrs. Jefferson had also become a member of the company and Hardinge and Mrs. Morris, both originally with Wignell in 1793, ac-

[12] See *Personal Recollections of the Stage*, by William B. Wood, p. 90.
[13] *Retrospections*, p. 258.

companied Wood to America, though Mrs. Morris was to appear only once during the season, on the occasion of her husband's benefit.

The season, which began on December 12, 1803 and ended on April 3, 1804, is noteworthy for the first production of *John Bull; or, The Englishman's Fireside* and *A Tale of Mystery*, which Durang asserts to have been "the first melodrama ever acted in Philadelphia." Wood had brought the manuscript of the comedy from England but Holcroft's "mixed drama of words and ten bars of music," as Durang describes it, had been previously acted in New York. The original music was by Dr. Busby, with accompaniments by Mr. Reinagle. The "piece," records Durang, "had a very profitable run;" and "it was well acted and well put upon the stage." Holland and his assistants, Robins and Master Hugh Reinagle, painted the scenery, Francis arranged the dances and Gibbons prepared the dresses.

The industry of the new "acting managers," Warren and Wood, is further reflected, during the season of 1803–04, in the first Philadelphia production of the farces of *The Wheel of Truth* and *Two Per Cent* (both by James Fennell) and the native "comic opera" of *The Tripolitan Prize*; the foreign comedies of *The Marriage Promise, The Maid of Bristol, Hear Both Sides, Delays and Blunders*; the "comic interlude" of *The Blue Devils*; the tragedy of *Mahomet*; the musical pieces of *A House to be Sold, Bonaparte Mistaken* and *Paul and Virginia*; the "pantomimical romance" of *The Knights of Calabria* and the "grand pantomimical spectacle" of *Raymond and Agnes*; *The Voice of Nature* (an adaptation anticipatory of Holcroft's *A Tale of Mystery*);[14] the romantic *A Tale of Terror, Count Benyowski* and *Blackbeard*, the last "pantomimical;" and the "historical play," *The Hero of the North.*

On June 20, 1804, a detachment of the Chestnut Street company opened the Southwark with the bill of *The Poor Gentleman* and *The Irishman in London* for a season lasting to July 18. On July 4, "in honor of the day," they produced, for the first time in Philadelphia, the *American Liberty in Louisiana* and, on July 18, also for the first time, the comedy of *Hearts of Oak* and the farce of *'Tis All a Farce.*

Story, a comedian of the London and Charleston theatres, also opened the Southwark; but, according to Durang, it was for the single night of October 3.

---

[14] Somewhat contradictory of Durang's claim for *A Tale of Mystery* is the fact that it was produced on January 20, 1804, while *The Voice of Nature*, also an adaption of a "melodrame," was produced on January 13, a week earlier.

On December 3, 1804, Mrs. Wignell and Reinagle resumed at the Chesnut. The first bill of the season of 1804–05, which ran to April 3, included the popular comedy of *John Bull*, with McKenzie, new to the company, playing the rôle of Peregrine. McKenzie was successful; and it must have been a victory for Wood, who had urged Warren to engage him, when McKenzie interpreted, to every one's delight, the difficult rôle of Sir Pertinax MacSycophant, a rôle which extended the powers of even the celebrated Cooke. During the season, the Seymours from the New York theatre and Taylor, originally from the Boston theatre, also appeared. On December 29, 1804, Cooper, more popular than ever after English triumphs, started a successful engagement of eleven nights, to be followed by another of four.

In the course of the season, only one American piece was produced for the first time. It was the patriotic *American Tars in Tripoli*. Among the new foreign pieces to be offered were the comedies of *The Sailor's Daughter, The Soldier's Daughter, Guilty or Not Guilty, Love Makes a Man, I'll Tell You What*; the farce of *The Counterfeit*; the tragedies of *Cleone* and *The Death of Louis XVI*; *The Paragraph, Love Laughs at Locksmiths* and *The Castle of Sorento* (all musical); the "grand pantomimical drama" of *La Perouse*; the melodrama of *The Wife of Two Husbands* and the "grand dramatic masque" of *Arthur and Emmeline*.

During the summer of 1805, Warren, whose wife had died, consoled himself with a trip to England, "as Mrs. Wignell's agent," *Durang* records, "to engage performers and transact other business." He returned in time for the opening of the Chesnut Street season of 1805–06, which extended from December 2 to April 9.

The players whom Warren secured were Cross and Mrs. Cunningham from the Royal Edinburgh Theatre, Bray from the Royal York Theatre and Mr. and Mrs. Woodham from the Covent Garden Theatre. Wood's opinion is that Mrs. Woodham was the "most valuable" of the new players. At all events, she danced and interpreted high comedy rôles in a fascinating way; and she was one of the players who helped to make this season what Durang asserts to have been "one of extraordinary success." Other attractive players were Harwood, one of Wignell's original company, now returned, after six years, to play Goldfinch on December 14, 1805; the famous Mrs. Melmoth, who, occasionally assisted in tragedies such as *The Distressed Mother, Mary Queen of Scots, Essex* and *Pizarro*; and there were Fennell and Cooper, both of whom appeared in engagements.

[9]

As compared with the list of new players, the list of new plays is unimpressive, though Dunlap's *Lewis of Monte Blanco* and Breck's *The Fox Chase*, native comedies, were produced, for the first time in Philadelphia, during the season of 1805–06 and Byrne's pantomime of *Cinderella* had an unprecedented run of ten nights following its American première on January 1, 1806. The new foreign comedies included *The School of Reform*, *Who Wants a Guinea?*, *The Honey Moon*, *The Blind Bargain* and *The Will for the Deed*. *Mary Queen of Scots* was the only foreign tragedy to be given for the first time during the season; there were three new musical pieces, *The Hunter of the Alps*, *Thirty Thousand* and *Matrimony;* a new pantomime, *The Brazen Mask*; and a new anonymous "melodrame" entitled *Captain Smith and the Princess Pocahontas*. It was produced as "never acted," on March 5, 1806, with "entire new scenery, designed by Mr. Holland, and painted by him and H. Reinagle. The music," according to an advertisement in the Aurora, was "composed and selected by Mr. Woodham."

In June a detachment of the Chesnut Street company appeared for a few nights at the Southwark, which had competed mildly with Mrs. Wignell and her partner when, in February, it had housed Manfredi and his three daughters for performances on the tight rope, ballets and "petite pantomimes." At the Southwark in June a "young gentleman of fine education and manly figure," as Durang describes him, made his début in the person of Cone, who played "juvenile tragedy and second gentlemen of comedy very respectably" and who, "flattered with his success,"[15] went with the company to Washington and Alexandria, still, on Durang's testimony, "a most excellent theatrical town."

On August 15, 1806, before the return of the company to Philadelphia, Mrs. Wignell became Mrs. Warren, marrying again, as Durang explains, "in order to give the right of government to one more resolute than herself."

Warren proved to be. Now that he was manager in fact as well as in name, he renovated the Chesnut for the season of 1806–07, which extended from December 1 to April 23; and secured the services of such new players as Mills (the brother of Mrs. Woodham), Mrs. Mills, Webster (a singer), and Bailey. Among the old favorites he engaged Fennell for a series of performances beginning on December 15.

His vigorous policy found expression, too, in another performance of *The Fox Chase* and in the American première of Barker's *Tears and Smiles*,

---

[15] *Durang*, I, XXXIX.

as well as in the Philadelphia première of Dunlap's *The Glory of Columbia*. On April 15, 1807, as a fitting climax, perhaps, to a season in which the "American drama," as Durang writes, had "received more than usual aid," the new manager singled out Lewis Hallam, the "father of the American stage," for a complimentary benefit in his first appearance at the Chesnut in the fifty-five years he had been on the Philadelphia stage.

Warren's initiative drew a compliment from The Theatrical Censor and Critical Miscellany, newly established and published every Saturday, which spoke of "a very agreeable variety . . . offered" this season "to the lovers of the drama."

This variety included the foreign comedies of *The School for Friends*, *The Man of the World*, *A Hint to Husbands*, *The Fingerpost*, *The Delinquent* and *The Fashionable Lover*; the farces of *We Fly by Night*, *The Weathercock* and *Easter Holidays*; the musical *Too Many Cooks*, *Youth*, *Love and Folly*, *The Cabinet*, *The Spanish Dollars*, *The Honest Yorkshireman* and *The Travellers*; and the melodramatic *Valentine and Orson* and *Theseus and Ariadne*.

On June 24, 1807, Warren & Reinagle opened the Chesnut for a season of eight nights lasting to July 10.

On July 22, Lewis Hallam permitted John Durang to use the Southwark "gratis," as his son records, "to perform in it as long as he could so employ it." The veteran himself played Petruchio, the Miller (in the *King and Miller of Mansfield*), 1st. Peasant and Alberto in *The Child of Nature*, with Mrs. Hallam in the rôle of Amanthis and Darby in *The Poor Soldier*. The company consisted first of Durang's own family and five others; later other players joined it, among them Messrs. Barrett, Wilmot, McKenzie, Johnson, Williams, Yeats, Master George H. Barrett, Mrs. Barrett and Mrs. Wilmot. "The business," *Durang* states, "afforded them all a good living."

Warren & Reinagle resumed at the Chesnut on December 7, 1807 for a season that was to run to April 21, 1808. Briers and Serson were now in the company. Cooper appeared for two engagements during the season; and Bernard for an engagement of seven nights, during which he interpreted the rôles of Lord Ogleby, Sir Robert Bramble, Sharp (in *The Lying Valet*), Lovegood (in *The Miser*), Brulgruddery, Abednego (in *The Jew and the Doctor*), Captain Ironsides (in *The Brothers*), Puff, Sir Peter Teazle, Nipperkin, Sheva (in *The Jew*), Shelty, Jack Junk (in *Reconciliation*) and Lovel.

[11]

Durang alludes to the bitter feeling which, at this time, prevailed against England for the "encroachments" on our commerce. The "retaliatory measures adopted by the American government," he writes, "led to an excitement unprecedented in our annals." Theatre audiences, pervaded by a factional spirit, were inflammable and unruly. "At the benefit season the actors catered" to this spirit; and Blissett, "whose benefits were not always a sure card (favorite as he was) thought it expedient to avoid the legitimate line and trust to the exciting causes of the day for a subject. He prevailed upon James N. Barker to write him a piece founded upon the local topics of the day."

The piece was *The Embargo; or, What News?* and, as it expressed the democratic sentiments of the day, it aroused no antagonism on March 16, though, as Durang points out, "nice political questions, where two large parties are nearly balanced, [had to] be warily tuched on the stage" of the period.

On April 6, however, Blisett's lack of discretion became evident. *The Embargo* had been inoffensive but its production seemed to act as an invitation to the rowdies to make themselves obnoxious. Their pretext was a vicious story circulated against Webster, the singer. The riot was serious. "Pugilistic contests occurred," states Durang, . . . "in the upper saloons and lobbies of the theatre . . . [Webster] could not show himself upon the stage at all. He was sure to be hissed and pelted off. Glass chandeliers were torn down and thrown at him, and lighted squibs were cast in[to] the pit."

The first American performance of Barker's *The Indian Princess* was interrupted and so the boomerang returned unfairly upon the author of *The Embargo.*

Ironically, too, for all the intensity of American feeling, there were as many as fourteen foreign pieces acceptably presented, for the first time in Philadelphia, during the season of 1807–08. These were the comedies of *The Curfew, Town and Country, Time's a Tell-Tale* and *The School of Arrogance*; the musical entertainments of *The Invisible Girl, Three and the Deuce* and *Love for Love I Promise Him*; the "musical drama" of *The Young Huzzar* and the operas of *The Soldier's Return* and *Of Age Tomorrow*; the pantomime of *Harlequin Dr. Faustus*; the sentimental *Adrian and Orrilla*, the melodrama of *The Fortress* and *Henry the Fifth.*

On June 28, 1808, Warren became a widower again. "Departed this life on Tuesday afternoon, at Alexandria, after a short but severe illness," ran an obituary in the American Daily Advertiser of July 2, "Mrs. Ann

[12]

Warren, the amiable consort of Mr. William Warren, Manager of the Philadelphia and Baltimore Theatres."

What with the loss of the former Mrs. Merry and the rise of the "starring system," which, as Durang asserts, was to have the "sad effect of destroying the stock nights," Warren was coming to depend, more and more, upon the competent Wood. "Nervous debility,"[16] unfortunately, had driven the latter abroad for his health; and, since Reinagle was mortally ill, Warren had to shoulder the burdens of management alone.

Possibly with the Webster riot in mind, his chief anxiety was the decorum of his theatre. Four days after its opening on December 7, 1808, he announced the establishment of the "Ladies Coffee Room," adding "that only such Gentlemen, as are in the party of Ladies, or who may wish to join such party, [would] consider [the] apartment as intended for their use." Seemingly as a hint to casuals from the drinking saloons, Warren concluded, "This intimation is with great deference submitted to the consideration of gentlemen generally, who in one moment it is presumed will observe, that ladies will exclude themselves from their visits here unless this regulation is complied with."[17]

Warren's efforts bore fruit. The season was brilliant, with visits from Cooper, who was accomplishing the miracle of acting twice a week in Philadelphia and twice in New York; from Mrs. Stanley of Covent Garden (she appeared as Lady Teazle, Roxalana, Lady Townly, Rosalind, Juliana and Violante) and from John E. Harwood.

These stars were expensive, of course, a drain on the treasury as well as on the morale of the regular company; but they arrived opportunely to offset a competition which proved to be the most serious of its kind since the destruction of Rickett's in 1799.

This was the competition of Pepin and Breschard, talented equestrians, for whom a building had been erected at the corner of Ninth and Walnut Streets. "The house was very spacious," as Durang describes it. "The dome over the ring was an immense affair; it had from the pit the appearance of being some eighty feet in height, and looked very oriental and magnificantly imposing."

In announcing their opening, Pepin & Breschard called themselves "Professors of the art of Horsemanship and Agility." It was their claim that they had, "within a year, arrived from Spain, [having] had the

[16] See *Recollections*, p. 121.
[17] USG of November 11, 1808.

honour of performing before the principal courts of Europe" and, "for six months, [of having] received the most unbounded marks of approbation from the inhabitants of New York and Boston."[18]   Their company, in Durang's words, "was numerous and well appointed.   Their study of horses was thoroughly broken and composed of splendid animals.   Their wardrobe was new, costly, and, indeed the best thing of the kind that had been seen in the country."   The bill of February 2, the opening night, consisted of "military exercises," "comic attitudes," "vaulting," and juggling, all on horseback, of course, concluding with a "horse Calmly wrapt in Flames," obviously some illusory effect.

Warren countered during the season, which ended on April 23, 1809, with two new American and twelve new foreign pieces.   *The School for Prodigals*, a comedy, and *The Wounded Hussar*, a musical afterpiece, both by J. Hutton, a Philadelphian, were given; the foreign comedies numbered three (*The World, Begone Dull Care*, and *A Word to the Wise*), the farces two (*Portrait of Cervantes* and *Retaliation*), the musical pieces, three (*Who Pays the Piper?* as translated by Bray, a member of the company, *Catch Him Who Can* and *A Sea-Side Story*); and the melodramas, three.   These last included *Tekeli, The Lady of the Rock* and *The Wood Demon* (by Lewis).   In addition, there were offered, for the first time, *Julius Caesar*, the "grand operatic romance" of *The Forty Thieves*, the tragedy of *Adelgitha* and *The Wanderer*, as translated from Kotzebue by Charles Kemble.

On September 21, 1809, the ranks of the veterans lost another member in the person of Alexander Reinagle.   "On Thursday evening last," lamented an obituary in The United States Gazette of September 25, "in the sixty-second year of his age," the courtly Reinagle passed away. "His talents as a musical composer," it was held, "were unrivaled in this country.   His intrinsick goodness of heart, and the mildness and urbanity of his manners endeared him to his friends, by whom his loss will be sincerely regretted."

Warren, bereft of wife and of friend, must have looked forward to Wood's anticipated return.

It took place in October, 1809; and it "found Master Payne," as Wood records in his recollections, "in the full tide of popular favor at Baltimore."[19]   Shortly after the opening of the Chesnut Street season of 1809–10, on November 20, Payne made his début in Philadelphia, follow-

[18] See USG of February 2, 1809.
[19] P. 127.

ing a successful appearance as Young Norval on this occasion, December 6, with an interpretation of the rôles of Frederick (in *Lovers' Vows*), Zaphna, Rolla, Tancred, Octavian, Selim (in *Barbarossa*), Hamlet and Romeo, rôles "suitable," as Durang claims, "to his youthful aspect" but in which Wood, seldom impressed by prodigies, found him occasionally absurd.

His engagement, however, was a triumph; and completely overshadowed that of the Infant Vestris, another prodigy, who made his début, on December 22, in dancing a pas seul composed by "Mr. Whale," evidently his father. Wood, fresh from London theatre-going, must have been amused at the ingenuousness of these performances, though Cooper's acting, in his two engagements of this season, and that of the Irish comedian, John Dwyer, who made a startlingly successful first bow at the Chesnut, on April 20, must have been comparable to the best of the acting just seen at the Haymarket.

The season, ending on April 27, 1810, brought an end to Warren's independent management, which was to be resumed only after a break with Wood in 1828. Friends had "proposed to [Wood] the plan of a purchase from Warren of a share in his property and management;" and the "means of payment were [soon] generously provided, terms adjusted, and an equal partnership formed."[20] During the season, offering no new native plays, Warren had contented himself, possibly until the partnership should become operative, with the production, for the first time in the city, of the foreign comedies of, *Is He a Prince?*, *Man and Wife* and *Grieving's a Folly*; the musical pieces of *Killing No Murder*, *Who Wins?*, *Wicklow Mountains*, *The Foundling of the Forest* and *The Africans*; the pantomime of *Mother Goose*; the melodrama of *Ella Rosenberg*; the romantic *Rugantino*, *The Caravan* and *Lodoiska*; and *The Blind Boy*, from Kotzebue.

Officially, the partnership of Warren & Wood, soon to be justly celebrated, began with the Baltimore autumn season of 1810, which ran from October 8 to November 22. At its outset, the Chesnut Street Company included Jefferson, Fennell, Francis, McKenzie, Blissett, Hardinge, Robins, Wilmot, Durang, Seymour, George Barrett, Jacobs, Taylor, Drummond, Downie, Harris, Cone, Calbraith, Briers, Lindsey, Allen, F. Durang, West (actor and scene painter), Jones, Master Scrivener; and Mesdames Twaits, Wood, Francis, Wilmot, Barrett, Seymour,

---

[20] See *Recollections*, p. 129, for details.

[15]

Jacobs, Jefferson, Downie, Melmoth, Morris, Durang, Miss E. White and Miss Pettit. Charnock was the prompter.

Fennell, in an engagement of nine nights, averaged $474, realizing $667, or $367 over expenses, on the occasion of his benefit. It was his first appearance in Baltimore in fourteen years; and, as Wood points out, "These successes [might be cited] as evidence of constancy in the audience, and proving satisfactorily that an abandonment of the wild projects by which Mr. Fennell's speculative fancy was allured and betrayed, and any attention to his proper profession, might have saved that actor from most, if not from all, of his subsequent distresses."[21]

As a prelude to an engagement in Philadelphia, Mrs. Beaumont of the London and Liverpool theatres, appeared for several nights, playing Madame Clermont in *Adrian and Orrilla* so successfully as to be pronounced by critics as equal to the original representative. However, she taxed Warren's patience by using the "stale artifice" of deferring her arrival in Baltimore for several days in order "to excite public curiosity;" and he candidly writes of her in his *Diary* that "she was tolerably received" in Philadelphia "upon the whole, tho' there were a great many Dissentients."[22]

There were to be no "dissentients," on the other hand, in the case of an erratic tragedian, who, "in his staid, gray surtout, his stiff hair brushed back" reminded Durang of "a retired half-pay [army] officer." This was George Frederick Cooke, who made his début on March 25 as Richard the Third.

Cooper had brought him to America and his managers, Cooper & Price, lent him to Warren & Wood for a sum finally amounting to $8809.16. As Richard, Shylock, Lear and especially as Iago, opposite Cooper as Othello, Cooke amazed the critics in the pit; and so captured the fancy of the town "that," as Durang reveals, "the back door of the theatre, in Carpenter street, was blocked up at ten o'clock in the morning to see him get out of his coach to attend the rehearsals."

Yet, even before Cooke's Richard took the town by storm, Warren & Wood's first season in Philadelphia had been "brilliant." Mrs. Twaits, Mrs. McKenzie, Calbraith and Dennison had all been financially successful in first appearances. The engagements of the Beaumonts and Fennell had been lucrative, both to the managers and to themselves; and the actors' benefits had been unusually good, although the foresight of

[21] *Recollections*, p. 131. See also *An Apology for the Life of James Fennell*.
[22] See reference to Warren's *Diary* in the Foreword, p. viii.

Warren & Wood in scheduling them before the arrival of Cooke may, in a measure, have accounted for the fact.

It was only to managers who could look ahead that the horizon must have seemed anything but rosy. Warren cheerfully resigned his rôle of Falstaff, on April 8, in order that Cooke might play it; but he must have joined with Wood in wondering how, in emergencies, they were going to succeed in paying such rates as Cooke received, while capable players such as Jefferson, Blissett and Cone were probably alarmed and somewhat disgruntled over the assumption by a visiting "star" of a rôle superbly played and belonging, as an inalienable right, to a member of the regular company.

What was more, the prosperity of the season of 1810–11 was to be shortlived. A small theatre in Apollo Street, a converted dwelling-house behind the old Southwark and called "The Apollo Street Theatre," opened on June 12, 1811 with a company including Webster and players from the regular Chesnut Street company; but it had to close its doors after an unsuccessful season of about six weeks.

The threat of war with England and resulting depression in commerce, as well as a terror caused by the burning of the Richmond Theatre, were to conspire against the success of Warren & Wood in their second Philadelphia season, which ran from September 9, 1811 to March 14, 1812. Pepin & Breschard, too, were shortly to resort to producing plays, as they had observed a waning in the popularity of their equestrian performances.

However, with the Chesnut "elegantly refitted, newly ornamented and considerably enlarged," Warren & Wood answered the challenge by engaging Mrs. Simpson of the Boston theatre, Mrs. Mason of the New York theatre (whose "merry arch smile," as Durang attests, made her Beatrice the "gay being" of Shakespeare's "conception"), Cone, Spiller of the Theatre Royal, Haymarket, and Duffy of the London and Dublin theatres. Their visiting stars were Cooper (who helped them fight the circus with players from the Park Theatre, New York), Cooke, Payne, Dwyer (before he was engaged by Pepin & Breschard), and the Darleys.

The competition of Pepin & Breschard began when, on January 1, 1812, they opened their doors with the bill of *The Rivals*, *The Poor Soldier* and an interlude of equestrian feats. Strickland, a young architect, "had arranged the stage" and painted a drop scene for their theatre, now called the Olympic. Fortune was kind to them, too, at the outset, when a group of malcontents from the Chesnut Street company, including

[17]

McKenzie, the Brays, Jacobs and others, sought employment with Pepin & Breschard.

Warren & Wood threw down the gauntlet, on the opening night of the Olympic, with the first American performance of *The Lady of the Lake*. No pains were spared to make the production effective. "Fourmanned and masted barges [sailed] toward the island [in the lake]. Above their pikes and axes appear[ed] the Bannered Pine of Sir Roderick. On the landing of the clan[a] Grand Chorus [sang] "Hail to the Chief, who in triumph advances!" Act II disclosed a grand cataract in the mountains. "A large rude bridge [spanned] a deep glen. On one side Roderick [sat] by his watch-fire, his men slumbering in groups around him. Brian [stood] on the frightful summit of a huge cliff. Day dawn[ed]; the centinels sound[ed]."[23]

The fight between the theatres went merrily on. Warren & Wood gained the upper hand, on February 15, when Duff of the Dublin and Boston theatres, rebuffed at the Olympic, made a triumphant début in the rôles of Macbeth and Jeremy Diddler. With McKenzie and Dwyer in charge of its stage department, the Olympic had already produced *The Winter's Tale*, for the first time in Philadelphia; and it was soon to forestall the production, at the Chesnut, of Barker's *Marmion* with the American première of Mrs. Ellis' play of the same name.

Although it had opened, too, nearly four months later than the Chesnut, the former circus offered as many as eighteen as against the Chesnut's eight new pieces. Numbered among the eighteen were the American pantomimes of *The Taking of Yorktown* and *American Generosity and Moorish Ingratitude*, obviously chauvinistic; the comedies of *A Bold Stroke for a Husband, Guerre Ouverte, The Gazette Extraordinary* and *The Impatient Lover*; the farces of *The Man of Fashion* and *Trial by Jury*; the foreign pantomimes of *The Escape of Adelina, The Life and Death of Harlequin, La Fille Hussar, The Battle of Lodi, Harlequin Highlander, Black Beard* (billed as "the Original from London" and "not that which was formerly performed at the Chesnut"), and *Telemachus*; and the melodrama of *The Exile*.

In some of the pantomimes there were "Combats with real Horses on the stage," since the Olympic had been a circus and still had facilities for equestrian performances; and this twofold repertory must have given the Olympic an advantage over the Chesnut and helped to prolong the

[23] Advertisement in the Aurora of January 1, 1812.

season of Pepin & Breschard to May 15, a month after Warren & Wood had left for Baltimore.

The rivalry had given rise to personal animosities. McKenzie, to avoid the consequences of breaking his contract, had spread the story that Wood had maligned the mechanics of the town. Disgraceful riots ensued in the Chesnut Street Theatre. Shortly after the opening of the Olympic, Warren remarks in his *Diary*, "A play and Farce at the Circus this evening. At the head of this Band stands Beaumont, Dwyer, McKenzie, the Wilmots—all formerly belonging to our Establishment. They allow it as their intention to ruin us—if possible. No doubt but they will do their best;" to which Warren adds, after the lapse of years, "The whole of this party went to destruction. Pepin kept a livery stable, McKenzie drowned himself in Boston, the Wilmots are dead, etc. etc."

During the summer of 1812 came the declaration of war with England.

The Olympic chose this unpropitious time to open, on June 29, for a brief season of six nights. Its success was to prove ephemeral, for its English, Scotch and Irish players and French and Spanish equestrians quarreled among themselves and Dwyer and McKenzie were temperamentally too dissimilar to get along with each other. Besides, their success, as Duff expressed it, had put them "on the high ropes" and, now that adversity threatened, they were to betray how little real business ability they had. To begin with, they made the cardinal mistake of failing to pay their actors; and so, on July 4, after lucrative performances of the patriotic *Bunker Hill* and a new piece entitled *The American Naval Pillar*, Wilmot, Fisher, Brown and Charnock retaliated by retaining the funds, which had been entrusted to their keeping. They were arrested and McKenzie, in closing the theatre with his benefit on July 17, announced disgustedly that he would make "his *last* appearance on *any* stage."[24]

Twaits took over the duties of Dwyer and McKenzie and the Olympic opened on September 25 with Breschard in charge of its equestrian department. Its opening bill included *Timour the Tartar*, now produced for the first time in Philadelphia. On October came a new piece entitled *Philadelphia Volunteers or Who's Afraid?* It was "performed with new dresses, scenery, &c.;" but a lack of patronage forced the Olympic to close, after Breschard's benefit, on October 15, 1812.

The Chesnut Street managers had meanwhile succeeded in reviving

[24] See *Durang*, I, XLIX.

[19]

"a theatrical spirit in the people, which," as Wood writes, "brightened [their] prospects." On their opening night of September 28 they produced *The Constitution or American Tars Triumphant*, a patriotic piece celebrating the first naval victory; and, during the season, which ran to April 24, 1813, they introduced, to the Chesnut Street audience, such excellent new players as Doyle of the New York theatres, Hilson (the comedian), Holman of the London and Dublin theatres and his daughter, "a great drawback to [whose] success," however, "was their too frequent appearance as lovers, and husband and wife, in characters where the relation as well as the text were unfavorable to effect."[25] Other stars of the season were Mrs. Whitlock, Cooper and Fennell.

Among its outstanding events was the first production,on January 1, 1813, of Barker's *Marmion*.

On November 30, 1812, the Southwark had opened its doors for a season to last until the middle of January. It was in charge of the handsome Beaumont, an indifferent actor but a manager of enterprise and tact. His purpose in opening the Southwark was primarily to introduce the Misses Abercrombie, young Dublin dancers and nieces of his wife, though there were other players whom he was planning to introduce to the Philadelphia audience: Mrs. Goldson of the Haymarket, for example; Jones of the New York theatre and Mrs. Riddle, billed as "of this city [Philadelphia]."

Durang reveals that the Abercrombies "excelled in light rustic ballets." On December 9 they captivated the Southwark audience, generally too coarse to appreciate their dainty refinement, in the American première of the ballet of *Little Red Riding Hood*. Other novelties at the old theatre included *The Naval Frolic*, also a ballet and by a "gentleman of Philadelphia" and the pantomime of *The Christmas Box; or, Harlequin in Philadelphia*. Beaumont also produced, for the first time, the melodrama of *The Sicilian Romance* and the comedy of *Right and Wrong*.

On January 21, 1813, his wife announced that, "in compliance with the repeated solicitations of her friends," "her benefit" would take place in the Olympic Theatre. Ever since December 2 Pepin & Breschard's converted circus had been advertised for sale "at Public Vendue." Its two "Glass Chandeliers, 268 Lamps, 5 Street Lamps, 10 Grecian Lamps, quantity of Lamp Glasses, three Pine Tables, Chairs, Sopha, Carpet, Andirons, Fender, Looking Glasses, three Stoves, &c." had been "seized

---

[25] *Recollections*, p. 176.

and taken in execution"[26] and were to be sold by the sheriff; but, meanwhile, the Beaumonts put the theatre to use. On January 26 they offered the "Comick Pantomime" of *Mother Bunch* and, on January 28, the "new Ballet" of *Little Fanny's Love*. Their season seems to have ended about February 2.

The Abercrombies, now that their fame was established, were engaged at the Chesnut, where, on April 9, 1813, they appeared in the first American production of the ballet of *Cinderella*.

Warren & Wood, after the Philadelphia season of 1812–13, went to Baltimore to occupy a newly erected theatre. Warren must have been keeping an eye on its erection, for, on April 16, 1813, he writes in his *Diary*, "On this morning I left Balt[imore] at 2. A.M. in the Expedition stage. Arrive in Philadelphia at $\frac{1}{2}$ past one next morning after being upset near Charleston."

For a man of Warren's avoirdupois, being upset was no idle matter; but it worred him less, probably, than the thought of having to proceed, in the face of chaotic business conditions, with the expensive project to which the Chesnut Street managers had committed themselves. However, all things considered, the succeeding Baltimore season of a month was satisfactory enough with its nightly average of $422, though the summer season in Washington was utterly ruined by a threat of attack from the British.

Meanwhile, a company called "The Theatrical Commonwealth" had begun to play at the Southwark on April 13, 1813. It was chiefly composed of dissatisfied players. With Twaits at its head, it included Caulfield, whose imitations were famous, Burke and his wife, whose voice overcame the odds of the "intensity of Sol's rays, the war, ragged paper money, and," as *Durang* adds, "the objectionable location and decayed state of the old South street theatre." On April 20 Leigh Waring of the Dublin and Liverpool theatres joined the commonwealth company.

On May 26 Twaits produced *The Force of Nature* (with the author, the elder Fennell, as Eugenius) and on June 9, for the first time in Philadelphia, Ioor's *The Battle of Eutaw Springs*.

The "commonwealth" had begun with an appeal for support against "the managerial powers" in charge of "the various metropolitan theatres of the country" and Twaits had pushed the campaign as vigorously as his wretched health would permit; yet, as *Durang* records, "Its efforts, however just and meritorious, met but with little assistance from our

[26] See The United States Gazette of December 2, 1812.

[21]

republican play-goers, from whom a sympathetic response was fondly anticipated."

The Southwark closed about June 9, 1813.

On July 9, 1813, a summer theatre was opened at the Columbian Garden, Market Street above Thirteenth. "Pantomimes were given by Manfredi and others, comic and sentimental songs," Durang writes, "eking out the evening's entertainment." The garden closed on October 2.

On August 30 Pepin & Breschard resumed as a circus at the Olympic. After appealing to the patriotic sentiments of the Philadelphia public with such pantomimes as *The Fall of York and the Death of General Pike* (by Joseph Hutton, a Philadelphian) and another announced as "a grand representation of Proctor's defeat by Gen. Harrison," and offering the usual equestrian exhibitions, the Olympic closed on December 4.

Returning from a fairly successful season in Baltimore, Warren & Wood opened the Chesnut on November 22 for the season of 1813–14.

The company included the managers, Duff, Greene, Bray, Jefferson, Hardinge, Doyle, Francis, Blissett, F. Durang, John Durang, Abercrombie, the Mesdames Whitlock, Wood, Mason, Duff, Bray, Seymour, Francis and the Misses Sophia Abercrombie and M. White.

Durang records that, among the plays presented for the first time this season, *The Ethiop* and *The Exile* were especially well liked; and Marmion, acted occasionally, "proved highly effective on the stage."

In *Marmion* the personable young Irishman, John Duff, clad "in burnished armor, covered with a flowing purple mantle," Durang reveals, fluttered the feminine hearts in the audience as he "delivered the message of his embassy in the most haughty and impassioned style, in King James' court."

The season closed on April 16, 1814.

On January 17, 1814, "The Theatrical Commonwealth" had returned to the Olympic from a season in New York. Its company now included Twaits, Waring, Clarke, Anderson, Fisher, Hathwell, Jacobs, Fennell, Jr., Burke, Caulfield, Pierson; and Mesdames Clarke, Jacobs and Burke.

Holman and his daughter appeared in *The Honey Moon* on the opening night; Dwyer and Fennell played engagements during the season (which was to be the last for the "Commonwealth") and Mrs. Placide and her daughter made their débuts in Philadelphia. There were produced, for the first time in Philadelphia, the comedy of *The Students of Salamanca* and the romantic play of *The Vintagers*. The "Commonwealth" failed on March 17, 1814.

On April 16, before leaving for Baltimore, Warren & Wood "made a new arrangement with the proprietors of the Philadelphia Theatre for a lease for five years from 26th July, 1814, at $5000 p[e]r ann[u]m, payable ½ yearly."[27] On the previous day, "news of the British fleet being in sight of Baltimore [had caused] the packet and steam boat line [to be] suspended;"[28] but the managers opened their new playhouse on April 20 and, in spite of the panic caused by the proximity of the British fleet and a lingering hostility to the theatre, took in an average of $419 a night during a season lasting until June 10.

Meanwhile the Vauxhall Garden, at the northeast corner of Broad and Walnut Streets, had captured the fancy of Philadelphians. It opened on May 11, 1814; and, seated beneath its variegated lights, its patrons could sip their refreshments and listen to the music of its band and the voices of McFarland, "late of the Boston theatre," Hardinge and others.

For the time being, at least, it would appear that Warren & Wood had outridden all serious opposition. Twaits died on August 25, 1814, between the Washington and Baltimore seasons of the Chesnut Street company; and, after performances by Villalave & Co., rope dancers, the Olympic closed on October 7. It was advertised to be sold at auction on November 29. It opened again on December 21, but it was only for a few nights. Perez & Co., also rope dancers, occupied it.

With the town once more to themselves, Warren & Wood set out to furnish it with the best talent obtainable during the season of 1814–15, which extended from November 28 to April 17. They engaged James Entwisle, who made his début on December 2 as Zekiel Homespun in *The Heir at Law* and Crack in *The Turnpike Gate*, Waring, Cooper and Bibby, who interpreted acceptably the difficult rôles of Richard the Third and Sir Archy MacSarcasm.

Outstanding events of the season were the first performance of Mrs. Carr's *The Return from Camp* on January 6 and the celebration, on February 13, of the ending of the War of 1812.

The treaty of Ghent had been signed on December 24, 1814; but its articles seemed, in no sense, to apply to the feuds that raged among the actors and between them and the managers. During the season of

[27] Warren's *Diary*.
[28] Warren's *Diary*.

[23]

1814–15, these feuds were apparently more distracting than the war itself. "Mrs. Hardinge not heard of since his benefit," Warren writes in the April 17 entry of his *Diary*. "He owes us $120. Mrs. Green[e] left the company without any previous notice. On the last night she made a speech and a very ludicrous one it was. She told the audience that 'she had always been the humblest of their slaves, had behav[e]d like a woman and actress' and thank'd them for the proofs they had given her of their gratitude. Jefferson has withdrawn his daughter—a dispute ab[ou]t going on in a chorus."

Financially, the season had been a little more satisfactory, with a nightly average of $581. The fact must have been consoling, for "the losses sustained" by Warren & Wood "at this period," Warren asserts in his *Diary*, "are not to be calculated. The extra expenses we were put to in the Carriage of our Wardrobe [were] at least $1000. [The] property Burn'd at French Town [was worth] $600. [The] expense of Stage Fire [was] rais'd to $12. Spermacetti Oil [is] $2.50 p[e]r Gallon, which before this was at 90 Cents. Firewood [is] almost double . . . Indeed I don't wish to witness such melancholy days again."

In a mood of divided loyalty, Warren concludes, "All might have been avoided had wisdom and not passion prevailed in the Councils of the nation."

While the Chesnut Street managers were following the summer circuit to Baltimore, Washington, Alexandria and back to Baltimore again, Vauxhall furnished most of the entertainment available to Philadelphians.

The Chesnut Street Theatre opened for the season of 1815–16 on November 27. Warren & Wood were now reaping the benefit of a return to peace. The spring season in Baltimore had averaged as much as $591 a night and, while the Washington season was disappointing, the Alexandria season and the autumn season in Baltimore had brought Warren & Wood back to Philadelphia with high hopes that were soon to be realized. Early in the season they introduced a group of new players, Johnson, Savage, McFarland, Mrs. Placide and Mrs. Claude; and efforts to make their bills as attractive as possible were rewarded when the production of *Zembuca* brought close to an average of $1000 a night for a run of nine performances.

Jefferson materially aided the success of this production by constructing intricate stage machinery. In referring to this service Wood writes in gratitude that Jefferson "felt himself amply repaid for the exercise of his varied talent, by the prosperity of the establishment of which, for twenty-five years, he continued the pride and ornament;"[29] but at this time the esprit de corps at the Chesnut was generally excellent, though a stray player or two might take it into his head to decamp.

The stock actors fared well in their benefits. Cooper, although his "terms were to divide after $400 p[e]r night, his benefit charges to be $300," was a gainer by $2746;[30] but, in an engagement averaging $900 for a period of eight nights, he added to the treasury of the Chesnut almost as much as he received.

The season of 1815–16, in fact, was the most successful since that of 1810–11, the first of Warren & Wood's management in Philadelphia. It closed on April 17, 1816.

During the summer months Vauxhall and the Columbian gardens furnished entertainment for the citizens of Philadelphia and "Day Francis, the Great, a conjurer and magician, gave exhibitions of sleight of hand, at the Masonic Hall, much to the gratification of the town."[31] On May 30 a concert was given by Messrs. Gilles and Etienne at the Olympic, to which the price of admission was unprecedentedly high at $2 for the boxes and $1 for the pit. At the time, Warren & Wood were playing in Baltimore to a satisfactory average of $524 a night.

On June 14, 1816, during this Baltimore season, James Fennell died in Philadelphia. Warren reveals that "he had been a wretched sot for many years past and consequently much distressed in his last days;"[32] but his example seems to have been lost on players like Savage, whom Wood had to discharge, on June 21, for resenting discipline and collaring the manager and tearing his shirt.[33]

Business in Washington and Alexandria was fair and in Baltimore, during the autumn season, it reached the gratifying nightly average of $559; but Warren & Wood stood in need of every penny they could clear above the $300 required for expenses, for they had taken the expensive step of contracting to have the Chesnut Street Theatre lighted by gas.

After signing bonds with a Dr. Kugler "relative to the Gas lights," Warren "left Phil[adelphi]a in the new Steam boat Baltimore, Cap[tain] Jenkins," at "one P.M.," arriving "at ½ past 6 . . . at Newcastle" and, leaving there "in the Stage" on Sunday, October 27, "at 2 A.M." went

[29] *Recollections*, p. 205.
[30] Warren's *Diary*, entry of February 3, 1816.
[31] *Durang*, I, LIV.
[32] Warren's *Diary*, entry of June 19, 1816.
[33] Warren's *Diary*, entry of June 21, 1816.

"on board the S[team] B[oat] Philadelphia, Cap[tain] Trippe, "at ½ past 5," to be landed "in Baltimore ab[ou]t 3 P.M."[34]

On the fatiguing journey, he was probably considering how he should break the news to Wood of a new threat to the supremacy of the Chesnut. J. West, English equestrian, had arrived in New York with his "celebrated circus corps, stage performers, and a splendid stud of different colored horses," the "first spotted horses," asserts Durang, to be "seen in this country;" and Warren must have anticipated their engagement at the Olympic, though his report on the activities of Pepin & Breschard could be reassuring.

They had begun at the Olympic on August 19 with their usual equestrian exhibitions, ballets and pantomimes. *Durang* records that they had met with only "sad reverses" when, near the end of their season, in November, 1816, the engagement of West gave the Olympic an advantage which it pressed against the Chesnut. Campbell, the clown of West's company, was "extremely clever," *Durang* states; and the novelty of West's equestrian melodramas drew throngs to the Olympic for a period of twenty-seven nights, beginning on November 28 and ending on January 4, 1817. Wood reveals that the receipts averaged $807 a night, a production of *Timour the Tartar* realizing as much as $1098.[35]

How he secured such specific information must remain a mystery though it may have come from the twenty-year-old Ferdinand Durang, a dancer in the Chesnut Street company, who, angry at Warren & Wood over the matter of a forfeit he felt to have been unjustly imposed upon him, applied to West for the job of playing the rôle of Timour, one difficult to fill from the ranks of noted actors, who were already under engagement. To the surprise of everybody, Durang made up in agility for what he lacked in histrionic talent and experience; and *Timour* left the audience breathless with surprise and delight.

"Ramparts were scaled by the horses, breaches were dashed into, and a great variety of new business was introduced," *Durang* records[36] "The horses were taught to imitate the agonies of death and they did so in a manner which was astonishing. In the last scene, where Zorilda, mounted on her splendid white charger, ran up the stupendous cataract

[34] Warren's *Diary*, entry of October 26, 1816. The entry of July 22, 1816, reads: "Am making arrangements with Dr. Kugler to light the theatre next season with Gas."

[35] On the fly-leaf of Volume I of the *Account Book* Wood has written a record of the receipts of twenty-seven of West's performances.

[36] I, LIV.

to the very height of the stage, the feat really astounded the audience. Perhaps no event in our theatrical annals," concludes *Durang*, "ever produced so intense an excitement as that last scene. The people in the pit and boxes arose with a simultaneous impulse to their feet, and, with canes, hands and wild screams, kept the house in one uproar of shouts for at least five minutes."

It was lucky for Warren & Wood that West's engagement came to an end on January 4, 1817, with his departure to Baltimore.

Curiosity to see what the gas lights were like, of course, must have brought a great many persons to the Chesnut four nights after its opening on November 25, 1816, though, in their homes, Philadelphians stuck conservatively, for many years, to their candles and whale-oil lamps. "The managers were happy to be the first to introduce the use of gas in lighting theatres in America," runs an advertisement in the Aurora of November 21, 1816; and they "flatter[ed] themselves that its superior safety, brilliancy and neatness will be satisfactorily experienced by the audience."

The receipts of the season, following the disturbing success of West, proceeded to a comfortable average of $596 a night, even after the novelty of the lights had worn off and the weather become so severe that the oak-fed stoves in the theatre hardly tempered its icy atmosphere.

Less lucky than the audience, who could repair to the drinking saloons in the building in quest of artificial warmth or sit huddled in great coats, beating a tattoo with their feet, the poor actors fell ill. Robertson, Barrett and Wood himself, were indisposed; and Warren records in his *Diary* that "Old Durang [remained] ill [for] 2 months."

The managers, however, were able to present, for the first time, Robertson and the Burkes; and to produce the tragedy of *Bertram* and the romantic melodrama of *Aladdin*, the latter with "great attention to scenery, costumes, machinery, &c."[37] During this season, too, they had the journalistic enterprize to commission Barker to dramatize John R. Jewitt's story of his experiences with the savages of Nootka Sound. The music was by Lefolle; and the principal rôle in the melodrama, that of the armourer of the ship Boston, was played by Jewitt himself. Indian dances were included in the production, which filled the boxes at the customary dollar and the pit and gallery at seventy-five and fifty cents.

Rokeby, by Mr. Kilty, the Chancellor of Maryland,[38] was the only

[37] *Durang*, I, LIV.
[38] Warren's *Diary*, entry of November 19, 1816.

[27]

other American play to be offered this season. It had not "go[ne] off well" in Baltimore in the fall of 1816 and in Philadelphia, on December 21, it drew the modest sum of $442.

The eventful season of 1816–17 closed on April 24.

While Warren & Wood were absent on their summer circuit, the usual entertainments were given in Philadelphia. The Southwark opened for a few dramatic performances; the circus began a ten-day season on July 2; and, at Vauxhall Garden, "John Huxtable gave exhibitions of fireworks" and John R. Jewitt sang songs "dressed in Nootka costume."[39]

To a man of Warren's two hundred and fifty odd pounds the strain of the summer seasons must have been equal to that of a winter in Philadelphia. "I [leave] Newcastle at 4 p.m.," he writes in his *Diary* on June 13, 1817. "On board the Steam Boat Phila[delphia] at ¼ past 7. Detain[e]d 5 Hours at F[rench] Town to stop a hole in the boiler. Did not arrive until dusk in Baltimore."

Meanwhile the gas, now installed in the Baltimore theatre, had proven another source of irritation. "On Friday during the last act of Aladdin," is Warren's comment on May 10, "the gas lights suddenly went out and left the audience for a short time in darkness. They bore it very patiently—in ½ an hour it was restor'd—and the piece concluded."

The Philadelphia managers must have regretted the installation of a system of lighting still in an experimental stage, for, on July 5, Warren complains, "We find the Gas lights have caus'd a heavy addition to our expences. Fixing the pipe has cost $2500."

In consequence, the average of $505 dollars a night realized this season represented a poor return on the investment; and, in addition, on June 16, just as it was beginning to seem that it hardly paid to open the Washington theatre, the "last ½ year's rent" on that playhouse, $202, had fallen due.[40] During a mid-summer visit to Philadelphia Warren husbanded the resources of the firm by "laying in firewood for the Theatre at [$]5.00 per Cord,"[41] returning to Baltimore in the autumn to help with the supervision of the work of completing the interior decoration of the Baltimore playhouse and to join with Wood in introducing Incledon, the singer, to the Baltimore public.

Anxious thoughts must have attended the managers on their return

[39] *Durang*, I, LV.
[40] Warren's *Diary*.
[41] Warren's Diary, entry of August 5, 1817.

[28]

to Philadelphia, for they were contemplating heavy expenditures during the season of 1817–18, which was about to begin.

"Very beautiful weather" greeted Warren, "on Board the steamboat Delaware;" but, if he had been as superstitious as some of his brother actors, he might have taken it as an ill omen "when, off the Lazarretto, the other steam boat Vesta hoisted a signal of distress" and Warren's boat was compelled to return "to Chester for her. [The Vesta] had broken her crank." Warren adds cheerfully, "[We] took her in tow— and arrived at Philadelphia at ½ past 2."[42]

The circus, under the management of Pepin & West, had been running since October 3, 1817. Aided by a few dramatic performers, it had produced *The Weathercock*, in which the ambitious Mrs. West played Variella, the pantomime, new to Philadelphians, of *The Deserter of Naples*, the spectacle of *The Secret Mine*; and it had revived *Timour the Tartar*. During this season at the Olympic, which ended on November 29, Pepin & West also offered *The Battle of Bunker's Hill*.

In the bill advertising their opening night of December 1, 1817, Warren & Wood assured the public that the troublesome gas lights had "received very great improvements" and made promises which they hastened characteristically to fulfill.

On December 3 they introduced Betterton from the Covent Garden Theatre; and, though Betterton was now too old to make a favorable impression, Incledon, the singer from the same theatre, who succeeded him, became instantly popular. Incledon's "pieces were generally strongly cast," *Durang* attests, "the company being *pat* in what is termed 'old English comic opera,' wherein the music, viz., songs, duets, trios, and concerted pieces, met the understanding of all, and mingled with easy and amusing dialogue, were rendered attractive."

Incledon's nightly average was $912; but Wood felt that it was a tribute to Incledon's vocal powers, for "his attempts at acting" were "slovenly and ineffective" and his audience seemed to care little whether his songs were appropriate, just as long as he sang them.

The celebrated Philipps began an engagement on January 5, 1818; and Incledon's precedent (as Wood alludes to it, his "little attention to 'keeping' ") must have proved an annoyance at first. Philipps, at all events, angered his public by refusing to include, in *The Siege of Belgrade*, the popular song of *Eveleen's Bower*. However, his "fine personal appearance . . . so strongly in contrast with Incledon's ungainly figure and

---

[42] Warren's *Diary*, entry of November 28, 1817.

[29]

manner"[43] helped him to win the battle for good taste. Incidentally, *Eveleen's Bower*, which he sang so acceptably, continued to be "strummed on every piano, whistled by the celebrated Black Bob, the oysterman, and sung by every serenader."[44]

Yet the success of the singers must have enriched them at the expense of the managers, for Warren protests that, while "the circus [was doing the Chesnut Street] little or no injury," the revenues of their own playhouse were being seriously drained by the operatic performances.[45]

Possibly he was exasperated by Philipps' attempt to force his hand as betrayed in "a great deal of puffing in the papers about" the singer. On January 12 Warren writes, "[Philipps] seems to be up to what the actors call Gammon. All these puffs emanate from himself; he has given Orders to the writers of them, to my knowledge." Whether ethical or not, the ruse helped to secure Philipps another engagement in February, after Cooper had shown, in a successful engagement of nine nights, that the popularity of the regular drama, as well as his own, was as great as it had ever been. Cooper was particularly attractive in the rôle of Malec, in *The Apostate*, produced for the first time in Philadelphia on January 23, 1817.

On March 6, 1818, the proprietors, or owners of the building, deceived possibly by the press of carriages about the doors of the Chesnut and its crowded pit and gallery, demanded a rental of $6000 a year. The season closed, on April 25, 1818, to a nightly average of $641; but Warren laments, in his *Diary*, that "the profit [had] not [been] much. . . . There remain[ed] in [the] Philadelphia Bank $2356 towards the ½ year's rent due in July."

The Olympic under the combined management of Pepin and Caldwell & Entwisle, newly from the South, had been offering equestrian and dramatic performances since April 16, 1818; and, before its "theatrical department," under Caldwell & Entwistle, dissolved on June 6, Warren & Wood had reached the middle of their spring season in Baltimore, which proved to be only moderately successful.

Washington was as disappointing as usual; and its heat must have done its part to make the problem of discipline, especially among the younger members of the corps, more difficult than ever. Warren writes on June 6 that, on the Saturday previous to his arrival, "some of the

[43] *Recollections*, p. 213.
[44] *Durang*, I, LV.
[45] Warren's *Diary*, "Retrospect" of season.

Wild lads in the Upper tier of Boxes [had] hiss'd MacFarland in the song, 'Girl of My Heart.' Pat was in a Rage and Challeng'd the dirty Blackguard. This occasioned a tumult. He swore he would not play any more. The part was given to Mr. Hughes but, on Monday after the rehearsal, he begged to be reinstated. As his name was still in the bills and *he had* a few partisans, we thought proper to grant his request. Wood said something for or rather against him, begging that he might be forgiven, fined him $50 for addressing the audience without leave— and so it rests at present."

The fine was heavy but it was for a serious offense. As Fennell points out in his autobiography, "the prospectus of a disturbance, or, as some call it, fun, [was] the most attractive bill that [could] be made out;"[46] and, if audiences were unruly just out of sheer exuberance, it was natural that they should welcome an excuse for engaging in a riot that would send the ladies in the theatre scurrying to their carriages.

During the Baltimore autumn season of 1818, the Darleys rejoined the Chesnut Street Company after an absence of six years; and Warren & Wood engaged Wheatley from the Theatre Royal, Dublin, and Mr. and Mrs. H. Wallack from the Hull and Drury Lane theatres. J. Wallack, the younger brother of H. Wallack, and Cooper were the stars.

Thus reinforced, Warren & Wood, closing the Baltimore theatre on November 2, hurried to Philadelphia, where, on November 5, they opened a season of one hundred and fifteen nights extending to April 30, 1819.

There were débuts aplenty during this season. On November 6 Hughes of the Boston theatre, on November 9 Wheatley and on November 10 Herbert of the Theatre, Brighton, made their first appearances. On December 26 Henry Wallack appeared, for the first time in Philadelphia, as Don Juan in *The Libertine*, a rôle to whose "witching charms," his "fine dashing look and manner, his figure and [style of] acting" were as well suited as they proved to be to the rôle of Rob Roy, in which the elder Wallack drew an appreciative house of $989 on January 1, 1819. James Wallack made his début, on January 8, as Rolla in *Pizarro*. As *Durang* records, "the audience were in perfect rapture with him;" and, in the rôles of Macbeth, Hamlet, Bertram, Shylock and Walter (in *The Children in the Wood*), he made such a "prodigous sensation" that he overshadowed Maywood (later the producer) and the Bartleys (all from Drury Lane), who made their débuts on February 2 and February 15

[46] See the odd and interesting book, *An Apology for the Life of James Fennell*, p. 406.

respectively. Warren & Wood secured James Wallack for a second and then a third engagement.

During the season they also presented Blissett (returned to the company after an absence of three years), Cooper and Duff.

Whether a season in which so many new players were added to the company and so many new stars appeared could be financially, as well as artistically, a success is a pertinent and interesting question. Its nightly average of $555 must have been inadequate, for the stars, whom the public demanded, were expensive.

It would have been Warren & Wood s policy, however, to present them, in any event. As Wood expresses it, "possessed, as [they] were of a virtual monopoly," they "were bound to offer to the supporters of [their] highly favored theatre the best talent which it was possible to procure;"[47] and, during the season of 1818–19, the Olympic had offered only feeble opposition. Following its spring season of 1817 Pepin had entered into an arrangement with Entwisle to open the Olympic in the autumn. Entwisle was to go to England to engage new performers, procure new pieces and such other novelties as he could obtain. Pepin opened the Olympic for a few weeks during the summer; and then closed "for the fall in the pleasing anticipation of the reception of the novelties and fresh actors which Mr. E. was to bring over."[48] He re-opened, as a circus, on October 4 and "theatrically," as Durang phrases it, on November 12.

Entwisle, however, returned with only the manuscript of *The Rendez-vous*, so Pepin's dreams evaporated. The Olympic closed on March 20, having operated during the last month only as a circus.

During the summer of 1819 Philadelphians flocked to the oriental theatre in the midst of the serpentine walks and flowered shrubbery of the Vauxhall Garden to see such pieces as *The Liar* and *Three Weeks after Marriage* and, now that Incledon and Philipps had whetted their appetite for music, to hear the sweet, if uncultivated tenor of Arthur Keene, a dashing young Irishman.

Warren & Wood had gone to Baltimore, where a disappointing season averaging only $376 a night was a prelude to a series of misfortunes about to overtake the Chesnut Street company. The threat of an epidemic of yellow fever kept them out of the Baltimore theatre in the fall.

During the Philadelphia season of 1819–20, which began on September

[47] *Recollections*, p. 132.
[48] *Durang*, I, LIX.

[32]

27 and ended on March 27, business conditions were so bad that the nightly receipts fell uncomfortably close to the necessary $300. Although, as Warren reveals in the November 17 entry of his *Diary* "the proprietors agree[d] to reduce the rent to $5000 this year," the managers were to "leave off" at the end of the season, "$6000 worse than [they] began."

Mrs. Entwisle, newly engaged, barely made expenses on her opening night. Keene, the Irish tenor, averaged less than $400 in five appearances; and received but little more than that amount for his benefit. Cooper was luckier, with an average of $529 for an engagement of seven nights, though his benefit was to only $575. The Bartleys, who also played an engagement, drew an average of only $290, for a period of seven nights. The town turned out in force, to receipts of $1041, on the occasion of Mrs. Bartley's benefit; but it may have been to view her "rotundity of figure," as Durang describes it, in "the dress of Hamlet." J. Wallack, who began an engagement in his attractive rôle of Rolla, after the Bartleys had departed for England, drew an average as low as $324 for a period of ten nights, though his benefit reached the sum of $1106.

The members of the regular company fared little better with their benefits. Jefferson, a great favorite, drew $775 and the elder Wallack $1165; but Wood drew as little as $317 and Warren suffered the humiliation of having a second benefit, for whose support he pleaded, fail like the first. Members of the company went to crazy lengths to cozen patronage. Mrs. Darley paraded her "amiable private character, whether as daughter, wife, mother or friend." Mrs. Entwisle "resorted to ill usage, tyranny & oppression to make [a] house" of $832, according to Warren's testimony, while Herbert, who excelled in the rôles of humorous old men, "got himself stuck up in all the print-shops as Richard," the rôle he attempted for his benefit, leading Warren to add, in his entry of March 10, "It won't do, after all . . . ."[49]

It is to the credit of the Chesnut Street managers that, despite the hard times, they managed to produce, for the first time in Philadelphia, the American plays of *She Would be a Soldier* and *Altorf*.

As a fitting climax to this season of heartbreak came an event foreshadowed by a fire which had destroyed Vauxhall Garden before the opening of the Chesnut. This was the burning of the Chesnut Street Theatre, "the first Old Drury," on April 2, 1820.

Wood writes in his autobiography, that the "destruction was by many

[49] Warren's *Diary*.

[33]

imputed to the malice of an incendiary" but that the "charge" was "liable to much doubt, as being wholly unsupported by any probable evidence." According to the February 26 entry of his *Diary*, however, Warren was "call[e]d up by an alarm of Fire at the Theatre ab[ou]t ½ past eleven. It proved to be Judge Tilghman's stable at our Back door in Carpenters street. Luckily, "Warren adds, the fire "did us no injury." There came a second alarm on March 22; and Warren contradicts his partner with the statment, "An attempt was made to set the Theatre on fire by introducing combustibles into the Hose House in Carpenter Street."

"The destruction was so complete," writes Wood, whatever its origin, "that [a] green-room mirror, a beautiful model of a ship, and the prompter's clock, were alone preserved. The expensive gas works shared the common fate. It is not generally known that the stockholder's property consisted of the walls alone [,the] scenery, lights, wardrobe, and other appointments having been purchased from them by the managers some years before. The loss was very great, as the property had been liberally augmented and improved through a long series of years. The most irretrievable part was the splendid English scenery presented to Wignell in 1793 by Richards, Hodges and Rooker, artists of the first reputation in their day. The wardrobe was of great extent, including the whole of the dresses from Lord Barrymore's theatre, as well as those from a French establishment recently purchased. The library and music were of an extent and value unknown to any other American theatre. Two grand pianos, costing 100 guineas each [, at one of which Reinagle used to preside,] a noble organ, used in the 'Castle Spectre,' and other chapel scenes, and models of scenery and machinery, imported at a large cost, swelled the sum of our misfortune."

It was a blow from which the managers never recovered, for "until within a few months of the disaster," Wood laments, "we had been guarded by insurance to a considerable amount, but the frequency of fires, as well as alarms, rendered the offices reluctant to venture on the risk of theatres and certain dangerous manufactories; and, while we were actively engaged in applications to different offices here and elsewhere, our policy expired."

It was a wise course for the insurance companies to follow, for, within a short space of time, the Washington and Park theatres were to suffer the fate of the "first Old Drury." On April 19, 1820, word reached Warren of the destruction of the Washington theatre. "On this evening at ½ past 8 P.M." he writes in his *Diary* of this fresh misfortune, "we received a letter from Mr. R. Weightman, stating that the Washington Theatre was burn't. At ½ past 8 in the morning it was discovered to be on fire. We lose another stock of scenery, lamps, &c."

The horizon looked bleak.

While the Columbian Garden, rechristened The Tivoli, was reaping the benefit of having the Vauxhall Garden and the Chesnut out of the way and, under Stanislas Surin, a former "professor of legerdemain," making money out of putting on farces and tight rope performances, Warren & Wood were playing to a losing average, in Baltimore, of $262 during the spring and $218 during the autumn season.

The only rift in the clouds was the fact that the Olympic was without a tenant and available to Warren & Wood, for the Philadelphia season of 1821–22, on easy terms. Of course, "the house having been originally constructed only with a view to circus purposes, and subsequently imperfectly changed to dramatic uses, required expensive improvements in every part. The performers' dressing-rooms, the green-room, and indeed," Wood states, "nearly every portion of the building needed alteration." It was necessary to remove the dome, which had spoiled the acoustics of the Olympic, rebuild its stage and construct a pit; but it proved a haven for the Chesnut Street Company, even though the Chesnut Street patrons turned up their noses at a theatre so recently a circus and at first declined to patronize it on the ground that it was unsafe.

The Olympic was now renamed the Walnut Street Theatre.

With Mr. and Mrs. Baker from England added to the company, Warren & Wood opened the Walnut on November 10, 1820. Among the players they introduced, during the season, were Mr. and Mrs. Williams (later Mrs. Robert C. Maywood), Mrs. Alsop, (daughter of the celebrated Mrs. Jordan, from Drury Lane) and Mr. and Mrs. Barnes from the Park Theatre. The season began with receipts as low as $175 and $245; and it was not until Cooper's benefit, on December 23, and the first performance of *Ivanhoe*, on January 1, 1821, that the amounts of $773 and $888 were realized.

On November 27 "a well grown young man, with a noble figure, unusually developed for his" sixteen years and with "features" that were "powerfully expressive"[50] had made his début as Young Norval to the modest sum of $319.75; and "acquitted himself" so well 'hat he was

[50] *Recollections*, p. 250.

[35]

engaged to repeat the performance on December 2 and to play Frederick in *Lover's Vows* on December 29. This was Edwin Forrest, who was destined to arise, as Durang puts it grandiosely, "in all his vigor and glory, while the star of Cooper was going down in fading grandeur." Forrest's benefit, which followed on January 6, was a failure with receipts of $215; but a heavy snowstorm and the imminent arrival of a celebrated English tragedian were definitely accountable, though Forrest's "reception in his native city" had been "cool" enough, writes Wood, to "have discouraged a less ardent and confident mind."

The English tragedian was Edmund Kean, who, after having survived unfavorable comparisons with Cooke and Fennell, had three successful engagements.

The season ended on April 28, 1821, to the inadequate average of $304.50, after stars and benefits had been paid and Kean, as Jaffier on the concluding night, had thrown the house into an uproar by an eccentric behavior that brought hisses and "apples, oranges, and other light missiles," Durang writes, from the Walnut Street audience.

On the whole, it had been far from a satisfactory season. There had been competition, too, in a little theatre in Prune Street, called "The Winter Tivoli," though it had amounted to little.

Fortunateiy, Kean behaved himself in Baltimore, where he attracted, during the spring season, the unusually large sum of $500 a night in an engagement of fourteen performances. His Richard inspired Herbert to try the rôle once more. Tradition gave an actor the right to choose his own rôle for his benefit; Warren was helpless; his only redress was to write in his *Diary* the rueful comment, "Herbert acts Richard ag[ai]n for his own amusement." Herbert's benefit failed, though the fact could hardly have consoled the manager for the "first time" his own "night," that of June 6, "ever failed in Baltimore."[51]

The receipts of the season, "after deducting Stars & Benefits,"[52] were under expenses.

During the season Warren "view[ed the] progress [being] made [on the] theatre [in the course of erection in Washington] at Brown's, formerly Davis' Hotel" and, on June 20, 1821, received word, as he also reveals in his *Diary*, of the completion of the playhouse.

Before occupying it, Warren & Wood, badly in need of money, tried the experiment of playing a short summer season in Philadelphia. On

[51] Warren's *Diary*.
[52] See the text of the *Account Book*.

the opening night, however, the first production of *Thérèse* brought only $271. Even the sharing principle which they put into force, as *Durang* reveals, "per share, in three nights, ten dollars," was inadequate to save the day; and, Warren & Wood, closing the Walnut on July 16, opened the new Washington playhouse on August 8.

Their first season within its walls brought a nightly average of only $134, so the managers might have been excused for returning to Baltimore with misgivings as to the success that would attend their efforts during the autumn season. The receipts fell under the amount needed for expenses; sickness among the players necessitated frequent changes in bills; but the season is noteworthy in that it introduced, to the Baltimore public, a famous English tragedian.

This was Junius Brutus Booth, who, following a now famous rivalry with Kean, had taken ship for America and arrived unheralded in the South.

On November 13, 1821, Warren & Wood opened the Philadelphia season, which was to extend to April 24, 1822. It was to be their last in the Walnut Street Theatre. Plans were now afoot to build a theatre to take the place of the one destroyed. In April of 1821, while Wood was in doubt of the wisdom of such a step, he was seriously considering an offer from New York to take charge of the Park; but Warren protested and old ties proved strong.

There was little to fear in the competition of the Prune Street Theatre, which opened on September 24 under Stanislaus Surin, now known as Stanislaus. Its company had been strengthened by Mr. and Mrs. Williams, Herbert and the Misses Durang, who, disgruntled at the sharing system used in the summer by Warren & Wood, had quit their company; and the Prune Street Theatre, before the opening of the Walnut, had been progressive enough to put on the melodrama of *The Forest of Rosenwald* for the first time in Philadelphia. But the theatre, which Durang describes as a long, narrow manufactory building, was much too small to menace the prestige that a newly built, large and fully equipped theatre would have.

Its prices, moreover, of 50, 37½ and 25 cents seemed too low to yield its manager an adequate margin of profit; and the withdrawal of the Williamses, Herbert and the Misses Durang was soon to suggest that the pay they received was neither sufficient nor reasonably certain. The authors Joseph Hutton and Augustus Stone and the tragedian Pelby were the best known, probably, of Stanislaus' company, which disbanded at the end of the season of 1821–22. .

[37]

At the beginning of this season, Warren & Wood presented the usual quota of new players. On November 15, Nichols, a singer from the London and Charleston theatres, appeared as Count Belino in *The Devil's Bridge*, anticipating the return of Philipps for a last engagement in Philadelphia. Mrs. Drake "from the Kentucky theatre" played Juliana on November 22, though to the disappointing sum of $261.

Old favorites also appeared. After an absence of two years, the Burkes rejoined the company; and it was planned to have J. Wallack start an engagement on November 30.

Wallack suffered a broken leg, however, on his way to Philadelphia; and the managers had to rely on Pelby (later to appear at the Prune Street Theatre) to interpret the rôles of Macbeth, Rolla, Bertram, Pierre and Brutus. Pelby tried industriously to please, giving clever imitations, on his benefit night, of his idol Kean. For all Pelby's efforts, though, the public signified their disappointment at the non-arrival of the younger Wallack by a support falling short of expenses.

At length, on January 1, 1822, upon the occasion of the first American production of *Undine*, Warren & Wood could feel, for the first time, that the patrons of "Old Drury" had not deserted them entirely. Receipts of $1032 rewarded the efforts that had gone into the production, for which the "whole of the Scenery, Machinery, Dresses and Decorations" were entirely new and the versatile Joseph Jefferson had helped to construct "a dark submarine grotto" and a "hugh Fish," upon which Gyblin, one of the characters in the "melodramatic romance," was seen to fly away. There were water and moonlight effects and a bridge which changed to "a car drawn by horses, resembling Phaeton's car" and an excellent cast including H. Wallack, Jefferson, Burke and the Darleys.

On February 2 William, brother of Edwin Forrest, made a first appearance, just prior to the beginning of Philipps' engagement on February 5. The début was financially a failure but it is of interest as being the début of a future manager of the Arch Street Theatre (constructed in 1828). In any event, Philipps' receipts were definitely lower than they would have been in weather more favorable.

The winter, as Warren reveals in his *Diary*, was very severe. Firewood, the precious "Oak at 9 doll[ar]s p[e]r Cord," was being hauled "over the river on the Ice." Many of the players fell ill.

Philipps was re-engaged on February 25; and the combination of a pleasant evening and the first performance of *The Barber of Seville* dre· a house of $669. Rossini's opera, *Durang* records, was "translated frc the Italian . . . and adapted to the English stage. The overture was by Bishop." The production made money for two nights more and then Philipps, for his benefit, appeared in *Fontainbleau* to receipts of $828.

The season seems now to have run its course. It was only March 29, but few profitable performances followed. The Walnut was unpopular. It must have been uncomfortable in winter; and Warren, writing in his *Diary* on March 2, must have been glad to note that "Strickland, the Architect, [had] contracted to build the [new Chesnut Street] Theatre for $45,000."

On December 12, 1821, Warren & Wood had answered an "urgent request of the stockholders" with "proposals" for the rebuilding of the Chesnut Street Theatre. The site, the same as that of the "first Old Drury," had been transferred, on January 31, 1822, from "the Trustees and Agents of the Proprietors of the (former) New Theatre" to "Joseph R. Ingersoll and Hartman Kuhn, Esquires, 'In trust for the Stockholders of the New Theatre.' " On February 4, 1822, these stockholders, acting on the proposals of Warren & Wood, decided to issue one hundred shares at $600 each.[53]

With work on the new Chesnut to begin during the summer, Warren & Wood opened the Holliday Street Theatre, where, during the spring of 1822, they presented the first French dancers to be seen in Baltimore. These were Tatin and Labasse. Receipts were disappointing; and Philipps, who followed the dancers, could barely attract the requisite $300. Cooper, in the best of his rôles, was even less fortunate; and the managers must, at this time, have been equally exasperated at Pelby, whom *Durang* reveals as dogging their footsteps in search of an engagement and at Dwyer, whom Warren, in his *Diary*, reports to have been "forced" on them by "Judge Hanson & Judge Warde."

It was "under a promise to make a House," states Warren. Dwyer was "to have ½ after $312." There is no record as to whether the amateur managers made up the difference when Dwyer's house came to only $287.

Warren's benefit failed again; and it is with absolute truth that he remarks in his *Diary*, "This town [Baltimore] once so profitable, is now good for nothing."

After the Washington summer season, Warren & Wood reopened the Holliday for what Wood asserts to have been "one of the most ruinous"

[53] See the printed copies of the *Proposals*, the *Fundamental Rules and Regulations and the Lease of the New Theatre*, in possession of the Historical Society of Pennsylvania.

[39]

seasons which they had "encountered," but one signalized by the American début of an English comedian who was a host within himself. This was Charles Mathews, whom an epidemic of yellow fever had led Stephen Price to release to Warren & Wood against the opening of the Park. Mathews began his engagement at the Holliday Street Theatre, Baltimore, on September 23, 1822; and, with *A Trip to Paris, Country Cousins, Travels in Earth, Air and Water, The Polly Packet* and *A Christmas at Brighton,* played to respectable receipts, in spite of a partial prevalence of yellow fever at Fells' Point, "a place immediately adjoining the city, a matter which created a considerable panic" and what Wood also reports to have been the "depressed state of the times."

Booth, following Mathews, played to losing receipts, so the managers, on their return to Philadelphia, must have hoped to reimburse themselves out of the receipts attracted by their new theatre.

By this time it was nearly completed. The Baltimore season ended on November 15, 1822; and on December 30 the new Chesnut Street Theatre was leased to Warren & Wood for a period of ten years. The rent was $3000 a year or $2000 less than it had been for the previous "Old Drury." According to a description on the back of a playbill for the opening night, the new theatre was attractive and comfortable.[54] It

[54] See picture of the theatre, frontispiece. On the back of the first night's bill is printed the following description of the building: "The approach to the boxes is from Chesnut street through a close arcade of five entrances opening into a vestibule 58 feet long, by 8 feet in width—communicating at each end with the box office, and a withdrawing ladies' room. From the vestibule are screen-doors, immediately opposite, and corresponding with the openings of the arcade, leading into spacious lobbies, warmed with fire-proof furnaces, and calculated to contain upwards of 1000 persons. Double flight of large stairways communicate with a spacious saloon and coffee rooms, together with the lobbies of second and third floors. The audience part of the house is described upon a semi-circle of 46 feet in diameter, containing 3 rows of boxes resting upon cast iron columns, and secured with iron sockets from the foundation to the dome—the whole being combined, laterally, with a strong wall, bounding the lobbies, and supporting the roof. The dress circle of the boxes is formed by a seat in advance of the columns, covered with a splendid canopy projecting from the front of the 2d row of boxes, in the style of the Covent Garden Theatre, London.

"The peculiar form given to this part of the house places the mass of the audience within 35 feet of the Stage—securing to them the important objects of distinct sound and perfect scenic view, an advantage which the best Theatres of Europe do not possess, although they may exceed it in magnitude.

"The dome is 46 feet in diameter rising six feet to the crown which is perforated and formed intc a ventilator, from which is suspended an elegant Chandelier 9 feet in diameter, containing 60 Patent Lamps enriched with appropriate ornaments.

was lighted, not with gas, but with "patent lamps." Its site had apparently cost a great deal more than had been anticipated; and the "patent lamps" were cheaper and much more practicable than the gas, which was still, after all, in an experimental stage.[55]

Certain of possessing their new theatre by "the first Monday in December, 1822," Warren & Wood had released the Walnut; and it had reverted to a circus, which also offered dramatic performances. It had been altered and rechristened the Olympic. On September 4, 1822, it had opened under the management of Price & Simpson, with Hugh Reinagle, the scenic artist, as acting manager and Drummond, formerly of the Chesnut Street Theatre, as stage manager. Its company was the equestrian troupe once headed by West, but now by Samuel Tatnall.

The Olympic closed on November 28, 1822.

With the Prune Street, renamed "The City Theatre" about to offer the only competition of any consequence they were to meet, Warren &

"The effect produced by this concentration of light, will be great inasmuch as the whole of the audience part of the house can be brilliantly illuminated without resorting to the detached lamps that have been in common use, and which is destructive to finish decoration.

"The Proscenium is 46 feet by 25 feet, an opening well calculated to exhibit the best exhibitions of the Drama. The tympanum immediately over the centre of the·Stage is chastely decorated with an appropriate design exhibiting the claims of Thalia and Melpomene to the genius of Shakespeare—over which is seen the motto 'To raise the genius and to mend the heart.' There are two doors of entrance to the Pit from Sixth street, through a passage 14 feet in width, which passage enters a lobby paved with brick, communicating with a bar-room and private stair way leading into the box-lobby on the western side of the building. The Pit floor is laid on a solid inclined plane of brick and mortar, and will accommodate 400 persons—The Orchestra will contain from 40 to 50 persons independent of the Musicians, and is to be approached from the box-lobby by a private stairway. The Gallery has its entrance from Carpenter street through a passage situated on the outside of the building, leading to a lobby and bar-room, and will contain 2[00] or 300 persons. It may be here proper to observe that the whole building will contain upwards of 2000 persons; and that the door-ways are numerous and wide, opening outwards into the three surrounding streets. The principal front is on Chesnut street, being 92 feet by 150, built of marble in the Italian style; the leading features of which are an Arcade supporting a skreen of composite columns and a plain entablature, flanked by two wings and decorated with niches and basso relievo's representing the Tragic and Comic masks with the attributes of Appolo [sic.]." For copy of bill see Harvard College Library.

[55] A notation in Volume I of the *Account Book*, which is headed "Expenses December 1822," includes the items, "Oil, 16 Gall[on]s p[e]r Night, 64 Gall[on]s, 90," "Wicks, 4" and "Lamp Glasses 5."

[41]

Wood might have entered lightheartedly upon their first season in the new playhouse, save for the one hundred and twenty free admissions in the hands of the stockholders and such misgivings as Wood may have felt as to the interference that might come from the five stockholders composing a "Board of Agents" to whom the other stockholders had delegated legal powers. In reference to this season, he was to write of "new influences" which "began to prevail" and to alienate him from Warren.

At its beginning, however, prospects were bright. The company had never been stronger. Wemyss, the English comedian, who joined it on November 26, 1822, felt that he had "a harder task" before him than he had anticipated after witnessing the efforts of the company at the Park. In his experienced eyes, the Chesnut Street company were "veteran actors, who understood their profession."[56]

In the company, besides the managers, were Henry Wallack, Jefferson, Burke, Francis, Wilson, T. Jefferson, J. Jefferson, D. Johnston, Darley, Barclay, Greene, Wheatley, Hathwell, Parker, Bignall, Murray, Andes, Scrivener; Mesdames Wood, Darley, Entwisle, H. Wallack, Lefolle, Burke, Francis, Jefferson, Anderson, Simpson, Greene, Murray; and the Misses Hathwell (Matilda, Henrietta and Louisa) and Parker. Lopez was the prompter.

During the season, Mrs. Entwisle and Mrs. Duff rejoined the company; and, according to Wemyss, Mr. and Mrs. Mestayer and family became members of it.

On December 6 Cooper played the first of what were to be nineteen performances. Durang calls his "arrangement" with the managers, during the season of 1822–23, an "ad libitum" one, with intervals which Cooper "filled up at the other cities." At forty-six the tragedian was still holding his own against such players as the younger Wallack and Francis Wemyss, whom Durang mistook for "one of old England's sprigs of nobility or gentry" as the comedian, newly arrived in the country, was coming out of Judd's Hotel, in South Third Street, wearing a "Bob Logic hat," a "green Bond street promenading coat, rounded at the skirts;" a "red waistcoat, with pocket flaps and bell buttons . . . salmon-colored stockinet pantaloons, fitting to the skin" and "Cossack polished boots."

Cooper was still so attractive, in fact, that, at the conclusion of an engagement of J. Wallack, beginning on January 17 and ending with a

[56] See *Twenty-Six Years of the Life of an Actor and Manager* by Francis Courtney Wemyss, Volume I, Chapter IX.

benefit of $1087 on January 29, there was a public request that the older and younger tragedian appear together.

On February 4 an engagement reminiscent of that of Cooke and Cooper in 1811 began with a somewhat meagre house of $539; but, extending through seven nights, ended with benefits of $863 and $1231 for Wallack and Cooper respectively.

The season had yet to include a surprising failure and an equally surprising success. The failure was Booth's. With receipts falling under expenses, his engagement was interrupted to make way for an engagement with Mathews.

The town was agog to see the comedian, who had taken New York by storm. Upon his arrival in America, Mathews, "one of the most irritable of *homos*," as Durang calls him, had been horrified by the plague which had caused the boarding up of all the streets above the Battery and the people of the city, in a desperate hope "to drive the blue devils away," to make carnival "above the fever barricades." However, after "Yellow Jack's final exit,"Mathews had, on November 27, begun his deferred engagement in New York.

His Philadelphia engagement started on February 24. His success was tremendous. In such rôles as Lord Duberly, Dr. Pangloss, Ollapod, Rover and Twineall, Wood asserts, Mathews refuted the charge that he was only a mimic, while in his own entertainments of song, recitation and impersonation he was conceded to be in a class by himself. Philadelphia had never seen lightning changes so featly performed as Mathews performed them in his seven rôles in *The Actor of All Work*.

After his departure, the season languished. Booth's interrupted engagement was to wretched receipts; and only the belated approval of *Tom and Jerry*, produced four times at the season's end, could console the managers for a nightly average of $420, after the "stars" and "benefits" had been paid. Even this slender advantage they had to resign to the Olympic, which, under Cowell, produced the popular "burletta," after which mixed drinks had been named, and used it "without intermission, to the close of [its] season."[57]

The time had come for the opening of the Holliday Street Theatre. Warren & Wood, after a season in which the "stars" and "benefits" had absorbed a quarter of their gross receipts, opened a spring season in Baltimore which was to average as little as $233. The Washington and Baltimore autumn seasons were even less successful, the latter despite

[57] See Wemyss' *Life*, I, Chapter IX.

[43]

the services of Hunter, a celebrated equestrian and tight rope performer.

Fleeing an unseasonable snowstorm, after appropriately presenting *The Tempest* Warren & Wood returned to Philadelphia, where they opened the Chesnut Street Theatre, on December 2, for the season of 1823–24. During the summer there had been tight rope and dramatic performances at Tivoli Garden and the Olympic put on its usual equestrian interludes and spectacles, together with some melodramas and farces, during a season running from May 1 to May 30.

The Chesnut Street season of 1823–24, which began on December 2, witnessed the first recognition of Booth's talents as an actor. Old favorites among the players were being displaced. Cooper, less attractive than he had been "in his more youthful days," Durang writes, "was declining in popularity." Fits of the gout were rendering Duff incapable of acting. "Poor old Jeff," as Durang alludes to the comedian, "was beginning to show great physical distress."

It was Booth's opportunity; and he improved it, on January 7, by a triumphant performance of Hamlet before a large and fashionable audience attending a "benefit for the Greek Fund."[58]

On January 21 Pearman, a singer from Covent Garden, was introduced in Philipps' famous rôle of Count Belino; but audiences preferred the rôle as sung and acted by the "original." Vincent de Camp, Drury Lane comedian and uncle of Fanny Kemble, was added in vain to Pearman's support. It was not until he appeared in the character of Jocoso, in Payne's comic opera of *Clari*, that Pearman was liked as a singer and actor.

Near the end of the season the managers engaged the well-known tragedian Conway and later, coupling him with Cooper, "produced some excitement," in the words of Durang, "as there was a desire expressed to behold these two noble-figured gentlemen in the same plays, and to draw comparisons of their relative merits."

During the season, which ended on May 19, 1824, there were given, for the first time in Philadelphia, the American melodrama of *Adelina* and the musical *Clari*, already mentioned. *Superstition*, the best of Barker's plays, was produced for the first time on any stage. The list of foreign pieces to be produced, for the first time in the city, included the farces of

[58] *Durang*, II, Chapter Sixteenth, explains that "associations were everywhere formed in this country to aid the [Greeks] with funds. This led to a benefit for the Greek fund at the Chesnut Street theatre."

Fire and Water and *Frightened to Death*; the tragedies of *The Bride of Abydos* and *Durazzo*; the "satirical, burlesque, operative parody" of *The Death of Life in London* (an inept sequel to *Tom and Jerry*;) and the "operatic, tragic, pantomimic, burletta, spectacular extravaganza" of *Don Giovanni*.

Wood asserts that the season was "marked by an injudicious [reduction in] prices, in imitation of the rates at the New York theatre." These "rates," he protests, "had never been approved either by our judgment or our experience. That greater numbers patronize the theatre because the prices are seventy-five, fifty and twenty-five cents, instead of a larger sum, had been emphatically disproved by our books; and a slight inclination to exclusiveness of the better class by making it too cheap, would of course be as prejudicial, as the reverse of this would confessedly be. Children were now admitted at half price . . ."[59]

Wood's ideas were generally sound. Even the policy of engaging expensive understudies, "leading exempts," as Durang sarcastically calls them, a policy for which the Chesnut Street managers were severely criticized, seemed justified this season. There was need of capable players to substitute for favorites on short notice. During the season of 1823–24, Duff had been ill "seventeen consecutive nights," as Wood reports; and again nine nights. "H. Wallack" had been ill "ten" and "Mrs. Duff, forty-three nights."

After a summer of negligible dramatic performances at the Chesnut, which opened from May 31 to July 5, and at the Tivoli and Vauxhall gardens, between which there raged a miniature "war of the theatres," the Olympic began a fall season on August 30 which ran to December 1. Price & Simpson's Philadelphia house was now under the direction of Joseph Cowell, who succeeded Wood as stage manager at the Chesnut when Warren's partner left the firm of Warren & Wood. Feats of horsemanship and performances of *Timour, the Tartar, The Cataract of the Ganges,* (in which real water doused a troop of calvary), the farce of *The Turnpike Gate* and the spirited *Tom and Jerry* were in Cowell's repertory.

Having played only the fall season in Baltimore, following a season in Washington of which Wood has left but a fragmentary record, the Chesnut Street company began the Philadelphia season of 1824–25 on December 4.

Booth and Cooper were the first stars of the season and they played

[59] *Recollections*, p. 299.

[45]

at least to moderate receipts; but Conway, who followed, was dogged by an habitual ill luck. He appeared to the proverbial "beggarly account of empty boxes." Clason, announced as from the Theatre Royal, Drury Lane, though a New Yorker by birth and, in the eyes of Durang, "a dashing fine figured, gentlemanly-looking man," had meanwhile appeared as Hamlet and, Wood writes, "with general approbation." J. Barnes and wife, secured in London by Price, were engaged to support the aging Cooper; and Watkins Burroughs, described by Wemyss as "of a minor order of stars, who afterwards found their way by dozens into the United States [but who] possess[ed] no talent above mediocrity," played Romeo, Frederick Friburg, Young Mirabel and several melodramatic characters, as Wood thought, in a satisfactory manner.

During this season, the American tragedy of *Ugolino*, attributed to Junius Brutus Booth, was produced for the first time on any stage; and the historical *La Fayette* (by Samuel Woodworth,) for the first time in Philadelphia. The list of foreign pieces to be produced, for the first time in the city, included the foreign comedies of *Sweethearts and Wives*, *Pigeons and Crows*, *A Woman Never Vext* and *Simpson & Co.*; the farces of *The Irish Tutor*, *Family Jars* and *Sponge Out of Town;* the tragedies of *Caius Gracchus* and *Alasco*; the "grand, romantic, operatic drama" of *Der Freyschutz* (in Durang's opinion, a "failure") and the spectacular *Cherry and Fair Star*, which captivated with a mirror bower scene and "shaking water" effects.

In the spring of 1825 the Walnut Street Circus put on its usual equestrian feats and dramas in a season running from May 1 to May 31, attracting large audiences, as "the taste of the masses was, at that time," *Durang* testifies, "eminently in favor of circus amusements." The Tivoli opened earlier; and, though *The Mountaineers*, *The Stranger* and other pieces in its repertory were inadequately given in its "al fresco atmosphere," it managed to prolong its season to the end of July.

Warren & Wood must at last have given up hope that the Baltimore theatre would ever pay the rent of the Chesnut again. Washington had turned out definitely to be a bad theatrical town, Wood noting that, this year, "The Washington season for the first time wholly failed."

Vastly more discouraging, however, was the vacillating policy which the "new influences," mentioned by Wood and apparently exercised through the "agents" of the stockholders, were forcing on the Chesnut Street managers. During the summer of 1824, as *Durang*, II, Chapter Twenty-First, reveals, "the prices of admission [had been] fixed at 75 cents boxes, pit 50 cents, gallery 25 cents," only to be restored to the old rates for the season of 1825–26. It was a confession that Wood was right in objecting to a change in the prices. Unfortunately, as Durang points out, "this was the first entering wedge to a radical alteration in the original scale" and it indicates the extent to which the "amateur or dilettante stage-management" was making Wood's "old friend and partner . . . very much less a real manager than he had been."

In explaining the rift that was to separate them in the summer of 1826, Wood asserts that, "while, as an ostensible manager," Warren "was still dealing with me, I found that we should certainly have, sooner or later, to encounter all the difficulties arising from want of candor and independence in relations where perfect candor and independence are qualities of capital necessity, and absolutely requisite either to success or comfort.

"It was impossible for me to be dealing in any way but in one way," continues Wood, "with my old friend Warren; and that was a direct, candid and independent one. While he was what he had been—while he could and did act out himself in the spirit and independence of himself—I could go on with him as I had always gone on, not only safely, but also with harmony, pleasure and success. When he was in any way the representative of interests, objects or schemes not really his own, yet presented as his, and so to be treated and considered by me, it was clear that there would be an end, sooner or later, of any harmony at all; and when harmony ceased, not only was success at an end, but bankruptcy and ruin met us in its place."

"I therefore told my old friend in the summer of 1825," Wood writes, "that the joint management, if it was about to be conducted on any judgment not his own—irresponsible and unknown to me—must end. I offered to buy him out myself, and so become sole manager. To this he objected, urging that the management had now become a source of certain and settled income, increasing gradually every year, and holding out a safe and comfortable prospect for him and his family in his advancing life.

"I then told him," Wood continues, "that he must become sole manager himself, or any rate that I must retire from the connection; which I informed him I should do at the end of a twelvemonth. Our articles of partnership required this amount of notice.

"For several months Mr. Warren did not suppose my purpose of retirement real. He 'hoped I would reconsider it,' urged his inability to undertake the toilsome details of management, a thing for which he

[47]

knew I was aware that he had a positive aversion, and which, with his heavy and lethargic figure, would become almost impossible, if from no other cause than from his difficulty of light and active motion.

"I considered the matter fully."

"The original influence, of which I have already spoken—not that of a hand unseen, guiding all, controlling all, while another figure was the representative, but that of a hand guiding nothing, and interfering with everything—had become more and more visible, and its effects were more and more injuriously felt."

"Finding me settled in my purpose of retirement," concludes Wood, "Mr. Warren joined me in arrangements for our separation. Easy terms were adjusted without difficulty, and in consideration of a sum agreed to be paid to me, a transfer of all my share of property in the different theatres, as well as in the lease of the Philadelphia house, having sixteen remaining years at $3000 a year, was duly executed . . . A condition made and insisted on by Warren was, that I should be bound to retain the situations held as actors by Mrs. Wood and myself as long as we continued on the stage in Philadelphia. To this I could make no objection."[60]

The autumn season following the decision of Warren & Wood to separate was as unprofitable as usual. With receipts in Baltimore falling under the nightly expenses, it was especially disturbing that the Walnut Street Circus, under Cowell, should be enjoying a successful season, which opened on August 29 and closed on December 1.

Cowell's company was fortified by James Kirby, a clown and painter from Drury Lane, and John Hallam, a comedian "from the Royal and Lincoln theatres," who, when Cowell leased the Walnut in 1827, was sent to England in search of talent for that theatre.

In 1825, there were other capable players who had been added to the corps of the Walnut. There was Collingbourne, for example, dancer, pantomimist and "actor of all work" who had been at the Royal Cobourg Theatre. During the season, Cowell had the enterprize to present a new melodrama by Collingbourne; and the company filled the house with performances of *Jacko*, in which Kirby played the monkey to perfection, and of the pantomime of *The Talking Bird*.

Warren & Wood opened the Chesnut for the season of 1825–26, their last Philadelphia season together, on November 21. Cooper, at its beginning, "the majesty of age" having replaced "the comeliness of his

[60] *Recollections*, Chapter XVII.

youth," still pleased in "classical personations."[61] In the middle of January Kean reappeared and, having weathered the storm of "rotten eggs, children's bullet buttons, and other small missles"[62] that first greeted him, because of alleged insults to America and a personal scandal at home, drew a nightly average of over $600 and well-earned applause in his usual rôles of Richard, Macbeth, Othello and Hamlet.

The season included engagements with Lydia Kelly (brought from London by Price) and Conway, ending brilliantly with the return of Edwin Forrest, after four years' absence. He had come from the Albany theatre managed by Gilfert. Durang writes that Forrest was no longer "a lad in years and appearance;" he had "grown in manly beauty and masculine expressiveness;" and, when he played Jaffier to Mrs. Duff's Belvidera in *Venice Preserved*, the ovation was so great that he was asked to play Rolla on the two nights that remained of the season.

During its course, there were produced, for the first time in Philadelphia, the comedy of *Charles the Second*, by Payne and Irving, and the American farce of *Exit in a Hurry*; the foreign comedies of *Smiles and Tears* and *The Hypocrite*; the "historical play" of *William Tell* and the "melodramatic romance" of *The Ninth Statue*.

From an artistic point of view the season had apparently been a success. However, there was a meagre average of $391 for one hundred and fifty one nights, which may have given Wood an excuse for shaking his head; and there is evidence that his opinion, later so candidly expressed, had undergone no change.

In view of actual accomplishments, Warren, on the other hand, was vexed at the attitude of lofty resignation which Wood could assume so irritatingly on occasion.

In writing his "retrospect" of the season, after its end on May 20, Warren asserts in his *Diary* that "this season has been productive and might have been more so but for the wayward conduct of my partner, who being ab[ou]t to leave the scheme has at times done everything he could to destroy the season—he wanted to make matters so uncomfortable that he thought I would throw the concern up in a pet and he might get it on any terms—yet the propos'd dissolution came from him— he then declar'd his intention of going to New York where he had higher views—said views after a time vanished—he then wished to back out— but I said no. We have paid a great many of the Old Claims, met all

---

[61] *Durang*, II, Chapter Twenty-Eighth.
[62] See Wemyss' *Life*, I, Chapter XI.

[49]

our engagements and I may say that the whole situation of our affairs is very much improv'd."

Thus at loggerheads, Warren & Wood began the last and most ruinous of their seasons in Baltimore. Kean was driven from the stage and his life threatened.

According to Durang's account, the tragedian was only in part to blame; yet, feeling beholden to Warren & Wood, he suggested a return to Philadelphia for a summer season. The offer was accepted; and an ensuing season of twenty-five nights, in view of torrid weather and the one hundred and fifty-one nights of entertainment recently given, was surprisingly successful. The engagement, Kean's last in Philadelphia, drew nearly $4000.

Following his departure, Edwin Forrest appeared in his first "star" engagement in the city. It was a coincidence, for the American tragedian had made his début, at the Walnut, about a month before Kean's.[63]

While the season of 1825–26 was in progress at the Chesnut, melodramas and "light singing farces," writes Durang, were being performed at the Tivoli Garden, converted into a circus bearing the name of "The Pavilion Circus;" and indifferently acted at the Washington Museum at No. 48 Market Street and later at the Pennsylvania Museum above Eighth on Market.

On August 7, 1826, Cowell began his autumn season at Simpson's circus, Walnut Street, bringing it to a close on December 2, just two days prior to the opening of the Chesnut, which was now under the sole management of Warren.

Following a losing season in Washington extending from August 31 to October 6, the Chesnut Street company had returned, without having opened the Baltimore theatre, for the Philadelphia season of 1826–27, which was to run from December 4 to May 20. At Warren's invitation Cowell left the employ of Simpson to accept the duties of stage manager in place of Wood. The company, in Durang's opinion "not up to its former strength in talent," consisted of Wood, the former manager, and his wife, of Warren, Jefferson, Cowell, Wemyss, William Forrest, Heyl, John Jefferson, C. Porter, Wheatley, Darley, Webb, Hathwell, John Hallam (who accompanied Cowell from the circus), J. Greene, Bignall, Hosack, Garner, Tayleure, Howard, Meer, Jones, Klett, Parker, Singleton; and Mesdames Jefferson, Joseph Jefferson (formerly Mrs. Burke),

[63] Forrest's début had been on November 27, 1820; Kean's, January 8, 1821.

Anderson, Francis, Cowell, Greene, Darley, Meer, Murray, the Misses Hathwell and Miss Parker.

Wood felt that the company, "viewed as a body, certainly presented the means of steady, if not of vast attraction;" and the stars whom Warren engaged to play during the season make an impressive list. There were the sprightly Miss Kelly who, in her comedy rôles, pleased her public with such interpolated songs as *Even as the Sun* and *Stay, Little Foolish Fluttering Thing*; and Cooper, Booth, Edwin Forrest and Henry Wallack. There were also Macready, the well-known tragedian from Drury Lane, who appeared as Macbeth, Hamlet, Virginius, William Tell, Damon, Pierre, Coriolanus and Petruchio; and Mrs. Knight of Drury Lane, "the archness and vivacity" of whose "acting," writes Wemyss, "greatly enhanc[ed] the pleasure derived from the sweet tones she warbled forth in her ballads" and, in the rôle of Kate O'Brian in Perfection, actually caused the pit to rise in acclamation, at the fall of the curtain, and demand "a repetition, a compliment so very unusual in those days, when the habit of calling for every actor at the close of an engagement was not in vogue, that it was appreciated as no mean honor."[64]

During her engagement, Mrs. Knight played Floretta in *The Cabinet*, Diana Vernon in *Rob Roy Macgregor*, Lucy Bertram, Rosina, Margaretta in *No Song No Supper*, Virginia in *Paul and Virginia*, Mary Copp in *Charles the Second*, Louisson in *Henri Quatre* and Fanny in *Maid and Wife*.

With such stars at his disposal, Warren was able to present, for the first time in the city, *The Comedy of Errors* (with the music); the comedies of *The Foundling, Teasing Made Easy* and *Old and Young*; the farces of *A Year in an Hour* and *Husbands and Wives*; the tragedy of *Sylla* and the "Hibernian melodrama" of *Brian Boroihme*.

"The season certainly appeared quite successful," comments Wood, "although, undoubtedly, it was grossly exaggerated from time to time. The receipts were, in some instances, large, but there were many very bad nights; and, admitting that our former terms with stars were still maintained, the receipts of their nights could have done little more than repay the losses on the failing ones."[65]

Nothing could have been more human, under the circumstances, than Wood's pessimism; but the fact is that Warren must have felt a few misgivings of his own. The "amateur management" was throttling him.

[64] See Wemyss' *Life*, I, Chapter XIII.
[65] *Recollections*, p. 343.

[51]

At the beginning of the season it had foisted on Warren the unpopular policy of reserving six boxes for "one hour on each day after the box-book opens, for those who [might] desire to take a whole box." Later, it had balked his plan to have his daughter Hetty follow up the success she had achieved on the occasion of her début.

The circumstances must have been galling to Warren; but, after the season ended on May 12, it was less the interference of the stockholders that seemed his greatest irritation, as he wrote the "retrospect" of the season, than the defection of Cowell, his stage manager, who had deserted him to go back to Simpson.

The season "began under favorable auspices [and] was generally productive," runs Warren's *Diary*. "I engaged Mr. Cowell as my acting manager; he promised much but I too late discovered that, in league with Simpson, to whom I never did any wrong, he was secretly acting against me. While receiving a salary he engag'd some of the performers of my theatre—to wit, Mestayer and Family, Porter, Singleton. The departures of these I regret not, except Green and wife. She [is] eminently useful and he valuable for low Irishmen—not good for much else . . . A blackguard without any gratitude; but let them go—my debts I have considerably diminished—some remain yet I hope another season will set me free."

In Baltimore, during the Spring season, the post vacated by Cowell was offered to Wemyss, who accepted it along with a commission to go to England in search of players. Wemyss was to be one of four agents who, in the year 1827, produced what Durang calls a mania in the minds of the English actors to immigrate to America. The others were John Hallam, representing Cowell and Simpson, who preceded Wemyss to London; Dr. Hart, representing Charles Gilfert, who had just built the first Bowery Theatre; and an emissary for the Boston managers.

Wemyss, sailing on June 20, 1827, carried out Warren's instructions in a characteristically capable manner. On the eve of departure he received supplementary instructions[66] from Richard Peters, Jr., one of the Board of Regents of the Chesnut but, interpreting them tactfully, he engaged for the season of 1827–28 such valuable players as the Slomans, S. Chapman (who was to become a manager) Southwell, Mercer, Rowbotham (also to become a manager) and Miss Emery, a singer as well-

[66] See Wemyss' *Life*, I, pp. 123–127, for documentary proof of Wood's contentions. It is contained in Warren's and Peters' letters, which are printed in full. Warren's instructions are as definite as Peters' are vague.

known and admired as Mrs. Austin, Willis whose knowledge of music and ability as a violinist were invaluable in the production of melodramas, Lewis (almost a genius as a stage mechanic), J. T. Norton (popular trumpeter of "the King's theatre, Italian opera house"), together with some useful dancers.

During Wemyss' absence there had been a summer season at the Chesnut lasting twelve nights. The Chesnut opened on June 30 and closed on July 26, 1827, offering a novelty in an engagement with Monsieur Achille and Mesdames Achille and Hutin, French dancers, and the new American play of *The Indian Prophecy*, by Custis, as a feature of the program of July 4.

At the same time, the Walnut had been in the midst of a season running from May 28 to July 25. Cowell, now a partner of Simpson, was using his regular circus troupe and stage performers while awaiting the return of Hallam. In Durang's opinion, "Messrs. Cowell & Simpson . . . understood well the nature of their Philadelphia operations. It was easy to employ the circus corps in circuits around our large country, and to gradually convert the Walnut into a regular dramatic house, where Simpson & Co. could profitably employ their European novelties and stars, to the exclusion of the Chesnut Street Theatre."

Before the end of the season Hallam returned with his recruits; and so, perceiving the advantage he had over Warren, as well as the fact that his "ring performances had decreased in public attractiveness," Cowell, detaching "the equestrian troupe from his dramatic corps . . . sent them on a traveling tour" and closed the Walnut to make alterations.

He converted "the ring into a spacious pit," *Durang* records, "and otherwise altered . . . opened the Walnut street house under the name of the 'Philadelphia Theatre,' on the 29th of August, 1827." During the season, which extended to November 3, Hamblin, Booth and Cooper appeared as stars.

Meanwhile, the Chesnut had opened on September 28 for a short season lasting until October 16. It was occupied by a French company from New Orleans to whom Warren, rather than have it "lying fallow," had leased it for performances of such operas as *Le Petit Chaperon Rouge* (*Little Red Riding Hood*) and *La Pie Voleuse* (*The Magpie and the Maid*).

Warren was criticised for this move, for "the éclat which attended the French company's most excellent representations," writes Durang, "certainly had a dampening effect upon the opening novelties" of the season of 1827–28, which began on October 29. Warren probably wished

[53]

to recoup himself, to whatever extent he could, for an expenditure, for "auxiliary aid," of "between five and six thousand dollars."[67]

It can be imagined with what anxiety Warren began a season upon which he had spent so much in advance. He must have doubted the wisdom as heartily as he objected to the ethics of discharging a "considerable number of [the] regular performers . . . not from any suggestion of either incompetency or decline, nor from any want of good conduct anywhere, but from the enormous expense which it was said the promised succession of new English performers had involved."[68]

By this time, however, Warren was at the mercy of the "amateur management," whose fantastic schemes, as Wood's record brings out, were to lead to a season of two hundred and two acting nights averaging only $295.

Artistically, as Wemyss asserts, the season was a success. Wood's successor "produced the dramatic spectacle of *Peter Wilkins, The Red Rover, Thirty Years of the Life of a Gambler*, and *The Gnome King*, four heavy scenery pieces in one season, dispatch," as Wemyss claims, "hitherto unknown in an American theatre; four new tragedies, two full operas, of three acts each; and one entirely original of one act; eighteen new farces; one musical comedy; one play (*The Usurper*) in five acts; and three domestic melodramas; in all, thirty-four new pieces, eleven revivals of pieces previously acted in Philadelphia, but almost forgotten."

To these achievements must be added an engagement, near the season's end, with Horn, Pearman and Mrs. Austin which the public had the bad grace to demand after the singers had been successful at the Park in English opera and in which Warren lost an additional $1000.

At the time, well acted comedies at the Walnut, which Cowell had opened on May 1, seemed more to the taste of the town. The Walnut closed before the month was over, but not before Warren had felt the competition of its prices of 50, 37½ and 25 cents.

The season at the Chesnut dragged on to a costly conclusion on June 21, 1828. As early as April 14, writes Durang, Wood had taken a farewell benefit at the Chesnut Street Theatre. The existence of a fragmentary record of a summer season in 1828 would seem to prove that he remained with the company longer than *Durang* records that he did; but Wood reveals in his autobiography that, at the very beginning of the season, he was "looking at the prospect about, around and before [him],

[67] See Wemyss' *Life*, I, Chapter XIV.
[68] *Recollections*, p. 347.

and expecting either that the theatre itself would sooner or later disappear from under [him] or that [he] might find it necessary to become disengaged from it, if it continued in name to exist."

Wood writes that he heard (just at what time he fails to state) of "a number of gentlemen [who], dissatisfied by what had already been done [at the Chesnut] and thinking that they saw a benefit to property about them, had entered upon the scheme of another theatre in Arch street."

"At this time," Wood continues, "every one supposed that the Walnut street house, never a good one for theatrical representations, was about to be demolished, and give way to private houses. The other project, therefore, went on. The stock was rapidly subscribed, and the edifice erected almost before Mr. Warren knew that it was certainly in progress. While debating on some other prospects, I received an invitation from the stockholders of the new building to become the lessee. I had great hesitation in accepting this offer. The whole new enterprise was in a measure irregular, although if, as every one supposed, the Walnut street house was about to be torn down, a new theatre would be requisite.

"It had, too, somewhat the aspect of a schism from the Chesnut street theatre, though it was so less, perhaps, than was believed.

"Under any circumstances, I well knew what it was to get a company of new performers into drill at short notice. Even good performers require to be familiar with one another before they can play easily and with proper correspondence. The growth of our old theatre had been, as a natural growth commonly is, gradual. It had therefore been sure. I knew as yet very imperfectly what company the Arch street theatre was likely to have; and I knew no more of the principal persons by whom the theatre was owned, and would of course in all great matters be controlled.

"Independent of this, I had, to great extent, built the Chesnut street theatre. It was a beautiful, convenient and excellent house. I had up to that time many pleasant associations with it, and I felt somewhat as if I was abandoning my own offspring.

"However, being quite unable to control the new course of operations there—certain that they would not only ultimately, but would very soon, end in failure—uncertain how long, even if I desired to remain, I could find it possible to do so—and not being doubtful that my retirement would be willingly received whenever offered, I accepted the offer so politely made me from Arch street.

"Mrs. Wood not long before had of necessity ended her connection with the Chesnut street managers, where her services, though always acceptable to the public, were neither rendered by her nor received by the direction as she could desire. I entered therefore upon my new management from necessity, and with feelings of reluctance and great doubt as to the issue. Still, as we were credibly informed that arrangements were in progress for pulling down the Walnut street house—a matter really resolved upon, though afterwards defeated or abandoned— and as it was certain that the Chesnut street theatre, under its new direction, was not likely to prove a formidable rival to us, the prospect was not entirely dark.

"We had had very numerous applications for engagements, and the prominent situations were filled by persons of good natural capacities. The important line of business formerly done by Warren was entrusted to an actor named Reese, of much ability. S. Chapman, who had quitted Warren from some dissatisfaction about salary, was appointed stage manager and director of the pantomimic and melo-dramatic departments, an office for which he had real ability. An inexperienced judge, however sagacious, would have said that we had in all respects a good theatrical community."[69]

In his version of what happened, Wood seems modestly inclined to undervalue his own prestige, which, in the meantime, had frightened Cowell into giving up the Walnut Street Theatre and Wemyss into refusing a partnership with Warren.

The Walnut, however, was rebuilt;[70] and Wood opened the Arch Street Theatre, on October 1, 1828, attractive and well equipped though it was,[71] with little anticipation of success. His detailed record of the

[69] *Recollections*, Chapter XVIII.

[70] See *Durang*, II, Chapter Forty-Five.

[71] In the United States Gazette of June 10, 1828, appears this article: "The following description of [the Arch Street Theatre] has been received, and may prove interesting to the lovers of the drama, and friends to the improvements of our city. Mr. Strickland, the architect, has contracted to complete it by the first of October, but from the great advancement of the building, and the number of persons employed, it is highly probable that it will be completed some time sooner, and opened by Mr. Wood, the manager, with a very powerful establishment.

"The dimensions of the Theatre now building in Arch street are 70 feet by 155 feet— The front, which is to be of marble, will consist of a Colonade between two wings formed by coupled columns 16 feet in height and 2 feet in diameter, supporting an Entablature and Balustrade of the Roman Doric Order.

"The entrances of the Vestibule and Lobbies of the Boxes are by a flight of marble steps 42 feet in length rising to the platform of the Colonade. Those to the Pit will

season's receipts revealed that he had the support of the public; but his autobiography and the account of Durang and Wemyss agree that his efforts, guided though they were by experience, were doomed to failure.

Wood's company all pulled "different ways." "Each desired to be the feature; and the course of stage business," Wood asserts, "instead of working smoothly, in correspondence and with ease, was irregular, disturbed and uncomfortable. Many of the performers . . . had come from minor establishments, where the absence of system and discipline had bred habits of neglect and insubordination, which were so fixed as to render vain any hope of reformation."

Wood had to fall back on the star system, "a miserable resort," as he calls it.

He secured expensive engagements with the dancers, Mlle. Celeste and her sister Constance, Holland, Lydia Kelly, Horn and Mrs. Austin (the singers,) Miss Rock and James Wallack, to whom "persons interested in the edifice and property," the ubiquitous amateur advisers, practi-

---

be through the wings. The Box Treasurer's offices will be contained in the wings; and the stair ways to the upper Lobbies will commence at each end of the vestibule.

"The ground plan of the Boxes will be in the form of a horse shoe 40 feet across its shortest diameter at the stage Box; rising in three tiers or rows, and containing three ranges of seats in each tier on the sides, and five in the circular front. These boxes will be bounded by a strong brick wall separating them from the lobbies which will be carried up through each tier to support and strengthen the roof of the building:—

"The supports of the boxes will consist of Cast Iron Columns fashioned in imitation of the Thyrsus of Bacchus—They will recede upwards of 4 feet from the front of the Boxes, and be founded on a strong stone wall forming the back of the Pit.—The first row or tier of Boxes will decline 2 feet from the circular front towards the stage:—and the Pit will extend under the first row of Boxes in the form of an alcove, and will command a fine view of the stage at all points. This part of the house will contain between 5[00] and 600 persons, and will be approached by two wide entrances paved with brick, leading directly from Arch Street.—The coffee room will be over the vestibule in front, and on a level with the second lobby floor.

"The stage will extend back to the depth of 155 feet from Arch street, where it will be increased in width 30 feet upon a ten feet wide alley, communicating with Sixth St.; this space will be occupied with a Scene room, dressing rooms, and carpenters' shop.— The entrances to the stage and gallery will be immediately from the above mentioned alley and sixth street.—The foundation walls will be of the most substantial stone work, and the superstructure of the best brick work 22 inches in thickness.—The side walls of the whole building will be carried up at this thickness to the square of the roof, where a Parapet wall will be raised, and coped with stone 2 feet above the Eaves.

"The building will contain, including the Pit, Boxes and Gallery, about 2000 persons."

[57]

cally forced him to pay the ruinous rate of "$200, certain, per night, what-
ever might be the receipts."[72]

It was a losing fight; and, "after trying the reduction of the prices of
admission," Wemyss writes, "in the middle of Mr. Wallack's engagement, the [Arch Street] theatre closed, [on December 22,] never to be
opened again under Mr. Wood's management, whose reign, in his new
theatre, had been a short and not a very merry one."[73]

A short after-season occurred when it reopened under the auspices of
Roberts, Willis and others, but a season to last only until December 29,
when the Arch was completely vanquished.

The competition of the Chesnut, with the prestige of "Old Drury" and
the strategy of Wemyss, had proved too vigorous. Warren, at the beginning of Wood's season, had used the effective ruse of renting the Chesnut, against the time when he should open it, to Davis' French Company,
which had enjoyed a prosperous season running from September 16 to
October 18 and an after-season beginning on October 28 and ending on
November 5.

Warren, following the opening of the Chesnut Street season, on November 13, 1828, had matched the Arch Street stars with Cooper, the
Slomans, Mrs. Knight, Herr Cline (the tight rope performer, who, appearing for the first time, had been "much admired") Clara Fisher and
the singers, Hunt and Miss Phillips.

In addition, he had presented, for the first time, *The Noyades*, the
musical farce of *The Invincibles* (with the part of Victoire, the Little
Corporal, fetchingly played by Mrs. Knight), *Cramond Brig* and the
domestic tragedy of *The Lear of Private Life*.

Defeating Wood, however, was of little satisfaction to Warren, for,
as *Durang* records, "the houses were not good, notwithstanding the almost nightly appearance of from four to five stars, in tragedy, comedy,
opera, farce." The sixty-one-year-old manager was eager to retire.
Even with Wood out of the way, there would be competition from the
Walnut Street Theatre, which was to open on January 4, 1829, under
the management of Inslee & Blake.

Wemyss writes that "Blake was unremitting in his exertions to
procure a good company for [his] opening . . . which the closing of the
Arch Street rendered an easier task than he had any right to expect."

Warren offered to sell out to Wemyss; and the stage manager induced

[72] *Recollections*, p. 351.
[73] Wemyss' *Life*, I, p. 162.

[58]

Lewis T. Pratt to join him in the speculation. They were to give Warren two thousand dollars, cash down, and to pay the rent of the Chesnut Street Theatre, allowing Warren "three thousand a year for the use of his theatrical property, including the rent of the Baltimore and Washington theatres." In addition, they were to pay him $40 a week for his services as an actor during "the continuation of the lease."[74]

Warren took his farewell benefit on December 30, playing the rôle of Falstaff in *The Merry Wives of Windsor*, which was ironically followed by the "grand romantic drama" of *Illusion*.

Under Pratt & Wemyss, the Chesnut struggled through a season ending on May 27, 1829.

"The drama," in the words of Wood, "was at sixes and sevens." As he asserts, in writing of this period, "Any history of the theatre, that is to say, any history of a continuous and regular management now comes to an end. . . . There had been a complete debacle, or breaking up of everything that had been . . . Permanence belonged now to nothing except failure, disorder and bankruptcy. The vitality of the theatre neither was nor can be destroyed, but its action was irregular, spasmodic and disordered."[75]

The conditions described by Wood were to last from the beginning of 1829 until May of 1831, when the new firm of Maywood & Co. assumed control of the Walnut Street Theatre. The interval was definitely a period of transition in the affairs of the Philadelphia stage. It was a period during which most of Wood's forebodings were realized.

Three theatres entered into a struggle in which the prices of admission were dangerously cut, stars were paid flat rates or a percentage of gross rather than net receipts and the courtesy and dignity of the old days were forgotten in attempts to forestall a rival's amusements. Managers, unable to stand the pace, went bankrupt one after another.

Pratt & Wemyss were the first to show signs of succumbing. Driven from Philadelphia by the enterprize of Inslee & Blake at the Walnut, they braved the hardships of a January snowstorm in a flight to Baltimore, where weather conditions perversely continued to hamper their efforts.

Before long, Inslee & Blake themselves encountered difficulties and, on April 14, 1829, failed at the Walnut.

Pratt & Wemyss re-opened the Chesnut, from April 9 to May 27; and then dissolved.

[74] See Wemyss' *Life*, Volume I, p. 164.
[75] *Recollections*, p. 353.

"The failure . . . was poor Warren's finishing stroke," as Durang asserts. "The terms of the lease of the Chesnut Street Theatre not having been fulfilled, the original and sub-lease made by Warren to Pratt & Wemyss, became null and void; the stockholders, [including the amateur management], re-entered and took possession of the theatre; and the whole of Mr. Warren's valuable theatrical property was sacrificed at 'one fell swoop,' under the Sheriff's hammer."

Pratt took charge of the Chesnut, after the failure of Pratt & Wemyss, only to go bankrupt after a season running from October 26, 1829 to March 20, 1830. Aaron J. Phillips suffered the same fate at the Arch after two seasons extending from April 15 to May 20, 1829 and August 31, 1829 to March 29, 1830.

S. Chapman & John Greene, at the Walnut, were at first successful, during the summer of 1829, when "they had their choice," as *Durang* reveals, "out of the débris of three companies." Their summer season, which ran from May 27 to July 29, was followed by a season, which, beginning on September 7, 1829 with Edmonds a member of the firm, ended disastrously on January 18, 1830. S. and W. Chapman now took over the Walnut for a fairly prosperous season extending from February 20 to August 4, 1830; but, after the sudden death of S. Chapman, the most talented of the family, on May 16, the theatre was destined to pass, after another season running from August 28 to December 18, 1830, into more capable hands.

Archer, Maywood & Walton took charge of the Arch for a single season, which started on August 30, 1830 and finished on May 3, 1831; and Lamb & Coyle, of whose absurd activities Wood has left a detailed and pathetic record, were the last of a list of eight managerial firms that succumbed, during this transition period of two and a half years, to the exorbitant demands of stars, over-competition and to what at times amounted to public indifference.

Demoralization of the managers was naturally accompanied by demoralization of the players. "It may . . . be imagined," writes Durang, "how [they] flew from one theatre to another in pursuit of employment. As one house shut, or failed to pay, away they ran in groups, to any person who had succeeded in newly leasing an abandoned theatre." The stock companies rapidly disintegrated.

The law of compensation, however, was at work. Now that the theatres were in trouble, the managers were more open-minded in the matter of experiments. On May 5, 1829, *Il Trionfo della Musica*, the

first "bona fide" Italian opera, as Durang calls it, to be acted in Philadelphia, was given at the Chesnut. New players were given a chance.
James E. Murdoch made the most of the opportunity; and, with a successful début at the Arch, on October 13, added his strength to a group
of actors and actresses who were soon to dispel the prejudice against
native talent.

By the end of 1830, in fact, that prejudice had vanished to such a
degree that Edwin Forrest was accounted a better actor than Charles,
the son of Edmund Kean, who made his first appearance at the Arch on
September 30.

Meanwhile, American drama had been coming into its own. During
the year 1829, there were produced, for the first time in Philadelphia,
The Disowned, The Sentinels and *William Penn* (all by Richard Penn
Smith) and *Rip Van Winkle* (by Kerr); and, during the year 1830,
Metamora (by Stone), *The Deformed, The Triumph at Plattsburg* and *The
Water Witch* (all by Smith), *Down East; or, The Militia Training* (attrib-
uted to Hackett), Kerr's *Gasperoni* and *Pocahontas* (by Custis). In the
first half of 1831, there were produced, for the first time in the city,
the anonymous *Miantonimoh* and George Pepper's *The Red Branch
Knight*.[76]

With the end of the period on May 7, 1831, when Maywood & Co.,
"the only management," as *Durang* points out, "assuming anything
like stability since the days of Warren & Wood," took charge of the Walnut, it seems logical that the firm of Jones, Duffy & Forrest should have
come into existence. The three "Williams," who opened the Arch on
August 29, 1831, were to win the distinction of being called by Durang
"the first legitimate American management in the large Atlantic cities."

Wood has left no record of Maywood & Co.'s first season at the Walnut extending from May 9 to July 30, 1831. Engaged by them on
September 16, 1831, however, and remaining in their employ throughout
the period of their competititon with Jones, Duffy & Forrest, he has
supplemented his account of the activities of his own firm with a very
interesting one of the activities of those of Maywood & Co. at a time
when "Old Drury" seemed about to regain its lost prestige.

[76] According to the valuable list of American plays in A. H. Quinn's *A History of the
American Drama, From the Beginning to the Civil War*, the plays in the above list that
were given for the first time on any stage include the following: *The Sentinels, William
Penn, The Deformed, The Triumph at Plattsburg, The Water Witch, Gasperoni* and
Pocahontas.

Wood was thirteen years younger than Warren and still able to make new conquests in rôles such as Jeremiah Bumps in *Turning the Tables*, produced at the Chesnut on November 5, 1831, or Mercutio, in support of the Kembles on October 14, 1832; or even to pass muster as a fifty-three-year-old Romeo opposite the radiant Fanny Kemble, on November 3 of the same year, in order that her father might electrify the town as Mercutio.

With Warren, of course, it was lamentably different. His strength was sufficient only for such public appearances as required the delivery of an "address as Sir John Falstaff;"[77] and his last engagement, Wood discloses, was to $210, $86 and $90. His benefit came to only $206, or about $100 under expenses.

Opposite the November 25, 1831 entry in his *Account Book*, Wood writes succinctly of this occasion, "This night his [Warren's] memory failed him entirely," while Wemyss expands in pathetic detail: "In the beginning of the fifth act [of *The Poor Gentleman*, Warren] suddenly laid his hand upon my shoulder, and said, 'Frank, lead me off the stage, for I do not know what I am talking about.' He finished the part, committing blunder upon blunder, until it became evident to the audience, who kindly cheered the last moments of his public career with their long continued approbation. He never acted again—and thus closed the theatrical life of William Warren, one of the greatest favorites, both as a man and an actor, the Philadelphia stage ever possessed."

"In these unforseen misfortunes," writes Durang, "divested of home and old friends," Warren "sought an asylum in Baltimore, and became the proprietor of a small inn, where he might have exclaimed, in the lines of Jack Falstaff, which he was wont to give so inimitably, 'Shall I not take mine ease in mine inn?' "[78]

There was little ease for Maywood & Co. and Jones, Duffy & Forrest, who had begun a spirited competition. Following the failure of Lamb & Coyle, the Walnut Street managers had taken over the Chesnut. They opened the Walnut for a season which began on August 27 and ended on October 15, 1831; and then Maywood & Co., opening the Chesnut for a

---

[77] Wemyss' Life, Volume I, p. 197, states that the last time Warren's name was announced was "at the Arch Street Theatre, on the 8th of December, [1831,] when he intended to take leave of the audience in an address, in the character of Falstaff. [However,] he was too ill to appear."

[78] Durang adds, I, LXVII: "In the old arm-chair, where he daily courted sleep and oblivion of worldly sorrow, he was found dead on the 19th of October, 1832, his head resting on a pillow before him."

season to run to December 9, announced, according to Wemyss, "the old standard" of prices, which they justified, asserts Durang, on the ground of having secured an engagement, "at very great expense," with the "great vocalist, Mr. Sinclair, of Drury Lane and Covent Garden."

Unfortunately for the Walnut, Sinclair, whom Wemyss calls the "wreck of his former self," failed to please. On the same evening, too, Edwin Forrest appeared at the Arch in his popular rôle of Metamora. The Sinclair engagement was doomed when, on October 24, Forrest brought "the pit—indeed, the entire male portion of the audience . . . to their feet" to give "at least nine cheers"[79] at the second act curtain of Robert Mongomery Bird's *The Gladiator*, produced in Philadelphia for the first time.

By 1831 the appeal of an American actor in American plays was more than sufficient to offset the appeal of a Sinclair or a Charles Kean. The managers of the Arch reveled in the name of "The American Theatre" given to it by "Colley Cibber," a noted critic. It was an asset to them and they felt, with "Colley Cibber," that they had earned a right to the title, "as most of [their] performers [were] Americans, and all the American plays [were] there first played that else would not see the light."[80]

In the company were W. Forrest, Murdoch and J. R. Scott, all natives of Philadelphia, the last an able foil to the American star, Edwin Forrest, who, with "the Delaware frozen over" and snowdrifts block-[ing] all the avenues in and out of the city,"[81] attracted crowds to his brother's theatre while Maywood & Co. were playing to receipts of $35, $54 and $75.

Maywood & Co. were floundering. After offering a prize of "$300 for the best American play (viz: a comedy), which shall have for its object the exhibition of the whole talent of a stock company," and, with the idea "that some Yankee feeling might subserve their views,"[82] after presenting Hackett in *The Lion of the West* and Kean in the American tragedy of *Waldimar*, the managers of the Chesnut turned to the English opera of *Cinderella*, which had been popular at the Park, only to resign the lion's share of the $940 realized from it, on November 28, to the singers, J. Jones and Mrs. Austin.

[79] *Durang*, III, Chapter Sixteenth.
[80] *Durang*, III, Chapter Sixteenth.
[81] *Durang*, III, Chapter Seventeenth.
[82] *Durang*, III, Chapter Twentieth.

[63]

Their next move was to engage Hamblin of the Bowery Theatre, who brought with him Miss Clifton, a native of Philadelphia, and George Jones to act in *Venice Preserved*, but to less than a third of expenses. Defeated in their first skirmish with "the three Williams," Maywood & Co. fled to the Walnut, which they opened on the next day, December 10, at the reduced rates of 50, 25 and 18¾ cents. Durang records their announcement that "they would play on alternate nights at either house, thus affording all classes an opportunity of enjoying themselves and consulting their finances, etc. This was an excellent managerial dodge," in his opinion, "to reopen a half-price theatre."

Jones, Duffy & Forrest, however, continued their successful opposition to the end of the Arch Street season on June 18, 1832. Dixon, the American "buffo singer," whom they engaged, and "Yankee" Hill, a member of the company, attracted greater receipts than Barrimore "of Drury Lane and the Park," whom Maywood & Co. secured "as stage director and arranger of melodramas, pantomimes, etc."

Luck played a part in the victory of the Arch. Wallace's version of Cooper's *Water Witch* was better liked than Taylor's, the Bowery version produced under Hamblin's direction at the Walnut; *Conrad, King of Naples*, written for Murdoch by Judge Conrad of Philadelphia, was a success; and a stroke of luck put into Duffy's hands *The Hunchback* by Knowles, currently popular in London.[83]

[83] "A simple history," states *Durang*, III, Chapter Nineteenth, "belongs to the introduction of the play of 'The Hunchback' in this country, which, as a dramatic record, we beg to give in our present sketches. Captain McMichael, (brother to Morton McMichael, Esq.), commanding a London trader out of the port of Philadelphia, (or Liverpool, we now do not remember,) was in London when this play was first produced and published. On the eve of returning home, he thought (as Miss Fanny Kemble had produced quite a sensation in Julia, and the play was a topic of conversation) he would purchase a copy for his brother, who at that period reviewed such matters as a critic, and took an interest in theatricals. On his arrival here he gave it to him. Mr. McMichael discerned the merits of the piece, and being a friend of Francis C. Wemyss, presented the play to him to be used for his benefit. The Arch Street Theatre was about closing for the season in June, and the benefit of Mr. Duffy being announced, he was at a loss for some novelty to attract an audience, everything like attraction being exhausted. Wemyss had a benefit also to come off. He offered "The Hunchback" to Duffy if he thought proper to take it. The only difficulty that offered itself was the time required to study it in, it being Friday, June 8, and on Monday the benefit. Duffy accepted it. The play on the Saturday was read in the green room. It was then taken apart, and four or five copyists put to work upon it. By 10 o'clock Saturday night the parts were all given out to the performers engaged in it, who had only that night and Sunday to study them in, for Monday night, June 11."

Maywood & Co., moving opportunely from Chesnut to Walnut, finally brought down the curtain on an unprofitable season of two hundred and seventy-eight nights, during the close of which the engagement of Thomas Rice, progenitor of "the Ethiopian opera," seems the only event that occasioned any public enthusiasm.

During the latter half of 1832 cholera kept the theatres closed until September 5 when the Arch began its season of 1832–33. The Chesnut opened on September 8, 1832.

During this season the policy of Jones, Duffy & Forrest was substantially the same as it had previously been. The Arch produced the new American plays of *Oralloossa, Giordano, Camillus* and *The Ancient Britain,* using Forrest as its "ace of trumps" to meet the competition of Maywood & Co.

That competition became spirited when, on October 10, the Kembles began an engagement at the Chesnut. On that night *Oralloossa* attracted receipts of $960, about the same amount as Kemble attracted at the Chesnut; but the *Account Book* reveals that the success of the English stars must have been a threat to the continued prosperity of the Arch.

On January 5, 1833, Maywood & Co., resigning the Chesnut to an Italian opera company, moved to the Walnut, where the Ravels (a family of remarkable gymnasts) continued to please and the Kembles to attract large receipts.

Both the Walnut and Arch, however, seem to have suffered from the competition of the Italian opera company, whose season ran from January 23 to March 16; and, with the average for one hundred and eight nights standing at $270, Maywood & Co. could hardly consider that they had won more than a doubtful decision.

The Walnut and the Arch closed on the same day, May 11.

On May 13 Maywood & Co. opened the Chesnut for a spring season lasting to June 28, 1833; and, on June 29, the same day as Jones, Duffy & Forrest opened the Arch, their rivals began a summer season at the Walnut ending July 27, twelve days after the close of the Arch's summer season.

Duffy & Forrest, without the aid of Jones, who had apparently left the management to resume a position as stock actor, began what was to be their last season on August 28, 1833. The Walnut, opening on August 31, presented in Tyrone Power the first of a series of English stars to whom Duffy & Forrest had only the latter's brother Edwin to offer as a counter attraction.

[65]

Nevertheless, their policy was vigorous.

On September 10 they anticipated Maywood & Co. in the successful production of *Mazeppa*. They closed the season on February 4 but, resuming on February 22, produced a new native drama called *Yorktown; or, The Surrender of Cornwallis*

Meanwhile, at the Chesnut, to which Maywood & Co. had moved on September 23 after closing the Walnut on September 21, Power, Mrs. and Mrs. Joseph Wood and the Kembles were playing to large receipts.

Competition between the Chesnut and the Arch was at fever heat when, on March 3, 1834, William Forrest died; and Duffy, who had neither the ability nor the tact of the tragedian's brother, must have felt himself incompetent to fight Maywood & Co. singlehanded.

The Arch closed about April 5, reopening for a summer season, which ran from June 2 to June 18 and during which it offered Bird's new American play of *The Broker of Bogota;* but it was a foregone conclusion that Maywood & Co. would now secure the lease of the theatre.

The *Account Book* records that, after a season at the Chesnut, which began on April 7 and ended on July 19, 1834, Maywood & Co. moved to the Arch for a season which began on August 23 and ended on October 11. With prices restored to $1, 50 and 25 cents, now that they had a monopoly, Maywood & Co. began at the Chesnut the last season of which Wood has kept a record.

A theatrical epoch was now drawing speedily to a close.

Securing the lease of the Walnut, Wemyss rechristened it "The American Theatre" and attacked the Chesnut as McKenzie and Cowell had done before him; but his activities are only a connecting link between the span of 1800 to 1835 and the period that follows.

From 1800 to 1826 the Chesnut had enjoyed the reputation of possessing the ablest troupe in the country and Philadelphia was universally reputed to be America's greatest theatrical center. Then came the dissolution, in 1826, of Warren & Wood, whose influence extended to the end of 1828; and the chaos of 1829, 1830 and 1831 that contributed to the ascendency of the Park.[84]

Before 1831 New York had become a theatrical center of greater importance than Philadelphia. "The town" that, in 1832, impressed Fanny Kemble as "perfect silence and solitude, compared with New York" had suffered from the disadvantage of having an inferior port

[84] See A. H. Quinn's *A History of the American Drama, From the Beginning to the Civil War*, pp. 201–203.

[66]

and fewer possibilities for expansion. It may have pleased the fastidious English actress with "its greater air of age;"[85] but neither Maywood nor Wemyss could secure the necessary stars as easily as the New York managers could, while Philadelphia, at the same time, lacked the large floating population of New York, whose patronage was lucrative to both Simpson of the Park and Hamblin of the Bowery.

Wood's last record is of the season at "Old Drury" that ran from October 13, 1834 to February 21, 1835. As he asserts, he now "retired from anything like management."[86] It is evident that he kept no record of theatrical performances beyond the last entry in the *Account Book*, for what he writes in his autobiography of the years following 1835 seems to be based on newspaper accounts, hearsay evidence or conjectures, as far as receipts and expenditures go.

Except for Cooper, he was the only one of "the old guard" who still trod the boards. Cooke, Mrs. Lefolle, Thomas Burke, Francis, Mrs. Young, John Jefferson, Joseph Jefferson, Edmund Kean, Duff, Warren: all had died. Mathews was to die before the end of the year.

Cooper, now verging on sixty, was following "professional circuits" that were to become "more provincial." *Durang* asserts that, after "the appearance of Kean in this country, Mr. Cooper's fame and popularity obviously declined. The arrival of numerous stars from London, in

[85] *Journal* of Frances Anne Kemble Butler, 1835; Volume 1, p. 139. Fanny Kemble's two volumes are a treasure-house for the novelist in search of "color," with their references to the "one-arched bridge at Fair Mount" looking "like a scarf, rounded by the wind, flung over the river;" to the evening parties with their inevitable "stewed oysters and terrapins;" and to the Park Theatre, with its stage "so dark" that "we," writes Miss Kemble, "are obliged to rehearse by candlelight" and with its "gold carving and red silk," which gave it a "rich and warm" appearance—albeit the mosquitoes infesting its stage "made dreadful havoc" with Miss Kemble's arms. Of course, it is Miss Kemble's impressions of the theatre that are the most valuable; and her impressions of the Park are particularly interesting because, although she is herself a star, she agrees with Wood that a theatre depends, for its ultimate success, upon the efforts of a good stock company. "It is fortunate for the managers of the Park Theatre," she asserts, "and very unfortunate for the citizens of New York, that the audiences who frequent that place of entertainment, are chiefly composed of the strangers who are constantly passing in vast numbers through this city. It is not worth the while of the management to pay a good company, when an indifferent one answers their purpose quite as well; the system upon which theatrical speculations are conducted in this country is having one or two 'stars' for the principal characters, and nine or ten sticks for the rest. The consequence is, that a play is never decently acted; and, at such times as stars are scarce, the houses are very deservedly empty."
[86] *Recollections*, p. 428.

every department of the drama, injured his prospects. The introduction of the opera, English and Italian—which, being almost a new species of amusement to our public, and of a fascinating character, absorbed the patronage of the fashionable world—depressed the legitimate acting drama. Shortly afterward the rising reputation of Edwin Forrest and other young actors bursting upon public admiration, Cooper gradually sunk behind the theatrical horizon, until his once brilliant rays were no longer visible. . . . The generations who gloated with admiration upon his beauty of person, and were charmed with his acting, had grown old with himself, and had ceased to visit theatres.' [87]

The Chesnut still stood; but its strength, like the strength of every great human institution, had lain in something less palpable than brick and mortar. The building known as "the second Old Drury" had risen almost literally, after the fire of 1820, upon the foundations of the first. Without Warren & Wood, however, it was a body without a soul.

Just as Philadelphia had ceased to be the theatrical center of America, "Old Drury" had ceased to be the theatrical center of Philadelphia. The epoch upon which Warren and Wood had left the stamp of their personalities had definitely passed and there had begun a new epoch in the history of the Philadelphia stage.

[87] I, LXIII.

THE DIARY OR DAILY ACCOUNT BOOK OF WILLIAM BURKE WOOD

WASHINGTON SEASON[, COMMENCING JUNE 18, ENDING AUGUST 27,] 1810

[Warren]

PREFACE—**July 4**: After *The Blind Boy*, an entertainment, *Columbia's Independence*, consisting of singing, dancing and recitations. NI **July 23**: NI announces the benefit of Mrs. and Master Barrett. In this entry Wood has written the word "dism[isse]d," which explains the omission of receipts. **August 2**: *The Sailor's Landlady*, a pantomimical dance composed by Mr. Francis. NI **August 21**: NI announces Paine as Tancred in *Tancred and Sigismunda*; but the *Account Book* is obviously accurate, as NI later announces the first performance of the play for August 27. "Hurry," part of a title in the entry of July 28, is illegible beyond the "H." It seems to be "Hurr." The players receiving a benefit on July 30 are Mr. and Mrs. Joseph Jefferson, parents of Thomas, John and Joseph, Jr. The "proprietors" mentioned in the entry of August 2 are the owners of the building. For an explanation of the whereabouts of the company between August 4 and 21, see the Alexandria Season of 1810.

June 18 [The] Busy Body & [The] Irish[man] in London   149.25

     21 Abaellino & Killing no Murder*   104.25

     23 Ella Rosenberg* & [The] Shipwreck   133.50

     25 Tekeli* & [The] Highland Reel   146.25

     28 [The] Foundling of [the] forest* & Raising the Wind   226.25

     30 [The] Child of Nature, Syl[vester] Dag[gerwoo]d & Who Wins[?]*   110.50

July 2 [The] Foundling of [the] for- 170.50
est & Lovers['] Quarrels*

4 [The] Blind Boy,* Interlude & 480.50
Too Many Cooks.
[See preface to this season.]

7 George Barnwell & [The] 40 341.25
Thieves

9 [The] West Indian & [The] 127.75
Agreeable Surprize

12 [The] Deaf Lover* & Blue 151.
Beard

14 Tekeli & False & true 106.50

16 Ella Rosenberg & [The] Lady 84.25
of [the] Rock*

19 [The] Child of feeling* & [The] 232.75
Poor Soldier

21 [The] Spoil'd Child & Mother 137 50
Goose*

Barretts 23 Jane Shore & [The] Sea-Side
Story
[See preface to this seaon.]

[Benefit of] 26 [The] Wonder* & Bluebeard 86.75
Wilmots

Francis 28 [The] Wanderer, [The] Catch 92.25
Club, [The] Old Maid,
Harl[equin] H[urry
Scurry]

[Benefit of Mr. & Mrs.] Jefferson	30 [The] Africans & [The] Caravan*	[The] 193.
Aug[ust] Ben[efit of the] Prop[rietors]	2d. [The] Mountaineers, Inter-[lude] & [The] Weather-cock [See preface to this season.]	60.25
	4 Pizarro* & Don Juan	153.25
Mr. Payne	21 Douglas & Who Wins[?] [See preface to this season.]	191.50
"	22 Lovers['] Vows & [The] Purse [Master Payne as Frederick in *Lovers' Vows*. NI]	215.25
P[ayne's] Ben[efit]	27 Tancred & Sigismunda* [See preface to this season.]	398.

ALEXANDRIA SEASON, [COMMENCING AUGUST 6, ENDING SEPTEMBER 25,] 1810.

[Warren]

PREFACE—**August 18**: An interlude consisting of songs, catches and glees, called *The Catch Club*. ADG **September 4**: After *Tekeli* a comic Scotch dance, composed by Mr. Francis, called *Shelty's Frolic*. ADG **September 8**: Between the plays, *Harlequin Hurry Scurry*. ADG **September 13**: ADG also announces Blissett as Souffrance in *Dicky Gossip*, a sketch in one act taken from *My Grandmother*. **September 25**: "D[itt]o" refers to *The Wood Demon*. Wood has written under the titles of the plays, "Pos[t]p[one]d on acc[oun]t of the Conflagration." NI records that, in Alexandria, "every building was burnt in the square, lying on Union Street and extending from Duke to Prince Streets, bordering on the river." Charnock, who shared the benefit of September 15, was also the prompter. In *Durang*, I, XLIV, we are told he "was a very excellent one, and a gentlemanly man. He had been originally a very respectable ship master, both in England and America." The players receiving a benefit on September 18 were the elder Jeffersons.

[71]

August	6	[The] Africans & [The] Village Lawyer	115.
Payne	8	Hamlet & Too Many Cooks	260.75
"	11	Pizarro & Fortune's frolic	180.75
"	14	Romeo & Juliet & Lovers['] Quarrels	130.
	16	Lovers['] Vows & [The] Shipwreck	212.
P[ayne's] Ben[efi]t	18	[The] Mountaineers, Inter-[lude] & Killing No Murder* [As Octavian in *The Mountaineers*. ADG See preface to this season.]	335.
	23	Ella Rosenberg* & Who Wins [?]*	75.75
	25	[The] Foundling [of the] forest* [The] Purse	142.
	28	[The] Blind Boy* & [The] 40 Thieves	163.50
	30	[The] Found[ling] of [the] forest & Half [an] hour after Sup[pe]r*	89.
Sep[tembe]r	1	[The] Deaf Lover & Mother Goose*	105.25

[Benefit of]   4 Tekeli, Interl[ude] & Blue 131.
  Down[ie] & Briers   Beard
                    [Downie as Edmund, Briers
                    as Officer in *Tekeli* and
                    Hassan in *Blue Beard*.
                    ADG See preface to this
                    season.]

[Benefit of   6 Columbus & [The] Caravan* 130.25
  Mr. and Mrs.]
  Francis

[Benefit of   8 [She] Stoops to Conquer, 207.50
  Mrs. and Master]   Int[erlude] & [The] Hun-
  Barrett   ter of [the] Alps
                    [Mrs. Barrett as Helena de
                    Rosalvi, with Master
                    Barrett as Felix, in *The
                    Hunter of the Alps*. Mas-
                    ter Barrett also as Young
                    Marlow in *She Stoops to
                    Conquer*. ADG See pref-
                    ace to this season.]

              11 Lodoiska* and [The] 40 172.75
                 Thieves

[Benefit of]   13 Wild Oats & Raising [the] 157.
  Cone & Bliss[ett]   Wind
                    [Cone as Rover, Blissett as
                    Sim in *Wild Oats*. ADG
                    See preface to this
                    season.]

[Benefit of   15 [The] West Indian & Don 139.75
  Mr.] Charn[ock]   Juan
  & [Mrs.] Seymour   [Charnock as a sailor, Mrs.
                    Seymour as Violetta in
                    Don Juan. ADG]

Benefit of   18 [The] Road to Ruin & [The]   428.50
Mr. & Mrs.   Poor Soldier
Jeff[erson]

           20 George Barnwell & Mother   68.75
           Goose

           22 [The] Agreeable Surprize &   95.
           [The] Wood Demon*

           25 [The] Highland Reel & D[itt]o
           [See preface to this season.]

BALTIMORE [AUTUMN] SEASON, [COMMENCING OCTOBER 8, ENDING NOVEMBER 22,] 1810.

[Warren & Wood]

PREFACE: As stated in the Foreword, p. vii, there are two versions of the record of this season. The interpolations from the Volume II version include: November 9—"Ben Charleston," which replaces "Charles ben" of the Volume I version. November 19: "Mrs. Beaumont," which replaces "Beaum" of Volume I. The Fennell beginning an engagement on October 8 is the elder Fennell. The allusion to the Charleston fire in the editorial note of November 9 is explained by an entry of the same date in Warren's *Diary*. The entry reads, "200 Houses burn'd."

Fennel[l] October 8 Othello & [The] Village 694.75
                        Lawyer
                        [As Othello. FG]

"   10 [The[Distress'd Mother &   426.25
                 Cath[erine] & Petruchio
                 [Fennell as Orestes in *The*
                 Distress'd *Mother*. FG]

"   12 King Lear & Sylv[ester] Dag-   550.
                 gerwood
                 [Fennell as Lear. FG]

"   13 Jane Shore & Don Juan   270.   1941
            [Fennell as Lord Hastings ——
            in *Jane Shore*. FG]

"   15 [The] Revenge & Killing No   437.50
            Murder
            [Fennell as Zanga in *The
            Revenge*. FG]

"   17 Macbeth & [The] Review   574.
            [Fennell as Macbeth. FG]

"   19 Richard 3d. & Who's the   415.25
            Dupe?
            [Fennell as Richard. FG]

"   20 Hamlet & [The] Invisible Girl 341.50 1768.25
            [Fennell as Hamlet. FG]   ——

"   22 [The First Part of] Henry 4th 560.25
            & Love a la mode
            [Fennell as Hotspur.   FG]

"   Ben[efit] 24 [The]   Gamester & [The] 667.
            Hunter of the Alps
            [Fennell as Beverly in *The
            Gamester*. FG]

          26 [The] Foundling of [the] forest 426.25
            & [The] Weathercock

Dwyer   27 [The] Way to Get Married & 397.25 2050.
            [The] Ag[reeable] Surprize   ——
            [As Tangent in *The Way to
            Get Married*. FG]

"   29 [The] West Indian & Who 436.50
            Wins[?]
            [Dwyer as Belcour. FG]

" 31 [The] Dramatist & Love 381.50
laughs at Lock[smith]s
[Dwyer as Vapid in *The
Dramatist*. FG]

" Novem[be]r 2 Laugh When you Can* & 264.75
[The] Shipwreck
[Dwyer as Gossamer in
Laugh When You Can.
FG]

" 3 [A] Cure for the Heartache & 298.50 1381.25
Ella Rosenberg ———
[Dwyer as Young Rapid in
A Cure for the Heartache.
FG]

" 5 Romeo & Juliet & [The] Liar 397.
[Dwyer as Mercutio and as
Young Wilding in *The
Liar*. FG]

" Ben[efit] 7 [The] Deserted Daughter & 656.
[The] High[land] Reel
[Dwyer as Cheveril in *The
Deserted Daughter*. FG]

Ben[efit of] 9 Town & Country & [The] 571.50
Charleston Blind Boy
[For the benefit of the
sufferers by the late fire at
Charleston. FG]

10 [The] Foundling of [the] forest 238.50 1863.
& Raising the Wind ———

12 De Mon[t]fort* & Modern 516.50
Antiques.

	14 [The] Iron Chest & [The] Lady of [the] Rock	317.75	
	16 Wild Oats & [The] 40 Thieves	391.	
	17 John Bull & Mother Goose	305.	1530.25
Mrs. Beaumont	19 Isabella & [The] Review [As Isabella. FG]	344.50	
"	20 Venice Preserv'd & Blue Beard [Mrs. Beaumont as Belvidera in *Venice Preserved*. FG]	414.	
"	21 Adrian & Orrilla & [The] Sultan [Mrs. Beaumont as Madame Clermont in *Adrian and Orrilla* and Roxalana in *The Sultan*. FG]	666.25	
	22 High life in the City* & Too many Cooks	653.50	2078.25
			$12612.

28 nights averaged $450

1ST. PHILADELPHIA SEASON, [COMMENCING NOVEMBER 26,] 1810, [ENDING APRIL 30,] 1811.

[Warren & Wood]

PREFACE: As stated in the Foreword, p. vii, there are two versions of the record of this season. The only interpolation from the Volume II version is "Warren's ben," see April 29, which replaces "W's ben." of the Volume I version. In the entry of March 27, it has been advisable to substitute "Richard 3d." for ditto marks which Wood has used to signify that the play was repeated.

[77]

The explanations of the references to this preface are as follows:
February 1—Calbraith as Zanga in *The Revenge*. Warren, in an entry
of the same date, asserts that this was Calbraith's first appearance on
any stage and that "he was greatly applauded." The version in Volume
II of the *Account Book* includes the notation, "F[ir]st App[ea]r[ance] of
C[albraith.]" **March 6**: Robins was a scene painter. **March 8**: Mrs.
Seymour in a song called *The Netting Girl*. A **March 11**: Master Whale
as Adolphe in *La Forêt Noire*. A **March 16**: Dennison as Gustavus.
Warren's *Diary*. According to A, it was his "first appearance on any
stage." **March 20**: "The public are respectfully informed that the
theatre is unavoidably closed until Monday on account of the indisposition of Mr. Cooke who has not yet sufficiently recovered but will posi-
tively make his first appearance on that evening." A of March 21.
April 10: A announces *Othello*; but Warren's *Diary* records that, with
Cooke and Wood ill, *The Merchant of Venice* was substituted, with G.
Barrett playing Bassanio. **April 17**: Wood has crossed out the ditto
marks but A announces Cook as Lear. **April 19**: Wood has crossed
out the ditto marks but A announces Cooke as Sir Pertinax MacSycophant in *The Man of the World*. **April 22**: Pullen was the treasurer
of the company. **April 30**: In *Durang* I, XLIV, Cooper is said to have
played Othello, with Cooke as Iago. It is the elder Jefferson, of course,
who received a benefit on February 18.

In *Recollections*, p. 132, Wood writes enthusiastically of the success of
this season; and Durang, in commenting on the receipts of the Cooke
engagements, asserts that "these were certainly great receipts for a time
when there was scarcely any population in the city much above Ninth
street. Spring Garden, "Durang points out, I, XLIV, "was only occupied by the victualers as grazing grounds; and Moyamensing was covered
with brick kilns and milk farms. Southwark and the Northern Liberties
were not one-fourth of the present size [c. 1855]; yet Philadelphia filled
two theatres, and successfully contended with Great Britain on the ocean
in two years afterwards."

Novem[be]r 26 [The] Way to Get Married &   782.75
[The] Agree[able] Sur-
prize

Mrs. Twaits' 1st.   28 Macbeth & [The] Prisoner at 1334.25
Large
[As Lady Macbeth. A]

Mrs. McKenzie['s] 30 [The] Child of Nature & Mod- 556.75
1st.   [ern] Antiques
                  [As Amanthis in *The Child
                     of Nature.* A]

Dec[embe]r 1 Adelgitha & Killing No Murder 588.75
                                      ——— 3262.50

           3 [The] Foundling of the forest 814.
              & Raising [the] Wind

[Mrs.] Beaum[on]t 5 Isabella & [The] Sultan 1090.50
                  [As Isabella and as Roxa-
                   lana in *The Sultan.* A]

      "   7 [The] Grecian Daughter & 953.50
                  [The] High[lan]d Reel
                  [Mrs. Beaumont as Eu-
                   phrasia in *The Grecian
                   Daughter.* A]

           8 Speed the Plough & Don Juan 799.50
                                        ——— 3657.50

      "   10 Adrian & Orrilla & [The] 842.25
                  Citizen
                  [Mrs. Beaumont as Madame
                   Clermont in *Adrian and
                   Orrilla* and Maria in *The
                   Citizen.* A]

      "   12 [The] Belle's Stratagem & Ella 557.75
                  Rosenberg
                  [Mrs. Beaumont as Letitia
                   Hardy in *The Belle's
                   Stratagem* and as Ella
                   Rosenberg. A]

Fennel[l]   14 King Lear & Who Wins[?] 1348.50
                      [As Lear. A]

[Mrs.] B[eaumont] 15 Romeo & Juliet & Fortune's 644.50
                       frolic   ——— 3393.
                       [As Juliet. A]

      "   17 Jane Shore & [The] Sultan 659.75
                       [Mrs. Beaumont as Jane
                       Shore and as Roxalana in
                       The Sultan. A]

Mrs. B[eaumont's] 19 [The] Will & [The] Maid of 960.
ben[efit]   the Oaks
                       [As Albina Mandeville in
                       The Will and Lady Bab
                       Lardoon in *The Maid of
                       the Oaks.* A]

B[eaumont]   21 Pizarro & [The] Weathercock 1004.67
                       [As Rolla in *Pizarro.* A]

F[ennell]   22 Richard 3d. & Of Age tomor- 566.75
                       row   ——— 3191.17
                       [As Richard. A]

B[eaumont]   24 [The] Mountaineers & [The]   564.50
                       Portrait [of] Cervantes
                       [As Octavian in *The Moun-
                       taineers.* A]

                   26 High life in the City* & [The] 1412.06
                       40 Thieves

F[ennell]   28 Othello & Too Many Cooks   728.50
                       [As Othello. A]

      "   29 [The First Part of] Henry 4th 571.
                       & Hit or Miss*   ——— 3296.06
                       [Fennell as Hotspur. A]

B[eaumont]   31 [The] Castle Spectre & [The] 575.75
        Review
        [As Osmond in *The Castle*
        Spectre. A]

1811. Jan[uar]y 1 Columbus & [The] Prisoner 1449.90
        at Large

Charles[ton]   2 [A] Cure for [the] Heartache 554.25
Ben[efit]   & Rais[in]g [the] Wind
        [A announces: "For the
        benefit of the sufferers by
        the late dreadful fire at
        Charleston."]

B[eaumonts]   4 [The] Stranger* & Tom 511.
        Thumb [the Great]
        [Beaumont as the Stranger,
        Mrs. Beaumont as Mrs.
        Haller. A]

        5 Columbus & [The] Deaf Lover 478.50
                —— 3568.35

B[eaumonts]   7 [The] School for Scandal & 519.50
        [The] Prize
        [Beaumont as Charles Sur-
        face, Mrs. Beaumont as
        Lady Teazle in *The School*
        for Scandal. A]

   "   9 Julia & Hit or Miss 565.
        [Beaumont as Montevole,
        Mrs. Beaumont as Julia. A]

F[ennell]   11 Hamlet & [The] Ghost 734.25
        [As Hamlet. A]

	12 Columbus & Who's the dupe?	918.50	
		———	2737.25
Mr. B[eaumont's] Ben[efi]t	14 Venice Preserv'd & Cath-[erine] & Petruchio [As Pierre in *Venice Pre-served.* A]	879.75	
F[ennell]	16 [The] Roman Father & Ways & Means [As Horatius, the Roman Father. A]	479.	
"	18 [The] Revenge & [The] Blind Boy [Fennell as Zanga in *The Revenge.* A]	641.75	
	19 [The] Foundling of [the] Forest & My Grandmother	442. ———	2442.50
F[ennell]	21 [King] Lear & Catch him Who Can [As Lear. A]	837.50	
"	23 Douglas & [The] Hunter of the Alps [Fennell as Glenalvon in *Douglas.* A]	414.75	
"	25 [The] Provok'd Husband & Love laughs [at Lock-smiths] [Fennell as Lord Townly in *The Provoked Husband.* A]	547.87	
	26 Columbus & [The] Weather-cock	597.25 ———	2397.37

"   28 Macbeth & [The] Spoil'd 414.25
Child
[As Macbeth. A]

"   30 Pizarro & [A] Budget of 685.75
blunders*
[Fennell as Rolla in *Pizarro*.
A]

Feb[ruar]y   1 [The] Revenge & [The] Lady 1266.
Calb[raith.]   of [the] Rock
[See preface to this season.]

2 George Barnwell & Columbus 709.75   3085.75
——————

F[ennell's]   4 [The] Distrest Mother & [A] 712.
Ben[efi]t   Bud[get] of blunders
[As Orestes in *The Distressed
Mother*. A]

6 [The] Doubtful Son* & [The] 452.30
Irishman in London

Wood['s] Ben[efit]   8 De Mon[t]fort* & [The] 40 1203.53
Thieves
[As De Montfort. A]

9 [The] Foundling [of the] forest 536.75   2904.58
& [A] Budget [of] ——————
Blunders

11 Venice Preserv'd & [The] 661.50
Irish Widow

13 [The] Doubtful Son & Blue 731.
Beard

[83]

15 [The] Robbers & Ella Rosen-   644.75
    berg

16 [The] Doubtful Son & La foret   172.75   2210.
    Noire   ————

[Benefit of]   18 [The] Deserted Daughter &   1403.
Jefferson   Matrimony
                      [To sing comic songs. A]

[Benefit of   20 [The] Foundling [of the] forest   391.06
Mr. & Mrs.]   & [The] Adopted Child
Barrett   [Barrett as Florian, Mrs.
                      Barrett as Unknown Fe-
                      male in *The Foundling of
                      the Forest.* A]

[Benefit of]   22 Abaellino & [A] Tale of Terror   826.30
Cone   [As Abaellino and Flodoardo
                      in *Abaellino.* A]

[Benefit of]   23 [The] Stranger & Oscar &   388.56   3008.92
Francis   Malvina   ————
                      [As Solomon in *The Stranger*
                      and Fingal in *Oscar and
                      Malvina.* A]

[Benefit of]   25 [The] Wheel of fortune &   801.44
McKenzie   Val[entine] & Orson
                      [As Sydenham in *The Wheel
                      of Fortune* and the Green
                      Knight in *Valentine and
                      Orson.* A]

[Benefit of]   27 [The] Road to Ruin, Dr.   959.
Blisset   Last['s Examination] &
                      [A] budget [of] blunders
                      [As Mr. Silky in *The Road to
                      Ruin* and as Dr. Last. A]

[84]

March [Benefit of Mrs.] Wilmot	1 Richard C[oeur] de Lion, [The] I[rish] Widow & [The] Span[ish] Barber [As Matilda in *Richard* *Coeur de Lion*, the Widow Brady and Rosina in *The* *Spanish Barber*. A]	785.	
[Benefit of Hardinge]	2 [The] Surrender of Calais & S[t.] Patrick's day [To sing comic songs. A]	425. ———	2970.44
[Benefit of] Mrs. Francis	4 [The] Merchant of Venice & [The] Old Maid	651.	
[Benefit of] Robins	6 Coriolanus & [The] Poor Soldier [See preface to this season.]	456.	
[Benefit of Mrs.] Seymour	8 Alexander [the Great] & [The] Chil[dren] in [the] Wood [See preface to this season.]	537.	
	9 John Bull & Val[entine] & Orson	353. ———	1997.
[Benefit of Master] Whale	11 Town & Country & La foret Noire [See preface to this season.]	764.	
[Benefit of Mrs.] Twaits	13 Adrian & Orrilla & High life below Stairs [As Kitty in *High Life Below* *Stairs*. A]	314.50	
[Benefit of Miss] White	15 [The] Poor Gentleman & [The] Spanish Barber [As Emily Worthington in *The Poor Gentleman*. A]	647.	

[85]

D[ennison]　　　16 Gustavus Vasa & [The] 40　575.　　2300.50
　　　　　　　　　　Thieves
　　　　　　　　　[See preface to this season.]

　　　　　　　　18 Columbus & [The] Recon-　208.
　　　　　　　　　ciliation

　　　　　　　　20 [The] Busy Body & [The] 40　304.　　46905.
　　　　　　　　　Thieves.

　　　　　　　　　　No play
　　　　　　　　　　d[itt]o
　　　　　　　　[See preface to this season.]

(Cooke.)　　　　25 Richard 3d. & [The] Review　1345.
　　　　　　　　　[As Richard. A]

　　　　　　　　27 [Richard 3d.] & Matrimony 1104.

　　　　　　　　29 [The] Man of the World & 1475.
　　　　　　　　　[The] Hunter of [the]
　　　　　　　　　Alps

　　　　　　　　30 [The] Merchant of Venice & 1160.　　5084.
　　　　　　　　　[A] Budget [of] Blunders

(Cooke)　April　1 Richard 3d. & [The] Adopted 1189.
　　　　　　　　　Child
　　　　　　　　[As Richard. A]

　"　　　　　　　3 [The] Man of the World & 1202.
　　　　　　　　　[The] Weathercock
　　　　　　　　[Cooke as Sir Pertinax Mac-
　　　　　　　　Sycophant in *The Man of
　　　　　　　　the World*. A]

　"　　　　　　　5 [King] Lear & Sylv[ester] 997.
　　　　　　　　　Daggerwood
　　　　　　　　[Cooke as Lear. A]

"   6 [A] New Way to pay old debts 1030.   4418.
         & Kill[ing] no Murder   ———
         [Cooke as Sir Giles Over-
         reach in *A New Way to
         Pay Old Debts.* A]

"   8 [The First Part of] Henry 4th 1020.
         & Of age tomorrow
         [Cooke as Falstaff. A]

"   10 [The] Merchant of Venice &   880.
         [The] Spoil'd Child
         [See preface to this season.]

"   11 Macbeth & Too Many Cooks   780.

"   13 Douglas & Love a la Mode   1196.   3876.
         [Cooke as Glenalvon in ———
         Douglas and Sir Archy
         Mac Sarcasm in *Love a la
         Mode.* A]

Ben[efit of]   15 Every man in his Humor* & 1356.50
Cooke   [The] H[ighland] Reel
               [As Kitely in *Every Man in
               his Humor.* A]

"   17 [King] Lear & Modern An-   668.75
         tiques
         [See preface to this season.]

"   19 [The] Man of the World &   948.50
         [The] Prisoner at Large
         [See preface to this season.]

"   20 Richard 3d. & S[t.] Patrick's 1000.
         day   ———   3973.75
         [Cooke as Richard. A]

[87]

Pullen's ben[efit]   22 [The] Castle Spectre & [The] 676.
Lady of [the] Rock
[See preface to this season.]

Calb[raith's]   24 [The] Robbers & [The] Chil- 823.
Ben[efit]   dren in [the] Wood
[As Charles de Moor in
The Robbers and Walter
in *The Children in the
Wood.* A]

C[ooke] & Cooper 26 Othello & [The] Old Maid 1504.
[Cooke as Iago, Cooper as
Othello. A]

"   27 [The] Gamester & Ways & 1189.
Means   —— 4192.
[Cooke as Stukely, Cooper
as Beverly in *The
Gamester.* A]

"   29 Venice Preserv'd & Don Juan 1312.
Warren's ben[efit]. Warren
as Priuli, Cooke as Pierre,
Cooper as Jaffier in *Venice
Preserved.* A]

Cooper's Ben[efit] 30 Othello & [The] Irish[man] in 1292.   2604.30
London
[See preface to this season.] ——————
$71052.

88 Nights.
Averaging $860

Baltimore Spring [Season, Commencing May 4, Ending
June 10,] 1811.

[Warren & Wood]

Preface: As stated in the Foreword, p. vii, there are two versions of
the record of this season. The interpolations from the Volume II version
include the names of the days of the week; and also "Calb," May 4,

[88]

"Mrs. McKen," May 10, "Mrs. Beaum," May 13, "enzie" of McKenzie, May 25, and "cis" of Francis and "braith" of Calbraith, May 29.

In the Volume I version Wood has written "& C" after the ditto marks of the June 1 entry. His reference is obviously to be interpreted as "and Cooper;" and the editorial note of that date records that Cooper must have played Othello. Wood has also written "C" after the ditto marks of the June 3 entry but FG makes no mention of Cooper. For June 4, however, FG announces Cooper; and, as the Volume II version includes his name in the entry of June 4, the ditto marks of the Volume I version possibly refer to Cooper. Warren's *Diary*, in an entry of about this time, reveals that "Cooke was so unwell last night from being intoxicated on the preceding evening that he could get through with the greatest difficulty—declares he will play no more." In his *Recollections*, p. 134, Wood asserts that, the day after this indiscretion, Cooke was "hoarse and could not act. We had to change the play," Wood adds. "Cooper, to save the house being closed, consented to play Hamlet." According to Warren's *Diary*, Cooke was still malingering on June 7, for "the play would have been *Richard*, but Cooke could not perform that character." The entry also states that Cooper played Antonio. On June 8—not June 9, as erroneously given in both versions of the season—Cooke paid for his folly. "The audience having been disappointed once," Wood explains in his *Recollections*, p. 134, "naturally would not come again, when [Cooke] was announced; and a part which many persons reckoned one of his best and which he had played in Philadelphia to $1475 and before in Baltimore to $801.72 he now played to $474."

Cooke was not the only player to give trouble, however, for one of the interesting details which Warren's *Diary* adds to the history of this season is that it started a day late because "as usual M'Kenzie came not." The *Diary* also reveals that Mrs. Beaumont played Ella as well as Letitia on May 15 and Maria in *The Citizen* as well as Elvira in *Pizarro* on May 17

	May		
Calb[rait]h	Saty.	4 [The] Merchant of Venice &	365.50
		[The] Agreeable Surprize	———
		[As Shylock. FG]	
	Mon.	6 [The] Revenge & [The] Blind	382.25
		Boy	

Wed.   8 [The] Foundling of [the] forest   358.50
       & Hit or Miss*

   Frid 10 [The] Child of Nature & [A]   462.
Mrs. McKen[zie]   Budget of Blunders*
          [As Amanthis in *The Child
          of Nature*. FG]

   Sat. 11 George Barnwell & [The] 40   333.25   1536.
       Thieves   ————

   Mon. 13 [The] Grecian Daughter & [A]   440.25
Mrs. Beaum[ont]   bud[get] of Blunders
          [As Euphrasia in *The Gre-
          cian Daughter*. FG]

"   Wed. 15 [The] Belle's Stratagem &   330.15
       Ella Rosenberg
       [Mrs. Beaumont as Letitia
       Hardy in *The Belle's
       Stratagem*. FG]

"   Frid. 17 Pizarro & [The] Citizen   526.50
       [Mrs. Beaumont as Elvira
       in *Pizarro*. FG]

"   Saty. 18 [The] Castle Spectre & Cath-   257.25   1554.15
       [erine] & Petruchio   ————
       [Mrs. Beaumont as Angela
       in *The Castle Spectre*. FG]

"   Mon. 20 [The] Honey Moon & Don   318.25
       Juan
       [Mrs. Beaumont as Juliana
       in *The Honey Moon*. FG]

"   Wed. 22 Columbus & Modern Antiques   598.75

   Frid. 24 Columbus & [The] Irish   350.50
       Widow

[Benefit of Mr. & Mrs.] Jefferson	Saty. 25	[The] Doubtful Son* & [The] Spanish Barber [Jefferson in comic song. FG]	474.75 1742.25

[Benefit of] Cone & McKenzie — Mon. 27 Abaellino & [A] Budget [of] Blunders [McKenzie in recitation. FG] — 261.50

[Benefit of Mrs.] Francis & Calbraith — Wed. 29 [The] Doubtful Son & Tekeli — 262.25

Cooke — Frid. 31 Richard 3d. & [The] Invisible Girl [As Richard. FG] — 825.75

[June]
" Saty. 1 Othello & [The] Old Maid [Cooke as Iago, Cooper as Othello. FG] — 773.50 2123.

" Mon. 3 [The] Man of the World & [The] Highland Reel [Cooke as Sir Pertinax Mac-Sycophant in *The Man of The World*. FG] — 801.75

" Tues. 4 Hamlet & [The] Ghost [Cooper as Hamlet. FG] — 320.

" Wedy. 5 Venice Preserv'd & [The] Scheming Lieut[enan]t [Cooke as Pierre, Cooper as Jaffier in *Venice Pre-served*. FG] — 938.

[91]

"   Friday 7 [The] Merchant of Venice &   858.25
         Love a la Mode
         [Cooke as Shylock and as
         Sir Archy McSarcasm in
         Love a la Mode. FG]

"   Saty. [8 The] Man of the World &   474.25   3392.25
         fortune's frolic   ———
         [Cooke as Sir Pertinax Mac-
         Sycophant. FG]

"   Mon. 10 [The First Part of] Henry 4th   901.75   901.75
         & Ways & Means   ———
         [Cooke as Sir John Falstaff, $11613.75
         Cooper as Hotspur. FG]
         23 Nights
         Averaged 504.75

PHILADELPHIA [SEASON, COMMENCING SEPTEMBER 9,] 1811, [ENDING MARCH 14, 1812.]

[Warren & Wood]

PREFACE: As stated in the Foreword, p. vii, there are two versions of the record of this season. The interpolations from the Volume II version include: October 11—"& Wedding Day." November 1: "Mr. Cooper's Ben," which replaces "Coop Ben" of the Volume I version. November 15: "0" in "724.05." November 23: "0" in "646.06." November 30: "0" in "571.07." December 13: "& Youth's Errors." January 1: "1812."

The explanations of the references to this preface are as follows: **November 30**—Ditto marks in the Volume I version indicate that Cooke must have played and ADA announces: "Mr. Cooke's last night. The public are respectfully informed that Mr. Cooke has consented to perform one night more for Wood's benefit." In an entry of the same date, Warren's *Diary* comments that "Wood prevailed on Cooke to play Sir Pertinax." **January 18**: Darley and the ditto marks under the name sometimes stand for Mr. and Mrs. Darley and sometimes for either one or the other. For example, according to A, Mrs. Darley played Lydia in *Love Laughs at Locksmiths* and Miss Dorillon in *Wives as They*

Were on January 17 and Amanthis in *The Child of Nature* and Morgiana in *The Forty Thieves* on January 18. According to A, she played Rosamonda in *Abaellino* (with Cooper as Flodoardo and Abaellino) on **January 22**, Juliet on January 24, Ophelia on January 27, Floranthe in *The Mountaineers* on January 29, Jessy Oatland in *A Cure for the Heartache* on January 31 and Miss Peggy in *The Country Girl* and Fatima in *Blue Beard* on February 3. **February 19**: Wood has written "D" after "Curfew." A advertises that Wood is to play Mr. H. in Mrs. Wood's benefit and ADA explains the "D" by announcing Duff as Fitzharding in *The Curfew*. **March 9**: Mr. Pullen was treasurer of the company.

Warren's *Diary*, *Durang* and Wood's *Recollections* contain many interesting details regarding the history of this season. In his entry of February 12, Warren identified "Js. Fennell" as "Fennell Jun[ior]," adding the caustic comment that he was "very bad indeed." The Jefferson receiving a benefit on February 17 was, of course, the elder Jefferson.

In *Recollections*, pp. 142–3 Wood points out that "there were various causes which combined to render the season . . . particularly disastrous and unproductive. An extreme commercial depression at this time prevailed, chiefly occasioned by the threatening aspect of our relations with England, which in a few months resulted in a declaration of war, and in an excited state of public feeling, always unfavorable to the success of theatrical representations. Then came the destruction of the Richmond Theatre, [December 26, 1811], with its dreadful consequences. [For detailed account, see *Durang* I, XLVII.] This awful event would alone have arrested for a season the current of the best fortune. It seemed to create a perfect panic, which deterred the largest portion of the audience for a long time from venturing into a crowd, either theatrical or other. But," asserts Wood, "the striking incident of the season at Philadelphia arose from the McKenzie riots." See the general introduction, p. 19.

Septem[be]r 9 Town & Country & [Of] Age   447.85
           tomorrow

          11 [The] Soldier's daughter &   339.
             [The] Review

          13 Pizarro & [The] Weathercock   367.

	14 Speed the Plough & Don Juan	277.50	1431.85
	16 Lovers['] Vows & [The] Highland Reel	339.	
	18 [The] Foundling of [the] forest & Mod[ern] Antiques	360.25	
	20 Much ado ab[out] Nothing & [A] Bud[get] of blunders	465.60	
	21 [The] Castle Spectre & Raising [the] Wind	217.50	1382.35
	23 [The] Heir at Law & Blue Beard	374.	
	25 Venoni* & [The] Citizen	285.	
Cooper	27 Richard 3d & [The] Irish Widow [As Richard. A]	565.	
"	28 Hamlet & Sylv[ester] Daggerwood [Cooper as Hamlet. A]	520.	1744.50
	30 [The] Stranger & Oscar & Malvina	392.95	
October	2 [The] Pilgrim* & [The] Deaf Lover	352.	
C[ooper]	4 Macbeth & [The] Invisible Girl [As Macbeth. A]	479.33	
"	5 [The] Honey Moon & Oscar & Malvina [Cooper as Duke Aranza in *The Honey Moon*. A]	508.31	1732.59

[94]

	7 [The] Merry Wives of Windsor & [The] Ghost	410.45	
	9 Abaellino & Don Juan	590.25	
C[ooper]	11 Adelgitha & [The] Wedding Day [As Michael Ducas in *Adelgitha*. A]	430.	
"	12 Rule a Wife [& Have a Wife] & [The] Prisoner at large [Cooper as Leon in *Rule a Wife*. A]	422.75 ———	1953.45
Dwyer	14 [The] West Indian & Fortune's frolic [As Belcour in *The West Indian*. A]	370.25	
"	16 Laugh When You Can & [A] Tale [of] Mystery [Dwyer as Gossamer in *Laugh When You Can*. A]	341.50	
C[ooper]	18 Othello & [The] Citizen [As Othello. A]	537.25	
"	19 [The] Merchant of Venice & Cath[erine] & Petruchio. [Cooper as Shylock and Petruchio. A]	494.53 ———	1743.53
D[wyer]	21 [The] Deserted Daughter & [The] Child[ren] in [the] Wood [As Cheveril in *The Deserted Daughter*. A]	390.	

[95]

"   23 Romeo & Juliet & [The] Liar   654.50
                               [Dwyer as Mercutio and
                               as Young Wilding in *The*
                               Liar. A]

C[ooper]   25 [The] Wheel of fortune & Ella   551.
                               Rosenberg
                               [As Penruddock in *The*
                               Wheel of Fortune. A]

C[ooper]   26 Venice Preserv[e]d & [The]   360.75   1956.25
                               Agree[able] Surprize   ———
                               [As Pierre in *Venice Pre-*
                               served. A]

D[wyer]   28 [The] Way to Get Married &   385.21
                               Tom Thumb [the Great]
                               [As Tangent in *The Way to*
                               Get Married. A]

"   30 Romeo & Juliet & [The]   301.
                               Review
                               [Dwyer as Mercutio. A]

Nov[ember]   1 Pizarro & Ella Rosenberg   767.50
Mr. Cooper's   [As Rolla in *Pizarro.* A]
Ben[efit]

C[ooper]   2 King John & Matrimony   529.25   1982.96
                               [As Falconbridge. A]   ———

Dwy[er']s Ben[efit]   4 [The] School for Scandal &   687.50
                               [The] Hunter of [the] Alps
                               [As Charles Surface in *The*
                               School for Scandal and
                               Felix in *The Hunter of the*
                               Alps. A]

D[wyer]   6 Every One has his fault & 488.62
              [The] Poor Soldier
              [As Sir Robert Ramble in
              Every One Has His Fault.
              A]

(Cooke)   8 Richard 3d. & fortune's frolic 917.
              [As Richard. A]

"   9 [The] Man of the World & 780.41 2873.53
              Tom Thumb [the Great] ———
              [Cooke as Sir Pertinax Mac-
              Sycophant in *The Man of
              the World.* ADA]

"   11 King Lear & Ways & Means 675.95
              [Cooke as Lear. A]

"   13 Macbeth & [The] Prisoner at 729.75
              Large
              [Cooke as Macbeth. A]

"   15 [The] Wheel of fortune & 724.05
              [The] Hunter of [the] Alps
              [Cooke as Penruddock in
              The Wheel of Fortune. A]

"   16 Richard 3d. & Matrimony 706.75 2836.40
              [Cooke as Richard. A] ———

"   18 [The First Part of] Henry 4th 632.25
              & [The] Irishman in
              London
              [Cooke as Falstaff. A]

"   20 [The] Merchant of Venice & 1177.75
              Love A la Mode
              [Cooke as Shylock and as
              Sir Archy MacSarcasm in
              Love a la Mode. A]

"   22 [The] Man of the World & 1115.50
[The] Devil to pay
[Cooke as Sir Pertinax Mac-
Sycophant in *The Man
of the World.* A]

"   23 [A] New Way to pay old debts   646.06   3571.56
& [A] Bud[get] of blunders   ———
[Cooke as Sir Giles Over-
reach in *A New Way to
Pay Old Debts.* A]

"   25 King John & [The] Adopted   546.88
Child
[Cooke as King John. A]

"   27 [The] Merchant of Venice & 1041.37
Love a la Mode
[Cooke as Shylock and Sir
Archy MacSarcasm. A]

C[ooke's] Ben[efi]t 29 Richard 3d. & Who's the 1121.89
dupe?
[As Richard. A]

Wood's B[enefit]   30 [The] Man of the World &   571.07   3281.21
[The] Lady of [the] Rock   ———
[See preface to this season.]

Decem[ber]   2 She Stoops to Conquer &   902.
[The] 40 Thieves

4 Venice Preserv'd & 2 Strings   397.25
to Y[ou]r Bow

6 [The] Wonder & [The] 40   353.45
Thieves

7 [The] Stranger & Catch him   333.89   1986.59
Who Can   ———

[98]

Payne	9 [The] Mountaineers & [A] Budget of blunders [As Octavian in *The Mountaineers.* A]	602.80	
	11 Mahomet & [The] Scheming Lieutenant	464.	
	13 Tancred & Sigismunda & Youth's Errors*	383.50	
	14 Douglas & Valentine & Orson	517.25	1967.55
	16 Hamlet & 2 Strings to your bow	458 75	
	18 Pizarro & [The] Old Maid	348.25	
	20 [The] Distress'd Mother & Blue Beard	369.50	
	21 Jane Shore & Valentine & Orson	288.37	1464.87
Payne's Ben[efit]	23 Alexander [the Great] & Killing no Murder [As Alexander. A]	539.87	
	24 Speed the Plough & R[aymond] & Agnes	170.50	
	26 [The] Chapter of Accidents & Columbus	434.50	
	27 Geo[rge] Barnwell & [The] 40 Thieves	406.25	1551.12
	30 [The] Foundling of [the] forest & [The] Mayor of Garrat	471.75	

[99]

1812. January 1 [The] Lady of the Lake* & 1201.50
           Ways & Means

           3 D[itt]o & 2 Strings to y[ou]r 446.75
           Bow

           4 [The] Robbers & Ella Rosen- 105.25 2225.25
           berg   ⸺

           6 [The] Lady of [the] Lake &   487.50
           [The] Soldier's Daughter

Simp[so]n   8 [The] Road to Ruin & [The] 166.70
           Weathercock
           [As Harry Dornton in *The
           Road to Ruin* and Trist-
           ram   Fickle   in   *The
           Weathercock.* A]

          10 [The] Lady of [the] Lake & 549.75
"   & Cooper   Rule a Wife [& Have a
           Wife]
           [Simpson as Michael Perez
           and Cooper as Leon in
           Rule a Wife. A]

"   "   11 Othello & Raising [the] Wind 278.50 1482.45
           [Simpson   as   Diddler   in   ⸺
           Raising the Wind, Cooper
           as Iago. A]

"   "   13 King Lear & [The] Honest 117.
           thieves
           [Simpson as Edgar, Cooper
           as Lear. A]

"   "   15 [The] Revenge & Columbus 254.
           [Simpson as Don Alonzo,
           Cooper as Zanga in *The
           Revenge.* A]

Darley & Co[oper] 17 Wives as they Were [& Maids   319.
                       as They Are] & Love
                       laughs [at Locksmiths]
                       [Darley as Captain Beldare
                       in *Love Laughs at Lock-
                       smiths*, Cooper as Sir
                       William Dorillon in *Wives
                       as They Were*. A]

  "   "   18 [The] Child of Nature & [The]   186.   876.
                       40 Thieves   ——————
                       [See preface to this season.]

  "   "   22 Abaellino & [Of] Age tomorrow 295.25
                       [See preface to this season.]

  "   "   24 Romeo & Juliet & [The] Lady   380.50
                       of [the] Lake
                       [Cooper as Romeo. A Mrs.
                       Darley as Juliet. TA]

  "   "   25 [The] Honey Moon & Blue   229.75   905.50
                       Beard   ——————
                       [Darley as Selim in *Blue
                       Beard*, Cooper as Duke
                       Aranza in *The Honey
                       Moon*. A]

  "   "   27 Hamlet & 3 Weeks after   144.
                       Marriage
                       [Cooper as Hamlet. A]

  "   "   29 [The] Mountaineers & [The]   291.45
                       Lady of the Lake
                       [Cooper as Octavian in *The
                       Mountaineers*. A]

[101]

D[arley] & Co[oper]	31 [A] Cure for [the] Heartache & Cath[erine] & Petruchio Simp[son's] Ben[efit. Simpson as Young Rapid in *A Cure for the Heartache*, Cooper as *Petruchio*. A]	305.50
" Feb[ruar]y	1 [The] School for Scandal & [The] 40 Thieves [Mr. &] Mrs. D[arley's] Ben[efit. Darley as Granem, Mrs. Darley as Morgiana in *The Forty Thieves* and as Lady Teazle, with Cooper as Charles Surface, in *The School for Scandal*. A]	260.75 ——— 1001.70
"	3 [The] Country Girl & Blue Beard [Darley as Belville in *The Country Girl*. A]	161.
	5 False & true & [The] Elopement*	142.50
Warren's ben[efit]	7 [The] Tempest & [The] Children in the Wood [As Caliban. ADA]	ʊ24.
	8 [The] Foundling of [the] forest & [A] Budget [of] blunders	74. 1001 ———
	10 [The] Bridal Ring* & [The] Lady of [the] Lake	276.

J[ame]s Fennel[l]   12 Douglas[, The] Elopement &   127.
                        [The] Invisible Girl
                        [As Young Norval in
                        Douglas. A]

                     14 [The] Tempest & [The] Bridal   199.
                        Ring

Duff's 1[st.]   15 Macbeth & Raising the Wind   123.   725.
app[earance]   [As Macbeth and as Did-   ——
                        dler in *Raising the Wind*.
                        A]

[Benefit of]   17 [The] Hero of the North &   667.
Jefferson   [The] Comet*
                        [To sing comic songs. A]

[Benefit of]   19 [The] Curfew & Mr. H.*   347.
Mrs. Wood   [See preface to this season.]

[Benefit of]   21 3 & [the] deuce, [The] Bridal 295.
Mrs. Twaits   Ring & Mr. H
                        [As Taffline in *Three and
                        the Deuce*. ADA]

[Benefit of   22 Man and Wife & [The] Wed-   267.   1576.
Mrs.] Mason   ding day   ——
                        [As Helen Worrett in *Man
                        and Wife*. ADA]

[Benefit of]   24 Secrets Worth Knowing &   321.
Cone   [The] Comet
                        [As Rostrum in *Secrets
                        Worth Knowing*. A]

[Benefit of Mr. &   26 3 & [the] Deuce, [The] Ap- 624.
Mrs.] Francis   prentice & Cinderella

[Benefit of]   28 [The] School of Reform &   748.
Blisset[t]   [The] Critic

[103]

[Benefit of]   29 3 & [the] deuce, [The] Ship-   539.   2232.
Hardinge   wreck & [Of] Age to-   ——·
                 morrow

        March   2 Alexander [the Great,] Sylv- 1101.
[Benefit of]   [ester Dagg[erwoo]d &
Duff   [The] Review
                 [As Alexander, as Sylvester
                   Daggerwood   and   as
                   Looney   Mactwolter   in
                   The Review. A]

[Benefit of]   4 3 & [the] Deuce, Sylv[ester]   984.50
Calb[raith]   Dagg[erwoo]d   &   Ella
                 Rosenberg
                 [As Storm in *Ella Rosen-*
                 berg. A]

[Benefit of   6 [The] Voice of Nature[, The]   347.25
Mrs. and Miss]   D[ouble] Disguise & [A]
Seymour.   Tale of Mystery
                 [Mrs. Seymour as Rose in
                 The Double Disguise, Miss
                 Seymour to sing. A]

[Benefit of   7 Hamlet Travestie,* Tekeli &   295.75   2728.50
Mr. and Mrs.]   [The] Honest Thieves   ———
Bray   [Bray as Hamlet and as
                 Abel Day in *The Honest*
                 Thieves. A]

[Benefit of]   9 John Bull & [The] Blind Boy   320.75
Pullen   [See preface to this season.]

Cone's 2d.   11 [The] Peasant Boy* & [The]   735.
[Benefit]   Fortress
                 [As Baron Montaldi in *The*
                 Peasant Boy. A]

Mason['s] 2d. [Benefit]	13 [The] Soldier's daughter & feudal times*	485.75	
	14 [The] Peasant Boy & High life below Stairs	190.25	1731.75
			$56947.46

108 Nights $527

Baltimore Spring [Season, Commencing March 23, Ending June 7,] 1812.

[Warren & Wood]

Preface: As stated in the Foreword, p. vii, there are two versions of the record of this season. The interpolations from the Volume II version include: The word "Spring" in the heading. April 20: "Benefit," which replaces "Ben" of the Volume I version. April 24: "Mr." in "Mr. Wood's Ben[efit]." April 27 and 29: "P" of "Payne," which replaces ditto marks of the Volume I version. May 1–June 7: The names of the days of the week. May 4: "ayne" of Payne. May 6: "ayne" of "Payne['s]." May 22: "Mr. Payne's," which replaces "Payne 2d." of the Volume I version.

The explanations of the references to this preface are as follows: **April 24**—According to FG which announces an "olio of singing, recitation and dancing," Mr. Wood is to recite an epilogue, "Dash on, keep moving," in the character of Young Rapid. **May 1**: FG announces, "After the play a grand military olio called *Soldier's Revels.* **May 2**: "In the course of *The Lady of the Lake*," states FG, "will be introduced a living elephant now in this city, richly caparisoned, attended by guards, drivers, etc." Warren notes in the May 2 entry of his *Diary*, "We give the owner of the elephant $80." **May 4**: "The public are respectfully informed that, in consequence of the indisposition of Mr. Payne, the play of *Hamlet* is unavoidably changed to *The Foundling of the Forest.*"

In this announcement FG explains "Ch[anged] from Hamlet," written between the titles of the plays in the entry of this date. Warren's *Diary* remarks, "The play was to have been Hamlet by Payne—who sent word he was ill." **May 8**: "Mr. Warren respectfully informs the public that, Mr. Bernard having arrived in the city, he has availed himself of the opportunity of engaging him for his benefit this evening. He will make his first appearance these eight years in *A School for Scandal*. A dis-

[105]

sertation on faults, including the faults of young misses, old maids, young wives and old husbands by Mr. Bernard. With Mr. H." FG The May 8 entry of Warren's *Diary* includes the notation, "Sir Peter by John Bernard." **May 18:** FG announces Blissett as Memmo in *Abaellino*; and, after the play, "an Olla Podrida consisting of Recitation, Song, Dance & Spectacle, in which will be introduced an Emblematical Transparency, designed and executed by Mr. Robins, representing Wisdom & Justice bearing a Scroll: 'Wisdom in our Councils, Strength in our Defenders, and Justice in our Cause.' "

The Jeffersons receiving a benefit on May 25 are the elder Jeffersons. On May 27 Warren's *Diary* refers to Duff as having acted Puff in *The Critic* as well as the three Singles. With the War of 1812 imminent, it is not surprising that, as Wood declares in his *Recollections*, pp. 171–2, "The theatre followed a downhill course throughout the Baltimore season, although strengthened by the engagement of Fennell and Payne, by *The Lady of the Lake* and other attractions. . . With nightly expenses exceeding $300," Wood declares of this season, "a large loss was sustained by the managers."

March 23	Town & Country & [The] Weathercock	268.
25	[The] Castle Spectre & Mr. H.*	259.
27	[The] Soldier's daughter & [A] Budget [of] blunders	197.50
28	[The] Bridal Ring, Syl[vester] dagg[erwoo]d & [The] Hon[est] thieves	186. 910.50
30	[The] Peasant Boy* & Val-[entine] & Orson	321.50
April 1	[The] Foundling of [the] forest & Mr. H.	314.
3	[The] Lady of the Lake* & [The] Citizen	503.50

	4 [The] Peasant Boy & [The] 40 Thieves	175.	1314.
Fennell	6 [The] Lady of [the] Lake & [The] Agreeable Surprize	359.	
Fennell	8 King Lear & [The] Invisible Girl [As Lear. FG]	228.	
	10 Columbus & Killing No Murder	164.	
F[ennell]	11 Macbeth & [The] Deaf Lover [As Macbeth. FG]	218.	969.
	13 [The] Wheel of fortune & [The] Lady of [the] Lake	333.	
Payne	15. Tancred & Sigis[munda,] Sylv[ester] Dag[gerwoo]d & Mr. H. [As Tancred. FG]	355.	
Payne	17 Lovers' Vows & Youth's Errors* [As Frederick in *Lovers' Vows*. FG]	315.	
"	18 George Barnwell & Tekeli	207.	1210.
Fen[nell's] Benefit	20 Douglas & Matrimony [As Glenalvon in *Douglas*. FG]	427.	
	22 [The] Gazette Extraordinary* & [The] Adopted Child	245.	

[107]

Mr. Wood's   24 [The] Hero of the North &   534.
Ben[efit]   [The] Comet*
                [See preface to this season.]

Payne   25 Pizarro & Tom Thumb [the   246.   1452.
                   Great]   ———
                [As Rolla in *Pizarro*. FG.]

P[ayne]   Mon. 27 Alexander [the Great] & 2 244.
                   Strings to Y[ou]r Bow
                [As Alexander. FG.]

P[ayne]   Wed. 29 Adelgitha & [The] Review   255.50
                [As Lothair. FG.]

            May
            Friday 1 He would be a Soldier, Inter- 475.50
                   lude & [The] Beehive*
                [See preface to this season.]

Elephant   Saty. 2 [The] Lady of the Lake &   711.   1686.
                   [The] Comet   ———
                [See preface to this season.]

Payne   Mon. 4 [The] Foundling of [the] forest 158.
                   [&] Mod[ern] Ant[ique]s
                [See preface to this season.]

Payne['s] 1st. Wed. 6 Venoni* & [The] Beehive   656.
Ben[efit]   [As Venoni. FG]

Warren's   Fri. 8 The School for Scandal &   504.
ben[efit]   [See preface to this season.]

Bern[ar]d   Saty. 9 [The] Battle of Hexham &   502.   1820.
                   Blue Beard   ———
                [As Gregory Gubbins in *The
                Battle of Hexham*. FG]

[Benefit of] Mon. 11 [The] Merry Wives [of Wind- 254.
  Francis   sor, The] Elopem[en]t [&
                    The] Day after [the]
                    Wedding*

[Benefit of Wed. 13 [The] Poor Gentleman, Ham- 322.
  Mr. and Mrs.]   [let] travestie* & [The]
  Bray   Day after [the] W[edding]

[Benefit of Fri. 15 [The] Deserted Daughter & 77.50
  Mrs.] Wood   [The] Blind Boy
  & [Mrs.] Twaits

[Benefit of] Saty. 16 Rule a Wife [& Have a Wife] 257.   910.50
  Cone   & [The] Comet   ———
                  [As Leon in *Rule a Wife*.
                  FG]

[Benefit of] Mon. 18 Abaellino & [The] Devil to 487.
  Bliss[ett] &   pay
  Robins.   [See preface to this season.]

Duff   Wed. 20 Macbeth & Raising the Wind 270.
                  [As Macbeth and as Diddler
                    in *Raising the Wind*. FG]

Mr. Payne's Frid. 22 Mahomet, [The] Mayor of 537.
  2d. ben[efit]   Garrat & Hamlet Trav-
                  istie
                  [As Zaphna in *Mahomet*.
                  FG]

D[uff]   Sat. 23 3 & [the] Deuce & Tekeli 257.   1551.
                  [As the three Singles in ———
                    Three and the Deuce and
                    as Count Tekeli. FG]

[Benefit of   Mon. 25 Every One has his fault & 756.
Mr. & Mrs.]   [A] Bud[get] of blunders
Jefferson   [Jefferson as Solus, Mrs.
                               Jefferson as Mrs. Placid
                               in *Every One Has His
                               Fault.* FG]

D[uff]   Wed. 27 3 & [the] Deuce & [The] 255.
                               Critic
                               [As the three Singles. FG]

"   Fri. 29 [The] Honey Moon & [The] 300.
                               Weathercock
                               [Duff as Duke Aranza in
                               The Honey Moon and
                               Tristam Fickle in *The
                               Weathercock.* FG]

"   Saty. 30 Venice Preserv'd, Sylv[ester] 143.   1454.
                               Dag[gerwoo]d & Youth's ——
                               Errors
                               [Duff as Pierre in *Venice
                               Preserved* and as Sylvester
                               Daggerwood. FG]

               June 2 3 & [the] Deuce, Sylv[ester] 229.
Duff's ben[efit]   Dag[gerwoo]d & Oscar &
                               Malvina
                               [As the three Singles. FG]

               Wed. 4 [The] Stranger & [The] Lady 187.
                               of the Lake

               Fri. 6 [The] Tempest & Ella Rosen- 355.
                               berg

               Saty. 7 [The] Robbers & Mother 153.   924.
                               Goose   ——   ——
                                                                   $14201.

44 Nights
Average $323

[110]

WASHINGTON SEASON[, COMMENCING JUNE 15, ENDING AUGUST 10,] 1812.

[Warren & Wood]

PREFACE—There is only one version of the record of this season, which was only two days old when, on June 18, war was officially declared against Great Britain.   It was a trying time for one of Warren's birth and he had to submerge his own prejudices in an effort to keep the hot-headed members of his company out of difficulties.   In the June 23 entry of his *Diary*, he writes as follows: "On this evening Gen[era]l Varnum, Sam Ringold and some other members of Congress called for some Tunes and the band took on themselves to disobey in one or two instances, upon which those gentlemen, being heated with wine, pelted them with nuts, apples and such things as were at hand.   De Luce and Young went round to them; some words and a blow passed.   In the end we had to dismiss the two musicians."

For **July 4** NI announces: "An occasional address written expressly for the occasion by a gentleman of the city, allusive to the present state of our country, called The United Freemen, will be delivered by Mr. Warren.   After the comedy will be presented, in honor of the day, a grand patriotic and appropriate olio in the Temple of Liberty, consisting of recitations, patriotic and comic songs, national dances, &c."   Despite those allurements, Warren, in the entry of July 4, laments, "We have very few ladies on this night.   There was a fracas took place in this Theatre on last anniversary which keeps them away.   Preparation is making to carry on the War.   Some are for it but the nation at large do not approve of this measure.   For our parts we calculate to be ruined by it."   Warren & Wood, however, were too resourceful in any emergency.   On **August 4** they made haste to substitute for the delicate repartee of *The School for Scandal*, already scheduled, the robust action of *Abaellino* and the spectacular effects of *Oscar and Malvina* "on ac-c[oun]t," as the August 4 entry of Warren's *Diary* discloses, "of the Indian Chiefs who visit the Theatre this evening."   To the right of his entry of this date Wood has written "Indians."

June 15 [The] West Indian & [The]   179.
Review

17 [The] Honey Moon & Raising   180.
[The] Wind

[111]

19 Rule a Wife [& Have a Wife] 201.   560.
—   & Ella Rosenberg   ——

21 [The] Stranger & [The] Comet* 194.

22 3 & [the] Deuce* & Kill[in]g 123.
   No Murder

24 [The] Peasant Boy & 3 146.
   W[ee]ks after Marriage

25 Romeo & Juliet & [The] Day 176.   639.
—   after [the] Wedding*   ——

27 [The] Point of Honor & [The] 367.
   40 Thieves

28 [The] Adopted Child & [The] 84.
   40 thieves

[July] 2 [The] Sold[ier's] Daughter & 184.
   [A] tale [of] Mystery

4 He W[oul]d be a Soldier* & 309.   944.
—   Olio   ——
   [See preface to this season.]

6 [A] Cure for [the] Heartache 104.
   & [The] Devil to pay

9 Wild Oats* & [The] Wed[ding] 83.
   day

11 [The] Foundling [of the] for- 115.   302.
—   est & [The] Deaf Lover ——

14 [The] Lady of [the] Lake* & 355.
   [The] Comet

16 Hamlet & Matrimony   93.

18 [The] Lady of [the] Lake &   175.50   623.50
—   [The] Citizen   ———

[Mr. & Mrs.   21 [The] Surrender [of] Calais,   93.
Wood's [night.]   [The] Man[ager in] distress & Syl[vester] Dag-
[gerwoo]d

[Benefit of Mrs.] 23 Speed the Plough & [The] 117.
M[ason] & [Mr.]   Sultan
Hard[inge]

[Benefit of Mr. & 25 [The] Wheel of Fortune & 103,   313.
Mrs.] Barrett   [The] Hunter of [the] Alps   ——

[Benefit of Mr.   [28] Pizarro & Cath[erine] & 143.
& Mrs.] Duff   Petruchio

[Benefit of Mr.   [30] Ham[let] Travestie, [The] 38.
& Mrs.] Bray   H[onest Thieves & Tekeli

Aug[ust] 1 Every One [has] his fault & 139.
[Benefit of Mr. &   [The] N[aval] Pillar*
Mrs.] Jeff[erson]

[Benefit of Mr. & 4 Abaellino & O[scar] & Mal- 207.
Mrs.] Francis   vina*
[See preface to this season.]

7 [The] Castle Spectre & Val- 198.
[entine] & Orson

10 She Stoops to Conquer &
[The] Lady of [the] Lake

PHILADELPHIA SEASON, COMM[ENCIN]G SEP[TEMBER] 28, 1812, [ENDING APRIL 24, 1813.]

[Warren & Wood]

PREFACE: As stated in the Foreword, p. vii, there are two versions of the record of this season. The interpolations from the Volume II version include: The heading of the season, "Mrs. Green" in the entry of October 5, "Mrs." in "Mrs. W[hitlock's] Ben[efit]" and "Recit[atio]n" in the entry of November 2, "& V. Law" in the entry of December 12, "F" of "F. Durang" in the entry of April 3, and "Suff[erer]s," which replaces "Suf[ferers]" of the Volume I version.

The explanations of the references to this preface are as follows: **October 2**—A announces "A Tribute to Departed Genius; Or, the tears of Thalia and Melpomene for the loss of the celebrated George Frederick Cooke. The stage will present an extensive view of a cathedral richly illuminated. At the upper end a statue of the immortal Shakespeare. Solemn Music. In the avenues persons properly habited, bearing mourning banners of Mr. Cooke's principal plays. In the front an elevated mourning platform on which will be exhibited Sully's full length picture of Mr. Cooke as Richard III. The Tragic and Comic Muse drooping over the bier. Comic Muse, Mrs. Mason. Tragic Muse, Mrs. Wood. The ceremony will conclude with A Monody, to be delivered by Mr. Duff, his second appearance this season." **December 11**: A also announces Miss Holman as Lady Contest in *The Wedding Day*. **December 19**: In *Recollections*, p. 186, Wood explains, "A learned elephant contributed in Philadelphia this season to the attraction of *Blue Beard*, now revived. "On the Christmas holidays," *Durang*, I, XLIX, adds, the elephant "lent his portly presence to the plays of *Barbarossa*," (see **December 23**), "and *The Forty Thieves*," (see December 28). **December 21**: "Early in December," writes Wood in *Recollections*, p. 173, "Cone made known his wish to retire once more from the drama. His request was complied with, and his benefit took place, contrary to usage, in the heart of the season; the receipts $460. In the course of a parting address to the audience, Mr. C. glanced at a want of public patronage, and a 'lack of advancement' in the theatre, as the causes of his secession. A useful actor, he maintained a highly respectable position; while in the theatre his cheerful disposition and correct deportment strongly recommended him to the respect and good wishes of his fellow actors." Warren, in the December 21 entry of his *Diary* is less friendly.

[114]

"Mr. Cone spoke an address," he writes, "the purport of which was that managers were tyrants and oppressors. He is a grateful youth. The benefit was granted to his necessities. He had no claim—thus he repays us." A announces Cone as Lothair but he must have played another rôle. *Adelgitha* is scratched out in the Volume II version and *The Foundling of the Forest* is substituted for it, while only the latter appears in the Volume I version. **January 8:** "At the request of many influential persons," Wood states in his *Recollections*, p. 188, "a night was appropriated in aid of 'The fund for the translation and publication of the Holy Scriptures into the Eastern languages'." In explanation of the meager receipts, Warren writes in the January 8 entry of his *Diary*, "The folks have no charity in that way." **January 20:** A announces a divertisement in which Monsieur Menardier, an amateur, will dance a Pas Seul, also an Allemande with Mrs. Bray. **February 24:** A announces ballet, *L'Amour Vient à Bout de Tout*; or, *La Précaution Inutile*. "The broad sword hornpipe by Miss C. Abercrombie, in which she will introduce the broad sword exercise." **March 13:** A announces *The Sailor's Daughter*, *The Day After the Wedding* and *Timour the Tartar*. The first and last appear in the Volume II version but are crossed out and, in place of the first, "[The] Honeymoon, Ballet & C[etera]" are substituted. The March 13 entry of Warren's *Diary* records that "Harding[e] and Mrs. Duff [were] sick." **March 15:** According to A, Mr. Duff is to give imitations of Mr. Kemble, Mr. Cooke, Mr. Elliston and Mr. Munden. **March 17:** A announces a comic dance called *The Shamrock*; *or, St. Patrick's Day in the Morning*; and, after *Lovers' Quarrels*, an entertainment consisting of dialogue, songs, dance and pantomime called *The Magician of the Enchanted Castle*. **March 19:** Robins was the principal scene painter. A announces "necromantic picture, this night only, to conclude with transparent portraits of Captains Hull, Decatur and Bainbridge." **March 29:** Doyle to sing *Mary Le Moor*. A also announces, in Act II of *The Foundling of the Forest*, "a characteristic ballet by six warriors, a pas de deux by the Misses Abercrombie and a combat between two boys habited as warriors."

In spite of what Wood terms in *Recollections*, p. 172, "the anxious state of all classes" the receipts of this season averaged $507.50. With the War of 1812 in progress Warren & Wood wisely opened the Chesnut "with a series of entertainments commemorative of the late brilliant naval victories," as *Durang*, I, XLIX records. "An occasional address

[115]

was delivered by Mr. Wood. *The Soldier's Daughter* was performed, and a new patriotic opera entitled *The Constitution; or American Tars Triumphant*, in the course of which was exhibited a grand naval column, on which was inscribed the names of Hull, Rogers, Decatur, Porter, Morris, and other distinguished naval characters. *The Pride of Columbia*, a new naval song, was sung by Mr. Hardinge. A grand emblematic portrait of Captain Hull was also exhibited, and a scenic representation of the chase and battle between the United States frigate Constitution and the British frigate Guerrière, and the capture of the latter, together with appropriate dances, composed by Mr. Francis, and a new song entitled *American Chronology.*" With *The Constitution*, already mentioned, *The Return from a Cruise, The Constitution Again* and other patriotic entertainments the managers overcame the odds that had compelled them to omit the Baltimore fall season of 1812. In the winter of 1813 the weather was a factor against which they had to contend. Warren complains in his February 20, 1813 entry that it had generally "been very much against the Theatre. This season," he writes, "the streets [have been] frequently in such a condition that it was impossible to walk in them."

Septem[be]r 28 [The] Soldier's Daughter &   690.
              [The] Constitution*

Duff's 1[st]   30 [The] Mountaineers & Raising   442.
app[earanc]e   the Wind
                  [As Octavian in *The Moun-
                  taineers* and Diddler in
                  Raising the Wind. A]

October 2 [The] Stranger, Monody [to] 391.
            Cooke & [The] Vill[age]
            Lawyer.
            [See preface to this season.]

Mrs. Duff's   3 [The] Castle Spectre & [The]   230.   1753.
1st [appearance]   Constitution   ———
                  [As Angela in *The Castle
                  Spectre*. A]

Mrs. Green   5 Pizarro & Love laughs [at   443.
Locksmiths]
[As Cora in *Pizarro*. A]

7 3 & [the] Deuce & [The] Mayor   667.50
[of] Garrat & [A] Tale [of]
Mystery

9 Hamlet & [The] Day after   405.50
[the] Wedding*

10 [The] Honey Moon & [The]   378.50   1894.50
40 Thieves   ——

12 Rule a Wife [& Have a Wife]   321.
& [A] Budget of blunders

14 Alexander [the Great] &   270.50
Darkness Visible*

16 Every One has his fault &   305.50
Val[entine] & Orson

17 Three & [the] Deuce & [The]   464.   1361.
40 Thieves   ——

Whitlock   19 Isabella & Killing no Murder   578.50
[As Isabella. A]

"   21 Douglas & Darkness Visible   387.50
[Mrs. Whitlock As Lady
Randolph in *Douglas*. A]

"   23 [The] Mourning Bride & [The]   358.50
Comet
[Mrs. Whitlock as Zara in
The Mourning Bride. A]

[117]

"   24 [The] Lady of the Lake &   414.50   1739.
                 [The] Citzen   ———

"   26 [The] Jealous Wife & [The]   479.
                 Devil to pay
                 [Mrs. Whitlock as Mrs.
                 Oakly in *The Jealous
                 Wife*. A]

"   28 Macbeth & [The] Day after   512.50
                 [the] Wedding
                 [Mrs. Whitlock as Lady
                 Macbeth. A]

"   29 [The] Carmelite & Darkness   349.
                 Visible
                 [Mrs. Whitlock as Lady St.
                 Valori in *The Carmelite*.
                 A]

                 31 3 & [the] Deuce, [The] Mayor   537.50   1878.
                 of Garrat, Catch him who   ———
                 [can.]

November   2 [The] Grecian Daughter, Reci-   721.
Mrs. W[hitlock's]   t[atio]n & [The] Fortress
Ben[efit]   [As Euprasia in *The Grecian
                 Daughter*. A also an-
                 nounces that, after the
                 play, Mrs. Whitlock is to
                 recite *The Standard of
                 Liberty*.]

                 4 [The] Foundling of [the] forest   580.
                 & [The] Beehive*

                 6 [The First Part of] Henry 4th   486.75
                 & [The] Apprentice

7 She Stoops to Conquer & 391.25 2189.
  [The] Lady of [the] Lake ——

9 [The] Sons of Erin* & [The] 641.50
  Beehive

11 [The] Belle's Stratagem & 377.50
  Tekeli

13 [The] Sons of Erin & [A] Bud- 538.50
  get of blunders

14 3 & [the] Deuce, Syl[vester] 442. 1999.50
  Dagg[erwoo]d & [The] ——
  Deaf Lover

Holman & D[aughte]r 16 Hamlet & [The] Ghost 548.
  [Holman as Hamlet. A]

" 18 [The] Provok'd Husband & 726.
  [A] Bud[get of] Blunders
  [Holman as Townly, Miss
  Holman as Lady Townly,
  in *The Provoked Husband.*
  A]

" 20 Venice Preserv'd & Darkness 549.50
  Visible
  [Holman as Jaffier, Miss
  Holman as Belvidera in
  Venice Preserved. A]

" 21 [The] Wonder & [The] Review 386. 2209.50
  [Holman as Don Felix, Miss ——
  Holman as Donna Vio-
  lante in *The Wonder.* A]

[119]

23 [The Earl of] Essex & [The] 407.
"   Beehive
[Holman as the Earl, Miss
Holman as the Countess
of Rutland. A]

"   25 Romeo & Juliet & Too Many 420.
Cooks
[Holman as Romeo, Miss
Holman as Juliet. A]

"   27 [The] Fair Penitent & Two 386.50
Strings to Y[ou]r bow
[Holman as Horatio, Miss
Holman as Calista in
The Fair Penitent. A]

"   28 Much ado about nothing & 494.50 1708.
[A] Tale [of] Mystery   ———
[Holman as Benedick, Miss
Holman as Beatrice. A]

"   30 Othello & Raising the Wind 532.50
[Holman as Othello, Miss
Holman as Desdemona.
A]

Dec[embe]r 2 [The] School for Scandal & 512.50
"   Ella Rosenberg
[Holman as Charles Surface,
Miss Holman as Lady
Teazle in *The School for
Scandal.* A]

"   4 [The] Honey Moon & [The] 386.50
Prisoner at Large
[Holman as Duke Aranza,
Miss Holman as Juliana
in *The Honey Moon.* A]

[120]

"   5 [The] Votary of Wealth &   367.50   1799.
         [The] Comet   ——————
         [Holman as Drooply, Miss
         Holman as Caroline in
         The Votary of Wealth. A]

"   7 Pizarro & [The] Wedding Day   726.25
         H[olman's] ben[efit. Hol-
         man as Rolla, Miss Hol-
         man as Cora in *Pizarro*.
         A]

"   9 Fontainville Forest & [The] 1252.75
         Sultan
         Miss H[olman's Benefit.
         Holman as Lamotte, Miss
         Holman as Adeline in
         Fontainville Forest and as
         Roxalana in *The Sultan*.
         A]

"   11 [The] Votary of Wealth & 1234.50
         [The] Return from [a]
         Cruise*
         [Holman as Drooply, Miss
         Holman as Caroline in
         The Votary of Wealth. A
         See preface to this season].

"   12 [The] Provok'd Husband &   563.75   3777.25
         [The] Return from [a]   ——————
         Cruise & [The] V[illage]
         Law[yer]
         [Holman as Townly, Miss
         Holman as Lady Townly.
         A]

         14 [The] Sons of Erin & Is he a   292.50
         Prince[?]

16 Town & Country & Don Juan   354.

18 Three & [the] Deuce, [The]   375.
     Day after [the] Wedding
     & [The] Beehive

Elep[hant]   19 [The] Dramatist & Blue Beard   692.   1713.
      [See preface to this season.]   ———

Cone['s] Ben[efit]   21 [The] Foundling of [the] forest   461.
       &   3   W[ee]ks   after
       Marriage
       [See preface to this season.]

Elep[hant]   23 Barbarossa & Matrimony   422.
       [See preface to this season.]

24 Abaellino & High life below   257.
     Stairs

26 W[illia]m Tell* & Hercules &   565.   1705.
     Omphale*   ———

Elep[hant's]   28 [The] Stranger & [The] 40   666.
Ben[efit]   Thieves
       [For the benefit of the Pro-
       prietors of the Elephant.
       A]

30 George Barnwell & Hercules   349.
     & Omphale

1813 Jan[uar]y   1 Marmion* &   Killing   No 1414.75
       Murder

2 d[itt]o & Fortune's frolic   357.25   2787.
                             ———

4 d[itt]o & [The] Honest Thieves   483.

	6 [The] Tempest & [The] Irish-man in London	267.	
Benefit of Mary[lan]d	8 Such things Are & [The] Agreeable Surprize [See preface to this season.]	227.50	
	9 3 & [the] Deuce & [The] Blind Boy	257.	1234.50
	11 Marmion & Tom Thumb [the Great]	578.	
	13 [The] Gazette Extra[ordinar]y & Oscar & Malvina	363.50	941.50
	15 [A of 14 and 15 announces for 15 The Merry Wives of Windsor and The Day after the Wedding.]		
	16 No performance.		
Wood's ben[efit]	18 Marmion & [The] Brazen Mask [As the Palmer in *Marmion*. A]	845.25	
	20 [The] Poor Gentleman, Di-vert[isement] & [The] Chil[dren] in [the] Wood [See preface to this season.]	245.	
Cooper	22 Richard 3d & Of Age to-morrow [As Richard. A]	465.	
"	23 [The] Robbers & [A] Budget of Blunders [Cooper as Charles de Moor in *The Robbers*. A]	731.50	2286.75

[123]

"   25 Much ado about Nothing & 463.25
              [The] Brazen Mask
              [Cooper as Benedick. A]

"   27 Rule a Wife [& Have a Wife] 489.
              & Paul & Virginia
              [Cooper as Leon in *Rule a Wife*. A]

"   29 Othello & Modern Antiques   304.
              [Cooper as Othello. A]

          30 Speed the Plough & Oscar & 198.50   1454.75
              Malvina   ———

" Feb[ruar]y 1 [The] Wheel of fortune & [The] 373.
              Blind Boy
              [Cooper as Penruddock in *The Wheel of Fortune*. A]

C[ooper's] Ben[efit] 3 [The] Robbers & Sprigs of 1130.
              Laurel
              [As Charles de Moor in *The Robbers*. A]

           5 Marmion & Darkness Visible   332.

           6 [The] Way to Get Married & 150.   1985.
              Too Many Cooks   ———

           8 [The] Merry Wives of Wind- 267.50
              sor & Mr. H.

         10 Timour [the Tartar]* & [The] 447.
              Children in the Wood

         12 [The] School of Reform, Ballet 411.
              & [The] Prize
              [Ballet, *Rural Grace*. A]

13 3 & [the] Deuce & Timour   419.50   1545.
[the Tartar]   ———

15 Marmion, Rural Grace &   466.
[The] Inv[isible] Girl

Warren's Ben[efit] 17 [The] Rivals & Timour [the   704.25
Tartar]
[As Sir Anthony Absolute in
The Rivals. A]

19 Right & Wrong,* [The] Mir-   375.
[aculous] Mill, All the
World['s a] Stage

20 3 W[ee]ks after Marr[ia]ge,   136.25   1681.50
[The] Mir[aculous] Mill   ———
& Timour [the Tartar]

22 Bunker Hill, [The] Constitu- 1031.75
tion Ag[ai]n* & [The]
Adopted Ch[il]d

Miss Aber-   24 [The] Jealous Wife, Ballet &   857.
[crombie']s   [The] Romp
ben[efit]   [See preface to this season.]

[Benefit of]   26 [The] West Indian & [A] Bud-   585.50
Mrs. Riddle   [get of] Blunders
[As Louisa Dudley in *The
West Indian.* A]

27 Laugh When you Can &   308.   2782.25
Timour [the Tartar]   ———

March 1 [The] Merchant of Venice &   278.50
[The] Constit[utio]n again

[125]

3 Julius Caesar, Ballet & [The]   310.50
   Deaf Lover
   [Ballet, *L'Amour Vient a*
   Bout de Tout. A]

5 [The] Follies of a day, Ballet &   371.
   [The] Critic
   [Ballet, *Mirth by Moonlight.*
   A]

6 Three & [the] Deuce & Timour   300.   1260.
   [the Tartar]   ———

8 [The] Curfew, Ballet & Paul &   257.
   Virginia
   [Ballet, *Mirth by Moonlight.*
   A]

[Benefit of]   10 Love Makes a Man, Ballet &   1271.
Jefferson   [The] Sleepwalker*
   [As Don Lewis in *Love Makes*
   a Man and Somno in *The*
   Sleepwalker; also to sing
   a comic song. Ballet,
   The Jovial Crew; or, The
   Humor of a Country
   Wake. A]

[Benefit of]   12 Wild Oats,* Ballet & [The]   556.
Mrs. Wood   Sleepwalker
   [Ballet, *Rural Grace.* A]

[Benefit of   13 [The] Honey Moon, Ballet,   528.   2612.
Mrs.] Mason   [The] day after [the]   ———
   Wedding
   [As Lady Elizabeth in *The*
   Day after the Wedding.
   See preface to this season.]

[126]

Duff   15 Coriolanus, Imitations & 1573.
      Netley Abbey
      [As Coriolanus and M'Ser-
      ape in *Netley Abbey*. A
      See preface to this season.]

[Benefit of]   17 Wild Oats, Lovers['] Quarrels, 588.50
Francis   Pantomime & c[etera]
      [As Sir George Thunder in
      Wild Oats. A See pref-
      ace to this season.]

[Benefit of]   19 [The] Sailor's daughter, Trans- 455.
Robins   p[arencie]s & [A] tale [of]
      Mystery
      [See preface to this season.]

[Benefit of   20 [A] Cure for [the] Heartache, 701.   3317.50
Mrs.] Green   Ballet & How to die [for   ——
      Love]*
      [Ballet, *The Shamrock*. A]

[Benefit of]   22 [The] Road to Ruin, Mirth by 689.50
Blissett   Moon[light] & How to
      die [for Love]

[Benefit of]   24 Richard 3ᵈ·, Ballet & [The] 949.50
Mrs. Duff   Weathercock
      [As Lady Anne. Ballet,
      Rural Grace. A]

[Benefit of]   26 [The] Clandestine Marriage, 425.
Francis   Ballet & Mr. H.
      [Ballet, *Arlequin dans la
      Lune, ou La Fête du Vil-
      lage*. A]

[Benefit of]   27 [The] Jealous Wife & How to 357.50   2421.50
Mr. Barrett   die for love   ——

[Benefit of]   29 [The] Found[lin]g of [the]   594.50
Doyle   forest, Ballet & [The]
                          Honest thieves
                          [See preface to this season.]

[Benefit of]   31 Town & Country, Ballet &   463.
Bray   [The] Lady of [the] Rock
                          [Ballet, *Little Red Riding
                          Hood*. A]

April 2 [The] Point of Honor, Ballet   733.25
[Benefit of]   & [The] Review
Hardinge   [As Looney Mactwolter in
                          The Review. Ballet, *Little
                          Red Riding Hood*. A]

[Benefit of]   3 He Would be [a] Soldier, Bal-   446.   2236.
F. Durang &   let & Val[entine] & Orson
Lindsley   [Durang to appear in sailor's
                          hornpipe.   Lindsley to
                          recite.   Ballet, *The
                          American Volunteer*; *or,
                          A Scene on the Frontier.*
                          A]

[Benefit of]   5 Wild Oats & Timour [the   487.50
Miss M. White   Tartar]

[Benefit of   7 Love Makes a Man, Ballet &   438.
Mrs. and Miss]   [The] Ag[reeable] Sur-
Seymour   prize
                          [Ballet, *Little Red Riding
                          Hood*. A]

                    9 [The] Point of Honor & Cin-   825.
                          derella

                    10 [The] Dramatist & Cinderella   384.   2134.50
                                                      ———

	12 Cinderella, How to die [for Love] & All the World's [a] St[a]ge	617.25	
Fennell	14 King Lear & Little Red R[iding] Hood [As Lear. A]	336.	
"	15 [The] Revenge & Cinderella [Fennell as Zanga. A]	401.75	
"	17 Douglas & Cinderella [Fennell as Glenalvon in Douglas. A]	317.	1672.
	19 [The] Heir at Law, Ballet & [The] Quadrupeds [of Quadlinburg*] [Ballet, *Easter Sports; or, Harlequin's Rambles.* A]	498.	
Fenn[ell's] ben[efi]t	21 Gustavus Vasa, Ballet & [The] Sleepwalker [As Gustavus. Ballet, *Easter Frolics.* A]	479.50	
Ben[efit of] Easton Suf- f[erer]s	23 [The] Wheel of Fortune & Cinderella [For the relief of the unfortunate sufferers by the late fire and sickness at Easton, Md.]	416.	
Pullen['s Benefit]	24 [The] Peasant Boy & [The] Critic	450.75	1843.25

$59860.

118 Nights.
Average 507.50

BALTIMORE SPRING [SEASON, COMMENCING MAY 10, ENDING
JUNE 10,] 1813.

[Warren & Wood]

PREFACE: As stated in the Foreword, p. vii, there are two versions of
the record of this season. The interpolations from the Volume II version
include the names of the days of the week, "bie" of "Abercrombie" in
the entry of May 28, "our" of "Seymour" in the entry of June 4 and
"cis" of "Francis" in the entry of June 7. For the entire entry of May 10
the text of the Volume II version has been used.

The explanations of the references to this preface are as follows: **May
10**—FG states that "The Theatre will open with an occasional patriotic
address." **May 19:** "After [*The Sons of Erin*], for the first time in this
city, will be performed the celebrated shawl dance, by the Misses Abercrombie." FG **May 22:** FG announces a new dramatic, patriotic olio,
commemorative of the victories of the Macedonia, Java and Peacock.
It is to consist of "Song, Dance and Spectacle, with New and Elegant
Transparent Portraits of Naval Commanders, &c." **May 24:** FG
announces an entertainment similar to that of May 22, entitled *Freemen
in Arms*. **May 28:** The Ballet is *The Shamrock*, in which, according
to FG, "will be introduced the favorite Wreath Dance by the Misses
Abercrombie and a variety of lilts, flings &c. by the Misses Abercrombie,
Mrs. Bray, etc." **June 4:** FG announces a ballet, wreath dance and
pas de deux by the Misses Abercrombie and that Mrs. Seymour is to
sing a hunting song. **June 8:** For an explanation of "Nav[al] Portraits,"
see the note of May 22.

In Volume I Wood has written the words "New Theatre" over the
record of this season and, in *Recollections*, p. 189, he explains that "the
liberality of the Baltimore public had induced the managers to form
contracts for erecting a building more convenient and worthy of their
patronage. In despite of the unfavorable state of the times, it became
necessary to proceed with the enterprise, at least so far as to make a
beginning under great disadvantages, and the new theatre was opened
May 10, [1813. For further details, see the general introduction, p. 21].
For the first night, and several succeeding ones, the accommodations for
the audience [were] confined to the lower boxes and the pit. . . . The
stair cases leading to the upper boxes and gallery were wholly unfinished."

More vexatious, however, than this handicap was the "great alarm
and anxiety" which Warren writes in his *Diary* on May 4, "prevail here

[130]

at present on ac[coun]t of the Enemy being so near. They have burnt
French Town and Havre de Grace." Warren adds, "We lost a new green
Curtain & a drop cloth intended for the theatre here—value $650."
On May 12 Warren writes, "The alarm has subsided, the fleet having
gone down the bay;" but the loss of the curtains had been a further
embarrassment to Warren & Wood, who had to summon painters from
Philadelphia in order "to present a few plays creditably." Wood in
Recollections, p. 191, quotes Warren as remarking wittily, "We ought
not to complain, as these were the only bays (baize) the English had yet
gained by the war."

May
Mon. 10 [The] West Indian & [The] 355.25
        Sleepwalker* & Address
        [See preface to this season.]

Wed. 12 [The] Mountaineers, R[ural] 436.
        Grace* & [The] Constitu-
        tion [& the Wasp]

Frid. 14 [The] Point of Honor, [Little 397.25
        Red] R[iding] Hood* &
        [The] Chil[dren] in [the]
        Wood.

Saty. 15 [The] Peasant Boy & Dark- 290.75 1479.25
        ness Visible*   ———

Mon. 17 [The] Jealous Wife, [Little 288.50
        Red] R[iding] Hood &
        [The] Invisible Girl.

Wed. 19 [The] Sons of Erin,* Ballet* & 388.75
        Tom Thumb [the Great.]
        [See preface to this season.]

Frid. 21 [The] Foundling of [the] 405.75
        forest & How to die for
        Love*

Saty. 22 Three & [the] Deuce, Olio   395.   1478.
[The] Mayor of Garrat ——
[See preface to this season.]

Mon. 24 Wild Oats, Olio & [The] 480.75
Review
[See preface to this season.]

Wood's   Wed. 26 Town & Country, [The] Jovial 346.75
[Benefit]   Crew & [The] Apprentice

[Benefit   Frid. 28 [The] Blind Boy, Ballet, [The] 479.
of the Misses]   Purse & [The] Agree[able]
Abercrombie   Surprize
[See preface to this season.]

[Benefit   Saty. 29 Richard 3d., [The] Shamrock 376.   1682.50
of Mr. and   & [The] Irish[man] in
Mrs.] Duff   London
[Duff as Richard and as
Murtoch Delany in *The
Irishman in London.* FG]

[Benefit   Mon. 31 [A] Tale [of] Mystery, [The] 259.75
of Mr. and   Hon[est] Thieves, [Little
Mrs.] Bray   Red] R[iding] Hood &
[The] Critic
[Bray as Abel Day in *The
Honest Thieves*, Mrs.
Bray to dance in *Little
Red Riding Hood.* FG]

June
[Benefit   Wed. 2 Every one has his fault   337.50
of Mrs.] Green   [The] Rival Soldiers
& [Mrs.] Mason   [Mrs. Green as Mary Tactic
in *The Rival Soldiers* and
as Miss Wooburn with
Mrs. Mason as Lady
Eleanor in *Every One Has
His Fault.* FG]

[Benefit   Frid.   4 He W[oul]d be a Soldier, ballet   185.
of Mrs.] Seymour   & Ella Rosenberg
& Barrett   [See preface to this season.]

[Benefit   Saty.   5 Love Makes a Man & How to   707.50   1489.75
of Mr. & Mrs.]   die for Love   ———   ———
Jefferson   [Jefferson to sing comic
                 song. FG]

[Benefit   Mon.   7 [The] Clandestine Marriage,   642.50
of] Francis &   Ballett & [A] Budg[et] of
Blissett   blunders
                 [Ballet, *La Triomphe de
                 l'Amour.* FG]

         Tues.   8 [The] Dramatist, Nav[al] Por-   181.75
                traits & All the World's
                [a Stage]
                [See preface to this season.]

         Wed.   9 [The]   Prisoner   at   Large,   858.
                Timour [the Tartar]* &
                [The] Romp

      Thursday 10   Right & Wrong* & Timour   637.50   2319.75
                [the Tartar]   ———   ———

                                           $8449.25

                   20 Nights
                 Average $422.

WASHINGTON SEASON[, COMMENCING JUNE 15, ENDING
SEPTEMBER 13,] 1813.

[Warren & Wood]

PREFACE: There is only one version of the record of this season. In Wood's entry of August 19, it has been advisable to change "Greens" to "Green" and, in his entry of August 24, "Barretts" to "Barrett" in order to maintain uniformity of style.

The explanations of the references to this preface are as follows: **June 19**—DNI announces that "a part of the evening's entertainments will be appropriated to a commemoration of our naval victories in a patriotic entertainment called *Freemen in Arms.*" See note for May 24 in preface to the Baltimore Spring Season of 1813. **July 5**: DNI announces a monumental tribute called *The Tears of Columbia.* "The stage will discover a national monument to the memory of General Z. M. Pike and the gallant and lamented Captain James Lawrence. A female figure in mourning representing Columbia leans despondently over one side of the tomb. The genius of Liberty advances and delivers an elegiac poem written by a gentleman of the city to the memory of the two lamented heroes." **July 13**: DNI of July 14 announces *Right and Wrong* and *The Romp* for July 15. There is no record in the *Account Book* of these performances and, on July 29, DNI announces *Right and Wrong* as "never having been performed here." On page one of DNI for July 15 appears this notice: "Theatre. To be sold to the highest bidder, on Saturday, the 24th inst. at Davis's Hotel, the Theatre in this city with the lots belonging thereto. N. L. Queen, Auctr." On July 17 DNI announces there will be no performance until further notice. Even in normal times, according to A. I. Mudd in an article entitled *Early Theatres in Washington City* (in Columbia Hist. Soc. Records, V, 1902, pp. 64–86) the theatre used by Warren & Wood had "not been a paying investment;" and now, as Warren in the July 13 entry in his *Diary* discloses, "After this night the theatre was closed in consequence of the British fleet standing up the Potowmach—to the great annoyance of the Government, who were evidently very much alarmed for themselves." **August 3**: Wood's date is evidently incorrect. At all events, DNI announces that these performances are "unavoidably postponed" until August 5. Warren, in the August 3 entry of his *Diary*, writes, "I learn that the play announced for this Evening was postponed on Acc[oun]t of the death of Miss Ch[arlo]t[te] Abercrombie, who died yesterday morning aged 16 yrs." Warren mentions *Timour the Tartar* as being given on August 5. In his September 4 entry he writes, "The British fleet have Sail[e]d down the Bay. We shall therefore open in Baltimore."

June
T[uesday] 15 [The] Birthday, R[ura]l Grace   245.75
        & [The] Comet

T[hursday] 17 [The] Sailor's D[aughte]r &   168.24
        [Little] R[ed] R[iding]
        Hood*

S[aturday] 19 [The] Blind Boy, N[aval] Vic-   325.
       tories & [The] Bee Hive*   ——
       [See preface to this season.]

T[uesday] 22 [The] Point of Honor, R[ural]   299.50
       Grace [&] All the World's
       [a] Stage

T[hursday] 24 Speed the Plough & [The]   241.25
       Sleepwalker*

S[aturday] 26 Ways & Means, N[aval] Vic-   264.25
   —   tories & [The] Ch[ildren]   ———
       in [the] Wood

T[uesday] 29 Town & Country & [The]   237.75
       Prize

July
T[hursday] 1 Mr. H.,* |Little] R[ed] R[id-   123.50
       ing] Hood & How to die
       for love*

S[aturday] 3 [The] Peasant Boy & Valen-   307.25
   —   tine & Orson   ———

M[onday] 5 W[illia]m Tell,* [The] Agree-   480.25
       able Surprize & C[eter]a
       [See preface to this season.]

T[hursday] 8 [The] Stranger & Modern An-   226.75
       tiques

S[aturday] 10 Alexander the Great* & [The]   230.75
   —   Beehive   ———

T[uesday] 13 Guerre Ouverte, [The] M[irac-   203.25
       ulous] Mill & [Of] Age
       tomorrow
       [See preface to this season.]

T[uesday] 27 [The] Follies of a day, [The]   121.
Purse & [The] Review

T[hursday] 29 Right & Wrong* & [The]   167.
Weathercock

S[aturday] 31 Macbeth & [The] Day after   243.25
— [the] Wedding   ————

August
T[uesday] 3 Timour the Tartar* & 3   224.
W[ee]ks after Marriage
[See preface to this season.]

Sat[urday] 7 Timour [the Tartar] & [The]   176.25
— Irishman in London   ————

T[uesday] 10 [The] Heir at Law & [The]   80.25
Critic

T[hursday] 12 [The] Glory of Columbia &   141.75
Cath[erine] & Petruchio

S[aturday] 14 [The] R[oad] to Ruin, H[ar-   122.50
ben[efit of Mr. &   lequin] H[urry] Scurry &
Miss] Aber[crombie]   [The] Sultan

T[uesday] 17 [The] Prov[oke]d Husband,   155.25
[Benefit of Mr.   [The] Const[itutio]n &
and Mrs.] Jefferson   D[arkness] Visible*

T[hursday] 19 [The] M[anager] in distress,   133.
[Benefit of Mr. &   [The] Dramatist & Inkle
Mrs.] Green   & Yarico

S[aturday] 21 [The] Soldier's Daughter &   122.
[Benefit of Mrs.]   [The] Critic   ————
Mason &
[Mr.] Harris

T[uesday] 24 Othello & [The] Day after 106.75
[Benefit of Mr. &   [the] Wedding
    Mrs.] Barrett   [Barrett as Othello. DNI]

T[hursday] 26 Youth's Errors,* [The] H[on- 139.50
[Benefit of] Bray   est] thieves & [The]
    & Francis   R[obber] of Genoa

S[aturday] 28 Adelgitha* & Lock & Key*   58.00
[Benefit of Mr.]
    Doyle &
    [Mrs.] Seymour

T[uesday] 31 Timour [the Tartar] & [The] 141.50
              Village Lawyer

Sep[tember]
T[hursday] 2 Blue Beard & [The] Pris[oner] 114.
              at Large

S[a]turday 4 [The] 40 Thieves & 2 Strings 143.
           —   to Y[ou]r Bow*   ——

M[onday]   6 [The] School of Reform & 129.75
              Her[cules] & Omphale*

W[ednesday] 8 [The] Gamester & Raising the 58.75
              Wind

F[riday]   10 [The] Wheel of fortune & for- 82.25
              tune's frolic   ——

Mon[day]   13 Bunker Hill, [The] Catch Club 171.75
              & [The] Adopted Child   ——

BALTIMORE AUTUMN [SEASON, COMMENCING OCTOBER 1, ENDING
NOVEMBER 18,] 1813.

BALTIMORE AUTUMN 1813.

[Warren & Wood]

PREFACE—**October 1**: FG announces, "On this evening the curtain
will rise to a national air and discover (for the first time here) an entire

[137]

new drop scene representing a splendid temple.   In the centre a Rostral
Column commemorative of the first seven naval victories achieved by
the navy of the United States.   The whole painted by Mr. Worrell and
assistants, expressly for the occasion.   After the play a monody on the
late Capt. Lawrence and Lieut. Burroughs, to be spoken by Mrs. Mason.
Between the play and the opera will be exhibited a grand naval transparency painted by Mr. Jefferson.   The Genius of America is seen seated
on a rock upon the borders of a lake, presenting to an infant figure of
Fame illustrative of the growing splendor of our naval band a portrait
of the youthful hero Commodore Perry.   In the perspective a distant
view of the enemy's captured fleet at the moment of its being taken
possession of by its valiant conqueror and surmounted by our national
flag."   **October 23**: FG announces "A variety of new dances composed
by Mr. Francis, among which are a flag dance by Miss Abercrombie and
a naval triple hornpipe."   This was Miss Sophia Abercrombie.   Her
sister Charlotte had died, as Warren's *Diary* reports, during the Washington season just passed.   Since the last Baltimore season "the theatre
had been completed," writes Wood in *Recollections*, p. 192; and this
season was "heralded in October by this Announcement.   The managers
respectfully inform the public that the interior of the building is now
completed and the *lobbies, coffee room, passages* and *discharging doors*
fitted up in the best manner.   The whole offering to the public a degree
of accomodation not exceeded by any theatre in the United States."

October	1	She Stoops to Conquer, Olio & [The] Heroes of the Lakes [See preface to this season.]	578.25	
Saty.	2	Three & [the] Deuce, [The] Purse & [A] Budget of Blunders	125.25 ———	703.50
Mon.	4	[The] Road to Ruin & [The] Heroes of the Lakes	230.75	
Wedy.	6	Abaellino & [The] Critic	411.50	
Frid.	8	Rule a Wife [& Have a Wife] & [The] Lady of the Lake	542.25	

Saty. 9 [The] Stranger & [The] Sleep-   162.50   1347.
walker   ─────

Mon. 11 [The] Provok'd Husband &   205.25
Killing No Murder

Wed. 13 Much Ado about Nothing   207.
& Don Juan

Frid. 15 'Tis all a farce, [The] Lady of   458.75
[the] Lake & [The] Mayor
of Garrat

Saty. 16 William Tell,* & Valentine   273.   1144.
and Orson   ─────

Mon. 18 [The] Robbers & [The] Beehive

Wed. 20 [The] Birthday & Timour   487.75
[the Tartar]

Frid. 22 [The] Heir at Law, [Little]   275.75
R[ed] R[iding] Hood & 3
W[ee]ks after Marr[ia]ge

Saty. 23 Geo[rge] Barnwell, Dance &   216.75   1371.25
[The] Robber of Genoa   ─────
[See preface to this season.]

Mon. 25 [The] Soldier[']s Daughter &   350.50
[The] Lady of the Lake

Wed. 27 [The] Wonder & Timour [the   290.75
Tartar]

Frid. 29 [The] Harper's Daughter* &   462.25
Of Age tomorrow

[139]

Saty. 30 Speed the Plough, [The] 223.50 1327.
M[iraculous] Mill & ———
Lovers['] Quarrels

Novem[ber] 1 [The] Poor Gentleman & 226.50
Tekeli

Wedy. 3 [The] Harper's Daughter & 406.50
Timour [the Tartar]

Frid. 5 [Count] Benyowsky & Dark- 376.50
ness Visible

Saty. 6 [The] School for Scandal & 254.50 1264.
How to die for love ———

Mon. 8 Romeo & Juliet & Mr. H. 331.25

Wed. 10 Marmion* & [The] Romp 840.75

·Frid. 12 Marmion & All the World's a 583.50
Stage

Saty. 13 [The] Privateer & [The] Devil 160.25 1915.75
to pay ———

Nov[embe]r 15 [Count] Benyowsky, Ballet 310.25
& Catch him Who Can
[Ballet, *The Miraculous
Mill*. FG]

Tues. 16 Marmion & Fortune's frolic 334.50

Wed. 17 [The] Honey Moon & Two 328.50
Strings to Your Bow

Thurs. 18 The Kiss & [The] Brazen 296.50 1269.75
Mask ——— ———

$10342.25

30 Nights
Averaged $344

[140]

PHILADELPHIA SEASON, COMMENCING NOVEM[BE]R 22D. 1813,
[ENDING APRIL 16, 1814.]

[Warren & Wood]

PREFACE—**November 22**: A announces "a display of naval pillars," a "pas seul" by Miss [Sophia] Abercrombie, a "naval dance" and a "naval procession." **November 27**: A announces "a Grand Display of Naval Pillars entwined with the names of Hull, Jones, Decatur, Bainbridge, Lawrence, Burroughs, Perry and Harrison;" also, dances and a naval procession. **December 1**: A announces "additional naval and patriotic entertainments" in honor of the "gallant Commodore Bainbridge," who is "to visit the theatre this evening." **December 6**: In an entry of this date Warren writes in his *Diary*, "Major General Harrison visits the Theatre this Evening." **January 8**: A announces "a new naval dance; the scene discovers Lake Erie and the fleet of Commodore Perry at anchor with the captured fleet of the enemy." **January 15**: The marginal note "C. Perry" occurs in the text of this entry. Warren notes in his *Diary* on this date: "Perry visits the Theatre this Evening." **January 29**: A announces that Cooper is to recite a monody "on the late lamented Captain Lawrence." **March 14**: On the occasion of the elder Jefferson's benefit Wood has written over the title "Transformation" the words "Perry's Victory." The Aurora throws no light on this reference, which may be to the "scene" mentioned in the note of January 8. **March 21**: A announces *The Shakespeare Jubilee*, "music, dialogue and spectacle, written by the late David Garrick in honor of the immortal bard." Francis is to direct the pastoral ballet *L'Amour Vient à Bout de Tout* and to sing with Blissett *The Warwickshire Thief*. **March 23**: Robins, according to A, contributes new scenery to *The Hero of the North*, with the assistance of H. Warren and T. Reinagle. **April 11**: A also announces Miss [Sophia] Abercrombie in a broad sword hornpipe in Act V of *The Kiss* and in *Easter Frolics*. **April 16**: Mr. Pullen was treasurer of the company.

Rumors of the enemy's movements kept disturbing the public during this season. In the April 15 entry of his *Diary*, Warren reports that "news of the British fleet being in sight of Baltimore the packet and steam boat line are suspended." Wood, however, in his *Recollections*, p. 182, recalls the figure of the ill wind in stating that "frequent [patriotic] celebrations proved a welcome aid to [the] exhausted treasury." "The

German drama," he points out, "at this time stood high in public favor. We may call it, indeed, the German season."

At the end of the record of this season Wood has written: "11 [nights] under [$] 300, 23 under 400, 5 under 250, 2 under 200." In the March 26, 1814 entry of his *Diary*, Warren contradicts Wood. "Mrs. Whitlock's N[igh]t," he records. "[The] Honey Moon & How to die for Love—chang[ed] from Isabella. Mr. Whitlock ill."

Novem[be]r 22 [The] Road to Ruin, Olio &   834.50
　　　　　　　　[The] Heroes of the Lakes
　　　　　　　　[See preface to this season.]

　　　　　　24 Three & [the] Deuce, [The]   651.50
　　　　　　　　Purse & [A] Budget of
　　　　　　　　blunders

　　　　　　26 Wives as they Were [& Maids   440.75
　　　　　　　　as They Are] & [The]
　　　　　　　　Critic

　　　　　　27 Romeo & Juliet, Scenery &   470.75   2397.50
　　　　　　　　Mr. H.   　　　　　　　　　　　———
　　　　　　　　[See preface to this season.]

　　　　　　29 Adelgitha & [The] Sleepwalker 616.25

Decem[be]r 1 [The] Wonder & Cinderella 1105.25
Bainbridge　　　[See preface to this season.]

　　　　　　　3 [The] Kiss,* Ballet & [The]   455.50
　　　　　　　　Wedding day
　　　　　　　　[Ballet, *Little Red Riding
　　　　　　　　Hood*. A]

　　　　　　　4 [The] Jealous Wife & [A] Tale 276.75   2453.75
　　　　　　　　of Mystery   　　　　　　　　　———

Gen[eral] Harrison 6 Macbeth & [The] Day after 999.75
　　　　　　　　the Wedding
　　　　　　　　[See preface to this season.]

[142]

8 Much ado about Nothing   261.25
    Cinderella

10 Marmion & [The] Sleepwalker   850.

11 Three & [the] Deuce, [The]   339.50   2450.50
    Mayor of Garrat & [The]   ———
    Robber of Genoa*

13 [The] Harper's Daughter*   673.50
    & [The] Mir[aculous] Mill
    & [The] Devil to pay

15 [The] Kiss, Syl[vester] Dag-   519.50
    gerwood &[The] High-
    land Reel

17 [The] School for Scandal &   470.25
    [The] Beehive

18 [The] Robbers & Cinderella   457.50   2120.75
                            ———

20 [The] Harper's Daughter &   366.50
    [Of] Age tomorrow

22 [The] Foundling of [the] forest   490.75
    & How to die for love

23 [The] Grecian Daughter &   227.
    Darkness Visible

24 Marmion & [The] Comet   549.50   1633.75
                            ———

27 [Count] Benyowsky* & [The]   981.25
    Lady of the Lake

29 Wild Oats & Valentine &   505.25
    Orson

[143]

31 Geo[rge] Barnwell & W[illia]m 449.
    Tell

[1814.] January   1 [The] Ethiop* & 'Tis all a farce 1607.25   3542.7.
                                                        ─────────

3 [The] Ethiop & Two Strings to 994.25
    your Bow

5 [The] Ethiop & [The] Children 806.25
    in the Wood

7 [The] Ethiop & [The] Weather- 772.75
    cock

8 [The] Privateer, Dance & 366.50   2939.75
    Three and [the] Deuce   ─────────
    [See preface to this season.]

Bar[ker's]   10 Marmion & [The] Rival 575.50
ben[efit]   Soldiers
                      [Benefit of James Nelson
                      Barker, the author of
                      Marmion. A]

Cooper   12 Hamlet & 3 Weeks after 788.50
                      Marriage
                      [As Hamlet. A]

"   14 Rule a Wife [& Have a 680.
                      Wife], Ballet & Killing
                      no Murder
                      [Cooper as Leon in *Rule a
                      Wife.* Ballet, *Little Red
                      Riding Hood.* A]

"   15 Richard 3rd. & [The] Hunter 971.50 3015.50
                      of the Alps
                      [Cooper as Richard. A See
                      preface to this season.]

[144]

" 17 [The] Virgin of the Sun & 638.50
[The] Sleepwalker
[Cooper as Rolla in *The
Virgin of the Sun*. A]

" 19 Pizarro & Fortune's frolic 640.
[Cooper as Rolla in *Pizarro*,
a sequel to *The Virgin of
the Sun*. A]

" 21 [The] Honey Moon & [The] 576.
Highland Reel
[Cooper as Duke Aranza in
The Honey Moon. A]

C[ooper's] 22 [The First Part of] Henry 4th 778. 2632.50
Ben[efit] & Catherine & Petruchio ——
[As Hotspur and Petruchio.
A]

Cooper 24 Venice Preserv'd & Hercules 291.50
& Omphale
[As Pierre in *Venice Pre-
served*. A]

" 26 Othello & Tom Thumb [the 402.75
Great]
[Cooper as Othello. A]

" 28 Abaellino & [A] Budget of 662.50
blunders
[Cooper as Abaellino and
Flodoardo in *Abaellino*.
A]

" 29 [The] Wheel of fortune, Mon- 402.75 1759.50
ody, All the World's [a] ——
Stage
[Cooper as Penruddock in
The Wheel of Fortune. A
See preface to season.]

[145]

31 [The] Ethiop & [The] Adopted 553.75
   Child

Feb[ruar]y   2 [The] Stranger & [The] Lady 378.
   of the Lake

4 Education* & [The] Beehive 368.

Wood's Ben[efi]t   5 [The] Ethiop & [The] Mayor 654.   1953.75
   of Garrat

Ben[efit of] J. N. B. 8 Marmion & [The] Span[ish] 948.25
   Barber
   [For explanation of J. N. B.
   see announcement in A:
   "Benefit of Jack Barker,
   author of *Marmion*."]

9 [The] Mountaineers & 3 & 223.50
   [the] Deuce

11 [The] Birthday, [Little] R[ed 198.50
   Riding] Hood & [The]
   Blind Boy

12 [Count] Benyowsky & [The] 289.   1659.25
   Toothache*   ————

14 [The] Ethiop & How to die 358.
   for Love

16 Education, Dance & [The] 402.75
   Toothache
   [Dance, *The Miraculous
   Mill.* A]

18 [The] Exile & [The] Village 980.
   Lawyer

[146]

19 [The] Exile & Killing no 457.   2197.75
    Murder   ——

21 [The Exile & [The] Toothache 621.25

22 [The] Soldier's Daughter & 390.25
    [The] Corsair

25 Education & Catch him Who 474.75
    Can

26 [The] Exile & [The] Hunter of 554.   2040.25
    the Alps   ——

28 [The] Exile & [The] Honest 426.
    Thieves

March 2 [The] Ethiop & 'Tis all a farce 338.25

4 Remorse* & [The] Sleepwalker 395.50

5 Education & [The] Corsair 265.50 1425.25
                       ——

7 [The] Exile & [The] Midnight 516.
    Hour

9 Marmion & Matrimony   194.

11 Remorse & [The] Midnight 223.75
     Hour

12 [The] Exile & Who's the 333.50 1267.25
    Dupe?   ——

[Benefit of]   14 Education & Transformation* 1241.
Jeff[erson]   [As Camelion in *Transfor-
                    mation* and to sing. A]

[Benefit of] Mrs. Wood	16 [The] Span[ish] Barber, [The] Follies of a day & Timour [the Tartar]	509.	
[Benefit of] Mrs. Mason	18 [The] Sons of Erin, [The] Day after [the] Wedding & Transform[ation] [As Lady Ann Lovel in *The Sons of Erin* and Lady Elizabeth in *The Day after the Wedding.* A]	629.50	
[Benefit of] Mr. Duff	19 [The] Iron Chest, [The] Sham- rock & [The] Irishman in Lond[on] [As Sir Edward Mortimer in *The Iron Chest* and Murtoch Delany in *The Irishman in London.* A]	1186.25 ———	3565.75
[Benefit of] Mr. Francis	21 Adrian & Orrilla & Shakes- peare Jubilee [See preface to this season.]	368.50	
[Benefit of] Robins	23 [The] Hero of the North & ['Tis] all a farce [See preface to this season.]	638.75	
[Benefit of] Mrs. Green	25 Town & Country & Timour [the Tartar] [As Rosalie Somers in *Town and Country* and as Liska in *Timour the Tartar*; also to sing. A]	828.50	
[Benefit of Mrs.] Whitlock	26 Isabella & How to die for Love [As Isabella and to recite. A]	270.75 ———	2106.50

Benefit of
Blissett

28 [The] Fortress, [The] Widow's 783.50
Vow & [The] Poor Soldier
[As Don Antonio in *The
Widow's Vow* and Baga-
telle in *The Poor Soldier.*
A]

[Benefit of]
Mrs. Duff

30 Abaellino & 3 & [the] deuce 806.25
[As Rosamonda in *Abael-
lino.* A]

April

[Benefit of] Mrs.
Francis

1 [The] Recruiting Officer & [A] 423.
Tale of Mystery
[As Rose in *The Recruiting
Officer* and Fiametta in *A
Tale of Mystery.* A]

[Benefit of] Bray

2 [The] Point of Honor, [The] 441.25 2454.
Toothache & [The] ——
Boarding House*
[As Simon Spatterdash in
The Boarding House; and
to sing. A]

[Benefit of]
Barrett

4 [The] Rivals & Lovers['] Quar- 475.
rels & [The] Jew & Doctor
[As Captain Absolute in
The Rivals. A]

[Benefit of]
Aber[crombie] &
[Mrs.] Seymour

6 [The] Peasant Boy, [The] 469.50
Robber of Genoa & [The]
Prisoner at Large
[Abercrombie as Vincent in
The Peasant Boy and Le
Terreur in *The Robber of
Genoa.* A]

[149]

[Benefit of] Doyle 8 [The]   Gamester & [The] 386.50
N[aval] Pillar & [The]
Review
[As Stukely in *The Gamester*
and as Looney Mac-
twolter in *The Review*. A]

[Benefit of] 9 [The] Jew, Ballet & [The] 741.   2072.
Hardinge Soldier's Return ——
[As Sheva in *The Jew* and as
Dermot O'Diddipole in
The Soldier's *Return*; also
to sing.   Ballet, *The
Shamrock*. A]

[Benefit of] Miss 11 [The] Kiss & Tekeli 933.75
Aber[crombie] [As Christine in *Tekeli*. A
See preface to this season.]

[Benefit of] Miss 13 [The] B[oarding] House & 466.
[M.] White Adrian & Orrilla
[As Caroline in *The Board-
ing House* and as Orrilla.
A]

Warren's [Benefit] 15 [The] Exile & [The] Forest of 963.
Hermanstadt*
[As the Governor of Tobolsk
in *The Exile* and Sir John
Falstaff in an epilogue
written by Mr. Merry. A]

Pullen's [Benefit] 16 Education & Ella Rosenberg 814.   3176.75
[See preface to this season.] ——   ————
$48864.75

84 Nights
averaged 581.75

[150]

BALTIMORE SPRING SEASON, [COMMENCING APRIL 20, ENDING JUNE 10,] 1814.

[Warren & Wood]

PREFACE—**April 23**: BP states that "in consequence of the non-arrival of a large part of the theatrical baggage, the managers are compelled to postpone the performance advertised for Saturday evening." In the April 23 entry of his *Diary* Warren writes, "postponed—waggons not come." **May 14**: According to BP, the "evening's entertainment will, as far as possible, be rendered appropriate and commemorative" of the capture of the brig Épervier by the American sloop of war Peacock, Captain Warrington. **May 28**: FG announces Miss [Sophia] Abercrombie and F. Durang in the *Minuet de la Cour*, which is to be introduced in a masquerade to be a part of the fourth act of *The Belle's Stratagem* and Miss Abercrombie as Red Riding Hood in the ballet of that name to be given "under the direction of Messrs. Abercrombie and Francis." In the course of the ballet, according to FG, "will be introduced a variety of dances and, for the first time this season, the favorite Pas de Deux of *Coolen* by Miss Abercrombie and Mr. F. Durang." FG also announces Miss Abercrombie as Little Pickle "with song" in *The Spoiled Child*. **June 4**: Duff is to recite *Bucks, Have at Ye All*. FG **June 8**: See the note for March 23, 1814 in the previous preface. Robins has painted scenery described in FG.

On June 1 it is the elder Jeffersons who receive the benefit. Miss E. Jefferson, who shares the benefit on June 6, is obviously Euphemia. The only other Miss E. Jefferson, Elizabeth, was born in 1810. In his *Recollections*, p. 189, Wood makes the mistake of stating that the new theatre was opened this season. In the *Account Book*, however, he has crossed out the words "New Theatre opened" and also the word "Address" written in the entry of April 20. The word has consequently been omitted from the printed text as well as "&" preceding it.

April
Wedy. 20 Education* & Who's the dupe? 326.50

22 [The] Robbers & Transforma- 300.50
tion*

23 (Postponed) 626.50
[See preface to this season.]

25 Education & [The] Highland 495.
Reel

27 [The] Day after [the] Wed- 446.25
[din]g, [The] Lady of the
Lake & ['Tis] All a farce

29 [The] Kiss & Transformation 312.

30 Marmion & Half an hour after 377.   1630.25
Supper   ——

May 2 [The] Recruiting Officer & 413.
Timour [the Tartar.]

4 Remorse* & [A] Budget of 508.
blunders

6 Education & [The] Toothache* 226.50

7 [The] Lady of [the] Lake & 262.25 1409.75
[The] Mid[night] Hour   ——

Wood's ben[efit]   9 Adrian & **Orrilla & [The]** 602.25
Forest of Hermanstadt*

11 [The] Foundling of **[the] forest** 277.
& [The] **Toothache**

13 Abaellino & **[The] Boarding** 311.75
House*

14 Reconciliation, Olio & [The] 148.50 1339.50
Corsair   ——
[See preface to this season.]

Warrens[']   16 [The] Wheel of fortune & 502.75
[Benefit]   Timour [the Tartar]

18 [The] Exile* & 'Tis all a farce   834.75

20 [The] Exile & [The] Sleep- 646.
    walker

21 Remorse & [The] Boarding 146.50 2130.
    House

23 [The] Exile & Mr. H.   531.50

25 [The] Exile & [The] Widow's 354.25
    Vow

[Benefit of]   27 [The] Sons of Erin & [The] 473.75
Mr. & Mrs. Blissett   Fortress

[Benefit of]   28 [The] Belle's Stratagem & 285.50 1645.
Mr. & Miss   [The] Spoil'd Child
Abercrombie   [See preface to this season.]

[Benefit of]   May 30 [The] Castle Spectre, Ballet & 450.25
Bray & Francis   [The] Boarding House
        [BP announces pantomi-
        mic interlude interspersed
        with song, dance, &c.
        called *Whitsuntide Frol-
        ics;   or,   Harlequin's
        Holiday.*]

[Benefit of   June 1 [The] Rivals & [The] High- 714.50
Mr. and Mrs.]   land Reel
Jefferson   [Jefferson as Bob Acres,
        Mrs. Jefferson as Lucy in
        The Rivals. FG]

[Benefit of Mr.   3 Othello & [The] Poor Soldier 372.
and Mrs.] Green   [Green as Iago, Mrs. Green
        as Desdemona. FG]

[Benefit of Mr. & Mrs.] Duff	4 [The] School for Scandal & [The] Beehive [See preface to this season.]	354.25	1891.

| [Benefit of Mrs.] Mason and [Miss] E. Jeff[er-son] | 6 [The] Jealous Wife & [The] A[greeable] Surprize [Miss Jefferson to sing *Nobody Coming to Marry Me*. FG] | 307.25 | |

| [Benefit of Mr.] Robins & [Mrs.] Wood | 8 [The] Hero of [the] North & How to die for Love [See preface to this season.] | 410. | |

| | 9 She Stoops to Conquer & Cinderella | 500.25 | |

| | 10 [The] Exile & Cinderella | 672.50 | 1890. |

$12562.

30 Nights
Averaged $419.

WASHINGTON SEASON, [COMMENCING JUNE 16, ENDING AUGUST 13], 1814.

[Warren & Wood]

PREFACE—**July 4**: DNI announces an interlude in honor of the day. It is to be an "Entertainment of Song, Dance & Spectacle." Wood has written "Share 6" after the entry of June 21. In an entry of the same date Warren records in his *Diary*, "Shar[e]d $6 each;" that is to say, both Warren and Wood must have received a profit of $6. This explanation may also be assumed for the following notations in the *Account Book*: "Share 12," in the entry of June 28; "Share 24," in that of July 4; "Share 18," in that of July 12; and "Share 12," in that of July 19. Wood has written the word "Share" in the entry of August 1 but no figure to indicate the amount of the share. It has been advisable to omit these notations from the printed text in order to keep it as readable as possible. Wood has interpolated in his entry of July 19 the word "alarm,"

[154]

which, Warren reveals in his entry of the same date, is "Alarm of the approach of J. Bull." In the August 18 entry of his *Diary*, Warren goes into detail: "The point of Honor &c. was given out for Saturday when the proceedings of the Company were stopped by the Capture of the City of Washington by the British Army under Ross and the subsequent capitulation of Alexandria to Captn. Gordon of the Sea Horse, British Frigate—they did not molest our property, which we recovered. The loss of it would have been a serious injury to us." The players, however, had more to face than the possible loss of their property. In moving from theatre to theatre, they endured the hardships, if not a few of the risks of the soldiers in the war. "I leave Baltimore in Steam boat," writes Warren in the June 13 entry of his *Diary*. "Rain. Tuesday at 5 at F[rench] Town—a Storm wind, NE. At 6 leave F[rench]Town. There being not sufficient number of Stages to carry the passengers (near 80), I and several Others Rode with the luggage in a baggage Waggon. At ½ past 12 PM we arrive at Newcastle—dripping wet from the Storm—at ½ past 8 I got Home."

Following his record of this season Wood has devoted two pages in Volume II to a record of "Disbursements for [the] Washington Theatre 1814." These include such items at "T. Reinagle, 4 days repainting &c[etera], [$]6;" "Bolts, locks & hinges [$]3" "Canvas & tar for Roof, [$]2.50;" "Waggon to Balt[imore], I p[ai]d, see receipt [$]20" and "Rent for Wash[ington] Theatre, [$]400.'

June 16 Adrian & Orrilla & [The] Day   57.75
       after [the] Wedding
             rainy

  18 [The] Stranger & How to die   171.50
       for Love
           fair & Cool

  21 [The] Point of Honor & Tim-   140.50   369.75
       our [the Tartar]
           d[itt]o

  23 [The] Iron Chest* & [The]   184.75
       Highland Reel
           fair & Cold

[155]

25 [The] Wonder & Valentine &   164.
—   Orson
           fair & Very Cold

28 [The] Honey Moon & Who's   137.   485.75
   the Dupe?   ——
           Warm & fair

30 [The] Foundling of [the] For-   90.50
   est & 'Tis all a farce*
           d[itt]o

July 2d. [The] Castle Spectre & [The]   148.
   Widow's Vow*
           Cool & Rain

Mon. 4th [The] Recruiting Officer, Olio   453.50   692.
   & Lovers['] Quarrels   ——
   [See preface to this season.]
           Hot & Cloudy

July 7th [The]   Privateer*   &   [The]   95.25
   Hunter of the Alps
           Cool & fair

9th [Count] Benyowsky* & [The]   312.
   Weathercock
           Cool & Cloudy

12th Pizarro & [The] Spoil'd Child   170.50   578.75
   remarkably Cool & fine

14 [The] Iron Chest & [The] For-   112.50
   est of Hermanstadt*
           Very Cool & fair

16 C[ount] Benyowsky & The   123.57
   Sultan
           Very Sultry & rain

[156]

19th Education* & Fortune's frolic   164.75   401.
       Cool & fair   ———

21 [The] Poor Gentleman & [The]   75.75
    Corsair
       Showery & Warm

23 Alexander the Great & [The]   83.75
    Boarding House*
       Warm & fine

26 No play.

28 [The] Exile* & The Purse   178.50
Violent Storm & rain all day & night   ———

July 30th [The] Exile & [The] Beehive   365.   704.
       fair & Warm

August   1 [The] Exile & [The] Schem-   120.
    [in]g Lieutenant
       Very Warm & fair

[Benefit of Mr.   4 [The] Kiss & [The] A[gree-   154.50
and Mrs.]   able] Surprize
Jefferson
       Hot & rainy

[Benefit of Mrs.]   6 [The] Sons of Erin* & [The]   139.
Mason & [Miss]   Devil to pay
Abercrombie
       Cloudy & Cool

[Benefit of] Mr.   9 Next door Neighbors, Animal   192.50   606.
& Mrs. Francis   Magnetism   &   [The]
     Toothache*   ———
       Fair & Cool

[157]

[Benefit of Mr.]   11 [The] Fortress, Matrimony & 128.50
  Barrett & [Mrs]   [The] Irishman in London
  Seymour   Fair & Warm

13 Town & Country & [The]
Children in [the] Wood
d[itt]o
25 Nights

BALTIMORE AUTUMN SEASON, [BEGINNING OCTOBER 12, ENDING
NOVEMBER 21,] 1814.

[Warren & Wood]

PREFACE—**October 14**: BP announces, "The profits of this night's performances will be appropriated to aid the fund for the defence of the city under the direction of the committee of vigilance and safety." **October 19**: BP announces, "Mr. Hardinge will sing a much admired new song written by a gentleman of Maryland in commemoration of the gallant defense of Fort McHenry called *The Star Spangled Banner* and a new grand scene will be exhibited for the first time representing the situation of the two fleets during the glorious victory achieved by the American fleet commanded by Commodore McDonough . . . painted expressly for the purpose by Mr. Grain, marine painter." Warren, in his *Diary*, also identifies the picture as a "painting of [the] Victory of Lake Champlain." **November 12**: Warren, in his entry of this date, refers to a "painting by Mons. Grain representing the bombardment of Fort McHenry."

A reference in the *Account Book* in the entry of November 16, "discd. Gilln" may mean "discharged Gillman" and, in the entry of November 18, another, "discd. C. Durang" may mean "discharged C. Durang," as Wood, for insubordination or some other cause, had occasionally to discharge players. Reports of the enemy's movements were still alarming the country-side. In the October 19 entry of his *Diary*, Warren reports that the "B[ritish] fleet are coming up the bay," and adds on November 16, "There has been some alarm this week by the appearance of a B[ritish] Frigate near Annapolis which as usual was magnified into a 74, &c. The water communication . . . has been suspended from Sunday. Today it is open'd again."

[158]

October 12 [The] Point of Honor & [The] 242.50
    Highland Reel

benefit of Defence 14 He would be a Soldier & [The] 480.
    review
    [See preface to this season.]

15 Adrian & Orrilla & How to die 130.75   853.25
    for Love   —————

17 She Stoops to Conquer & 301.50
    Cinderella

19 [Count] Benyowsky, Grain's 508.50
    Picture & Killing no
    Murder
    [See preface to this season.]

21 [The] Soldier's Daughter & 213.75
    Tom Thumb [the Great]

22 [The] Honey Moon & 175.   1198.75
    Cinderella   —————

C[ooper]   24 Richard 3d. & [The] Tooth- 641.
    ache
    [As Richard. FG]

"   26 Othello, [Little] R[ed Riding] 461.
    Hood & ['Tis] All a farce
    [Cooper as Othello. FG]

"   28 [The] Wheel of fortune & Two 256.25
    Strings [to your Bow]
    [Cooper as Penruddock in *The*
    Wheel of Fortune. FG]

"   29 [The] Revenge & [A] Tale of 330.   1688.25
    Mystery   —————

[Cooper as Zanga in *The Revenge*. FG]

"   31 [The] Robbers & [The] Comet   402.25
[Cooper as Charles de Moor
in *The Robbers*. FG]

"   Nov. 2 Rule a Wife [& Have a   374.25
Wife] & [A] Budget of
Blunders
[Cooper as Leon in *Rule* a
Wife. FG]

"   4 Romeo & Juliet & [The] Sleep-   233.25
walker
[Cooper as Romeo, FG]

"   5 Macbeth & Who's the Dupe?   382.50   1392.25
[Cooper as Macbeth, FG]   ———

       7 Venice Preserv'd & [The] Pris-   318.75
oner at large

       9 [The] Merchant of Venice &   460.25
Cath[erine] & Petruchio

C[ooper's]   11 Hamlet & [The] Critic   779.75
Ben[efi]t   [As Hamlet.   FG]

       12 [The] Fortress, Picture, Olio   421.75   1980.50
& [The] Weathercock   ———
[See preface to this season.]

       14 [The] Exile & Fortune's frolic   459.75

       16 [The] Exile & [The] Sultan   325.25

       18 [The] Ethiop & [The] Tooth-   690.
ache

19 d[itt]o & [The] Irishman in   49,3.25   1967.25
London   ———

21 d[itt]o [& The] Poor Soldier   771.25   771.25
                                           ———
                                           $9851.5
24 Nights
Average 410

PHILADELPHIA SEASON[, COMMENCING NOVEMBER 28,] 1814 & [ENDING APRIL 17,] 1815.

[Warren & Wood]

PREFACE—**February 3:** Warren has written in his *Diary*, "Major Gene[ra]l Brown attends the Theatre." **February 22:** The war ended December 24, 1814 and A announces, "There will be exhibited the Temple of Concord. In the center of the stage is seen the Altar of Peace ornamented with appropriate devices and inscriptions. An ode on the return of peace to be spoken by Mr. Wood. A new military and naval pas de deux by F. Durang and Miss [Sophia] Abercrombie. Warren records in his *Diary* that "the Washington Society meet in the Theatre to hear the oration in memory of Gen[eral] Washington." **March 3:** Warren records that "Bibby from N[ew] York plays Richard; and *Durang* I, LII, that he also played Sir Archy MacSarcasm in *Love à la Mode.* With respect to Bibby, Warren and Durang seem to contradict each other. In the March 15 entry of his *Diary*, Warren asserts "this young Gentleman is a native of New York and celebrated there for his imitation of the late G. F. Cooke (of whom he was a great admirer). In private Society from this circumstance he was induced by his friends to perform a few nights in the City of his nativity where his success was such that we were warranted in making this engagement." *Durang*, in I, LII, states that Bibby was "from the English theatres" and that, "although a good actor, [he] made no extraordinary sensation." Warren more generously comments, "He has been well received." **March 13:** In this entry Wood has written "1 B" over "Love à la Mode" and "2" over "The Wedding Day." The figures may indicate the order in which the plays were given. The "B," according to Warren's *Diary*, stands for Bibby, who appeared as Sir Archy MacSarcasm in *Love à la Mode*. **March 25:** A announces, "The new grand scene of the Temple of Concord in which will

[161]

be performed the Minuet de la Cour & Allemande by Mr. Francis and Miss [Sophia] Abercrombie. Favorite ballad, *Black Ey'd Susan*, by Mr. Steward; Flag Hornpipe, by Mr. F. Durang." **March 27**: A announces a "Beautiful View of the Passaic Falls, drawn upon the spot and painted expressly for this occasion by Robins, principal scene painter." **April 14 [15]**: In this entry Wood has crossed out the name Pullen and substituted Fennell who, according to Warren's *Diary*, "has absolutely become a pauper." In his entry of April 14 Warren has written, "My night much injured by the unprecedented begging for Fennel[l]." *Durang*, I, LII, reveals that it was Fennell's "last appearance on the stage" and that the "effort was in vain; he broke down during the performance —energy, voice and memory, all gone. He died soon afterward." **April 16 [17]**: Pullen was the treasurer of the company.

There are a few items in the *Account Book* it has been necessary to omit from the printed text. Wood has written vertically, from the entry of November 28 to that of December 12 inclusive, the words "Mr. Duff Sick," which Warren, in the December 3 entry of his *Diary* explains more fully in the comment, "Duff ill—he has not performed yet." Wood has written "C. F." in his entry of March 23 and "E. M." in his entry of March 27 but the sources consulted have yielded no explanation of these letters, which may be the initials of players. Waring, who appeared on December 17, Warren, in his *Diary*, pronounces "a wretched actor in a wretched state of Health;" and the Jefferson receiving a benefit on March 20 is the elder Jefferson.

Novem[be]r 28 She Stoops to Conquer & 755.
[The] Poor Soldier

30 Town & Country & Killing No 215.
Murder

December 2 [The] Heir at Law & [The] 630.
Turnpike Gate

3 [The] Robbers & [The] Review 537.   2137.

5 [Count] Benyowsky & [The] 493.
Beehive

7 Wild oats & Valentine & 539.75
  Orson

9 Adrian & Orrilla & [The] 415.25
  Sleepwalker

10 [The] Recruiting Officer & 293.50 1741.50
  [The] Highland Reel   ————

12 [The] Foundling of the Forest 439.75
  & [The] Toothache

14 [The] Point of Honor, [The] 550.25
  Hole in the Wall* & [The]
  Purse

16 [The] Ethiop & [The] Hole in 608.
  the Wall

Mr. Waring's 1[st] 17 Columbus & 3 & [the] Deuce 577.   2175.
app[ea]r[ance.]   [As Harry Herbert in ————
  Columbus. A]

19 [The] Ethiop & 'Tis all a farce 445.

21 How to die for Love, 3 & [the] 508.
  deuce & [The] Hole in the
  Wall

23 [The] Exile & Mr. H. 574.25

24 Pizarro & [The] Comet 631.   2158.25
  ————

26 Peter the Great* & [The] 1123.25
  Camp* & [The] Tooth-
  ache

28 Speed the Plough & [The] 709.
  Camp

[163]

30 Education & [The] Camp   413.25

31 [The] Exile & [A] Budget of   495.50   2741
Blunders   ——

[1815.] January   2 [The] Renegade* & [The] Hole 1100.
in the Wall

4 [The] Renegade & [The] Bee- 545.75
hive

6 [The] Renegade & [The] Re- 531.75
turn from Camp*

7 George Barnwell & 3 & [the] 490.50   2668.
Deuce   ——

9 Romeo & Juliet & [The] 548.75
Widow's Vow

11 [The] West Indian & [The] 637.50
Forest of Hermanstadt

13 [The] Ethiop & Darkness 299.
Visible

14 He would be a Soldier & [A] 269.50   1754.75
Tale of Mystery   ——

16 [The] Students of Salamanca* 598.50
& [The] Poor Soldier

18 [The] Students of Salamanca 375.50
& [The] Highland Reel

20 [The First Part of] Henry 4th 651.50
& [The] Devil to pay

21 [The] School for Scandal & 424.50 2050.
    Tom Thumb [the Great] ————

23 [The] Jealous Wife & Matri- 275.
    mony

25 Who Wants a Guinea? & 398.50
    Killing no Murder

27 Abaellino & [The] Widow's 326.50
    Vow

28 Who Wants a Guinea [?] & 297.50 1297.50
    [The] Critic ————

C[ooper]   30 Othello & [The] Weathercock 773.50
    [As Othello. A]

Feb[ruar]y 1 Rule a Wife [& Have a Wife] 730.50
C[ooper]   & [The] Shipwreck
    [As Leon in *Rule a Wife.* A]

"   Gen[eral] 3 Richard 3rd. & Two Strings to 705.50
    Brown   Your Bow
    [Cooper as Richard. A See
    preface to this season.]

"   4 Hamlet & [The] Day after the 446.50 2656.
    Wedding ————
    [Cooper as Hamlet. A]

"   6 [The] Honey Moon & [The] 680.
    Boarding House
    [Cooper as Duke Aranza in
    The Honey Moon. A]

"   8 Macbeth & Transformation 656.25
    [Cooper as Macbeth. A]

[165]

"   10 Pizarro & [The] Sleepwalker 597.50
                              [Cooper as Rolla in *Pizarro*.
                              A]

C[ooper's] Ben[efit] 11 [The] Mountaineers & Cath- 714.50   2648.25
                              [erine & Petruchio   ———
                              [As Octavian in *The Moun-
                              taineers* and as Petruchio.
                              A]

Cooper   13 Alexander [the Great] & 3 & 701.
                              [the] Deuce
                              [As Alexander. A]

                          16 [The] Castle Spectre & Miss in 597.25
                              her Teens

"   17 Abaellino & Transformation 498.
                              [Cooper as Abaellino and
                              Flodoardo in *Abaellino*.
                              A]

"   18 Romeo & Juliet & [The] 374.   2170.25
                              Critic   ———

Cooper's Ben[efit]   20 Hamlet & Raising the Wind 809.50
                              [As Hamlet. A]

                          22 [The] Man of 10000, Olio & 820.
                              [The] Agreeable Surprize
                              [See preface to this season.]

                          24 John Bull & Love & Money 227.50

                          25 [The] Exile & Ways & Means 204.50   2061.50
                                                                  ———

                          27 [The] Poor Gentleman & [The] 299.50
                              Fortress

	March	1	Who's the Dupe[?]—[The] Miller and [his] Men* & [The] Devil to pay	753.50
Bibby		3	Richard 3d. & [The] Boarding House [See preface to this season.]	666.25
		4	[The] Midnight Hour & [The] Miller & his Men	348.50 2067.75
Benefit [of the] Poor		6	Who Wants a Guinea[?] & Fortune's frolic	543.
B[ibby]		8	[The] Man of the World & [A] Budget of blunders [As Sir Pertinax MacSycophant in *The Man of the World*. A]	873.25
W[ood's] Benefit		10	King Henry 4th, 2 part & Timour [the Tartar] [As the Prince of Wales. A]	636.
		11	[The] Road to Ruin & [The] Miller & his Men	486. 2538.25
		13	[The] Children in [the] Wood, Love a la Mode & [The] Wedding day [See preface to this season.]	508.
B[ibby's] Ben[efit]		15	[The] Man of the World & [The] Review [As Sir Pertinax MacSycophant. A]	540.
		17	[The] Stranger & Turn Out*	307.75

[167]

18 Douglas & [The] Miller   452.50   1808.25
     [his] Men   ———

[Benefit of]   20 [A] Bold Stroke for [a] Hus- 1184.50
Jefferson.   band, [The] Catch Club
               & Turn out
               [As Don Caesar in *A Bold*
                  Stroke and Gregory in
                  Turn Out. A]

[Benefit of Mrs.]   22 Tamerlane & [The] Sultan   500.
Mason.   [As Arpasia in *Tamerlane*
                and Roxalana in *The*
                Sultan. A]

[Benefit of] Duff   23 Alfonso & Tekeli   764.25
               [As Alfonso and Tekeli. A]

[Benefit of]   25 Deaf & Dumb & Inkle &   458.50   2907.25
Francis   Yarico & Interlude   ———
               [See preface to this season.]

[Benefit of]   27 Speed the Plough, [Little]   602.50
Robins   R[ed] R[iding] Hood &
               [The] Lady of the rock
               [See preface to this season.]

[Benefit of   29 Man & Wife, Love laughs at   679.25
  Mrs.] Green   Lock[smiths]

[Farewell Benefit   31 Zorinski & [The] Anatomist 1112.50
of] Blissett   [As Monsieur Le Medecin
               in *The Anatomist.* A]

         April   1 Adelmorn, Sylv[ester] Dag-   530.   2924.25
[Benefit of]   g[erwoo]d & Of age to-   ———
Mrs. Duff   morrow

[Benefit of]   3 [A] Cure for the Heartache &   713.50
Barrett   [The] Blind Boy

[168]

[Benefit of] Hardinge	5 Every one [has] his fault & No Song no Supper [As Robin in *No Song No Supper*. A]	531.25	
[Benefit of] Entwisle	6 [The] School of Reform & [The] Farmer [A announces Masonic Olio of singing and recitation in which Entwisle is to participate.]	463.	
[Benefit of Mrs. & Miss] Seymour	7 [The] Kiss & Catch him who Can	432. ———	2139.75
[Benefit of] Miss Aber[crombie]	9 Love Makes a Man & [The] Hunter of [the] Alps [As Florella in new comic ballet under her direction called *The Village Ghost; or, The Cooper Outwitted*; also, with Mr. F. Durang, in minuet and strathspey and in pas de deux. A]	871.	
[Benefit of] Miss White	11 Education & [The] Spoil'd Child [In occasional address written by a lady of this city. A]	514.25	
[Benefit of] Warren.	13 [The] Prisoner at Large, [The] Lady of [the] Lake & 3 W[ee]ks af[ter] Marriage	718.75	
[Benefit of] Fennell	14 King Lear & [The] Boarding House [As Lear. A See preface to this season.]	1369.75 ———	3495.75

[169]

[Benefit of]   16 [The] Rivals & How to die for   928.75 47069.
Pullen   Love
                [See preface to this season.]
                81 Nights $581

BALTIMORE SPRING SEASON, [COMMENCING APRIL 21, ENDING JUNE 10,] 1815.

[Warren & Wood]

PREFACE—**May 15**: BP announces "A favorite pas de deux called *La Petite Trompeuse* by F. Durang and Miss [Sophia] Abercrombie. **May 22**: BP announces, "After *The Man of 10,000* will be exhibited a splendid scene representing the *Temple of Discord*. This magnificent scene displays several ranges of brilliant columns, the whole extent of the stage, from which are suspended banners inscribed in letters of gold with the names of the distinguished naval and military characters who have rendered eminent services in the late war. In the center of the stage the Altar of Peace, ornamented with appropriate devices. On the right a transparency of a female figure representing Britannia. Both these admired figures painted by an eminent artist. Over the altar wave the standards of both nations. On the pedestal are names of the American commissioners at Ghent. A pas de deux, Messrs. E. and C. Durang; *The Patriotic Baker; or, A Fig for Invasion,* by Mr. Entwisle; a new military and naval pas de deux by Mr. F. Durang and Miss [Sophia] Abercrombie." Warren notes in his *Diary*, "Wood ill. Barrett plays his part—that of Barrett played by Entwisle." **May 26**: BP announces "Comic Song, *My Dearie*, Mr. Entwisle. Favorite Hunting Song, *Tantivy*, by Mrs. Seymour." **May 29**: BP announces that pantomime, *Hercules and Omphale*, is to be under the direction of Francis. **May 31**: According to BP, Steward is to sing the much admired song called *The Star Spangled Banner* and with the [elder] Jefferson, see June 2, the duet *All's Well*. Mrs. Mason is to speak the epilogue of *The Soldier's Daughter*. **June 3**: BP announces "a masonic address by Brother Duff." **June 7**: Robins is the principal scene painter. Warren's *Diary* reveals that, on May 27, Miss A[bercrombie was] ill [and] did not perform;" and that, on June 5, Blissett's benefit was "advertis[e]d as his farewell benefit with a quantity of puffing in the papers setting forth his great deservings and the irreparable loss he will be to the concern."

It has been advisable to omit a notation, "Season averaged [$]591.20[,]

[170]

Ben[efits] averaged 616.30," which Wood has written to the right of the heading of this season.

Friday 21 [The] Heir at Law & [The] Turnpike Gate	594.50	
22 [The] West Indian & [The] Toothache	282.50	$877.
April 24 Town & Country & [The] Hole in the Wall*	$543.50	
26 Who Wants a Guinea? & [The] Hunter of [the] Alps	547.50	
28 [Count] Benyowsky & [The] Anatomist*	512.50	
29 Every One has his fault & 'Tis all a farce	390. ———	1993.50
May 1 [The] Ethiop & Ways & Means	668.50	

B[ibby]
3 [The] Man of the World & [A] Budget of Blunders [As Sir Pertinax MacSycophant in *The Man of World*. BP]   805.50

"
5 Richard 3d. & Fortune's frolic [Bibby as Richard.   BP]   701.50

6 [The] Students of Salamanca* & [The] Review   317.50   2493.
———

8 [The] Foundling of the Forest & Turn Out*   621.50

[171]

	10	Love a la Mode, Raising the Wind & Tom Thumb [the Great]	495.50	

B[ibby's] ben[efit] 12 [The] Merchant of Venice & Turn Out [As Shylock. BP] 797.

13 [The] Exile & [The] Anatomist 627.   2541.

Warren's [Benefit] 15 [The First Part of] Henry 4th, Dance & [The] Shipwreck [See preface to this season.] 951.75

17 [A] Bold Stroke for [a] Husband & Ella Rosenberg 470.

19 [The] Midnight Hour, [The] Mayor [of] Garrat & [The] Miller & his Men* 633.50

20 [The] Wonder & [The] Miller & his Men 391.25 2446.50

Wood 22 [The] Man of 10,000,* Olio & Transformation [See preface to this season.] 658.

24 [The] Renegade* & [The] Spoil'd Child 548.

[Benefit of Mr.] Entw[isle] & [Mrs.] Seym[ou]r 26 [The] School of Reform & [The] Children in the Wood [See preface to this season.] 427.

[Benefit of Mr.] Harris & [Miss] Aber[crombie]	27 Abaellino & Timour [the Tartar] [Miss Abercrombie in pas seul. BP]	618. ——	2251.
[Benefit of] Mr. & Mrs. Francis	29 Secrets Worth Knowing & Hercules & Omphale [See preface to this season.]	325.25	
[Benefit of Mr.] Stew[ar]d. & [Mrs.] Mason	31 [The] Soldier's Daughter & Rosina [See preface to the season.]	650.50	
[Benefit of] June Mr. & Mrs. Jefferson	2 [The] Clandestine Marriage & [The] Prisoner at Large	843.50	
[Benefit of] Mr. & Mrs. Duff	3 [The] Wheel of fortune & [The] Forest of Hermanstadt [See preface to this season.]	473. ——	2292.25
[Benefit of] Mr. & Mrs. Blissett	5 Adelmorn & [The] Poor Soldier	620.	
[Benefit of Mr.] Robins & Mrs. W[oo]d	7 Alexander [the Great] & [The] Highland Reel [See preface to this season.]	596.50	
	9 [The] Dramatist & [The] Lady of the Lake	926.25	
	10 Peter the Great* and ditto	699. ——	2841.75 ———

$17736.

30 nights
Average 591.25

[173]

WASHINGTON & ALEX[ANDRI]A SEASON[, COMMENCING JUNE 20, ENDING SEPTEMBER 25,] 1815.

[Warren & Wood]

PREFACE—**July 4**: DNI announces, "A national scene, being a spirited representation of the battle and victory on Lake Erie achieved by the gallant Commodore Perry; painted by Mr. Grain, marine painter. The celebrated song of *The Star Spangled Banner*, by Mr. Steward. After which will be exhibited the Temple of Concord. This scene displays several ranges of banners inscribed in letters of gold with the names of distinguished naval and military characters who have rendered eminent services during the late war. In the center of the stage is seen the Altar of Peace supporting the genius of America; around it, entwined, are the names of the American Commissioners of Ghent. A new military and naval pas de deux by Mr. Harris and Miss [Sophia] Abercrombie. Epilogue to *The Soldier's Daughter* by Mrs. Mason. Comic song, *My Dearie*, by Mr. Entwisle. **August 10**: DNI announces "A Scotch panto-mimical dance called *The Scheming Sisters*."

It has been necessary to omit from the printed text the following notations: "Share [$]13," in the entry of June 25; "11," in that of July 1; "27," in that of July 8; "16," in that of July 15; "20," in that of July 22; "13," in that of July 29; "24," in that of August 5; "9," in that of August 12; and "16," in the entry of August 19. Warren verifies that these represent Wood's "share" of the profits made. In the July 1 entry of his *Diary*, for example, Warren sets down "shar[e]d $11," exactly the amount that Wood records.

In the text of this season it has been advisable to substitute "The Tennessee Hunter" for the word "d[itt]o" which Wood has written in the August 5 entry and immediately under "The Tennessee Hunter" in his entry of August 3. In order to maintain uniformity of text it has also been advisable to substitute Duff for Duffs in the entry of August 8.

For references to the performances in Alexandria, see p. 177, under the caption "Alexandria."

June 20 Barbarossa & No Song no 203.25
Supper

22 [The] School of Reform & [Of] 133.
Age tomorrow

[174]

25 [The] H[ighland] Reel, [The]   256.
—   Hole in the Wall* & [The]   ——
    Widow's Vow

27 Richard 3d. & [The] Turnpike 326.50
    Gate*

29 [The] Jealous Wife* & [The] 106.75
    Prize

July 1 [The] School for Scandal & 151.
    Miss in her Teens   ——

4 [The] Hero of [the] North, 472.
    Interlude & [The] P[oor]
    Soldier
    [See preface to this season.]

6 Macbeth & [The] Shipwreck 178.75

8 [The] Mountaineers & [The] 207.75
—   B[oarding] House   ——

11 [The] Hole in [the] Wall, [The] 156.50
    Miller & [his] Men* &
    [The] Purse

13 [The] Curfew* & [The] Review 214.50

15 3 & [the] Deuce & [The] Miller 228.50
—   & [his] Men   ——

18 [The] Merchant of Venice & 208.
    Rosina

20 Abaellino & Turn Out*   210.75

22 Peter the Great* & High Life 233.50
—   [below Stairs]*   ——

[175]

25 Adelmorn & Turn Out   161.75

27 Othello & [A] Budget of Blun- 182.25
    ders

29 [The] Exile & [The] Village 144.
    Lawyer   ———

Aug[ust] 1 Speed the Plough & [The] 142.75
    Devil to Pay

3 [The] Ten[n]essee Hunter,* 370.
    Turn Out & [A] Bud[get
    of] Blunders

5 [The Tennessee Hunter,] Kill- 241.
    ing no Murder & [The]
    Toothache

Aug[ust] 8 Fortune's frolic, [The] L[ady] 241.50
[Benefit of Mr. and   of [the] Lake & 3 & [the]
Mrs.] Duff   deuce

[Benefit of Mr. 10 [A] Bold Stroke [for a] Hus- 96.
and Mrs.] Francis   b[an]d,* Dance & [My]
    Grandmother
    [See preface to this season.]

[Benefit of Mr. 12 As you like it & Blue Beard 192.75
and Mrs.]   ———
Entwisle

[Benefit of] 15 [The] Dramatist & Val[entine] 148.50
Harris &   & Orson
Anderson

[Benefit of Mr. 17 Every one [has] his fault, 208.
and Mrs.]   [Little] R[ed Riding]
Jeff[erson]   Hood & Transformation*

Stock 19 [The] Kiss & [The] Critic 241.

ALEXANDRIA

[Warren & Wood]

PREFACE—**August 24**: ADG announces, "After *The Mountaineers* will be exhibited *The Temple of Concord.*" See the note for July 4 in the preceding preface. **September 12**: ADG announces, "Mr. Steward and Mrs. Placide are extremely sorry to inform the Ladies and Gentlemen of Alexandria and its vicinity, that on account of the severe indisposition of Mr. Harris, the Farce of *Turn Out*, intended for representation this Evening, for their Benefit, is changed to that of *My Grandmother; or, The Living Picture*: which, they trust, will give satisfaction." According to ADG, Steward is to sing *The Star Spangled Banner* and to play Woodby in *My Grandmother*; Mrs. Placide to sing *Tarry Awhile with Me, My Love* and to play Florella in *My Grandmother*. **September 21**: ADG announces, "In the course of the Farce, the Comic Songs of *Manager Strut* and *Honey & Mustard* by Mr. Jefferson." This is the elder Jefferson.

As in previous instances, notations as to amounts of "shares" have been omitted from the printed text. These include "[$]21," in the entry of August 26; "27," in that of September 1; "10," in that of September 9; "12," in that of September 16; and "12," in the entry of September 23.

Aug[ust] 24	[The] Mountaineers, Inter- lude & Turn Out* [See preface to this season.]	247.
26	[The] Exile & [The] Hole in — [the] Wall*	409. ——
29	3 & [the] Deuce & [A] Bud- [get] of Blunders	259.50
31	[The] Miller & [his] Men & Matrimony	294.50
Sept[ember] 1	Timour [the Tartar]* & Killing — no Murder	282.75 ——
[Benefit of Mr. & Mrs.] Entw[isle] 5	[The] Lady of [the] Lake* & [The] Turn[pike] Gate	111.75

[Benefit of Mr.   7 Macbeth & [The] Beehive*   296.75
& Mrs.] Anderson

[Benefit of Mr.   9 Richard 3d. & [The] Tooth- 357.75
& Mrs.] Duff   —   ache*

[Benefit of Mr.]   12 [The] Exile & [My] Grand- 208.
Stew[ar]d &   mother
[Mrs.] Placide   [See preface to this season.]

[Benefit of Mr.]   14 [The] H[oney]moon & Val- 274.50
Aber[crombie] &   [entine] & Orson
[Mrs.] Seym[ou]r

[Benefit of Mr.]   16 How to die for love,* [Of] Age 230.50
Hath[well] &   —   tom[orrow] & [The] Ship- ———
[Mrs.] Simp[son.]   wreck

[Benefit of Mr.   19 [The] H[ighland] Reel, [Little] 234.25
& Mrs.] Harris   R[ed] R[iding] Hood* &
[The] Poor Soldier

[Benefit of Mr.   21 Every one [Has His] fault, 417.75
& Mrs.]   [Little] R[ed Riding]
Jeff[erson]   Hood & Transformation*
[See preface to this season.]

[Benefit of Mr.   23 [A] Bold Stroke [for a] Hus- 367.50
& Mrs.]   —   band* & [The] Lady of ———
Franc[is.]   [the] Lake

Entw[isles'] 2d.   25 Lovers' Quarrels, No Song no 295.75
Sup[per] & Turn Out

BALTIMORE [AUTUMN] SEASON, COMMENCING OCTOBER 2, [ENDING
NOVEMBER 23,] 1815.

[Warren & Wood]

PREFACE—**October 16**: Warren, in his *Diary*, notes that "Horton [has]
run away." **October 28**: Warren writes, "Mr. Savage plays Durimel
[in *The Point of Honor*]; only passable."

[178]

In his *Diary* Warren records the following: On October 2 Mrs. Placide also played Caroline in *The Prize*. On October 4 McFarland also played Looney Mactwolter in *The Review*. "Madam Aira," who appeared on October 9, was, Warren writes, "a Spanish Lady from Madrid." Wood, in *Recollections*, pp. 204–5, accounts for her engagement by stating that "during this season a vessel destined for Havana was by stress of weather compelled to make harbor in Baltimore. Among the passengers was Signora Aria [, *sic*] a beautiful woman and accomplished dancer, engaged for the Cuban theatres. The vessel requiring repairs, which occasioned a detention of several days, an application was received through the Spanish consul for the engagement of this distinguished artiste. The performance fully confirmed all that had been said of her talents, although the peculiarity of her dances at first promised no favorable conclusion. One of these resembled what we have since received under the title of the Bolero, and startled not a little some of the audience, at that time wholly unused to the style since so favorably received. . . . So divided were the audience as to the decency of the exhibition, that at the close of the evening a strong remonstrance was forwarded to the managers against a repetition of her performance. The bills announcing her re-appearance being by this time posted through the city, and a strong counter-remonstrance having reached us, it was resolved to conclude her engagement as originally designed. The receipts of the second night [Oct. 11 according to BP], reached $781, proving very satisfactorily that the public were at least divided on the subject." Wood, however, admits rather ruefully that "the number of ladies on the second night was unusually small." In the October 14 entry of his *Diary*, Warren pronounces "Mr. Johnson very bad," having recorded, in his entry of October 13, that Mr. Johnson played Timour as well as the baron. In his entry of October 21 Warren writes that Mrs. Francis plays Sedona [in *The Exile*]. The farce would have been the Hole in the Wall else." In his November 6 entry Warren corroborates Wood's notation, "Mr. Johnson absent," with the notation, "Mr. Johnson run off—his name in the bill.

[October]
Mony. 2 The Wonder & the Prize   586.50
Mrs. Placide's 1st.   [As Donna Violante in *The*
App[ea]r[ance]   *Wonder.* BP]
                                      Clear and fine

[179]

Wed. 4 Man & Wife & the Review   514.
Mr. McFarland's 1st.   [As O'Dedimus in *Man and*
Wife. BP]
Very fine & Warm

Frid. 6 [The] Mountaineers & Rosina   566.50
Mrs. Claude's 1st.   [As Rosina. BP]
fine & Warm

Sat. 7 [The] Exile & [The] day after   687.50   2354.50
the Wedding
Warm & rainy all day

Mon. 9 [The] School for Scandal &   861.50
Signora Aira—   Transformation
1st. Night   [In a Spanish dance. BP]
fine & Warm.

Wed. 11 [The] Iron Chest & [The]   788.50
Mr. Jackson['s] 1st.   Highland Reel
[As Wilfred in *The Iron*
Chest. BP]
Very fine & Warm

Frid. 13 [The] Curfew & Timour [the   735.50
Mr. Johnson['s] 1st.   Tartar]
[As Baron Hugh de Tracy in
The Curfew. BP]
fine.

Saty. 14 Turn Out & [The] Lady of the   658.   3043.50
Lake
fine & Warm

Mon. 16 Adrian & Orrilla & Love   517.25
laughs at locksmiths
Changed to Abaellino &
[The] Review. Wood ill.
Horton absconded. [See
preface to this season.]
Cloudy & threatening

Wed. 18 Speed the Plough & [The]   622.50
Mr. Philips 1st.   Shipwreck
                    [As Henry in *Speed the
                    Plough*, BP]
                          fair & Warm

Frid. 20 Romeo & Juliet & Past 10   882.
                    O'Clock*
                    Very fine & Clear

Saty. 21 [The] Exile & [The] Hole in   569.   2590.75
                    the Wall
                    Mrs. Jeff[erson] ill—farce
                    chang[e]d to [The] Prize
                    in conseq[uenc]e.
                          fine & Clear

Mon. 23 Douglas & Past 10 O'Clock   689.75
Mr. Philips 2d.   [As Young Norval in *Doug-
                    las*. BP]
                          fine & Cool

Wed. 25 [A] Cure for the Heartache &   587.
                    [The] Miller & his Men
                          fine & Cool

Frid. 27 [A] Bold Stroke for a Husband   358.
                    & [The] Fortress
                    Cold & lowering

Saty. 28 [The] Point of Honor, [Little]   402.75   2039.59
Mr. Savage['s] 1st.   R[ed] R[iding] Hood &
                    Sprigs of Laurel
                    [See preface to this season.]
                    Clear & Very Cold

Mon. 30 [The] West Indian & [The]   502.25
                    Hole in the Wall
                          Mild & fair

[181]

Novem[be]r

Wedy. 1st. Adrian & Orrilla & Lock &   519.
      Key
           Cool & fair

Frid. 3 [The] Wedding day, [The]   633.75
      Lady of the Lake & [The]
      Irishman in London
           foggy & Mild

Saty. 4 [The] Foundling of [the] Forest   372.50   2027.50
      & Sprigs of Laurel
           foggy & Mild

Mon. 6 Jane Shore & 3 & the Deuce   532.25
      Mr.   Johnson   absent.
      [BP announces him as Sir
      Richard Ratcliffe in *Jane
      Shore.*]
           Cloudy & rain

Wedy. 8 [The] Exile & [The] Weather-   430.50
      cock
           Clear & Cold

Frid. 10 Debtor & Creditor* & Of Age   659.25
      tomorrow
           Clear & Cold

Saty. 11 [The] Road to Ruin & Ella   409.   2030.
      Rosenberg
           Cold and fine

Mon. 13 Debtor & Creditor & Raising   337.25
      the Wind
           Clear & Cold

Wed. 15 Alfonso & Past 10 O'Clock   643.50
           Mild & fine.

Frid. 17 Othello & [The] Turnpike 478.75
Gate
Cool & fair

Saty. 18 3 Weeks after Marriage, [The] 421.75 1881.25
Lady of the Lake & [The]
Devil to pay
Dull & Cold

Mon. 20 George Barnwell & Turn Out 603.75
Dull & Mild

Tuesy. 21 How to die for Love, 3 & [the] 325.25
Deuce & [The] Shipwreck
Dull & Warm

Wed. 22 Zembuca* & Lock & Key 1138.25
fine & Warm

Thurs. 23 Zembuca & [The] Comet 1094.75 3162.
fine & Cool ————
$19127.

32 Nights Averaged $398.

PHILADELPHIA SEASON, COMMENCING 27TH NOVEMBER, 1815[, ENDING
APRIL 16, 1816.]

[Warren & Wood]

PREFACE—**March 30**: Mr. Robins was the principal scene painter.
April 10: A announces "At end of *Pizarro* [the songs of] *Fresh and Strong
the Breezes Blowing*, by Miss Seymour [; and] *Tantivy*, by desire, Mrs.
Seymour." **April 16**: Pullen was the treasurer of the company.

In his *Diary* Warren records that, on February 9, Mrs. Williams also
played Little Pickle in *The Spoiled Child*. On March 6 he writes, "Mr.
Bartow from New York, an amateur, plays Hamlet—he insures us $600—
he was wretched." Warren evidently means that Mr. Bartow has agreed
to pay Warren & Wood the difference between the receipts and the
amount of $600. On March 9 Warren states that Mrs. Burke also played
Little Pickle. On March 16 a notation in the *Account Book*, "Mr.

[183]

Bartow, who made this house up $500," refers to an arrangement like that mentioned by Warren on March 6. On April 15, Warren records that Miss White appeared as Athanasia in *Count Benyowski*. In the April 13 entry of his *Diary* Warren writes, "Chang[e]d to [The] Poor Soldier. Mrs. Entwisle refused to play Helen," in which he may be referring to the rôle of Helena in *The Hunter of the Alps*. In the text of the *Account Book* the numbers 2 to 6, February 10 to February 17 inclusive, refer unquestionably to Mrs. Williams' appearances. *Durang*, I, LIII records that she played Mrs. Oakley in *The Jealous Wife*, see February 14; and Albina Mandeville in *The Will*, see February 16.

Wood, in *Recollections*, p. 198, recalls that "The Philadelphia season of 1815 afforded a grateful vicissitude," as he explains, "from the gloomy history of former years." In the April 16 entry of his *Diary* Warren exults, "And thus concludes the most prosperous season we ever knew. . . . We have been enabled to pay our arrears to the proprietors of $3700 and $1400 to Pullen and other arrearages which our bad season in the year of the Richmond fire and losses during the war brought upon us." Warren also records, with characteristic sympathy, that "Mrs. Duff has not acted since the 17th of February. Francis & [the elder] Jefferson," he adds, are "still unable to perform." See February 24.

Novem[ber]
    Mon[day] 27 [The] West Indian & [The] 1151.25
         Review
                Rainy & Cold

    Wed[nesda]y 29 [The] Mountaineers & [The] 883.75
         Prize
                Dull & Cold

Decem[be]r
    Frid[ay] 1 Alfonso & [The] Romp 756.25
                Clear & Cold

    Sat[urda]y 2 Three & [the] deuce & [The] 777.50 3568.75
         Miraculous Mill & [The] ——————
         Miller & [his] Men
                Clear & Cold

Mon. 4 Romeo & Juliet & Past 10 1117.25
    O'Clock*
        Clear & Cold

Wed. 6 [The] Foundling of the Forest 1005.75
    & Past 10 O'Clock
        Cloudy & mild

Frid. 8 Debtor & Creditor* & [The] 829.50
    Devil to pay
        Very Cold

Saty. 9 [The] Exile & [The] Day after 709. 3661.50
    [the] Wedding
        Very Cold

Mon. 11 [The] Robbers & Turn Out 858.50
        Very Severe

Wed. 13 Adrian & Orrilla & Past 10 698.
    O'Clock
        Snow

Frid. 15 [The] School for Scandal & 635.50
    Sprigs of Laurel
        Rain

Saty. 16 How to die for Love, [The] 940.50 3132.50
    L[ad]y of [the] Lake &
    [The] Hole in the Wall
        Rain all day

Mon. 18 Macbeth & [The] Weather- 825.50
    cock
        Cold & fair

Wed. 20 [The] Stranger & [The] For- 909.50
    tune of War*
        Cloudy

[185]

Frid. 22 Adelmorn & [The] Fortune of 552.50
War
Clear & Mild

Saty. 23 She Stoops to Conquer & 795.50 3083.
[The] Lady of the Lake
Heavy Rain

Tues. 26 Jean de Paris,* Lovers['] Quar- 1213.
rels & Val[entine] & Orson
Very Cold & fine

Wed. 27 Jane Shore & Jean de Paris 558.50
Very Cold

Frid. 29 Speed the Plough & [The] 815.50
Hunter of the Alps
Snow

Saty. 30 [The] Exile & Of Age to- 424. 3010.
morrow
Dull & Snow

1816. January
Mon. 1 Zembuca* & Turn Out 1764.25
Clear & Cold

Wed. 3 Zembuca & [The] Comet 1100.25
Clear & Cold

Frid. 5 Zembuca & Past 10 O'Clock 1006.50
Snow all day

Saty. 6 Zembuca & [The] Fortune of 815. 4685.50
War
Clear

Mon. 8 Zembuca & [The] Beehive 839.75
Clear & Very Cold

[186]

Wed. 10 Zembuca & Lock & Key   743.50
           Very Cold

Frid. 12 Zembuca & Jean de Paris   573.50
           Clear & Cold

Sat. 13 George Barnwell & [The] Lady 821.25   2978.
        of [the] Lake
              Cold

Mon. 15 Zembuca & [The] Highland 479.75
        Reel
           Snow & very Cold

        Wed. 17 [The] Forest of Bondy,*[& 1036.75
Wood's Benefit   The] Span[is]h Barber
        great Thaw & Rain till Evening

Frid. 19 [The] Forest of Bondy, [Little] 493.
        R[ed] R[iding] Hood &
        [The] Agreeable Surprize
           Clear & Cold

Cooper   Saty. 20 Hamlet & 3 Weeks after 986.   2995.50
        Marriage
        [As Hamlet. A]
           fine & Clear

"   Mon. 22 Richard 3rd & Fortune's frolic 829.50
        [Cooper as Richard. A]
           Clear & Cold

"   Wed. 24 [The] Honey Moon & 3 & [the] 895.50
        deuce
        [Cooper as Duke Aranza in
        The Honey Moon. A]
           Clear

"   Frid. 26 Macbeth & Ways & Means   656.50
               [Cooper as Macbeth. A]
                       Dull & Cold

"   Saty. 27 [The] Iron Chest & [The] 695.   3076.50
               Turnpike Gate
               [Cooper as Sir Edward
               Mortimer in *The Iron
               Chest.* A]
                       Snow & Rain

"   Mon. 29 Othello & [The] Widow's Vow 767.50
                       Clear & Cold

"   Wed. 31 [The] School for Scandal & 1261.50
               Cath[erine] & Petruchio
                       Mild & fine

       Feb[ruar]y
       Frid. 2 Rule a Wife [& Have a Wife] 900.75
               & Ella Rosenberg
                       Clear & fine

                Saty. 3 Much ado [about Nothing] 1146.50 4076.25
       C[ooper's] Benefit   & [The] Shipwreck
               [As Benedick. A]
                       Mild & Clear

       Mon. 5 [The] Belle's Stratagem & 594.50
               Raising the Wind
                       Mild & Clear

       Wed. 7 [The] Kiss & [The] Lady of 430.
               the Lake
                       Very Cold

[188]

Frid. 9 [The] Soldier's Daughter & 673.
Mrs. W[illiams]   [The] Spoil'd Child
    [As the Widow Cheerly in
    The Soldier's Daughter.
    A]
          Very Cold

" 2 Saty. 10 [The] Wonder & [The] Prize 494.   2191.50
    [Mrs. Williams as Donna
    Violante in *The Wonder.*
    A]
          Cold

" 3 Mon. 12 [The] Honey Moon & [The] 651.50
    Devil to pay
    [Mrs. Williams as Juliana
    in *The Honey Moon* and
    as Nell in *The Devil to
    Pay.* A]
          Clear & Mild

4 Wed. 14 [The] Jealous Wife &[The] 580.
    Irishman in London
          Very Cold

5 Frid. 16 [The Will & [The] Romp 596.50
          Cold

6 Saty. 17 [The] Mountaineers & [The] 416.50 2243.50
    Irish Widow
          Thaw & Very rainy

Mon. 19 [The] Belle's Stratagem & 1131.50
[Mrs.] Williams'   [The] Spoil'd Child
Benefit   [As Letitia Hardy in *The
    Belle's Stratagem* and
    Little Pickle in *The
    Spoiled Child.* A]
          Mild & fine

Wed. 21 [The First Part of] Henry 4th   395.75
& Valentine & Orson
Storm of Rain

Thurs. 22 Columbus & [The] Beehive   1036.50
fine & Mild

Frid. 23 Zembuca & Fortune's frolic   490.50
Mild & fair

Saty. 24 Pizarro & Raising [the] Wind   592.   3646.25
Chang[e]d   from   [The]
Comet. Jeff[erson] ill.
[A announces *The Comet.*]
Rain & dull

Mon. 26 Wild Oats & [The] Forest of   442.50
Bondy
fair & Mild

Wed. 28 [The] Magpie & [the] Maid* 1188.50
[Benefit of] Warren   & Turn Out
Very fair

March
Frid.   1 [The] Magpie & [the] Maid &   730.50
[The] Children in the
Wood
Mild & fine

Saty.   2 [The] Magpie & [the] Maid &   548.50   2910.
3 & [the] Deuce

Mon.   4 [The] Magpie & [the] Maid &   641.50
[The] Critic
Rain all day

Mr. Bartow   Wed.   6 Hamlet & [The] Prisoner at   768.50
Large
[As Hamlet. A]
fine & Cool

Mrs. Burke   Fri.   8 [The] Foundling of the Forest   668.
& my Grandmother
[As Rosabella in *The Foundling of the Forest.* A]
Clear & Very Cold

"   Saty.   9 No Song no Supper, Past 10   529.75   2607.75
O'Clock & [The] Spoil'd
Child
[Mrs. Burke as Margaretta
in *No Song No Supper.*
A]
Clear & Cold

"   Mon. 11 Rosina, [The] Wedding Day &   669.75
[The] Devil to pay
[Mrs. Burke as Rosina and
as Nell in *The Devil to
Pay.* A]
Cloudy & Cold

Mrs. Burke's   Wed. 13 [The] Hero of [the] North & 1206.50
Ben[efit]   Paul & Virginia
[As Frederica Rubenski in
The Hero of the North
and as Virginia. Also to
sing a hunting song. A]
fine & Mild

Frid. 15 [The] Magpie & [the] Maid &   580.25
'Tis all a farce
fine & Cold

Mr. Bartow Saty. 16 Romeo & Juliet & [The] Sultan 435.   2891.50
[As Romeo. A]

Mon. 18 [The] Magpie & [the] Maid &   1249.
Zembuca
                                   Snow & Cold

[Benefit of] Wed. 20 [The] Battle of Hexham &   1618.
Jefferson   Love, Law & Physic*
                              Cloudy & Wet

[Benefit of]   Frid. 22 [The] Family Legend* & [The]   616.
Mrs. Wood   Poor Soldier
                                 Some Snow

[Benefit of] Saty. 23 Which is the Man[?] & [The]   657.25   4140.25
Mrs. Entwisle   Citizen
                           Mild & Very fine

[Benefit of] Mon. 25 Alexander [the Great] & [The] 1145.50
Mr. Duff.   Children in the Wood
                     [To sing comic song. A]
                              Very fine

[Benefit of] Wed. 27 [The] Family Legend, All in   666.
Mr. Francis   good humor & Frolics of
                     fancy
                             fine & Mild

[Benefit of]   Frid. 29 [The] Point of Honor, Matri- 1320.75
Mr. Barrett   mony & Tekeli
                              Very fine

[Benefit of] Saty. 30 [The] Devil's Bridge & Rais- 753.50   3885.75
Mr. Robins.   ing the Wind
                     [See preface to this season.]
                            Rain & Snow

                April
[Benefit of] Mon. 1 King Lear & Mr. H.   716.50
Mrs. Duff

                            Rain & Thunder

[Benefit of]   Wed.   3 Abaellino & [The] Padlock   484.50
  Mrs. Claude.   [To sing. A]
                                     Very fine

[Benefit of]   Frid.   5 [The] Rivals & Love Laughs   606.
  Mr. Entwisle   at Locksmiths & [The]
                         Day after [the] Wed[din]g
                                              Rain

[Benefit of]   Saty.   6 Man and Wife, [Little] R[ed]   759.50   2566.50
  Mr. McFarland.   R[iding] Hood & Matri-
                         mony
                         [As O'Dedimus in *Man and
                         Wife* and O'Cloghorty in
                         Matrimony. A]
                                     Heavy Rain

Benefit of   Mon.   8 [The]   Gamester   &   [The]   700.50
  Mr. Steward.   Farmer
                      [To sing. A]
                                     Very fine

[Benefit of   Wed. 10 Pizarro, [The] Purse & [The]   701.25
  Miss &] Mrs.   Miraculous Mill
  Seymour.   [See preface to this season.]
                                     fine & Cool

          Thursd. 11 [The] Mask'd Friend, [The]   585.50
[Benefit of]   Highland Reel & [The
  Mrs. Harris   Scheming] Milliners
                      [As Janette in *The Schem-
                      ing Milliners* and in new
                      pas seul. A]
                                     Storm of rain all day

[Benefit of   Saty. 13 Speed the Plough & [The]   916.50   2903.75
  F. Durang &   Hunter of the Alps
  Misses C. & K.]
  Durang.
                                     Clear

[193]

Mon. 15 Count Benyowsky & Rosina   923.50
Miss White

                                              Clear

Tues. 16 [The] Wheel of Fortune & 1008.50 1932.
[Benefit of] Pullen.   [The] Fortress   ———   ———
                     [See preface to this season.] Doll[ar]s 66287.75

83 Nights, averaging $796.
21 Benefits Averaged 949 Doll[ar]s.

BALTIMORE SPRING SEASON, COMMENCING [APRIL 19, ENDING
JULY 4, 1816.]

[Warren & Wood]

PREFACE—**May 22**: FR announces, "The public are respectfully informed that the managers will offer the profits of this night in aid of the
fund for the relief of the widows and families of the brave men who fell
in the defence of this city." **June 24**: ACDA announces, "After
Alexander the Great a ballet dance called *Auld Robin Gray's Wedding*;
Jemmy's Return. A Scotch pas seul by Mrs. Harris; a double hornpipe
by Mr. Durang and Miss M. Durang. An Irish lilt by all the characters." **June 26**: According to ACDA, Messrs. Jefferson, McFarland
and Steward are to sing a glee, *Life's a Bumper* at the end of act one of
The Review. **June 28**: ACDA announces that Entwisle is to sing the
comic song, *The Beauty*, and Mrs. Entwisle is to recite *Collins' Ode*.

In his entry of June 3 Wood has written, "Whit [suntide] Mon[day]"
and "Mrs. Young's 1st." It has been necessary to omit these notations
from the printed version. Warren, in his *Diary*, reveals that Mrs.
Young's "first appearance" was "as Virginia." The players receiving
a benefit on July 3 were undoubtedly the elder Jeffersons.

April
Frid. 19 Speed the Plough & Matri-   501.
         mony
                     Very Cold.

Saty. 20 [The] Mask'd Friend* & [The] 471.
         Lady of the Lake
                          fine & Cold

Mon. 22 [The] Rivals & [The] Hunter   684.75
       of the Alps
                    Very fine

Wed. 24 Zembuca & [The] Wedding   759.50
       day
                        fine

Frid. 26 Zembuca & [The] Sultan   524.50
                     very fine

Saty. 27 Abaellino & [The] Highland 396.   2364.75
       Reel
                        fine

Mon. 29 [The] Magpie & the Maid* & 811.75
       [The] Beehive
                        fine

May
Wed. 1 [The] Magpie & the Maid & 723.25
       Mr. H.
                     Warm

Frid. 3 [The] Magpie and the Maid & 588.50
       [The] Miller and his Men
                     fine

Saty 4 [The] Exile and [The] Day 521.50 2045.
       after the Wedding
                    Sultry

Mon. 6 [The] Robbers & Love, Law & 570.50
       Physic*
                     fine

Wed. 8 [The] Point of Honor & [The] 535.50
       Fortune of War*
                 very fine

[195]

Frid. 10 [The] Magpie & the Maid &   613.75
Love, Law & Physic
                                fine

Sat. 11 Zembuca & [The] Fortune of 311.   2030.75
War
                                Rain

Mon. 13 [The] Honey Moon & [The] 407.
Miller & his Men
                                fine

Wedy. 15 Alfonso & Paul & Virginia 535.50
Very Cold

Fridy. 17 Lovers['] Quarrels, Jean de 659.
Paris* & My Grand-
mother
                          Very Cold

Saty. 18 [The] Lady of the Lake & Past 311.   1912.50
10 O'Clock
                          very Cold

Mony. 20 [The] School for Scandal & 399.
Transformation
                                fine

Ben[efit]   Wedy. 22 [The] Voice of Nature & [The] 754.
fund N[orth] Point   Fortress
                   [See preface to this season.]
                                Warm

Fridy. 24 [The First Part of] Henry 4th 453.
& Love, Law & Physic
                                Rain

Sat. 25 [The] Magpie & [the] Maid &   384.   1990.
         Zembuca
                        Storm of Rain

Mon. 27 [The] Gamester & Turn Out   445.50
                                fine

Wed. 29 [The] Forest of Bondy* & 1000.
         [The] Devil to pay
                                fine

Frid. 31 [The] Forest of Bondy & [The] 568.75
         Poor Soldier
                                very fine

June
Sat.   1 [The] Forest of Bondy & [The] 226.75   2241.
         Follies of a day
                                Rain

Wood's   Mon 3 [The] Virgin of the Sun, Ballet 695.50
[Benefit]   & Paul & Virginia
                     [Ballet the Scots Minuet
                     from *Marmion*, by F.
                     Durang   and   Harris.
                     ACDA]
                                Warm

Wed.   5 [The] Castle Spectre & [The] 422.50
         Romp
                                Warm

Frid. 7 [The] Family Legend* & [The] 470.50 ·
         Agreeable Surprize
                        Very Cold.

Saty. 8 [The] Magpie & [the] Maid & 269.
         [The] Critic
                                Cold

[197]

Mon. 10 [The] Farmer's Wife* & [The]   500.25
Warrens [Benefit]   Spoil'd Child
                         [As Cornflower in *The*
                         Farmer's Wife. ACDA]
                                         Very Cold.

Wed. 12 Wild Oats & Ella Rosenberg   299.25
                                   fine

Fri. 14 Pizarro & [The] Hole in the   438.50
        Wall
                            Warm

Saty. 15 [The] Peasant Boy, [The   289.50   1527.50
Warren & Wood   Scheming] Milliners &
 & Harris   Timour [the Tartar]
                         fine & Cool

Mon. 17 Othello & [A] Tale of Mystery   459.25
[Benefit of]
Mr. & Mrs. Young
                            Mild & Cloudy

Wed. 19 [King] Lear & [The] Hunter   605.50
[Benefit of]   of the Alps
 Mr. & Mrs. Duff
                            Warm

Frid. 21 [The] Foundling of [the] Forest   335.50
[Benefit of]   & Tekeli
 Savage & Legg   [Legg as Florian, the
                        foundling. ACDA]
                                    fine

Sat. 22 [A] Cure for [the] Heartache   356.   1756.25
[Benefit of] Steward   & [The] Turnpike Gate
 & Barrett   [Steward to sing, Barrett as
                        Young Rapid in *A Cure
                        for the Heartache.* ACDA]

Mon. 24 [The] Road to Ruin & [The]   220.
[Benefit of Mrs.]   Adopted Child
   Seymour &   [See preface to this season]
   [Misses] C. & K
   Durang.

                            Sultry

       Wed. 26 Adelmorn & [The] Review   536.75
[Benefit of   [See preface to this season.]
   Mr.] McFarl[an]d
   & [Mrs.] Lefolle

                   Cool & Cloudy

       Frid. 28 [The] Belle's Stratagem &   383.   1139.75
[Benefit of]   [The] Blind Boy
   Mr. & Mrs.   [See preface to this season.]
   Entwisle

                      Mild & fine

      July
      Mon.   1 [The] Way to Get Married &   526.25
[Benefit of Mr. &]   [The] Farmer
   Mrs. Francis

                 Cloudy & very Cold

       Wed.   3 [The] Battle of Hexham &   928.
[Benefit of]   [The] Weathercock
   Mr. & Mrs.   [Jefferson to sing comic
   Jefferson   song. ACDA]
                    Mild & fine

      Thurs.   4 Columbus & Sprigs of Laurel 1196.37 ——————
                                  $23087.62

                 Very fine & mild
        44 Nights averaging $524.50
         Benefits Averaging 485.

WASHINGTON SEASON[, COMMENCING JULY 11, ENDING AUGUST 24,] 1816.

[Warren & Wood]

PREFACE—July 27: An olio consisting of recitation and singing. DNI "d[itt]o," July 23, refers, of course, to *The Magpie and the Maid*; "d[itt]o," August 8, 10, 13, 15, 17, 19, to "fine," August 6; and "d[itt]o," August 24, to *Zembuca*. It has been advisable to substitute "Young" for "Youngs" in Wood's entry of August 10, "Entwisle" for "Entwisles" in Wood's entry of August 13 and "Jefferson" for "Jeffersons" in Wood's entry of August 19, in order to maintain consistency of style. In his record of this season Wood has included the amounts representing his share of the profits. To the right of July 11, 13, 16, he has written "Share [$]18;" of July 18, 20, 23, "Share—22;" of July 25, 27, 29, "Share—20;" of August 1, 3, 6, "Share—27;" of August 8, 10, 13, "Share—17;" of August 15, 17, 19, "Share—16;" and of August 22, 24, "Share—30" and the total, "$150."

July 11 [The] Peasant Boy & [The] 219.25
      Romp   fine

13 [The] Foundling of [the] For- 241.25
    est & Love, law &
    physic*
              Rain

16 [The] Way to get Married & 192.50
    [The] Spoil'd Child   ——
             Cloudy

18 [The] Hunter of [the] Alps, 280.   933.
    [The] Day after [the] ——
    Wed[din]g & past 10
    O'Clock*
              fine

20 [The] Magpie & [the] Maid* & 321.75
    Turn Out
             fine

23 d[itt]o & Love, law & physic   326.25

fine

25 [The] Castle Spectre & [The]   282.50
    Devil to pay

Rain

27 Paul & Virginia,* Olio, & 3   237.50
—   Weeks after [Marriage
[See preface to this season.]

Rain

29 [The] Forest of Bondy* &   359.75
    [The] Weathercock

Cloudy

August 1st She Stoops to Conquer &   336.25
    [The] F[orest] of Bondy

fine

3 Geo[rge] Barnwell & [The]   331.
—   T[urnpike] Gate

fine

6 [The] Magpie & [the] Maid &   217.50
    Past 10 O'Clock

fine

8 [The] Battle [of] Hexham* &   210.87
    Raising [the] Wind

d[itt]o

[Benefit of Mr.   10th Man & Wife* & Ella   337.87
& Mrs.] Young   Rosenberg

d[itt]o

[Benefit of Mr.   13 Adelgitha & [The] Shipwreck   230.
and Mrs.]
Entwisle

d[itt]o

[201]

[Benefit of Mr.   15 [The] Rivals & [The] Farmer*   254.50
and Mrs]
Francis
                                            d[itt]o

[Benefit of]   17 [A] Cure for [the] Heartache   246.
Bar[rett] &   & Cath[erine] & Petru-
[Mrs.] Harris   chio
                                            d[itt]o

[Benefit of Mr.   19 [The] Honey Moon & [The]   337.25
& Mrs.]   Fortune of War*
Jefferson   d[itt]o

                    22 Zembuca* & [The] Romp   450.

                    24 d[itt]o & Matrimony   373.
                                            ⸻

ALEXANDRIA SEASON[, COMMENCING AUGUST 31, ENDING
SEPTEMBER 26,] 1816.

[Warren & Wood]

PREFACE: To the right of the entries for September 5, 7 and 10, Wood has
written "Share [$]17;" to the right of the entry for September 14, "Share
12;" and to the right of the entry for September 21, "Share 12" and, under
it, the total, "$191." In the entry of September 14 Wood has written
"Scrivr. & Mrs. Bloxton," unquestionably meaning "Benefit of Scrivener
and Mrs. Bloxton."

August 31 [The] M[agpie] & [the] Maid*   230.
            & Love, Law & Physic*

Sept[ember] 2 Adelgitha & past 10 O'Clock*   228.

            [3 The] Forest of Bondy* & [The]   213.
            Romp

[202]

                    5 Zembuca* & [The] day after 370.
                    [the] Wedding
                                        Cloudy

            Saty.   7 Zembuca & [The] Weather-   278.
                    cock
                                        d[itt]o

            Tues. 10th [The] F[orest] of Bondy & 116.
Ben[efi]t [of]   P[aul] & Virginia
  Aber[crombie]   Rain
  & Harris

            Thurs. 12 [The] Batt[le of] Hexham* & 382.37
[Benefit of]   [The] M[agpie] & [the]
  Mr. & Mrs.   Maid
  Jefferson

            Saty. 14 [The] Rivals & [The] Fortune 221.16
                     of War

            Tues. 17 [The] Soldier's Daughter &   441.25
[Benefit of]   Timour [the Tartar]
  Mr. & Mrs.
  Entwisle

            Thur. 19 [The] Way to Get Married &   282.
[Benefit of] Barrett &   [A] Tale of Mystery
  T. Jeff[erson]

[Benefit of] Saty. 21 Town & Country & [The]   348.
  Mr. & Mrs. Young   Romp   ——

            Tues. 24 [The] F[oundling] of [the]   345.
[Benefit of]   Forest & Turn out
  Hathwell & Willis

            Thurs. 26 [The] School for Scandal & 509.
[Benefit of]   [The] Spoil'd Child
  Mr. & Mrs. Francis
                                        ————————————
                                        D[ollar]s 3933.68

                    [203]

BALTIMORE AUTUMN SEASON[, COMMENCING OCTOBER 1, ENDING NOVEMBER 21,] 1816.

[Warren & Wood]

PREFACE: In the entry of October 16 Wood has written "Mr. Harris died at 6 this morning." Warren notes in his *Diary*, "This morning at 6 o'clock died after an illness of 2 years & ½ Joseph Harris of our Company. Tuesday attended the funeral of Joseph F. W. Harris."

<table>
<tr><td>Tuesday</td><td></td><td></td><td></td><td></td></tr>
<tr><td>October 1st.</td><td>She Stoops to Conquer & [The] Miller & [his] Men</td><td>460.25</td><td></td></tr>
<tr><td></td><td>fine</td><td></td><td></td></tr>
</table>

Tuesday
October 1st. She Stoops to Conquer &   460.25
          [The] Miller & [his] Men
                  fine

Wed. 2 [The] Magpie & [The] Maid &   263.50
         Rosina
                fine

Frid. 4 [The] Honey Moon & [The]   583.50
Mrs. G[ilfert]   Beehive
         [As Juliana in *The Honey Moon*. ACDA]
               fine

"   Saty. 5 Romeo & Juliet & Raising the   370.50   1677.75
         Wind
         [Mrs. Gilfert as Juliet. ACDA]
               fine

"   Mon. 7 [The] Gamester & Love, Law   441.50
         & Physic
         [Mrs. Gilfert as Mrs. Beverly in *The Gamester*. ACDA]
               fine

"   Wed. 9 Much ado about Nothing &   488.50
              [A] Budget of Blunders
              [Mrs. Gilfert as Beatrice.
              ACDA]
                          fine

"   Frid. 11 [The] Castle Spectre & My   334.
              Grandmother
              [Mrs. Gilfert as Angela in
              The Castle Spectre.
              ACDA]
                         cloudy

"   Saty. 12 Pizarro & [The] Weathercock   459.50   1723.50
              [Mrs. Gilfert as Elvira in   ———
              Pizarro. ACDA]
                         Rain

             Mon. 14 [The] Provok'd Husband &   799.25
Ben[efit of Mrs.   Cath[erine] & Petruchio
Gilfert]   [As Lady Townly in *The Pro-*
              voked Husband and as
              Catherine. ACDA]
                         fine

             Wed. 16 Columbus & [The] Toothache   537.
                         fine

             Frid. 18 [The] Mask'd Friend &   296.50
              Zembuca
                         fine

Cooper   Saty. 19 Hamlet & Lovers['] Quarrels   959.75   2592.50
              [As Hamlet. ACDA]
                         fine

C[ooper]   Mon. 21 Rule a Wife [& Have a Wife]   593.50
              & [A] Tale of Mystery
              [As Leon in *Rule a Wife.*
              ACDA]
                         Rain

[205]

"   Wed. 23 Adelgitha & Of Age tomorrow 663.50
              [Cooper as Michael Ducas
                 in *Adelgitha*. ACDA]
                                    fine

"   Frid. 25 Bertram & [The] Review   937.50
               [Cooper as Bertram. ACDA]
                         Rain at Night

"   Saty. 26 Macbeth & Matrimony   617.50   2812.
                         fine & Cool   ———

"   Mon. 28 [The] Merchant of Venice &   531.
               Cath[erine] & Petruchio
               [Cooper as Shylock. ACDA]
                                    fine

"   Wed. 30 Bertram & Turn Out   404.50
               [Cooper as Bertram. ACDA]
                                    fine

November
"   Frid. 1 Richard 3rd. & [The] Hunter 723.50
                of the Alps
                [Cooper as Richard. ACDA]
                                    Cold

       Saty. 2d. Coriolanus & How to die for 511.50 2170.50
                 love   ———
                 [Cooper   as   Coriolanus.
                 ACDA]
                                    fine

       Mon. 4th Othello & [The] Hole in the   435.
                Wall
                [Cooper as Othello. ACDA]
                                    Warm

                       [206]

Wed. 6th Alexander [the Great] & For- 524.50
tune's frolic
Clear & Cold

Frid. 8th [The] Iron Chest & [The] 458.50
Prisoner at Large
fine

Saty. 9th [The] Robbers & 3 & [the] 788.50
C[ooper]'s Benefit   Deuce
[As Charles de Moor in *The
Robbers.* ACDA]
Cold

Mrs. Burke Mon. 11 [The] Foundling of [the] forest 488.50
& [The] Padlock
[As Rosabelle in *The Found-
ling of the Forest* and
Leonora in *The Padlock.*
ACDA]
Cold

"   Wed. 13 No Song no Supper, [The] 398.50
Devil to Pay & Of Age
tomorrow
[Mrs. Burke as Margaretta
in *No Song No Supper*,
Nell in *The Devil to Pay*
and Maria in *Of Age
Tomorrow.* ACDA]
fine

"   Frid. 15 2d. Rosina & [The] 1st. 461.50
Dramatist
[Mrs. Burke as Rosina and
as Marianne in *The
Dramatist.* ACDA The
numbering probably re-
fers to the order of
presentation.]
fine

[207]

" Saty. 16 [The] Hero of [the] North & 397.50 1748.
          [The] Spoil'd Child
          [Mrs. Burke as Frederica
          Rubenski in *The Hero
          of the North* and Little
          Pickle in *The Spoiled
          Child*. ACDA]
                                    fine

                Mon. 18 [The] Mountaineers & Paul 970.
Mrs. B[urke's]   & Virginia
ben[efit.]   [As Agnes in *The Moun-
                       taineers* and as Virginia.
                       ACDA]
                                    fine

        Tuesdy. 19 Rokeby* & [The] Comet   509.75
                                    fine

        Wed. 20 [The] Woodsman's Hut* & 701.50
                [The] Highland Reel
                               Cloudy

        Thurs. 21 [The] Woodsman's Hut & 840.50 3021.75
                  [The] Lady of the Lake   ————————
                                            $17,950.50
                                    fine
                    average 559 per night

PHILADELPHIA SEASON, COMMENCING NOVEMBER 25TH, 1816, [ENDING
                    APRIL 24, 1817.]

                    [Warren & Wood]

PREFACE—**December 24**: In his entry of this date Wood has written
"CD," which is probably explained by an announcement in A to the
effect that Miss C. Durang is to dance a pas seul. **Januany 2**: After
"[The] Belle's Stratagem" Wood has written "ch[an]g[e]d fr[om] T[own] &
Country, Wood ill." In his *Diary* Warren writes, "The play changed

from Town & Country, Wood being hoarse." **January 13**: A announces, "A new comic piece, in one act, called *Personation*; *or Fairly Taken In*. The whole of the characters by Mr. Jefferson [the elder] and Mrs. Wheatley. **March 3**: In this entry Wood has written "[The] Iron Chest." He has then crossed out the title and written below it, "Chang[e]d to [The] Gamester." A of March 1 announces Cooper as Sir Edward Mortimer in *The Iron Chest*. Warren discloses, in his *Diary*, that the "play" was "changed to The Gamester" because "Mrs. Entwisle" was "not ready in Helen." **April 3**: A announces, "The evening's entertainment to conclude with the Musical olio of *The Catch Club*." **April 24**: Mr. Pullen was the treasurer of the company. With regard to the rôles played by Mrs. S. Wheatley, Warren reveals that, on December 16, she "appear[ed] in Letitia Hardy [in *The Belle's Stratagem*] and Zorilda [in *Timour the Tartar*.]"

During this season Warren and Wood had to face the handicaps of severe weather and, as Wood recalls in his autobiography p. 207, "the most formidable opposition [they] had ever experienced." In the February 5 entry of his *Diary* Warren writes, "Night one of the Sharpest of the season. Sleighs ply between Market Street and the Jersey shore to carry passengers across." Wood's benefit, on February 24, Warren notes, was "postponed on account of the Snow Storm." Wood identifies "the formidable opposition" as "a powerful equestrian and melodramatic corps, conducted by Mr. West of the London amphitheatre." For an account of this rivalry, see the general introduction p. 26.

In spite of this "strong counter attraction," however, Wood asserts, "our season of $569 may be considered highly prosperous." The excellence and novelty of their performances were undoubtedly the factor contributing most to Warren & Wood's success in meeting the competition of Mr. West's company; but there was another factor which must have helped to attract audiences this season to the Chesnut Street Theatre. This was the introduction of gas lights which, according to *Durang*, I, LIV, the bills of the opening night asserted were being used in an American theatre for the first time. For further details, see the general introduction, p. 25.

[November]
    Mon. 25 She Stoops to Conquer & 1113.50
           Rosina
                              fine

Wed. 27 [The] Foundling of the For- 788.50
       est & Raising [the] Wind
                       fine

Frid. 29 Pizarro & [The] Weathercock 609.50
               Rain all day

Sat. 30 Zembuca & past 10 O'Clock 586.25 3097.75

                 Very fine

December
Mon. 2 [The] Mountaineers & [The] 595.50
Mrs. Burke's 1st.   Spoil'd Child
          [As Agnes in *The Moun-*
          taineers and Little Pickle
          in *The Spoiled Child.* A]
                     Cold

Wed. 4 [The] Rivals & no Song no 487.50
       Supper.
               Clear & Cold

Frid. 6 Romeo & Juliet & Love, Law 480.
       & Physic
                   Mild

Saty. 7 [The] Magpie & [the] Maid & 600.25 2063.25
       3 & [the] deuce
                Very mild

Mon. 9 Bertram* & [The] Agreeable 820.50
       Surprize
                  Cloudy

Wed. 11 [The] School for Scandal & 486.50
       Paul & Virginia
               Rain all day

Frid. 13 Adrian & Orrilla & [The] 447.
Miller & his Men

Rain

Saty. 14 Bertram & Turn Out   384.75 2138.75

Cold & fine

Mon. 16 [The] Belle's Stratagem & 526.
Mrs. Wheatley   Timour [the Tartar]

fine

Wed. 18 [The] Honey Moon & Timour 465.50
Mrs. W[heatley]   [the Tartar]

Mild

"   Frid. 20 [The] Jealous Wife & [The] 403.25
Spoil'd Child

fine

"   Saty. 21 Rokeby* & [The] Devil to 442.50 1837.25
pay

Cold

"   Mon. 23 [The] Soldier's Daughter & 380.25
[The] Lady of the Lake

Cold

"   Tues. 24 Geo[rge] Barnwell & [The]   393.50
P[oor] Soldier
[See preface to this season.]

Thurs. 26 [The] Fortune of War & [The] 1043.50
Woodsman's Hut*

Very mild

Frid. 27 Wild Oats & d[itt]o   598.50
Warm & fine

[211]

Saty. 28 3 & [the] Deuce & d[itt]o   313.50   2729.25
                         ——

                Cold & fine

Mon. 30 Speed the Plough & d[itt]o 376.50
                         fine

1817. Jan[uar]y
     Wed. 1 Aladdin* & She Stoops to 1470.25
           Conquer
                  fine

     Thurs. 2d. Aladdin & [The] Belle's Strat- 498.
           agem
           [See preface to this season.]
                  fine

     Frid. 3 Aladdin & [The] School of 556.50
           Reform
               Rain at night

     Saty. 4 Aladdin & [The] Magpie & 401.50   3302.75
           [the] Maid   ——
               at Night Fair

     Mon. 6 Aladdin & [The] Wonder   560.
                     dull

     Wed. 8 Man & Wife & Bombastes 501.
Mrs. W[heatley]   [Furioso]*
                     Cold

     Frid. 10 [The] Will, Bombastes [Furi- 408.
Mrs. W[heatley]   oso] & [Of] Age tomorrow
                     fine

    "   Saty. 11 Alfonso & [The] Prize   341.50   1810.50
                                ——

                Very Cold

Mon. 13 [The] Provok'd Husband, 627.25
Ben[efit of] Mrs.   Personation & Turn Out
W[heatley]   [See preface to this season.]
     Cold

Wed. 15 [The] Busy Body & [The] 40 1042.75
     Thieves
     fine

Frid. 17 Town & Country, & [The] 40 431.50
     Thieves
     Warm

Cooper   Saty. 18 Hamlet & [The] Day after 727.50
     [the] Wedding
     [As Hamlet. A]
     very Cold

Cooper   Mon. 20 Macbeth & Ways & Means 619.25
     [As Macbeth. A]
     very Severe

"   Wed. 22 [The] Honey Moon & Paul & 599.75
     Virginia
     [Cooper as Duke Aranza in
     The Honey Moon. A]
     Cold

"   Frid. 24 Richard 3d. & High life below 780.75
     Stairs
     Mild

"   Saty. 25 [The] School for Scandal & 625.   2624.75
     Cath[erine] & Petruchio ——
     [Cooper as Charles Surface
     in *The School for Scandal*
     and as Petruchio. A]
     fine & Mild

[213]

"   Mon. 27 Bertram & [The] Hunter of   768.50
              the Alps
              [Cooper as Bertram. A]
                  fine & Sleighing

"   Wed. 29 Coriolanus & How to die for   499.
              Love
              [Cooper as Coriolanus. A]
                  very Cold & Sleigh[in]g

"   Frid. 31 Rule a Wife [& Have a Wife]   539.50
              & [The] Padlock
              [Cooper as Leon in *Rule a
              Wife.* A]
                  d[itt]o   d[itt]o

       Feb[ruar]y
C[ooper]   Saty. 1 Pizarro & Transformation   726.50   2533.50
              [As Rolla in *Pizarro.* A]
                  fine & Sleigh[in]g

"   Mon.   3 Othello & Killing no Murder   580.
              [Cooper as Othello. A]
                  Very Cold & Sleigh[in]g

"   Wed.   5 Bertram & [The] Fortune of   625.25
              War
              [Cooper as Bertram. A]
                  Very Severe

"   Frid.   7 Alexander [the Great] & [The]   427.75
              Midnight Hour
              [Cooper as Alexander.]
                  Cold

"   Saty.   8 [The] Robbers & Mr. H.   785.75   2418.75
              [Cooper as Charles de Moor
              in *The Robbers.* A]
                  Mild

[214]

"   Mon. 10 Much ado about Nothing &   400.75
                [The] Poor Soldier
                [Cooper as Benedick. A]
                        Very Cold

"   Wed. 12 [The First Part of] Henry 4th   738.50
                & [The] Irishman in
                London
                [Cooper as Hotspur. A]
                        Very Severe

"   Frid. 14 Julius Caesar & Past 10   634.50
                O'Clock
                        the Coldest I remember

"   Saty. 15 [The] Castle Spectre & [The]   505.   2278.75
                Review
                [Cooper as Osmond in *The
                Castle Spectre*. A]
                        very Severe

"   Mon. 17 [The] Wheel of fortune &   945.50
C[ooper's] Ben[efit]   [The] Liar
                [As Penruddock in *The
                Wheel of Fortune* and
                Young Wilding in *The
                Liar*. A]
                        Cold & Rain

        Wed. 19 3 & [the] deuce & Aladdin   476.50
                        Mild & thaw

        Frid. 21 Columbus & Of age tomorrow   235.
                        Heavy rain & thaw

        Saty. 22 Gustavus Vasa & Zembuca   651.   2308.
                        Mild & fine

[215]

Wood's Ben[efi]t	Mon. 24 [The] Suspicious Husband & Blue Beard postp[one]d on acc[ount of] Storm		
Cooper	Wed. 26 Bertram, [Little] R[ed] R[id- ing] Hood & [The] Bee- hive [As Bertram. A] fine	611.	
C[ooper] Poor	Frid. 28 [The] Mountaineers & All the World's a Stage [As Octavian in *The Moun- taineers*. A announces benefit for poor.] Storm of Rain	851.50	

March

C[ooper]	Saty. 1 Hamlet & [The] Ghost [As Hamlet. A] Cold & Snowy	404.	1866.50
C[ooper]	Mon. 3 [The] Gamester & [The] Comet [As Beverly in *The Gamester*. A See preface to this season.] Mild & fine	625.50	
[Benefit of] Wood	Wed. 5 [The] Suspicious Husband & Blue Beard very fine	993.50	
	Frid. 7 Guy Mannering* & [The] Critic Very fine	592.	
	Saty. 8 The Kiss & [The] 40 Thieves fine	320.50	2530.50

Mony. 10 Guy Mannering & [The] Mid- 304.50
night Hour

Foggy

[Benefit of] Wed. 12 [The] Ethiop & My Land- 830.50
Warren lady's Gown*

Snow

Fridy. 14 [The] Curfew & [The] Wood- 160.
man's Hut

Snow

Saty. 15 [The] Farmer's Wife* & [A] 311.50 1606.50
Tale of Mystery

fine

Mon. 17 [The] Lady of the Lake, L[ov- 756.50
ers'] Quarrels & Blue
Beard

Cloudy

Wed. 19 [The] Point of Honor, Matri- 385.
mony & Tekeli

Very Cold

Frid. 21 [The] Busy Body & [The] 721.50
Armourer's Escape*

fine

Saty. 22 Abaellino & d[itt]o 339.75 2202.75

very mild

Mon. 24 [The] Stranger & d[itt]o 301.50
Jewitt['s] Ben[efit] [Benefit of Mr. J. R. Jewitt,
author of *The Armourer's
Escape.* A]

Rain

[217]

Wed. 26 [The] Man of 10,000, Bomb- 1337.50
[Benefit of]   astes [Furioso] & What
Jefferson   Next?*

                     fine

Frid. 28 [The] Provoked Husband & 767.50
[Farewell Benefit of]   [The] Farmer
Mrs. Entwisle

                     fine

Saty. 29 [The] West Indian & Ella 717.25   3123.75
[Farewell night of]   Rosenberg
Mr. Duff

                     fine

[Benefit of] Mon. 31 [The] Siege of Belgrade & 859.25
Mrs. Burke   [The] Blind Boy

                 Very fine

April
[Benefit of] Wed. 2 The Man[age]r in distress, 860.75
Barrett   [The] W[ay] to Get Mar-
                  ried & 3 Weeks after
                  Marriage

                     fine

Thurs. 3 [The] Tempest, 1/2 hour after 392.50
[Benefit of] Francis   Supper & [The] Catch
                  Club
                  [See preface to this season.]
                  cloudy

Sat. 5 King Lear, Miss in her Teens 601.   2713.50
[Farewell benefit   & [The] Sleepwalker
of] Mrs. Duff

                     fine

[Benefit of] Mon. 7 [The] Surrender of Calais, & 387.75
Mrs. Claude   Robin Hood

                 very fine

[Benefit of] Wed. 9 [The] Grecian Daughter & 453.50
Robertson   [The] Highland Reel

                                   fine

[Benefit of] Frid. 11 [The] Heir at Law, Married 615.75
Entwisle   Yesterday* & [The] Turn-
              pike Gate

                           Cool & fine

[Benefit of] Saty. 12 [The] Road to Ruin & Two 353.25   1810.25
Burke   Strings to your bow
            [As Silky in *The Road to*
            Ruin and Lazarillo in
            Two Strings to Your Bow.
            A]

                                   fine

[Benefit of] Mon. 14 John Bull & Love laughs at 998.25
McFarland   locksmiths
            [As Dennis Brulgruddery in
            John Bull and Captain
            Beldare in *Love Laughs at*
            Locksmiths. A]

                        Very Mild

[Benefit of] Wed. 16 Macbeth & [The] Jew & 482.
Steward   Doctor

                      fine & Warm

[Benefit of Frid. 18 [A] Cure for [the] Heartache 355.25
Mrs.] Bloxton [&   & [The] Adopted Child
Miss Seymour]

                      Very Cold

[Benefit of] Saty. 19 Speed the Plough & Lock & 663.50   2499.
Mrs. Harris   Key

                      Very Cold

[219]

[Benefit of] Mon. 21 [A] Bold Stroke for a husband 442.25
  Abercrombie   & Valentine & Orson
                       fine

       Wedy. 23 [The] Poor Gent[leman] & All 637.
[Benefit of]   the World's a Stage
  Mrs. Francis

                      fine

     Thursday 24 [The] Dramatist & [The] 688.50 1767.75
[Benefit of]   Agreeable Surprize
  Pullen   [See preface to this season.]
                      Dull

                             $51,886.75

87 Nights averaging 596 each
24 Benefits averaged 687 each
20 Under Charges

BALTIMORE [SPRING] SEASON, COMMENCING APRIL 28, [ENDING JULY 4,] 1817.

[Warren & Wood]

PREFACE—**June 16**: ACDA announces, "The whole of the characters [in *Personation*] by Mr. Burke and Mrs. Wheatley. **June 18**: According to Warren's *Diary*, "Mrs. Wheatly continues lame—unable to act this night—Mrs. Burke plays Nell [in *The Devil to Pay*]." **June 28**: ACDA announces "An interlude consisting of singing and dancing under the direction of Mr. Francis called *The Sailor's Return; or,All Alive at Fell's Point*. In the course of the ballet, *Tally Ho!* by Mrs. Claude. T[homas] Jeff[erson] is the eldest son of Mr. and Mrs. [Joseph] Jefferson who received a benefit on June 27. **July 1**: ACDA announces "The grand French bravoura of *Est-il Un Sort Plus Glorieux*, from the opera of *La Belle Arsène*, by Mrs. Burke. A pas seul by Mrs. Harris; hunting song, by desire, *The Morn Unbars the Gates of Light*, by Mrs. Burke; the favorite song of *Are Ye Fair as Opening Roses*; and the much admired masquerade song from the opera of *My Grandmother, On the Lightly Sportive Wing*, by Mrs. Burke. A pas de deux by Mr. F. Durang and Mrs. Harris."

[220]

Warren's *Diary* adds to Caldwell's rôle of Belcour announced by ACDA for May 31 the rôles of the Singles in *Three and the Deuce*. In his entry of June 1 Warren writes of this actor, who becomes later the widely known James H. Caldwell, "Mr. C. was well received; but, in my opinion, he is a very queer actor." It is evident from a notation in the April 28 entry of Warren's *Diary*, "the Theatre lighted with gas," that Warren & Wood had been sufficiently satisfied with the new means of lighting the theatre in Philadelphia to try it in Baltimore. For comment on the extent to which it was satisfactory consult the general introduction, p. 28.

[April]

Mon. 28 [The] Honey Moon & [The] 482.
       Comet
                     fine

Wed. 30 [The] Mountaineers & [The] 510.50
       Spoil'd Child
                     fine

May

Frid. 2 [The] Busy Body & [The] 642.50
       Woodman's Hut
                     fine

Saty. 3 [The] Heir at Law & What 322.   1957.
       Next?*
                     fine

Mon. 5 [The] Provok'd Husband & 447.
       Love laughs at Lock-
       smiths
                     fine

Wed. 7 [The] Midnight Hour & Alad- 700.
       din*
              Storm of rain

Frid. 9 [The] Magpie & [the] Maid 708.50
       & d[itt]o
                     fine

[221]

Saty. 10 [The] Man of 10,000 & [Little] 293.   2148.50
Red R[iding] Hood &
Bombastes [Furioso]*
fair

Cooper   Mon. 12 Hamlet & [The] Day after the 964.25
Wedding
[As Hamlet. ACDA]
very Cool

"   Wed. 14 Bertram & [The] Hunter of 514.50
the Alps
[Cooper   as   Bertram.
ACDA]
Cold

"   Frid. 16 Much ado about nothing & 556.50
Lock & Key
[Cooper   as   Benedick.
ACDA]
Very Cold

"   Saty. 17 [The] Gamester & [The] 444.50 2479.75
Woodman's Hut
[Cooper as Beverly in *The
Gamester*. ACDA]
Mild

"   Mon. 19 Richard 3d. & Miss in her 604.
teens
[Cooper as Richard. ACDA]
fine

"   Wed. 21 [The First Part of] Henry 4th 619.50
& Married Yesterday*
[Cooper as Hotspur. ACDA]
fine

[222]

"   Frid. 23 [The] Honey Moon & Paul &   428.50
                Virginia
                [Cooper as Duke Aranza in
                The Honey Moon. ACDA]
                               Rain

"   Saty. 24 Macbeth & Married Yester-   458.50   2110.50
                day
                [Cooper   as   Macbeth.
                ACDA]
                             Warm

                Mon. 26 Pizarro & How to die for Love   947.
C[ooper's] Ben[efit]   [As Rolla in *Pizarro*. ACDA]
                             Warm

                Wed. 28 [The] Siege of Belgrade & My   330.75
                Landlady's Gown*
                             Dull

[Benefit of]   Frid. 30 [The] School of Reform &   713.50
   Warren   [The] 40 Thieves
                             fine

Caldwell   Sat. 31 [The] West Indian & 3 &   272.75   2264.
                [the] Deuce
                [As Belcour in *The West*
                Indian. ACDA]
                             fine

          June
Cal[dwell]   Mon. 2 Romeo & Juliet & [The] Liar   494.75
                [As Romeo and as Young
                  Wilding   in   *The Liar*.
                ACDA]
                      Rain at night

[223]

[Benefit of] Wed. 4 [The] School for Scandal & 756.50
  Stew[ar]d. &   [The] Review
  McFarland   [McFarland as Carleless in
          The School for Scandal.
          ACDA]
                    Rainy

[Benefit of] Frid. 6 [The] Suspicious Husband & 706.
  Wood   Blue Beard
                Mild & fine

         Saty. 7 [The] Foundling of [the] forest 256.   2213.25
Caldwell['s] Ben[efit]   & 3 & [the] Deuce
          [As Florian the foundling.
          ACDA]
                 fine

[Benefit of] Mon. 9 [The] Jealous Wife & Turn 527.25
  Mr. & Mrs.   Out
  Entwisle
             Rainy till Night

        Wed. 11 [The] Belle's Stratagem & 387.50
Mrs. W[heatley]   [The] Prize
          [As Letitia Hardy in *The
          Belle's Stratagem* and
          Caroline in *The Prize.*
          ACDA]
                 fine

    "   Frid. 13 [The] Will & of Age tomorrow 200.50
          [Mrs. Wheatley as Albina
          Mandeville in *The Will*
          and Maria in *Of Age
          Tomorrow.* ACDA]
                 fine

"   Saty. 14 [The] Wonder & [The] Lady 285.50 1399.75
                of the Lake
                [Mrs. Wheatley as Donna
                Violante in *The Wonder*
                and Blanche of Devon in
                The Lady of the Lake.
                ACDA]
                                      fine

                Mon. 16 [The] Soldier's Daughter, Per- 387.50
Mrs. W[heatley's]   sonation & [The] Spoil'd
  Ben[efit]   Child
                [As Widow Cheerly in *The
                Soldier's Daughter* and
                Little Pickle in *The
                Spoiled Child.* ACDA
                See preface to this season.]

W[heatley]   Wed. 18 [The] Critic, Aladdin & [The] 402.50
                Devil to pay
                Mrs. W[heatley] ill [See
                preface to this season.]
                                      Rainy

"   Frid. 20 Guy Mannering* & Blue 425.
                Beard
                [Mrs. Wheatley as Meg
                Merrilies in *Guy Man-
                nering* and Irene in *Blue.
                Beard.* ACDA]
                                      Rainy

                Saty. 21 Columbus & Robin Hood 230.
[Benefit of]
  Rob[ertso]n &
  [Mrs.] Lefolle
                          Rain & Thunder
                        [225]

[Benefit of] Mon. 23 [The] Rivals & Timour [the 312.
Mr. & Mrs.   Tartar]
Francis

          Cool & fine

Ben[efit of] Wed. 25 [The] Point of Honor, 3 387.50
Barr[ett &]   W[ee]ks after Marriage &
F. Durang   [The] Blind Boy
          Cool & fine

[Benefit of] Frid. 27 Guy Mannering, Miss in her 543.25
Mr. & Mrs.   teens & [The] Irish Widow
Jeff[erson]

       a Shower at Night

[Benefit of   Saty. 28 Alfonso & [The] Agreeable 175.50   1418.25
Mrs.] Claude and   Surprize
T. Jeff[erson]   [See preface to this season.]
           fine

    Mon. 30 Alexander [the Great], Sylv- 659.
[Farewell benefit of]   [este]r Daggerwood &
Mr. & Mrs. Duff   [The] Day after [the]
       Wedding
           fine

    Tuesday
    July 1 [The] Birthday, Tekeli & Olio 496.50
Benefit of] Mr. &   [See preface to this season.]
Mrs. Burke

           fine

[Benefit of Wed. 2 [The] Road to Ruin & Valen- 492.
Mr.] Aber[crombie]   tine & Orson
& [Mrs.] Harris   [Mrs. Harris in pas de trois
      and minuet and straths-
      pey from *Marmion.*
      ACDA]
         Very fine

Frid. 4 Manuel* & Aladdin   1117.50 ———
                                      $20202.
40 Nights averaging 505 D[ollar]s.
Benefits Averaged.

WASHINGTON SEASON[, COMMENCING JULY 12, ENDING SEPTEMBER 25,] 1817.

[Warren & Wood]

PREFACE—**August 28**: DNI announces "Mr. Thompson, in imitation of Mr. Kean, the English actor, will perform three of the principal scenes in *Richard the Third.*"

Wood has written, in the July 17 entry, "Share $20;" in the July 26 entry, "Share;" in the August 2 entry, "Share $20;" in the August 11 entry, "Share $15;" in the August 16 entry, "Share $10;" in the August 24 entry, "Share $15;" and in the August 28 entry, "Share $10." In the August 30 entry Wood has written "profit 53.25" and "Share $4." Part of the profit may have gone to the players sharing the benefit. In the September 2 entry Wood has written "profit 204.31;" in the September 4 entry, profit "133.71;" in the September 6 entry, "profit 25.56" and "Share $12," the other half apparently going to Warren; in the September 9 entry, "profit 173.42;" and in the September 13 entry, "profit $76" and "Share $12," the difference between $24, his and Warren's shares, apparently going to the players receiving the benefit. In the September 20 entry Wood has written "Share $12" and, in the entry of September 25, "Share $7."

July 12 [The] Birthday & No Song   158.
        no Supper

Tues. 15 Abaellino & [The] Spoil'd 258.
        Child

Thurs. 17 Guy Mannering & Miss in 183.75   599.75
        her Teens   ———

Saty. 19 [The] Heir at Law & My   195.75
        Grandmother

Tues. 22 Zembuca & Of age tomorrow   252.50
                                fair

Thurs. 24 Bertram & [The] Devil to pay   65.75
                            dreadful Storm

Saty. 26 Guy Mannering & My Land-   204.25   718.25
                lady's Gown*   ———

Tues. 29 Bertram & Lock & Key   218.75

Thurs. 31 [The First Part of] Henry 4th   217.75
                & [The] Prize

August
  Saty.   2 Ways & Means & [The] 40   452.25   888.75
                    Thieves   ———

Tues. 5th [The] Magpie & [the] Maid &   174.75
                Married Yesterday*

Thurs.   7 [The] Midnight Hour & [The]   195.
                40 Thieves

Mon. 11 [The] Forest of Bondy & Turn   88.
                Out

Wed. 13 John Bull & Paul & Virginia   176.

Frid. 15 [The] Robbers & [The] Agree-   122.75
                able Surprize

Saty. 16 [The] Forest of Bondy & Love   139.
                Laughs [at Locksmiths]

Tues. 19 Aladdin & [The] Prisoner at   293.
                Large
                        Rain at Night

Thurs. 21 Aladdin & [The] Irishman in 212.50
London

Saty. 24th Aladdin & [The] Point of 249.48
Honor   ———

26 [The] Busy Body & Bomb- 225.25
astes [Furioso]*

Thurs. 28 [The] Miller & [his] Men, 212.
Scenes of Richard [3d.]
& [The] Village Lawyer
[See preface to this season.]

Saty. 30 Pizarro & Rosina   208.25
Ben[efit of] Mr.
Willis & Scrivener

[September]
Tues. 2d. [The] Road to Ruin & Blue 358.75
[Benefit of] Mr.   Beard
& Mrs. Burke

Thurs. 4 She Stoops to Conquer & 287.25
[Benefit of] Mr.   [The] Woodman's Hut*
& Mrs. Jefferson

Saty. 6 Columbus & [The] Chil[dren] 177.75
[Benefit of] Hath-   in [the] Wood
well & [Mrs.]
Lefolle

Tues. 9 Macbeth & [The] Liar*   324.
[Benefit of] Barrett   [Barrett as Macbeth, Rob-
& Robertson   ertson as Macduff. DNI]

Thurs. 11 [The] School for Scandal & 145.75
[Benefit of] T.   [The] H[ighland] Reel   ———
Jeff[erson] &
Mrs. Anderson

Saty. 13 Town & Country & Val[en- 229.
[Benefit of Mr.]   tine] & Orson
  Abercrombie &
  Mrs. Harris

Tues. 16 Speed the Plough & [The] 107.
        Woodman's Hut

Thurs. 18 Manuel* & [The] Review 141.

Saty. 20th [The] Busy Body & Cinder- 167.75
        ella*

Tues. 23d. [A] Cure for [the] Hearthache 135.25
        & [The] Blind Boy

Thurs. 25 [The] Broken Sword, [The] 445.75
Mr. & Mrs.   Old Maid & [The] Ghost
  Francis' Night
                                    ————
                                    $7033.50
        33 Nights Averaging $213.50.

BALTIMORE AUTUMN SEASON, COMM[ENCIN]G OCTOBER 1ST., [ENDING
        NOVEMBER 26TH.,] 1817.

[Warren & Wood]

PREFACE—**November 12**: ACDA announces "End of the first act of
The Irishman in London (for the first time here) George A. Stevens'
celebrated ballad called *The Storm*. Description of a hurricane, ship
in distress, &c. In the character of a ship-wrecked sailor, by Mr. Incledon." In the entry of this date Warren's *Diary* records that "Incledon
sings the Storm." It must have been a very successful performance,
for Wood lists the ballad in his entry of November 12. **November 21**:
ACDA announces, *The Feast of Apollo*, a musical olio consisting of songs,
duets and glees. "To be sung by Messrs. Incledon, Jefferson, Francis,
McFarland, Mr. Taylor—from the Covent Garden Theatre, his 1st.
appearance here—and Mr. Clifton of this city, who has kindly offered
his assistance. The songs, duets and glees to be accompanied on the
piano forte by Messrs. Clifton and Taylor."

In ACDA "The managers respectfully inform the public that during the recess [preceding this season,] this theatre has been completely finished and the dome, boxes &c. splendidly decorated under the direction of Messrs. H. Warren, Reinagle and assistants and now offers to the public a theatre at least equal in elegance and accomodation to any in the United States."

October

Wedy.	1	Town & Country & [The] Highland Reel	440.25
		Dull	
Frid.	3	[The] Clandestine Marriage & My Grandmother	529.75
		fine	
Saty.	4	[The] Magpie & [the] Maid & Aladdin	306.50 1276.50
		fine	
Mon.	6	[The] Provok'd Husband & [The] Deuce is in him*	328.75
		fine	
Wed.	8	[The] Ethiop & All the World's a Stage	423.50
		fine	

Cooper Frid. 10 Venice Preserv'd & Love, Law 681.50
& Physic
[As Pierre in *Venice Preserved*. ACDA]
fine

" Saty. 11 Hamlet & Married Yesterday 412.75 1846.50
[Cooper as Hamlet. ACDA]
fine

[231]

"   Mon. 13 Bertram & My Landlady's   470.50
             Gown
             [Cooper as Bertram ACDA]
                   fine

"   Wed. 15 Richard 3d. & [The] Old Maid   518.50
             [Cooper as Richard ACDA]
                   Cool

"   Frid. 17 [The] Curfew & How to die for   465.75
             Love
             [Cooper as Fitzharding in
              The Curfew. ACDA]
                   fine

"   Saty. 18 Pizarro & Mr. H.   427.50   1882.25
             [Cooper as Rolla in *Pizarro*.
             ACDA]

"   Mon. 20 [The] Mountaineers & Cath-   519.75
             [erine] & Petruchio
             [Cooper as Octavian in *The*   519.75
             Mountaineers. ACDA]
                   fine

"   Wed. 22 [The First Part of] Henry 4th.   617.75
             & Zembuca
             [Cooper as Hotspur. ACDA]

Cooper   Frid. 24 [The] Apostate & [The] Bee-   944.50
             hive
             [As Malec in *The Apostate*.
             ACDA]
                   fine

"   Saty. 25 [The] Apostate & Miss in her   322.50   2404.50
             teens
             [Cooper as Malec in *The*
             Apostate. ACDA]
                   fine

Mon. 27 [The] Orphan & [The] Liar   853.
C[ooper's] Ben[efit]   [As Chamont in *The Orphan.*
ACDA]
Rain at Night

Wed. 29 [The] West Indian & Aladdin   427.50
fine & Cold

Fridy. 31 Abaellino & Killing no   295.
Murder
Dull

November
Saty.   1 Columbus & [The] Spoil'd   186.75   1762.25
Child
Storm all day

Mon.   3 Manuel & the Prize   375.50
fine

Wedy.   5 [The] Foundling of the forest   375.50
& High life below Stairs
fine

Fridy.   7 [The] Robbers & the Comet   332.50
Warm & fine

Saty.   8 [The] Stranger & [The] 40   393.50   1476.50
Thieves
Very Warm

Incledon   Mon. 10 [The Benevolent] Quaker, Mr.   919.50
H. & [The] Waterman
[Incledon as Steady in *The
Benevolent Quaker* and
Tom Tug in *The Water-
man.* ACDA]
Sultry

[233]

" Wed. 12 [The] Poor Soldier, [The] 744.
Turnpike Gate & [The]
Irishman in London
[Incledon as Patrick in *The
Poor Soldier* and Henry
Blunt in *The Turnpike
Gate*. ACDA See preface
to this season.]
Warm

" Fridy. 14 Love in a Village, [The] Storm 734.50
& [The] Ghost
[Incledon as Hawthorn in
Love in a Village. ACDA]
Cool

Incledon Saty. 15 Rosina, [The] Devil to pay & 437.50 2835.50
[The] Midnight Hour
[As Belville in *Rosina* and
Sir John Loverule in *The
Devil to Pay*. ACDA]
Rain all day

" Mon. 17 [The] Mayday Dower, [The] 374.25
Voice of Nature & Lock
& Key
[Incledon as Steady in *The
Mayday Dower* and Cap-
tain Cheerly in *Lock and
Key*. ACDA]
Rain all day

" Wed. 19 [The] Banditti of [the] Forest 545.
or [The] Castle of Anda-
lusia & All the World's a
Stage
[Incledon as Don Caesar in
The Banditti. ACDA]
very Cold

[234]

Benefit [of   Frid. 21 Inkle & Yarico, [The] Sons of   939.50
    Incledon]   Apollo & Sailors on Shore
               [See preface to this season.]
                         very Cold

"   Saty. 22 [The] Maid of the Mill, [The]   318.50   2177.25
               S[ons of] Apollo &
               L[over]s' Quarrels
               [Incledon as Giles in *The*
                 Maid of the Mill. ACDA]
                           Cold

"   Mon. 24 Rosina, Ella Rosenberg &   363.
               [The] Farmer
               [Incledon as Belville in
                 Rosina and Captain Val-
                 entine in *The Farmer*.
                 ACDA]
                           fine

       Wednes. 26 [The] Fair American* & Blue   907.50
               Beard   ———
                               $16932.25
                       Cold

33 Nights averaged $513
Incledon averaged (Without Benefit) 549.

PHILADELPHIA SEASON, COMMENCING MONDAY DECEMBER [1,] 1817[,
ENDING SATURDAY, APRIL 25, 1818.]

[Warren & Wood]

PREFACE—**December 2**: In the "opening bill for the Chesnut Street
Theatre," quoted in *Durang*, I, LV, occurs an allusion to a young gentleman who will "make his 4th appearance, on any stage, in the character
of Macbeth." "On the 2d. of December," states *Durang*, "the young
gentleman alluded to above, who was to make his fourth appearance on
any stage, did so. He was afterwards known as Jacob Woodhull and
was long a member of the old Park company." Warren writes in his

Diary, "A Mr. Woodhull acted Macbeth—tolerable." **December 15:** "The afterpiece on this evening," states *Durang,* I, LV, erroneously, it would appear, for December 13, "was *The Poor Soldier,* in which Incledon played Patrick, singing all the original music and introducing Dibdin's song, *Oh, What a Charming Thing's a Battle!* and *Henry Blunt."* **January 28:** Wood has written under the title "Killing No Murder," "Mr. Jeff[erson] ill." **February 18:** A announces, "For the first time, a celebrated French ballet called *Pygmalion; or, The Animated Statue,* in which Monsieur Giraud, from the Grand Opera at Paris, will make his first appearance on this stage." **March 9:** *Recollections,* p. 214, states that Finn's "houses were 'Hamlet,' $440, 'Shylock' $321, [see **March 14**] 'Iron Chest' $406, [see **March 16,**] 'Mountaineers' $406 [, see **March 18,**] and benefit, 'Macbeth,' $360 [, see **March 25**]." *Durang* I, LV, states that Finn played Sir Edward Mortimer in *The Iron Chest* and Octavian in *The Mountaineers,* to which Warren, in his entry of March 18, adds the rôle of Baron Welinghoerst [*sic*] in *Of Age Tomorrow.* A announces, "Finn, from the Theatres Royal, Drury Lane and Edinburgh, will make his first appearance on this stage." **March 27:** In this entry Wood has written "Heir at Law," crossed out the title and substituted "Birthday" for it. He has also written what is obviously an explanation, "Changed —Mrs. Anderson ill." A announces *The Heir at Law* in place of *The Birthday.* **April 1:** Warren, in his entry of this date, writes, "Mr. White, Zanga [in *The Revenge*]. He was queer." **April 13:** A announces "a characteristic ballet composed by Mr. Francis" and "Scotch Minuet and Strathspey taken from *Marion* as composed by Mr. Francis." **April 17:** A also announces that McFarland is to sing and dance. **April 25:** Mr. Pullen was the treasurer of the company.

Recollections, p. 213, adds to the rôles already listed as having been played by Philipps those of Lord Aimworth in *The Maid of the Mill,* see January 9, and Young Meadows in *Love in a Village,* see January 10; and *Durang,* I, LV, Prince Orlando in *The Cabinet,* see February 6 and Lionel, see February 11. In the April 18 entry of his *Diary,* Warren states that the bill was *The Peasant Boy, Little Red Riding Hood* and *Raising the Wind.* He explains that "the farce was to have been Past 10 O'Clock but [that it was] changed on account of my indisposition." According to a proposed cast in the *Account Book,* Warren was to have played Sam Squib.

"This season," asserts *Durang* I, LV, "may be deemed the dawn of English opera with us or at least its revival." Wood explains, p. 211, that "the arrival of Incledon and Philipps enabled [Warren & Wood] to present at Philadelphia, in 1817, an agreeable variety of entertainment in the performance of English opera."

Warren's "retrospect" of the season is considerably less enthusiastic than Wood's. "Those singers," is the verdict in his *Diary*, "have ruined our season which would have been profitable to us—without them." Warren's pessimism may have been due, in a measure, to the unusually heavy expenses incurred in offering, as A of December 1 announces, "a greater degree of novelty in performers and new Dramas than in former seasons" and in improving the gas lights and "refitting" the coffee rooms.

December

	Mon.	1	Town & Country & [The] Bee-hive	768.50
			Mild & fine	
Woodhull	Tues.	2	Macbeth & Love, Law & Physic	418.
			[See preface to this season.]	
			Rain all day	
	Wed.	3	[The] Clandestine Marriage & [The] 40 Thieves	663.25
			Cold	
	Thurs.	4	[The] Magpie & [the] Maid, Married Yesterday & Bombastes [Furioso]	264.50
			Cold	
	Frid.	5	[The] Provok'd Husband & [The] Prize	376.25
			Very Cold	
	Saty.	6	[The] Ethiop & High life below Stairs	466.50 2957.
			Cold	

Incledon   Mon. 8 Rosina, [The] Birthday & 1340.
Lock & Key
[As Belville in *Rosina* and
Captain Cheerly in *Lock
and Key*.]
fine

"   Wed. 10 Love in a Village & Mr. H. 1161.25
[Incledon as Hawthorn in
Love in a Village. A]
fine

"   Frid. 12 [The] Mayday Dow[e]r, [The] 719.25
Fortune of War & [The]
Waterman
[Incledon as Steady in *The
Mayday Dower* and Tom
Tug in *The Waterman.*
A]
Rain all day

"   Saty. 13 [The] Maid of the Mill & [The] 612.   3832.50
Midnight Hour
[Incledon as Giles in *The
Maid of the Mill.* A]
Dull & rain

"   Mon. 15 [The] Poor Soldier, [The] 727.25
Voice of Nature & [The]
Turnpike Gate
[See preface to this season.]
rain

"   Wed. 17 [The] Banditti of the Forest & 951.50
How to die for Love
[Incledon as Don Caesar in
The Banditti. A]
Cold

[238]

"   Frid. 19 As You like it & Rosina   872.50
                 [Incledon as Amiens. A]
                      Cold

       Saty. 20 Inkle & Yarico, [The] Old 1020.25   3571.50
In[cledon's] Benefit   Maid & [The] Devil to ———
               pay
               [As Captain Campley in
               Inkle and Yarico. A]
                     Very Cold

      Mon. 22 Richard 3rd. & Aladdin   585.50
                      Cold

      Wed. 24 [The First Part of] Henry 4th   689.75
               & Zembuca
                      Mild

      Frid. 26 [The] Broken Sword,* [The]   604.75
               Wedding day & [My]
               Landlady's Gown
                      fine

       Saty. 27 George Barnwell & [The] 763.25   2643.25
               Broken Sword
                      fine

      Mon. 29 [The] West Indian & [The]   408.50
               Broken Sword
                      Rain

      Wed. 31 Wild Oats & Valentine &   433.50
               Orson
                      fair

1818. January
      Thurs. 1 [The] Conquest of Taranto* & 1162.
              Love, Law & Physic
                      fine

Frid. 2 d[itt]o & [The] Wedding Day   406.
       fine

Saty. 3 d[itt]o & All the World's a   332.50   2742.50
       Stage
                              Cold

Philip[p]s   Mon. 5 [The] Devil's Bridge* & [The]   870.
                     Old Maid
                     [As Count Belino in *The
                     Devil's Bridge*. A]
                              fine

P[hilipps]   Wed. 7 [The] Devil's Bridge & [The]   931.
                     Irishman in London
                              fine

P[hilipps]   Frid. 9 [The] Maid of the Mill & [The]   984.75
                     Review
                              Snow

P[hilipps]   Saty. 10 Love in a Village & [The]   615.   3400.75
                     Comet
                              Wet

P[hilipps]   Mon. 12 Brother & Sister,* Mr. H. &   1120.50
                     [The] Poor Soldier
                     [As Don Sylvio in *Brother
                     and Sister* and Patrick
                     in *The Poor Soldier*. A]
                              fine

P[hilipps']   Wed. 14 [The] Siege of Belgrade &   953.
                     How to die for love
                     [As Seraskier in *The Siege
                     of Belgrade*. A]
                              Cold

[240]

"   Frid. 16 Love in a Village & Modern   860.
                 Antiques
                              fine

           Saty. 17 [The] Maid of the Mill & 1302.75
P[hilipps'] Benefit   Brother & Sister
                          very fine

C[ooper]   Mon. 19 Venice Preserv'd & [The]   704.75
                  Sleepwalker
                  [As Pierre in *Venice Pre-*
                  served. A]
                              fine

"   Wed. 21 Bertram & [The] Apprentice   729.
                  [Cooper as Bertram. A]
                              fine

"   Frid. 23 [The] Apostate* & [My] Land-   883.25
                  lady's Gown
                  [Cooper as Malec in *The*
                  Apostate. A]
                              fine

"   Saty. 24 Hamlet & [The] Spoil'd Child   725.50   3042.50
                  [Cooper as Hamlet. A]
                       drizzling rain

"   Mon. 26 [The] Curfew & Catherine &   596.75
                  Petruchio
                  [Cooper as Fitzharding in
                  The Curfew and as Petru-
                  chio. A]
                            rainy

"   Wed. 28 [The] Orphan & Killing no   598.75
                  Murder
                  [Cooper as Chamont in *The*
                  Orphan. A See preface to
                  this season.]
                            rainy

"   Frid. 30 Richard 3rd. & [The] Hunter   664.
                of the Alps
                [Cooper as Richard. A]
                                        Cold

"   Saty. 31 Bertram & [The] Fortune of   276.75   2127.25
                War
                [Cooper as Bertram. A]
                                        Snow

    February
           Mon. 2 [The] Apostate & [The] Liar   988.75
C[ooper's] Ben[efi]t   fine

P[hilipps]   Wed. 4 [The] Devil's Bridge & [The   817.
                King &] Miller of Mans-
                field
                [As Count Belino in *The
                Devil's Bridge*. A]
                                        Cold

           Friday 6 [The] Cabinet & Fortune's   713.
                frolic
                                        fine

P[hilipps]   Saty. 7 [The] Maid of the Mill & 'Tis   396.50   2915.25
                all a farce
                                        very fine

P[hilipps]   Mon. 9 [The] Cabinet & High life   399.50
                below Stairs
                                        Very Cold

P[hilipps]   Wed. 11 Lionel & Clarissa & [The]   684.50
                Sultan
                                        Cold

P[hilipps]   Frid. 13 [The] Devil's Bridge & [The]   891.
                Prisoner at Large
                                        Very Mild

                        [242]

P[hilipps]   Saty. 14 [The] Duenna & [The] Poor 731.   2706.
                   Soldier

                            Rainy

           Mon. 16 Lionel & Clarissa & Brother & 1373.
P[hilipps'] Benefit   Sister
                            fine

Giraud   Wed. 18 [The] School for Scandal, 561.50
                   Pygmalion* & Lovers'
                   Quarrels
                   [See preface to this season.]
                   Snow at night

           Frid. 20 [The] Merry Wives of Wind- 512.75
                   sor & Aladdin
                         Mild

Giraud   Saty. 21 Romeo & Juliet, Pygmalion & 395.50 2812.25
                   Married Yesterday
                          fine

          Mon. 23 [The] Surrender of Calais & 590.
                   Blue Beard
                     Cold & Dull

          Wed. 25 [The] Foundling of [the] Forest 346.75
                   & [The] Deaf Lover
                      Thaw

          Frid. 27 [The] Conquest of Taranto & 284.50
                   Killing no Murder
                          fine

        Saty. 28th [The] Robbers & Aladdin   447.50 1668.75
                    Mild & fine

      March
          Mon. 2 Abaellino & [The] Highland 259.75
                  Reel
                     Rainy

[243]

Wed. 4 [The] Stranger & [The] Inn- 670.
Wood's ben[efit]   keeper's Daughter*
                         Violent Storm

Frid. 6 [The] Lady of the Lake, [The] 548.75
                         Ghost & Blue Beard
                         Very Cold

Saty. 7 Speed the Plough & [The] 391.50 1870.
                         Innkeeper's Daughter
                         Cold

Finn   Mon. 9 Hamlet & 'Tis all a farce. 440.
                         [See preface to this season.]
                         Cold

Wed. 11 She Stoops to Conquer & [A] 340.50
                         Tale of Mystery
                         Mild & fine

Frid. 13 [The] Faro table* & [The] 40 529.75
                         Thieves
                         Mild & fine

Finn   Saty. 14 [The] Merchant of Venice & 321.50 1631.75
                         [The] Deaf Lover
                         [See preface to this season.]
                         fine

"   Mon. 16 [The] Iron Chest & [The] Inn- 406.
                         keeper's Daughter
                         [See preface to this season.]
                         Very Cold

"   Wed. 18 [The] Mountaineers & Of Age 314.50
                         tomorrow
                         [See preface to this season.]
                         Cold

Thursy. 19 [The] Road to Ruin & Paul &   253.50
Virginia
Very fine

Saty. 21 [The] Virgin of the Sun &   394.50   1368.50
[The] 40 Thieves
Cold & Windy

Mon. 23 [The] Snow Storm* & Easter   1129.50
[Benefit of] Warren   frolics & [The] Spanish
Barber
Cold & Threatening

Wed. 25 Macbeth & Raising the Wind   342.75
Mr. Finn's Ben[efi]t   [See preface to this season.]
fine

Frid. 27 [The] Birthday & [The] Snow   433.50
Storm
[See preface to this season.]
fine

Saty. 28 [The] Magpie & [the] Maid &   319.75   2224.75
[The] Lady of the Lake
fair

Mon. 30 [Count] Benyowsky & [The]   276.75
Padlock
Rain & Cold

April
Wed. 1 [The] Revenge & [The] Show-   580.75
White's 1st.   Storm
app[ea]r[ance]   [See preface to this season.]
Cold

Friday 3 [The] Slave* & [The] Inn-   366.75
keeper's Daughter
fine

[245]

Saty. 4 [The] Slave & [The] Snow 246.50 1470.25
Storm

Rain

[Benefit of] Mon. 6 Every one [has] his fault & 1406.50
Jefferson [The] Dead alive
[To sing. A]
fine

[Benefit of] Wed. 8 How to Grow rich & Turn Out 1043.25
Mr. & Mrs. Burke
Drizzly at Night

[Benefit of] Frid. 10 [The] Point of Honor, [The] 1056.75
Mr. Barrett Liar & [The] Blind Boy
fine

[Benefit of] Saty. 11 Othello & Lock & Key 775.50 4582.
Mr. Betterton [As Othello. A]
fine

[Benefit of] Mon. 13 [The] Secret & [The] Fortress 655.50
Mr. & Mrs. [See preface to this season.]
Francis fine

Wedy. 15 Pizarro & my Grandmother 617.
[Benefit of]
Robertson fine

[Benefit of] Frid. 17 Who Wants a Guinea[?] & 815.
McFarland Val[entine] & Orson
[As Sir Larry MacMurrah
in *Who Wants a Guinea?*
A See preface to this
season.]
Rain at night

Saty. 18 [The] Peasant Boy, [Little] 402. 2489.50
[Benefit of] R[ed] R[iding] Hood &
Mrs. Harris past 10 O'Clock
Cold

[246]

[Benefit of   Mon. 20 [The] Heir at Law & Ella   370.50
Mr.] Aberc[rombie]   Rosenberg
& [Mrs.] Carter   fine

                Wed. 22 Town & Country & Tom   470.
[Benefit of]   Thumb [the Great]
Mrs. Anderson   fine

Benefit of   Frid. 24 [The] Slave & [The] Agreeable   388.50
the Poor.   Surprize
                                        very fine

[Benefit of] Saty. 25 [The] School of Reform, [The]   582.50
Pullen   Blue Devils & [The]   ———
                       Romp
                       [See preface to this season.]
                                        fine

                                                    $55835.75

            87 Nights Averaging $641.50
            18 Benefits averaged 837.

WASHINGTON WINTER SEASON[, COMMENCING JANUARY 24,
            ENDING MARCH 14,] 1818.

                [Caldwell & Co.]

PREFACE: During this season the Washington Theatre was used by another company, as Wood reveals in a notation in the *Account Book.* Wood has written this notation, "Mess[rs.] Caldwell & Co.," under and to the right of "Washington Winter Season 1818" and again between the entries of February 24 and 26. In *Durang* I, LVI is a list of the members of this company and also a brief account of its activities. According to the March 2, 1818 entry of Warren's *Diary*, Warren & Wood "received $227 from Caldwell for the rent of the Washington Theatre which," explains Warren, "we have let them have for 10 p[e]r Cent of the Receipts."

    The explanations of the references to this preface are as follows: **February 12**: WG announces, "Tyke in *The School of Reform* by a

                    [247]

gentleman of Washington, his first appearance on any stage." **February 24**: DNI announces, "The managers, ever anxious to please the patrons of the theatre, by presenting every species of novelty which offers itself for their amusement, respectfully announce to the citizens of Washington, Georgetown and their vicinities that they have engaged the celebrated Indian juggler, Jena Jama, from Madrass, recently from London, and subsequently from New York, Philadelphia, Baltimore &c. for one night only. Jena J‸m‸ will exhibit his wonderful and surprising feats with cups and balls, four brass balls, balancing with tops, balancing with swords, East Indian sports, Chinese castle, exercise of Hercules, surprising feats with a twenty pound stone." **February 27**: According to DNI, the juggler has consented to stay in Washington to perform one night longer, "prompted to do it by the unexampled applause bestowed on him on Tuesday evening."

To the left of the entry of January 24, Wood has written "1 [st.] night." Wood spells the name of the juggler "Sena Sam."

[January]
[Saturday 24] [The] Honey Moon & For-   206.66
            tune's frolic

[Mon. 26] [The] Foundling of [the] forest   223.75
        & [The] Liar
[27] Bertram [&] No Song No   145.
    Supper

[29] [The] West Indian & Turn   263.81
    Out

[30] [The] Apostate & 3 & [the]   218.22
    Deuce

[31] [The] Soldier's Daughter &   45.22
    Rosina

[February 2] Hamlet & [The] Turnpike   206.87
        Gate

[4] Laugh When You Can & [The]   158.50
    P[oor] Soldier

[248]

[5] Paul & Virginia, [The] Liar   157.
[&] Zembuca

[6] Othello & [The] Sleepwalker   150.

[9] Romeo & Juliet & 'Tis all a   75.50
farce

[10 A Cure for the Heartache &
Rosina]

[12] [The] School of Reform & [Of]   167.50
a 1st. app[ea]r[ance]   Age tomorrow
[See preface to this season.]

Brown   [13] [A] Cure for [the] Heartache   238.50
& [The] Irish[man] in
London
[Brown of the Theatre Royal, Covent Garden, is
engaged for three nights
and will make his first
appearance in America
on Friday evening. DNI]

"   [16] She Stoops to Conquer &   224.50
Turn Out
[Brown as Tony Lumpkin
in *She Stoops to Conquer*.
DNI]

"   17 Town & Country & Love   214.38
Laughs [at Locksmiths]
[Brown as Hawbuck in
Town and Country and
Risk in *Love Laughs at
Locksmiths*. WG]

[19] [The] Belle's Stratagem &   127.75
[The] Day after [the]
Wedd[in]g

[249]

[20] Guy Mannering & [The]   88.10
     Weathercock

[23] [The] Glory of Columbia &   145.50
     [The] American Captive

Jena Jama   [24] [The] Point of Honor & [The]   251.38   3308.
     Poor Soldier   ————
     [See preface to this season.]

Feby. 26 Rosina, [The] Liar & [The]   217.50
Incledon   Turnpike Gate
     [As Count Belville in *Rosina*
     and Henry Blunt in *The
     Turnpike Gate*. DNI]

     27 Jena Jama   214.50
     [See preface to this season.]

     28 [The] Way to Get Married &   237.
     M[arried] Yesterday

March 3 Speed the Plough & [The]   152.
     Devil to pay

     5 Venice Preserv'd & ['Tis] All   79.
     a farce

     6 Adelgitha & Don Juan   130.50

     [7 George Barnwell & Catherine
     & Petruchio]

     9 [The] Foundling of the Forest   99.50
     & Fortune's frolic

     12 Timour [the Tartar] & [The]   573.97
     Wonder

13 d[itt]o & [The] Devil to pay   374.81

14 d[itt]o & Tekeli   493.88
                                    _____
                                    $5880.81
29 Nights averaging $202.88

BALTIMORE SPRING SEASON, [COMMENCING APRIL 29, ENDING JULY 4,] 1818.

[Warren & Wood]

PREFACE—**May 11**: In this entry Wood has written over a title, "[The] School for Scandal," which he has crossed out, the notation, "Changed to The [Faithful] Slave, Mr. Francis ill." **May 18**: In this entry Wood has written over a title, "[The] Apostate," which he has crossed out, the notation, "Chang[e]d, Mr. Cooper's hand Cut." ACDA announces, "The public are respectfully informed that Mr. Cooper (in consequence of a severe cut received on Saturday night) is wholly unable to complete his engagement at present." **June 29**: Over the title "Castle Spectre" Wood has written "Chang[e]d to Speed the Plough. Mrs. Wood ill." In his entry of the same date Warren writes, "Mrs. Wood ill from the agitation of Saturday's tumult." In the June 27 entry of his *Diary* Warren reveals that "Mrs. Harris resorted this evening to the stale artifice of 'the tyran[n]y and oppression' to make her Benefit—and by various lies contriv'd to raise a tumult in the House at night. Wood endeavored to pacify them by his Eloquence and assertions that the calumnies were groundless, but in vain. Previous to the Farce he led Mrs. Harris forward to disavow her knowledge of the Hand bill which had been industriously circulated by her friends in the afternoon; but she spoke not and cried so abundantly that it made matters worse. The event was that 74 dollars were thrown on the Stage as a charitable subscription for the 'poor Widow.' How are we fallen!" **July 1**: Warren records in his *Diary*, "Mrs. Wood ill. Mrs. Wood, Mrs. Anderson and Mrs. Lefole [*sic*] all laid up." According to ACDA, *The Merchant of Venice*, with Blissett as Shylock, was to have been played. Wood, in his July 1 entry, has crossed out "Merchant of Venice" and written over it "Road to Ruin, Toothache."

On May 22 Warren's *Diary* records that Herbert also appeared as

[251]

Lazarillo in *Two Strings to Your Bow*. The players receiving a benefit on June 26 were undoubtedly the elder Jeffersons but Warren's *Diary* records that their eldest son Thomas also appeared. He was "Winlove in [the] farce [, *We Fly by Night*.]"

April
Wedy. 29 [The] Heir at Law & My Grand-   309.50
mother
very Cold

May
Frid. 1 [The] Virgin of the Sun &   481.50
Zembuca
fine & Mild

Saty. 3 [The] School of Reform &   205.50
Tom Thumb [the Great]
Rain all day

Mon. 4 [The]   Fair   American   &   420.25
Aladdin
Cloudy & Cold

Wedy. 6 [The] Midnight Hour, [The]   555.50
Broken Sword & [The]
Romp
Cloudy

Frid. 8 [The First Part of] Henry 4th   450.25
& Blue Beard
fine

Saty. 9 [The] Secret & [The] Broken   319.75   1745.75
Sword
fine

Mon. 11 The [Faithful] Slave & [The]   671.50
Wood's Ben[efit]   Forest of Bondy
[See preface to this season.]
fine

[252]

Wedy. 13 [The] Snow Storm,* [The]   436.50
        Sleepwalker & Lovers[']
        Quarrels
              Showery

Cooper   Frid. 15 Hamlet & The Sultan   547.
        [As Hamlet. ACDA]
             fine

"   Saty. 16 Richard 3d. & [The] Hunter 218.50   1873.50
        of [the] Alps
        [Cooper as Richard. ACDA]
          Violent Storm all day

Mon. 18 [The] Fair American & [The] 322.25
        40 Thieves
        [See preface to this season.]
           Rain all day

Wed. 20 [The] Surrender of Calais & 536.
        [The] Snow Storm
             fine

        Frid. 22 Speed the Plough & 2 Strings 501.75
Herbert 1st.   to your Bow
  app[ea]r[ance]   [As Sir Abel Handy in *Speed*
        the Plough. ACDA]
             fine

Saty. 23 [The] Voice of Nature, Mar- 294.75   1654.75
        ried Yesterday & [The]
        Broken Sword

Mon. 25 [The] Stranger & [The] Snow 468.75
        Storm
             fine

Wed. 27 Pizarro & [The] Snow Storm 323.75
          Showery & bad

[253]

Philipps   Frid. 29 [The] Devil's Bridge* & [The]   722.25
Sultan
[As Count Belino in *The
Devil's Bridge.* ACDA]
fine
"   Saty. 30 [The] Devil's Bridge & Mr. H.   460.   1974.75
[Philipps as Belino. ACDA]
fine
June
"   Mon.   1 Love in a Village & How to die   620.75
for Love
[Philipps as Young Meadows
in *Love in a Village.*
ACDA]
Warm

"   Wedy.   3 [The] Cabinet* & [The] Wed-   673.25
ding day
[Philipps as Prince Orlando
in *The Cabinet.* ACDA]
Warm

"   Frid.   5 [The] Maid of the Mill &   548.50
Matrimony
[Philipps as Lord Aimworth
in *The Maid of the Mill.*
ACDA]
Warm

"   Saty.   6 Brother & Sister,* [Little]   386.50   2229.
R[ed] R[iding] Hood &
[The] Poor Soldier
[Philipps as Don Sylvio in
Brother   and   Sister.
ACDA]
Warm

"   Mon.   8 [The] Devil's Bridge & Miss   598.50
in her teens
[Philipps as Belino. ACDA]
Warm

P[hilipps']
Ben[efit]

Wedy. 10 Lionel & Clarissa* & Brother   817.50
     & Sister
     [As Lionel and Don Sylvio.
     ACDA]
          very Warm

[Benefit of]
Warren

Frid. 12 [The] Innkeeper's Daughter,*   637.
     [A] Bud[get] of Blunders
     & [The] Mayor of Garrat
          Sultry

Saty. 13 [The] Innkeeper's Daughter,   172.25   2225.25
     [The] Snow Storm &
     [The] Village Lawyer
          Very Warm

P[hilipps] Mon. 15 [The] Duenna & [The] Tooth-   373.50
     ache
     [As Carlos in *The Duenna.*
     ACDA]
          fine & Cool

P[hilipps] Wedy. 17 Love in a Village & [The]   295.50
     Poor Soldier
     [As Young Meadows and as
     Patrick in *The Poor Sol-
     dier.* ACDA]
          Cool fine

P[hilipps] Frid. 19 [The] Devil's Bridge & [A]   405.50
     Budget of blunders
     [As Belino. ACDA]
          Cool, fine

P[hilipps'] ben[efit]

Saty. 20 [The] Maid of the Mill & Love   347.50   1422.
     Laughs at Locksmiths
     [As Lord Aimworth and as
     Captain Beldare in *Love
     Laughs.* ACDA]
          Very Cool

[255]

Mon. 22 [The] School for Scandal & 540.25
[Benefit of]   [The] Review
McFarl[and] &   [McFarland as Careless in
[Mrs.] Lefolle   *The School for Scandal.*
                        ACDA]
                                Showery

Wedy. 24 John Bull & [The] Romp   467.
[Benefit of] Mr. &   [Burke as Dan, Mrs. Burke
Mrs. Burke   as Mary Thornberry in
                        John Bull. ACDA]
                                Very Warm

[Benefit of]   Frid. 26 He would be a Soldier & We 353.25
Mr. & Mrs. Jefferson   fly by night
                                Very Warm

Saty. 27 Town & Country & [The] 315.50 1676.
[Benefit of Mr.]   Toothache
Aber[crombie] &   [Mrs. Harris in broad sword
[Mrs.] Harris   hornpipe and in pas de
                        trois with the Misses
                        Durang. ACDA]
                                Warm

Mon. 29 [The] Castle Spectre & Turn 258.25
[Benefit of] Fran-   Out
[cis] & Barrett   [See preface to this season.]
                                Very Warm

July
Wedy. 1 [The] Road to Ruin, [The] 309.50
[Benefit of Mr.]   Toothache & [The] Chil-
Bliss[ett] &   [dren] in [the] Wood
Mrs. Wood   [See preface to this season.]
                                very pleasant

Frid. 3 How to Grow rich,* [Little 349.75
[Benefit of the]   Red] R[iding] Hood &
Misses Durang   Tom Thumb [the Great]
& Hathw[el]l
                                Warm

[256]

Saty. 4 [The] Conquest of Taranto* & 743.50
        [The] Blue Devils*   ———
                                      $17,418.50
                        Warm
Mr. Philipps' average without Ben[efi]ts. 508.20
       39 Nights averaging 446.50

WASHINGTON SEASON[, COMMENCING JULY 11, ENDING
        AUGUST 29], 1818.

            [Warren & Wood]

PREFACE—**August 29**: Wood has written under this entry, "Sold this Benefit to Hughes for $100." In the July 16 entry, he has written "Share $10;" in the July 23 entry, "2d. Share $20;" in the July 30 entry, "3d. Share $25;" in the August 6 entry, "4th Share $20;" in the August 13 entry, 5th Share "$12;" in the August 20 entry, "6th Share $12;" and, above the name "Scrivener" in the August 24 entry, the notation "½ this night." In his entry of this date, Warren writes in his *Diary*, "Scrivener's ½ Ben[efit]."

        July
Saty. 11 [The] Poor Gentleman & [A] 181.75
          Budget of Blunders
                  Very hot

Tuesday 14 [A] Tale of Mystery, [The] 114.
          Toothache & [The] Chil-
          [dren] in [the] Wood
                  Violent Storm

Thurs. 16 [The] Fair American* & [The] 224.
          Hunter of [the] Alps
                  Cool & fine

Saty. 18 [The] Surrender of Calais & 200.25
          [The] Mayor of Garrat
                  Warm

Tues. 21 Romeo & Juliet & [The] day 314.25
          after the Wedding
                  fine

            [257]

Thurs. 23 Of Age tomorrow, [The]   224.
         Broken Sword [& The]   ———
         Village Lawyer
                 Showery

Saty. 25 [The] Foundling of [the] For-   260.
         est & We fly by Night*
            Drizz[lin]g Rain

Tues. 28 [The] Snow Storm* & Cath-   397.
         [erine] & Petruchio
             fine & Clear

Thurs. 30 [The] Devil's Bridge* & [The]   248.75
         Irishman in London   ———
             Very Warm

August
     Saty.   1 [The] Snow Storm & Turn Out   207.
                         fine

Mon[da]y   3 Geo[rge] Barnwell & [The] 40   301.50
         Thieves

Tues.   4 [The] Conquest of Taranto* &   191.25
         [A] Budget of Blunders

Thurs.   6 [The] Innkeeper's Daughter*   173.50
[Benefit of]   [& The] H[ighland] Reel
T. Jefferson &
Mrs. Anderson   fine

Saty.   8 [The] Merchant of Venice &   276.50
[Benefit of]   [The] Anatomist*
Bliss[ett] & Finn
                         Rainy

[Benefit of] Tues. 11 [The] Stranger & Mr. H.   243.50
Mr. & Mrs
Francis
                     very fine

Thurs. 13 [The] Castle Spectre & Paul &   176.25
[Benefit of]   Virginia
  Mr. & Mrs. Darley

                                    Very fine

Saty. 15 [The] Honey Moon & [The]   193.50
[Benefit of   Poor Soldier
  Mr.] Aber[crombie]
  & [Mrs.] Harris

                                    Some rain

Tues. 18 [The] Exile & [The] Agreeable   270.25
[Benefit of] Mr. &   Surprize
  Mrs. Jeff[erso]n

                              fine at night

Thurs. 20 Bellamira* & Two Strings to   310.
[Benefit of]   Y[ou]r bow
  Hughes & Herb[ert]

                                    fine

Saty. 22 [A] Cure for [the] Heartache &   189.
[Benefit of]   Tom Thumb [the Great]
  Hath[well] &
  [Mrs.] Lefolle

Mon[da]y 24th [The] Conquest of Taranto &   205.50
Scrivener   Love Laughs [at Lock-
                              smiths]

Thurs. 27 [The] School for Scandal &   246.50
                [The] B[roken] Sword

Saty. 29 [The] Virgin of [the] Sun &   377.50
Wood's ben[efit]   [The] Blue Devils*
                [See preface to this season.]

BALTIMORE AUTUMN SEASON, COMMENCING SEPT[EMBER] 2ND., [ENDING NOVEMBER 2ND.,] 1818.

[Warren & Wood]

PREFACE—**September 12**: ACDA announces, "The public are respectfully informed that this day being the anniversary of the battle of Baltimore and the bombardment of Fort McHenry the profits of the performance will be appropriated in aid of the fund for the widows and families of the brave men who fell on that day." James Wallack, who made his first appearance in Baltimore on September 25, was the younger brother of Henry Wallack, who made his first appearance on September 30 and who, according to *Recollections*, p. 227, interpreted the rôle of Don Juan in *The Libertine*, see October 31 and November 2, after having made a very inauspicious start in that of Othello.

Sept[ember]
Wed.	2	[The] Poor Gentleman & Lock	247.50	
Mr. Darley['s] 1st. ap[pearance]		& Key [As Captain Cheerly in *Lock and Key*. ACDA] pleasant		
Frid.	4	Romeo & Juliet & [A] Budget	347.75	
Mrs. Darley's 1st. [appearance]		of Blunders [As Juliet. ACDA] Very fine		
Saty.	5	[The] Virgin of the Sun & [The] Irishman in London Violent Storm	139.50	734.75
Mon.	7	[The] Conquest of Taranto & We fly by Night fine	292.25	
Wed.	9	[The] Busy Body & Aladdin fine	298.	
Frid.	11	[The] Stranger & [The] Snow	410.	
Mr. Wheatly 1st. app[ea[r[ance]		Storm [As the Stranger. ACDA] fine		

[260]

Saty. 12 Gustavus Vasa & Sprigs of   735.   1735.25
Ben[efit] of   Laurel
Mon[umen]t fund   [See preface to this season.]
                        fine

Mon. 14 [The] School for Scandal &   263.75
Cath[erine] & Petruchio
Warm & fine

Wed. 16 How to Grow Rich & Blue   301.75
Beard
                        fine

Frid. 18 [The] Exile & [A] Budget of   476.50
Blunders
               Cool & fine

Saty. 19 Bellamira* & Love, Law &   333.50   1375.50
Physic
                      Rain

Mon. 21st. [The] Fair American, [Little]   268.50
R[ed Riding] Hood &
[The] Blue Devils
                        fine

Wed. 23 Who Wants a Guinea [?] &   399.75
[The] Snow Storm
                        fine

Fridy. 25 Macbeth & [The] Village   624.
Mr. [J] Wallack   Lawyer
           [As Macbeth. ACDA]
                        fine

"   Saty. 26 Pizarro & [The] Spoil'd Child   388.   1680.25
[Wallack as Rolla in *Pizarro*.
ACDA]
                    fine

[261]

"   Mon. 28 Hamlet & [The] Agreeable   422.50
               Surprize
               [Wallack as Hamlet. ACDA]
                                fine

"   Wed. 30 Coriolanus &   My   Grand-   392.75
               mother
               [Wallack   as   Coriolanus.
               ACDA]
                                fine

               October
"   Frid.   2 [The] Mountaineers & Sprigs   305.
               of Laurel
               [Wallack as Octavian in *The
               Mountaineers*. ACDA]
                                drizzling

"   Saty.   3 Pizarro & [The] Comet   344.   1464.25
               [Wallack as Rolla. ACDA]
                                dull

               Mon.   5 Richard 3d. & No Song no   654.
Ben[efit of] W[allack]   Supper
               [As Richard.   ACDA]
                                fine

               Wedy.   7 [The] Iron Chest & [The]   334.
               Kaleidoscope*
                                fine

               Frid.   9 Bellamira & [The] Kaleido-   334.
               scope
                                fine

               Saty. 10 Who Wants a Guinea [?] &   296.25   1618.25
               [The] 40 Thieves
                                fine

Mon. 12 [The] Exile & [The] Sleep- 383.25
    walker
           rain at Night

Wedy. 14th. George Barnwell & [The] 429.75
    Snow Storm
           rain & dull

Frid. 16 [The] Merry Wives of Wind- 426.50
    sor & the Sultan
           fine

Saty. 17 As You like it & [The] Romp 244.50 1484.
           fine

Mon. 19 [The] Honey Moon & [The] 40 327.50
    Thieves
           fine

Cooper   Wed. 21 Macbeth & [The] Kaleido- 695.50
    scope
    [As Macbeth. ACDA]
           fine

"   Frid. 23 Hamlet & All the World's a 462.50
    Stage
    [Cooper as Hamlet. ACDA]
           fine

"   Saty. 24 Alexander [the Great] & Dark- 361.25
    ness Visible
    [Cooper   as   Alexander.
    ACDA]
           fine

"   Mon. 26 Richard 3d. & [The] Beehive 516.50 2035.79
    [Cooper as Richard. ACDA]
           fine

Wed. 28 [The] Gamester & [The] Liar   878.
C[ooper's] Ben[efi]t   [As Beverly in *The Gamester*
                          and Young Wilding in
                          The Liar. ACDA]
                                          fine

Frid. 30 Othello & Married Yesterday   467.50
Mr. H. Wallack's   [As Othello. ACDA]
1st. app[earance]
                                          fine

Saty. 31 [The] Midnight Hour & [The]   421.50   2283.50
         Libertine*
                                          fine

November
Mon. 2 Where to find a friend* &   933.50
        [The] Libertine
                                          fine   ———

Wed. 4   36 nights averaging $421. $15,156.

Philadelphia Season, Commencing 5th November 1818[, Ending
April 30, 1819.]

[Warren & Wood]

Preface—**November 7**: In this entry Wood has written "Mrs. Darley
& Mr. Bliss[ett] 1st." A announces Mrs. Darley as Juliana in *The Honey
Moon* and Mr. Blissett as Jacques in *The Honey Moon* and Dr. Dablancour
in *A Budget of Blunders*. **November 26**: A announces, "In the course
of the after-piece will be introduced a beautiful living white camel from
Africa caparisoned in the Eastern style and bearing four riders." Warren
writes in his *Diary*, "We give $50 for the use of a Camel this evening."
December 7: A announces *Speed the Plough* and *Paul and Virginia*.
In the entry of this date Warren's *Diary* records that "Barrett left the
rehearsal—said he was ill and could not play." Warren adds, "Change to
the Exile and Lock and Key." **December 12**: A announces, "The
Managers respectfully inform the public that they have engaged (for
one night) on Saturday, the five Wyandot Indian Chiefs, who will perform

[264]

many of their National Dances, a War Speech, &c." Warren records in his *Diary*, "Cooper $522.50, Indians 50." **January 30:** A announces "After the play (by particular desire) Mr. Wallack will give imitations of several of the most distinguished London performers." **February 8:** A announces, "Mr. & Mrs. Bartley from the Theatre Royal, Drury Lane. Mrs. Bartley as Belvidera in *Venice Preserved*. She will recite Collins' *Ode on the Passions*, accompanied by appropriate music." **February 17:** Under this entry Wood has written, "Gen[era]l Jackson." According to A, "The Managers respectfully acquaint the public that Major General Jackson will visit the theatre this evening." A news item explains that "General Jackson and his suite left Washington and arrived at Baltimore the same evening on their way to Philadelphia, New York and West Point." **March 1:** Bartley as Captain All-Clack in *The Invisible Girl* and James Megrim in *The Blue Devils*. Mrs. Bartley as Madam Clermont in *Adrian and Orrilla* and in the recitation of a poem written expressly for her by Thomas Moore entitled *A Melologue*, expressive of the effects of national music upon national character, in the course of which will be introduced the airs of Greece, Switzerland, Spain, Ireland and America." A **March 3:** A announces Bartley as Guiscard in *Adelgitha* and Sir Adam in *The Wedding Day*. A announces Mrs. Bartley as Adelgitha, as Lady Contest in *The Wedding Day*; and in the recitation of *A Melologue*, to be repeated in consequence of the great applause it received on Monday night. **March 9:** A announces, "By particular desire Mr. Duff will give imitations of celebrated performers; Mr. Kemble as Hamlet; Mr. Cooke in Richard the Third; Mr. Munden as Sir Abel Handy; Mr. Holman in Jaffier." According to *Durang*, I, LVIII, Duff also appeared as Octavian in *The Mountaineers*. **March 12:** Duff as Count Belino in *The Devil's Bridge*, in which he will sing *Behold in his Soft, Expressive Face, Though Love is Warm Awhile, Is There a Heart that Never Loved?*, *Fancy's Sketch* and *William Tell, the Patriot of Switzerland*. **March 19:** According to A, "The profits will be respectfully offered in aid of the funds of the Grand Lodge of the state of Pennsylvania." **March 29:** Francis as Blackman in *Next Door Neighbors* and Forge in *Harlequin's Invasion*. He is to offer a pas de deux composed by himself. Mrs. Francis as Miss Harlowe in *The Old Maid* and Dolly Snip in *Harlequin's Invasion*. A According to a playbill of March 29, 1819 in possession of the Historical Society of Pennsylvania, Francis and Darley are to appear as old women, "with Songs," in Harlequin's Invasion. **April 10:** A announces the bill of April 21 and later

[265]

its postponement. **April 21**: Mr. Pullen was the treasurer of the company. **April 28**: Wood has written under the title "[The] Poor Gent[lema]n," the notation, "Chang[e]d from [She] Stoops to Conquer, Mrs. Ent[wisle] ill." According to A, Warren appeared as Hardcastle in *She Stoops to Conquer*. A playbill of April 28, 1819, however, announces Warren as Sir Robert Bramble in *The Poor Gentleman*. "The original epilogue [is to] be spoken by Mr. Hughes, Mr. Burke, Mr. Warren, Mr. Jefferson, Mr. Wood, Mrs. Darley and Mrs. Francis." The playbill is in possession of the Historical Society of Pennsylvania.

In the entry of November 10 Warren's *Diary* records that Herbert also appeared as Robin Roughhead in *Fortune's Frolic*. Durang, I, LVIII, adds to the rôles already mentioned as having been played by Bartley the rôles of Evander (*The Grecian Daughter*), Puff, Sir Fretful Plagiary (*The Critic*) and Petruchio and to Mrs. Bartley's rôles the rôles of Mrs. Haller (*The Stranger*) and Katherine.

November

	Thurs.	5	[The] School for Scandal & Lock & Key	732.50
			fine	
Mr. Hughes' 1st.	Frid.	6	[The] Conquest of Taranto & [The] Wedding Day [As Valentio in *The Conquest of Taranto*. A]	392.50
			Rain	
	Saty.	7	[The] Honey Moon & [A] Budget of Blunders [See preface to this season.]	959.50 2084.50
			Cold	
Mr. Wheatley['s] 1st.	Mon.	9	[The] Merchant of Venice & [The] Snow Storm [As Shylock. A]	679.50
			fine	
Mr. Herbert['s] 1st.	Tues.	10	John Bull & Fortune's frolic [As Job Thornberry in *John Bull*. A]	345.
			fair	

[266]

Wed. 11 Pizarro & [The] Kaleidoscope*   478.50
             Rain

Thursd. 12 [The] Merry Wives [of Wind-   503.50
             sor] & Blue Beard
                                    fair

Frid. 13 [The] Apostate & [The] Kalei-   532.
             doscope
                                    fair

Saty. 14 Who Wants a Guinea[?], Love   475.50   3014.
             among the Roses* & [The]
             Blue Devils
                                    fine

Mon. 16 [The] Robbers, Love among   579.75
             the roses & Turn Out
                                    fine

Tues. 17 Town & Country & [The] 40   447.
             Thieves
                                    fine

Wed. 18 Where to find a friend,*   413.50
             [Little] R[ed] R[iding]
             Hood & [The] Toothache
                         Rain all day

Frid. 20 [The] Exile & [A] Budget of   860.75
             blunders
                                    fine

Saty. 21 [The] Busy Body & [The]   469.50   2770.50
             Magpie & [the] Maid
                                    fair

Mon. 23 [The] Exile & Darkness Visible   509.50
                                    fair

[267]

Tues. 24 [The First Part of] Henry 4th 434.
    & Blue Beard
        fine

Wed. 25 Bellamira,* Ballet & [The] 552.50
    Village Lawyer
    [Ballet, *Love among the
    Roses*. A]
        fine

Thurs. 26 [The] Stranger & [The] 40 446.75
Camel   Thieves
    [See preface to this season.]
        fine

Frid. 27 [The] Virgin of the Sun & 329.
    [The] Anatomist
        rainy

Saty. 28 Bellamira & Turn Out 465. 2736.
        dull

Mon. 30 [The] Way to Get Married & 432.25
    [The] Broken Sword

Decem[be]r 1 [The] Foundling of [the] forest 387.50
    & Love, Law & Physic
        dull

Wed. 2 [The] Exile & We fly by Night 363.50
        Cold

Thurs. [3] Bellamira & [The] Broken 344.50
    Sword
        fine

Frid. 4 [The] Slave & [The] Snow 402.50
    Storm
        fair

Saty. 5 Where to find a friend & [The] 513.50 2543.75
    Lady of the Lake
                Rain

Mon. 7 [The] Exile & Lock & Key 393.50
    [See preface to this season.]
                Cold

Tues. 8 Wild Oats & [The] Magpie &
    [the] Maid Given up,
    Barrett ill. [A an-
    nounces: "On account of
    the indisposition of Mr.
    Barrett there will be no
    performance."]

C[ooper] Wed. 9 Macbeth & [The] Spoil'd 1023.50
    Child
    [As Macbeth. A]
                fine

Thurs. 10 [The] Honey Moon & [The] 410.75
    Broken Sword
                dull

Frid. 11 Hamlet & Matrimony 554.75
                rainy

Saty. 12 Richard 3d. & Wyandot 903. 3288.50
    Indians
    [See preface to this season.]
                Cold

Mon. 14 Romeo & Juliet & [The] 470.
    Agreeable Surprize
                Cold

Tues. 15 Jane Shore, Love among the 547.50
    Roses & [My] Grand-
    mother
                Cold

Wed. 16 [The] Mountaineers & Cath-   449.
[erine] & Petruchio
Cold

Frid. 18 [The] Green Man* & [A]   945.50
Budget of blunders
fine

Saty. 19 Alexander [the Great] & Blue   387.50   2799.50
Beard
Cold

Mony. 21 Pizarro & [The] Liar   964.50
C[ooper's] Ben[efi]t   [As Rolla in *Pizarro*. A]
very fine

C[ooper]   Wed. 23 [The] Green Man & Zembuca   1113.
[As the Green Man. A]
very Cold

"   Thurs. 24 Bellamira & [The] Lady of the   620.
Lake
[Cooper as Amurath in
Bellamira. A]
Cold

Saty. 26 [The] Libertine,* [The] For-   535.23
tune of War & no Song
no Supper

Mon. 28 George   Barnwell   &   [The]   434.50
Libertine
Snow

Tues. 29 Speed the Plough & [The]   349.50
Libertine
Sleigh[in]g & fine

Wed. 30 Wild Oats & [The] Libertine 253.50
Rain

Thurs. 31 How to Grow Rich & [The] 200.25
Magpie & [the] Maid
dull

1819. January
Frid. 1* Rob Roy [Macgregor]* & 989.50
Zembuca
fair

Saty. 2 Rob Roy [Macgregor] & How 469.50
to die for love
Cold

Mon. 4 Fazio* & Darkness Visible 292.50
fine Sleig[hin]g

Wed. 6 Rob Roy [Macgregor] & [The] 441.50
dead alive
Cold

Frid. 8 Pizarro & [The] Review 710.25
[J.] Wallack [As Rolla in *Pizarro*. A]
Snow

" Saty. 9 Macbeth & Turn Out 412.50
[Wallack as Macbeth. A]
drizzling

" Mon. 11 Hamlet & [The] Mayor of 567.50
Garrat
[Wallack as Hamlet. A]
fair

Wallack Wed. 13 Bertram & [The] Sleeping 889.75
draught*
[As Bertram. A]
fine

[271]

"   Frid. 15 Coriolanus & [The] Sleeping   652.50
             Draught
             [Wallack as Coriolanus. A]
                 fine

"   Saty. 16 [The] Merchant of Venice &   670.25
             [The] Chil[dren] in [the]
             Wood
             [Wallack as Shylock and as
             Walter in *The Children in*
             the Wood. A]
                 fine

      Mony. 18 Pizarro, Sylv[ester] Dagg[er- 1520.50
"   Ben[efi]t   woo]d & [The] Weather-
             cock
             [Wallack as Rolla and as
             Sylvester   Daggerwood.
             A]

"   Wedy. 20 Othello & [The] Sultan   415.50
             [Wallack as Othello. A]
                 dull

"   Frid. 22 Richard the Second* & [The]   515.
             Sleeping Draught
             [Wallack a; Richard. A]
                 dull

"   Saty. 23 [The] Wonder & [The] Chil-   563.
             [dren] in [the] Wood
             [Wallack as Don Felix in
             The Wonder and Walter
             in *The Children in the*
             Wood. A]
                 fine

"   Mon. 25 Romeo & Juliet & All the   518.50
             World's a Stage
             [Wallack as Romeo. A]
                 fine

Wed. 27 [The] Mountaineers & My   897.50
   Aunt*
   [Wallack as Octavian in
   The Mountaineers and
   Dashley in *My Aunt.* A]
         fine

"   Frid. 29 Pizarro & My Aunt   870.
   [Wallack as Rolla and
   Dashley. A]
         fine

"   Saty. 30 Richard 3d., Imitations &   718.
   Lovers['] Quarrels
   [Wallack as Richard. A
   See preface to this season.]
         fine

Feb[ruar]y
   Mon. 1 Hamlet & Love a la Mode   819.75
Benefit [of   [As Hamlet and as Sir
Wallack]   Archy MacSarcasm in
   Love a la Mode. A]
         fine

Maywood Tues. 2 [The] Merchant of Venice &   308.50
   Miss in her Teens
   [As Shylock. A]
         fine

"   Wedy. 3 Othello & My Uncle*   269.
   [Maywood as Othello. A]
         fine

"   Thurs. 4 [The] Iron Chest & [The]   281.
   Review
   [Maywood as Sir Edward
   Mortimer in *The Iron
   Chest.* A]
         fine

[273]

Maywood   Frid. 5 A New Way to pay old debts   249.50
                    & My Uncle
                    [As Sir Giles Overreach in
                    *A New Way to Pay Old
                    Debts.* A]
                                    fine

           Sat. 6 King Lear & High life below   414.
Ben[efit of   Stairs
Maywood]   [As Lear and as Lovel in
                    High Life below Stairs.
                    A]
                                    fine

Bartleys   Mon. 8 Venice Preserv'd, Collins' Ode   679.
                    & [The] Weathercock
                    [See preface to this season.]
                                    Rain

   "   Wed. 10 [The First Part of] Henry 4th   325.50
                    & [The] Sleeping draught
                    [Bartley as Falstaff. A]
                                    fine

   "   Frid. 12 (Postponed Mrs. B. ill)
                    [A announces Mrs. Bartley
                    in *Isabella* and the com-
                    edy of *Raising the Wind.*]

   "   Saty. 13 [The] Green Man, [The] In-   420.
                    visible   Girl   &   [The]
                    Adopted Child
                    [Bartley as the Green Man,
                    Captain All-Clack in *The
                    Invisible Girl* and Michael
                    in *The Adopted Child.* A]
                                    Snow

"   Mon. 15 Isabella & Raising the Wind   602.
               [Mrs. Bartley as Isabella.
               A]
                                          Cold

"   Wed. 17 Fazio & My Uncle   822.
               [Mrs. Bartley as Bianca in
               Fazio. A See preface to
               this season.]
                                          Cold

"   Frid. 19 [The] Jealous Wife & Ode to   778.50
               [the] Passions & Ways &
               Means
               [Bartley as Oakly, Mrs.
               Bartley as Mrs. Oakly in
               The Jealous Wife. Bart-
               ley as Sir David Dun-
               der in Ways and Means,
               Mrs. Bartley to recite
               Collins' Ode. A]
                                          Cold

"   Saty. 20 [The] Green Man, [The] In-   427.50
               visible Girl & [The]
               Adopted Child
               [Bartley as the Green Man,
               Captain All-Clack and
               Michael. A]
                                          fine

         Mon. 22 Bunker Hill & [The] Miller   624.
Wash[ington's]   and his Men
  B[irth]day
                                          fair

         Wed. 24 [The] Grecian Daughter &   981.75
Mrs. B[artley's]   [The] Critic
  ben[efit.]   [As Euphrasia in The Gre-
               cian Daughter. A]
                                          Very fine

[275]

Thurs. 25 [The] Stranger & Cath[erine] 443.75
& Petruchio
Rain

" Frid. 26 [The] Provoked Husband & 463.25
[The] Adopted Child
[Bartley as Lord Townly,
Mrs. Bartley as Lady
Townly in *The Provoked
Husband*. Bartley as
Michael in *The Adopted
Child*. A]
fair

Saty. 27 Deaf & Dumb, & Ways & 312.75
[Mr. & Mrs.] Means
B[artley] [Mrs. Bartley as Julio in
Deaf and Dumb. A]
fine

March
" Mon. 1 Adrian & Orrilla, [The] In- 838.25
v[isible] Girl, [A] Melo-
logue & [The] Blue Devils
[See preface to this season.]
fair

Wed. 3 Adelgitha, [A] Melologue & 792.50
Mr. B[artley's] [The] Wedding Day
B[enefit] [See preface to this season.]
fine

Duff Thurs. 4 King Lear & 3 & [the] Deuce 490.50
[As Lear and the three
Singles in *Three and the
Deuce*. A]
fine

"   Frid.   5 [The] Wheel of Fortune & 3 &   283.50
                  [the] Deuce
                  [Duff as Penruddock in *The*
                  Wheel of Fortune and the
                  three Singles. A]
                                        fair

          Saty.   6 (Mr. Duff hoarse: postponed.)
                  [A announces *The Devil's*
                  Bridge and *A Tale of*
                  Mystery.]

"   Mon.   8 Bellamira & [The] Broken   340.50
                  Sword
                  [Duff as Montalto in *Bella-*
                  mira. A]
                                        fair

          Tues.   9 [The] Mountaineers, Imita- 434.50
Duff['s] ben[efit]   tion[s] & [The] Mayor of
                  Garrat
                  [See preface to this season.]
                                        fair

Maywood   Wed. 10 King Lear & [The] Prize   234.50
                  [As Lear. A]
                                        fine

Duff   Frid. 12 [The] Devil's Bridge & [A] 375.
                  Budget of Blunders
                  [See preface to this season.]
                                        Snow

"   Saty. 13 [The] Ethiop & Cath[erine] & 332.50
                  Petruchio
                  [Duff as the Ethiop and
                  Petruchio. A]
                                        fair

[277]

Mon. 15 (No play.)

"   Tues. 16 [The] Devil's Bridge & 3 &   528.
                [the] Deuce
                [Duff as Count Belino in
                The Devil's Bridge. A]
                                    Snow

        Wed. 17 (No play.)

        Thurs. 18 Accusation* & [The] Sleeping   386.
                Draught
                                    fine

        Frid. 19 [The] Poor Gentleman & [The]   950.
Masonic benefit   Miller & [his] Men
                [See preface to this season.]
                                    fine

        Saty. 20 Accusation & My Uncle   188.50
                                    fine

        Mon. 22 Accusation & of Age To-   234.50
                morrow
                                    fine

[Benefit of] Wed. 24 [The] Rivals & Is he Alive?*   995.75
    Jefferson   [As Bob Acres in *The Rivals*
                and Bang in *Is He Alive?*
                A]
                                    Rain

        Friday 26 [The] Heir at Law & Paul &   814.
[Benefit of]   Virginia
    Mrs. Burke   [As Cecily Homespun in
                The Heir at Law and as
                Virginia. A]
                                    Rain

[278]

[Benefit of] Saty. 27 [A] Cure for [the] Heartache, 423.
Mr. Barrett   Dr. Last['s Examination]
                     & [The] day after [the]
                     Wedding
                     [As Young Rapid in *A Cure
                     for the Heartache* and
                     Colonel Freelove in *The
                     Day after the Wedding.*
                     A]
                                          fine

[Benefit of] Mon. 29 Next Door Neighbours, [The] 469.50]
Mr. & Mrs.   Old Maid & Harl[equin's]
Francis   Invasion
                     [See preface to this season.]
                                          Rain

[Benefit of] Wed. 31 [The] West Indian & Who's 450.
H. Wallack   Who?*
                     [As Major O'Flaherty in
                     The West Indian and
                     Charles Headstrong in
                     Who's Who? A]
                                          fine

              April
[Benefit of] Frid. 2 [The] Natural Son & of Age 831.
Mr. Blissett   tomorrow
                     [As Dumps in *The Natural
                     Son,* and Molkus in Of
                     Age Tomorrow. A]
                                          fine

[Benefit of] Saty. 3 Every one has his fault & 294.
Mr. Burke   [The] Romp
                     [As Placid in *Every One Has
                     His Fault* and Watty
                     Cockney in *The Romp.* A]
                                          mild

[279]

[Benefit of]   Mon.   5 [The] Point of Honor, Who's   681.75
Hughes   Who[?] & [The] Forest
                            of Bondy
                            [As the Chevalier de St.
                            Franc in *The Point of
                            Honor* and Captain Aubri
                            in *The Forest of Bondy.*
                            A]
                                                      fair

                Wedy.   7 [The] Slave, [The] Scotch   463.
[Benefit of]   Ghost & for Freedom
Mrs. [H.] Wallack   Ho!*
                            [As Fanny in *The Scotch
                            Ghost* and Lisette in *For
                            Freedom Ho!* A]
                                                      fair

                Fridy. 9 C[oun]t Benyowsky, Ballet   423.50
[Benefit of]   & [The] High[land] Reel
Mrs. Harris   [Ballett, *The Scotch Ghost*,
                            in which Mrs. Harris is to
                            play Jemmy and to dance.
                            Mrs. Harris as Moggy
                            McGilpin in *The High-
                            land Reel.* A]
                                                      fair

                Saty. 10 (postponed, Mrs. Lefolle ill.)
[Benefit of] Pullen   [See preface to this season.]

                Mony. 12 Pizarro, Ballet & Who's Who[?]   863.
J. Wallack   [As Rolla in *Pizarro.* A
                            Ballet, *Love among the
                            Roses.*]
                                                      Very fine

Wallack   Wedy. 14 Richard 3d. & [The] Highland   408.50
                            Reel
                            [As Richard. A]
                                                      fine

[280]

"   Frid. 16 [The] Honey Moon & Paul &   418.
                 Virginia
                 [Wallack as Duke Aranza in
                 The Honey Moon. A]
                                       Rain

"   Saty. 17 Barbarossa & 3 & [the] Deuce   448.50
                 [Wallack as Achmet in *Bar-*
                 barossa and the three
                 Singles in *Three and the*
                 Deuce. A]
                                       Rain

"   Mon. 19 [The] Gamester & [The] Chil-   439.
                 dren in the Wood
                 [Wallack as Beverly in *The*
                 Gamester and Walter in
                 The Children in the Wood.
                 A]
                                       Rain

          Wedy. 21 Accusation & [The] Miller &   567.50
Pullen's ben[efi]t   [his] Men
                 [See preface to this season.]
                                       fine

Wallack   Frid. 23 [The] School for Scandal & 3   527.50
                 & [the] Deuce
                 [As Charles Surface in *The*
                 School for Scandal and
                 the three Singles. A]
                                       fine

"   Saty. 24 Town & Country & Love a la   314.50
                 mode
                 [Wallack as Reuben Glen-
                 roy in *Town and Country*
                 and Sir Archy MacSar-
                 casm in *Love a la Mode.*
                 A]
                                       fine

[281]

Mon. 26 Alexander [the Great] & My   588.50
W[allack's] Ben[efi]t   Aunt
    [As Alexander and as Da-
        shall in *My Aunt.* A]
            fine

Wedy. 28 [The] Poor Gent[lema]n &   708.50
[Benefit of] Warren   Barmecide*
    [See preface to this season.]
            fine

Frid. 30 Brutus* & Barmecide   1308.50
[Benefit of] Wood   [As Brutus. A]
            fine

115 nights averaging 555   ————
22 Benefits   767 $63828.50

Mr. & Mrs. Bartley's average 556 for 11 nights.
Mr. Wallack's   "   640 for 12 d[itt]o
    "   488 for 7 d[itt]o
Cooper's   "   675 for 8.

BALTIMORE [SPRING] SEASON, COMMENCING MAY 3RD., [ENDING
JUNE 21ST.,] 1819.

[Warren & Wood]

PREFACE—May 29: ACDA announces Blissett as Richmond, Herbert
as Richard. June 5: The players who received the benefit are the elder
Jeffersons. ACDA announces that Jefferson is to sing. June 16:
According to ACDA, Mrs. Bartley is to play Hamlet and to recite *Collins'
Ode.* In his *Diary,* Warren pronounces "Mrs. B[artley]'s Hamlet very
queer." In the June 12 entry of his *Diary,* he records that "Mr.
B[artley]" also played Megrim in *The Blue Devils.*

May
Mon. 3 [The] Stranger & [The] Sleep-   381.50
        ing Draught*
            fine

[282]

Wed. 5 [The] Poor Gentleman & [The] 426.75
Libertine
fine

Frid. 7 Next door Neighbours & [The] 332.25
Forest of Bondy
rain

Saty. 8 [The] West Indian & Who's 265. 1405.50
Who?*
Very Rainy

Mon. 10 Accusation* & [The] Sleeping 489.25
Draught
[ACDA announces *A Bud-
get of Blunders* in place of
The Sleeping Draught.]
Cloudy & Show[er]y

Wed. 12 [The] Green Man* & [The] 449.50
Sleeping Draught
Very Cold

Frid. 14 Brutus* & My Grandmother 919.25
Cold & Rain

Saty. 15 Accusation & Paul & Virginia 205.50 2063.50
Rainy

Mon. 17 [The] Exile & My Uncle* 299.50
Storm of rain

Wed. 19 Brutus & Who's Who? 512.50
fine

Frid. 21 [The] Wonder, Love Among 353.
Wood's ben[efit;] [the] Roses & My Uncle
Mrs. Entwisle['s] [Mrs. Entwisle as Donna
Ist. app[ea]r[ance] Violante in *The Wonder.*
ACDA]
fine

[283]

Saty. 22 Rob Roy [Macgregor]* & 361.50 1526.50
[The] Village Lawyer
fair

Mon. 24 Rob Roy [Macgregor] & Blue 335.75
Beard
fine

Wed. 26 Barmecide,* [The] Wedding 437.25
Warren['s] Ben[efit] Day & Ella Rosenberg
fine

Frid. 28 Pizarro, [Little] R[ed] R[iding] 356.25
Mrs. Entw[isle's] Hood & Turn Out
ben[efit]
fine

Saty. 29 Richard 3d. & Of Age 472.50
[Benefit of] tomorrow
Bliss[ett] & [See preface to this season.]
Herbert

show[er]y at night

Mon. 31 Deaf & Dumb, [The] Sail[or's] 312.
[Benefit of] Mr. & Landlady & [The] Broken
Mrs. Francis Sword
Rainy

June
[Benefit of] Wed. 2 Brutus & Tekeli 526.50
Hughes & [Mrs.]
Harris
fine

Frid. 4 [The] Merchant of Venice, 273.50
[Benefit of] Mr. & [The] S[cotch] Ghost &
Mrs. [H] Wallack Tom Thumb [the Great]
[Mrs. H. Wallack in Scots
Pas Seul in *The Scotch
Ghost* and in pas de deux
with Mrs. Harris. ACDA]
Warm & fair

[284]

Saty. 5	Rob Roy [Macgregor] & [The]	395.50
[Benefit of] Mr. & Mrs. Jefferson	Prisoner at Large [See preface to this season.] Warm	

Mon. 7	Adrian & Orrilla & [The]	307.75
[Benefit of] Mr. & Mrs. Burke	Weathercock [Mrs. Burke as Lothaire in *Adrian and Orrilla* and Variella in *The Weather- cock.* ACDA] Very Warm	

Bartleys	Wed. 9 Venice Preserv'd, Collins' Ode	230.50
	& [The] Review [Mrs. Bartley as Belvidera in *Venice Preserved.* ACDA] Thunder Storm	

"	Frid. 11 [The] Green Man, [The] In-	232.75
	v[isible] Girl & [The] Adopted Child [Bartley as the Green Man. ACDA] Mild & fine	

"	Saty. 12 [The] Grecian Daughter, [A]	239.
	Melologue & [The] Blue Devils [Bartley as Evander, Mrs. Bartley as Euphrasia in *The Grecian Daughter.* ACDA] Cool & fine	

"	Mon. 14 Fazio* & Ways & Means	347.50
	[Bartley as Sir David Dunder in *Ways and Means.* ACDA] Cool & fine	

[285]

	Wed. 16	Hamlet, Collin's Ode & [The]	541.50
Mrs. B[artley's]		Adopted Child	
benefit		[See preface to this season.]	
		Warm	

Frid. 18 [The] Anatomist, Barmecide   122.
     & [The] Romp

                               fair

Saty. 19 (No Play)

Mon. 21 Jane Shore, New Scene of   417.
Balt[i]m[ore] & Sigesmar
[the Switzer]*
["After the tragedy will be
exhibited, for the first
time, an entire new scene
representing Baltimore in
the year 1752. Copied
accurately from the print
recently published from
an accurate drawing.
The scene executed by
Mr. H. Warren, Mr. T.
Reinagle and assistants."
ACDA]

                              —— $10,542.75

28 Nights Averaging 376.50

PHILADELPHIA SEASON, COMMENCING SEPTEMBER 27, 1819[, ENDING MARCH 27, 1820.]

[Warren & Wood]

PREFACE—**October 18**: Arthur Keene to sing *Scots Wha Hae wi' Wallace Bled* and as Paul, in which he will sing a duet with Mrs. Burke, *See from the Ocean Rising* and the songs, *Vast Is the Swelling Tide of Joy, Boldly I Come to Plead the Cause* and *The Wealth of the Cottage.* DP **October 25**: Keene as Carlos in *The Duenna*, in which he will sing *Had I a Heart for Falsehood Fram'd, Ah, Such a Pair Was Never Seen, Love's Young Dream* from Moore, Sir John Stevenson's Irish Melodies and *Gentle Maid, Ah*

Why Suspect Me? After the opera, by particular desire, *Thine Am I, My Faithful Fair,* composed by Mr. Whitaker. DP **October 27**: Keene as Count Belino in *The Devil's Bridge,* in which he will sing *Behold His Soft Expressive Face, Though Love is Warm Awhile, Is There a Heart that Never Loved?, Fancy's Sketch,* and *William Tell, the Patriot of Switzerland,* composed by Braham. Keene as Masetto in *The Libertine,* in which he will sing *When Women Warm Us,* and duets with Mrs. Burke, *Now Place Your Hand in Mine, Dear, The Purest Flame This Bosom Warming* and *I Love Thee.* DP **November 3**: DP announces, "For such of the poor as have suffered by the late calamity." **December 11**: DP announces Bartley as Oakley, Mrs. Bartley as Mrs. Oakley in *The Jealous Wife;* Bartley as James Megrim in *The Blue Devils.* For comment on Mrs. Bartley's recitation of *A Melologue,* see the preface to the previous Philadelphia season, March 1 and 3, 1819. **December 15**: DP announces Bartley as Macbeth and as Sir Charles, with Mrs. Bartley as Lady Racket, in *Three Weeks after Marriage* Mrs. Bartley is also to play Lady Macbeth and to recite *Collins' Ode on the Passions* "with appropriate music." **January 3**: According to *Durang* I, LXI, Warren appeared as Leonato in *Much Ado About Nothing,* as Falstaff in *The First Part of Henry the Fourth* and as Falstaff in a comic epilogue called *More Sack.* **February 4**: DP announces that the "proceeds will be submitted to the Mayor of Savannah, in aid of the sufferers by the late Dreadful Calamity." **February 28**: The word "Life" in the title should be "Reign." DP announces Jefferson as Gregory Gubbins in *The Battle of Hexham* and in comic songs. His son, "T. Jefferson," is to fill the rôle of Warwick on the same evening; and, on March 15, he receives a benefit. **March 18**: DP announces Crampton as Sir Patrick O'Neil in *The Irish Widow* and Scotsman in *The Register Office.* He is also to sing. King is to play Landry in *The Forest of Bondy.* **March 22**: DP announces Mr. and Mrs. H. Wallack's benefit, with H. Wallack as Rob Roy and as Jemmy in *The Scotch Ghost.* According to DP, he is also to dance. Mrs. H. Wallack is to dance and to play Fanny in *The Scotch Ghost.*

Sickness and hard times combined to make this season one of the most disappointing in the career of the Chestnut Street company. In the November 27 entry of his *Diary,* Warren writes, "Wood and Hughes both ill;" but, according to the *Account Book,* "Hughes" was already "ill" on November 22. There is a notation to that effect in Wood's entry of the same date and ditto marks under it signify that Hughes remained ill on November 24, 26 and 27. The notation, "Mr. Hughes ill" is

[287]

repeated in the entry of November 29 and also in the entries of December 1 and 13. Ditto marks in the entries of December 15, 17 and 18 signify that Mr. Hughes was still sick. "Francis" was "ill" on February 5, "Mr. Wallack [sic]" was "ill" on February 25 and "Jeff[erson]" was "Sick" on March 25. The notations as to the state of the weather make it apparent that the actors may have suffered from its sudden changes from "fair" to "thaw & Rain" and "Violent Snow Storm" and back again to "fair," "slight rain" and "Snow at night."

Wood, Durang and Warren all tell of the even severer handicap of the hard times, which, in spite of the "numerous novelties" proving "that there was no want of provocation to public support," led to "an important falling off" in patronage, Wood writes in *Recollections*, p. 233, after Cooper's benefit on November 27. More specifically, *Durang*, I, LXI, reveals that "during the latter part of 1819, while the Bartleys were playing," see December 9," the business got extremely poor. On the eleventh week of the season half salaries or in ratio were paid. This was on Saturday, December 18, when the comedy of *The Green Man* was played. . . . . On New Year's Eve, there being no suitable audience present to approve or disapprove, the house was dismissed." In his entry of this date Wood notes, "postponed on account of Sleighing." He explains, in *Recollections*, p. 236, "in regard to sleighing, particularly on fine moonlight nights, the experience of this year confirms that of former years, and proved that this amusement cost the theatre at least $150 per night." Durang continues: "On Saturday, January 1, full salaries were paid in proportion of three nights per week. The next pay day brought again half salary. On the fifteenth week, January 15, half salaries were paid. Thus the half salaries went on till about the 12th of February, when a proposition was made to the company that, if the receipts of the theatre thereafter should be equal to the expenses, the whole of the salaries should be paid. If not, the actors were to receive in such proportions as the funds in the treasury warranted."

In the February 4 entry of the *Account Book* there is a notation, "new arrangement" evidently referring to the "proposition" of which Durang writes.

Following a second benefit on March 24 even more disappointing than a first on January 3, Warren opines that "this season has been wretched beyond all former precedent. . . . The times are very bad," he writes, "business of every description being exceedingly dull and the merchants breaking hourly. The cargoes which arrive in port won't bring their original cost, which doubtless is the prime cause of our lack of business. The New York, Boston & Charleston theatres suffer as much or indeed more than we. They have put the performers upon half salaries also."

Sept[ember]

Mon. 27 Every One has his fault & 451.50
Barmecide
very Warm

Wed. 29 Much ado about Nothing & of 318.75
Mrs. Entw[isle's]   age tomorrow
1st. app[earance]   [As Beatrice. A]
Rain

October

Frid. 1 My Uncle, Sigesmar [the 357.75
Switzer]* & [A] Budget of
Blunders
fine

Saty. 2 Rob Roy [Macgregor] & [The] 374.75   1502.75
Irishman in London
fair

Mon. 4 [The] Exile & [The] Wedding 343.50
Day
fair

Wed. 6 Brutus & Who's Who? 394.50
Very Hot

Frid. 8 [The] Stranger & [The] Snow 324.50
Storm
Warm & fair

Saty. 9 [The] Robbers & Paul & 295.50   1358.
Virginia
Storm of rain

[289]

	Mon. 11 [The] Devil's Bridge & [The]	476.50	
[Arthur] K[eene]	Village Lawyer		
	[As Count Belino in *The Devil's Bridge.* DP]		
	fine		

"	Wed. 13 Brutus & [The] Poor Soldier	322.50	
	[Keene as Patrick in *The Poor Soldier.* DP]		
	Very Cold		

	Frid. 15 [The] Heart of Mid-Lothian,*	638.	
	[The] Romp & [The] Sleeping draught		
	fair		

	Saty. 16 [The] Poor Gentleman & [The]	238.50	1675.50
	Broken Sword		
	fair		

	Mon. 18 [The] Heart of Mid-Lothian	350.75	
Keene	& Paul & Virginia		
	[See preface to this season.]		
	Cold		

	Wed. 20 Guy Mannering & Who's	440.75	
K[eene]	Who?		
	[As Harry Bertram in *Guy Mannering.* DP]		
	Cold		

	Frid. 22 [The First Part of] Henry 4th	473.	
	& Sigesmar [the Switzer]		
	Cold		

	Saty. 23 [The] Sold[ier's] Daughter &	273.50	1538.
	Zembuca		
	fair		

[290]

K[eene]   Mon. 25 [The] Duenna & [The] Mayor 294.50
                  of Garrat
                  [See preface to this season.]
                             fine & Cool

          Wed. 27 [The] Devil's Bridge & [The] 427.25
K[eene's] Ben[efit]   Libertine
                  [See preface to this season.]
                             fine

          Frid. 29 Wanted a Wife* & Ella 472.25
                  Rosenberg
                             fine

          Saty. 30 Jane Shore & Love Laughs at 262.50 1676.75
                  Locksmiths
                             fair

     November   [The] Foundling of the forest 365.50
      Mon. 1   & Sigesmar [the Switzer.]
                             fair

          Wed. 3 [The] Follies of a day & [The] 516.50
Ben[efit of]   Heart of Mid-Lothian
Balt[more] Poor   [See preface to this season.]
                             fair

          Frid. 5 Wanted a Wife & [The] Forest 420.25
                  of Bondy
                             fine

          Saty. 6 Rob Roy [Macgregor] & [The] 360.   1662.25
                  Anatomist
                             fair

          Mon. 8 Town & Country & [The] 336.75
                  Miller & his Men
                             fair

[291]

Wed. 10 Wanted a Wife & [The] 302.50
Broken Sword
fair

Frid. 12 [The] School for Scandal & 344.75
[The] Anatomist
fair

Saty. 13 [The] Bride of Abydos* & 190.50 1174.50
[The] Sleeping Draught
fair

Cooper   Mon. 15 Brutus & [A] Budget of 687.50
Blunders
[As Brutus. DP]
fair

"   Wed. 17 Macbeth & Of age tomorrow 382.75
[Cooper as Macbeth. DP]
Rain

"   Frid. 19 Marmion & [The] Weather- 969.
cock
[Cooper as Marmion. DP]
fine

"   Saty. 20 Richard 3d. & [The] Wedding 253.75 2293.
Day
[Cooper as Richard. DP]
fair

"   Mon. 22 Marmion & Raising the Wind 423.50
[Cooper as Marmion. DP]
fine

"   Wed. 24 Hamlet & [The] Ghost 486.50
[Cooper as Hamlet. DP]
Cold

"   Frid. 26 Bertram & [The] Review   511.75
                 [Cooper as Bertram. DP]
                              fine

        Saty. 27 Brutus & [The] Liar   575.75   1997.
Cooper's ben[efit]   [As Brutus and as Young
                 Wilding in *The Liar*.
                 DP]
                            Mild

        Mon. 29 [The] Green Man, Love   360.75
                 among [the] Roses &
                 Lock & Key
                            fair
December
        Wed. 1 [The] Merry Wives [of Wind-   286.50
                sor] & [A] Tale of Mystery
                            fair

        Frid. 3 Fazio & [A] Roland for an   245.50
                Oliver*
                            fine

        Saty. 4 Wanted a Wife & [The] Heart   238.75   1131.50
                of Mid-Lothian
                            fine

        Mon. 6 Rob Roy [Macgregor] & [The]   288.75
                Libertine
                            fair

Bartleys   Wed. 8 [The] Grecian Daughter, Ode   409.75
                to [the] Passions & [The]
                Adopted Child
                [Bartley as Evander, Mrs.
                Bartley as Euphrasia in
                The Grecian Daughter.
                Bartley as Michael in
                The Adopted Child. DP]
                            fair

"   Frid. 10 Adrian & Orrilla, Love   256.
am[on]g [the] Roses &
Ways & Means
[Bartley as Sir David
Dunder in *Ways and
Means*, Mrs. Barley as
Madame Clermont in
Adrian and Orrilla. DP]
Cold

"   Saty. 11 [The] Jealous Wife, [A] Melo-   286.75   1242.
logue & [The] Blue Devils
[See preface to this season]
Clear

"   Mon. 13 Douglas & the Critic   286.50
[Bartley as Old Norval,
Mrs. Bartley as Lady
Randolph in *Douglas*.
Bartley as Sir Fretful
Plagiary and Puff in *The
Critic*. DP]
Clear

"   Wed. 15 Macbeth, [Collins'] Ode & 3   380.25
Weeks after Marriage
Mr. B[artley's] ben[efi]t
[See preface to this season.]
Cold

"   Frid. 17 [The] School for Scandal &   344.75
[The] Adopted Child
[Bartley as Sir Peter, Mrs.
Bartley as Lady Teazle in
The School for Scandal.
Bartley as Michael in
The Adopted Child. DP]
fine

[294]

"   Saty. 18 [The] Green Man & [The]   203.50   1215.
                 Wedding Day
                 [Bartley as the Green Man
                 and as Sir Adam with
                 Mrs. Bartley as Lady
                 Contest in *The Wedding
                 Day*. DP]
                                        fine

B[artleys]   Mon. 20 Jane Shore & Ways & Means   203.50
                 [Bartley as Dumont, Mrs.
                 Bartley as Jane Shore.
                 Bartley as Sir David
                 Dunder in *Ways and
                 Means*. DP]
                                        fair

            Wed. 22 Hamlet & [The] Invisible Girl 1041.
Benefit [of]   [Mrs. Bartley as Hamlet
Mrs. B[artley]   and in rentations. DP]
                                        fine

            Thurs. 23 Guy Mannering & Sigesmar   160.50
                 [the Switzer]
                                        fair

            Frid. 24 She W[oul]d be a Soldier* &   435.   1838.
                 [The] Fortune of War
                                 Rainy

            (Christmas)

            Mon. 27 She W[oul]d be a Soldier &   811.50
                 [The] Miller & [his] Men
                                        fine

            Wed. 29 Geo[rge]   Barnwell,   Love 225.50
                 among the Roses & My
                 Grandmother
                                 fair

                        [295]

Frid. 31 Speed the Plough & Turn Out
postponed on account of Sleighing

[1820.] January
Saty. 1 [The] Falls of Clyde,* Where   697.
Shall I dine[?]* & [The]
40 Thieves
Sleighing & very Cold

Mon. 3 [The] School of Shakespeare*   427.50
Warren's benefit.   & Where Shall I dine[?]
[See preface to this season.]
fair

Wed. 5 Altorf* & Turn Out   660.50
(Cooper played Altorf.)
fair

Frid. 7 Education & [The] Lady of   243.50
the Lake
fair

Saty. 8 She Would be a Soldier &   294.   1625.50
Where Shall I dine?
thaw & Rain

[J.] Wallack Mon. 10 Pizarro & [The] Weathercock   397.50
[As Rolla in *Pizarro*. DP]
Violent Snow Storm

"   Wed. 12 Coriolanus & [The] Highland   219.50
Reel
[Wallack   as   Coriolanus.
DP]
Sleighing & Cold

"   Frid. 14 [The] Mountaineers & 3 &   348.   965.
[The] Deuce
[Wallack as Octavian in *The
Mountaineers* and as the
three Singles. DP]
d[itt]o

[296]

Saty. 15 (No performance.)

Mon. 17 (Postponed on acc[ount of] Storm.)

" Wed. 19 [The] Carib Chief* & Raising 457. the Wind [Wallack as Omreah in *The Carib Chief.* DP] Cloudy

" Frid. 21 [The] Carib Chief & Turn Out 330. [Wallack as Omreah. DP] fair

" Saty. 22 Brutus & Where Shall I dine? 231.50 1018.50 [Wallack as Brutus. DP] Slight rain

" Mon. 24 Bertram & [The] Children in 261. the Wood [Wallack as Bertram and as Walter in *The Children in the Wood.* DP] fine

" Wed. 26 Marmion & [The] Devil to 263.50 pay [Wallack as Marmion. DP] Snow at Night

" Frid. 28 Pizarro & [The] Falls of Clyde 422.75 [Wallack as Rolla. DP] Dull

" Saty. 29 [The] Honey Moon & [The] 338.50 1285.75 Heart of Mid-Lothian [Wallack as Duke Aranza in *The Honey Moon.* DP] Rain

[297]

Mon. 31 Pizarro, Sylv[ester] Dagger- 1106.
Benefit [of]   wood & My Aunt
Wallack   [As Rolla, Sylvester Dag-
                        gerwood and as Dashall in
                        My Aunt. DP]
                                    Very fine
        February
        Wed. 2 (No performance.)
                [DP announces "a favorite
                play" and *The Inn-
                keeper's Daughter.*]

        Frid. 4 [The] Way to Get Married & 572.50
Benefit of Savannah   [The] Innkeeper's Daugh-
                        ter
                [See preface to this season.]

        Saty. 5 Speed the Plough & [The] 162.75 1841.25
                Anatomist
                                    fair

        Mon. 7 Fredolfo* & Where Shall I 164.
                dine[?]
                                    rain

        Wed. 9 Fredolfo & [The] Innkeeper's 169.75
                Daughter
                                    rainy

        Frid. 11 [The] West Indian & Helpless 317.50
Wood's Benefit   Animals*
                [As Belcour in *The West
                Indian.* DP]
                                    fine Sleighing

        Saty. 12 [The] Point of Honor, H[elp- 154.50 805.75
                less] Animals & [The]
                Toothache
                                    Rain

[298]

Mon. 14 [The] Road to Ruin & [The] 209.50
Magpie & [the] Maid
fine

Wed. 16 Where to find a friend & [The] 164.50
Innkeeper's Daughter
foggy

Frid. 18 [The] Castle Spectre & [A] 208.
Budget of Blunders
Very fine

Saty. 19 [The] Poor Gentleman & Ella 116.50   693.50
Rosenberg
Clear

Mon. 21 (No performance.)

Tues. 22 She Would be a Soldier & 1178.50
Robinson Crusoe*
very fair

Wed. 23 [A] Roland for an Oliver, 185.50
Helpless Animals &
Robinson Crusoe
fair

Frid. 25 [The] Mountaineers & Lock & 143.75
Key
Rain

Saty. 26 [A] Short Reign & [a] Merry 137.50   1645.25
One* & Blue Beard
fine

[Benefit of] Mon. 28 [The] Battle of Hexham & [A] 775.75
Jefferson   Short Life & [a] Merry
One
[See preface to this season.]
Snow at Night

[299]

March

	Wed.	1 [The] Mask'd friend, Belles	262.50
[Benefit of]		without Beaux* & Mr. H.	
Mrs. Wood		[As Barbara Turnbull in *The Masked Friend* and Lady Lucretia in *Belles without Beaux*. DP] Rain and Snow at Night	

	Frid.	3 [The] Ethiop & [The] Spoil'd	618.50
[Benefit of]		Child	
Mr. & Mrs. Burke		[Burke as Old Pickle, Mrs. Burke as Little Pickle in *The Spoiled Child*. DP] fine	

	Saty.	4 Abaellino, Love among [the]	213.75
[Benefit of]		Roses & Belles Without	
Mr. & Mrs. Darley		Beaux	
		fair	

	Mon.	6 She Stoops to Conquer, [The]	832.50
[Benefit of]		Day after [the] Wed[din]g	
Mrs. Entwisle		& Bomb[astes] Furioso	
		[As Miss Hardcastle in *She Stoops to Conquer* and Lady Elizabeth in *The Day after the Wedding*. DP] fair	

	Wed.	8 (Postponed on account of
[Benefit of] Mr. &		Weather.)
Mrs. Wallack		[DP announces *Rob Roy Macgregor*, *The Scotch Ghost* and *the Ruffian Boy*.]

[300]

[Benefit of]   Frid. 10 Richard 3d. & Who's Who?   481.75
Mr. Herbert   [As Richard. DP]
                                 fair

         Saty. 11 Wild Oats & [A] Budget of 546.
[Benefit of]   Blunders
Mr. Blissett   [As Sim in *Wild Oats* and
                   Dr. Dablancour in *A*
                   Budget of Blunders. DP]
                                 fine

         Mon. 13 Adelgitha & [The] Jew of 307.50
[Benefit of]   Lubeck*
Hughes   [As Michael Ducas in *Adel-*
                   githa and as the Jew. DP]
                                 dull

         Wed. 15 [The] Rivals, [The] Ren- 247.25
[Benefit of]   dezvous* & [A] Roland
T. Jefferson   for an Oliver
                   [As Captain Absolute in
                   The Rivals and Smart in
                   The Rendezvous. DP]
                                 fair

[Benefit of   Frid. 17 Columbus & Robinson Crusoe 492.75
Mrs.] Carter &
[Mrs.] Bloxton
                                 fair

         Saty. 18 [The] Irish Widow, [The] 378.75 1426.25
[Benefit of]   R[egiste]r Officer & [The]
Crampton & King   Forest of Bondy
                   [See preface to this season.]
                                 fine

         Mon. 20 (Postponed on acc[oun]t [of]
[Benefit of] H.   Rain & Jeff[erson] ill.)
Warren & T.
Reinagle

[301]

Wed. 22 Rob Roy [Macgregor, The] 1165.50
2d. night,   Scotch Ghost & [The]
H. Wallack   Ruffian Boy*
                              [See preface to this season.]
                                       fair

Frid. 24 [The] Merry Wives [of Wind- 274.50
Warren's 2d.   sor] & [The] Falls of Clyde
ben[efi]t   [As Falstaff. DP]
                                  fair

Saty. 25 (No performance.)

Mon. 27 [The] Soldier's Daughter & 627.50
[Benefit of]   [The] Ruffian Boy
Pullen   [See preface to this season.]
                              fair   _____

                                         $39,148.
98 Nights averaged $399.50
Benefits averaged.

BALTIMORE [SPRING] SEASON, [COMMENCING APRIL 3, ENDING
JULY 4,] 1820.

[Warren & Wood]

PREFACE—**April 28**: ACDA announces the sword hornpipe by Miss K. Durang and, for the first time on this stage, "the celebrated sailor's hornpipe" by Mrs. [H.] Wallack, in character, "as performed in Philadelphia with great applause." **May 1**: ACDA announces, "The managers have the pleasure to inform the public that the company of Regular Blues, commanded by Capt. Huber, and the military band attached to Major Pinkney's Rifle Corps have politely volunteered their appearance on this occasion." **June 19**: ACDA announces a terpsichorean divertisemento commencing with *L'Amour et Marriage*, a pas de deux by the Misses Durang. In the course of the dance the celebrated Irish piper will play on the union pipes the airs of *Robin Adair, Jesse, the Flower O'Dumblane*, &c. In the course of *The School of Reform*, by particular request, the story of the Dutch milkman and the monkey and the Dutch song called *The Trumpeter Speaks with His Horn*, by Mr. Blissett.

[302]

June 23: ACDA announces "Miss Durang" as Lubin, "Miss K. Durang" as Little Red Riding Hood; "Miss Hathwell" as Andrew in *The Lady of the Rock* and Janet, with "Miss H. Hathwell" as Colinette in *Little Red Riding Hood*. According to ACDA, both "Miss Hathwell" and "Miss H. Hathwell" are to dance. Miss Seymour is to play Anna in *Little Red Riding Hood* and Laura in *Belles Without Beaux*. For information regarding the Durangs and Hathwells, see the index to players. **June 24**: ACDA announces Francis as Gaffer Totterton in *The Miraculous Mill* and Mrs. Francis as Bendetta in *The Voice of Nature*. Mr. Francis is also to sing. The Misses Durang, Hathwell and Seymour are to appear in "Minuet à Quatre and Strathspey composed by Francis." **June 26**: ACDA announces Carter as Lord Duberly's servant in *The Heir at Law* and Cook in *The Devil to Pay*, Mrs. Carter as Caroline Dormer in *The Heir at Law* and Lucy in *The Devil to Pay*. **June 30**: ACDA announces a comic song, *How to Nail 'Em*, by Mr. Jefferson. Mrs. Burke is to sing the celebrated hunting song of *Awake, Ye Dull Sluggards, Awake!* There are to be a pas seul by the Misses Durang and "the favorite comic ballet in character" called *Oh Cruel; or, the Wandering Melodists*, with Mr. Jefferson as the Female Ballad Singer and Mr. Blissett as the Fiddler. The players receiving the benefit are the elder Jeffersons.

In the entry of May 31 Wood has written "Mr. & Mrs. Entwisle decamped." In his entry of the same date, Warren writes, "Mrs. Entwisle left the company—no warning." It has been advisable to omit two of Wood's notations from the printed version. These are "Mr. Jefferson Sick in Phil[adelphia]," which Wood has written vertically across the entries of April 3 to April 17 inclusive; and "Philadelphia Theatre destroyed on 2d. April," which Wood has written over the entry of April 3. For an account of the fire to which Wood is alluding, see the general introduction, p. 34.

April

Mon. 3 Wild Oats & [The Ruffian   290.75
         Boy*

                          Snow

Wed. 5 Rob Roy [Macgregor] & [The]   245.50
       Ruffian Boy

                          Cold

[303]

Frid. 7 Speed the Plough & [The] 206.25
Innkeeper's Daughter
Cold

Saty. 8 [The] Rivals & [The falls of 197.75 940.25
Clyde*
Cold

Mon. 10 [The] Point of Honor & [The] 258.75
Innkeeper's Daughter
fair

Wed. 12 (Postponed. .Mr. H. Wallack & Mrs. Entwisle
Sick.)

Frid. 14 [The] Way to Get Married & 307.75
[The] Falls of Clyde
fine

Sat. 15 Brutus & [The] Romp 228.50 895.25
Rain

Mon. 17 [The] Soldier's Daughter & 411.50
Ben[efit] of Battle   Sigesmar [the Switzer]
Widows   [The public are respectfully
informed that the profits
of this night's entertainments will be offered in
aid of the fund for the
relief of the widows and
and families of the brave
men who fell in defense
of Baltimore. ACDA]
fair

Wed. 19 Fazio & a Roland for an 257.50
Oliver*
fair

Frid. 21 [The] Heart of Mid-Lothian* 315.75
         & Mr. H.
                    Warm

Saty. 22 Where to find a friend & [The] 145.50   1130.
         Falls of Clyde
                    fair

Mon. 24 [The] Heart of Mid-Lothian & 221.50
         [A] Roland for an Oliver
                    fine

Wed. 26 Wanted a Wife,* Love among 282.50
         the Roses & [The] Mayor
         of Garrat
                very fine

Frid. 28 Every one has his fault, 520.
Wood's Benefit   Dances & Belles Without
         Beaux*
         [See preface to this season.]
                Very fine

Saty. 29 [The] Foundling of the forest 131.50 1155.50
         & Bombastes [Furioso]
                    dull

May
Mon. 1 She would be a Soldier,* Olio 908.75
        & [The] Fortune of War
        [See preface to this season.]
               Very fine

Wed. 3 [The] West Indian & [The] 160.50
        Rendezvous*
                   dull

Frid. 5 She would be a Soldier & 363.50
        Where Shall I dine?*
                 dull

Saty. 6 Pizarro, [The] Scotch Ghost 294. 1726.75
Benefit [of Mr. & & Where Shall I dine?
Mrs.] H. Wallack
                                            Rain

Mon. 8 [The] Fair American & [The] 162.50
          Highland Reel
                                    fair

Wed. 10 [The] Wedding Day, [A] Short 231.50
          Reign & [a] Merry one* &
          [A] Roland for an Oliver
                                    dull

Frid. 12 [The] Clandestine Marriage & 407.50
Warren's Benefit   Helpless Animals*
          [As Mr. Sterling in *The
          Clandestine   Marriage.*
          ACDA]
                                    fair

Saty. 13 Adrian & Orrilla & [The] 120.50 922.
          Rendezvous
                                    fair

Mon. 15 [The] Castle Spectre & Help- 230.50
          less Animals
                                    fair

Wed. 17 [A] Short Reign & [a] Merry 334.25
          One & Robinson Crusoe*
                              drizzling

Frid. 19 [The] Steward* & [The] 210.
          Anatomist
                                    dull

Saty. 20 [The] Stranger & Turn Out 119.75 894.50
                                    dull

[306]

Whitsuntide
Mon. 22 [The] Steward & Robinson 199.50
   Crusoe
      fine

Wed. 24 Rob Roy [Macgregor] & Help- 221.50
   less Animals
      Cloudy

Cooper Frid. 26 Macbeth & [The] Toothache 515.50
   [As Macbeth. ACDA]
      rainy

" Saty. 27 [The First Part of] Henry 4th 351. 1287.50
   & Where Shall I dine?
   [Cooper as Hotspur.
   ACDA]
      fine

" Mon. 29 Richard 3rd. & [A] Budget of 283.50
   Blunders
   [Cooper as Richard. ACDA]
      fine

" Wed. 31 Alfonso & my Grandmother 227.
   [Cooper as Orsino in *Al-*
   fonso. ACDA]
      Rain
  June
" Frid. 2 [The] Revenge & [The] Hunter 302.50
   of the Alps
   [Cooper as Zanga in *The*
   Revenge. ACDA]
      Rain

" Saty. 3 Marmion & [The] Romp 466.75 1279.75
   [Cooper as Lord Marmion.
   ACDA]
      dull

[307]

Benefit [of] Cooper Mon. 5 Brutus & Cath[erine] & 534.50
        Petruchio
        [As Brutus and Petruchio.
        ACDA]
            Showery

C[ooper] Wed. 7 Bertram & Love Laughs at 246.50
        Locksmiths
        [As Bertram. ACDA]
            fine

C[ooper] Frid. 9 Rule a Wife and Have a Wife 297.
        & Paul & Virginia
        [As Leon. ACDA]
           Warm & fair

C[ooper] Saty. 10 Hamlet & [The] Blue Devils 230. 1308.
        [As Hamlet. ACDA]
          Very Warm

     Mon. 12 She Stoops to Conquer & 137.
        [The] Broken Sword
            Rain

Benefit of Wed. 14 Town & Country & Miss in 176.
[Baltimore] Gen[era]l her Teens
Dispensary
          Very Warm

     Frid. 16 Abaellino & [The] Poor Soldier 90.25
            Warm

     Saty. 17 [The] Poor Gentleman & [The] 74.50 477.75
        Weathercock
          fine & Cool

[Benefit of] Mon. 19 [The] School of Reform, Olio 334.50
Herbert &   & Of Age tomorrow
Blissett   [See preface to this season.]
            fine

Wed. 21 [The] Battle of Hexham & No   127.50
[Benefit of]   Song No Supper
Mr. & Mrs.   [Darley as Crop in *No Song*
Darley   *No Supper* and the First
                Robber, with Mrs. Darley
                as Queen Margaret, in
                The Battle of Hexham.
                ACDA]
                     fair & Warm

Frid. 23 [The] Lady of the Rock,   102.
[Benefit of the]   [Little] R[ed] R[iding]
Misses Durang,   Hood & Belles W[ithout]
Hath[well] &   Beaux
Seymour   [See preface to this season.]
                      Warm

Saty. 24 [The] Voice of Nature, [The]   97.75   767.25
[Benefit of] Mr.   Old Maid & [The] Mirac-
& Mrs. Francis   ulous Mill
               [See preface to this season.]
                      Warm

[Benefit of   Mon. 26 [The] Heir at Law & [The]   142.50
Mr. and Mrs.]   Devil to pay
Carter & C[harles]   [See preface to this season.]
Ward

                      Very Cool

Wed. 28 [The] Folli⌐s of a day, [The]   76.
[Benefit of]   Scotch Ghost & [The]
Wheatley &   Pris[one]r at Large
[Mrs.] Bloxton   [Mrs. Bloxton as Female
                Attendant in *The Follies*
                of a Day and Rachel in
                The Prisoner at Large.
                ACDA]
                      fair

[309]

[Benefit of]   Frid. 30 [The] Spanish Barber, Olio &   347.25
Mr. & Mrs.   Who's the Dupe?
Jefferson   [See preface to this season.]
                               Very Warm

          July
          Saty. 1   Fredolfo,* & [The] Irishman   74.   639.75
[Benefit of] Hughes   in London
& Burke   Hughes as Count Wallen-
                   berg in *Fredolfo*, Burke as
                   Murtoch Delany in *The
                   Irishman   in   London.*
                   ACDA]
                               Hot & Clear

          Mon. 3 She W[oul]d be a Soldier &
[Benefit of Mrs.]   Rosina (Postponed.)
Lefolle & T.
Jeff[erson]

          Tues. 4 [The] Glory of Columbia &   417.50
                   Sprigs of Laurel   ———·—
                               Warm
                                              $13,636.25
          52 Nights averaging $262.25

BALTIMORE [AUTUMN] SEASON, COMMENCING SEPTEMBER 12th, [ENDING
          NOVEMBER 3RD.,] 1820.

          [Warren & Wood]

PREFACE—**September 12**: ACDA announces that the profits are to be
devoted in aid of the fund for the relief of the widows and families of
the brave men who fell in defense of the city.   **October 25**: In this
entry Wood has written "Changed to Thursday, Cooper ill" and Warren,
in his *Diary*, explains, "Postpon'd. Cooper not able to act—from
a fever."

Wood has written vertically across the entries of September 13, 15
and 16, "Sick list Commences." In *Recollections*, p. 247, he states,
"So large was our sick list in the autumn season of 1820 that three of
the first five nights' performances were unavoidably postponed."

[310]

It has been necessary to omit a few miscellaneous notations from the printed text. These notations are: "Mr. Hathwell lame, by coming by land," written over the entry of September 12; and "See Agreement No. 4," written after "No performance" in the entry of October 11.

September

Tues. 12	She Stoops to Conquer &	334.50	
Ben[efit of]	[The] Agreeable Surprize		
Battle fund	[See preface to this season.]		
	Very Cool		

Wed. 13

Frid. 15	[The] Iron Chest & Of Age	162.50	497.
Mr. Williams' 1st	Tomorrow		
app[earance]	[As Wilford in *The Iron*		
	Chest. ACDA]		
	very Cool		

Sat. 16

Mon. 18	[The] Road to Ruin & [The]	202.50
Mrs. Baker's 1st.	Innkeeper's Daughter	
[appearance]	[As Sophia Freelove in *The*	
	Road to Ruin. ACDA]	
	Very Warm	

Wed. 20	As You Like it & [The] Scotch	213.75
Mrs. Williams	Ghost & Helpless Animals	
	[As Rosalind. ACDA]	
	Very fine	

Frid. 22	Man and Wife & Ella Rosen-	174.50
	berg	
Mrs. Young's 1st.	[As Helen Worrett in *Man*	
[appearance]	*and Wife*. ACDA]	
	Very Cool	

Saty. 23	[The] Point of Honor & Where	88.	678.75
	Shall I dine[?]		
	fine		

[311]

Mon. 25 [The] Castle Spectre & [The] 178.
Anatomist
fine

Wed. 27 Town & Country & [The] 193.75
Falls of Clyde
fine

Frid. 29 Henri Quatre* & Where Shall 278.50
I dine?
fair

Saty. 30 Henri Quatre & [A] Budget of 105.50   755.75
Blunders
fair

October
Mon. 2d. Rob Roy [Macgregor] & Of 99.
age tomorrow
(Election Day)
Heavy Rain

Wedy. 4 Geo[rge] Barnwell & [The] 143.
Broken Sword
Mr. Jeff[erson] ill. [ACDA
announces *A Short Reign
and a Merry One* in place
of George Barnwell.]
dull & Rain

Frid. 6 Pizarro & Belles Without 173.50   415.50
Beaux
fine & Cool

Saty. 7 No performance.

Mon. 9 [The] Way to Get Married 117.50
& [The] Innkeeper's
Daughter
Warm

Wed. 11 No performance.

Frid. 13 a Short Reign & C[eter]a 242.50
Helpless Animals & Belles
Without Beaux
fine

Saty. 14 [The] Heart of Mid-Lothian & 57.75 417.75
[The] Review
Heavy rain

Mon. 16 [A] Cure for the Heartache & 103.50
Turn Out
fine & Cool

Wed. 18 Ivanhoe* & [The] Agreeable 393.50
Surprize
fine

Cooper Frid. 20 Brutus & [The] Wedding Day 259.50
[As Lucius Junius. ACDA]
Very fine

" Saty. 21 Othello & High life below 206.50 963.
Stairs
[As Othello. ACDA]
fine

22d. (Hughes & Mrs. Young left
the Theatre.)

C[ooper] Mon. 23 [The] School for Scandal & 263.75
Cath[erine] & Petruchio
[As Charles Surface and
Petruchio. ACDA]
Mild

" Wed. 25 Virginius* & Where Shall I 328.75
dine?
[See preface to this season.]
Very Cold & fair

[313]

" Frid. 27 [The] Mountaineers & Rosina 234.75
     [Cooper as Octavian in *The
     Mountaineers*.]   Miss
     Seymour's 1st. app[ear-
     ance. ACDA announces
     her as Rosina.]
                   very Cold

" Saty. 28 Virginius & [A] Budget of 164.50   991.75
     Blunders
     [Cooper   as   Virginius.
     ACDA]
                        Cold

     Mon. 30 Macbeth & Turn Out   414.75
Cooper's Benefit   [As Macbeth. ACDA]
                             fine

November
     Wed. 1 [The] Village Lawyer & [The] 373.75
           Vampire* & Rosina
                             fair

     Frid. 3 Wild Oats & [The] Vampire 403.50   1192.
                     fine   ———
                                       $5911.50

     Cooper averaged With Ben[efits] 7 nights $260.
          27 Nights averaged $218.75
               after paying Cooper.
     Mr. Hathwell did not play till 18 October.

PHILADELPHIA SEASON, COMMENC[ING] 10TH NOVEMBER, 1820[, ENDING
                    APRIL 18, 1821.]

                 [Warren & Wood]

PREFACE—**November 27**: Wood has written in this entry, "Changed
to [A] B[udget] of Blunders, Mrs. Wood ill." According to a playbill of
November 27, 1820 in possession of the Historical Society of Pennsyl-

                        [314]

vania, Mrs. Wood was to have played Lady Racket in *Three Weeks after Marriage*. DP announces "a young gentleman of this city" as Young Norval; and *Recollections*, pp. 250–1, states that Edwin Forrest appeared on November 27, 1820 in *Douglas*. **December 2**: Warren writes in his *Diary*, "Forrest acts Young Norval. The Boy pleases very much." **December 29**: Warren writes in his *Diary*, "Mast[e]r For[r]est plays Frederick" in *Lovers' Vows* **February 5**: DP announces Mrs. Alsop as Donna Violante in *The Wonder*, with a song called *Felix Dearest*, accompanied by herself on the harp; and as six characters in *The Actress of All Work*. **March 7**: DP announces, "The orchestra will perform a national olio called *The Columbiad*, intended as an overture to a new farce, never performed, called *The Author's Night; or, The Bailiffs Outwitted*, by H. McMurtrie, M.D."

According to *Durang*, I, LXV, Williams appeared, on November 11, as Frederick in *The Poor Gentleman* and Baron Wellinghoerst in *Of Age Tomorrow*. According to the same authority, "Mrs. Barnes, during [her] engagement, played . . . Paul in [*The*] *Wandering Boys*," see the entry of March 5. In the entries of January 20, 22, 24, 26, 27 and 29, Wood has used a parenthesis, instead of ditto marks, to indicate that Kean was appearing. The tragedian's rôles were Macbeth, Lear, Leon (*Rule a Wife*), Bertram and Reuben Glenroy (*Town and Country*).

Sickness among the players handicapped the managers during this season. Vertically across the entries of April 9, 11, 13, 14 and 16, Wood has written the notation "Mrs. Darley ill from 2d. Feb[ruar]y to the End of the Season" and throughout the manuscript, from the entry of February 2 to the last entry of the season, various references to her illness.

The managers had also to contend with adverse business conditions. In consequence, as *Durang*, I, LXXIII, reveals, "in March, 1821, the nineteenth week of the season, the actors were not paid in full; on the twentieth week, there was one-third salary; twenty-first and twenty-second weeks, one-third. This was in consequence of an agreement between the actors and managers." Wood alludes to this "agreement" in a notation, "Benefits p[ai]d but ½ Salary," written over the notation, just quoted, regarding Mrs. Darley's illness. Following his record of the Baltimore Spring Season of 1821, Wood has made a notation of the sums of money "Paid on Star Engag[emen]ts . . . from 10 Nov[embe]r, 1820 to June, 1821." This notation, which is interesting in view of the fact that the sums were paid while the receipts were averaging only $418.50 a night, is as follows: "Mr. Cooper, 821.37; For[r]est, 39; Mr.

[315]

Kean, 5747.12; Mrs. Alsop, 309.87; Mrs. Barnes, 243.37; McMurtrie [, the author of *The Author's Night*,] 366; Warren's Ben[efi]t, 87; Mr. Barnes, 175; Mr. Kean, 1450 [; total, $] 9238.73."

During this season, one of the causes of a falling-off in patronage was a dislike of the Walnut Street Theatre, to which Warren & Wood had to move after a fire had destroyed the Chesnut Street Theatre on April 2, 1820. See the general introduction, p. 35.

[Walnut Street Theatre

[November]

	Frid. 10 Wild Oats & [The] Agreeable Surprize	459.75	
	Very Cold		
Williams' 1st. app[earance]	Saty. 11 [The] Poor Gentleman & Of Age tomorrow	175.50	
	Snow		
Mrs. Williams' 1st. app[earance]	Mon. 13 As You Like it & Rosina [As Rosalind. DP]	308.75	
	Cold		
	Wed. 15 [The] Road to Ruin & [A] Budget of Blunders	338.50	
	Cold		
	Frid. 17 Henri Quatre* & Where Shall I dine?	397.50	
	Cold		
	Saty. 18 a Short Reign and a Merry One & [Little] Red R[id-ing] Hood & High life bel[ow] Stairs	245.50	1290.25
	Mild		
	Mon. 20 Henri Quatre & Turn Out	232.50	
	fair		

[316]

Wed. 22 [The] Wonder & [The] 360.50
         Vampire*
                   Mild

Frid. 24 Henri Quatre & [The] Vampire 293.50
                   Mild

Saty. 25 Rob Roy [Macgregor] & [The] 309.75   1196.25
         Anatomist
                   Cold

         Mon. 27 Douglas, [Little] R[ed] R[iding] 319.75
Forrest['s] 1st.   Hood & 3 Weeks after
                Marriage
             [See preface to this season.]
                 Very Cold

Wed. 29 [The] Busy Body & [The] 247.75
         Vampire
                   Cold

         December
         Frid. 1 [The] Iron Chest & Helpless 214.50
                Animals
                 Very Cold

         Saty. 2 Douglas & [The] Ruffian Boy 378.75
E. Forrest['s] 2d.   [See preface to this season.]
app[earance]
                   Mild

Mon. 4 [The] Foundling of the Forest 190.75
         & Belles Without Beaux
               Storm all day

Wed. 6 [The] Heart of Mid-Lothian, 325.50
         Love among [the] Roses
         & [The] Ruffian Boy
                   fair

[317]

Frid. 8 The Steward* & [The] 294.50
Vampire

rain

Saty. 9 Rob Roy [Macgregor] & Belles 194.   914.75
Without Beaux

Rain

Mon. 11 She Stoops to Conquer & 264.25
[The] Magpie & [the]
Maid

Rainy

Wed. 13 Wanted a Wife & Love 146.50
am[on]g [the] Roses &
High life below stairs

Rainy

Cooper   Frid. 15 Virginius & Where Shall I 646.
dine?
[As Virginius. DP]

rain all day

C[ooper]   Saty. 16 Macbeth & [The] Wedding 359.
Day
[As Macbeth. DP]

dull

C[ooper]   Mon. 18 Virginius & Turn Out   495.75
[As Virginius. DP]

rain

Tues. 19 (Postponed, Wood ill.)
[DP announces *Othello* and
The Anatomist]

C[ooper]   Wed. 20 Bertram & [The] Review   385.
[As Bertram. DP]

fair

[318]

C[ooper]   Thurs. 21 Hamlet & [The] Anatomist   240.50
                     [As Hamlet. DP]
                               Rain

C[ooper]   Frid. 22 Richard 3d. & [The] Hunter 314.50
                     of the Alps
                     [As Richard. DP]
                               Cold

           Saty. 23 Virginius & Cath[erine] & 773.50 2209.25
Benefit [of] Cooper   Petruchio
                     [As Virginius and Petru-
                     chio. DP]
                               Cold

           Tues. 26 [The] Fate of Calas* & Killing 193.75
                     no Murder
                               Snow

           Wed. 27 George Barnwell, [The] Scotch   149.75
                     Ghost & [The] Ruffian
                     Boy
                               Cold

           Frid. 29 Lovers['] Vows & the Ghost 258.59
Forrest['s] 3d.   [See preface to this season.]
                               Rain

           Saty. 30 (No performance.)   597.

1821. January
          Mon. 1 Ivanhoe* & [The] Agreeable 888.75
                     Surprize
                               fair

          Wed. 3 [The] Robbers & Raising the 147.
                     Wind
                        very Cold

[319]

Frid. 5 Ivanhoe & [The] Adopted 170.
Child
fine

Saty. 6 [The] Mountaineers & [The] 215.50 1421.25
Forrest's Benefit— Village Lawyer
4th night [As Octavian in *The Mountaineers.* DP.]
Snow

Mon. 8 Richard 3d. & Killing no 1178.75
Mr. [Edmund] Murder
Kean [As Richard. DP]
fair

" Wed. 10 Othello & Where Shall I 837.50
dine[?]
[Kean as Othello. DP]
Cold

" Frid. 12 [The] Merchant of Venice & 1241.
Turn Out
[Kean as Shylock. DP]
Cold

" Saty. 13 Hamlet & [The] Ghost 718. 3975.25
[Kean as Hamlet. DP]
Storm of Snow

K[ean] Mon. 15 Richard 3d. & [A] Budget of 833.
Blunders
[As Richard. DP]
Cold

" Wed. 17 Brutus & [The] Hunter of the 897.
Alps
[Kean as Brutus. DP]
Cold

[320]

Frid. 19 [A] New Way to pay old debts 1397.
[Kean's] 1st.   & [The] Wedding day
Ben[efi]t   [As Sir Giles Overreach in
A New Way to Pay Old Debts. DP]

fair

Sat. 20 Macbeth & [The] Village 615.50 3742.50
Lawyer

Cold

Mon. 22 King Lear & Raising the Wind 1351.

Cold

Wed. 24 Rule a Wife & Have a Wife & 699.50
[The] Adopted Child

very Cold

Frid. 26 Bertram & High life below 650.75
Stairs

Cold

Saty. 27 Town & Country & [The] 675. 3376.25
Dead Alive

Cold

Mon. 29 King Lear & [The] Comet 889.50

Cold

Wed. 31 Othello & [The] Review 1199.37
Mr. Kean's 2d.   [As Othello. DP]
Benefit

Warm

February
Kean   Frid. 2 [The] Merchant of Venice & 400.50
[The] Dead Alive
[As Shylock. DP]

Mild

[321]

" Saty. 3 [The] Iron Chest & [The] 727.25 3216.62
Anatomist
[Kean as Sir Edward Mor-
timer in *The Iron Chest.*
DP]
Rain

Mon. 5 [The] Wonder & [The] Actress 393.
[Mrs.] Alsop of all Work*
[See preface to this season.]
fair

" Wed. 7 [The] Country Girl & [The] 377.
Devil to pay
[Mrs. Alsop as Miss Peggy
in *The Country Girl* and
Nell in *The Devil to Pay.*
DP]
fair

" Frid. 9 As You like it & [The] Actress 322.50
of all Work
[Mrs. Alsop as Rosalind and
as six characters in *The
Actress of All Work.* DP]
fair

Saty. 10 [The] Child of the Mountain* 218.75 1311.25
& [The] Review
mild & fine

Mrs. Alsop Mon. 12 [The] School for Scandal & 297.75
[The] Romp
[As Lady Teazle in *The
School for Scandal* and
Priscilla Tomboy in *The
Romp.* DP]
fine

[322]

"   Wed. 14 [The] Belle's Stratagem &   179.75
              [The] Day after the
              Wedding
           [Mrs. Alsop as Letitia
              Hardy in *The Belle's
              Stratagem* and Lady
              Elizabeth in *The Day
              after the Wedding.* DP]
                               Rain

"   Frid. 16 The Rivals & Matrimony   65.50
              [Mrs. Alsop as Lydia
              Languish in *The Rivals*
              and Clara in *Matrimony.*
              DP]
                          Snow Storm

"   Saty. 17 [The] Midnight Hour, For- 135.   678.
              tune's frolic & [The] Devil
              to pay
              [Mrs. Alsop as Flora in *The
              Midnight Hour* and Nell in
              The Devil to Pay. DP]

           Mon. 19 [The] Will, [The] Actress of all 619.50
Ben[efi]t [of]   Work & Killing no
Mrs.] Alsop   Murder
              [As Albina Mandeville in
              The Will and as six char-
              acters in *The Actress of
              all Work.* DP]
                            very fair

Mrs. Barnes Wed. 21 Romeo & Juliet & Raising the 187.50
              Wind
              [As Juliet. DP]
                              fair

           Thurs. 22 She W[oul]d be a Soldier & 522.75
W[ashington's]   Sprigs of Laurel
Birthday
                           rainy
                    [323]

Frid. 23 Isabella & of age tomorrow   156.75
Mrs. B[arnes]   [As Isabella. DP]
                                    dull

"   Saty. 24 (No performance.)   1486.50

Mon. 26 [The] Castle Spectre & Ella   186.75
Mrs. B[arnes]   Rosenberg
                       [As Angela in *The Castle
                       Spectre* and as Ella Rosen-
                       berg. DP]
                                    Rain

"   Wed. 28 Jane Shore & [The] Broken   141.50
               Sword
               [Mrs. Barnes as Jane Shore
               and as Myrtillo in *The
               Broken Sword*. DP]
                                    Rain

March
"   Frid. 2 [The] Honey Moon & [The]   193.50
               Falls of Clyde
               [Mrs. Barnes as Juliana in
               The Honey Moon and
               Ellen Enfield in *The Falls
               of Clyde*. DP]
                                    very fair

"   Saty. 3 [The] Stranger & [The] Day   169.50   691.25
               after the Wedding
               [Mrs. Barnes as Mrs. Hal-
               ler in *The Stranger* and
               Lady Elizabeth in *The
               Day after the Wedding*.
               DP]
                                    Cold & dull

[324]

Mrs. B[arnes'] Mon. 5 Douglas, [The] Actress of all   492.50
Ben[efit]   Work* & [The] Wander-
                     ing Boys
                     [As Young Norval in
                     Douglas and as six char-
                     acters in *The Actress of
                     All Work*. DP]
                                              fair

Author's Benefit Wed. 7 [The] Child of the Mountain   791.50
                       & [The] Author's Night*
                       [See preface to this season.]
                                              fine

Warren's Benefit Frid. 9 [The] Exile & Tom Thumb   319.50
                       [the Great]
                       [As the Exile. DP]
                                              fair

              Saty. 10 Speed the Plough & Sprigs of   169.75   1773.25
                       Laurel
                                              fine

              Mon. 12 [The] Exile & Lovers[']   74.
                      Quarrels
                                              fair

              Thurs. 15 [The] Merry Wives of Windsor   190.75
                        & [The] Dead Alive
                                              fine

Barnes   Frid. 16 [The] Rivals & [The] Turn-   104.50
                       pike Gate
                       [As Sir Anthony Absolute
                       in *The Rivals* and Crack
                       in *The Turnpike Gate*.
                       DP]
                                   Thunder at Night

[325]

    "   Saty. 17 [The] Steward & Fortune's   71.75   441.
frolic
[Barnes as Item in *The
Steward* and Robin Rough-
head in *Fortune's Frolic.*
DP]
Severely Cold

Barnes   Mon. 19 [The] School for Scandal &   105.50
[The] Poor Soldier
[As Sir Peter Teazle in *The
School for Scandal* and
Darby in *The Poor
Soldier.* DP]
very Cold

    "   Wed. 21 Laugh When You Can &   107.50
Sprigs of Laurel
[Barnes as Bonus in *Laugh
When You Can* and Nip-
perkin in *Sprigs of Laurel.*
DP]
fine

    "   Frid. 23 She Stoops to Conquer &   138.50   351.50
[The] Turnpike Gate
[Barnes as Tony Lumpkin
in *She Stoops to Conquer*
and Crack in *The Turn-
pike Gate.* DP]
fair

    "   Saty. 24 (No performance.)

              Mon. 26 [A] Bold Stroke for a Hus-   350.50
Barnes' Benefit   band, Collins' Ode & [A]
Mogul Tale
[Barnes as Don Caesar,
Mrs. Barnes as Olivia in

*A Bold Stroke for a Hus-
band.* Barnes as Johnny
Atkins in *A Mogul Tale.*
DP.]

Cold

Wed. 28 Exchange no Robbery* &   600.50
[Benefit of] Jefferson   Love among [the] Roses &
                              Who's the Dupe[?]
                              [As Sam Swipes in *Ex-
                              change no Robbery* and
                              Old Doily in *Who's the
                              Dupe?* DP]

fair

Frid. 30 [The] Heir at Law, [Little]   102.50
[Benefit of] Mrs.   R[ed] R[iding] Hood &
Baker [&] Misses   [The] Spoil'd Child
[C. & K.] Durang   [Mrs. Baker as Cicely
                        Homespun in *The Heir
                        at Law*, Miss C. Durang
                        as Lubin in *Little Red
                        Riding Hood* and Little
                        Pickle in *The Spoiled
                        Child*. Miss K. Durang
                        as Little Red Riding
                        Hood. DP]

fair

Saty. 31 (No performance.)   1053.50

April
[Benefit of] Mon. 2 Ivanhoe & Inkle & Yarico   197.
Mr. Herbert   [As Isaac in *Ivanhoe.* DP]

fair

[Benefit of] Wed. 4 Richard 3d. & [A] Tale of   384.50
Mr. & Mrs.   Mystery
Williams   [Mrs. Williams as Richard.
                DP]

fine

[327]

[Benefit of] Frid. 6 [The] Clandestine Marriage & 110.50   692.
Mr. & Mrs.   [The] Highland Reel
Francis

                                          dull

           Saty. 7 (No performance)

[Edmund] Mon. 9 Richard 3d. & Matrimony 613.50
Kean   [As Richard. DP]

                                          dull

"   Wed. 11 Othello & [The] Comet   528.50
                  [Kean as Othello. DP]

                                          dull

"   Frid. 13 Riches* & [The] Broken Sword 523.50
                  [Kean as Luke in *Riches*.
                  DP]

                                          fine

"   Saty. 14 King   Lear   &   Lovers['] 412.50   2078.
                  Quarrels
                  [Kean as Lear. DP]

                                          fair

"   Mon. 16 [The] Iron Chest & Inkle & 537.75 2615.75
                  Yarico
                  [Kean as Sir Edward Mor-
                  timer in *The Iron Chest*.
                  DP]

                                          fine

Benefit [of] Wed. 18 Venice Preserv'd & [The] Deaf 1005.75
Mr. Kean   Lover
                  [As Jaffier in *Venice Pre-
                  served*. DP]

                                        fine   ————

                                              $37345.87

89 nights averaging 418.50
after Stars and Benefits averaged 304.50

BALTIMORE [SPRING[SEASON, COMMENCING APRIL 23D., [ENDING JUNE 22,] 1821.

[Warren & Wood]

PREFACE—**June 1:** After the ditto marks in this entry occurs the notation, "Wood's Benefit." ACDA announces Wood as Prince John, with H. Wallack as Sir Brian de Bois, in *Ivanhoe*. **June 15:** The players receiving this benefit are unquestionably the elder Jeffersons. ACDA announces that Mr. Jefferson is to sing. In the entry of April 23 Wood has written "Hath[well] ill" and, in the entries of April 25, 27 and 29, ditto marks to signify that the actor is still on the sick list. After his record of this season, Wood has written: "N. B. Benefits Were at ½ Salary. Mrs. Darley absent the whole Season, 34 nights & 40 in Phil[adelphia]. My Benefit p[ai]d full Charges. All the rest only ½."

[April]

[Edmund] Kean	Mon. 23	Richard 3d. & Where Shall I dine? [As Richard. ACDA] Hath-[well] ill. Very fair	789.75
"	Wed. 25	Othello & [The] Wedding Day [Kean as Othello. ACDA] fine	611.50
"	Frid. 27	[The] Merchant of Venice & [The] Hunter of the Alps [Kean as Shylock. ACDA] fair	799.62
"	Saty. 28	[A] New Way to pay old Debts* & [The] Comet [Kean as Sir Giles in *A New Way to Pay Old Debts.* ACDA] fine	696.75 2897.62

[329]

Kean Mon. 30 King Lear & Lovers['] 929.75
      Quarrels
      [As Lear. ACDA]
           fair

    May
"   Wed. 2 Macbeth & [The] Deaf Lover 630.75
      [Kean as Macbeth. ACDA]
           Rain

"   Frid. 4 [The] Iron Chest & Fortune's 602.50
      frolic
      [Kean as Sir Edward Mor-
      timer in *The Iron Chest.*
      ACDA]
          fair & Cold

"   Saty. 5 Brutus & [The] Ghost 430.50 2593.50
      [Kean as Brutus. ACDA]
           fair

"   Mon. 7 Hamlet & [The] Village 652.75
      Lawyer
      [Kean as Hamlet. ACDA]
           fair

"   Wed. 9 Town & Country & [The] 633.25
      Dead Alive
      [Kean as Reuben Glenroy
      in *Town and County.*
      ACDA]
           fair

"   Frid. 11 Bertram & Raising the Wind 570.75
      [Kean as Bertram. ACDA]
           fair

"   Saty. 12 Riches* & High Life below   495.50   2352.25
                Stairs
                [Kean as Luke in *Riches*.
                ACDA]
                                    Warm

            Mon. 14 Othello & Who's the Dupe?   782.50
Mr. Kean's Benefit   [As Othello. ACDA]
                                    fine

Kean   Tues. 15 Richard 3d. & [A] Budget of 654.50
                Blunders
                [As Richard. ACDA]
                                    dull

            Wed. 16 [The] Wonder & [The] Actress 219.25
[Mrs.] Alsop   of all Work*
                [As Donna Violante in *The
                Wonder and six char-
                acters in *The Actress of
                All Work*. ACDA]
                                    rainy

"   Frid. 18 [The] Country Girl & [The]   158.50
                Devil to pay
                [Mrs. Alsop as Miss Peggy
                in *The Country Girl*.
                ACDA]
                                    Rain

"   Saty. 19 (No performance)   1814.75

            Mon. 21 As You Like it & [The] Day   197.75
                after [the] Wedding
                                    fair

            Wed. 23 [The] Rivals & [The] Romp   162.75
                                    Rain
                    [331]

Frid. 25 [The] Belle's Stratagem & Is   155.75
He Jealous [?]*
Rain

Sat. 26 Rosina, [The] Midnight Hour   106.50   622.75
& Turn Out
Rain

Mon. 28 [The] Will & [The] Actress of   303.50
Benefit [of Mrs.]   all Work
Alsop   [As Abina Mandeville in
                      The Will. ACDA]
                                fair
Wed. 30 Rob Roy [Macgregor] & [The]   202.75
H. Wal[lack]   Adopted Child
                  [As Rob Roy Macgregor.
                  ACDA]
                                Warm

June
"   Frid. 1 Ivanhoe & Killing No Murder   316.75
              [See preface to this season.]
                                fair

"   Saty. 2 [The] Mountaineers & [The]   93.50   916.50
              Review
              [H. Wallack as Octavian in
              The Mountaineers and
              Looney Mactwolter in
              The Review. ACDA]
                                fair

"   Mon.   4 Therese* & [The] Anatomist   140.
              [H. Wallack as Carwin
              in *Therese*. ACDA]
                                fair

[332]

Wed. 6 Pizarro & Raising the Wind 171.50
          [H. Wallack as Rolla.] War-
          ren's Ben[efit. ACDA
          announces him as Las
          Casas in *Pizarro*.]
                                    fair

"   Frid. 8 Therese & [The] Dead Alive 138.25
          [H. Wallack as Carwin in
          Therese. ACDA]
                                    fine

"   Saty. 9 [The] Foundling of [the] forest 60.   509.75
          & [The] Deaf Lover
          [H. Wallack as Florian, the
          foundling. ACDA]
                      Rain & Thunder

          Mon. 11 [The] Warlock of [the] Glen,* 327.75
H. Wall[ack's]   Love am[on]g [the] Roses,
Benefit   Syl[vester] Dag[gerwood]
                    & E[llen] Rosenberg
                    [As Andrew in *The Warlock
                    of the Glen*. ACDA]
                                    fair

          Wed. 13 She Stoops to Conquer & [A] 97.75
                    Tale of Mystery
                              Showery

[Benefit of] Frid. 15 [The] Warlock of the Glen, 317.
Mr. & Mrs.   Exchange no Robbery*
Jefferson   [See preface to this season.]
                              very fine

          Saty. 16 [No performance)   742.50

[Benefit of] Mon. 18 Richard 3d. & [The] Poor 218.
Blisset & Herbert   Soldier
                    [Herbert as Richard. ACDA]
                              very fine
                    [333]

[Benefit of] Wed. 20 Romeo & Juliet & [The] High- 159.
Mr. & Mrs.   land Reel
Williams   [Williams as Romeo, Mrs.
                       Williams   as   Juliet.
                       ACDA]
                                     fair

         Frid. 22 Too late for Dinner* & [The] 199.50   576.50
                Vampire
                       fair   ————
                                 $12,726.12
           34 Nights Averaging $734
        after deducting Stars & Benefits 265.75

PHILADELPHIA SUMMER SEASON, COMMENCING 2D. JULY[, ENDING
16TH JULY,] 1821.

[Warren & Wood]

PREFACE—**July 4**: In this entry Wood has written "Chang[e]d from Too
late for dinner & [The] R[ival] Sold[ie]r[s.]" In his entry of this date
Warren records, "Obliged to Change both play & Farce. Jefferson ill.
Play'd [The] Warlock of the Glen & [The] Adopted Child." To the
right of the entries of July 2, 4 and 6 Wood has noted "Shares $15 each;"
to the right of the entries of July 9, 11 and 13, "Shares $10 Each;" and,
to the right of the entry of Jul: 16, "Share $4 Each." Below his record
of the season Wood has written "21 Shares" and "$49 performers
on Sal[ar?]y."

          July
       Mony. 2 Therese* & [The] Deaf Lover 271.50
                        Rain

        Wed. 4 [The] Warlock of the Glen, 276.50
                    Olio & [The] Adopted
                    Child
                    [See preface to this season.]
                        very Cold

        Frid. 6 [The] Road to Ruin & [The] 126.   672.
                    Wedding day
                       very Cool

Mon. 9 Therese & [The] Spoil'd Child   113.75
                              fair

Wed. 11 Too late for Dinner* & [The]   146.75
                 Irishman in London
                                    fine

Frid. 13 Rob Roy [Macgregor] & [The]   234.75
                 Warlock of the Glen
                                    fair

Mon. 16 [The] Vampire & Too late   216.00
                 for Dinner
                                    fair   —————
                                              $1385.25

7 Nights averaged $197.75

WASHINGTON [SEASON, COMMENCING AUGUST 8, ENDING
OCTOBER 9,] 1821.

[Warren & Wood]

PREFACE—**August 8**: DNI announces, "The new theatre at Washington
will be opened by an occasional address to be spoken by Mr. Wood."
For an account of the destruction of the Washington theatre by fire
on April 19, 1820, see the general introduction, p. 35. **September 25**:
Wood has written in this entry, "Francis relinquished." DNI of the
same date announces Mrs. Francis as Miss Hebe Wintertop, with various
songs, duetts, &c. in *The Dead Alive*."

Over his record of this season Wood has written "Washington, New
Theatre, Opened Wed[nesda]y, 8th August, 1821;" and, in the entry of
August 11, "Share $7;" in the entry of August 18, "Share $8 each (that
is, for himself and Warren;) in the entry of August 25, "Share $7;" in
the entry of September 1, "Share $6;" and, in the entry of September
6, "Share $5."

On the page preceding his record of this season Wood has written the
names of the members of the "Company at Washington 1821." They
are Messrs. "Warren, Wood, Jefferson, Francis, H. Wallack, Wheatley,
Burke, Robertson, Nichols, Hathwell, Scrivener, Darley, Baker, Parker,

[335]

Murray, Johnston, J. Jefferson;" Mesdames "Wood, Jefferson, Francis, H. Wallack, Burke, Darley, Lefolle, Bloxton, Baker;" and "Miss Seymour" and the "Misses Hathwell," (see the index to players).

In Volume II of the *Account Book*, Wood has included an "Inventory of Scenery at Washington [,] Rec[eive]d from J. Caldwell at Alexandria 27[th] July [,] 1821." This "inventory" includes such items as "1 Cave," "1 Horizon," "Pantaloon's House," "Juliet's Balcony," "Capulet's Tomb," "Hot House for [The] W[ay] to Get Married" and "Bridge (H[eart] of Mid Lothian.)"

August
Wedy. 8 Address, She Stoops to Con- 114.
quer & [The] Spoil'd
Child
[See preface to this season.]
fine

Frid. 10 Venice Preserv'd & Where 124.
Shall I dine?*
fine

Saty. 11 [The] Road to Ruin & Belles 122.50   360.50
Without Beaux*
Warm

Tuesday 14 [A] Short Reign & [a] Merry 98.
One,* [The] Scotch Ghost
& [The] Chil[dren] in the
Wood
Warm

Thurs. 16 She W[oul]d be a Soldier* & 165.50
[The] Romp
very hot

Saty. 18 [The] Robbers & [The] Poor 172.   435.50
Soldier
excessive Heat

[336]

Tuesy. 21 Rob Roy [Macgregor] & [The] 122.50
Wedding Day
Cool

Thursy. 23 Wild Oats & Too late for 129.50
dinner*
Cool

Saty. 25 Town & Country & Helpless 99.50 351.50
Animals*
Cool

Tues. 28 Isabella & [The] Warlock of 156.50
the Glen*
Cool

Thurs. 30 [The] Foundling of the Forest 116.25
& [The] Highland Reel
fair & Warm

September
Saty. 1 [The] Vampire,* My Grand- 106. 378.75
mother & [The] Devil to
pay
Dull

Tues. 4 Henri Quatre* & [The] Comet 94.50
fair

Thurs. 6 [The] Poor Gentleman & 98.50
Rosina
fine

Saty. 8 Romeo & Juliet & [The] Deaf 146.50 339.50
Lover
Warm

Mon. 10 Speed the Plough & [The] 46.50
Weathercock
Warm

[337]

Tues. 11 [The] Castle Spectre & For-   57.75
    tune's frolic
        Excessively hot

Thurs. 13 [The] Fair American & Of Age   85.25
    Tomorrow
          Cool

Saty. 15 [The] Iron Chest & [The]   138.50
    Adopted Child
        Cool

Tues. 18 Pizarro & [The] Agreeable   136.50
    Surprize
        Cool

Thurs. 20 [The] Mountaineers & [The]   63.75
    Adopted Child
        Rain

Saty. 22 [The First Part of] Henry 4th   254.50   454.75
    & [The] Irishman in
    London
        Cool

Tues. 25 [The] Heir at Law & [The]   75.
    Dead Alive
    [See preface to this season.]
        dull

        Thurs. 27 [The] Way to get Married,   151.50
[Benefit of]   Olio & Miss in her Teens
Mr. & Mrs. Burke
        very fine

        Saty. 29 Abaellino & [The] Review   111.25
[Benefit of]
Mr. Nichols &
Mrs. Baker   fair

[338]

[October]

Tues. 2nd. [The] Clandestine Marriage &   313.50
[Benefit of] Mr. &   [The] Spanish Barber
Mrs. Jefferson

                       very fine

Thurs. 4th. Richard 3d. Syl[vester] Dag-   173.
[Benefit of]   g[erwoo]d & Bombastes
Mr. & Mrs.   Furioso
H. Wallack   [Wallack as Richard and
                 Sylvester Daggerwood.
                 DNI.]

                       fair

Saty. 6 Jane Shore & No Song no   108.
[Benefit of]   Supper
Mr. & Mrs. Darley [Darley as William in *Jane*
                 Shore and Crop in *No*
                 Song No Supper. Mrs.
                 Darley as Jane Shore.
                 DNI]

                       fair

Tues[da]y [9] [The] Merry Wives of Wind-   313.50
              sor* & [A] Budget of
              Blunders

                  Cold & fair

                            $3894.25

29 Nights Averaging $134.08

BALTIMORE [AUTUMN] SEASON, COMMENCING OCTOBER 12TH., [ENDING
NOVEMBER 9TH,] 1821.

[Warren & Wood]

PREFACE—**October 13**: See the preface to the Baltimore Autumn Season, 1820, September 12, for an explanation of "Monument fund." **October 15**: In this entry Wood has written "Chang[e]d from Isabella, Mrs. Wood Sick." **October 22**: In his entry of this date, Warren records in his *Diary*, "Play chang[e]d from [The] Honey Moon—Wallack ill." According to ACDA, he was to have played Duke Aranza. **November 3**: In this entry Wood has written, "Anatomist, Ch[an]g[e]d to Anatomist, Mr. Burke Sick." The afterpiece was evidently to have been *Helpless Animals* with Burke in the rôle of Martin.

Under his record of this season Wood has written "Tues[day] 6. Mr. [H.] Wallack ill & the farce Chang[ed] to F[ortune's] Frolic." It follows that *Too Late for Dinner* was supplanted in the bill of November 7.

It has been advisable to omit other notations from the printed version. These include: "Miss Sey[mour?], Mrs. Lefolle, Mrs. Baker" in the entry of October 12; "d[itt]o," referring to Mrs. Lefolle, in the entry of October 13; "Mrs. Baker," in the entry of October 15; "Lefolle (paid 2 nights,) and ditto marks referring to Mrs. Baker, in the entry of October 17; "d[itt]o" referring to Lefolle and ditto marks referring to Mrs. Baker, in the entry of October 19; "d[itt]o" referring to Lefolle, in the entry of October 20; "Lefolle," in the entry of October 22; "p[ai]d 2 nights," Mr. & Mrs. H. W[allack?,] Miss Seymour [, whom ACDA announces as Anne Page in *The Merry Wives of Windsor*,] Mrs. Lefolle & Mrs. Baker," in the entry of October 24; "Mrs. Baker," in the entry of October 28; and "Mrs. Baker" and "Miss Seymour Sick," in the entry of October 27. From this last notation it might be inferred that these references are usually to the illness of players. In Wood's entry of October 29 there are a "d[itt]o" referring to "Mrs. Baker" and a "d[itt]o" to "Miss Seymour." In this entry there also occurs the notation "p[ai]d 3 nights." Other notations it has been advisable to omit are "d[itt]o" referring to Mrs. Baker and "d[itt]o" referring to Miss Seymour, in the entry of October 31; "d[itt]o" referring to Miss Seymour in the entry of November 1; "d[itt]o" referring to "Mr. Burke Sick" of the previous entry, followed by "& Blissett," in the entry of November 5; "d[itt]o" referring to Blissett and "p[ai]d 5 nights," in the entry of November 6; and "p[ai]d 4 nights," in the entry of November 9.

Under his record of this season Wood has written: "Nov. 3. Mrs. Jeff[erson] refused L. Allworth 6 lengths & 6 lines intended for Tuesday 6th (but Chang[e]d for Burke's illness. Tues. 6. Mr. Wallack ill & the farce Chang[ed] to [Fortune's] Frolic."

October
Friday 12 [The] West Indian & [The] 116.
Review
Storm all day

Saty. 13 [The] Fair American & Of Age 150.50   266 50
Ben[efit] of   tomorrow
Monument fund   [See preface to this season.]
                         fine

Mon. 15 [The] Road to Ruin & Help- 217.50
        less Animals
        [See preface to this season.]
                         fair

Wed. 17 [The] Point of Honor & [The] 190.50
        Ruffian Boy
                         Cool

Frid. 19 [The] Follies of a Day, Miss in 224.50
        her Teens & Paul &
        Virginia
                         fine

Saty. 20 Speed the Plough & [The] 124.50   757.
        Spoil'd Child
                         fine

Mon. 22 [The] Honey Moon & Where 187.50
        Shall I dine?
        Chang[e]d to S[he Stoops]
        to Conquer. Mr. H.
        Wallack sick. [See pref-
        ace to this season.]
                         fair

Wed. 24 [The] Merry Wives of Wind- 287.75
        sor & Paul & Virginia
                         fine

Frid. 26 [A] Short Reign & [a] merry 218.50
        one, Belles With[out]
        Beaux & [The] Poor
        Soldier
                         fine

[341]

Saty. 27 Wild Oats & [The] Children in   182.50   876.25
the Wood
fine

Mon. 29 Isabella & [The] Romp   287.5C
mild & fine

Wed. 31 Henri   Quatre   &   [The] 321.
Anatomist
rain

November
Booth   Thurs. 1st. Richard 3d. & My Grand- 383.25
mother
[As Richard. ACDA]
fine

"   Frid. 2 [The] Iron Chest & [The] 315.50
Devil to pay
[Booth as Sir Edward Mor-
timer in *The Iron Chest.*
ACDA]
fine

Booth   Saty. 3 Othello & Helpless Animals 303.50 1610.75
[As   Othello. ACDA See
preface to this season.]
rain

"   Mon. 5 King Lear & [The] Ghost 360.50
[Booth as Lear. ACDA]
rain

"   Tues. 6 Town & Country & Too late 194.50
for Dinner
[Booth as Reuben Glenroy.
ACDA]

[342]

Ben[efi]t   Wed.   7 [The] Mountaineers & Turn   525.50
[of Booth]   Out
                [As Octavian in *The Moun-*
                taineers. ACDA]
                         fine

        Frid.   9 Wallace*&Valentine&Orson   964.50
                               —————

             Rain & Thunder

                                    $5555.50

19 Houses average (after deducting Mr. Booth's $406.) $271

PHILADELPHIA SEASON COMMENCING NOVEMBER 13, 1821, [ENDING
APRIL 26, 1822.]

[Warren & Wood]

PREFACE—**November 27**: *Durang*, II, Introductory, states, "On Tuesday evening, Nov[ember] 27, a benefit was given to the widow Baker and her children... Her husband had died in the summer at Washington, D. C. They both had been members of the company." **November 30**: In this entry Wood has also written the notation, "Mr. Wallack's accident." In DP appears this notice: "With great regret the managers have to announce the postponement of Mr. Wallack's engagement. On his journey to this city the carriage was overturned and he received so severe an injury as to render him wholly incapable of any professional exertion at present. Due notice will be given of his appearance here." In the November 30 entry of his *Diary*, Warren writes, "Wallack was to have open[e]d in Hamlet but was upset near Brunswick on his way thither— his leg broken and much Hurt." **December 1**: In this entry Wood has also written, "Mr. H. Wallack went to Brunswick;" and Warren adds, in his *Diary*, "No play—Wallack gone off to visit his Brother." In the entries of December 3 and 5 Wood has written "Mr. Wallack absent" and, in the entries of December 7 and 8, "d[itt]o d[itt]o," signifying that Mr. Wallack was still absent. See the comment on the entry of March 6. **December 19**: DP announces that there will be present deputations from the tribes of Grand Panis, Panis Republic, Panis Loups, O'Mahars, Kanzas, and Ottoes. **December 22**: DP "respectfully informs the

[343]

public that the Indian chiefs now in this city will visit the theatre this evening." See December 19. **January 28:** "During this season," states *Recollections*, p. 275, "occurred the frightful and well remembered destruction . . . by fire . . . of the Orphan Asylum, in which calamity more than twenty of its inmates perished. In the moment of the highest sympathy a benefit was offered and accepted. The public in their most generous feelings gave us a noble response, and from an assemblage as much distinguished by its brilliancy as its numbers, the large sum of $1760 was received. . . . Attached to the theatre as I have been for 47 years," Wood continues, "this is the only instance I [have] ever witnessed of a full house. On this memorable night every seat was occupied, from the orchestra to the remotest part of the gallery." **February 9:** To the right of the notation, "no performance," Wood has written, "Mr. Philipps' concert for Orphan Asylum." In the February 9 entry of his *Diary*, Warren alludes to "a Concert by Phillips [*sic*] assisted by the Company for the Ben[efi]t of the Orphan Asylum that gave $645." **February 20:** In this entry of the *Account Book* occurs the notation, "Wheatley's 1st app[ea]r[ance] since Sick." DP announces him as Rashleigh Osbaldistone in *Rob Roy Macgregor*. **March 6:** In this entry Wood has written, "Changed to [The] P[risoner] at Large (Mr. H. Wallack absent.")" In his *Diary*, Warren writes in exasperation, "Wallack went to see his brother and wrote not to insert his name until he sent word. He does as he pleases—we had to Change the after piece to the Pris[o]n[er] at Large." A playbill of March 6, 1822, in possession of the Historical Society of Pennsylvania, announces H. Wallack as Sir Hulbrand Ringstettin in *Undine*. In his March 8 entry Wood has written "(H. Wallack)" and, in his March 11 entry, "absent (H. Wallack.)" **March 22:** DP announces, "In the course of [*The Forty Thieves*] will appear a Living Elephant, (the largest animal of the kind ever exhibited in America), superbly caparisoned, with Riders, &c. in the Asiatic style." In his entry of March 23, Warren writes in his *Diary*, "The Elephant ag[ai]n—the Elephant [$]100, Phillips [*sic*, $]118." **April 5:** After "Frid. 5," Wood has written "(Good friday) Thursday.)" DP announces the bill for April 4. **April 8:** DP announces, "In act second, scene first of *The Snow Storm*, a winter view of the cottage and out houses of Peterhof. In this scene will be introduced a miniature carriage drawn by four dogs in complete harness with driver, &c. The most extraordinary trained animals of the kind perhaps ever exhibited." In his *Diary*, Warren writes that "these 4 dogs drew a carriage from Har-

[344]

risburg. We give $25 to shew 'em." **April 10:** This is the elder Jefferson. A playbill of April 10, in possession of the Historical Society of Pennsylvania, announces Jefferson as Don Lewis in *Love Makes a Man* and Ruttekin in *Robin Hood.* He is also to sing *Manager Strut* and *Sammy Sugarplumb and Polly Chitterlings.* **April 12:** Another playbill in possession of the same society announces H. Wallack as Baron Montaldi, with Mrs. Wallack as Marinetta in *The Peasant Boy.* Wallack is also to appear as Beggar, Friar, Flodoardo and Prince of Milan in *Rugantino* and Mrs. Wallack to dance. **April 15, 17, 19:** "The Managers respectfully inform the public that they have engaged Monsieur Labasse (pupil and member of the Royal Academy of Paris) and Monsieur Tatin." DP announces them in a "new Grand Ballet." *Durang,* II, Introductory, states that, on November 29, Smith played Captain Flash in *Miss in Her Teens* as well as Octavian.

"During this year," states *Recollections,* p. 277, Warren & Wood "suffered severely from sickness. Jefferson, Francis, Wheatley, and others were unable to appear for a third of the season." It has been necessary to omit from Wood's record a great many references to the illness of players and also to their absences.

At this time there seems to have been a weakening in the morale of the company. The Walnut Street Theatre was possibly as little liked by the players as by the public and business was even poorer than it had been during the previous Philadelphia season. Wood has written "Mr. Francis absent" in his entries of March 15 and 18 and the explanation, "Mr. Francis Sick" in his entry of March 20; but, in his entry of November 19, he has simply referred to the fact that "Mrs. H. Wallack [was] absent at Night & sent no excuse," in his entry of November 24, that "Miss Seymour [was] absent and not sick all night" and, in his entry of December 22, that "Blissett [was] absent all night." There is no record of any penalties exacted for these offences; and it must have exasperated Wood if policy compelled him to overlook them to a certain extent.

Under his record of this season, Wood has written: "6 nights at Close were to be ½ Sal[ar]y for a Week of 3 Nights—for all above $12 p[e]r W[ee]k & ⅔ for all Under."

[Walnut Street Theatre]

November

Tuesy. 13 [The] West Indian & [The]   368.
      Review

                fair

Wedy. 14 [The] Point of Honor, Help- 145.50
less Animals & Too late
for Dinner
                fair

Thurs. 15 [The] Devil's Bridge & [The] 265.50
Spoil'd Child
                dull

Fridy. 16 Wallace* & Of Age tomorrow 263.25
                Rain

Saty. 17 Rob Roy [Macgregor] & [The] 321.   1363.25
Ghost
                Dull

Mon. 19 Henri   Quatre   &   [The] 180.
Anatomist
                Cold

Tues. 20 Wallace & Valentine & Orson 320.50
                dull

Wed. 21 Wild Oats & [The] Vampire 181.50
                dull

Thurs. 22 [The] Honey Moon & Valen- 261.
Miss Drake's   tine & Orson
app[ea]r[ance]   [As Juliana in *The Honey
Moon*. DP]
                fine

Frid. 23 [The] Merry Wives of Wind- 170.
sor & [The] Ruffian Boy
                dull

Saty. 24 Isabella & Paul & Virginia 80.50 1193.50
                Rain

Mon. 26 Macbeth & Where Shall I 180.75
Mr. Pelby's 1st.   dine?
                 [As Macbeth. DP]
                            fair

Tues. 27 [The] Poor Gentleman & 460.
Mrs. Baker's benefit   Valentine & Orson
                 [See preface to this season.]
                            fine

Wedny. 28 She Stoops to Conquer & 188.50
                 Therese
                            fair

Thurs. 29 [The] Mountaineers & Miss 147.75
Master [George   in her teens
Frederick]   [As Octavian in *The Moun-*
Smith   *taineers.* DP]
                            dull

Frid. 30 Hamlet & Fortune's frolic
[J] Wallack   No performance. [See pref-
                 ace to this season.]

Decem[ber]
Saty. 1 Rob Roy [Macgregor] & Belles   977.
                Without Beaux
                Postponed. [See preface to
                this season.]

Mon. 3 Pizarro & My Grandmother 363.50
                            fair

Wed. 5 Bertram & [A] Budget of 163.75
                Blunders
                            Rain

Frid. 7 Pizarro & [The] Romp   258.
                            fair

Saty. 8 [The] Clandestine Marriage &   151.50   936.75
[The] Poor Soldier
Rain

P[elby]   Mon. 10 Venice Preserv'd & [The]   177.50
Highland Reel
[As Pierre in *Venice Preserved.* DP]
fine

Tues. 11 Rob Roy [Macgregor] & Belles   191.50
Without Beaux
fair

Wed. 12 Brutus & Cath[erine] & Petru-   360.75
Pelby['s] Ben[efit]   chio
[As Brutus and Petruchio. DP]
fine

Thurs. 13 [The] Devil's Bridge & [The]   70.75
Weathercock
Heavy rain

Frid. 14 Damon & Pythias* & Paul &   159.75
Virginia
Very Cold

Saty. 15 [A] Short Reign & [a] Merry   107.50   1067.75
One & Therese
Cold

Mon. 17 Damon & Pythias & [The]   206.55
Children in the Wood
Snow

Tues. 18 [The] School for Scandal &   95.50
[The] Comet
dull

Indians   Wedy. 19 Damon & Pythias & [The]   544.50
Poor Soldier
[See preface to this season.]
fair

Thurs. 20 [The] Foundling of the forest   66.50
& [The] Deaf Lover
heavy rain

Frid. 21 Damon & Pythias, Exhibition   147.50
of Small Sword & [My]
Grand Mother
Rain

Saty. 22 [The] Warlock of the Glen,   393.50   1454.
Indians   [The] Devil to pay &
Valentine & Orson
[See preface to this season.]
Rain

Mon. 24 [The] Robbers & Love Laughs   213.50
at Locks[miths]
Cold

Wed. 26 [The] Miller's Maid,* Turn   311.50
Out & [The] Libertine
Cold

Thurs. 27 Town & Country & [The]   120.50
Miller's Maid
Cold

Frid. 28 George Barnwell & [The]   129.50   775.
Warlock of [the] Glen
fair

Saty. 29 (No performance.)

Mon. 31 Romeo & Juliet & [The] Dead   113.75
Alive
fair

[349]

[1822.] Jan[uar]y

Tues. 1 Undine* & [The] Irishman in 1032.50
London
fair

Wed. 2 Undine & [The] Point of 300.75
Honor
fair

Frid. 4 Damon & Pythias & Undine 325.50
very Cold

Saty. 5 (No performance.)   1772.50

Mon. 7 Wallace & Undine   401.50
Very Mild

Wed. 9 She Would be a Soldier & 351.50
Undine
fair

Frid. 11 Damon & Pythias & [The] 40 178.50
Thieves
fair

Saty. 12 Undine, [The] Village Lawyer 187.
& [A] B[udget] of
Blunders
fine

Mon. 14 De Mon[t]fort & [The] 40 479.75
Wood's Benefit   Thieves
[As De Montfort. DP]
Very Cold

Wed. 16 [The] Green Man & [The] 205.25
Magpie & [the] Maid
Cold

[350]

Frid. 18 [The] Follies of a day, Undine 206.50
    & [The] Wedding day
            Rain

Saty. 19 Speed the Plough & [The] 131.   1022.50
    Falls of Clyde
          fog & Rain

Mon. 21 [The] Iron Chest & [The] 162.25
    Libertine
            dull

Wed. 23 Alexander [the Great] & [The] 275.50
Warren's Benefit   Rendezvous
    [As Clytus in *Alexander the
    Great.* DP]
          very Cold

Frid. 25 Usef Caramalli* & [The] Dead 261.75
    Alive
        Very Severe

Sat. 26 (No performance.)   699.50

Mon. 28 [The] Voice of Nature, [The] 1745.25
Ben[efit] of the   Rendezvous & [The] 40
Orphan Asylum   Thieves
    [See preface to this season.]
        Thaw & Wet

Wed. 30 Usef Caramalli & St. Patrick's 167.50
    Day
            Rain

Feb[ruar]y
  Frid. 1 Wallace & Love Laughs at 110.50
    Locksmiths
           dull

[351]

[William]   Saty. 2 Mahomet & [The] Anatomist 150.25 2173.50
For[r]est   [Master Forrest as Zaphne
            in *Mahomet.* DP]
                       fine

P[hilipps] Mon. 4 [The] Devil's Bridge & High 765.75
           life below Stairs
           [As Count Belino in *The Devil's Bridge.* DP]
               Cold & Wet

"   Wed. 6 Love in a Village & [The] 421.50
           Comet
           [Philipps as Young Meadows in *Love in a Village.* DP]
               Snow

"   Frid. 8 [The] Cabinet & [The] Falls of 503.50
           Clyde
           [Philipps as Prince Orlando in *The Cabinet.* DP]
               fair

"   Saty. 9 (No performance)   1689.75
           [See preface to this season.]

"   Mon. 11 [The] Devil's Bridge & 408.
           Modern Antiques
           [Philipps as Count Belino. DP]
               fair

"   Wed. 13 Brother & Sister[, The] Wedding 495.50
           day & [The] Poor Soldier
           [Philipps as Don Sylvio in *Brother and Sister* and Patrick in *The Poor Soldier.* DP]
               Wet

"   Frid. 15 Guy Mannering & Turn Out   311.25
                 [Philipps as Harry Bertram
                 in *Guy Mannering*. DP]
                            Sleighing

         Saty. 16 (No performance.)   1214.75

         Mon. 18 [The] Maid of the Mill & Love 508.25
Benefit [of] Philipps   Laughs [at Locksmiths]
                 [As Lord Aimworth in *The*
                 Maid of the Mill. DP]
                 Snow Storm all day & night

         Wed. 20 Rob Roy [Macgregor] & [The]   140.50
                 Prisoner at Large
                 [See preface to this season.]
                            Wet & Sleighing

         Frid. 22 Marion   &   Sigesmar   [the 570.75
Wash[ingto]n's   Switzer]
B[irth]day
                            very fine

         Saty. 23 (No performance.)   1221.50

P[hilipps] Mon. 25 Lionel & Clarissa & Modern 207.50
                 Antiques
                 [As Lionel, DP]
                            Cold

P[hilipps] Wed. 27 [The] Maid of the Mill & [A] 181.75
                 Tale of Mystery
                 [As Lord Aimworth in *The*
                 Maid of the Mill. DP]
                            fine

         March
P[hilipps] Frid. 1 [The] Barber of Seville* & 669.75
                 St. Patrick's Day
                 [As Count Almaviva in *The*
                 Barber of Seville. DP]
                            fair

[353]

Saty. 2 (No performance.)   1058.70

P[hilipps]   Mon. 4 [The] Barber of Seville & Ella   677.50
Rosenberg
[As Count Almaviva. DP]
fair

P[hilipps]   Wed. 6 [The] Barber of Seville &   651.50
Undine
[See preface to this season.]
fine

P[hilipps]   Frid. 8 [The] Barber of Seville & [The]   421.50
Review
[As Count Almaviva. DP]
dull & Cold

Saty. 9 (No performance.)   1750.50

Benefit [of]   Mon. 11 Fontainbleau & Brother &   828.50
Philipps   Sister
[As Henry in *Fontainbleau*
and Don Sylvio in *Brother
and Sister.* DP]
fair

Thurs. 14 Marion & [The] Wandering   103.50
Boys
Cold

Frid. 15 (No performance.)

Saty. 16 [The First Part of] Henry 4th   208.50   1140.50
& Undine

P[hilipps]   Mon. 18 [The] Barber of Seville & [The]   230.50
Wandering Boys
[As Count Almaviva. DP]
fair

[354]

P[hilipps]   Wed. 20 [The] Cabinet & Ella Rosen-   168.50
              berg
              [As Prince Orlando in *The
              Cabinet*. DP]
                                          dull

Elephant   Frid. 22 [The] Follies of a day & [The]   224.
              40 Thieves
              [See preface to this season.]
                                          Rain

P[hilipps]   Saty. 23 [The] Devil's Bridge & For-   191.25   814.25
              tune's frolic
              [As   Count   Belino. DP]
              Elephant
                                          fair

P[hilipps]   Mon. 25 [The] Russian Imposter* &   357.25
              [The] Ghost
              [As Risberg in *The Russian
              Imposter*. DP]
                                          fine

P[hilipps]   Wed. 27 [The] Russian Impostor &   330.50
              [The] Wandering Boys
              [As Risberg. DP]
                                          warm

P[hilipps]   Frid. 29 Fontainbleau & [The] Adopted   152.25
              Child
              [As Henry in *Fontainbleau*.
              DP]
                                          Cold

P[hilipps]   Saty. 30 [The] Russian Impostor & All   182.   1023.
              the World's a Stage
              [As Risberg. DP]
                                          fine

[355]

April

P[hillips] Mon. 1 [The] Duenna & Love Laughs 389.50
[at Locksmiths]
[As Don Carlos in *The Duenna* and Captain Beldare in *Love Laughs*. DP]
fine

Wed. 3 [The] Robbers & [The] 119.75
Vampire
fair

Frid. 5 [The] H[oney] Moon & [The]
F[alls] of Clyde dismissed
[See preface to this season.]

Saty. 6 Alfonso & All the World's a
Stage

Mon. 8 [The] Snow Storm, Little 206.50
4 Dogs & Carriage R[ed] R[iding] Hood &
Sigesmar [the Switzer]
[See preface to this season.]
fine

[Benefit of] Wed. 10 Love Makes a Man & Robin 720.
Jefferson Hood
[See preface to this season.]
Rain

Ben[efi]t [of Frid. 12 [The] Peasant Boy, Love 587.
Mr. & Mrs.] among [the] Roses &
Wallack Rugantino
[See preface to this season.]
fine

Saty. 13 (No performance.)

[356]

Labasse & Tatin	Mon. 15 Too late for Dinner, Jealousy in [a] Seraglio* & All the World's [a] Stage [See preface to this season.] dull	299.50
"	Wed. 17 Therese, Jealousy in [a] Seraglio & Miss in her Teens [See preface to this season.] fine	351.50
"	Frid. 19 [The] Honey Moon, Jealousy in [a] Seraglio & [The] Adopted Child [See preface to this season.] all day Rain	320.
	Saty. 20 (No performance.)	971
Mrs. Burke's [benefit]	Mon. 22 Rob Roy [Macgregor] & High life below Stairs [To sing. DP] fine	632.
	Tues. 23 [The] Spy* & [The] Highland Reel [USG announces as last night of season.] fair	629.50
	Fridy. 26 [The] Spy & [The] Highland Reel [DP states: In consequence of the general demand of the audience, *The Spy*, a second time, and *The Highland Reel*.] fair	310.

$29025.25

91 Nights averaging 309.75.
Without Stars & Benefits.

[357]

OLD DRURY OF PHILADELPHIA

BALTIMORE [SPRING] SEASON, COMMENCING APRIL 26, [ENDING JULY 4,] 1822.

[Warren & Wood]

PREFACE—**May 1**: In this entry Wood has written "Ch[an]g[e]d to [The] W[edding] Day, Jeffer[son] ill." The May 1 entry of Warren's *Diary* explains that "Jeff[erson] has the gout. [The] farce would have been Miss in Her Teens." **May 10**: In this entry Wood has written, "Changed from Ballet, Labasse absent." Warren's *Diary* explains, "Labasse & Tatin should have danc'd but did not come." ACDA announces them in *Jealousy in a Seraglio*. In his May 1 entry Wood has also written "Mr. Darley," who, Warren's *Diary* explains, has "gout." **May 11**: In this entry Wood has written "Ch[ange]d to [The] Spoil[e]d Child, H. Hathwell ill." Warren writes in his *Diary*, "[The] Hunter of the Alps Chang[e]d to [The] Spoil[e]d Child, Miss H. Hathwell ill—every night we have to change." According to his entry of May 10 and to ACDA, *The Hunter of the Alps* was to have been given on that date instead of *Undine*. **May 17**: ACDA announces "Mons. Labasse and Tatin's 2nd. night." See May 13. **May 22** and **25**: According to ACDA, *La Belle Peruvienne*, a "new grand Ballet of Action," is to be "produced under the immediate direction of Mons. Labasse," who is to appear as the European. **June 10**: ACDA announces Labasse as the French Officer in *The Capricious Widow*, a comic ballet, and as Fenando in *The Siege of Tripoli*, a ballet of action. He is also to dance with Mrs. [H.] Wallack. **July 4**: ACDA announces, "There will be exhibited a patriotic transparency designed and executed by Mr. H. Warren for the occasion, representing an American soldier expiring in the moment of victory. His comrade points out to him the success of the American arms on the hill, where the star-spangled banner is proudly flying. At the feet of the dying hero lies his broken musket. He lifts up his head at the shouts of victory, waving his cap in triumph as the American Eagle hovers over him, bearing a scroll inscribed 'American Independence.' And an olio of dance and song: song, *Hail Liberty!* by Mr. Darley; a pas seul, by Mrs. H. Wallack; a pas de deux, by Miss Seymour and Miss Hathwell; song, *The Soldier Tir'd of War's Alarms*, by Mrs. Burke; song, *The Star Spangled Banner*, by Mr. Nichols. To conclude with a scroll dance, the characters displaying scrolls of Washington, Defenders of Baltimore, Honor the Brave, a Soldier's Gratitude, &c." In the text of this season there are many references, obviously to illness, which it has been necessary to omit from the printed version. In the May 3 entry of his *Diary* Warren explains one of these references, "Mrs. Burke sick," which is in the May 3 entry of the *Account Book.* Warren's entry runs, "Mrs. Burke hoarse, Miss Seymour plays Rosina." In Wood's June 14 entry occurs the notation, "Mr. Parker in Phil[adelphia.]" Warren states, in the June 7 entry of his *Diary*, that Dwyer also played Young Wilding in *The Liar.* In Volume I of the *Account Book* Wood has made an interesting notation regarding "Benefit Charges. Spring 1822." It reads: "Arrangement at Baltimore, after the Close of the regular Season. Extract. $700 for 4 nights will enable us to pay ½ Salary to the principal performers and ¾ to the smaller Salaries. Should the receipts be more than 700 p[e]r w[ee]k of 4 nights, we shall pay in proportion—securing, however, ultimately the above sums for the remainder of the season. See the agreement."

	April	
	Frid. 26 [The] Honey Moon & Too late	243.75
Mrs. Simpson	for dinner	
	[As Hostess in *The Honey Moon*. ACDA]	
	fair	
	Saty. 27 No performance.	243.75
Mrs. Burke		
	Mon. 29 [The] Robbers & [The] Wandering Boys*	306.50
	fair	
	May	
	Wed. 1 [The] Spy* & Love among [the] roses & Miss in her teens	378.50
	[See preface to this season.]	
	fine	
	Frid. 3 Wallace & Rosina	218.50
	fair	

[359]

Sat. 4 [The First Part of] Henry 4th   159.75   1063.25
& Fortune's frolic
Rain

Mon. 6 [The] Point of Honor & [The]   183.
Falls of Clyde
Cold & fair

Wed. 8 Sigesmar [the Switzer] &   481.
Undine*
Warm

Frid. 10 Undine, Little R[ed] R[iding]   250.
Hood & [The] Spoil'd
Child
[See preface to this season.]
fine

Sat. 11 Undine, [The] Hunter of the   110.75   1024.75
Alps & Love among [the]
Roses
[See preface to this season.]
fine

Labasse   Mon. 13 Love Laughs [at Locksmiths],   345.
Jealousy in a Seraglio* &
[The] Adopted Child
[As Alonzo in *Jealousy in a
Seraglio*. ACDA]
fair

Dwyer   Wed. 15 Laugh When You Can, Reci-   287.75
tation & [The] Romp
[As Gossamer in *Laugh
When You Can* and in
comic recitation, *Bucks
Have at Ye All*. ACDA]
fair

[360]

L[abasse]   Frid. 17 [The] Spy & Jealousy in [a]   303.75
            Seraglio
            [See preface to this season.]
                                      Rain

P[hilipps] Saty. 18 [The] Devil's Bridge & [The]   300.25   1236.75
            Wedding day
            [A Count Belino in *The*
            Devil's Bridge. ACDA]
                                      Warm

P[hilipps] Mon. 20 [The] Barber of Seville* & All   443.50
            the World's a Stage
            [As Count Almavira in *The*
            Barber of Seville. ACDA]
                                      fine

L[abasse]   Wed. 22 Wild Oats & [La] Belle Peru-   284.50
            vienne*
            [See preface to this season.]
                                      fine

P[hilipps] Frid. 24 [The] Barber of Seville &   350.
            Sigesmar [the Switzer]
            [As   Count   Almavira.
            ACDA]
                                      very mild

L[abasse]   Saty. 25 [The] Vampire & La Belle   124.50   1202.
            Peruvienne
            [See preface to this season.]
                                      Cold

            Mon. 27 [The] Enterprize* & [The]   354.75
            Ghost
                                      Warm

P[hilipps] Wed. 29 Fontainbleau & St. Patrick's   270.50
            day
            [As Henry in *Fontainbleau*.
            ACDA]
                                      Warm

            [361]

Thurs. 30 Ella Rosenberg, [The] Capri-   163.50
Tatin's Benefit   cious Widow* & Modern
                           Antiques
                           [As the Italian Abbé in *The*
                           Capricious   Widow.
                           ACDA]
                                                   Rain

P[hilipps]   Frid. 31 [The] Cabinet & [The] Ren-   280.50   1069.25
                      dezvous
                      [As Prince Orlando in *The*
                      Cabinet. ACDA]
                                            Warm

                  June
                  Mon. 3 [The] Maid of the Mill &   593.
Philipps' Benefit   Brother & Sister
                          [As Lord Aimworth in *The*
                          Maid of the Mill and Don
                          Sylvio in *Brother and*
                          Sister. ACDA]
                                    not very Warm

Pelby   Wed. 5 Pizarro & [The] Devil to pay   345.
                     [As Rollo in *Pizarro*. ACDA]
                                         Very Cool

             Frid. 7 [The] West Indian & [The]   220.50
Benefit [of] Dwyer   Liar
                      [As Belcour in *The West*
                      Indian. ACDA]
                                          Mild

             Sat. 8 [The] Miller's Maid* & Val-   98.   257.50
                     [entine] & Orson
                                      Warm

Benefit [of]
Labasse

Mon. 10 Helpless Animals, [The] Ca-   181.50
p[ricious]   Widow,   My
Grandm[other] & [The]
Siege of Tripoli
[See preface to this season.]
Warm

Wed. 12 Damon & Pythias & [The] 40   225.50
Thieves
Changed to Therese. Mrs.
Wood, [announced by
ACDA   as   Calanthe,
beloved of Pythias,] ill.
fine & very Cool

Frid. 14 [The] Enterprize & [The]   114.50
Rendezvous
remarkably (very) Cool

Pelby

Saty. 15 [The] Mountaineers & [The] 113.75   635.25
Poor Soldier
[As Octavian in *The Mountaineers.* ACDA]
fine & Cool

C[ooper]

Mon. 17 Macbeth & [The] Dead Alive 314.50
[As Macbeth. ACDA]
fine

C[ooper]

Wed. 19 Bertram & [The] Highland 236.50
Reel
[As Bertram. ACDA]
very fine

C[ooper]

Frid. 21 [The] Gamester & of Age 255.25
tomorrow
[As Beverly in *The Gamester.*
ACDA]
fine

[363]

C[ooper]   Sat. 22 Richard 3d. & [The] Ghost 195.25   1001.75
                     [As Richard. ACDA]
                           fine

              Mon. 24 Virginius & Cath[erine] &   396.75
benefit [of] Cooper   Petruchio
                     [As Virginius and Petruchio.
                     ACDA]
                           very hot

              Wed. 26 [The] Pirate* & [The] Wander- 124.50
Warren's benefit   ing Boys
                           fine

              Frid. 28 Damon & Pythias* & [A] Bud- 240.25
[Mr. & Mrs. H.]   get of Blunders
   Wallack's Benefit   [Mrs. H. Wallack in pas
                       seul. ACDA]
                                 Cool

              Saty. 29 Rob Roy [Macgregor] & Blue 151.75   913.25
[Mr. & Mrs.]   Beard
   Burke's [Benefit]
                                 Hot

              July
              Mon. 1 Love Makes a Man & Robin   258.50
[Mr. & Mrs.]   Hood
   Jefferson's   [Jefferson to sing comic
   [Benefit]   song. ACDA]
                                 Hot

              Wed. 3 Hamlet & [The] Wandering   339.
                      Boys
Pelby's benefit   [As Hamlet. ACDA]
                               Very Warm

              Thurs. 4 Marion,* Olio & Sprigs of 311.50
                      Laurel   ———
                      [See preface to this season.]
                                 Hot   10,555.75

              40 nights averaging 263.50
                      [364]

WASHINGTON SEASON[, COMMENCING JULY 9, ENDING
SEPTEMBER 21,] 1822.

[Warren & Wood]

PREFACE: To the right of the entry of July 15 Wood has written "Share
$7;" to the right of the entry of July 20, "Share $7;" to the right of the
entry of July 27, "Share $7;" to the right of the entry of August 3,
"Share $12.50;" and, to the right of the entry of August 6, "Share [$]12."

July	[9] [The] Rivals & [The] Review	98.25
	[11] [The] Busy Body & [My] Grandmother	68.50
	[15] [The] Highland Reel & [The] Rendezvous	75.
	[16] Marion* & [The] Prisoner at Large	106.50
	[17] [The] Heir at Law & [The] Wandering Boys*	101.75
	[20] [The] Birthday & [The] Midnight Hour	66.75
	[23] Marion & [A] B[udget] of Blunders	93.
	[25] Therese* & Modern Antiques	72.75
	[27] Ways & Means, [Modern Antiques] & [The] Wand-[erin]g Boys	123.75
	[30] Who's the Dupe [?] & [The] 40 Thieves	95.25

B[ooth]   [August 1] Richard 3d & [The Rendez- 237.50
vous]
[As Richard. DNI]

"   [3] [The] Iron Chest & [The 150.50
Spoiled Child]
[Booth as Sir Edward Mor-
timer in *The Iron Chest.*
DNI]

"   [6] King Lear & [The Devil to 214.
Pay]
[Booth as Lear. DNI]

"   [8] Town & Country & [The 167.
Weathercock]
[Booth as Reuben Glenroy
in *Town and Country.*
DNI]

[13 Hamlet & The Mayor of
Garrat]

[15 The Heart of Midlothian* &
Turn Out]

[17 She Would Be a Soldier & No
Song No Supper]

[20 The School for Scandal &
Love Laughs at Lock-
smiths]

[22 Therese & Of Age Tomorrow]

[24 Pizarro & Miss in Her Teens]

[27 Bertram & The Comet]

[366]

[29 Othello & Raising the Wind]

[31 Alexander the Great & The Prize]

[September 3 Macbeth & The Rendezvous]

[5 The Honey Moon & The Dead Alive]

[7 The Wheel of Fortune & Catherine & Petruchio]

[12 Virginius* & The Highland Reel]

[14 She Stoops to Conquer & The Wandering Boys]

[17 Every One Has His Fault & Robinson Crusoe*]

[19 The Soldier's Daughter & Paul & Virginia]

[21 A Cure for the Heartache & The Ruffian Boy*]

BALTIMORE [AUTUMN] SEASON, COMMENCING MON[DA]Y, SEPT[EMBER] 23D., [ENDING NOVEMBER 15,] 1822.

[Warren & Wood]

PREFACE: September 23, 25, 27, 30; October 2, 4, 5, 8. See *Recollections*, pp. 282–3, the general introduction, p. 40, and particularly *Durang*, II, Chapter Ninth, for an account of Charles Mathews' performances. October 16: ACDA announces the usual benefit for those who fell in defense of the city. See the preface to the Baltimore Autumn Season, 1822, July 4, for a description of the "patriotic transparency."

[367]

ACDA also announces, "A pas seul by Mrs. H. Wallack; polacca, *Soldier, Rest*, by Mrs. Burke; song, *The Star Spangled Banner*, Mr. Darley; a song by Mrs. Anderson. To conclude with a scroll dance, the characters displaying scrolls of Washington, Defenders of Baltimore, Honor to the Brave, a Soldier's Gratitude, &c." **October 18:** In this entry Wood has written, "Chan[ge]d from [The] Two Foscari, Darley ill." Warren records in his *Diary*, "Darley could not play—something the matter with his great toe." **November 4:** ACDA announces that Booth, as Jerry Sneak, "will introduce a comic song." **November 6:** ACDA announces *The Children in the Wood* in place of *Modern Antiques.* **November 13:** According to ACDA, "Mr. Jefferson respectfully informs the public that in consequence of the very sudden and a severe indisposition of a principal performer his benefit was unavoidably postponed from Wednesday until this evening, Thursday 14." Mrs. Entwisle is to play Queen Margaret, with Jefferson as Gregory Gubbins, in *The Battle of Hexham.* Jefferson is also to play Crusoe. This is obviously the elder Jefferson, as the sons, Thomas and John, seem to be consistently identified by the initials of their first names.

There are many references apparently to illness in the record of this season and it has been advisable to follow the rule of omitting them from the printed version. A notation, "H. Wallack," in the entry of November 1, may mean, however, that he appeared as Macduff, see ACDA, rather than that he was ill. Vertically across the entries of November 11, 13 and 15 Wood has written "Benefits at ½ Salary." See the notation, "Benefit Charges, Spring 1822" in the preceding Baltimore preface.

[September]

	Mon. 23 [A] Trip to Paris*	752.75
Mathews	[See preface to this season.]	
	fine	

	Wed. 25 [A] Trip to Paris	385.50
M[athews]	[See preface to this season.]	
	light Rain	

	Frid. 27 Country Cousins*	468.50
M[athews]	[See preface to this season.]	
	Storm	

Saty. 28 [The] Wonder & [The] Day	126.50	1733.25

Mrs. Ent[wisle's]   after [the] Wedding
1st. app[ea]r[ance]   [As Donna Violante in *The*
                       Wonder. ACDA]
                       rain all day

       Mon. 30 [Travels in] Earth, Air &   489.50
M[athews]   Water*
               [See preface to this season.]
                          fair

Oct[obe]r
      Wed. 2 [The] Poor Gentleman & [La] 471.
M[athews]   Diligence*
              [See preface to this season.]
                          fair

       Frid. 4 [The] Heir at Law & [The] 431.
M[athews]   Polly Packet*
              [See preface to this season.]
                          fair

       Saty. 5 [The] Road to Ruin & [A] 222.50   1614.
M[athews]   Christmas at Brighton*
              [See preface to this season.]
                          fine

       Tues. 8 [The] Youthful days [of] Mr. 579.50
M[athews]   Mathews* & Mons[ieur]
              Tonson*
              [See preface to this season.]
                          fair

      Thurs. 10 Who Wants a Guinea[?] & 313.75
Wood's Ben[efit]   [The] Agreeable Surprize
M[athews]   [Mathews   as   Solomon
              Gundy in *Who Wants a*
              Guinea? and Lingo in
              The Agreeable Surprize.
              ACDA]
                     rain all day

[369]

Frid. 11 Loves Makes a Man & the   87.75
          Ghost
                    dull

M[athews]   Saty. 12 Ways & Means, My Grand-   309.   1290.
                    mother   &   Mons[ieur]
                    Tonson
                    [As Sir David Dunder in
                    Ways and Means and
                    Morbleu in *Monsieur
                    Tonson.* ACDA]
                                Rain

              Mon. 14 [The] Road to Ruin & [The] 1001.50
Benefit [of]   Sleepwalker
Math[ews]   [As Goldfinch in *The Road
                    to Ruin* and Somno in *The
                    Sleepwalker.* ACDA
                                Cool

              Wed. 16 Marion, Olio & [The] Review   116.50
Ben[efit] fund of   [See preface to this season.]
Monument

              Frid. 18 Douglas & Undine   133.50
                    [See preface to this season.]
                                Warm & fine

              Saty. 19 (No play.   Mr. Darley ill.)

Booth   Mon. 21 Richard 3d & [The] Weather-   237.50
                    cock
                    [As Richard. ACDA]
                                Cool

  "   Wed. 23 Bertram & the Comet   147.50
                    [Booth as Bertram. ACDA]
                                Very Cool

"   Frid. 25 King Lear & [The] Spoil'd   222.25
               Child
               [Booth as Lear. ACDA]
                         very Cool

"   Saty. 26 [The] Iron Chest & Miss in   124.50   731.75
               her Teens
               [Booth as Sir Edward Mor-
               timer in *The Iron Chest*.
               ACDA]
                         Cool

"   Mon. 28 Othello & [The] Blue Devils   237.75
               [Booth as Othello. ACDA]
                         fine & Cool

"   Wed. 30 A New Way to pay Old Debts   207.
               & [The] Adopted Child
               [Booth as Sir Giles Over-
               reach in *A New Way to
               Pay Old Debts*. ACDA]
                         fair

         November
"   Frid. 1 Macbeth & [The] Dead Alive   188.
               [Booth as Macbeth. ACDA]
                         fine

"   Saty. 2 [The] Mountaineers & Modern 123.50   756.25
               Antiques
               [Booth as Octavian in *The
               Mountaineers*. ACDA]
                         fine

         Mon. 4 Hamlet & [The] Mayor of   269.50
Booth's Benefit   Garrat
               [As Hamlet and as Jerry
               Sneak in *The Mayor of
               Garrat*. ACDA See pref-
               ace to this season.]
                         fine

[371]

Wed. 6 [The] Two Pages of Frederick   141.
[the Great] & Love
am[on]g [the] Roses &
M[odern] Antiques
Ch[ange]d [to The] C[hil-
dren in the] Wood. H.
Hath[well] ill. [See preface to this season.]

Frid. 8 [The] Two Foscari* & Help-   163.75
less Animals
fine

Saty. 9 [The] Two Foscari, & [The]   92.75
Two Pages [of Frederick
the Great]
rain

[Benefit of   Mon. 11 Alexander [the Great], Sylv-   179.50
Mr. & Mrs. [H.]   [ester] Dag[gerwoo]d &
Wallack   [The] Rendezvous
[H. Wallack as Alexander,
as Sylvester Daggerwood
and in a pas de deux with
Mrs. H. Wallack. Mrs.
H. Wallack as Parisatis
in *Alexander the Great*,
as Mrs. Daggerwood and
in an Irish lilt. ACDA]
very fine

Wed. 13 [The] Battle of Hexham &   438.25
[Benefit of] Mr. &   & Robinson Crusoe
Mrs. Jefferson   Ch[ange]d to Thurs[day.]
Mrs. Ent[wisle] ill. [See
preface to this season.]
Cool

Frid. 15 [The] Wood Demon & [The]   216.75   834.50
Wandering Boys   ———
[Mrs.] Darley [as Una,] T.
Jeff[erson as Willikind
and Mrs.] And[erson as
Clotilda in *The Wood
Demon*. ACDA]
                fine
                                                  $8878.25

30 Nights Averaging $237
Without Stars & Benefits.

PHILADELPHIA SEASON[,] COMMENCING 2d. DEC[EMBE]R, 1822, [ENDING
April 30, 1823.]

[Warren & Wood]

PREFACE—**December 2**: *Durang*, II, Chapter Third, records, "The new
Chesnut street theatre opened for the first time December 2d., 1822,
with an occasional address, written by Charles Sprague, Esq. of Boston,
and delivered by Mr. Wood with his usual excellence." For a description of the new theatre, see the general introduction, p. 43. In this
entry Wood has written "T. Jeff[erson]," who, according to Wemyss,
in *Life*, p. 74, played the part of Sir Benjamin Backbite in *The School for
Scandal*. **December 11**: In *Life*, p. 77 and *Durang*, II, Chapter Fifth,
it is stated that J. Jefferson played Peter in *The Dramatist*. There is
no mention in DP or USG of T. Jefferson. **January 29**: DP announces
that, "between the acts of the play and farce, Wallack will give imitations of celebrated performers." **February 12**: According to DP,
Wallack will give imitations of several performers. **February 15**:
Durang records, II, Chapter Sixth, "On the 15th of February was given
the first benefit offered in our recollection to the Fire Department of
Philadelphia." **March 7**: DP announces Mathews will play Jack
Rover "with imitations. In the fourth act he will recite part of Hamlet's
advice to the players after the manner of Kemble, Cooke, Young, Kean
and Incledon." He is to play all the characters in *The Actor of All Work*
except Velinspec, which Burke is to play. **March 10, 13, 15, 17, 19,**

[373]

21, 26. For an account of Mathews' performances, see *Recollections*, pp. 282–3, the general introduction, pp. 40, 43, and particularly *Durang*, II, Chapter Ninth. **April 11:** Wood spells the name "Simmson." DP announces "Zanga in *The Revenge* by a young gentleman who has never appeared on the stage." Wood, in *Recollections*, p. 294, alludes to "another Zanga [who] made a first and only appearance." **April 16:** DP announces, "At the request of many friends H. Wallack has consented, for the 1st. time in public, to attempt imitations of the following celebrated actors: Mr. Kemble as Coriolanus. Mr. Kean as Richard III. Mr. Booth as Sir Edward Mortimer. Mr. Mathews as Goldfinch. Mr. J. Wallack as Dashall. Mrs. H. Wallack will appear in an Italian dance."

Once more it has been advisable to omit many references, obviously to illness, from the printed text. Between the entries of January 25 and 27 Wood has written, at the conclusion of a series of references to the illness of Mrs. Lefolle, the notation, "Mrs. Lefolle died Sunday 26." Wood's references to T. Jefferson, in the entries of December 4, 5, 6, 7, 9, 11, may have been to the illness of the eldest son of Jefferson, Sr. At all events, contradicting Wemyss—see the comment on the entry of December 2—*Durang*, II, Chapter Fifth, asserts that "Mr. Thomas Jefferson made his first appearance in four years as Frank," in *Modern Antiques*, on December 13.

Durang and Warren's *Diary* supply stray bits of relevant information regarding this season. *Durang* II, Chapter Fifth, records that Mrs. Tatnall played Adelgitha on January 8. According to the *Diary*, Cooper played Hamlet on January 10; and, on January 24, the bill was *The Gamester* and *The Blue Devils*. Wemyss, in *Life*, p. 83 states that Mathews also played Goldfinch in *The Road to Ruin* on February 24. A playbill of March 27, 1823, in possession of the Historical Society of Pennsylvania announces Mathews as John Lump, as well as Caleb Quotem, in *The Review* which is to be given on March 29. In spite of the combined attraction of Wemyss, Junius Brutus Booth and Charles Mathews, who made their first appearance in Philadelphia, and of James Wallack, who had sufficiently recovered from his accident to return to the stage, this season was "not a profitable one to the management." As *Durang* continues in II, Chapter Eleventh, "The attractive days of an excellent stock company had passed away; a resort had to be made to stars, who absorbed all the profits."

[Chesnut Street Theatre]

[374]

December

Mon.　2 [The] School for Scandal, Ad- 1178.50
　　　　dress & [The] Wand-
　　　　[erin]g Boys
　　　　[See preface to this season.]
　　　　　　　　Cool

　　　Wed.　4 Damon & Pythias, Address & 478.25
T. Jeff[erson]　　Where Shall I dine?
　　　　　　　　very Severe

　　　Thurs.　5 Venice Preserv'd & of Age 173.
T. Jeff[erson]　　Tomorrow
　　　　　　　　Cold

C[ooper]　Frid.　6 Virginius & [The] Spoil'd 928.
T. Jeff[erson]　　Child
　　　　　　[As Virginius. DP]
　　　　　　　　Cold

C[ooper]　Saty.　7 [The] Honey Moon & [The] 433.　　3190.75
T. Jeff[erson]　　Child[ren] in [the] Wood
　　　　　　[Cooper as Duke Aranza
　　　　　　in *The Honey Moon*. USG]
　　　　　　　　Rain

　　　Mon.　9 [The] Soldier's Daughter & 444.50
Mrs. Ent[wisle's]　　[The] Wandering Boys
1st. app[earance.]　[Mrs. Entwisle as the
T. Jeff[erson]　　Widow Cheerly in *The
　　　　　　Soldier's Daughter*. DP]
　　　　　　　　fair

　　　Wed. 11 [The] Dramatist & [The] 393.75
Mr. Wemyss' 1st.　　Comet
app[earance.] T.　[Wemyss as Vapid in *The
Jeff[erson　　*Dramatist*. See preface
　　　　　　to this season.]
　　　　　　　　fine

[375]

C[ooper]   Frid. 13 Damon & Pythias & Modern   707.50
                     Antiques
                     [As Damon. DP]
                                              dull

C[ooper]   Saty. 14 Pizarro & [The] Rendezvous   620.50   2166.25
                     [As Rolla in *Pizarro*. DP]
                                              dull

C[ooper]   Mon. 16 Much ado about Nothing &   409.50
                     [The] Blue devils
                     [As Benedick. DP]
                                              fair

C[ooper]   Tues. 17 Virginius & Miss in her Teens   764.50
                     [As Virginius. DP]
                                              dull

             Wed. 18 Wild Oats & [The] 2 Pages   225.
                     of Frederick the Great*
                                              Cold

             Frid. 20 [The] Apostate & [The] Spoil'd   483.25
Mrs. T[atnall]   Child
                     [As Florinda in *The Apos-
                     tate* and Little Pickle in
                     The Spoiled Child. DP]
                                              Rain

             Saty. 21 [The] Belle's Stratagem &   307.50   2189.75
                     [The] Two Pages of Fred-
                     erick [the Great]
                                              Rain

             Mon. 23 Guy Mannering & [The] Day   249.50
[Mrs.] T[atnall]   after [the] Wedding
                     [As Meg Merrilies in *Guy
                     Mannering* and Lady
                     Elizabeth in *The Day
                     after the Wedding*. USG]
                                              fair

[376]

Tues. 24 Rob Roy [Macgregor] & [The]   268.75
Prize
                Cold

Thurs. 26 The Spy & [The] 2 pages [of   383.50
Frederick the Great]
              fine

C[ooper]   Frid. 27 Macbeth & Who's the Dupe?   563.50
[As Macbeth. DP]
              dull

C[ooper]   Saty. 28 [The First Part of] Henry 4th   508.   1973.25
& [The] Wandering Boys
[As Hotspur. DP]
              Snow

Mon. 30 Damon & Pythias & [The]   793.25

C[ooper's] Ben[efi]t   Highland Reel
[As Damon. DP]

1823. January   2   1
Wed. 1 [The] Wood Demon & ['The]   484.
Law of Java*
         dreadful Storm

C[ooper]   Frid. 3 Virginius & [The] Prize   623.37
[As Virginius. DP]
         Cold & dull

C[ooper]   Saty. 4 [The] Robbers & [The] 2 pages   291.   2191.62
of Frederick [the Great]
[As Charles de Moor in *The
Robbers*. DP]
         Rain

Mon. 6 [The] Law of Java & [The]   393.75
Wood Demon
         fair

[377]

Wed. 8 Adelgitha & [The] Highland   503.25
Mrs. T[atnall]   Reel
                            fine

C[ooper]   Frid. 10 Hamlet & [The] Mock Doctor   503.75
                            fair

C[ooper]   Saty. 11 Remorse & 3 Weeks after   339.50   1640.25
                     Marriage
                     [As Don Alvar in *Remorse*.
                     DP]
                            fair

C[ooper]   Mon. 13 Bertram & [The] Wood   240.
                     Demon
                     [As Bertram. DP]
                            Cold

C[ooper]   Wed. 15 [The] Revenge & [The] Wan-   423.50
                     dering Boys
                     [As Zanga in *The Revenge*.
                     DP]
                            Cool

            Thurs. 16 [The] Apostate & [The] Spoil'd   262.50
Mrs. T[atnall]   Child
                     [As Florinda in *The Apostate*
                     and Little Pickle in *The
                     Spoiled Child*. DP]
                            Cold

[J.] W[allack] Frid. 17 Pizarro & [The] Mock Doctor   706.25
                     [As Rolla in Pizarro. DP]
                            mild & fine

W[allack]   Saty. 18 Coriolanus & Who's the   428.50   2060.75
                     Dupe?
                     [As Coriolanus. DP]
                            mild & fine

[378]

W[allack]   Mon. 20 Fraternal Discord* & [The]   381.75
Chil[dren] in the Wood
[As Captain Bertram in
Fraternal Discord and
Walter in *The Children
in the Wood*. DP]
        fair

W[allack]   Tues. 21 Much ado ab[ou]t Nothing &   361.
[The] Chil[dren] in [the]
Wood
[As Benedick and Walter.
DP]
        fair

W[allack]   Wed. 22 [The] Mountaineers & My   378.25
Aunt
[As Octavian and as Dashall
in *My Aunt*. DP]
        Rain

W[allack]   Thurs. 23 Pizarro & [The] Devil to pay   618.50
[As Rolla. DP]
        Rain

C[ooper]   Frid. 24 [The] Gamester & Lock &   343.50
Key—[The] Blue Devils
[USG announces *The
Gamester*, with Cooper as
Beverly, and *The Blue
Devils*.]
        dull

C[ooper]   Saty. 25 Othello & [The] Rendezvous   237.25   2320.25
[As Othello. DP]
Snow & Rain all day

Mon. 27 Brutus & [The] 2 Pages [of   424.50
C[ooper's] Benefit   Frederick the Great]
[As Brutus. DP]
        Snow

[379]

Wed. 29 Hamlet, Imitations & My 1087.75
W[allack's] Ben[efit]   Aunt
                            [As Hamlet and as Dashall
                            in *My Aunt*. DP See pref-
                            ace to this season.]
                                                    fine

C[ooper]   Frid. 31 Virginius & [The] Phre- 570.75
                      nologist*
                      [As Virginius. DP]
                                              dull

             February
C[ooper]   Saty. 1 Richard 3d. & [The] Phre- 289.   2372.
                     nologist
                     [As Richard. DP]
                                              Cold

             Mon. 3 Bellamira & [The] Spoil'd 1013.25
Benefit [of] Mrs.   Child
T[atnall]   [As Bellamira and as Little
                     Pickle in *The Spoiled
                     Child*. DP]
                                              fair

C[ooper] & Tues. 4 Venice Preserv'd & 3 Weeks 539.50
W[allack]   after Marriage
                   [Cooper as Pierre, Wallack
                   as Jaffier in *Venice Pre-
                   served*. DP]
                                              fair

" Wednesday 5 Douglas & [A] Tale of Mystery 475.62
            [Cooper as Glenalvon, Wal-
            lack as Young Norval in
            Douglas. DP]
                                          Cold & fair

"   Frid. 7 Othello & [The] Prisoner at   689.50
          Large
          [Cooper as Iago, Wallack as
          Othello. DP]
                 very Cold

"   Saty. 8 Julius Caesar & [The] Day 935.50   3653.37
          after [the] Wedding
          [Cooper as Antony, Wallack
          as Brutus. DP]
                 very severe

"   Mon. 10 King John & [The] A[greeable] 349.50
          Surprize
          [Cooper as John, Wallack as
          Falconbridge. DP]
                 Cold

          Wed. 12 Julius Caesar, Imitations & 863.50
W[allack's] Ben[efit]   My Aunt
          [Cooper as Antony, Wal-
          lack as Brutus and as
          Dashall in *My Aunt*. DP
          See preface to this season.]
                 fair

          Frid. 14 Rule a Wife [& Have a Wife] 1231.50
C[ooper's] Ben[efit]   & Cath[erine] & Petruchio
          [Cooper as Leon, Wallack as
          Michael Perez in *Rule a*
          Wife. Cooper as Petru-
          chio. DP]
                 Snow Storm

          Saty. 15 Rob Roy [Macgregor,] Fire & 448.75   2893.25
Benefit [of] fire &   Water* & [The] Day after
Hose Comp[anies]   [the] Wedding
          [See preface to this season.]
                 Cold

[381]

B[ooth]   Mon. 17 Richard 3d. & [The] Spoil'd   264.75
Child
[As Richard. DP]
             very Cold

B[ooth]   Wed. 19 The Iron Chest & [The]   247.75
Citizen
[As Sir Edward Mortimer
in *The Iron Chest*. DP]
             dull

B[ooth]   Frid. 21 A New Way to pay old debts   300.25
& [The] Dead Alive
[As Sir Giles Overreach in
*A New Way to Pay Old
Debts*. DP]
             dull

           Saty. 22 W[illia]m Tell, Olio & [The]   344.50   1157.25
Wandering Boys
           Warm & fine

Mathews   Mon. 24 [The] Road to Ruin & Mon- 1189.50
s[ieur] Tonson*
[As Morbleu in *Monsieur
Tonson*. DP]
          Snow all day

"   Wed. 26 [The] Poor Gentleman & [The]   855.50
Sleepwalker
[As Ollapod in *The Poor
Gentleman* and Somno in
The Sleepwalker. DP]
             dull

"   Frid. 28 [The] Heir at Law & Mon- 1099.75
s[ieur] Tonson
[Mathews as Dr. Pangloss
in *The Heir at Law* and as
Monsieur Tonson. DP]
          Very Cold

[382]

March
"   Saty.   1 Who Wants a Guinea[?] & 1199.   4343.75
[The] Actor of all Work*
[Mathews   a   Solomon
Gundy in *Who Wants a
Guinea?* and as seven
characters in *The Actor of
All Work.* DP]
Mild

"   Mon.   3 Ways & Means, [A] Day at an   827.75
Inn & [The] A[greeable]
Surprize
[Mathews as Sir David
Dunder in *Ways and
Means*, Buskin in *A Day
at an Inn* and Lingo in
The Agreeable Surprize.
DP]
Cold

"   Wed.   5 Rob   Roy   [Macgregor] &   728.50
Mons[ieur] Tonson
[Mathews as Bailie Nicol
Jarvie in *Rob Roy* and as
Monsieur Morbleu. DP]
Rain

Frid.   7 Wild Oats & [The] Actor of 1083.75
Benefit [of]   all Work
Mathews   [Mathews as Jack Rover in
Wild Oats. DP See pref-
ace to this season.]
fine

"   Saty.   8 [The] Heir at Law & Monsieur 492.50   3132.50
Tonson
[Mathews as Dr. Pangloss
and Monsieur Tonson.
DP]
fair

[383]

"   Mon. 10 [A] Trip to Paris* & [La] 1387.25
          diligence*
          [See preface to this season.]
                                      Cold

"   Thurs. 13 Country Cousins*   811.50
          [See preface to this season.]
                                      dull

          (No performance.)

"   Saty. 15 [A] Trip to Paris [& La 746.50 2945.25
          Diligence]
          [See preface to this season.]
                                      fair

M[athews] Mon. 17 Mail Coach adventures* & 800.25
          [The] Polly Packet*
          [See preface to this season.]
                                      fine

"   Wed. 19 [The] Road to Ruin & [A] 491.50
          Christmas at Brighton*
          [Mathews a Goldfinch in
          The Road to Ruin. DP
          See preface to this season.]
                                      mild

          Frid. 21 [The] Youthful Days [of Mr. 986.50
Mr. M[athews']   Mathews]*
Ben[efit]   [See preface to this season.]
                                      fine

          No performance.   2278.25

M[athews] Mon. 24 Wild Oats & [La] Diligence 364.
          [As Jack Rover in *Wild
          Oats.* DP]
                                      fine

          [384]

M[athews]   Wed. 26 [The] Youthful Days [of Mr. 387.25
               Mathews]
            [See preface to this season.]
                     Rain & Snow

M[athews] Thurs. 27 Such things Are & [A] Christ- 302.37
            [mas] at Brighton
            [As Twineall in *Such Things
            Are.* DP]
                         fine

         Saty. 29 [The] Review, [The] Polly 1312.25 2365.87
3d. Ben[efi]t [of]   Packet   &   Mon[sieur]
  M[athews]   Tonson
            [As Caleb Quotem in *The
            Review* and as Monsieur
            Morbleu. DP]
                         fair

        Mon. 31 [The] Two Foscari* & Val- 451.50
Ben[efit of] Wood.   [entine] & Orson
  Mrs. Simpson   [Wood as Francis Foscari,
            Mrs. Simpson as Marina.
            DP]
                       fair

        April
B[ooth]   Wed. 2 King Lear & [The] Romp   237.50
            [As Lear. DP]
                       fair

B[ooth]   Frid. 4 Town & Country & [The] 296.75
            Citizen
            [As Reuben Glenroy in
            Town and Country. DP]
                       fine

B[ooth]   Saty. 5 [The] Mountaineers & Ella 167.75 1153.50
            Rosenberg
            [As Octavian in *The Moun-
            taineers.* DP]

[385]

Ben[efit of] Mon. 7 [The] Distrest Mother & [The] 492.75
Booth Mrs.   Mayor of Garrat
Duff['s] 1st.   [Booth as Orestes, Mrs.
ap[pearance]   Duff as Hermione in *The*
                        Distrest Mother. Booth
                        as Jerry Sneak in *The*
                        Mayor of Garrat. DP]
                        Violent Storm of Rain

Ben[efit of] Wed. 9 [The] Man[ager] in distress, 402.50
Warren   Guy Fawkes* & [The
                      King and] Miller of
                      Mansfield
                      [As the Miller. DP]
                                             fine

          Frid. 11 [The] Revenge & [The] War- 177.50
Mr. Simpson's 1st.   lock of the Glen
                       [See preface to this season.]
                                             dull

          Saty. 12 Pizarro & [The] falls of Clyde 358.50 1426.25
Mrs. Tatnall's   [As Elvira in *Pizarro* and
Benefit   Ellen Enfield in *The*
                       Falls of Clyde. DP]
                                             fair

[Benefit of] Mon. 14 [The] Brothers, My Grand- 697.50
Jefferson   mother & [A] Roland for
                       [an] Oliver
                       [As Sir Benjamin Dove in
                       The Brothers, Dicky Gos-
                       sip in *My Grandmother*
                       and Fixture in *A Roland*
                       for an Oliver. DP]
                                             fine

Wed. 16 Therese, Is he jealous?*   &   493.75
[Benefit of Mr. and   [The] Blind Boy
  Mrs.] H. Wallack   [Wallack as Carwin, Mrs.
                      Wallack as Countess de
                      Morville in Therese and
                      Mrs. Belmour in *Is He
                      Jealous?* DP See preface
                      to this season.]
                                     fine

Frid. 18 [The] Devil's Bridge & Tekeli   494.50
[Benefit of Mr.   [Burke as Pietro, Mrs.
  & Mrs.] Burke   Burke as Count Belino in
                      The Devil's Bridge. Burke
                      as Conrad, Mrs. Burke as
                      Christine in *Tekeli.* DP]
                                     fair

Saty. 19 [The] Jealous Wife & 3 & [the]   375.50   2091.25
[Benefit of Mrs.]   Deuce
  Entwisle. Duff['s]   [Mrs. Entwisle as Mrs.
  1st. app[earance]   Oakly, Duff as Oakly in
                      The Jealous Wife. DP]
                                  Rain

Mon. 21 Alexander   [the   Great,]   242.
[Benefit of] Wilson.   L[overs'] Quarrels & [The]
  Mrs. Duff['s] 2d.   Hunter of [the] Alps
                      [Wilson as Alexander and as
                      Felix in *The Hunter of the
                      Alps.* Mrs. Duff as
                      Statira in *Alexander.* DP]
                                Warm

Wed. 23 Speed the Plough & [The]   328.75
                      Wandering Boys
                      Ticket night [for the benefit
                      of the door keepers, police

[387]

officers, and others em-
ployed in the theatre.
DP]
fine

Frid. 25 Tom & Jerry* & Turn Out   782.75
       fine

Saty. 26 Tom & Jerry & [The] Comet   501.50   1855.
       fine

Mon. 28 Tom & Jerry & [The] Two   630.25
       Pages of Frederick [the
       Great]
       fine

Wed. 30 [The] North American* &   669.35
       Tom & Jerry
            drizzling   ————
                     $50765.
91 Nights Averaging 555.50
d[itto] without Stars & Ben[efi]ts, $420.75

BALTIMORE [SPRING] SEASON, COMMENCING MAY 5, [ENDING
JUNE 21,] 1823.

[Warren & Wood]

PREFACE—June 20: Warren writes in his *Diary*, "Farce changed to
The Comet, H. Wallack ill—said so." ACDA announces him as
Hardy Knute in *The Wood Demon*. It has been advisable to omit a
number of notations from the printed text of this season. These notations include "Mr. Wilson absent" in the entry of May 5 and "d[itt]o"
referring to it in the entries of May 7, 9, 10, 12. They also include many
references obviously to the illness of players. In the entry of June 6,
Wood has written "18 nights," and, under "284.50" the total of [$]4868.87,
thus far received. He has also written "Mrs. Entwisle refused a Gray."
In this notation he may be alluding to the rôle of Alice Gray in *The Bride
of Lammermoor*, to be played on June 11. In the June 6 entry Wood
has also written "New Arrangement. See Agreement" and under the

notation and vertically across the entries of June 9 to June 21 inclusive, the explanatory notation, "½ Sal[ar]y to principals & ¾th to Small." On another page in Volume I, Wood has recorded the terms of "Mr. Duff's Engag[ement in] Balt[imore, beginning] June 9th, 1823." The entry reads: "Your Compensation for the remainder of the Season, in proportion with the other performers, and in Washington Mrs. D & you begin with a Star Eng[agement] for 6 nights to Share after [$]110 p[e]r night & Ben[efi]t at 110, then be on Shares for the rest of the time."

May

Mondy. 5 [The] Dramatist & [The] 126.
Wandering Boys
fair

Wedy. 7 Romeo & Juliet & [The] Day 256.50
[Mr. & Mrs.] D[uff]   after the Wedding
[Duff as Romeo, Mrs. Duff
as Juliet. ACDA]
Cool

"   Frid. 9 Venice Preserv'd [&] 3 and the 257.25
Deuce
[Duff as the three Singles
in *Three and the Deuce*;
Mrs. Duff as Belvidera in
Venice Preserved. ACDA]
Cool

"   Saty. 10 [The] Foundling of the forest 141.25   781.
& Fire & Water*
[Duff as Bertrand in *The
Foundling of the Forest.*
ACDA]
fine

"   Mon. 12 [The] Distrest Mother & 258.50
Therese
[Duff as Orestes, Mrs. Duff
as Hermione in *The Dis-*

[389]

trest Mother; Mrs. Duff as
Mariette in *Therese.*
ACDA]

Rain

Wed. 14 [The] Law of Java* & Who's 216.50
the Dupe?

fine

Friday 16 Damon & Pythias & [The] 252.50
[Mr. & Mrs.] D[uff]   Warlock of the Glen
[Duff as Matthew, Mrs.
Duff as Adela in *The
Warlock of the Glen*; Mrs.
Duff as Calanthe in
Damon and Pythias.
ACDA]

fine

Saty. 17 (No performance)   727.50

Mon. 19 Tom & Jerry* & Fire & Water 634.75
Mrs. Burke   [As Kate in *Tom and Jerry.*
ACDA]

Warm

Wed. 21 Tom & Jerry & L[overs'] 350.75
Quarrels

Warm

Frid. 23 Damon & Pythias & Adeline* 214.75
Wood's Benefit

Cool

Saty. 24 Tom & Jerry & My Grand- 210.75 1411.
mother

Warm

Mon. 26 Isabella & [The] Magpie & 643.50
Mrs. Duff's Benefit   [the] Maid

[390]

[As Isabella and as Annette
in *The Magpie and the
Maid*. ACDA]
fine

Wed. 28 Tom & Jerry & [The] Ren-   263.75
dezvous
Cool, fair

Frid. 30 Zembuca & [The] Romp   140.62
Cool

Saty. 31 Pizarro & [The] Dead Alive 105.62   1153.5
[Mr. & Mrs.] D[uff]   [Duff as Rolla, Mrs. Duff as
Cora in Pizarro. ACDA]
Cold

June
Mon. 2d. Guy Mannering, [The] Man-   211.62
[Mr. & Mrs.] Duf[f]   [age]r in distress & [The]
Day after [the] Wedding
[Duff as Dick Hatteraick,
Mrs. Duff as Meg Mer-
rilies in *Guy Mannering*.
ACDA]
Cool & fine

Wed. 4 [The] Apostate & [The] Irish-   299.75
Duff's ben[efi]t.   man in London
[As Malec in *The Apostate*
and Murtoch Delany in
The Irishman in London.
ACDA]
fine

Frid. 6 [The] North American* &   284.50
Tom & Jerry
fair

[391]

Mon. 9 [The] Robbers & [The] Man- 160.75
[Mr. & Mrs.] D[uff]   ager in Distress
                        [Mrs. Duff as Amelia in
                        The Robbers. ACDA]
                                    fair

Wed. 11 [The] Bride of Lammermoor* 190.
        & [The] 2 pages of Fred-
        erick [the Great]
                    fine

Frid. 13 [The] Jealous Wife & Tekeli 98.37
[Mr. & Mrs.] D[uff]   [Duff as Oakly in *The
                        Jealous Wife* and as Count
                        Tekeli. ACDA]
                                    Warm

Saty. 14 Rob Roy [Macgregor] & [The] 86.75   535.12
[Mr. & Mrs.] D[uff]   Rendezvous
                        [Mrs. Duff as Helen in *Rob
                        Roy Macgregor*. ACDA]
                                    Very hot

[Benefit of] Mon. 16 Tom & Jerry & [The] High- 76.
Wemyss & [Mrs.]   land Reel
Anderson   [Wemyss as Corinthian
                        Tom, Mrs. Anderson as
                        Kate in *Tom and Jerry*.
                        ACDA]
                                    fair

[Benefit of] Wed. 18 Jane Shore & Tom & Jerry 218.50
Mr. & Mrs. H.   [Wallack as Lord Hastings
Wallack   in *Jane Shore* and as Jerry
                       Hawthorn, with Mrs.
                       Wallack as *Jane*, in *Tom
                       and Jerry*. ACDA]
                                    Hot

[392]

Frid. 20 [The] Brothers & [The] Wood 233.50
[Benefit of] Mr.   Demon
& Mrs. Jefferson   Changed to [The] Comet.
                       Wallack ill. [See preface
                       to this season.]
                                        very Warm

Saty. 21 [The] Lady of the Lake & No 154.75
[Benefit of] Mr.   Song No Supper
& Mrs. Burke.   [Burke as John of Brent,
[Mrs.] D[uff].   Mrs. Burke as Blanche of
                       Devon and Mrs. Duff as
                       Lady Ellen Douglas in
                       The Lady of the Lake;
                       Burke as Endless and
                       Mrs. Burke as Marga-
                       retta in *No Song No
                       Supper*. ACDA]
                                           Hot
                                                  —— 1218.62

18 nights of the regular season averaged
$270. After Stars & Benefits, $253.

The After Season of 8 nights averaged 152.25
After Benefits were paid, $141.90

Average of the 26 nights
$233.

WASHINGTON SEASON[, COMMENCING JUNE 26, ENDING
SEPTEMBER 18,] 1823.

[Warren & Wood]

PREFACE—**July 5**: Neither DNI nor WG was published on July 4 and
neither announces any plays on July 5. The record of this season is
fragmentary; and though Wood records the sum of "[$]94.25," he records
no titles for July 5. **July 29**: According to DNI, however, "The managers are gratified in being able to announce the arrival of Mr. Jefferson.

In consequence of their wish to gratify their friends and enable Mr. Jefferson to appear as early as possible, the farce of *The Children in the Wood*, advertised for this evening, July 29, is changed to *Who's the Dupe?* Old Doily, his 1st. appearance this season, Mr. Jefferson."

In the entry of July 12, Wood has written "Duff[']s ben[efi]t." DNI announces Duff as Rolla in *Pizarro* and as Sylvester Daggerwood. It has been advisable to omit four other notations from the printed version. These are three amounts of shares ("$15," written to the right of the dates June 26, 28 and July 1; "[$]20," written to the right of the dates, July 3, 4, 5, 8 and 10; and [$]9, written to the right of the dates, July 15, 17, 19 and 22;) and the notation, "Mr. C[ooper] Shared (after $100 Each night) [$]59.37."

Such record as exists of the performances of this season is in Volume II of the *Account Book*. In Volume I there is a record of the terms of "Mr. Booth's Eng[agement] for Washington [,] 1823." The entry reads: "Acts 5 nights—the Receipts of 4 nights to be divided *nightly* after [$]110 Charges—the 5th, his Benefit at 110 Charges, and to be on a Monday Night. This Eng[agement] to Commence the 3d. Week of the Washington Season."

June
Thurs. 26 [The West Indian & Fortune's   57.25
Frolic]
[According to DNI and
WG, postponed to 27.]

Saty. 28 [The Apostate & The Day   38.75
after the Wedding]

July
Tues. 1 [Isabella & The Irishman in   87.50
London]

Thurs. 3 [Romeo & Juliet & Of Age   63.25
Tomorrow]

Frid. 4 [The Spy* & The Purse]   96.25

Saty. 5 [See preface to this season.]

[394]

Tues. 8 [The Foundling of the Forest   88.75
          & Fire & Water*]

Thurs. 10 [Venice Preserved & No Song
          no Supper]

Saty. 12 [Pizarro, Sylvester Dagger-
          wood & Is He Jealous?*]

15 [The Spy & The Rendezvous]

17 [Richard 3d. & Fire & Water]

19 [Othello & Lovers' Quarrels]

Tues. 22 [Town & Country & Raising
          the Wind]

Thursday 24 [King Lear & Where Shall I
          Dine?]

26 [A New Way to Pay Old
          Debts & How to Die for
          Love]

29 [Adeline* & The Children in
          the Wood]
          [See preface to this season.]

31 [Therese & The Comet]

August 2d. [A Cure for the Heartache
          & The Children in the
          Wood

[5 Rob Roy Macgregor & The
          Village Lawyer]

[7 The Manager in Distress &
          Tom & Jerry*]

[395]

Cooper   9   Virginius & [The Village Law-   118. 25
yer]
[As Virginius. DNI]

12   Rule a Wife [& Have a Wife]   90.
& [Where Shall I Dine?]

14   Damon & Pythias* [& Is He   166. 25
Jealous?]

16   Macbeth & [Lovers' Quarrels]   134. 25

[19   The Mountaineers & Catherine & Petruchio]

[21   Tom & Jerry & The Blue
Devils]

[23   The Manager in Distress &
Tom & Jerry]

[26   The Ghost & Tom & Jerry]

[28   Rob Roy Macgregor & Three
& the Deuce]

[30   A Roland for an Oliver* &
The Wandering Boys]

[September   2   The Merchant of Venice &
The 2 Pages of Frederick
the Great*]

[4   Zembuca & The Lady & The
Devil*]

[6   The Dramatist & The Magpie
& the Maid]

[9 The Law of Java & The 2
Pages of Frederick the
Great]

[11 The Lady of the Lake & The
Libertine]

[13 The Blind Boy, Little Red
Riding Hood & The
Highland Reel]

[16 The Wonder & Monsieur
Tonson*]

[18 St. Patrick's Day & The
Wood Demon]

BALTIMORE [AUTUMN] SEASON, COMMENCING SEPTEM[BE]R 24, [ENDING
NOVEMBER 19], 1823

[Warren & Wood]

PREFACE—September 24: "The managers respectfully inform the public
that Mr. Hunter, late of the Royal Amphitheatre, London, and the
Olympic Theatre, Philadelphia, is engaged for a few nights and will
appear on this evening. This celebrated equestrian and tight rope
performer will go through his wonderful feats on the tight rope. He will
dance with wooden shoes and with baskets on his feet, together with
various other feats in which he has been considered unequalled by any
other performer in Europe." ACDA In this entry Wood has also
written the notation, "Francis." September 25: "D[itt]o" in the entry
refers to Hunter, who repeats his performance of September 24. In
this entry Wood has also written the notation "d[itt]o," referring to
Francis, and the notation "Mrs. Anderson," whom ACDA announces
as Leonora in *Lovers' Quarrels*. September 26: Hunter repeats his performance of September 24 and 25 except that he dances "with a boy on
his shoulders." ACDA. In this entry Wood has also written the notation, "d[itt]o," referring to "Mrs. Anderson," in the entry of September
25. September 27: "D[itt]o" in this entry refers to Hunter who "will,
for the 1st. time here, perform the wonderful feat of the Polander's
Ladder. He will ascend a Ladder which falls to pieces and leaves him
on a single pole Fourteen Feet High, where he will stand upon his head,

[397]

turn round, &c., &c. He will also perform his feats on the tight rope."
September 29: Hunter repeats his performance of September 27. October 1: ACDA announces Mrs. Battersby as Juliana in *The Honey Moon*
and Widow Brady in *The Irish Widow*. Hunter is to perform a variety
of new feats on the tight rope and to dance with two boys tied to his feet.
November 17: In this entry Wood has crossed out "Mon[day]" and,
under it, written "Tues[day]." He has also written the explanation,
"Postponed to Tuesday on acc[ount of] Snow Storm." ACDA announces that the performances intended for Monday are postponed until
November 18 in consequence of the extreme inclemency of the weather
and that Francis is to play Skiff in *The Brothers* and Old Brummagem
in *Lock and Key* and Mrs. Francis is to play Lady Dove in *The Brothers*.

It has been necessary to omit four notations from the printed text of
this season. These include: "Mrs. Battersby arrived this morn[in]g,"
which Wood has written to the left of the entry of October 1; and "Mr.
Duff's Commencement this day," which Wood has written to the left of
the entry of October 4. The second notation is explained by an announcement in ACDA to the effect that "Mr. Duff and Mr. H. Wallack
are engaged" and that Duff is to play Jerry and Baron Wellinghoerst in
Of Age Tomorrow. Wood has written the third of the four notations to
the left of the entry of October 20. It is "Mr. Perkins' 1st app[earance]."
ACDA announces that he is to appear as Baron Longueville in *The Foundling of the Forest* and as *Zembuca*. To the left of the entry of October 21
Wood has written the fourth notation, "The Review," which Warren
explains in an entry of the same date. Warren's *Diary* reads, "He
Would be a Soldier and the Poor Soldier. The Review. The Governor
and the Military attend the Theatre."

Sept[ember]

Hunter	Wed. 24	She Stoops to Conquer, Tight Rope & Fire & Water [See preface to this season for explanation of every reference to Hunter.] very Cool	182.50
H[unter]	Thurs. 25	[The] Poor Gentleman & d[itt]o & Lovers['] Quarrels Cold	88.25

[398]

H[unter]	Frid. 26 Wild Oats, Tight Rope & [My] Grandmother Cold	83.25	
H[unter]	Saty. 27 Speed the Plough, d[itt]o & [The] Prize Cold	104.75	458.75
H[unter.] Ben[efit of the] mon[umen]t fund	Mon. 29 [The] Fair American & Sprigs of Laurel [In aid of the fund for the relief of the indigent widows and children of the brave men who fell in defense of the city. ACDA] fine & Cold	130.75	

October

Hunter's Benefit	Wed. 1 [The] Honeymoon, Ascension & [The] Irish Widow Mrs. Battersby's Ist. ap-p[earance.] [See preface to this season.] fine	218.75	
	Frid. 3 Riches, Ode to the Passions & [The] Mock Doctor mild & fine	120.75	
	Saty. 4 Tom & Jerry & of Age tomorrow Warm	191.25	661.50
B[rown] & Mrs. D[uff]	Mon. 6 [The] Distrest Mother & 3 & [the] Deuce [Brown as Orestes, Mrs. Duff as Hermione in *The Distrest Mother*. ACDA] fair	209.25	

[399]

Tues. 7 [The] Soldier's Daughter &   92.25
         [The] Critic
                      fair

         Wed. 8 Damon & Pythias & [The] 200.25
B[rown] & [Mrs.]   Rendezvous
   D[uff]   [Brown as Damon, Mrs.
                   Duff as Calanthe in
                   Damon and Pythias.
                   ACDA]
                         Mild

Thurs. 9 Pizarro & No Song No Supper 120.25
                       Warm

Frid. 10 Laugh When You Can &   116.50
         [The] Vampire
                      Cool

Saty. 11 Tom & Jerry & [The] Blind 214.75   954.25
         Boy
                      Cold

B[rown]   Mony. 13 King John* & Turn Out   208.75
             [As King John. ACDA]
                         Mild

Tues. 14 Mod[ern] Antiques, [The]   250.
         Death of L[ife] in Lon-
         don* & [The] Dead Alive
                      Cold

         Wed. 15 Damon & Pythias, Ode to 200
Benefit [of] B[rown]   [the] Pass[ions], The]
                   S[cotch] Ghost & Matri-
                   mony
                   [Brown as Damon and in
                   recitation of the Ode.
                   ACDA]
                        fair

Thurs. 16 Rob Roy [Macgregor] & St.   79.
Patrick's day
                        Rain

Frid. 17 Isabella & 3 & [the] Deuce   84.50
                        fine

Saty. 18 Tom & Jerry & [The] Death of 153.50   975.75
Life in London
                        Cold

Mrs. Duff's   Mon. 20 [The] Foundling of [the] forest 329.75
Benefit   & Zembuca
                 [As Unknown Female in *The
                 Foundling of the Forest.*
                 ACDA]
                        fair

Tues. 21 He Would be a Soldier, Olio 570.75
                 & [The] Poor Soldier
                 [The gun hornpipe by Miss
                 Hathwell; song, *Soldier,
                 Rest!* by Mrs. Burke; a
                 pas seul by Mrs. Wal-
                 lack; patriotic epilogue
                 by Mrs. Battersby.
                 ACDA]
                        Storm of Thunder

Wed. 22 [The] Road to Ruin & Tekeli 142.50
                        fair

Thurs. 23 Tom & Jerry & Ella Rosen- 202.50
                 berg
                        Cool

Frid. 24 [The First Part of] Henry 4th 224.50
                 & Is he Jealous?
                        fine

[401]

Saty. 25 Douglas & Cath[erine] &   98.50
          Petruchio
              Dull

       Mon. 27 Julius Caesar* & Lovers['] 307.
Wood's Benefit   Quarrels
           [As Brutus. ACDA]
              fine

     Tues. 28 [The] School for Scandal & [A] 120.
           Tale of Mystery
              fair

      Wed. 29 [The] Wheel of fortune & 53.75
Mr. & Mrs.   [The] Wandering Boys
  Brown's ben[efit]   [Brown as Penruddock in
           The Wheel of Fortune and
           Count de Croissy in *The*
           Wandering Boys. Mrs.
           Brown and Mrs. H. Wal-
           lack as Paul and Justin,
           the wandering boys.
           ACDA]
              Rain

     Thurs. 30 Every One has his fault & 288.75
[Benefit of] Mr.   Blue Beard
  & Mrs. Jefferson   [Jefferson as Solus, Mrs.
           Jefferson as Mrs. Placid
           in *Every One Has His*
           Fault; Jefferson as Shac-
           atac in *Blue Beard*.
           ACDA]
              fine

     Frid. 31 Virginius & [The] Blue Devils 124.50
H. W[allack]   [As Virginius. ACDA]
              fine

Nov[embe]r

H. W[allack]	Saty. 1st.	[The] Wonder & [The] Two Pages of frederick [the Great] [As Don Felix in *The Wonder*. ACDA] Rain all day	57.75	949.75
Warren's benefit	Mon. 3	[The] Merry Wives of Windsor & [The] Devil to pay [As Falstaff. ACDA] Very Cold	194.50	
W[allack]	Tues. 4	[The] Merchant of Venice & [The] Libertine [As Shylock. ACDA] fair	160.	
W[allack]	Wed. 5	The Spy & [The] Wandering Boys [As Harvey Birch in *The Spy* and Count de Croissy in *The Wandering Boys*. ACDA] Rain	148.75	
	Thurs. 6	Joan of Arc* & Tom & Jerry heavy Rain	150.25	
W[allack]	Frid. 7	Alexander [the Great] & Too late for Dinner [As Alexander and as Frank Poppleton in *Too Late for Dinner*. ACDA all day, heavy Rain	66.	
W[allack]	Saty. 8	Macbeth & Who's the Dupe? [As Macbeth. ACDA fine	162.	881.50

[403]

Mon. 10   Much ado ab[ou]t Nothing &   155.50
Wallack's Benefit   [The] Two pages [of Fred-
erick the Great]
[As Benedick and as Fred-
erick in *The Two Pages.*
ACDA]
Rain all day

Tues. 11   Abaellino & [The] Lady &   105.25
[Benefit of]   [The] Devil*
Wemyss & [Mrs.]   [Wemyss as Wildlove, Mrs.
Anderson   Anderson as Zaphyrina
in *The Lady and the Devil*
and Rosamunda in *Abael-
lino.* ACDA
Rain

Wed. 12   Guy Mannering & [The] 40   205.25
[Benefit of]   Thieves
Mr. & Mrs. Burke   [Burke as Dandie Dinmont,
Mrs. Burke as Julia Man-
nering in *Guy Mannering*;
Burke as Mustapha, Mrs.
Burke as Morgiana in
The Forty Thieves. ACDA
Cold

Thurs. 13   [The] Belle's Stratagem &   86.25
[Benefit of]   Mons[ieur] Tonson
Mr. & Mrs.   [Darley as Courtall, Mrs.
Darley   Darley as Letitia Hardy
in *The Belle's Stratagem*;
Darley as Monsieur Mor-
bleu in *Monsieur Tonson.*
ACDA
Cold

Frid. 14   [The] Devil's Bridge & [The]   89.25
[Benefit of]   Peasant Boy
Mr. Duff [&]   [ACDA announces *The
Mrs. Wallack   Children in the Wood* and

[404]

Mrs. Wallack as Mari-
netta in *The Peasant
Boy.*]

Cool

Saty. 15   Hamlet & [The] Irish Widow   160.25   802.25
[Benefit of   [Mrs. Battersby as Hamlet,
Mrs.] Battersby   Mr. Johnston as Laertes;
& [Mr.] Johnston   Mrs. Battersby as Widow
                Brady in *The Irish
                Widow.* ACDA]

fine

Mon. 17   [The] Brothers & Lock & Key   116.
[Benefit of]   Postponed to Tuesday on
Mr. & Mrs. Francis   acc[ount of] Snow Storm.
                [See preface to this season.]

fair

Wedy. 19   The Tempest & [The] Lady   453.
              and [the] Devil   ——

Cold

$7821.75

46 Nights Averaging $170.
after Stars & Benefits —

WASHINGTON SEASON[, COMMENCING SEPTEMBER 1, ENDING
OCTOBER 8,] 1824.

[Warren & Wood]

PREFACE—**September 22:** DNI announces the bill for September
23. At the end of the record of this season, Wood has written: "7
Sept[ember,] Share $6; 14 [September, Share $]6; 21 [September, Share
$]4.25; 28 [September, Share $]5.25; 5 Oct[ober, Share $]6; 7 [October,
Share $]4.50; "and the total," [$]32.25. Following his record of this
season, Wood has devoted two pages to an "Inventory of the Washington
Theatre," dated "Nove[mbe]r 1824." It contains such items as "Cut
Wood," "Front Wood," "Back Wood," "Green Chamber," "Drapery

[405]

Palace," "One Horizon," "5 Rock Peices [sic,"] "3 rows smooth water," "Juliet's Balcony," "1 rain box," "1 coffin," "1 spike peice [sic,"] "1 Trick door," and "Canvas for Richard's Tent."

Sept[ember]	1 [The] Birthday & [The] Agreeable Surprize	88.
	3 Speed the Plough & L[ittle] R[ed] R[iding] Hood	91.75
	6 John Bull & Lovers['] Quarrels	91.
Caldw[ell]	7 Hamlet & [Little] R[ed] R[iding] Hood [As Hamlet. DNI]	69.25
C[aldwell]	10 [The] Honey Moon & [The] Blue Devils [As Duke Aranza in *The Honey Moon*. DNI]	102.75
C[aldwell]	11 [The] Dramatist & 3 & [the] Deuce [As Vapid in *The Dramatist*. DNI]	62.50
C[aldwell's] benefit	13 Damon & Pythias & [The] Liar [As Damon. DNI]	162.
	15 [The] Mid[night] Hour, L[ove] am[on]g [the] Roses & [The] Agreeable Surprize	44.25
	16 [The] Merry Wives [of Windsor] & Love am[on]g [the] Roses	117.
	[18 Rob Roy Macgregor & The Ghost]	

20 [The] Hunter of [the] Alps,   40.25
[The] Wed[ding] day &
[The] Scotch Ghost

21 Rob Roy [Macgregor] & For-   97.
tune's frolic

22 [The] Plains of Chippewa &   116.50
[The] Pris[oner] at Large
[See preface to this season.]

25 [The] Rivals & [The] Ghost   81.

27 Therese & [The] Irishman in   50.
London

28 [The] Magpie & [the] Maid &   74.
[The] Highland Reel

30 [The] Wood Demon & [The]   70.25
Mock Doctor

Oct[obe]r 1 Rob Roy [Macgregor] & [Har-   47.
lequin] Hurry Scurry

2 [The] School for Scandal &   99.25
[The] Comet

[Benefit of]   4 [The] Brothers & Turn Out   168.50
Mr. Jeff[erson] &
Mrs. Anderson.

5 [The] Poor Gentleman and   50.
[The] Blue Devils

[Benefit of]   7 [The First Part of] Henry 4th   114.75
Mr. Warren   & [Harlequin] Hurry
Scurry

8 La Fayette* & [The] Devil to   132.75
pay

[407]

PHIL[ADELPHIA] SEASON, COMM[ENCIN]G OCT[OBER] 29, 1827[, ENDING JUNE 21, 1828.]

[Warren]

PREFACE—**November 26**: ADA announces Mr. Delarue as Sylvester Daggerwood, "by desire, in which he will give imitations of the following performers: Mr. Kean, Mr. Booth, Mr. Barnes, Mr. M'Cready, Mr. E. Forrest, Mr. Hilson, and Mr. S. Chapman as Colonna." **November 27**: ADA announces Brown as Appius Claudius and "a young gentleman of this city, his 1st. appearance on any stage," as Virginius. The advertisement apparently explains a notation, "a 1st. app[earance] this was," which Wood has written after "Brown." **January 2**: USG announces Hackett as Sylvester Daggerwood, "with imitations of celebrated performers and his celebrated Yankee story of Jonathan and Uncle Ben." According to *Durang*, II, Chapter Thirty-Eighth, he also played Monsieur Morbleu in *Monsieur Tonson*. **January 3**: Wemyss, in *Life*, p. 138, asserts that Mrs. Sloman played the rôles of Isabella, Mrs. Haller, Belvidera, Jane Shore, Juliet, Mrs. Oakley and Lady Townly. **January 25**: According to USG Miss George was to have played Count Belino and Cowslip in *The Agreeable Surprize*. **January 29**: Wemyss, in *Life*, p. 154, states that McCahen also played Murtoch Delany in *The Irishman in London*. **February 13**: In this entry Wood has written "Miss K[elly] sick, Mrs. Darley played." According to USG, Miss Kelly was to have "personated" six characters in *The Actress of All Work*. **March 21**: ADA announces Miss Rock as Miss Dorillon in *Wives as They Were* and all the characters in *Winning a Husband*, except the added ones of Sir Roderick Strangeways, to be played by Hutchings, and Davy, to be played by Jefferson, Jr. **March 26**: In this entry Wood has written the notation "Forrest not come." Through USG, "The manager [Warren,] respectfully informs the public that having seen an advertisement in the Boston papers announcing Mr. E. Forrest for Monday evening, and the distance rendering it almost impossible for Mr. Forrest to be here in time to fulfill his engagement, he has announced *The Red Rover*; but, should Mr. E. Forrest arrive, immediate notice will be given and a favorite play substituted, in which he will sustain the principal character." **March 27**: *Durang*, II, Chapter Forty-One, states that Celeste played Julio in *Deaf and Dumb*. **April 5**: Wood's bill is "Fazio & Red Rover." However, he has written under "Fazio," "Ch[ange]d to Ella Rosenberg, Miss Emery absent." ADA announces

Miss Emery as Bianca in *Fazio*. **April 7**: USG announces that, in the course of the evening, Mr. Sloman is to sing. **April 14**: *Durang*, II, Chapter Forty-One, records that Wood played Robert Guiscard in *Adelgitha*. **April 17**: Southwell appeared as Conlath in *Malvina*. *Durang*, II, Chapter Forty-One. **April 18**: According to *Durang*, II, Chapter Forty-One, "At the benefit of Mr. S. Chapman, his brother William Chapman, a most excellent low comedian from the Bowery Theatre, acted Marall. The afterpiece was *The Two Gregories*, the two Gregories by the two Chapmans. The Panorama scene from *The Red Rover*, with *The Turnpike Gate*, Crack, Mr. W. Chapman. Receipts $413." **April 22**: USG announces that Miss Hawthorn is to dance, Master Kneass to make "his first appearance on any stage" as Richard, and Miss Workman to play Kitty in *High Life Below Stairs*, in which she is to dance a mock minuet with Mr. Jefferson, Jr." **May 2**: A playbill of this date, in possession of the Library Company of Philadelphia, Ridgway Branch, announces Cooper as Pierre and E. Forrest as Jaffier, and, for "to-Morrow Evening," **May 3**: Cooper as Brutus and E. Forrest as Mark Antony. **May 6**: *Durang*, II, Chapter Forty-One, tells of this appearance of Plantou, a dentist, "who made himself a laughing stock." Warren, in the May 6 entry of his *Diary*, contents himself with the comment, "A Mr. Plantou plays Richard in Broken English." **May 12**: ADA announces Mrs. Austin as Mandane, Horn as Artabanes and Pearman as Arbaces in *Artaxerxes*. **June 16**: ADA announces Miss Fisher as Helen Worrett in *Man and Wife* and Louisa in *The Dead Shot*. In this entry, however, Wood has written, "Horton ill. Ch[ange]d to [The] 4 Mowbra[ys] & [The] D[ay] after [the] W[edding.]" **June 21**: According to USG, Sloman is to sing "the following comic songs: *What are Ye Mortals Made Of?*, *D'Ye Give It Up?*, *Jerry Smart's Trip in Search of Sweet Kitty Clover*, *Betsy Baker* and *Major Longbow*; *or, 'Pon My Soul It's True, What Will You Lay It's a Lie?*

It has been necessary to omit a few notations of importance from the printed version of this season.

In the entry of October 29, Wood has written "Mrs. Braun, Mr. Southwell, Miss Hawthorn, Mr. and Miss Kerr." According to *Durang*, II, Chapter Thirty-Sixth, Mrs. Braun sang, "with variations, *Hope Told a Flattering Tale*, composed by Madame Catalini; Southwell appeared as Romeo, Miss Hawthorn executed a pas seul and Mr. and Miss Kerr also danced. In his October 30 entry Wood has written "Mr. Hutchings, Mr. Mercer, Mr. Norton, Mr. Braun." *Durang*, II, Chapter Thirty-

Sixth, records that Hutchings appeared as Captain Bellville, with Mercer as Mr. Bellville in *Rosina*, Mercer also as Frederick in *The Poor Gentleman*; and Norton in trumpet solos. In his October 31 entry Wood has written "Miss Emery, Mr. S. Chapman." According to *Durang*, II, Chapter Thirty-Sixth, Miss Emery appeared as Belvidera and S. Chapman as Pierre, "who made his first appearance in this character in consequence of the sudden indisposition of Mr. Wood." This last statement explains a notation, "Sick untill 8th. Rec[eived] ½ sal[ar]y on 12th." which Wood has written between the entries of November 12 and 14.

In the printed version of this season it has been advisable to omit a few allusions to sickness and a number of notations referring to financial matters,

[Chesnut Street Theatre]

M[onday] 29 Romeo & Juliet & Is he 610.
            Jealous[?]
                                        fair

T[uesday] 30 [The] Poor Gen[tleman] & 115.
            Rosina
                                        fair

W[ednesday] 31 Venice Pres[erv']d & [The] 270.
            Y[oung] Widow
                                        fair

Nov[ember]
T[hursday] 1 Guy Mann[erin]g & [The] 140.
            Sp[oil']d Child
                                        fine

F[riday] 2 Hamlet & [The] Romp   120.
                                        fine

S. 3 [The] Mount[aineers] & How 120.
            to die [for love]
                                        fine

M. 5 Richard [3d.] & [My] Grand- 130.
            mother
                                        fair

T[uesday]   6 Fazio & [The] Shipwreck   140.
                 fine

W.   7 W[illia]m Tell & [The] Y[oung]   200.
         Widow

                        Rain

T[hursday]   8 [The] Wonder & [A] R[oland]   220.
                 for [an] Oliver

                        fair

F.   9 Fazio & Bombastes [Furioso]   300.
         fine

S. 10 W[illia]m Tell & [The] D[ay]   190.
         after [the] Wed[ding]

                        fine

M. 12 [The] Rencontre & [The]   325.
         M[agpie] & [the] Maid

                        Rain

T[uesday] 13 Evadne* & Where Shall I   250.
                 dine[?]

                        fine

Horn & [Mrs]. W. 14 Love in a Village & [The]   600.
   Knight   Y[oung] Widow
                        [Horn as Young Meadows,
                        Mrs. Knight as Rosetta
                        in *Love in a Village*.
                        ADA]

                        fine

   T[hursday] 15 Rob Roy [Macgregor] & [The]   750.
H[orn] & [Mrs.]   V[illage] Lawyer
   K[night]

                        fine

[411]

F. 16 [The] Cabinet & F[ortune's] 530.
Frolic
fine

S. 17 Evadne & [The] Rencontre   350.   2805.
fair

M. 19 Evadne & [The] Rencontre 402.
[See preface to this season.]
fine

T[uesday] 20 Fazio & L[ove,] L[aw] & Physic 325.
Mr. Norton's   [To play fantasia on French
ben[efit]   horn. ADA]
fine

W. 21 G[uy] Mannering & Abon 1050.
Mrs. Knight's   Hassan
ben[efit]   [As Julia Mannering and as
Zulima in *Abon Hassan*.
ADA]
fine

T[hursday] 22 [The] Jealous Wife & [The] 280.
H[ighland] Reel
fair

F. 23 Evadne & [The] Rencontre 250.
fine

S. 24 Town & Country & Cherry 220.
Bounce
Cold

Mr. Delarue   M. 26 [The] Serjeant's Wife,* Syl- 350.
[vester] Dagg[erwoo]d &
Abon Hassan
[See preface to this season.]
fine

[412]

Brown   T[uesday] 27 Virginius & My Spouse & I   400.
                    [See preface to this season.]
                                              fine

        W. 28 Fazio & Simpson & Co.   160.
               ch[ange]d to W[illia]m Tell
               & C[herry] Bounce. Mrs.
               Anderson sick.
                                              fine

    T[hursday] 29 Abon Hassan, [My] Spouse &   110.
                  I & [The] Serj[eant's]
                  Wife
                                             Rain

        Frid. 30 Douglas & Love L[aw] &   130.
                 Physic
                                              fine

December
        Sat. 1 Evadne & My Spouse & I   150.   1300.
                                             Cold

        Mon. 3 [The] Haunted Tower & [The]   668.
Horn & Mrs.   Serj[eant's] Wife
   K[night]   [Horn as Lord William,
                     Mrs. Horn as Adela in
                     The   Haunted   Tower.
                     ADA]
                                              fine

        Tue. 4 Bellamira & [The] Romp   220.
                                             Rain

        Wed. 5 [The] S[iege] of Belgrade &   700.
Horn's ben[efit]   Turn Out
                    [Horn as Seraskier in *The
                     Siege of Belgrade.* ADA]
                                             Rain

                        [413]

Th. 6 Bellamira & Abon Hassan

102.

fair

Mrs. Sloman F. 7 Isabella & My Spouse & I   700.
[As Isabella. ADA]

fine

Saty. 8 [The] Stranger & C[herry] 310.
Bounce.

Rain

Mrs. Austin M. 10 Love in [a] Village & [The] 430.
Ghost
[As Rosetta in *Love in a
Village*. ADA]

dull

T[uesday] 11 Venice Preserv'd & 102*   730.
Mrs. S[loman]   [As Belvidera in *Venice
Preserved*. ADA]

Cold

Mrs. A[ustin] W. 12 G[uy] Mannering & 102   405.
[As Lucy Bertram in *Guy
Mannering*. ADA]

fair

T[hursday] 13 Jane Shore & [The] Rencontre 1108.
Mrs. [Sloman]   [As Jane Shore. ADA]

fair

F. 14 Rosina, Simpson & Co. & N[o] 300.
Song No S[upper]

dull

S. 15 Romeo & Juliet & Bombastes 708.   3681.
[Furioso]

dull

Mon. 17 [The] Gamester & Fish out of 1038.
Mrs. S[loman's]   Water
Ben[efit]   [As Mrs. Beverly in *The*
                         Gamester. ADA]
                                                    dull

Tues. 18 Henri   Quatre   [The]   Ser-   280.
Mrs. Austin   j[eant's] Wife
                         [As Florence St Leon in
                         Henry Quatre. ADA]
                                                    dull

Wed. 19 [The] Jealous Wife & Fish out   600.
Mrs. S[loman]   of Water
                         [As Mrs. Oakly in *The*
                         Jealous Wife. ADA]
                                                    dull

Thurs. 20 Rob Roy [Macgregor] & 102   160.
Mrs. A[ustin]   [As Diana Vernon in *Rob*
                         Roy Macgregor. ADA]
                                                    dull

Frid. 21 [The] Provok'd Husband &   740.
Mrs. S[loman]   Family Jars
                         [As Lady Townly in *The*
                         Provoked Husband. ADA]
                                                    dull

Sat. 22 Charles 2d & Simpson & Co.   250.
Mrs. A[ustin]   [As Mary Copp in *Charles*
                         the Second. ADA]
                                                    Cold

Mon. 24 Rosina & Bellamira   260.
Mrs. A[ustin]   [As Rosina. ADA]
                                                    Cold

T[uesday] 25 Geo[rge] Barnwell & Don   740.
                         Giovanni
                                                    dull

[415]

Wed. 26 The Usurper* & C[herry]   630.
           Bounce
                              · dull

         Thurs. 27 Jane Shore & Family Jars   850.
Mrs. S[loman]   [As Jane Shore. ADA]
                              Sleet & Rain

         Frid. 28 Artaxerxes & [The] Irish-   480.
Mrs. A[ustin's]   [man] in London
Ben[efi]t   [As Mandane in Artaxerxes.
                     ADA]
                              fair

         Sat. 29 [The] Gamester & Deaf as a   475.   3435.
Mrs. S[loman]   post
                     [As Mrs. Beverly in *The
                     Gamester*. ADA]
                              fair

         M. 31 Isabella & Dead as a post   1040.
Mrs. S[loman's]   [As Isabella. ADA an-
Ben[efit]   nounces *Family Jars* in
                     place of *Deaf as a Post*]
                              fair

         January
T[uesday] 1 Peter Wilkins & My Spouse   706.
            & I
                              dull

         W. 2 Peter Wilkins, Stories & Mr.   720.
Mr. Hacket[t]   Tonson
                     [See preface to this season.]
                              Rain

         T[hursday] 3 [The] Stranger & Paul Pry 1108.
Mrs. Sloman's   [See preface to this season.]
ben[efit]
                              fair

[416]

    F. 4 [The] Usurper & [The] Ser- 130.
       geant's Wife
           dull

Mr. Forrest S. 5 Brutus & [The] Romp 492. 4196.
           dull

Forrest Mon. 7 Damon & Pythias & [The] 630.
       Spoil'd Child
       [As Damon. ADA]
           dull

F[orrest] Tues. 8 W[illia]m Tell & Sprigs of 350.
       Laurel
       [As William Tell. ADA]
           Rain

    Wed. 9 Virginius & Abon Hassan 550.
F[orrest's] Ben[efit] [As Virginius. ADA]
           fine

    Thurs. 10 [The] Marriage of Figaro & 418.
Miss George   [The] L[ady] & [the] Devil
       [As Susanna in *The Mar-*
       riage of Figaro. ADA]
           dull

    Frid. 11 Peter Wilkins & Simpson & 340.
       Co.
           dull

    Sat. 12 [The] Marriage of Figaro & 250.
Miss George   Ella Rosenberg
       [As Susanna. ADA]
           dull

    Mon. 14 [The] Cabinet & Love, Law & 300.
Miss George   Physic
       [As Floretta in *The Cabinet.*
       ADA]
           Dull

[417]

Tues. 15 Peter Wilkins & [The] Iron   460.
Chest
fine

Wed. 16 [The] Padlock, 'Twas I & 102   280.
Miss G[eorge]   [As Leonora in *The Padlock*
and Georgette in *'Twas I.*
ADA]
Dull

Thurs. 17 Pizarro & My Grandmother   260.
Brown['s] 2[nd.]   [As Rolla in *Pizarro*. USG]
app[earance]
fair

Frid. 18 [The] Haunted Tower & 'Twas   300.
Miss G[eorge]   I
[As Adela in *The Haunted
Tower* and Georgette in
'Twas I. ADA]
dull

Sat. 19 [The] Apostate & Peter   360.   1960.
Wilkins
fair

Mon. 21 [The] Siege of Belgrade & No   201.
Miss G[eorge]   Song N[o] Supper
[As Margaretta in *No Song
No Supper*. USG]
C^ld

Tues. 22 John Rock & [The] Ren-   1^0.
contre
Cold

Wed. 23 [The] Apostate & Paul &   175.
Miss G[eorge]   Virginia
[As Virginia. USG]
fine

[418]

Thurs. 24 John Rock & P[eter] Wilkins 260.
fine

Frid. 25 [The] Devil's Bridge & [The] 120.
A[greeable] Surprize
Miss G[eorge] ill. Mr.
Heyl [as Count] Belino
[in *The Devil's Bridge.*
See preface to this
season.]
Rain

Saty. 26 Peter Wilkins & Don Giovanni 180.   1126.
Rain

Mon. 28 Inkle & Yarico, 'Twas I & 744.
Miss George's   [The] 100 £ Note
Ben[efit]   [As Wowski in *Inkle and
Yarico*, Georgette in
'Twas I and Harriet
Arlington in The £100
Note. ADA]
fine

Tues. 29 Douglas & [The] I[rishman] 470.
McCahen's 1st.   in London
ap[pearance]   [As Young Norval in
Douglas. USG See pref-
ace to this season.]
fine

Wed. 30 Bellamira & John Rock   130.
fine

Thurs. 31 Peter Wilkins, [The] Ren- 125.
dezvous & Cherry Bounce
fine

[419]

Feb[ruar]y

Frid. 1 Damon & Pythias, Tom & 300.
Jerry & [The] High[land]
Reel

fine

Saty. 2 [The] Wonder & [The] Village 475. 2244.
Miss K[elly] Lawyer
[As Donna Violante in *The
Wonder*. USG]

Rain

Mon. 4 Much Ado [about Nothing] & 599.
Miss K[elly] My Spouse & I
[As Beatrice. ADA]

dull

Tues. 5 [The] Inconstant & Abon 256.
Mr. Bur[roughs] Hassan
[As Young Mirabel in *The
Inconstant*. USG]

Rain

Wed. 6 [The] Belle's Stratagem & 456.
Miss K[elly] [The] Prize
[As Letitia Hardy in *The
Belle's Stratagem*. ADA]

Rain

Thurs. 7 [The] Stranger & the Cossack 125.
Mr. Bur[roughs] [& the Volunteer]*
[As the Stranger. ADA]

dull

Frid. 8 Wives as they Were [& Maids 460.
Miss K[elly] as They Are] & Turn Out
[As Miss Dorillon in *Wives
as They Were* and Marian
Ramsay in *Turn Out*.
ADA]

Very fine

Sat. 9 [The] Jealous Wife & the Cos- 440.   2336.
Miss K[elly]   sack [the Volunteer]
                     [As Mrs. Oakly in *The
                     Jealous Wife*. ADA]
                                    dull

Mon. 11 She Would & [She] W[oul]d 470.
Miss K[elly]   Not & [The] Prize
                     [As Hippolita in *She Would
                     and She Would Not* and
                     Caroline in *The Prize*.
                     ADA]
                                    fine

Tues. 12 Tom & Jerry & [The] Review 315.
Mr. Burr[oughs]   [As Jerry and as Caleb
                     Quotem in *The Review*.
                     ADA]
                               fine & Cold

Wed. 13 She Stoops to Conquer & 260.
                     [The] Acress of all W[or]k
                     [See preface to this season.]
                                    dull

Thurs. 14 Tom & Jerry & Of Age to- 190.
Mr. Bur[roughs]   morrow
                     [As Jerry. USG]
                                    Rain

Frid. 15 [The] Honey Moon & Simp- 270.
Miss K[elly]   son & Co.
                     [As Juliana in *The Honey
                     Moon*. USG]
                                    Rain

Saty. 16 As You Like it & Therese 360.   1865.
Miss K[elly]   [As Rosalind. ADA]
                                    fine

[421]

Mon. 18 [The] School for Scandal &   896.
Miss Kelly's   Ladies at Home
Ben[efit.]   [As Lady Teazle in *The*
            School for Scandal and
            Mrs. Banter in *Ladies at*
            Home. ADA]
                  Heavy Storm

Tues. 19 [The] Bride of Abydos & [The]   350.
Mr. Burr[ough's]   Sleep Walker
Ben[efit]
                    fine

Wed. 20 [The] Will & Old & Young   840.
Miss C[lara] Fisher   [As Albina Mandeville in
            The Will and every char-
            acter in *Old and Young.*
            ADA]
                Warm & fine

Thurs. 21 [The] Red Rover* & Cherry   704.
            Bounce
                    fine

Frid. 22 [The] Red Rover & Sprigs of   602.
W[ashington's]   Laurel
Birthday
                    fine

Saty. 23 [The] Belle's Stratagem &   906.   4298.
Miss C[lara] F[isher]   [The] Acress of all Work
            [As Letitia Hardy in *The*
            Belle's Stratagem and as
            every character in *The*
            Actress of All Work.
            ADA]
                  fine

Mon. 25 [The] School for Scandal & 620.
Miss F[isher]   Old & Young
[As Lady Teazle in *The
School for Scandal* and as
every character in *Old
and Young*. ADA]
Cold

Tues. 26 [The] Red Rover & [The] 100 540.
£ Note
fine

Wed. 27 Douglas & [The] Spoil'd Child 590.
Miss F[isher]   [As Young Norval in
Douglas. USG]
fair

Thurs. 28 [The] Red Rover & [My] 380.
Grandmother
fair

Frid. 29 [The] Rivals & [The] Romp 920.
Miss F[isher]   [As Lydia Languish. USG]
fair

March
Sat. 1st. [The] Merchant of Venice & 510.   3560.
Is he Jealous[?]
fine _____

Mon. 3 Lovers' Vows & [The] Dead 1234.
Miss F[isher's]   Shot
Ben[efit]   [As Amelia in *Lovers' Vows*
and Louisa in *The Dead
Shot*. ADA]
fair

Tues. 4 W[illia]m Tell & [The] Dead 302.
C[lara] Fisher   Shot

[423]

[As William Tell and
Louisa. ADA]

fine

Wed. 5 [The] Wand[erin]g Boys, [The] 340.
Miss F[isher] Rendezvous & [The]
Young Widow
[As Paul in *The Wandering
Boys*, Sophia in *The Ren-
dezvous* and Aurelia Fair-
love in *The Young Widow*.
ADA]

fine

Thurs. 6 [The] Country Girl & [The] 488.
Miss F[isher] Actress of all Work
[As Miss Peggy in *The
Country Girl* and as every
character in *The Actress
of All Work*. ADA]

fair

Frid. 7 John Rock & [The] Ten 1128.
Miss F[isher] Mowbrays
[As the ten Mowbrays.
USG]

fine

Saty. 8 [The] Ten Mowbrays & [The] 960. 4452.
Hig[hlan]d Reel
Miss F[isher's] [As the ten Mowbrays and
Benefit as Moggy McGilpin in
The Highland Reel. ADA]

fine

Mon. 10 [The] Belle's Stratagem & 385.
Miss Rock Winn[in]g a Husband
[As Letitia Hardy in *The
Belle's Stratagem* and as

[424]

eight characters in *Win-
ning a Husband*. ADA]
fair

Tues. 11 [The] Red Rover & Rais[in]g 250.
the Wind
Rain

Miss Rock

Wed. 12 [The] Soldier's Daughter & 275.
[The] 100 £ Note
[As the Widow Cheerly in
The Soldier's Daughter
and Harriet Arlington in
The £ 100 Note. ADA]
fair

Thurs. 13 [The] Red Rover & [The] 330.
Village Lawyer
fair

Miss Rock

Frid. 14 [The] Provok[']d Husb[an]d & 402.
Winn[in]g a Husband
fine

Miss Rock

Saty. 15 [The] Honey Moon & [The] 320.   1962.
Actress of all Work
Rain

Miss Rock

Mon. 17 Know y[ou]r own Mind & 335.
Therese
[As Lady Bell in *Know Your
Own Mind*. USG]
fine

Mad[emoiselle]
Celeste

Tues. 18 Abon Hassan, Dances, 'Twas 375.
I & S[ylvester] Dagg[er-
woo]d
[In grand pas seul. USG]
fine

[425]

Wed. 19 [The] Bride of Lammermoor   280.
Miss Rock   & [The] Citizen
                       [As Lady Ashton in *The
                       Bride of Lammermoor* and
                       Maria in The Citizen.
                       ADA]
                                              fine

Thurs. 20 [The] Red Rover, Dances &   420.
Mad[emoiselle]   [The]   I[rishman]   in
Celeste   London
                       [In grand pas seul. USG]
                                              fine

Frid. 21 Wives as they Were [& Maids   280.
Miss Rock   as They Are] & Winn[in]g
                       a Husband
                       [See preface to this season.]
                                              fine

Sat. 22 [The] Bride of Lamm[ermoo]r   200.   1890.
                       & Turn Out
                                              fine

Mon. 24 Know y[ou]r own Mind &   651.
Miss Rock['s]   Clari
benefit   [As Lady Bell in *Know
                       Your Own Mind* and as
                       Clari. ADA]
                                              fine

Tues. 25 [The] Broken Sword, Rosina   260.
Mad[emoiselle]   [&] Where Shall I dine[?]
Celeste   [As Myrtillo in *The Broken
                       Sword* and Julio in *Deaf
                       and Dumb.* ADA]
                                              fine

[426]

Wed. 26 [The] Red Rover & R[aising 190.
the] Wind
[See preface to this season.]
fine

Thurs. 27 Deaf & Dumb, Dances & 540.
Mad[emoiselle]   [The] Broken Sword
Celeste['s] Benefit   [See preface to this season.]
fine

Frid. 28 Charles 2d. & [The] 100 £ 116.
Note
Very Warm & fine

Sat. 29 [The] Sleepwalker, [The] 100 240.   1997.
Mr. Roberts   £ Note & Family Jars
[As Somno in *The Sleep-
walker*, Delph in *Family
Jars* and Billy Black in
The 100 £ *Note*. USG]
fine

Mon. 31 Gambler's fate & [The] Romp 580.
Rain

April
Tues. 1 Gambler's fate & 195.
fine

Wed. 2 Gambler's fate & 180.
fine

Thurs. 3 Gambler's fate & 'Tis all a 145.
farce
fine

Frid. 4 (Good Friday. No performance.)

[427]

Sat. 5 Ella Rosenberg & [The] Red   255.   1355.
Rover
[See preface to this season.]
fine

Mon. 7 [The] Innkeeper's D[aughte]r, 1052.
Warren['s] Benefit   [The] P[risoner] at Large
Mr. Sloman   & [The] Fish out [of]
Water
[See preface to this season.]
fair

Tues. 8 The Serf & [The] Innkeeper's 120.
D[aughte]r
fine

Wed. 9 Gambler's fate & Sprigs of 130.
Laurel
fine

Thurs. 10 [The] Serf & [The] Red Rover 170.
fine

Frid. 11 [The] Lie of the day & Who's 810.50
Jefferson's Benefit   Who?
fine

Sat. 12 Barbarossa & [The Agreeable 351.
Brown's ben[efit]   Surprise]
McCahen's 1st.   [Brown as Barbarossa, Mc-
app[earance]   Cahen as Selin. USG]
fine

Mon. 14 Adelgitha, Ballet & Mr. H.   626.50
Wood's ben[efi]t   [See preface to this season.]
Heavy Snow all day

Tues. 15 Peter Wilkins & [A] Budget of 188.50
[Benefit of]   blunders
Mr. Heyl   [As Peter Wilkins. USG]
fair

[428]

Wed. 16 Folly as it flies & 3 finger'd   307.
[Benefit of] Mrs.   Jack
And[erson] &
J. Jeff[erson]

                                        fine

[Benefit of] Thurs. 17 Malvina* & [The] Lie of a day   568.
Mr. Southwell   [See preface to this season.]

                                        fine

Frid. 18 [The] Vampire, [The] 2 Greg-   413.
[Benefit of] Mr.   ories & [The] Turnpike
S. Chapman,   Gate
W. Chap[man]   [See preface to this season.]

                                        fine

Sat. 19 [The] Road to Ruin & [The]   631.   2734.
[Benefit of] Miss   Rencontre
E. Jeff[erson]

                                        Rain

Mon. 21 [The] School of Reform, [The]   517.
Mr. & Master   Cossac[k] & [The] Adopted
Mercer['s Benefit]   Child

                                        Rain

Tues. 22 Richard 3d. & H[igh] life   579.
[Benefit of] Miss   below Stairs
Hawthorn.   [See preface to this season.]
M[aste]r Kneass
& Miss Workman

                                        fair

Wed. 23 [The] Foundling of [the] Forest   372.
[Benefit of] Mr.   & Tom Thumb [the
Watson   Great]

                                        fine

[429]

Thurs. 24 Fazio & [The] Innkeeper's 250.
Daughter
Ticket night. [For the
benefit of the Door-
keepers, &c. USG]
fine

Cooper   Frid. 25 Macbeth & [A] Budget of 655.
Blunders
[As Macbeth. USG]
Rain

Cooper   Saty. 26 Virginius & [The] Day after 218.   2591
[the] Wedding
[As Virginius. ADA]
Rain

Cooper   Mon. 28 Damon & Pythias & [The] 350.
Romp
[As Damon. ADA]
fair

Tues. 29 [The] Vampire, [The] 100 £ 150.
Note & Who's Who?
dull

Wed. 30 Othello & 'Tis all a farce 734.
For[r]est & Cooper   [Forrest as Iago, Cooper as
Othello. ADA]
fair

May
Thurs. 1 Crazy Jane, Tom Thumb 432.
Miss Emery's   [the Great] & Matrimony
ben[efit]   [As Crazy Jane. USG]
fine

Frid. 2 Venice preserv'd & [My] 284.
Cooper & Forrest   Spouse & I
[See preface to this season.]
Rain

[430]

Saty. 3 Julius Caesar & [The] H[igh- 432. 2382.
land] Reel
[See preface to this season.]
Dull

Mon. 5 Othello & Who's Who? 573.
Forrest's Ben[efit.] C[ooper as Iago] & F[orrest
as Othello. ADA]
fine

Plantou Tues. 6 Richard 3d. & Where Shall I 148.
dine[?]
[See preface to this season.]
fair

Wed. 7 Artaxerxes & [The] Vampire 452.
Horn, Pear[man] & [Horn as Artabanes, Pearman
Mrs. Austin as Arbaces and Mrs
Austin as Mandane in
Artaxerxes. USG
fine

Thurs. 8 Evadne & Deaf as a Post 536.
Wemy[s]s' Ben[efit.]
Mr. & Mrs
Sloman
fine

Frid. 9 [The] Marriage of Figaro & 410.
3 Singers Therese
fine

Sat. 10 Gambler's fate & Family Jars 90. 2209.
Mrs. Sloman sick.
fair

Mon. 12 Artaxerxes, C[herry] Bounce 288.
Mrs. Austin, Horn & [The] Rendezvous
& P[earman] [See preface to this season.]
fine

[431]

Tues. 13 Jane Shore & [The] Fish out   184.
Mr. & Mrs. Sloman,   of Water
Mr. Rowbotham['s]   [First night of] Mrs. Slo-
1st.   man['s engagement; 1st.
            [of] Mr. R[owbotham,
            who, according to USG,
            is to play Dumont in
            Jane Shore.]
                          fine

Wed. 14 [The] Broken Sword & For-   80.
            tune's frolic
            Miss   Jeff[erson]   Sick.
            Ch[ange]d from [The]
            M[arriage] of Figaro
                          fine

Thurs. 15 Foscari* & Deaf as a post   194.
Mr. & Mrs.   [Mr. Sloman as Tristram
S[loman]   Sappy in *Deaf as a Post*,
            Mrs. Sloman as Camilla
            in *Foscari*. USG]
                          fine

Frid. 16 [Der] Freyschutz & L[overs'] 359.
Horn, P[earman] &   Quarrels
[Mrs.] Austin   [Horn as Casper, Pearman
            as Rodolph and Mrs.
            Austin as Linda in *Der*
            Freischutz. ADA]
                          fine

Sat. 17 Foscari & [The] Turnpike   127.   1132.
Mr. & Mrs.   Gate
S[loman]   [Sloman as Crack in *The*
            Turnpike Gate, Mrs. Slo-
            man as Camilla in
            Foscari. ADA]
                        Warm

Mon. 19 Der Freyschutz & [The] Ren- 267.
Horn's benefit   dezvous
          [As Casper in *Der Frei-schutz*. ADA]
                    fair

Tues. 20 Isabella & [The] Lottery 612.
Mr. Sloman's   Ticket*
ben[efit]   [As Wormwood in *The Lottery Ticket*. ADA]
                    fine

Wed. 21 [The] Marriage of Figaro & 143.
Horn, P[earman] &   [The] Village Lawyer
Mrs. Austin   [Horn as Count Almaviva, Pearman as Figaro and Mrs. Austin as Countess Almaviva. ADA]
                    Rain

Thurs. 22 [The] Gamester & [The] Lot- 120.
Mr. & Mrs. Sloman tery Ticket
Mr. Robotham['s]   [Sloman as Stukely, Mrs.
2d.   Sloman as Mrs. Beverly in *The Gamester*. Sloman as Wormwood in *The Lottery Ticket*. ADA]
                    fair

Frid. 23 [The] Barber of Seville & [The] 186.
Pearman's ben[efit.] Blue Devils
          [Pearman as Figaro. ADA]
                    fine

Sat. 24 [The] Honey Moon & [The] 170.   1498.
Ben[efit of the]   Fish out of Water
Greek fund.   [Cooper as Duke Aranza,
Cooper & Mrs.   Mrs. Sloman as Juliana
Sloman   in *The Honey Moon*. ADA]
                    fine

[433]

Mon. 26 Artaxerxes & [The] Barber of 375.
Mrs. Austin's   Seville
Ben[efit]   [As Mandane in *Artaxerxes*
                       and Rosina in *The Barber
                       of Seville*. ADA]
                                Rain

Tues. 27 R[omeo] & Juliet, Song & 125.
Mr. & Mrs. Slom[an]   Quite Correct
& Sig[nor]
Angrisani.
                                      fine

Wed. 28 Foscari & Intrigue   375.
Mrs. Sloman's   [As Camilla in *Foscari* and
ben[efit.]   Ellen in *Intrigue*. ADA]
                                      fine

Thurs. 29 [The] Innkeeper's D[aughte]r 55.
Sig[nor]   & [The] Adopted Child
Ang[risani]   [In comic grotesque dance.
                       USG]
                                Rain

Frid. 30 Abon Hassan & 'Twas I   90.
Sig[nor]   [In dance between play
A[ngrisani]   and farce. USG an-
                     nounces *Pizarro* in
                     place of *Abon Hassan*.]
                                      fine

Saty. 31 Tom & Jerry & [The] Blue 85.   1105.
Sign[or]   Devils
A[ngrisani]   [In.dance. USG]
                                Rain

June
Mon. 2 [She] Stoops to Conquer & 147.
Mr. Sloman   Quite Correct

[434]

[As Tony Lumpkin in *She
Stoops to Conquer* and
Grojan in *Quite Correct*.
ADA]
                                    Rain

Tues.   3 Clari & [The] Ghost   65.
Sig[nor] Ang[ri-   [To appear in grotesque
sani's] Ben[efit]   dance. ADA]
                                          fine

Wed.   4 [The] Rivals, Songs & Animal   354.
Mr. Sloman's 3d.   Magnetism
Ben[efit]   [As Bob Acres in *The Rivals*
                         and La Fleur in *Animal
                         Magnetism*. ADA]
                                          Hot

Thurs.   5 Charles [the] 2d & [The] Romp   60.50
                                          fine

Frid.   6 [The] Ten Mowbrays & 'Twas   360.
Miss Fisher   I
                      [To personate ten different
                         characters in *The Ten
                         Mowbrays*. USG]
                                          fine
Saty.   7 No performance.   987.50

Mon.   9 [The] Country Girl & [The]   243.
Miss [Clara] Fisher   Actress of all Work
                      [To personate six different
                         characters in *The Actress
                         of All Work*. USG]
                                  Cool & fine

Tues. 10 [The]   Gnome   King*   &   425.
                      Lovers['] Quarrels
                                          fine

[435]

Wed. 11 As You Like it & [The] Spoil'd 114.
Miss [Clara] Fisher   Child
      [As Rosalind and as Little
      Pickle in *The Spoiled
      Child.* USG]
                  Warm

Thurs. 12 [The] Gnome King & [The] 345.
      Blue Devils
                  Hot

Frid. 13 Paul Pry & [The] Romp   195.
Miss [Clara]   [As Phoebe in *Paul Pry* and
Fisher   Priscilla Tomboy in *The
      Romp.* ADA]
                  Warm

Saty. 14 [The] Gnome King & Cherry 260.   1582.
      Bounce
                  Hot

Mon. 16 Man & Wife & [The] Dead 290.
Miss Fisher's   Shot
Ben[efit]   [See preface to this season.]
                  Hot

Tues. 17 [The] Gnome King & [The] 180.
      Ghost
                  Warm

Wed. 18 [The] Gnome King & [The] 160.
      100 £ Note
                  Rain

Thurs. 19 [The] Gnome King & Who's 140.
      Who[?]
                  fine

Frid. 20 [The] Gnome King &   150.
      [USG also announces *The
      Warlock of the Glen.*]
                  fair

ARCH STREET THEATRE

Saty. 21 Must Be Buried,* [The]   435.   1355.
Warren's Ben[efit]   G[nome] King &
Mr. Sloman   [See preface to this season.]
                      fair

$77276.50

202 Nights Averaged $382.50
After Stars & Ben[efits] 295.25

ARCH STREET THEATRE, OPEN'D OCT[OBE]R 1st., [CLOSED DECEMBER 29,] 1828.

[Wood]

PREFACE: Neither *Durang* nor *Recollections* includes a complete list of the members of the first Arch Street company. The *Account Book*, however, in its entry of October 8, records a weekly "Payment of Performers ['] Salaries." It has been necessary to omit the notation from the printed text; but, as it contains as complete a list as it is possible to secure of Wood's players, as well as the weekly salaries they received, it is interesting and important. The notation reads: "Mr. & Mrs. Wood, [$]56; Mr. & Mrs. Roberts, 68; Mr. & Mrs. Stone, 50; Mr. & Mrs. Blake, 60, Mr. Chapman, 46.67; Mr. & Mrs. Green, 40; Mr. Boyle, 38; Mr. Scott, 37; Mr. Duffy, 25; Mr. & Mrs. Blakely, 25; Mr. & Mrs. Murray, 20; Mr. Page, 20; Mr. Knight, 20; Mr. Sefton, 20; Mrs. Roper, 20; Mr. Kelly, 16; Mr. Isherwood, 15; Mr. Bignall, 14; Miss Southwell, 12; Miss Armstrong, 10; Mr. Eglee, 8; Mrs. Maywood, 25; Mr. & Mrs. Nelson, 13; Mr. Golden, 12; Mr. Conway, 12; Mr. Garson, 8; Mr. Thompson, 7; Mr. Lyon, 6; Miss Garson, 4; Mrs. Lee, 4." According to a notation in Wood's entry of October 22, a "Mrs. Fairfield" received "$7" for performing; and, according to another in Wood's entry of November 5, a "Mr. & Mrs. Wells" received "$45." Both of these notations have been crowded out of the printed text but they must be mentioned in connection with the notation in the entry of October 8. In his entry of October 4, Wood includes a notation of the "Payment of [the] Band to the 8th." This notation, though omitted from the printed text for the usual reason, is of sufficient importance to be printed in toto, as it contains a list of the members of the Arch Street band, together with the amounts of their weekly salaries. The notation reads: "Mr. Willis, [$]26.50; Mr. Krollman, 16; Mr. Hansen, 14; Mr. Kober, 12; Mr. Schmetz,

[437]

11; Mr. Gertz, 10; Mr. Carr, 10; Mr. Fiot, 10; Mr. Conter, 10; Mr. Clements & Mr. Brennan each $9, 18; Mr. De Marbias & Mr. Wolfe each $8, 16; Mr. Cross 5, Mr. Moran 4." In Wood's entry of October 22 a "Mr. Johnson" is mentioned as receiving "$9" for performing in the band. In the entry of November 5 occurs the notation, "Greenlund in place of Getz and $2 added to Salary[;] Schmeling [in place] of Bren-[n]an and $3 added to Salary[:] Worrell Salary added 10." In Wood's entry of November 26 a   Breck" is mentioned as having received "$7," evidently for playing in the band. All of these notations have been crowded out of the printed text, as well as the following: "Paid Mad'lle Celeste in full to Octr. 11th, Tickets & Cash, 252.25," in the entry of October 10; "Paid Mr. Holland in full, 130.00," in the entry of October 11; "Miss Southwell's Salary withheld this Week, 12; "Paid Mr. Horn for himself and Mrs. Austin, Cash, 850.00," in the entry of November 12; and "Paid Miss Rock in full as p[e]r receipt on file, 309.50," in the entry of November 24. Less relevant notations omitted from the printed text have to do with "Bills paid," including bills for "Coals," "Extra posting long Bills," "Charcoal," "Molasses for paint-room," etc. and "Payment to Servants," such as a "Housekeeper," "Hairdresser." "Machinist," "Box door keeper," etc. Wood's notations reveal that he spent, between October 4 and 8, the sum of $1572.14 in salaries to the players and the band and for miscellaneous necessities. It is easy to understand, in view of these expenses, why it was impossible for Wood to pay the rates demanded by stars. For further details regarding the Arch Street venture, see *Recollections*, Chapter XVIII. For a description of the theatre, see the general introduction, p. 56; and for an account of the conclusion of the 1828 season, see the general introduction, p. 58.

[Arch Street Theatre]

[October 1] [The] Honey Moon, prize
Address & Three & [the]
Deuce
[USG announces: "Arch
Street Theatre. The
public is respectfully informed that the theatre
will be opened this even-
ing, October 1, 1828 with
a prize address written by

a gentleman of this city
to be spoken by Mr.
Wood."]

Box	Certificates	80.50	
	Cash	603.00	
Pit	Cash	269.31	
Gal[ler]y	Cash	74.	1026.81

October 2nd. Sweethearts & Wives & Of Age
tomorrow

Box	Certificates	6.00	
	Cash	154.00	
Pit	Cash	86.75	
Gal[ler]y	Cash	23.00	
			296.75

3d. [The] Poor Gentleman & [The]
Day after the Wedding

Box	Certificates	24.00	
	Cash	150.00	
Pit	Cash	100.75	
Gal[ler]y	Cash	22.00	
			296.75

4th Venice Preserv'd & the Lottery Ticket

Box	Certificates	12.00	
	Cash	166.00	
Pit	Cash	160.00	
Gal[ler]y	Cash	56.75	394.75

6th Deaf and Dumb & [The] Lottery Ticket

Box	Certificates	6.00	
	Cash	140.00	
Pit	Cash	110.00	
Gal[ler]y	Cash	32.25	288.25

7th [The] Soldier's Daughter &
   Matrimony

Box	Certificates	8.00	
	Cash	163.25	
Pit	Cash	120.00	
Gal[ler]y	Cash	21.00	312.25

8th Sweethearts & Wives & [A]
   Day after the Fair

Box	Certificates	20.00	
	Cash	162.50	
Pit	Cash	112.25	
Gal[ler]y	Cash	27.00	321.75

9th Matrimony & [The] Whim[s]
   of a Comedian

Box	Certificates	6.00	
	Cash	156.50	
Pit	Cash	111.50	
Gal[ler]y	Cash	21.25	295.25

Mad[emoise]lle   10th [The] 100 £ Note & Valentine
Celeste's Night   & Orson
                    [As Valentine. USG]

Box	Certificates	21.00	
	Cash	244.50	
Pit	Cash	195.50	
Gal[ler]y	Cash	43.25	504.25

Mr. Holland's   11th [The] Whims of a Comedian &
Night   Valen[tin]e & Orson
                 [Mr. Holland will present an
                 entertainment called *The
                 Whims of a Comedian*,
                 consisting of ventril-

oquism, &c. The whole
of the performance will be
recited, acted, sung and
gesticulated by Mr. Hol-
land alone. USG]

Box	Certificates	15.00	
	Cash	163.50	
Pit	Cash	158.00	
Gal[ler]y	Cash	58.00	**394.50**

13th [The] Belle's Stratagem &
[The] 100 £ Note

Box	Certificates	55.00	
	Cash	244.50	
Pit	Cash	204.50	
Gal[ler]y	Cash	34.75	538.75

14th Adelgitha & the Lottery
Ticket

Box	Certificates	none	
	Cash	77.00	
Pit	Cash	83.25	
Gal[ler]y	Cash	26.50	186.75

15th Much ado about Nothing &
of Age tomorrow

Box	Certificates	44.00	
	Cash	205.50	
Pit	Cash	137.50	
Gal[ler]y	Cash	16.75	403.75

16th [The] Foundling of the Forest
& [The] Irishman in
London

[441]

Box	Certificates	17.00	
	Cash	89.00	
Pit	Cash	63.50	
Gal[ler]y	Cash	18.25	187.75

17th Wives as they Were [& Maids as They Are] & the Prize

Box	Certificates	47.00	
	Cash	203.00	
Pit	Cash	141.25	
Gal[ler]y	Cash	15.75	407.00

18th [The] Wonder & Family Jars

Box	Certificates	4.00	
	Cash	129.75	
Pit	Cash	172.50	
Gal[ler]y	Cash	30.00	336.25

20th [The] Jealous Wife & Turn Out

Box	Certificates	27.00	
	Cash	214.25	
Pit	Cash	169.25	
Gal[ler]y	Cash	27.00	437.50

21st. Adelgitha & [The] 100 £ Note

Box	Certificates	none	
	Cash	94.00	
Pit	Cash	95.75	
Gal[ler]y	Cash	19.25	209.00

22d. As you like it & [The] Lady & the Devil

Box	Certificates	18.00	
	Cash	191.75	
Pit	Cash	153.25	
Gal[ler]y	Cash	19.50	382.50

23d. [The] Robbers & [The] Irish
  Valet

Box	Certificates	9.00	
	Cash	88.75	
Pit	Cash	197.50	
Gal[ler]y	Cash	38.50	333.75

Miss Kelly's
Night

24th She Stoops to C[onquer],
  Ladies at home & [The]
  Lottery ticket
  [As Miss Hardcastle in *She
  Stoops to Conquer* and
  Mrs. Baxter in *Ladies
  at Home.* USG.]

Box	Certificates	80.00	
	Cash	324.50	
Pit	Cash	243.75	
Gal[ler]y	Cash	36.00	**684.25**

25th [The] Honey Moon & [The]
  Irish Valet

Box	Certificates	4.00	
	Cash	83.25	
Pit	Cash	109.25	
Gal[ler]y	Cash	32.75	229.25

27th [The] Soldier's Daughter &
  Ladies at Home

Box	Certificates	20.00	
	Cash	159.75	
Pit	Cash	116.00	
Gal[ler]y	Cash	23.00	**318.75**

28th [The] Robbers & Too late for
  Dinner

Box	Certificates	4.00	
	Cash	111.00	

[443]

Pit	Cash	140.00	
Gal[lery]	Cash	35.75	290.75

29th [The] Jealous Wife & [The]
Day after the Wedding

Box	Certificates	39.00	
	Cash	252.25	
Pit	Cash	214.00	
Gal[ler]y	Cash	26.00	531.25

30th Paul Pry & Three & [the]
Deuce

Box	Certificates	8.00	
	Cash	75.75	
Pit	Cash	62.25	
Gal[ler]y	Cash	16.25	162.25

Miss Kelly's
2nd Night

31st [The] School for Scandal &
[The] Rendezvous
[As Lady Teazle in *The
School for Scandal* and
Sophia in *The Rendez-
vous*. USG]

Box	Certificates	61.00	
	Cash	230.50	
Pit	Cash	219.25	
Gal[ler]y	Cash	39.50	550.25

Novem[be]r 1st. Guy Mannering & Family
Jars

Box	Certificates	6.00	
	Cash	87.50	
Pit	Cash	101.25	
Gal[ler]y	Cash	27.00	221.75

3d Guy Mannering & [The] Irish
Valet

Box	Certificates	13.00
	Cash	164.25

Pit	Cash	154.50	
Gal[ler]y	Cash	27.00	358.75

4th John Bull & [The] Irishman in
   London

Box	Certificates	none	
	Cash	113.50	
Pit	Cash	108.25	
Gal[ler]y	Cash	16.25	238.00

5th [The] Lord of the Manor &
   Family Jars

Box	Certificates	4.00	
	Cash	149.75	
Pit	Cash	149.00	
Gal[ler]y	Cash	18.50	321.25

6 King Lear & [The] Lottery
   Ticket

Box	Certificates	4.00	
	Cash	108.00	
Pit	Cash	109.25	
Gal[ler]y	Cash	34.50	255.75

7th [The] Beggar's Opera & [The]
   100 £ Note

Box	Certificates	39.00	
	Cash	412.00	
Pit	Cash	261.25	
Gal[ler]y	Cash	44.25	756.50

8th [The] Beggar's Opera & [The]
   Day after [the] Wedding

Box	Certificates	9.00	
	Cash	130.25	
Pit	Cash	165.00	
Gal[ler]y	Cash	34.50	338.75

Mrs. Austin's
Night

10th Native Land & [The] Rendezvous

[As Coelio in *Native Land.* USG]

Box	Certificates	63.00	
	Cash	190.75	
Pit	Cash	167.75	
Gal[ler]y	Cash	33.50	455.00

11 Paris & London & Matrimony

Box	Certificates	18.00	
	Cash	296.00	
Pit	Cash	270.50	
Gal[ler]y	Cash	66.25	650.75

Mr. Horn's
Night

12th Native Land & Rob Roy [Macgregor]

[USG announces his benefit and Horn in the rôle of Aurelio de Monlanto in *Native Land.*]

Box	Certificates	39.00	
	Cash	133.00	
Pit	Cash	138.50	
Gal[ler]y	Cash	24.75	335.25

13th Paris & London & Too late for Dinner

Box	Certificates	14.00	
	Cash	60.00	
Pit	Cash	101.00	
Gal[ler]y	Cash	19.50	194.50

14th [The] Belle's Stratagem & [The] Sleep Walker

Box	Certificates	none

	Cash	43.00	
Pit	Cash	40.00	
Gal[ler]y	Cash	4.25	87.25

15th Wives as they Were [&
    Maids as They Are] &
    Paris & London

Box	Certificates	none	
	Cash	103.00	
Pit	Cash	153.00	
Gal[ler]y	Cash	27.00	283.00

17th Romeo & Juliet, Paris &
    London

Box	Certificates	30.00	
	Cash	114.75	
Pit	Cash	200.25	
Gal[ler]y	Cash	36.50	381.50

18th Sweet Hearts & Wives &
    Timour [the Tartar]

Box	Certificates	8.00	
	Cash	82.75	
Pit	Cash	146.50	
Gal[ler]y	Cash	42.25	279.50

19 [The] School for Scandal &
    Timour [the Tartar]

Box	Certificates	15.00	
	Cash	114.50	
Pit	Cash	128.00	
Gal[ler]y	Cash	27.25	284.75

20th [The] Robbers & Timour [the
    Tartar]

Box	Certificates	none	
	Cash	43.00	
Pit	Cash	57.00	
Gal[ler]y	Cash	21.75	121.75

[447]

21 She Stoops to Conquer & Paris
    & London

Box	Certificates	12.00	
	Cash	61.75	
Pit	Cash	69.25	
Gal[ler]y	Cash	15.25	158.25

22d [The] Bride of Lammermoor
    & Paris & London

Box	Certificates	none	
	Cash	34.00	
Pit	Cash	59.50	
Gal[ler]y	Cash	17.75	111.25

Miss Rock's Night 24 the Will & Winning a Husband
[As Albina Mandeville in
The Will and as seven
characters in *Winning a
Husband*. USG]

Box	Certificates	150.00	
	Cash	182.75	
Pit	Cash	183.25	
Gal[ler]y	Cash	21.50	537.50

Mr. Blake's Night 25 [The] Dramatist & [The]
Young Widow

Box	Certificates	22.00	
	Cash	77.00	
Pit	Cash	129.75	
Gal[ler]y	Cash	12.00	240.75

26th Hamlet & Mr. H.

Box	Certificates	26.00	
	Cash	138.50	
Pit	Cash	168.00	
Gal[ler]y	Cash	33.50	366.00

27th George Barnwell & Timour
[the Tartar]

Box	Certificates	12.00	
	Cash	56.75	
Pit	Cash	96.75	
Gal[ler]y	Cash	31.75	197.25

28 Pizarro & [The] Young Widow

Box	Certificates	50.00	
	Cash	114.25	
Pit	Cash	184.75	
Gal[ler]y	Cash	30.25	379.25

[USG announces the following: 29, Richard III & The Lottery Ticket; December 1, Pizarro & The Sleep Walker; 2, Marion & The Rendezvous; 3, Much Ado About Nothing & My Aunt; 4, John Bull & Three and the Deuce; 5, Macbeth & The Irish Tutor; 6, Pizarro & My Aunt; 8, The Wonder & The Children in the Wood; 9, The Cabinet & Family Jars; 10, The School for Scandal & The Children in the Wood; 11, The Cabinet & The Irishman in London; 12, Brutus & My Aunt; 13, The Spy & The Adopted Child; 15, Bertram & The Adopted Child; 16, Much Ado About Nothing & Hypolitus, the Wild Boy*; 17, Speed the Plough & Raising the Wind; 18, Two last acts of Richard III & The Prize & The Hunter of the Alps; 19, Who Wants a Guinea? & The Manager in Distress & Nature and Philosophy; 20, Who Wants a Guinea? & The Manager in Distress & Nature and Philosophy; 22, The School for Scandal & The Adopted Child; 24, The Honey Moon & The Innkeeper's Daughter; 25, Douglas & The Lottery Ticket & The Day after the Fair; 27, The Point of Honor & Jamie of Aberdeen & The Lottery Ticket; 29, Alexander the Great & Buskin's Frolics & The Turnpike Gate.]

PHIL[ADELPHIA] SUMMER SEASON[, COMMENCING] JULY 3,
[ENDING JULY 18,] 1828.

[Warren]

PREFACE—**July 7**: Madame Labasse, Monsieur Barbere and Madame Rosalie are dancers. See *Durang* II, Chapter Forty-Two. In his entry of this date Warren records in his *Diary* that the plays, *My Spouse and I*

[449]

and *Father and Son*, were given. *Father and Son* is evidently the same as *The Rock of Charbonnière*, which ADA announces and *Durang*, II, Chapter Forty-Two mentions as having been given on July 7.

Wood's record of this season is fragmentary. Warren's *Diary*, however, reveals that, on July 9 and 11, *The Red Rover* and *Father and Son* were given. In an entry of July 18 Warren writes, "The dancer's Benefit and [The] Day after [the] Wedding, [The] Spoil'd Child." At the end of Wood's meagre record occurs the notation, "[$]700 in the Week. Dancers had ½." Warren, in an entry of July 20, adds the information, "This spec[ulation] of the dancers proved by no means profitable. The Company as usual much dis[s]atisfied. The dancers get $343.

[Chesnut Street Theatre]

July

Thurs. 3 [The] Point of Honor & Must   48.
be buried
                                    fine

Frid. 4 [The] Gnome King & Sprigs   276.
of Laurel

Mon. [7 Madame] La Basse[, Mon-   178.
sieur] Barbere & [Mad-
ame] Rosalie
[See preface to this season.]

Wed. [9]   d[itt]o   90.
[ADA announces *The Red
Rover* & *The Rock of
Charbonniere.*]

[Thursday] 10   d[itt]o
[ADA announces *How to
Die for Love* & *The Rock
of Charbonniere.*]

[Friday] 11   d[itt]o
[ADA announces *The Red
Rover* & *The Rock of
Charbonniere.*]

[450]

[14 The Death of Napoleon Bonaparte* & Tom & Jerry]

[15 The Wandering Boys & Must
Be Buried]

[16 The Rendezvous & Bom-
bastes Furioso]

[17 The Review & Is He Jealous?]

[18 The Day after the Wedding
& The Spoil'd Child]

[PHILADELPHIA SEASON, COMMENCING OCTOBER 18, 1830, ENDING
APRIL 9, 1831.]

[Lamb & Coyle]

PREFACE—October 22: According to *Durang*, III, Chapter Second, Miss
Kelly played Miss Dorillon in *Wives as They Were*. **October 29:** USG
announces, "Mr. Roberts will deliver his celebrated imitations." **December 4:** To the left of this entry Wood has written "Mrs. Sharpe,
Flynn, Booth," whom USG announces as Hamlet, "Mrs. Knight,"
whom USG announces as Kate O'Brian in *Perfection*; and "Mr. Cuddy,"
whom USG announces in a "musical mélange." **December 6:** USG
announces Hackett as Monsieur Morbleu in *Monsieur Tonson* and Major
Joe Bunker in *Down East*, "in which character he will introduce the
entire new Yankee story of *How to Sell a Fox Skin*." According to
Durang, III, Chapter Third, Mrs. Sharpe appeared as Lady Townly in
The Provoked Husband. **December 13:** To the left of this entry Wood
has written "Mrs. Sharpe," whom USG announces as Emma in *William
Tell* and Mrs. Simpson in *Simpson & Co.*, which USG announces in
place of *A Roland for an Oliver*; "Mr. Blake," whom USG announces as
Michael in *William Tell* and Bromley in *Simpson & Co.*; "Master Russell," whom USG announces as Albert; and E. "Forrest," whom USG
announces as William Tell. Master Russell, "the American Roscius,
a child only eight years old," is to sing *The Pilgrim of Love*, accompany-
ing himself on the piano forte. **December 17:** To the left of this entry
Wood has written "Thorne," whom USG announces as Hecate and as

[451]

Somerville, with songs, in *Turn Out*, "Blake" whom USG announces as Macduff, "Mrs. Hackett," whom USG announces as Marian Ramsay in *Turn Out*; and E. "Forrest," whom USG announces as Macbeth. **December 20**: To the left of this entry Wood has written "Aikin," whom USG announces as Sir Archy MacSarcasm in *Love à la Mode*, "Blake," whom USG announces as Cassio; and "[Mrs.] Sharpe," whom USG announces as Emilia. **December 29**: According to USG, Hackett is also to appear as Major Joe Bunker—see the entry of December 6—and Mrs. Hackett, in the part of Don Giovanni, to sing *Like the Gloom of Night Retiring*. **December 31**: USG announces Blake as Colonel Lambert in *The Hypocrite* and St. Lawrence in *Touch and Take*, Hackett as Mawworm in *The Hypocrite* and as *Rip Van Winkle*. USG announces that Blake will recite *Bucks, Have at Ye All*, after which "the Indian Chiefs, Grizzle Bear, Little Wave, Big Wave, etc. will appear on the stage and will perform their characteristic War Dance, War Song and Ceremony of Scalping." **January 4**: In his entry of this date, Warren writes in his *Diary*, "I play Sir Abel [Handy, in *Speed the Plough*.]" **January 29**: *Durang*, III, Chapter Fifth, states that Miss Kelly also appeared as Kate O'Brian in *Perfection*. **February 5**: ADA announced Finn as Timothy Quaint in *The Soldier's Daughter* and Gregory in *Turn Out*; Miss Kelly as Widow Cheerly in *The Soldier's Daughter* and Marian Ramsay in *Turn Out*; and Dwyer as Frederick Heartall in *The Soldier's Daughter*. **February 14**: To the left of this entry Wood has written, "[Madame] Hutin & [Monsieur] Barbere," celebrated Parisian dancers, whom ADA announces; "Cuddy" and "Miss Kelly." According to ADA, Cuddy is to play a "grand fantasia" on the flute, introducing the Irish air of *Gramarche* and a national American melody composed expressly for the occasion. **February 16**: To the left of this entry Wood has written, "Kelly, Dancers, Cuddy, Archer, Mr. & Mrs. Rowb[otham], Fisher." According to *Durang*, III, Chapter Fifth, Miss Kelly played Olivia; Archer, Don Julio; Rowbotham, Don Carlos; Mrs. Rowbotham, Minetto; and John Fisher, Don Vincentio in *A Bold Stroke for a Husband*. Mrs. Rowbotham also played Umba in *La Perouse*. "The French dancers assisted." **February 17** and **19**: The "dancers," of course, are Madame Hutin and Monsieur Barbere. **February 21**: In this entry Wood has written the title "Man & Wife," and, under it, "Ch[ange]d to [The] Wonder." ADA announces Miss Kelly as Helen Worrett in *Man and Wife* but obviously she appeared as Donna Violante in *The Wonder*. See February 17. ADA also announces for February 21, "Last night of

Madame Hutin and Monsieur Barbere." **February 22**: According to *Durang*, III, Chapter Fifth, "Miss Kelly acted Juliana in *The Honey Moon*." *Durang* also states that Madame Hutin's benefit was on **February 23**; and that she "played Myrtillo in *The Broken Sword* in broken English." **February 24**: In the entry of February 23 and 24 there are ditto marks referring to "Dancers Kelly" in the entry of February 22. ADA announces that Miss Kelly appeared as Lady Bell in *Know Your Own Mind*. C. Durang was the prompter. **March 3**: After the title "[The] S[chool] for Scandal" Wood has written "Changed to [The] Foundling of [the] forest." ADA, however, announces Mrs. Gilfert as Lady Teazle. **March 8** and **11**: See entry of March 5. **March 12**: ADA announces a "young gentleman of this city," his "1st. appearance on any stage," an Achmet in *Barbarossa*. **March 16**: Wood has partly crossed out "Is he Jealous?" and written under it "Ch[ange]d to Perfection." ADA announces Mrs. Knight as Alexina in *The Exile*. **March 19**: ADA also announces that Mrs. Knight is to sing. ADA of March 15 announces, "Mr. Cuddy [, the flute player,] is engaged and will perform in the orchestra, which will be augmented during Mrs. Knight's engagement." Cuddy often accompanied the singers, "mounted behind the scenes in the carpenter's gallery, with his flute echoing [their] cadenzas." See *Durang*, III, Chapter Fifth. **March 24**: ADA announces Hackett as Mr. Industrious Doolittle in *The Times* and Major Joe Bunker in *Down East*, "in which character he will introduce the entire new story of *How to Sell a Fox Skin*." **March 26**: Coyle was co-manager with Lamb. **April 9**: To the left of this entry Wood has written "Barton, Mrs. Gilfert, Siamese boys, Mrs. Duff." ADA announces Barton as Robert Guiscard in *Adelgitha* and as Petruchio, Mrs. Gilfert as Catherine and Mrs. Duff as Adelgitha. ADA also announces, "After the play Chang & Eng, the Siamese boys, will appear with their conductor."

As to Miss Kelly's rôle on October 22, *Durang*, III, Chapter Second, asserts that it was that of Miss Dorillon in *Wives as They Were*. To the left of the entry of January 19 Wood has written "Finn" and then almost erased the name. *Durang*, III, Chapter Fifth, erroneously states that this was "Mr. H. Finn's first night" and that he "appeared as Lord Ogleby in *The Clandestine Marriage*." Wood has also written to the left of this entry, "58 rec[eive?]d & tickets taken."

In writing of this season, *Durang* III, Chapter Sixth, asserts that "after the first eighty nights, the actors only received one-half and often

[453]

one-quarter of their weekly stipends." Several references to "half salary" which it has been necessary to omit from the printed text of this season attest to the truth of Durang's statement.

[Chesnut Street Theatre]

October

	M[onday] 18 [The] Heir at Law, [The] L[ottery] Ticket & [The] Young Widow	299.50	

T[uesday] 19 [The] Devil's Bridge & [The] L[ady] & [the] Devil [Plumer as Count Belino, Mrs. Plumer as Countess Rosalvina in *The Devil's Bridge* and Zephyrina in *The Lady and the Devil*. ADA]	137.50	

[Mr. & Mrs.] Plumer

W[ednesday] 20 Much ado [about Nothing] 166.75
Miss Kelly   & Rosina
                [As Beatrice. ADA]

T[hursday] 21 Damon & Pythias & Winn- 272.87
Cooper   [in]g a Husb[an]d
                [As Pythias. ADA]

F[riday] 22 Wives as they Were [& 166.50
Miss K[elly]   Maids as They Are] &
                [The] Prize
                [See preface to this season.]

Sat[urday] 23 Macbeth & [The] Poor Soldier 337.50   1380.62
Cooper   [As Macbeth. ADA]

Miss K[elly]   M. 25 [The] Jealous Wife & Walk for 224.
                a Wager
                [As Mrs. Oakly in *The Jeal-
                ous Wife*. USG]

Cooper　　　　T. 26 Rule a Wife [& Have a Wife]　193.25
　　　　　　　　　　& Seven's the Main
　　　　　　　　　　[As Leon.　USG]

Miss K[elly]　　W. 27 [The] School for Scandal &　194.
　　　　　　　　　　[The] P[oor] Soldier
　　　　　　　　　　[As Lady Teazle in *The
　　　　　　　　　　School for Scandal.* USG]

Cooper　　　　T. 28 [The] Revenge & [The] H[igh-　204.
　　　　　　　　　　land] Reel
　　　　　　　　　　[As Zanga in *The Revenge.*
　　　　　　　　　　USG]

Miss K[elly]　　F. 29 She Stoops to Conq[uer,] Pop-　245.
　　　　　　　　　　p[in]g the Question* &
　　　　　　　　　　Imitations
　　　　　　　　　　[As Miss Hardcastle in *She
　　　　　　　　　　Stoops to Conquer.* USG
　　　　　　　　　　See preface to this
　　　　　　　　　　season.]

　　　　　　Sat. 30 Virginius, Imitations, [The]　318.　　1378.
Ben[efit of] Cooper　　　Actress of all Work &　——
　　　　　　　　　　Popp[in]g [the] Question
　　　　　　　　　　[As Virginius. USG]

　　　Novem[be]r
Miss K[elly]　M. 1 [The] Wonder & [The] Dead　106.75
　　　　　　　　　　Shot
　　　　　　　　　　[As Donna Violante in *The
　　　　　　　　　　Wonder.* USG]

Mrs. Duff　　　T. 2 [The] Stranger & Popping the　199.87
　　　　　　　　　　Question
　　　　　　　　　　[As Mrs. Haller in *The
　　　　　　　　　　Stranger.* USG]

Ben[efi]t [of]　W. 3 All in the Wrong & No Song　245.
　　Miss K[elly]　　　No Sup[per]
　　　　　　　　　　[As Lady Restless in *All in*

[455]

the Wrong and Dorothy
in *No Song No Supper*.
USG]

Rainy

Ben[efi]t [of]   T. 4 Henri Quatre & Don Giovanni   213.
Mr. Plumer   [As Frederick St. Leon in
                         Henry Quatre and as Don
                         Giovanni. USG]

                    F. 5 Venice   Preserv'd   &   [The]   134.
Mr. White's 1st.   Highland Reel
[appearance.]   [White as Jaffier, Mrs. Duff
Mrs. Duff   as Pierre in *Venice Pre-
                         served*. USG]

Mrs. D[uff]   S. 6 Isabella & Don Giovanni   259.75   3917.25
                       [As Isabella. USG]

Ben[efi]t [of]   M. 8 Inkle & Yarico & Y[outh,]   228.
Mrs. Plumer   L[ove] & folly
                       [As Yarico and as Ari-
                       nette in *Youth, Love and
                       Folly*. USG]

Mrs. D[uff]   T. 9 Adrian & Orrilla & [The] Wed-   117.50
                       ding Day
                       [As Madame Clermont in
                       Adrian and Orrilla. USG]

                 W. 10 Guy Mannering & Youth,   277.37
[Mrs.] K[night] &   L[ove] & folly
[Madame] Feron   [Mrs. Knight as Julia Man-
                       nering, Madame Feron as
                       Lucy Bertram in *Guy
                       Mannering*. USG]

                 T. 11 Jane Shore & [The] Falls of   214.
                       Clyde

                                                Rain

F. 12 Aladdin* & Of Age tomorrow 220.

[Mrs.] K[night]   [Mrs. Knight as Aladdin,
[Madame] F[eron]   Madame Feron as Nour-
                  mahal in *Aladdin* and
                  Maria in *Of Age Tomor-
                  row.* USG]

                              Rain

Mr. Cooper.   S. 13 [The] Gamester & [The] Mag- 397.   5371.12
Benefit [of]   pie & [the] Maid
Mrs. Duff.   [Cooper as Beverly, Mrs.
                  Duff as Mrs. Beverly in
                  The Gamester and An-
                  nette in *The Magpie and
                  the Maid.* USG]

                        Heavy Rain

M. 15 Aladdin & Gretna Green   373.62

[Mrs.] K[night] &   [Mrs. Knight as Aladdin
[Madame] F[eron]   and as Betty Finikin in
                  Gretna Green. Madame
                  Feron as Nourmahal in
                  Aladdin. USG]

Mrs. D[uff]   T. 16 [The] Boh[emian] Mother, 187.
            Popping the Question &
            Raising the Wind
            [As Mathilde in *The Bo-
            hemian Mother.* USG]

W. 17 [The] Cabinet, 1st. Act & 252.37

[Mrs.] K[night] &   Aladdin
[Benefit of   [Mrs. Knight as Aladdin,
Madame] F[eron]   Madame Feron as Mour-
                  mahal and as Floretta in
                  The Cabinet. USG]

Mrs. D[uff]   T. 18 [The] East Indian & [The] 170.90
            Sleepwalker
            [As Zorayda in *The East
            Indian.* USG]

[457]

F. 19 Perfection, Concert & [The] 420.
Mrs. Knight's Invincibles
Ben[efit.] [Mrs. Knight as Kate
[Madame] F[eron] O'Brian in *Perfection*
and Victoire in *The In-
vincibles*. USG announces
concert of vocal and in-
strumental music, in
which Mrs. Knight,
Madame Feron and Mr.
Cuddy are to appear.]

S. 20 Aladdin & Gretna Green 425. 7100.
Mr. Cuddy's [Cuddy to play grand fan-
Ben[efit.] tasia on the flute. Mrs.
[Mrs.] K[night] & Knight as Aladdin and as
[Madame] F[eron] Miss Betty Finikin in
Gretna Green. Madame
Feron as Nourmahal in
Aladdin. USG]

Mrs. Sharpe M. 22 [The] School for Scandal & 109.
'Twas I
[As Lady Teazle in *The
School for Scandal* and
Georgette Clairville in
'Twas I. USG]

Mrs. D[uff] & T. 23 [The] East Indian & Perfec- 307.
Mrs. K[night] tion
[Mrs. Duff as Zorayda in
The East Indian, Mrs.
Knight as Kate O'Brian
in *Perfection*. USG]

Mrs. Sharpe W. 24 [The] Jealous Wife & [The] 80.
Sleepwalker
[As Mrs. Oakly in *The Jeal-
ous Wife*. USG]
Rain

[458]

Mrs. D[uff]   T. 25 Home, Sweet Home* & [The] 170.
Mrs. K[night]   Boh[emian] Mother
              [Mrs. Duff as Mathilde in
                The Bohemian Mother,
                Mrs. Knight as Madame
                Delmance in *Home, Sweet
                Home.* USG]
                              Rain

Mrs. K[night] F. 26 Aladdin & Perfection   162.
              [As Aladdin and Kate
              O'Brian. USG]

          S. 27 Adelgitha & [The] Invincibles 200.   8128.
Mrs. Knight &   [Mrs. Knight as Victoire in
Mrs. Duff   *The Invincibles*, Mrs.
              Duff as Adelgitha. USG]
                              Rain

          M. 29 [The] Apostate & Turn Out   249.
Mrs. K[night.]   [Mrs. Knight as Marian
Ben[efit of]   Ramsay in *Turn Out.*
Mrs. D[uff.]   Mrs. Duff as Florinda in
              The Apostate. USG]
                            Rain

        T. 30 Home, Sweet Home, Perfec- 185.
              tion & Gretna Green
                            Rain
      Decem[be]r
[Mrs.] Sharpe W. 1 [The] Avenger [of Sicily] & 172.
              [The] 100 £ Note
              [As Stella di Procida in *The
                Avenger of Sicily.* USG]
                            fine

Ben[efi]t [of] T. 2 12th Night, 5[th] Act [of] 259.
Roberts   Richard [3d.] & Family
              Jars

[As Sir Andrew Aguecheek
and as Old Delph in
Family Jars. To imitate
Mr. Kean as Richard.
USG]

fair

Mrs. Flynn   F. 3 Richard 3d. & [The] Young 366.
Mrs. S[harpe]   Widow
Booth   [Booth as Richard. Mrs.
                     Flynn as Lady Anne and
                     as Amelia Fairlove and
                     Captain Swagger in *The
                     Young Widow.* Mrs.
                     Sharpe as Queen Eliza-
                     beth. USG]

               S. 4 Hamlet & Perfection   813.   2030.
Ben[efi]t [of Mrs.]   [As Kate O'Brian in *Per-*
Knight   *fection.* USG See pref-
                     ace to this season.]

               M. 6 [The]   Provok'd   Husband, 728.
Mr. Hackett Mrs.   Down   East* & Mon-
Sharpe's Ben[efi]t   s[ieur] Tonson
                     [See preface to this season.]

Booth   T. 7 [The] Distrest Mother, Pop- 141.
                     p[in]g [the] Question &
                     [The] Rendezvous
                     [As Orestes in *The Distrest
                     Mother.* USG]

Mrs. Sharpe   W. 8 Damon & Pythias & [The] 389.
[Mr. E.] Forrest   Avenger [of Sicily]
                     [Mrs. Sharpe as Calanthe,
                     Forrest as Damon. Mrs.
                     Sharpe as Stella di Procida
                     in *The Avenger of Sicily.*
                     USG]

Booth   T. 9 [The] Merchant of Venice & 194.
                 [The] Avenger [of Sicily]
                 [As Shylock. USG]

[Mrs.] Sharpe F. 10 Metamora & Raising the 433.
Forrest   Wind
                 [Forrest as Metamora, Mrs.
                 Sharpe as Nahmeokee in
                 Metamora. USG]
                                     fine

          S. 11 [The] Iron Chest & Clari 217
Benefit [of] Booth   [As Edward Mortimer in
                 The Iron Chest. USG]

          M. 13 W[illia]m Tell & [A] Roland 701.
Mr. Lamb's ben[efi]t.   for an Oliver
                 [See preface to this season.]
                                  Rain

          T. 14 Sertorius* & [The] Hunter of 312.
Ben[efit of] Booth   the Alps
                 [As Sertorius. USG]

Forrest   W. 15 Pizarro & Popping the Ques- 194.
                 tion
                 [As Rolla in Pizarro. USG]

Booth Blake   T. 16 Sertorius & 3 & [the] Deuce 224.
                 [Booth as Sertorius, Blake
                 as the three Singles.
                 USG]

Ben[efit of]   F. 17 Macbeth & Turn Out 283.
Mrs. Sharpe   [As Lady Macbeth. USG
                 See preface to this season.]

Ben[efit] of   S. 18 Sertorius & Teddy the Tiler* 180.   1783.
[the] poor. Booth   [Booth as Sertorius. USG]

[461]

[Benefit of]   M. 20 Othello & Love a la Mode   1041.
Forrest   [As Othello. USG See pref-
                       ace to this season.]

Ben[efi]t [of]   T. 21 Bertram & Too late for Dinner 122.
Booth   [As Bertram. USG]

[Mr. & Mrs.]   W. 22 [The] Yankee in England,   100.
Hackett   [The] Romp & My
                       Grandmother
                       [Hackett as Solomon Swap
                       in *The Yankee in Eng-
                       land.* Mrs. Hackett as
                       Priscilla Tomboy in *The
                       Romp* and Florella in *My
                       Grandmother.* USG]

Flynn Booth   T. 23 King Lear & Too late for   94.
Benefit [of]   Dinn[er]
Mrs. Flynn   [Flynn as Edgar and as
                       Frank Poppleton in *Too
                       Late for Dinner.* Booth
                       as Lear, Mrs. Flynn as
                       Cordelia. ADA]

Mr. and Mrs.   F. 24 [The] Times, Teddy the Tiler 184.
Hackett   & [Of] Age tom[orrow]
                       [Hackett as Industrious
                       Doolittle, Mrs. Hackett
                       as Miss Amelia Traffic in
                       The Times and Maria in
                       Of Age Tomorrow. USG]

Blake   S. 25 Touch & Take, [The] Water 697.   2082.
                       Witch* & Family Jars
                       [As Sir Lawrence in *Touch
                       and Take.* USG]

Mr. Barnes Ben[efi]t   M. 27 Paul Pry & [The] Comedy of   513.
[of] Hackett.   Errors
                         [Barnes as Colonel Hardy
                           in *Paul Pry* and as Dro-
                           mio of Syracuse. Hack-
                           ett as Paul Pry and as
                           Dromio of Ephesus.
                           USG]

Warren   T. 28 [The First Part of] Henry 4th   240.
                           & [The] Water Witch
                           [As Falstaff. USG]

Hacketts   W. 29 [The] Times & Don Giovanni   258.
                           [Hackett as Industrious
                           Doolittle, Mrs. Hackett
                           as Amelia Traffic in *The*
                           Times and as Don Gio-
                           vanni. USG See pref-
                           ace to this season.]

Ben[efi]t [of]   T. 30 [A] Cure for [the] Heartache,   118.
Mrs. Willis   4th Act [of] Richard 3[d.]
                           & Lovers['] Quarrels
                           [As Jesse Oatland in *A Cure*
                           for the Heartache. USG]

Hackett   F. 31 [The] Hypocrite, 2[nd.] Act   309.
Indians Blake's   [of] Rip Van Winkle &
Ben[efi]t   Touch & Take
                           [See preface to this season.]

        1831. January
               S. 1 Tom & Jerry & Jacko [the   297.   1690.
                           Brazilian Ape]

Ben[efit of]   M. 3 [The] Harper's Daughter &   194.
Wood   X. Y. Z.
                           [As Baron Casimir in *The*
                           Harper's Daughter. ADA]
                                     fair

[463]

Warren   T.   4 Speed the plough & Jacko   126.
                           [the Brazilian Ape]
                           [See preface to this season.]

               W.   5 Sweethearts & Wives, [The]   87.
                           Sleepwalker & Jacko [the
                           Brazilian Ape]

             T.   6 [The] Merry Wives [of Wind-   394.
Warren's Ben[efi]t   sor] & How to die for
                           Love
                           [As Falstaff. USG]

Ben[efi]t [of]   F.   7 [The] East Indian, Two Eyes   97.
Mrs. Young   between two* & Deaf as
                           a post
                           [As Zorayda in *The East
                           Indian* and Lidda in *Two
                           Eyes Between Two*. USG]

C. Kean   S.   8 [The] Merchant of Venice,   297.   1195.
                           Jacko[, the Brazilian Ape
                           &] 2 Eyes between 2
                           [As Shylock. USG]

             M. 10 [The] Suspicious Husband &   296.
Wemyss' Ben[efi]t   Free & Easy*
                           [As Jack Meggott in *The
                           Suspicious Husband* and
                           Sir Charles Freeman in
                           Free and Easy. ADA]

C. Kean   F. 11 Richard 3d. & Free & Easy   130.
                           [As Richard. ADA]

C. Kean   W. 12 Town & Country & XYZ   60.
                           [As Reuben Glenroy in
                           Town and Country. USG]

C. Kean   T. 13 [A] New Way to pay old debts   80.
                & Teddy the Tiler
                [As Sir Giles Overreach in
                *A New Way to Pay Old
                Debts.* ADA]

C. Kean   F. 14 Richard the Second & Where   41.
                Shall I dine?
                [As Richard. ADA]

C. Kean   S. 15 Pizarro   607.
                No performance on ac-
                c[oun]t of Snow.

            Mon. 17 Brutus & [The] Hunter of 107.
Ben[efi]t [of]   [the] Alps
  C. Kean   [As Brutus and as Felix in
                The Hunter of the Alps.
                ADA]

Miss K[elly]   T. 18 No performance. Miss K. ill

            W. 19 No performance. Mr. Finn
                not arrived.   Checks
                given.

Miss K[elly]   T. 20 Wives as they Were [& 112.
                Maids as They Are] &
                [The] Warlock of the
                Glen
                [As Miss Dorillon in *Wives
                as They Were.* ADA]

Finn   F. 21 [The] Clan[destine] Marriage 118.
                & [The] Master's Rival
                [As Lord Ogleby in *The
                Clandestine Marriage.*]
                ADA]

Miss K[elly]   S. 22 As You Like it & [The] War- 131.   468.
                lock of [the] Glen
                [As Rosalind. ADA]

Finn   M. 24 [The] Hypocrite & 102   92.
              [As Mawworm in *The Hypo-*
              crite and Philip Garbois
              in *102.* ADA]

Miss K[elly] T. 25 [The] Belle's Stratagem &   107.
              Jacko [the Brazilian Ape]
              [As Letitia Hardy in *The*
              Belle's Stratagem. ADA]

Finn   W. 26 Paul Pry & [The] Falls of   124.
              Clyde
              [As Paul Pry and as Donald
              in *The Falls of Clyde.*
              ADA]

Miss K[elly] T. 27 [The] Will & [The] Wandering 108.
              Boys
              [As Albina Mandeville in
              The Will. ADA]

Finn   F. 28 [The] Poor Gentleman & [The] 106.
              Master's Rival
              [As Ollapod in *The Poor*
              Gentleman and Paul
              Shack in *The Master's*
              Rival. ADA]

Ben[efi]t [of] S. 29 Know Y[ou]r Own Mind &   272.   809.
Miss K[elly]   Perfection
                [As Lady Bell in *Know*
                Your Own Mind. ADA
                See preface to this
                season.]

Finn   M. 31 [The] Clan[destine] Marriage 96.
              & [The] Happiest day of
              my life
              [As Lord Ogleby in *The*

Clandestine Marriage and
Mr. Gilman in *The Hap-
piest Day of My Life.*
ADA]

February

Finn   T. 1 102[,The] Hypocrite & How 147.
to die for love
[As Mawworm in *The Hypo-
crite.* ADA]

Benefit [of] W. 2 Montgomery* & Tom & Jerry 441.
Finn   [As Sergeant Welcome
Sobersides in *Montgom-
ery* and Bob Logic in *Tom
and Jerry.* ADA]

[Miss] Kelly T. 3 [The] School for Scandal & 131.
Finn Dwyer   [The] Sleepwalker
[Miss Kelly as Lady Teazle.
Finn as Sir Peter and
Dwyer as Charles Sur-
face in *The School for
Scandal.* ADA]

Jones' Ben[efi]t F. 4 Twelfth Night & [The] Prize 163.
[As Sir Toby Belch. ADA]

Finn [Miss] S. 5 [The] Soldier's Daughter & 164.   1142.
Kelly Dwyer   Turn Out
[See preface to this season.]

[Miss] Kelly M. 7 [The] Way to Keep him & 202.
Finn   Ladies at home
[Miss Kelly as the Widow
Belmour in *The Way to
Keep Him* and Mrs.
Banter in *Ladies at
Home.* Finn as Sir Bash-
ful Constant in *The Way
to Keep Him.* ADA]

[467]

[Miss] Kelly   T.   8 Sweethearts & Wives, Simp-   150.50
Finn   son & Co. & Tom Thumb
               [the Great]
               [Miss Kelly as Eugenia in
               Sweethearts and Wives
               and as Mrs. Simpson.
               Finn as Billy Lackaday
               in *Sweethearts and Wives*.
               ADA]

            W.   9 Hamlet & [The] Prize   161.
Ben[efi]t [of] Finn   [As Hamlet and as Dr. Leni-
               tive in *The Prize*. ADA]

            T. 10 Married & Single, [The] D[ay]   150.
Finn   [Miss] Kelly   after [the] Wedding &
               [The] Happiest day of
               my life
               [Finn as Beau Shatterly in
               Married and Single and
               Gillman in *The Happiest
               Day of My Life*. Miss
               Kelly as Lady Elizabeth
               in *The Day after the Wed-
               ding*. ADA]

            F. 11 [The] Way to keep him &   144.
Finn   [Miss] Kelly   Ladies at home
               [Finn as Sir Bashful Con-
               stant in *The Way to Keep
               Him*, Miss Kelly as the
               Widow Belmour and
               Mrs. Banter. ADA]

            S. 12 [She] Stoops to Conquer &   290.   1097.50
Miss Kelly's 2d.   High life below Stairs
Ben[efi]t Finn   [Miss Kelly as Miss Hard-
               castle in *She Stoops to
               Conquer* and Miss Kitty

[468]

in *High Life Below Stairs*.
Finn as Tony Lumpkin
in *She Stoops to Conquer*
and Lovel in *High Life
Below Stairs*. ADA]

Lamb's Benefit	M. 14	Know y[ou]r own Mind & La perouse [See preface to this season.]	433.

Dwyer's Ben[efi]t | T. 15 | [The] Way to Get Married & [The] Mid[night] Hour. [As Tangent in *The Way to Get Married*. ADA] | 141.75

Coyle's ben[efi]t | W. 16 | [A] Bold Stroke for [a] Husband, Dancers & La Perouse. [See preface to this season.] | 243.25

[Miss] Kelly Dancers | T. 17 | Wives as they Were [& Maids as They Are] & High life below Stairs [Miss Kelly as Miss Dorillon in *Wives as They Were* and Kitty in *High Life Below Stairs*. ADA See preface to this season.] | 41.

[Miss] Kelly | F. 18 | [The] Wonder & La Perouse [As Donna Violante in *The Wonder*. ADA] | 52.

[Miss] Kelly Dancers | S. 19 | Much ado [about Nothing] & La Perouse [Miss Kelly as Beatrice. ADA See preface to this this season.] | 117.   1028.

[469]

M. 21 [The] Wonder & [The] Sleep-   98.
[Miss] Kelly   Dancers   walker
                [See preface to this season.]

Ben[efi]t [of   T. 22 [The] Honey Moon & She   139.50
Madame] Hutin   W[oul]d be a Soldier
[Miss] Kelly   Dancers   [See preface to this season.]

W. 23 Man & Wife & [The] Broken   98.
[Miss Kelly   Dancers]   Sword
                [Miss Kelly as Helen Wor-
                rett in *Man and Wife*.
                ADA   See preface to this
                season.]

C. Durang's   T. 24 Know y[ou]r own Mind &   64.75
ben[efi]t   [The] Prisoner at Large
                [See preface to this season.]

Miss K[elly]   F. 25 [The] Honey Moon & [La]   77.
Benefit [of]   Perouse
Barbere   [Miss Kelly as Juliana in
                The Honey Moon. Mon-
                sieur Barbere to dance.
                ADA]

Ben[efit of]   S. 26 [The] Provok'd Husb[an]d &   465.50   942.75
Miss Kelly   C[herry] & F[air] Star
                [As Lady Townly in *The
                Provoked Husband* and
                as Cherry. ADA]

Mrs. Gilfert   M. 28 Jane Shore & Cherry & Fair   151.50
                Star
                [As Jane Shore. ADA]

            March
Mrs. G[ilfert]   T. 1 [The] Stranger & La Perouse   107.25
                [As Mrs. Haller in *The
                Stranger*. ADA]

[470]

Mrs. G[ilfert] W.   2 [The] Provok'd Husband &   97.
C[herry] & F[air] Star
[As Lady Townly in *The
Provoked Husband.* ADA]

Mrs. G[ilfert] Th.   3 [The] Foundling of [the] for-   84.50
est & [The] 2 Thomsons
[See preface to this season.]

Fr.   4 [The] Suspicious Husband &   74.
C[herry] & F[air] Star

Saty.   5 [The] Master's Rival, Rope   94.50   608.75
Villalave family   Dancers & [The] Lottery
Ticket
[ADA announces first night
of Italian family on the
corde testa.]

Mon.   7 [The] Gamester & [The] Lot-   218.50
Mrs. Gilf[ert's]   tery ticket
Ben[efit]   [As Mrs. Beverly in *The
Gamester.* ADA]

Villalave   Tues.   8 Animal Magnetism, Ital[ian]   144.25
family & Deaf as a post
[See preface to this season.]

W. Chapman   W.   9 [The] Slave & [The] Comedy   279.
Robert's Ben[efit]   of Errors
[W. Chapman as Dromio of
Syracuse. Roberts as
Fogrum in *The Slave* and
as Dromio of Ephesus.
ADA]

Th. 10 Cheap Living & La Perouse   276.
Wemyss' ben[efi]t   [As Sponge in *Cheap Living.* ADA]

[471]

Villalave   F. 11 [The] Lottery ticket, Rope   114.50
                      Dancers & Val[entine] &
                      Orson
                      [See preface to this season.]

Mr. Gamble's   S. 12 Barbarossa, R[ope] Dancers   166.   1198.25
1st app[earance]   & Deaf as a post
                      [See preface to this season.]

                 M. 14 Henri Quatre & Perfection   192.50
Mrs. Knight['s] 1st.   [As Louison in *Henri Quatre*
                      and Kate O'Brian in *Per-
                      fection*. ADA]

                 T. 15 Home, Sweet Home, [The] 2   202.
    "   2d.   Thomps[ons] & Gretna
                      Green
                      [Mrs. Knight as Madame
                      Germance in *Home, Sweet
                      Home*, and Betty Finikin
                      in *Gretna Green*. ADA]

                 W. 16 [The] Exile & Is he Jealous?   276.
    "   3   [See preface to this season.]

                 Th. 17 [The] Exile & Turn Out   187.
    "   4   [Mrs. Knight as Alexina in
                      The Exile and as Marian
                      Ramsay in [The] *Turn
                      Out*. ADA]

                 F. 18 [The] Exile & Gretna Green   160.50
    "   5   [Mrs. Knight as Alexina
                      and Betty Finikin. ADA]

                 S. 19 Home Sweet Home & [The]   192.50   1210.50
    "   6   Invincibles
Mr. Cuddy   [Mrs. Knight as Madame
                      Germance and as Victoire
                      in *The Invincibles*. ADA
                      See preface to this season.]

[472]

Mon. 21 Two friends & Fontainbleau 478.
Mrs. Knight's [As Rose in *Two Friends*
ben[efi]t and Dolly Bull in *Fon-*
tainbleau. ADA]

Tues. 22 [The] Exile & [The] Invin- 170.87
Mrs. K[night] vincibles
[As Alexina and Victoire.
ADA]

Wed. 23 Charles 2d., Perfection & 165.
Mrs. K[night] [The] Prisoner at Large
[As Mary Copp in *Charles*
the Second and Kate
O'Brian in *Perfection.*
ADA]

Thurs. 24 [The] Times, Down East & 248.
Mr. Hackett Fam[ily] Jars
[See preface to this season.]

Cuddy's 2d. F. 25 Two friends & [The] Invin- 170.
Benefit cibles
[To perform fantasia on the
flute. ADA]

S. 26 Maid or Wife & Rip Van 320.
Coyle['s] 3d. Ben[efi]t Winkle
Hacket[t] & Mrs. [Hackett as Rip van
Knight Winkle, Mrs. Knight as
Fanny in *Man and Wife.*
ADA See preface to this
season.]

M. 28 Paul Pry & [The] Master's 218.
Barnes & Hackett Rival
[Barnes as Colonel Hardy in
Paul Pry and Paul Shack
in *The Master's Rival.*
Hackett as Paul Pry.
ADA]

[473]

Tues. 29 [The] Comedy of Errors, Per- 290.
Hackett's Ben[efi]t   fection & Lock & Key
                            [As Dromio of Ephesus.
                            ADA]

Wed. 30 Hamlet & [The] Turnpike 170.75
Mr. Barton's   Gate
1st [appearance]   [As Hamlet. ADA]

Thurs. 31 W[illia]m Tell & [The] Review 210.75
Mr. A. Adams   [Mr. A. Adams as William
Mrs. Young's   Tell. ADA]
2d. Ben[efi]t.

                April
Mr. Barton   F. 1 Macbeth & Where Shall I dine 163.
Mrs. Gilfert   [?]
                       [Barton as Macbeth, Mrs.
                       Gilfert as Lady Macbeth.
                       ADA]

"   S. 2 King Lear & [The] Rendez- 234.   1286.50
                       vous
                       [Barton as Lear, Mrs. Gil-
                       fert as Cordelia. ADA]

                Mon. 4 Werner & [The] Hunter of 539.50
Woods 2d. ben[efi]t   [the] Alps
                       [As Gabor in *Werner* and
                       Felix in *The Hunter of
                       the Alps*. ADA]

A. Adams   Tue. 5 Virginius & [The] Midnight 145.40
                       Hour
                       [As Virginius. ADA]

Barton   Wed. 6 Werner & Raising the Wind 145.
                       [As Werner. ADA]

[474]

Thur. 7 Damon & Pythias & [The] 257.50
A. Adams   Children in the Wood
Woodhull's ben[efi]t   [Adams as Damon, Wood-
                        hull as Pythias. ADA]

F. 8 Pizarro & [The] Weathercock 123.
Barton's ben[efi]t   [As Rolla in *Pizarro* and
                      Tristram Fickle in *The
                      Weathercock*. ADA]

Sat. 9 Adelgitha, Cath[erine] & Pe- 850.   2070.40
Lamb's Ben[efi]t   truchio & [The] Siamese
                    Boys
                    [See preface to this season.]

                                            $33960.90
147 Nights av[erage]d $231.
After S[tars] & Ben[efi]ts 151.75

[PHILADELPHIA] SUMMER SEASON[, COMMENCING APRIL 11, ENDING
JULY 28, 1831.]

[Lamb & Coyle]

PREFACE—**April 11:** See the entry of April 9 and the preface to the preceding season. **April 12:** To the left of this entry Wood has written "Mrs. Page, Mrs. Duff, Barton." ADA announces Mrs. Page as Little Pickle in *The Spoiled Child*, Mrs. Duff and Mrs. Haller and Barton as the Stranger. **April 20:** Between the pairs of ditto marks Wood has written "Siamese." **April 21** and **22:** In this entry Wood has also written ditto marks referring to "Siamese" in the entry of April 20. It has been advisable to substitute "Mrs. Duff, Adams, Siamese Twins" for three pairs of ditto marks. **April 25:** ADA announces Mrs. Duff as Desdemona and Cooper as Othello; also, "a new ballet called *The Village Fête*." **April 26:** In this entry Wood has written the title, "Matrimony" and, under it, "not played, Brown absent." **April 28:** In this entry Wood has also written two pairs of ditto marks referring to "Cooper" and "Mr. & Mrs. Barrett" of the previous entry. Master Kneass is to sing; Miss Kerr to dance, according to ADA; and Barrett to appear as George St. Germain, with Mrs. Barrett as Amelia, in *Thirty*

[475]

Years; or, The Life of a Gambler and as Mr. Belmour, with Mrs. Barrett as Harriet; in *Is He Jealous?* **May 5**: In this entry Wood has also written, "4 Twins, Mr. & Mrs. Barrett, Kelly." According to ADA, "the Two Double Twins aged 7 years will make their 1st. appearance in this city." They are to sing, "accompanied on the Piano Forte by Master Roberts." Barrett is to play four characters in *Brag's a Good Dog*, "written expressly for" him. Mrs. Barrett is to play Rosina, with Kelly as Suckling, in *Education*. **May 14**: In this entry Wood has also written "W. Chap[man's] 1[st.] app[earance] Mr. Gallott." ADA announces W. Chapman as Alexis in *The Ethiop* and Risk in *Love Laughs at Locksmiths*. **June 14**: In this entry Wood has also written "Lamb's benefit." ADA announces "Mr. Lamb's farewell benefit" and, according to USG, "The Boston City Guards accompanied by the Brigade Band will be present on the occasion." **June 17**: Through ADA "The managers beg leave to announce to the patrons of the Chesnut Street Theatre that they have appointed this evening for the benefit of the sufferers by the late fire at Fayetteville. The ladies and gentlemen of the company have generously volunteered their services on the occasion, reserving only the unavoidable expenses of the night." **July 14**: USG announces Roberts as the Cobbler in *The Forty Thieves* and Papirius in *State Secrets*. "Mr. Potter, the celebrated juggler, will perform many pleasing feats. Mr. Potter will partake of a cold collation of hot coals. Mr. Hess will perform on the Corde Volante." DC also announces *Down East; or, The Militia Muster* with Roberts as Major Joe Bunker and *The Master's Rival* with Roberts as Paul Shack. **July 16**: In this entry Wood has also written "Mrs. Stirking's [?] ben[efit]." **July 19**: A word in the second title is illegible. **July 26**: Wood has written under "[The] Miller & [His] Men" the notation "Ch[an]g[e]d to [The] I[rishman] in London."

To the left of the entry of May 18 Wood has written "left the Theatre." In *Recollections*, p. 360, Wood states that he "lingered with this falling establishment until the tenth of May." Durang, III, Chapter Seventh, writes that the "Chesnut Street Theatre, sunk as deep as the Atlantic cable in pecuniary tribulations, was now a dead letter. Its advertisements no longer appeared, although the company struggled on from night to night through July for mere bread and cheese. Maywood & Company, who had now in silence obtained its lease for the coming year, did all they could to close it up. But Lamb & Coyle's lease being unexpired, the distressed Thespians held on to it, acting and living in the theatre till the 28th of July, 1831, when the curtain fell on this eventful management, which might be personified as Chaos."

[Chesnut Street Theatre]

April

Mon. 11	Brutus & Touch & Take	345.	

Mrs. G[ilfert] [Mrs. Gilfert as Tulia,
Mr. Adams Adams as Brutus. ADA
Siamese [boys] See preface to this
season.]

Tues. 12 [The] Stranger & [The] Spoil'd   315.
ben[efi]t [of] Child
Siamese [twins] [See preface to this season.]

Wed. 13 [The] Fair American & [The]   192.
Brown's ben[efi]t Irish[man] in London
[As Clod in *The Fair American* and Murtoch Delany in *The Irishman in London*. ADA]

Thurs. 14 [The] School for Scandal &   169.50
Mrs. Gilfert's Therese
[Benefit] [As Lady Teazle in *The School for Scandal* and Mariette in *Therese*. ADA]

Fri. 15 [The] Busy Body & Alp the   198.25
Green's Ben[efi]t Renegade
[As Sir Francis Gripe in *The Busy Body*. ADA]

Sat. 16 [The] Gamester, [The] Roman   189.75   1409.50
Barton's ben[efi]t Actor & [The] Day after [the] Wedding
[As Beverly in *The Gamester*, Paris in *The Roman Actor*

[477]

and Colonel Freelove in
*The Day after the Wed-
ding.* ADA]

Mon. 18 [The] Wept of W[ish-ton-] 370.
Mrs. D[uff] Adams['] Wish & [The] Boh[emian]
Ben[efit] Mother
[Mrs. Duff as Narrah Mat-
tah; Adams as Conau-
chet in *The Wept of Wish-
ton-Wish.* Mrs. Duff as
Mathilde in *The Bohe-
mian Mother.* ADA]

Tues. 19 [The] Wept [of Wish-ton- 107.50
"   " Wish] & [The] Falls of
Clyde
[Mrs. Duff as Narrah Mat-
tah, Adams as Conan-
chet. Mrs. Duff as Ellen
Enfield in *The Falls of
Clyde.* ADA]

Wed. 20 [The] Wept [of Wish-ton- 163.50
"   " Wish] & [The] M[agpie]
& [the] Maid
[Mrs. Duff as Narrah Mat-
tah, Adams as Conan-
chet. Mrs. Duff as An-
nette in *The Magpie and
the Maid.* ADA See pref-
ace to this season.]

Thurs. 21 [The] Road to Ruin & [The] 117.50
Mrs. Moreland Broken Sword
[Mrs. Moreland as Myr-
tillo in *The Broken Sword.*
ADA See preface to this
season.]

[478]

Frid. 22 Pizarro & [The] Turnpike 144.50
[Mrs. Duff Adams   Gate
   Siamese Twins]   [Mrs. Duff as Elvira,
                Adams as Rolla in *Piz-
                arro*. ADA See preface
                to this season.]

Sat. 23 [The] Exile, Siamese [twins] & 152.50 1055.50
Siamese ben[efi]t.   Fortune's frolic
              [See preface to this season.]

Mon. 25 Macbeth, Ballet & [The] Ren- 185.50
Mrs. D[uff] Cooper   dezvous
              [See preface to this season.]

Tues. 26 C[herry] & fair Star & Mr. H. 46.
              [See preface to this season.]

Wed. 27 Rule a Wife [& Have a 130.50
Cooper Mr. & Mrs.   Wife], Ballet & [The]
   Barrett   Invincibles
              [Cooper as Leon, Barrett as
              Michael Perez, Mrs. Bar-
              rett as Estifania in *Rule a
              Wife* and as Victoire in
              The Invincibles. Ballet,
              The Village Fête. ADA]

Thurs. 28 Gambler's fate & Is he Jeal- 226.
Miss Kerr &   ous[?]
   Master Kneass'   [See preface to this season.]
   Ben[efi]t

Frid. [29] Virginius & [A] Race for a 131.50
[Cooper Mr. &   dinner
   Mrs. Barrett]   [Cooper as Virginius, Mrs.
              Barrett as Virginia, Bar-
              rett as Sponge in *A Race
              for Dinner*. ADA]

Sat. [30] [The Second Part of] Henry   182.50   901.50
Cooper's ben[efi]t   4th & Perfection
[As Falstaff. ADA]

May
Mon. 2 [The] Two friends & [The]   263.25
Elephant Mr. & Mrs.   Elephant of Siam
Barrett   [ADA announces elephant,
Mademoiselle de Jick.
Barrett as Ambrose, Mrs.
Barrett as Elinor in *The
Two Friends*. ADA]

Tues. 3 [The] 100 £ Note & [The]   149.62
"   "   Elephant of Siam
[Barrett as Montmorency,
Mrs. Barrett as Harriett
Arlington in *The £ 100
Note*. ADA]

Wed. 4 Perfection & [The] Elephant   237.25
"   "   [of] Siam
[Barrett as Charles Paragon,
Mrs. Barrett as Kate
O'Brian in *Perfection*.
ADA]

Thurs. 5 Education, Twins, Brag's a   480.50
Mrs. Page's ben[efi]t   good dog [but Hold Fast's
a Better]
[As Ellen in *Education*.
ADA   See preface to this
season.]

Fri. 6 [The] Two friends & [The]   212.50
[Elephant]   Elephant [of] Siam
[Mr. & Mrs.Barrett]   [Barrett as Ambrose, Mrs.
Barrett as Elinor. ADA]

Sat.   7 Is he Jealous [? & The] Ele-   275.75   1618.87
"   "   phant [of] Siam
              [Barrett as Belmour, Mrs.
              Barrett as Harriett in *Is
              He Jealous?* ADA]

Mon.   9 [The] Gambler's fate, [The]   189.87
Mrs. Barret's   Purse & Nature & Phil-
ben[efi]t.   osophy
              [As Amelia in *The Gambler's
              Fate* and Colin in *Nature
              and Philosophy*. ADA]

Elephant   Tues. 10 No Song no Supper & [The]   191.75
              Elephant of Siam

Wed. 11 [The] Purse & [The] Elephant   139.50
"   Benefit   [of Siam]
              [For benefit of the elephant,
              Madame de Jick. ADA]

Thurs. 12 [A] New Way to pay old debts,   84.50
Mrs. Moreland's   Ballet & Mr. H.
ben[efi]t W.   [Mrs. Moreland as Flora in
Isherwood   ballet, *Offering to the
              Graces*.   W. Isherwood as
              Sir Giles Overreach in *A
              New Way to Pay Old
              Debts*. ADA]

Frid. 13 [The]   Invincibles   &   [The]   62.50
              Elephant of Siam

Sat. 14 [The] Ethiop & Love Laughs at   405.50   1073.62
Mrs. Duff's   Lock[smith]s
ben[efi]t   [See preface to this season.]

Mon. 16 [The] Ethiop, [A] Tale of the   100.75
              Sea & Elephant

[481]

Mr. Palmer Tues. 17 [The] Merchant of Venice & 69.75
Sprigs of Laurel
[As Shylock. ADA]

Wed. 18 Blue Beard & [The] Review 116.75

Thurs. 19 [The] Elephant of Siam & 60.50
[The] Review

Frid. 20 [The] Busy Body & [The] 39.75
Romp

Sat. 21 Black-Ey'd Susan& [A] Tale of 56.75 6444.25
Mr. Gallot's   the Sea
ben[efit].   [As William in *Black-Eyed*
Susan and Jack Junk in
A Tale of the Sea. ADA]

Mon. 23 Miantonimoh & Gretna Green 110.50
Mrs. Duff   [Mrs. Duff as Narrah Mat-
A. Adams'   tah, Adams as Conauchet
in *Miantonimoh*; or, *The*
Wept of Wish-ton-Wish.
USG]

Tues. 24 [The] Stranger & Love Laughs 119.50
"   "   [at Locksmiths]
[Mrs. Duff as Mrs. Haller,
Adams as the Stranger.
USG]

Wed. 25 Damon & Pythias & [The] 100.25
"   "   Boh[emian] Mother
[Mrs. Duff as Mathilde in
The Bohemian Mother,
Adams as Damon. USG]

"   Thurs. 26 Isabella & [The] Falls of Clyde 109.75
[Mrs. Duff as Isabella and
as Ellen Enfield in *The*
Falls of Clyde. USG]

[482]

Frid. 27 Pizarro & Love Laughs [at 136.50
"   "   Locksmiths]
[Mrs. Duff as Elvira, Adams
as Rolla in *Pizarro.* USG]

Saty. 28 Evadne & [The] Honest 138.   714.50
"   A. Adams'   Thieves.
Ben[efi]t   [Mrs. Duff as Evadne,
Adams as Lodovico. USG]

Mon. 30 [The] Apostate & Black Ey'd 103.
Susan

Tues. 31 [The] Romp & [The] Vampire   78.

June
Mr. Finn   Wed. 1 [The] Heir at Law & [The]   69.
100 £ Note
[As Dr. Pangloss in *The
Heir at Law* and *Billy
Black* in *The £ 100 Note.*
USG]

"   Thurs. 2 Paul Pry & [The] Master's   63.
Rival
[Finn as Paul Pry and as
Paul Shack in *The Mast-
er's Rival.* USG]

"   F. 3 [The] Hypocrite & 102   72.50
[Finn as Mawworm in *The
Hypocrite* and Philip Gar-
bois in *102.* USG]

"   S. 4 Sweethearts & Wives & [The]   75.50   461.
Happiest day of my life
[Finn as Billy Lackaday in
Sweethearts and Wives
and Mr. Gilman in *The
Happiest Day of My Life.*
USG]

[483]

Mr. Finn   Mon. 6 [The] Clan[destine] Marriage 88.50
                    & [The] 2 Gregories
                    [As Lord Ogleby in *The
                    Clandestine Marriage* and
                    as Gregory. USG]

"   Tues. 7 Roses & Thorns* & [The] 2 83.
                    Thomsons
                    [Finn as Sir V. Verjuice in
                    Roses and Thorns and as
                    William Thomson. ADA]

        Wed. 8 [The] 2 Thom[son]s, [The] 2 143.50
"   Benefit   Gregories, [The] 2 Pauls,
                    [&] 2 Acts of [The] Hypo-
                    crite
                    [Finn as William Thomson,
                    as Gregory and as Paul
                    Shack in *The Two Pauls.*
                    ADA]

        Thurs. 9 Rip Van Winkle & The Prize 72.
Finn & Hackett   [Finn as Dr. Lenitive in *The
                    Prize* and Hackett as Rip
                    Van Winkle. USG]

"   " Frid. 10 Paul Pry & Mon[sieur] Ton- 74.
                    son
                    [Finn as Paul Pry and
                    Hackett as Monsieur
                    Morbleau in *Monsieur
                    Tonson.* USG]

"   " Sat. 11 Zembuca & Too late for 57.   518.
                    Dinner
                    [Finn as Buffardo in *Zem-
                    buca* and Twill in *Too
                    Late for Dinner.* USG]

Finn   Mon. 13 [The] Clan[destine] Marriage   68.
                 & [The] Beggar on Horse-
                 back
                 [As Lord Ogleby and as Sadi
                 in *The Beggar on Horse-
                 back.* USG]

"   Tues. 14 102, [The] Beggar on Horse-   66.
                 back & [The] Invincibles
                 [Finn as Philip Garbois in
                 102 and as Sadi in *The
                 Beggar on Horseback.*
                 USG   See preface to this
                 season.]

"   Wed. 15 [The] Hunter of the Alps, Of   53.
                 age tomorrow & family
                 Jars
                 [Finn as Frederick in *Of
                 Age Tomorrow.* USG]

         Thur. 16 She Stoops to Conquer &   323.50
Finn's benefit   [The] 100 £ Note
                 [As Tony Lumpkin in *She
                 Stoops to Conquer* and
                 Billy Black in *The £ 100
                 Note.* USG]

         Frid. 17 Zembuca & No Song No   49.50
Ben[efi]t [of]   Supper
    Fayetteville   [See preface to this season.]

         Sat. 18 [The] Lady of the Lake &   32.75   592.75
                 [The] M[idnight] Hour

         Mon. 20 [The] Bride of Abydos & [The]   51.25
                 Warlock of [the] Glen

[485]

A. Allen   Tues. 21 [The] Road to Ruin & A[ni-   49.
                  mal] Magnetism
                  [As Goldfinch in *The Road
                  to Ruin* and Doctor Bolus
                  in *Animal Magnetism*
                  ADA]

               Wed. 22 Venice Preserv'd & Raising   103.50
[Benefit of]   the Wind
   Murdock   [As Jaffier in *Venice Pre-
                  served* and Diddler in
                  Raising the Wind. USG]

             Thurs. 23 Richard 3d. & [The Spoil'd   92.
Coyle's benefit   Child]
                  [As Richard. USG]

               Frid. 24 Douglas & [The] Lady of [the]   61.
Master Wills   Lake
                  [As Young Norval in *Doug-
                  las*. ADA]

               Sat. 25 [The] Bride of Abydos & [The]   79.   435.75
                  Spectre Bridegroom

               Mon. 27 Abaellino, Scenes of [The] Iron   39.
Porter's Ben[efi]t   Chest & [The] Innkeeper's
                  Duaghter
                  [As Flodoardo and Abael-
                  lino. USG]

               Tues. 28 [The] Heart of Midlothian &   49.
Jones' Ben[efi]t   [The] Village Lawyer
                  [As Dumbledikes in *The
                  Heart of Midlothian* and
                  Justice Mittimus in *The
                  Village Lawyer*. USG]

McDougall's
Ben[efi]t

Wed. 29 [The] Red Rover & [The]   123.
Blind Boy
[As Scipio Africanus in *The Red Rover*. USG]

W. Isherwood's
ben[efi]t

Thurs. 30 Brutus & [The] Red Rover   53.
[As Brutus and the Red Rover. USG]

July

Rice's ben[efi]t
Palmer

Frid. 1 Othello & Teddy the Tiler   66.
[Rice as Cassio, Palmer as Othello. USG]

Andrew Allen's
benefit

Sat. 2 Patriotic Banquet & C[eter]a   83.50   413.50

Mon. 4 Columbus & [The] Flying   180.
Dutchman

Tues. 5 [The] Flying Dutchman &
[The] S[pectre] Bride-
groom
(Dismissed.)
_____

9819.25

73 Nights averaging $134
During the 220 nights there
were 77 Benefits

The whole season of 220 nights
am[oun]t[e]d to $43780, making
an average of $199 per night.
Reopened.

Roberts A. Adams

Thurs. 7 Pizarro & [The] Sleepwalker   80.
[Roberts as Somno in *The Sleepwalker*, Adams as Rolla in *Pizarro*. USG]

[487]

"   Frid.   8   Sweethearts & Wives & [The]   13.
L[ottery] Ticket
[Roberts as Billy Lackaday
in *Sweethearts and Wives*
and Wormwood in *The
Lottery Ticket.* USG]

"   Sat.   9   [The] Flying Dutchman &   72.
[The] Turnpike Gate
[Roberts as Peter von Bum-
mel in *The Flying Dutch-
man* and Crack in *The
Turnpike Gate.* USG]

Mon. 11   W[illia]m Tell & Therese   60.75
Mr. Pearson   [Pearson as William Tell,
Riley's Bene[fi]t   Riley as Carwin in
Therese. USG]

Tues. 12   Rob Roy [Macgregor] & [The]   62.
F[lying] Dutchman

Wed. 13   [The] Irish Widow[, The] 40   41.
C. Green's benefit   Thieves [&] Rumfustian
[As Whittle in *The Irish
Widow*, Alibaba in *The
Forty Thieves* and as
Rumfustian USG]

Thurs. 14   [The] 40 Thieves; State Se-   55.50
Roberts' 4th   crets; Potter, the Juggler;
   Benefit Potter   Hess, Rope Dancer
   Hess   [See preface to this season.]

Frid. 15   No performance.

Sat. 16   El Hyder & Fortune's frolic   55.50
Potter-Hess   [See preface to this
season.]

Mon. 18 No performance.

	Tues. 19 Douglas & 3 . . . Ears	37.
Miss Kerr's	[See preface to this season.]	
ben[efi]t		

Wed. 20 No performance.

	Thurs. 21 How to die for Love & [The]	79.87½
Watson's	Flying Dutchman &	
ben[efi]t	[The] Phil[adelphia] Mar-	
	ket	
	[As Trick in *How to Die for*	
	Love and Peter in *The*	
	Flying Dutchman. DC]	

Fri. 22 No performance.

	Sat. 23 D[amon] & Pythias & [The?]	42.
Mrs. Smith's	Butchers &	
ben[efi]t		
Murstack[?] & Gilman		

Mon. 25 No performance.

	Tues. 26 [The] Miller & [His] Men &	58.
Dixon's ben[efi]t	[The] Irish Tutor	
	[See preface to this season.]	

Wed. 27 No performance.

	Thurs. 28 [The] Lady of the Lake &	25.
Miss Hamilton's	[The] Y[oung] Widow	
ben[efi]t		

[PHILADELPHIA SEASON, COMMENCING AUGUST 27, ENDING
OCTOBER 15, 1831.]

[Maywood & Co.]

PREFACE—**September 3**: USG announces Madame Feron, Madame
Brichta and Signor Angrisani, singers. According to *Durang*, III, Chapter Thirteenth, Madame Feron played Diana Vernon in *Rob Roy Mac-*

[489]

gregor. **September 7:** USG announces that Madame Feron, Madam Brichta and Signor Angrisani will sing. According to *Durang,* III, Chapter Thirteenth, Madame Feron played Julia Mannering. **September 17:** USG announces *Der Freischutz* and *Lovers' Quarrels.* According to *Durang,* III, Chapter Fourteenth, Madame Brichta played Rose in *Der Freischutz* and Rosina in *The Barber of Seville.* If *Tancredi* were given Madame Brichta probably appeared as Tancredi. *Durang,* III, Chapter Fourteenth, contradicting the *Account Book* states that the Italian opera was "compressed into one act" for the night of September 14. **October 8:** USG announces *Der Freischutz,* with Mrs. Austin as Linda; a "musical mélange" in which Cuddy and Norton are to take part; and *'Tis All a Farce.* **October 10 and 11:** USG also announces that Cuddy is to perform a fantasia on the flute. **October 12:** USG also announces Mrs. Austin, Cuddy and Norton in a "musical mélange." **October 13:** USG announces a benefit "in aid of the Polish Fund."

Inside the cover of Volume VII of the *Account Book,* in which Wood has kept his record of this season, he has written the notation, "Engaged on Monday 12th," which obviously explains why he has begun with the entry of September 16, about three weeks after the opening of the Walnut Street Theatre. *Durang,* III, Chapter Fourteenth, states that, on "the 16th of September, Mr. W. B. Wood was engaged for a limited period, and made his first appearance as Lothario, in *The Fair Penitent.*"

Walnut Street [Theatre]

[August 27 The Heart of Mid-Lothian &
Raising the Wind]

[29 Paul Pry & The Sleepwalker]

[30 The Heart of Mid-Lothian &
Turn Out]

[31 The School of Reform &
Charles the Twelfth]

[September 1 Wreck Ashore, Matrimony &
The Colonel's Come]

[2 Fraternal Discord & The
Devil to Pay]

[490]

[3 Rob Roy MacGregor, Grand
Concert & A Lovers'
Quarrels]
[See preface to this season.]

[5 The Marriage of Figaro &
Raising the Wind]

[6 Paul Pry & Sprigs of Laurel]

[7 Guy Mannering, Grand Con-
cert & A Day after the
Wedding]
[See preface to this season.]

[8 Fraternal Discord & The
Agreeable Surprize]

[9 John of Paris, Grand Concert
& Wreck Ashore]

[10 The Hebrew* & Fish out of
Water]

[12 The School for Scandal & the
4th & 5th Acts of Paul
Pry]

[13 The Slave & the 1st. & 2nd.
Acts of The Marriage of
Figaro]

[14 The Heart of Mid-Lothian &
The Young Widow]

[15 Tancredi* & The Spectre
Bridegroom]

F. 16 [The] Fair Penitent [& Turn   126.
Out]
                            Storm

S. 17 Tancredi &   462.
Ben[efi]t [of]   [See preface to this season.]
Mad[ame] Brichta

M. 19 As You Like it & [The Actress 492.
C[lara] F[isher]   of All Work]
                         [As Rosalind and as six
                         characters in *The Actress
                         of All Work*. USG]

T. 20 [The] Found[ling] of [the] 187.
                         Forest[, Incantation
                         Scene from Der Frei-
                         schutzl] & [The Lottery
                         Ticket]

W. 21 Romeo & Juliet [& The Spoil'd 260.
C[lara] F[isher]   Child]
                         [As Juliet and as Little
                         Pickle in *The Spoiled
                         Child*. USG]

" T. 22 A B[old] Stroke for [a] hus- 226.
                         band [& Perfection]
                         [Clara Fisher as Donna
                         Olivia in *A Bold Stroke for
                         a Husband* and Kate
                         O'Brian in *Perfection*.
                         USG]

" F. 23 [The] Will & [The Dead Shot] 240.
                         [Clara Fisher as Albina
                         Mandeville in *The Will*
                         and Louisa in *The Dead
                         Shot*. USG]

Booth   S. 24 Richard 3d. [& The Turnpike 640.   2045.
                         Gate]
                         [As Richard. USG]

[492]

M. 26 Much ado [about Nothing & 214.
C[lara] F[isher's]   The] 2 pages [of Frederick
Ben[efi]t   the Great]
   [As Beatrice and one of the
   pages. USG See note,
   September 28.]
   Violent Rain

Booth   T. 27 Othello & ['Tis] All a farce   376.
   [As Othello. USG]

W. 28 She W[oul]d & [She] Would   290.
C[lara] F[isher]   Not & Husband at Sight
   [As Hypolita in *She Would
   and She Would Not* and
   Catherine in *Husband at
   Sight.* USG announces
   Miss Fisher's benefit,
   deferred from Monday,
   owing to "the inclemency
   of the weather."]

B[ooth]   T. 29 Hamlet & Is he jealous[?]   320.
   [As Hamlet. USG]

B[ooth]   F. 30 A New Way to p[lay] old debts   230.
   & [The Prize]
   [As Sir Giles Overreach in
   *A New Way to Pay Old
   Debts.* USG]

October
Mercer['s] 1st.   S.   1 Macbeth & F[ortune's] Frolic   290.   1720.
B[ooth]   [Mercer as Hecate and Mal-
   colm and as Robin
   Roughhead in *Fortune's
   Frolic.* Booth as Mac-
   beth. ADA]

[493]

Mrs. Pindar   M. 3 [The] B[ride] of Lammermoor 170.
              & [The] Broken Sword
              [As Lady Ashton in *The*
              Bride of Lammermoor and
              Myrtillo in *The Broken*
              Sword. USG]

          T. 4 K[ing] Lear & [The] L[ottery] 285.
"   & Booth   Ticket
              [Booth as Lear, Mrs. Pindar
              as Cordelia. USG]

"   " W. 5 R[omeo] & Juliet & [The] 2 175.
              Gregories
              [Booth as Romeo, Mrs.
              Pindar as Juliet. USG]

"   T. 6 Richard 3d. & [The Wedding 220.
              Day]
              [Mrs. Pindar as Lady Con-
              quest in *The Wedding*
              Day. USG]

          F. 7 [The] C[astle] Spectre, 2nd. 125.
" Benefit   act [of The] Sleepw[alke]r,
              4th Act [of] Douglas &
              [The] Rendezvous
              [As Angela in *The Castle*
              Spectre, Young Norval in
              Douglas and Sophia in
              The Rendezvous. USG]

         S. 8 Der Freyschutz, [The] Comet 380.   1355.
Austin   [See preface to this season.]
  Cuddy Norton
         M.10 G[uy] Mannering & [The] 220.
" " "   A[greeable] Surprize
              [Mrs. Austin as Julia Man-
              nering. USG See pref-
              ace to this season.]

	T. 11 [John of Paris & The Highland	200.
" " "	Reel]	
	[Mrs. Austin as the Princess of Navarre in *John of Paris*. USG See preface to this season.]	

Ben[efi]t [of	W. 12 [The] Tempest [&] no Song	310.
Mrs.] Austin	[No Supper]	
⸰	[Mrs. Austin as Ariel and as Margaretta in *No Song No Supper*. USG] [See preface to this season.]	

	T. 13 [The] Hero of Scotland* &	201.
Polish Ben[efi]t	[Turn Out]	
	[See preface to this season.]	

	F. 14 [The] Robbers & [The] H[igh-	364.
Wood's Ben[efi]t	land] Reel	
	[As Charles de Moor in *The Robbers*. USG]	

| | S. 15 [The] Hero of Scotland [& The | 390. | 1705. |
| | Sleepwalker] | |

[PHILADELPHIA SEASON COMMENCING OCTOBER 17, ENDING DECEMBER 9, 1831.]

[Maywood & Co.]

PREFACE—**December 2**: ADA announces *Cinderella* in place of *Rob Roy Macgregor*. Wood has written the title "Cinderella" but crossed it out and written under it "Rob Roy [Macgregor]."   To the left of this entry he has written the notation, "Mrs. Austin Sick" and ditto marks referring to it to the left of the entries of December 3, 5 and 6.   In the entry of December 7 he has written the notation, "Austin Sick;" and ditto marks referring to it in the entry of December 8.   On this date, according to *Durang*, III, Chapter Twenty-First, "the managers of the Ches-

[495]

nut Street Theatre announced the opening of the Walnut Street Theatre for the balance of the winter season." See the preface to the next season.

[Chesnut Street Theatre]

[October]

Sinclair	M. 17 Rob Roy [Macgregor & The] Col[onel']s Come [As Francis Osbaldistone in *Rob Roy Macgregor*. USG]	640.	
Finn	T. 18 Paul Pry & [The] M[aster's] Rival [As Paul Pry and as Paul Shack in *The Master's Rival*. USG]	201.	
S[inclair]	W. 19 [The] Cabinet & [The] H[igh-land] Reel [As Prince Orlando in *The Cabinet*. USG]	470.	
F[inn]	Th. 20 M[arried] & Single & [The Highland Reel] [As Dean Shatterly in *Married and Single* and Shelty in *The Highland Reel*. USG]	194.	
S[inclair]	F. 21 G[uy] Mann[erin]g & No[!] [As Henry Bertram in *Guy Mannering* and Frederick in *No!* ADA]	450.	
F[inn]	S. 22 [She] Stoops to Conquer [& The Prize] [As Tony Lumpkin in *She Stoops to Conquer* and Dr. Lenitive in *The Prize*. USG]	200.	2155.

[496]

S[inclair] M. [24 The] Slave, No! & [The] L[ot- 460.
     tery] Ticket
     [As Malcom in *The Slave*
     and Frederick in *No!*
     USG]

F[inn]   T. [25] [The] S[chool] for Scandal & 107.
     [The] May Queen
     [As Sir Peter Teazle in *The*
     School for Scandal and
     Caleb Pipkin in *The May*
     Queen. ADA]

S[inclair] W. [26] Rob Roy [Macgregor] & Mi- 320.
     das
     [As Francis Osbaldistone
     and as Apollo in *Midas*.
     USG]

     T. [27] 102, Snakes in [the] Grass, 220.
F[inn's] ben[efit] [The] Bashful Man [&
     The] 2 Thomsons
     [As Philip Garbois in *102*,
     Mr. Janus in *Snakes in*
     the Grass, Blushington in
     The Bashful Man and as
     William Thomson, 2nd.
     USG]

Sinc[lair] F. [28] G[uy] Mann[erin]g & Midas 240.
     [As Henry Bertram in *Guy*
     Mannering and Apollo in
     Midas. USG]

Hackett S. [29 The] Lion of the West [& The 480. 1827.
     Colonel's Come]
     [As Colonel Nimrod Wild-
     fire in *The Lion of the*
     West. USG]

M. 31 [The] Lord of [the] Manor, 710.
Sincl[air's] Ben[efi]t   No[!] & Midas
[As Trumore in *The Lord of
the Manor*, Frederick in
No! and Apollo in *Midas*.
USG]

Nov[ember]
H[ackett]   T. 1 [The] Lion of [the] West & 405.
[The Master's Rival]
[As Colonel Nimrod Wild-
fire in *The Lion of the
West*. USG]

H[ackett]   W. 2 [The] Lion of [the] West & Rip 376.
V[an] Winkle
[As Colonel Nimrod Wild-
fire and Rip van Winkle.
USG]

H[ackett]   T. 3 [The] Lion of [the] West & 320.
[The] 2 Gre[gorie]s
[As Colonel Nimrod Wild-
fire. USG]

H[ackett's]   F. 4 [The] Lion of [the] West & 360.
ben[efi]t   Jon[athan] in England
[As Colonel Nimrod Wild-
fire and as Solomon Swap
in *Jonathan in England*.
USG]

S. 5 [The] Robbers & Turn[in]g 149.   2290.
[the] tables*

Master Burke M. 7 Paul Pry & [The] I[rish] Tutor 522.
[As Paul Pry and as Terry
O'Rourke in The Irish
Tutor. USG]

[498]

"   T. 8 [The] M[erchant] of Venice   351.
           [&] Whirligig Hall
           [As Shylock and as six char-
           acters in *Whirligig Hall.*
           USG]

Master Burke W. 9 [The] H[eir] at Law & [The]   345.
           Review
           [As Dr. Pangloss in *The
           Heir at Law* and Looney
           Mactwolter in *The Re-
           view.* USG]

"   T. 10 Richard 3d. & [The] Weather-   270.
           cock
           [Master Burke as Richard
           and as Tristram Fickle in
           The Weathercock. USG]

"   F. 11 Speed the plough & [The]   404.
           Irish[man] in London
           [Master Burke as Sir Abel
           Handy in *Speed the
           Plough* and Murtoch De-
           lany in *The Irishman in
           London.* USG]

"   S. 12 John Bull & [The] March of   440.   2332.
           intellect
           [Master Burke as Dennis
           Brulgruddery in *John
           Bull* and as six characters
           in *The March of Intellect.*
           USG]

      M. 14 Douglas & L[ove] a la mode   410.
           [Master Burke as Young
           Norval in *Douglas* and
           Sir Callaghan O'Bral-
           laghan in *Love a la Mode.*
           USG]

[499]

"   T. 15 [The] Poor Gent[lema]n &   360.
[The] March of Intellect]
[Master Burke as Ollapod
in *The Poor Gentleman*
and as six characters in
The March of Intellect.
ADA]

"   W. 16 Hamlet & [The] I[rish] T[utor]   350.
[Master Burke as Hamlet
and as Terry O'Rourke
in *The Irish Tutor.* USG]

"   T. 17 Speed the plough & [Whirligig   360.   1480.
Hall]
[Master Burke as Sir Abel
Handy in *Speed the
Plough* and as six char-
acters in *Whirligig Hall.*
USG]

F. 18 Man & Wife & [The] P[oor]   806.
Master B[urke's]   Soldier
ben[efit]   [As Cornelius O'Dedimus in
Man and Wife and Pat-
rick in *The Poor Soldier.*
USG]

Warren   S. 19 [The First Part of] Henry 4th   210.   2496.
[& The] 2 Gregories
[As Falstaff. USG]

"   M. 21 [The] S[chool] for Scandal &   86.
[The] T[urnpike] Gate
[Warren as Sir Peter Teazle
in *The School for Scandal.*
USG]

"   T. 22 [The] Rivals & [Animal Mag-   90.
netism]

[Warren as Sir Anthony Absolute in *The Rivals.*
USG]

C. Kean	W. 23	Richard 3d. & Turning [the] Tables [As Richard. USG]	135.
"	Th. 24	[A] New Way to pay old debts & [The] H[ighland] Reel [Kean as Sir Giles Over-reach in *A New Way to Pay Old Debts.* USG]	140.
Warren's benefit	F. 25	[The] Poor Gent[leman] & [The] Colonel's Come [As Sir Robert Bramble in *The Poor Gentleman.* USG]	206.

C. Kean   S. 26 Waldimar* & [The] L[ottery]   270.   927.
                    Ticket
                    [As Waldimar. USG]

Jones & Austin	M. 28	Cinderella* & T[urning the] Tables [Jones as Felix, Mrs. Austin as Cinderella. USG]	940.
C. Kean	T. 29	Waldimar & T[urn] Out [As Waldimar. USG]	94.
J[ones] & [Mrs.] A[ustin]	W. 30	Cinderella & [The] Prize [Jones as Felix, Mrs. Austin as Cinderella. USG]	670.

Decem[ber]

C. Kean's benefit	Th. 1	Hamlet & [The] 2 Gregories [As Hamlet. USG]	140.

[501]

Jones   F. 2 Rob Roy [Macgregor] & [The] 124.
         Jenkins
         [See preface to this season.]

"   S. 3 G[uy] Mann[er]ing [&] A[ni- 109. 2077.
         mal] Magnetism
         [Jones as Henry Bertram in
         Guy Mannering. USG]

     M. 5 [The] F[oundling] of [the] 35.
         forest & [The] Sleep-
         w[alker]

     T. 6 [The] Heir at Law & R[aising 54. 89.
         the] Wind

     W. 7 V[enice] Preserv'd & [The] 75.
Hamblin Jones   Weathercock
Miss Clifton   [Hamblin as Jaffier, Miss
         Clifton as Belvidera in
         Venice Preserved. Jones
         as Tristram Fickle in *The
         Weathercock.* USG]

     T. 8 [The] Robbers & ['Tis] All a 42.
         farce

     F. 9 Cinderella & [The] Jenkins 402. 904.
[Mrs.] Austin Jones   [Mrs. Austin as Cinderella,
         Jones as Felix. USG]

[PHILADELPHIA SEASON, COMMENCING DECEMBER 10, 1831, ENDING
JULY 28, 1832.]

[Maywood & Co.]

PREFACE—**December 17**: To the left of this entry Wood has written
the notation, "Hamblin ill at End of 2 Act & the Evil Eye & R[aising]
the Wind Substituted." Wemyss in *Life*, p. 200, writes of this occasion:
"I must not forget to mention a row which took place on the 17th of

December, at the Walnut Street Theatre, in consequence of Mr. Hamblin breaking down in the character of Richard the Third, his old enemy, the asthma, preventing him from proceeding beyond the third act. An apology was made to the audience, who quietly sat out the new piece of 'The Evil Eye;' but when the curtain rose upon the farce of 'Raising the Wind,' in which I had to perform Jeremy Diddler, the audience gave strong proof of their determination to see the last two acts of 'Richard the Third.' From the violent disapprobation, I ventured to expostulate with Mr. Rowbotham upon the folly of attempting to proceed; but he asked me if I was afraid—I said 'No; but the ladies are.' 'Go on!' said he. 'Up with the curtain,' said I. But no sooner had we commenced the second act, and the determination of the management to proceed in spite of opposition became manifest to the audience, then some gentleman blackguard, (aside) threw a large piece of plaster extracted from the roof of the pit passage, with some force upon the stage. It fell at the feet of Mrs. Charles Green, who was acting Peggy, and whose face miraculously escaped the contact. Her husband, who was on the stage, representing the character of Old Plainway, in an instant seized the offending missile, and hurled it back upon the audience with the emphatic phrase, that the man that threw it, was a blackguard and a coward. A general row ensued, in which stoves were overturned, hot coals distributed, and the melee ended by leaving actors and audience in the dark, the lights being rapidly extinguished." **December 26**: According to *Durang*, III, Chapter Twenty-First, "Miss Hughes, a vocalist of London name and of acknowledged ability . . . made her first appearance as Julia Mannering." **July 19**: An editorial in USG of July 19, 1832 explains that the day has been set apart for humiliation, fasting and prayer, "in direct reference to the approach of the disease [cholera] whose ravages have been so fearful in a neighboring city."

In the text of this season "C" and "W" have been printed after the titles to signify Chesnut Street Theatre and Walnut Street Theatre respectively. "The two theatres," now under the management of Maywood & Co, "were simultaneously open, or one was shut and the other open, or the twain were in full blast, as circumstances governed." See *Durang*, III, Chapter Twenty-Second. Durang asserts that this "course of policy militated seriously against the interests of both houses." "In their valedictory at the end of this season," states *Durang*, III, Chapter Twenty-Second, Maywood & Co. "spoke of it as a 'severe and disastrous winter.' An idea may be formed when the nightly expenses were over

[503]

$300, the receipts per contra hardly averaging $175, involving a nightly loss of $125."

It has been necessary to substitute "Mrs. Austin & Jones," in Wood's entry of December 22, for two pairs of ditto marks referring respectively to "Mrs. Austin's" in the entry of December 19 and "Jones" in the entry of December 21.

W[alnut] Street [Theatre and Chesnut Street Theatre]

[December]

H[amblin] & Miss C[lifton]	S. 10	Macbeth & [The] 2 Gregories [W] [Hamblin as Macbeth, Miss Clifton as Lady Macbeth. USG]	305.		904.
[Mrs.] A[ustin] & [Jones]	M. 12	Cinderella & How to die for Love [C] [Mrs. Austin as Cinderella, Jones as Felix. USG]	450.		
H[amblin] & Miss C[lifton]	T. 13	Pizarro & [The] 2 Gregories [W] [Hamblin as Rolla, Miss Clifton as Elvira in *Pizarro.* USG]	140.		
[Mrs.] A[ustin] & J[ones]	W. 14	Cinderella [& The Lottery Ticket C] [Mrs. Austin as Cinderella, Jones as Felix. USG]	520.		
H[amblin] & Miss C[lifton]	T. 15	Venice Preserv'd & [The] Evil Eye [W] [Hamblin as Jaffier, Miss Clifton as Belvidera in *Venice Preserved.* USG]	110.		1220.
Mrs. A[ustin] & Jones	F. 16	Cinderella & Touch & Take [C] [Mrs. Austin as Cinderella, Jones as Felix. USG]	490.		

H[amblin]   S. 17 Richard 3d. [& The] Evil Eye   140.   1850.
               [W]   —
               [As   Richard.   USG   See
               preface to this season.]

Mrs. Austin's M. 19 Cinderella & N[o] Song N[o]   480.
   Ben[efi]t   Supper [C]
               [As Cinderella and as Mar-
               garetta in *No Song No
               Supper*. USG]

               T. 20 Bertram & [The] E[vil] Eye   90.
               [W]

               W. 21 Cinderella & [The] Jenkins   490.
Jones' Ben[efi]t   [C]
               [As Felix. USG]

[Mrs. Austin   T. 22 Cinderella & How to die [for 270.
   & Jones]   Love C]
               [Mrs. Austin as Cinderella,
               Jones as Felix. USG]

               F. 23 [The] Water Witch & L[overs'] 240.
                     Quar[rel]s [W]

               S. 24 [The] W[ater] Witch & F[or-   250.
                     tune's] Frolic [W]

               S. 24 Bertram & [The] L[ottery]   64.   1884.
Miss C[lifton's]   Ticket [C]   —
   Ben[efi]t   [As Imogine in *Bertram*.
               USG]

Miss Hughes   M. 26 G[uy] Mannering & Is he   180.
                     Jealous[? C]
               [See preface to this Season.]

[505]

26 Geo[rge] Barnw[ell] & [The] 604.
W[ater] Witch [W]

T. 27 Alexander [the Great] & [The] 202.
W[ater] Witch [W]

Sinclair & W. 28 Rob Roy [Macgregor] & No[!] 172.
Miss H[ughes] [C]
[Sinclair as Francis Osbaldi-
stone, Miss Hughes as
Diana Vernon in *Rob Roy
Macgregor*, Sinclair as
Frederick in *No!* USG]

T. 29 My Aunt, [The] W[ater] 120.
Witch & Down East [W]

" F. 30 [The] Lord of the Manor & 130.
Midas [C]
[Sinclair as Trumore, Miss
Hughes as Annette in
The Lord of the Manor.
Sinclair as Apollo in
Midas. USG]

S. 31 [The] W[ater] Witch, D[own] 191. 1599.
East [& The] Review [W] ——

January
M. 2 [Love in a Village & Rosina C]

[2 The Innkeeper's Daughter &
Tom & Jerry W]

T. 3 [The Sleepwalker & The
Water Witch W]

[4 My Aunt & The Innkeeper's
Daughter W]

[506]

[5 The Water Witch & Jocko,
the Brazilian Ape W]

[6 Is He Jealous & Jocko, the
Brazilian Ape & Raising
the Wind W]

[7 The Hero of Scotland & Jocko,
the Brazilian Ape W]

[9 Wives As They Were and
Maids As They Are &
The Spoil'd Child C]

[9 Washington* & Jocko, the
Brazilian Ape W]

[10 Washington & Pitcairn's
Island W]

[11 Perfection, the Dead Shot &
The Actress of All Work
C]

[11 The Innkeeper's Daughter,
Fortune's Frolic & Pit-
cairn's Island W]

[12 The Hero of Scotland & Pitcairn's Island W]

[13 A Bold Stroke for a Husband
& A Husband at Sight C]

[13 Paul Jones & Pitcairn's Island
W]

[14 Cinderella & The Two Gregories C]

[507]

[14 The Young Widow, The,
    Spectre Bridegroom &
    Jocko, the Brazilian Ape
    W]

[16 All in the Wrong & The Four
    Mowbrays C]

[16 The Press Gang* & The
    Spectre Bridegroom W]

[17 Cinderella & Family Jars C]

[17 The Press Gang & Jocko, the
    Brazilian Ape W]

[18 Cinderella & The Jenkins C]

[18 The Recluse of the Hulk &
    Jack Robinson & His
    Monkey W]

[19 Cinderella & The Lottery
    Ticket C]

[19 The Recluse of the Hulk, The
    Rendezvous & Jack
    Robinson & His Monkey
    W]

[20 Cinderella & Everybody's
    Husband C]

20 Paul Jones & Jocko, the
    Brazilian Ape W

[21 My Aunt, The Water Witch,
    The Spectre Bridegroom
    & Pitcairn's Island W]

[21 Cinderella & Everybody's
Husband C]

[23 Love Makes a Man & The
Prize C]

[24 Speed the Plough C]

[24 The Midnight Hour, Everybody's Husband, Poli-
chinelle Vampire & The
Prize W]

[25 Every One Has His Fault &
The Devil to Pay C]

[26 Macbeth, Polichinelle Vampire
& The Two Gregories W]

[27 The Heir at Law & The Poor
Soldier C]

[28 The Mountaineers & Harlequin & Mother Goose
W]

[30 The Poor Gentleman & The
Temple of Fire C]

[31 The Foundling of the Forest
& Harlequin & Mother
Goose W]

[February 1 Paul Pry & Harlequin &
Mother Goose W]

[2 The Hero of Scotland & Harlequin & Mother Goose
W]

[509]

[3 The Rivals & The Turnpike
Gate C]

[3 The Castle Spectre & Harlequin & Mother Goose
W]

[4 The Hero of Scotland, The
Old Soldier of the Revo-
lution & Harlequin &
Mother Goose W]

[6 The Comedy of Errors,
Therese & Two Strings
to Your Bow C]

[7 The Old Soldier of the Revo-
lution, Harlequin &
Mother Goose & The
Rendezvous W]

[8 High Ways & By Ways, Turn
Out & Polichinelle
Vampire C]

[9 The Old Soldier of the Revo-
lution, Meg Murnock &
Harlequin & Mother
Goose W]

[10 The Good Natured Man &
High Ways & By Ways
C]

[11 The Forty Thieves, High
Ways & By Ways & Har-
lequin & Mother Goose
W]

[13 The Old Soldier of the Revo-
lution, Meg Murnock &
Harlequin & Mother
Goose W]

[14 Charles the Second & The
Forty Thieves W]

[15 Therese & Industry & Idleness W]

[16 George Barnwell & Industry
Idleness W]

[17 The Young Widow, Turn Out
& Industry & Idleness
W]

[18 Meg Murnock, The Navi-
gator, High Ways & By
Ways & Industry & Idle-
ness W]

[20 The Fair Penitent & Industry & Idleness W]

[21 The Blue Devils, The Navi-
gator, The Jenkins & In-
dustry & Idleness W]

[22 Pizarro & Fortune's Frolic C]

[24 The Spoil'd Child, The Dream
of Christopher Colum-
bus, Matrimony & Har-
lequin & Mother Goose
W] .

[25 Julius Caesar & The Forty
    Thieves W]

[27 The Adopted Child, The
    Deuce Is in Her & Per-
    fection C]

[28 William Tell & High Ways &
    By Ways C]

[29 The Deuce Is in Her, The
    Adopted Child & The
    Grenadier C]

[March   1 The Exile & Mother Goose C]

[2 Gretna Green, Mother Goose
   & The Grenadier C]

[3 The Hunter of the Alps,
   Mother Goose & The
   Spectre Bridegroom C]

[5 Two Friends, The Deuce Is
   in Her & Mother Goose
   C]

[6 Mother Goose, Catherine &
   Petruchio & High Ways
   & By Ways C]

[9 Napoleon* C]

[10 Napoleon & The Rendezvous
    C]

[12 The Peasant Boy & The
    Grenadier C]

[512]

[13 Napoleon & The Turnpike
Gate C]

[14 Napoleon & Turn Out C]

[15 Napoleon & Simpson & Co.
C]

[16 Napoleon & The Spoil'd Child
C]

[17 Napoleon & St. Patrick's Day
C]

[19 Richard the Third & St.
Patrick's Day C]

[20 Napoleon & Simpson & Co. C]

[21 A New Way to Pay Old Debts
& The Midnight Hour C]

[22 Napoleon & The Irishman in
London C]

[23 Othello & Turn Out C]

[24 Napoleon & Lovers' Quarrels
C]

[26 Richard the Third &
Amateurs & Actors C]

[27 Napoleon & St. Patrick's Day
C]

[28 Napoleon & The Spoil'd Child
C]

[29 Napoleon & The Hunter of
the Alps C]

[30 Napoleon & The Irishman in
London C]

[31 Napoleon & Matrimony C]

[April 2 Cinderella & The Adopted
Child C]

[3 Napoleon C]

[4 Cinderella & The Rendezvous
C]

[5 Cinderella & Cramond Brig
C]

[6 Cinderella & How to Die for
Love C]

[7 The Peasant Boy & Short
Stages C]

[9 Cinderella & Short Stages C]

[10 The Carmelite & Simpson &
Co. C]

[11 Cinderella & St. Patrick's
Day C]

[12 Eugene Aram & The Bold
Dragoons* C]

[13 Cinderella & The Lottery
Ticket C]

[14 Tancred, King of Sicily &
The Bold Dragoons C]

[16 Cinderella & John of Paris C]

[17 The Hypocrite, the 5th Act of
Richard the Third & The
Bold Dragoons C]

[18 Cinderella, No! & Der Freischutz C]

[19 Cinderella, No! & John of
Paris C]

[21 The Hypocrite & The Bold
Dragoons W]

[23 Napoleon & Family Jars W]

[24 Napoleon & Matrimony W]

[25 Napoleon & St. Patrick's Dav
W]

[26 A New Way to Pay Old Debts
& The Bold Dragoons W]

[27 Napoleon & The Spoil'd Child
W]

[28 Richard the Third & Lovers'
Quarrels W]

[30 Hamlet & The Happiest Day
of My Life W]

[May   1 The Flying Dutchman, Dom-
inique, It Is the Devil*
W]

[3 Othello & No! W]

[4 It Is the Devil, the 5th Act of
Richard the Third & The
Young Widow W]

[5 Macbeth & The Spectre
Bridegroom W]

[7 King John & William Thomson W]

[8 The Iron Chest & The Bold
Dragoons W]

[9 Brutus, No! & The Review W]

[10 The Flying Dutchman &
Napoleon W]

[11 Rob Roy Macgregor & William Thomson W]

[12 Richard the Third & The
Happiest Day of My
Life W]

[14 Hamlet & The Highland Reel
W]

[15 Pizarro & The Bold Dragoons
W]

[16 A New Way to Pay Old Debts
& The Spectre Bride-
groom W]

[17 Masaniello & The Irishman
in London W]

[18 Town & Country & Catherine
& Petruchio W]

[19 Masaniello & St. Patrick's
Day W]

[21 Masaniello & How to Die for
Love W]

[22 Douglas & The Flying Dutchman W]

[23 Masaniello & Charles the
Second W]

[24 Pizarro & The Spectre Bridegroom W]

[25 Family Jars, the Bold Dragoons & Jocko, the Bra-
zilian Ape W]

[26 Hernani & The Highland
Reel W]

[28 Hernani & The Happiest Day
of My Life W]

[29 Masaniello & Jocko, the Brazilian Ape W]

[30 William Thomson, the Review
& Jocko, the Brazilian
Ape W]

[31 William Tell & The Spectre
Bridegroom W]

[June 1 Masaniello & Jack Robinson
& His Monkey W]

[517]

[2 Victorine* & Jocko, the Brazilian Ape W]

[4 The Lion of the West & Of
Age Tomorrow W]

[5 Victorine, Family Jars & The
£ 100 Note W]

[6 The Hero of Scotland & Masaniello W]

[7 Victorine & The Master's
Rival W]

[8 The Will & The Actress of All
Work W]

[9 The Africans & The Spectre
Bridegroom W]

[10 The Africans & The Lottery
Ticket W]

[12 Winning a Husband & Victorine W]

[13 The Gamester & The Bold
Dragoons W]

[14 Wives As They Were & Maids
As They Are & The Bo-
hemian Mother W]

[15 Jane Shore & Turn Out W]

[16 The Peasant Boy & The Miller & His Men W]

[18 Jane Shore & The Master's Rival W]

[19 The Miller & His Men & Masaniello W]

[20 Hamlet & Down East W]

[21 The Miller & His Men & Victorine W]

[22 Macbeth & The Happiest Day of My Life W]

[23 The Flying Dutchman & Tom & Jerry W]

[25 Victorine & Masaniello W]

[26 The Flying Dutchman & Tom & Jerry W]

[27 The Miller & His Men, Separation & Reparation & The Spoil'd Child W]

[28 Cherry & Fair Star & The Master's Rival W]

[29 A New Way to Pay Old Debts & Touch & Take W]

[30 Richard the Third & The Happiest Day of My Life W]

[July 2 The Hunter of the Alps & Cherry & Fair Star W

[3 King Lear & The Lottery
Ticket W]

[4 The Plains of Chippewa &
Cherry & Fair Star W]

[6 Julius Caesar & The Review
W]

[7 How to Die for Love & Victorine W]

[9 Turning the Tables & Cherry
& Fair Star W]

[10 The Forty Thieves & The
Master's Rival W]

[11 The Irishman in London &
Masaniello W]

[12 The Good Natured Man &
Don Giovanni W]

[13 Turning the Tables & Masaniello W]

[14 Rob Roy Macgregor & The
Bohemian Mother W]

[16 The £ 100 Note & Masaniello
W]

[17 The East Indian & Victorine
W]

[18 Turning the Tables & Guy
Mannering W]

[19 See preface to this season.
W]

[20 The Good Natured Man, No!
& Midas W]

[21 The Master's Rival & Blue
Beard W]

[23 Turning the Tables, The Beggar's Opera & Midas W]

[24 The Merchant of Venice &
Don Giovanni W]

[25 Education & The Sleepwalker
W]

[26 The Lottery Ticket, Cherry &
Fair Star & The Dumb
Girl of Genoa W]

[27 The Fair American & Bluebeard W]

[28 The Slave & Whirligig Hall
W]

[PHILADELPHIA] SEASON, COMM[ENCING] SEPT[EMBE]R 8, 1832, [ENDING
JANUARY 2, 1833.]

[Maywood & Co.]

PREFACE—**September** 13 and 20: The Ravel family, according to
Durang, III, Chapter Twenty-Third, were from Paris; and included ten
persons, professors of gymnastics. "The spectacle consisted of rope
dancing, herculean feats, and pantomime ballets, in four parts, in which
young Gabriel Ravel . . . sustained the principal characters. This corps
of pantomimists, rope dancers and gymnasts, probably was the most
extraordinary and universally enduring popular novelty that ever came

[521]

to this country from the old world." **October 4**: USG announces Gabriel Ravel as Monsieur Molinet and Mrs. Ravel as Nanette in *Monsieur Molinet*. **October 6**: USG announces Gabriel as Godenski, Antoine as Lovenski and Madame Ravel as Betsy in *Godenski*. **October 9**: USG announces Gabriel as Harlequin, Antoine as Pierrot, Jerome as Doubearde and Madame Ravel as Isabella in *The Golden Palm Leaf and Magic Mirror*. **October 11**: USG announces Gabriel as the Chevalier Lourdant, Antoine as Colin and Mlle. Émilie Ravel as Babet in *La Fête Champêtre*. **October 13**: ADA announces "the last appearance this season of the Ravel family" in a "grand wrestling gladitorial scene. After which herculean feats. After which, by request, the pantomimic ballet of *Monsieur Molinet*; or, *A Night of Adventures*. Mons. Molinet, Gabriel Ravel. The whole to conclude with *Buskin at Home* and *Tableau of the Robbers*; or, *a Burglary at Night*." USG announces Madame Ravel as Nanette in *Monsieur Molinet*. **October 20**: USG announces *The Happiest Day of My Life* in place of *The Riever's Ransom*. **December 20**: See the Philadelphia Season of 1822–3, April 23. **December 28**: USG announces Maywood as Master Walter in *The Hunchback*. In this entry Wood has written ditto marks referring to the Kembles. These marks and another pair of ditto marks in the December 29 entry have been crowded out of the printed version. According to USG, Kemble is to play Sir Thomas Clifford, with Miss Kemble as Julia, in *The Hunchback*, and Petruchio, with Miss Kemble as Catherine on December 28. **January 1**: Pratt was a member of the firm of Maywood & Co.

To the left of the entry of September 18 Wood has written "Ravel family," which it has been advisable to omit in view of the fact that the name is mentioned in the entry. It has been necessary to substitute "Miss Vincent" in the entry of September 28 for ditto marks referring to the name of that actress in the entry of September 26. It has been advisable to omit the notation, "Ravels," which Wood has written in the entries of October 2, 4, 6, 9, 11 and 13, for the reason just given; and also to omit ditto marks, in the entry of October 5, referring to "Ravels" in Wood's entry of October 4. It has also been advisable to omit "W. Warren died at Baltimore aged 66," in Wood's entry of October 19; "Warren's ben[efit] declined," in Wood's entry of November 6; and "Mrs. Roberts died," in Wood's entry of December 3. For an explanation of why Warren's family refused this benefit, see Wemyss' *Life*, pp. 211–213.

[Chesnut Street Theatre]

[522]

Sept[ember]

    Saty. 8 Napoleon & [The] L[ottery] 290.
          Ticket

     M[onday] 10 Masaniello & [The] Spectre 260.
Sinclair   Bride[groom]
[Madame] Feron   [Sinclair as Masaniello,
          Madame Fearon as El-
          vira in *Masaniello*. ADA]

    T[uesday] 11 Victorine & Turning the 180.
          tables

  W[ednesday] 12 Masaniello & An[imal] Mag- 260.
          netism

    T[hursday] 13 Cath[erine] & Petruchio & 308.
          Ravel family
          [See preface to this season.]

    F[riday] 14 Masaniello & [Of] Age tomor- 230.
          row

    S[aturday] 15 [The] M[aster's] Rival & 550.   2078.
          Ravels

Sinc[lair] &   M. 17 Cinderella & No[!]   330.
[Madame] Feron   [Sinclair as Felix in *Cin-* 330.
          derella and Frederick in
          No! Madame Feron as
          Cinderella. USG]

    T. 18 Ravels & [The] M[idnight] 340.
          Hour

  "   W. 19 Cinderella & Turning the 270.
          tables
          [Sinclair as Felix, Madame
          Feron as Cinderella.
          USG]

[523]

T. 20 Simpson & Co. & Ravels   360.
[See preface to this season.]

"   F. 21 Cinderella, Midas & Ravels   320.
Mad[ame] Feron's   [Sinclair as Felix, Madame
ben[efi]t   Feron   as   Cinderella.
Sinclair as Apollo, Mad-
ame Feron as Mysa in
Midas. USG]

S. 22 [The] Happiest Day [of my   510.   2130.
Life] & Ravels

M. 24 [2nd. & 3rd. acts of] Mas-   550.
Ravels Sinclair's   aniello, Cram[ond] Brig &
ben[efi]t M[adame]   [3rd. act of] Cind[erella &
Feron   Ravel family]
[Sinclair   as   Masaniello,
Madame Feron as Prin-
cess in *Masaniello*. Sin-
clair as Felix, Madame
Feron   as   Cinderella.
USG]

Ravels   T. 25 Cocomba, [The] Jenkins [&]   390.
Ravels
[Jerome Ravel as Zerbero,   •
Gabriel Ravel as Co-
comba. USG]

Miss Vincent   W. 26 Clari & Perfection   260.
[As Clari and Kate O'Brian
in *Perfection*. USG]

T. 27 1st. Act [of] Masaniello, No! &   620.
Sin[clair] & Feron   Jacko [the Brazilian Ape]
Gab[riel] Ravel's   [Sinclair   as   Masaniello,
ben[efi]t   Madame Feron as Princess in *Masaniello*. Gab-
riel Ravel as Jacko. USG]

[524]

F. 28 [The] Child of Nature & 140.
[Miss Vincent]   Therese
[As Amanthis in *The Child of Nature* and Mariette in *Therese*. USG]

S. 29 [The] Good Nat[ured] Man, 240.   2200.
Rice's ben[efit]   Songs & [The] B[old] Dragoons
[As Jim Crow. Also to sing three of his most popular extravaganzas. USG]

October
Miss Vincent M. 1 Romeo & Juliet & [The] 225.
          Review
[As Juliet. USG]

Ravels T. 2 [The] Jenkins, Ravels & Turn- 380.
          ing [the] Tables

W. 3 Rob Roy [Macgregor] & [The] 180.
Sinclair &   Dead Shot
[Madame] Feron   [Sinclair as Francis Osbaldi-stone and Madame Feron as Diana Vernon in *Rob Roy Macgregor*. USG]

Ravels T. 4 Ravels, Buskin at Home & 375.
          [The] Spec[tre] Bride-groom
[See preface to this season.]

F. 5 John of Paris, [The] Day after 230.
[Sinclair & Feron]   [the] Wedd[in]g & [The] Young Hussar
Sinclair as John of Paris, Madame Feron as Prin-

[525]

cess of Navarre and as
Caroline in *The Young
Hussar*. USG]

Ravels	S. 6 [The] Wanderer & Ravels	370.	1760.
	[See preface to this season.]		

Sinclair   M. 8 [The] Beggar's Opera & John   210.
[Madame] Feron   of Paris
    [Sinclair as Captain Mac-
    heath, Madame Feron as
    Polly Peachem in *The
    Beggar's Opera*. Sinclair
    as John, Madame Feron
    as Princess of Navarre.
    USG]

Ravels   T. 9 [The] B[old] Dragoons, Ravels   130.
    & [The] L[ottery] Ticket
    [See preface to this season.]

    W. 10 Hamlet & [The] 2 Thoms[o]ns   750.
Mr. C. Kemble   [As Hamlet. USG]

[Benefit of]   T. 11 Ravels & [The] Wanderer   240.
Ravels   [See preface to this season.]

Miss Kemble   F. 12 Fazio & [The] Colonel's Come   800.
    [As Bianca in *Fazio*. USG]

Ravels   S. 13 [The] M[idnight] Hour, Rav-   350.   2480.
    els, [Monsieur] Molinet,
    Attitudes & [The] Rob-
    bers['] Tableau
    [See preface to this season.]

Kembles   M. 15 Romeo & Juliet & Turn Out   960.
    [Kemble as Romeo, Miss
    Kemble as Juliet. USG]

T. 16 Napoleon & How to die for   200.
love

"   W. 17 [The] School for Scandal &   940.
[The] Bold Dragoons
[Kemble as Charles Surface,
Miss Kemble as Lady
Teazle in *The School for
Scandal*. USG]

T. 18 Buskin [at Home, The]   125.
S[pectre] Brideg[roo]m &
Cherry & F[air] Star

"   F. 19 Venice Preserv'd & [The] 2   820.
Gregories
[Kemble as Pierre, Miss
Kemble as Belvidera in
Venice Preserved. USG]

"   S. 20 Much ado [about Nothing] &   800.   3845.
[The] Riever's Ransom
[Kemble as Benedick, Miss
Kemble as Beatrice.
USG See preface to this
season.]

Kembles   M. 22 [The] Stranger & Cramond   805.
Brig
[Kemble as the Stranger,
Miss Kemble as Mrs.
Haller. USG]

"   T. 23 Fazio & Turning the Tables   640.
[Kemble as Giraldi, Miss
Kemble as Bianca in
Fazio. USG]

[527]

"   W. 24 [The] Hunchback & [The]   900.
Jenkins
[Kemble as Sir Thomas
Clifford, Miss Kemble as
Julia in *The Hunchback*.
USG]

"   T. 25 [The] Gamester & [The]   880.
Pris[oner] at large
[Kemble as Beverly, Miss
Kemble as Mrs. Beverly
in *The Gamester*. USG]

"   F. 26 [The] Hunchback & [Deaf as   850.
a Post]
[Kemble as Sir Thomas
Clifford, Miss Kemble as
Julia. USG]

              S. 27 [The] Provok'd Husband &   860.   4935.
Miss K[emble's]   [The] 2 Gregories
ben[efi]t   [Kemble as Lord Townly,
Miss Kemble as Lady
Townly in *The Provoked
Husband*. USG]

Mr. & Miss   M. 29 [The] Hunchback & Mod[ern]   900.
K[emble]   Antiques
[Kemble as Sir Thomas
Clifford, Miss Kemble as
Julia. USG]

"   T. 30 Much Ado [about Nothing]   720.
& [The] Riever's Ransom
[Kemble as Benedick, Miss
Kemble as Beatrice.
USG]

"   W. 31 [The] Hunchback & [The]   800.
             Pris[oner] at Large
             [Kemble as Sir Thomas
             Clifford, Miss Kemble as
             Julia. USG]

Novem[be]r

        T.   1 [The] Inconstant & [The]   900.
Mr. K[emble's]   M[idnight] Hour
ben[efit]   [Kemble as Young Mirabel,
             Miss Kemble as Bizarre
             in *The Inconstant.* USG]

"   F.   2 Venice Preserved & [The]   530.
             H[appiest] day of my life
             [Kemble as Jaffier, Miss
             Kemble as Belvidera in
             Venice Preserved. USG]

"   S.   3 Romeo & Juliet & [The] L[ot-   820.   4770.
             tery Ticket
             [Kemble as Mercutio, Miss
             Kemble as Juliet. USG]

Mr. Horn &   M.   5 Cinderella   &   Mod[ern]   260.
   Miss Hughes   Antiques
             [Horn as Felix, Miss Hughes
             as Cinderella. USG]

        T.   6 Simpson & Co. & [The] Peas-   45.
             ant Boy

"   "   W.   7 Masaniello & [The] Jenkins   220.
             [Horn as Masaniello, Miss
             Hughes as Elvira. USG]

"   "   T.   8 Masaniello & [St. Patrick's   90.
             Day]
             [Horn as Masaniello, Miss
             Hughes as Elvira. USG]

"   "   F. 9 John of Paris, [The] Gude   130.
                Man & No S[ong] No
                Supper
                [Horn as John, Miss Hughes
                as Princess of Navarre.
                Horn as Robin, Miss
                Hughes as Margaretta in
                No Song No Supper.
                USG]

"   "   S. 10 Cinderella & [The Irishman in   110.   855.
                London]
                [Horn as Felix, Miss Hughes
                as Cinderella. USG]

Horn   M. 12 Cinderella & Love in Wrinkles   250.
  Miss Hughes'   [Horn as Felix, Miss Hughes
  Ben[efit]   as Cinderella. Horn as
                Count Adolphe, Miss
                Hughes as Countess de
                Sterloff in *Love in
                Wrinkles.* USG]

"   "   T. 13 Cinderella & Love in Wrinkles   210.
                [See note, November 12.]

             W. 14 Pizarro & My Aunt   360.
J[ames] Wallack   [As Rolla in *Pizarro* and
                Dick Dashall in *My Aunt.*
                USG]

             T. 15 Der Freyschutz, Mus[ical]   280.
Horn['s] Ben[efi]t   Melange & Turning [the]
Miss Hughes   tables
                [Horn as Casper, Miss
                Hughes as Linda in *Der
                Freischutz.* USG]

             F. 16 Hamlet & [The] Jenkins   140.
[James Wallack]   [A[s] Hamlet. USG]

[530]

"   S. 17 [The] Rent day & my Aunt   350.   1590.

       [Wallack as Martin Hey-
        wood in *The Rent Day*
        and Dick Dashall in *My*
        Aunt. USG]

J. Wallack   M. 19 [The] Rent Day & [The]   480.
       Adopted Child
       [As Martin Heywood in
        The Rent Day and
        Michael in *The Adopted*
        Child. USG]

"   T. 20 [The] Rent day & Victorine   210.
       [Wallack as Martin Hey-
        wood. USG]

"   W. 21 [The] Brigand* & [The] Col-   190.
       onel's Come
       [Wallack as Allesandro
        Massaroni in *The Bri-*
        gand. USG]

"   T. 22 [The] Rent day & [The]   240.
       Chil[dre]n in the Wood
       [Wallack as Martin Hey-
        wood and as Walter in
        The Children in the Wood.
        USG]

"   F. 23 [The] Brigand, [The] Adopted   270.
       Child & [The] L[ottery]
       Ticket
       [Wallack as Allesandro
        Massaroni and Michael.
        USG]

"   S. 24 [The] Brigand & [The] Rent 510.   1890.
                      Day
                      [Wallack as Allesandro
                      Massaroni and Martin
                      Heywood. USG]

Wallack   M. 26 My Own Lover* & [The] Chil- 388.
                      [dren] in [the] Wood
                      [As Don Vincent in *My Own
                      Lover* and Walter in *The
                      Children in the Wood.*
                      USG]

"   T. 27 St. Patrick's day, [The] Rent 240.
                      day & My Aunt
                      [Wallack as Martin Hey-
                      wood in *The Rent Day*
                      and Dick Dashall in *My
                      Aunt.* ADA]

"   W. 28 My Own Lover & [The] 160.
                      Brigand
                      [Wallack as Don Vincent
                      and Allesandro Massa-
                      roni. USG]

                  T. 29 Education & [The] Bold 230.
Wood's benefit   Dragoons
                      [As Count Villars in *Educa-
                      tion* and Leon Sabretash
                      in *The Bold Dragoons.*
                      USG]

[Wallack]   F. 30 [The] Rent day & Spring & 370.
                      Autumn
                      [As Martin Heywood and
                      as Rattle in *Spring and
                      Autumn.* USG]

December
" S. 1 Pizarro & Spring & Autumn 290. 1678.
[Wallack as Rolla and Rat-
tle. USG]

M. 3 [The] Rent day, [The] Wolf 590.
Wallack's ben[efi]t & [the] Lamb & [The]
Brigand
[As Martin Heywood, Al-
lesandro Massaroni and
as Bob Honeycomb in
The Wolf and the Lamb.
USG]

T. 4 [A] Cure for [the] Heartache & 80.
St. Patrick's day

Kembles W. 5 Romeo & Juliet & [A] D[ay] 440.
after [the] Wedding
[Kemble as Mercutio, Miss
Kemble as Juliet. USG]

T. 6 [The] Good N[autre]d Man 45.
& [The] Irish[man] in
London

" F. 7 [The] Inconstant & 'Tis all a 600.
farce
[Kemble as Young Mirabel,
Miss Kemble as Bizarre
in *The Inconstant.* USG]

" S. 8 [The] Stranger & Anim[al] 560. 2315.
Magnetism
[Kemble as the Stranger,
Miss Kemble as Mrs.
Haller. USG]

Kembles M. 10 Isabella & [The] Happiest day 540.
of my life

[533]

[Kemble as Biron, Miss
Kemble as Isabella. USG]

T. 11 [The] Wanderer & Masaniello   90.

"   W. 12 K[ing] John & [The] Prisoner 520.
at large
[Kemble as Falconbridge,
Miss Kemble as Con-
stance. USG]

T. 13 [The] F[oundling] of the forest   60.
& deaf as a post

"   F. 14 [The] Hunchback & How to 900.
die for love
[Kemble as Sir Thomas
Clifford, Miss Kemble as
Julia in *The Hunchback*.
USG]

"   S. 15 Fazio & [The] B[old] Dragoons 440.   2550
[Kemble as Giraldi, Miss
Kemble as Bianca in
Fazio. USG]

Kembles   M. 17 Macbeth & [The] 2 Thomsons 720.
[Kemble as Macbeth,
Miss Kemble as Lady
Macbeth. USG]

Miss T. 18 Masaniello & [The] Scape-   90.
Kerr's benefit   grace
[As Fenella in *Masaniello*
and Tucker in *The Scape-
grace*. USG]

"   W. 19 [The] Wonder & ['Tis] All a 800.
farce

[534]

[Kemble as Don Felix, Miss
Kemble as Donna Viol-
ante in *The Wonder*.
USG]

	T. 20 [The] Hypocrite & [The] 40	200.
Ticket Night	thieves	
	[See preface to this season.]	

" F. 21 [The] Hunchback & [The] 620.
Spectre B[ride]groom
[Kemble as Sir Thomas
Clifford, Miss Kemble as
Julia in *The Hunchback*.
USG]

" S. 22 [The] Stranger & [The] Col- 510. 2960.
[onel']s Come
[Kemble as the Stranger,
Miss Kemble as Mrs.
Haller. USG]

M. 24 [The] Merchant of Venice & 950.
Miss Kemble's [The] A[greeable] Sur-
ben[efi]t prize
[As Portia. USG]

Kembles T. 25 Macbeth & Highways & By- 900.
[ways]
[Kemble as Macbeth, Miss
Kemble as Lady Mac-
beth. USG]

" W. 26 [The] S[chool] for Scandal & 780.
C[atherine] & Petruchio

T. 27 Much ado ab[out] Nothing 850
Kemble's benefit & C[atherine] & Petruchio
[As Benedick and Petru-
chio. USG]

[535]

F. 28 [The] Hunchback & Cath-   880.
Maywood's ben[efi]t   [erine] & Petruchio
                         [See preface to this season.]

Kembles   S. 29 [The] Wonder & Highways &   550.   4910.
                     byways
                     [Kemble as Don Felix, Miss
                     Kemble as Donna Viol-
                     ante in *The Wonder.*
                     USG]

               M. 31 [The] Rent day, Rose d'   310.
Mrs. Rowbotham's   Amour & 1st. act [of]
ben[efi]t   Tom & Jerry
                     [Sue in *Tom and Jerry.*
                     USG]

1833. Jan[uar]y
J. R. Scott   T. 1 T[own] & Country, Buskin's   340.
   Pratt's ben[efi]t   Frolic & R[ose] d'Amour
                        [Scott as Reuben Glenroy
                        in *Town and Country.*
                        USG   See preface to this
                        season.]

ben[efi]t [of]   W. 2 Sweethearts & Wives, 2[nd.]   980.
   Roberts   & 5[th] Acts [of] Alexander
                      [the Great & The] Hypo-
                      crite
                      [As Billy Lackaday in
                      Sweethearts and Wives,
                      Alexander and as Maw-
                      worm in *The Hypocrite.*
                      USG]

                                         $44586.

99 Nights average $451.
After Stars & C[eter]a (17395) $273.

[PHILADELPHIA SEASON, COMMENCING JANUARY 5, ENDING MAY 11, 1833]
[January]

[Maywood & Co.]

PREFACE—**January 9**: USG announces Gabriel Ravel as the Chevalier Lourdant in *La Fête Champêtre*. *Durang*, III, Chapter Twenty-Eighth, states that Jean Ravel played Old Man; Antoine Ravel, Colin; and Mlle. Émilie Ravel, Babet. **January 10**: USG announces *The Invisible Harlequin* with Gabriel Ravel as Harlequin and *The Conscript and the Soldier* by the Infant Ravels. **January 12**: In this entry Wood has written ditto marks referring to the notation "Ravels" in the entry of January 10. USG announces the Ravel Family in a performance on the Cord in two parts. "After which Herculean Feats by M. Jean Ravel, preceded by Academical Positions, copied from the first Models of Rome. To be followed by the Grand Wrestling Gladiatorial Scene by the young Gabriel and Antoine Ravel. Concluded with *Mons. Molinet.*" **January 15**: To the left of the date Wood has also written the notation "Ravels." USG announces the family in Godensky and, in the course of the evening, a "grand ascension from stage to gallery" by Gabriel Ravel. **January 17**: In this entry Wood has written ditto marks referring to the notation "Ravels" crowded out of his entry of January 15. In the next entry he has written ditto marks referring to the notation "Burke" in the entry of January 14. USG announces the Ravel Family in *The Death of Abel* for January 17, also an "Imitation of the Carnival of Venice" and "Three Chinese," a pas de trois on three cords. **January 19**: USG announces a "pantomimic ballet entitled *Godensky*. After which the highly interesting interlude called *The Conscript and the Soldier* (by the infant Ravels) To conclude with 1st. time in this city, a Grand Mythological Pantomime called *Vulcan and Cyclops.*" ADA announces Jean Ravel as Grivotish, an innkeeper, and Madame Ravel as Betsy in Godensky; and a "Grand Ascension on 2 Cords by Grabriel & Madame Ravel amidst Brilliant Fire Works!" **January 22**: USG announces the Ravels in *Monsieur Molinet* and *The Death of Abel*. **January 24**: USG announces the "last night" of the Ravel Family, who are to appear in *Jocko*, "Academical Positions," the "Grand Wrestling Gladiatorial Scene." "The Conscript and the Soldier" and "The Tableau of the Robbers." USG also announces *The Spoiled Child*. **March 8**: USG announces *Luke the Labourer, The Forty Thieves* and *Der Freischutz*. It has been advisable to delete "&," which occurs after

[537]

Wood's title. **March 27**: USG announces *The Sailor's Return* in place of *The Purse* with Walton as Will Steady. **April 2**: In this entry Wood has also written the notation "Francia." USG announces, "Monsieur Oliver Francia will appear and go through his astonishing performances." *Durang*, III, Chapter Twenty-Eighth, identifies him as a "performer in posturing, attitudes, and pantomimical mysteries, and academical exercises on a column." He was, according to *Durang*, "from the Port St. Martin's Theatre, Paris." **April 22**: In this entry Wood has written, "Sin[clair,] Reyn[oldso]n, Miss Hughes" and "Ch[an]g[e]d, Sinclair Sick, to [. . .]" USG announces Sinclair as Fra Diavolo, Reynoldson as Lord Goslington and Miss Hughes as Zerlina. **April 23**: In this entry Wood has written the notation "Hill" to the right of "Wilkinson." **April 26**: USG announces the second and third acts of *The Barber of Seville*. **April 27**: USG announces the second act of *Jonathan in England*, the first and second acts of *The Green Mountain Boy*, the first and second acts of *The Inquisitive Yankee* the first act of *The Forest Rose*, and *Family Jars*. **May 1**: In this entry Wood has written four pairs of ditto marks referring to "Sin[clair,] Reyn[oldson,] Miss Hughes," in the entry of April 29, and "Wilkinson" in the entry of April 30. USG also announces the second and third acts of *The Barber of Seville* and *Paul Pry*, "compressed in two acts." According to USG Reynoldson was to appear as Figaro in *The Barber of Seville* and Robin in *No Song No Supper*, Miss Hughes as Rosina in *The Barber of Seville* and Margaretta in *No Song No Supper*; and Wilkinson was to appear as Paul Pry.

It has been advisable to omit from the printed text a few financial notations; and, in the entry of February 21, to substitute "Madame Feron & Mr. Walton" for ditto marks referring to the names of those players in the entry of February 19. It has also been advisable to omit the notation "Sleighing," which Wood has written vertically, to the left of the entry of February 28; the notation, "Mrs. Cooper died at New York" in Wood's entry of March 19 and to substitute "Hamblin, Booth, Miss Vincent" in the entry of April 11 for three pairs of ditto marks referring to the names of those players in the entry of April 8. It has also been advisable to omit the notation, "Mrs. Gilfert died" which Wood has written to the right of his entry of April 19; the notation, "played Rover for Mr. Wemyss' ben[efit, at the Arch,]" which Wood has written to the left of the entry of April 22; and the notation "Mr. Roberts died at Charleston," which Wood has written to the left of his entry of April 26. See *Durang*, III, Chapter Twenty-Eighth, for an obituary of Mrs. Gilfert, ADA of April 22, 1833 for the announcement of Wood as Rover at the Arch Street Theatre and the comment on the entry of May 17, in the preface to the season beginning May 13 and ending June 28, 1833, for details regarding the benefit given the Roberts children.

[Walnut Street Theatre]

	S[aturday] 5 [The] Wanderer & Masaniello	270.	
Ravels	M. 7 Sweethearts & Wives, [The] death of Abel* & [Monsieur] Molinet [Gabriel Ravel as Monsieur Molinet. USG]	240.	
	T. 8 [The] Spy & St. Patrick's day	270.	
"	W. 9 [The] Good Natured Man & Ravels [See preface to this season.]	230.	
"	T. 10 [A] Cure for [the] Heartache & Ravels [See preface to this season.]	220.	
Master Burke	F. 11 S[peed] the plough & [The] Irish Tutor [As Sir Abel Handy in *Speed the Plough* and Terry O'Rourke in *The Irish Tutor*. USG]	320.	
	S. 12 [The] Robbers & Ravels [See preface to this season.]	370.	1920.
Burke	M. 14 John Bull & Whirl[igig] Hall [As Dennis Brulgruddery in *John Bull* and as six characters in *Whirligig Hall*. USG]	330.	

[539]

	T. 15 C[herry] & f[air] Star, Ravels 340. [& The] S[pectre] Bride- groom [See preface to this season.]	
"	W. 16 Douglas & L[ove] a la mode 170. [Master Burke as Young Norval in *Douglas* and Murtoch Delany in *The Irishman in London.* USG]	
	T. 17 Simpson & Co., Ravels [& 270. The] D[ay] after [the] Wedding [See preface to this season.]	
"	F. 18 Man & Wife & [The] March 250. of intellect [As Cornelius O'Dedimus in *Man and Wife* and as characters in *The March of Intellect.* USG]	
Benefit [of] Ravels	S. 19 [The] Peasant Boy, Vulcan & 805. Venus* & c[eter]a [See preface to this season.]	2165.
Burke	M. 21 [The] Poor Gentleman & 240. B[arney] Brallaghan [As Ollapod in *The Poor Gentleman* and Barney Brallaghan. USG]	
Ravels	T. 22 C[herry] & fair Star & Ravels 290. [See preface to this season.]	
Burke's benefit	W. 23 2[nd.] & 3[r]d. Acts [of The] 440. Hypocrite, Love a la	

mode [&] B[arney] Bral-
lagh[an]
[As Mawworm in *The Hypo-
crite*, Sir Callaghan in
Love a la Mode and as
Barney. USG]

Ravels   T. 24 Jocko [the Brazilian Ape,]   320.
Ravels, L[overs'] Quar-
rels & C[eter]a
[See preface to this season.]

Kembles   F. 25 Macbeth & [The] Scapegrace   320.
[Kemble as Macbeth, Miss
Kemble as Lady Mac-
beth. USG]

"   S. 26 [The] Stranger & How to die   540.   2150.
for love
[Kemble as the Stranger,
Miss Kemble as Mrs.
Haller. USG]

Kembles   M. 28 [The] Hunchback & [The]   740.
Jenkins
[Kemble as Sir Thomas
Clifford, Miss Kemble as
Julia in *The Hunchback*.
USG

"   T. 29 [The] Inconstant & [The]   480.
Riever's Ransom
[Kemble as Young Mirabel,
Miss Kemble as Bizarre
in *The Inconstant*. USG]

"   W. 30 Fazio & [The] Promissory   620.
Note
[Kemble as Giraldi, Miss
Kemble as Bianca in
Fazio. USG]

[541]

T. 31 [The] Hunchback & [The]   380.
       Hunter of [the] Alps
       [Kemble as Sir Thomas
       Clifford, Miss Kemble as
       Julia. USG]

February

"   F. 1 Much ado [about Nothing] &   520.
       Masaniello
       [Kemble as Benedick, Miss
       Kemble   as   Beatrice.
       USG]

"
Miss Kemble's   S. 2 [The] Gamester & [The] Jew   900.   3640.
benefit   & [the] D[octo]r
       [Kemble as Beverly, Miss
       Kemble as Mrs. Beverly.
       USG]

M. 4 [The] Merchant of Venice &   980.
Kemble's ben[efi]t   [Catherine & Petruchio]
       [Kemble as Shylock and
       Petruchio, Miss Kemble
       as Portia and Catherine.
       USG]

T. 5 [The] Robbers & Masaniello   75.

Finn   W. 6 Paul Pry & [The] Master's   120.
       Rival
       [As Paul Pry and as Paul
       Shack in *The Master's
       Rival* USG]

"   T. 7 [The] Hypocrite & [The] May 140.
       Queen
       [Finn as Mawworm in *The
       Hypocrite* and Caleb Pip-
       kin in *The May Queen*.
       USG]

"   F.   8 102, Snakes in [the] Grass &   120.
[The] 2 Gregories
[Finn as Philip Garbois in
102, Janus in *Snakes in
the Grass* and Gregory in
The Two Gregories. USG]

"   S.   9 Richard 3d. & [The] 100 £   120.   1555.
Note
[Finn as Richard and as
Billy Black in *The £
100 Note.* USG]

Finn   M. 11 [The] Clan[destine] Marriage   118.
& W[illia]m Thomson
[As Lord Ogleby in *The
Clandestine Marriage* and
as W[illia]m Thompson,
2nd. USG]

"   T. 12 Sweethearts & Wives & 1st.   125.
& 2[nd.] Act [of] Tom &
Jerry
[Finn as Billy Lackaday in
Sweethearts and Wives and
Bob Logic in *Tom and
Jerry.* USG]

"   Benefit   W. 13 Montgomery & [The] Mast-   102.
er's Rival
[Finn as Serjeant Welcome
Sobersides in *Montgom-
ery* and Paul Shack in
The Master's Rival. USG]

T. 14 [The] Goodnatured Man &   60.
C[herry] & F[air] Star

[543]

Finn's 2d.   F. 15 [She] Stoops to Conquer &   90.
Ben[efi]t   [The] £ 100 Note
                    [As Tony Lumpkin in *She
                    Stoops to Conquer* and
                    Billy Black in *The £ 100
                    Note*. USG]
                              a Snow Storm

              S. 16 [The] Wanderer & Napoleon 130.   625.

              M. 18 [The] Hut of [the] Red Moun- 155.
                    tain & Turn Out

              T. 19 [The] Barber of Seville & of 210.
Mad[ame] Feron &   Age tomorrow
  Mr. Walton   [Madame Feron as Rosina
                    in *The Barber of Seville*
                    and Maria in *Of Age
                    Tomorrow*. Walton as
                    Figaro in *The Barber of
                    Seville* and Baron Welling-
                    hoerst in *Of Age Tomor-
                    row*. USG]

Dr. Rice   W. 20 [The] Hut of [the] Red Moun- 270.
                    t[ai]n, Jim Crow & [The]
                    S[pectre] Bridegr[oom]
                    [As Jim Crow. USG]

              T. 21 Der Freyschutz & John of 180.
[Madame Feron &   Paris
  Mr. Walton]   [Madame Feron as Linda
                    in *Der Freischutz* and
                    Princess of Navarre in
                    John of Paris. Walton
                    as Adolphe in *Der Frei-
                    schutz*. USG]

Hill   F. 22 Jon[athan] in England, Jim   460.
                             Crow & Napoleon
                             [As Solomon Swap in *Jona-*
                             than in England. USG]

                         S. 23 Rob Roy [Macgregor], Jim   240.   1515.
                             Crow & [The] Young
                             Hussar

Hill Rice   M. 25 [The] Green Mountain Boy,*   220.
                             Jim Crow [& The] Prom-
                             [issory] Note
                             [Hill as Jedediah Home-
                             spun in *The Green Moun-*
                             tain Boy. Rice as Jim
                             Crow. USG]

                         T. 26 Cinderella & L[overs'] Quar-   210.
[Madame] Feron   rels
   & Walton   [Madame Feron as Cin-
                             derella, Walton as Felix.
                             USG]

                         W. 27 [The] Hut of [the] Red Moun-   440.
Rice's benefit Hill   tain, J[im] Crow, [The]
                             L[ottery] Ticket [&]
                             Y[ankee] Story
                             [Rice as Jim Crow and as
                             Wormwood in *The Lot-*
                             tery Ticket. Hill to
                             deliver a popular story
                             called *Zephaniah at the*
                             Tea Party; or, The Yankee
                             in Trouble. USG]

                         T. 28 Cinderella & St. Patrick's day   110.

March

Hill's Ben[efi]t	F. 1	[The] G[reen] Mountain Boy [&] 4[th &] 5[th] Acts [of] Jon[athan] in Engla[nd] [As Jedediah Homespun and as Solomon Swap in *Jonathan in England.* USG]	260.	
Mad[ame] Feron's ben[efi]t	S. 2	1[st]Act of Cinderella, 2[nd.] of Masaniello [&] 3[r]d. [of] D[er] Frey-schutz [As Elvira in *Cinderella* and Linda in *Der Freischutz.* ADA]	90.	1339.
Roberts' 2d. Ben[efit]	M. 4	Education & Cram[on]d Brig [As Suckling in *Education.* USG]	240.	
	T. 5	Henri Quatre & Turn Out	80.	
	W. 6	[The] Hut of [the] Red Mountain & [The] I[rishman] in London	70.	
Hamblin Miss Vincent	T. 7	Romeo & Juliet & How to die for love [Hamblin as Romeo, Miss Vincent as Juliet. USG]	220.	
	F. 8	[The] Hut of [the] Red Mountain [See preface to this season.]	80.	
" "	S. 9	[The] Hunchback & [The] Purse [Hamblin as Sir Thomas	304.	994.

Clifford, Miss Vincent as
Julia in *The Hunchback.*
USG]

Hamblin &   M. 11 Jane Shore & [The] Hunter of 220.
Miss V[incent]   the Alps
                    [Hamblin as Lord Hast-
                    ings, Miss Vincent as
                    Jane Shore. USG]

            T. 12 [The] Hut of [the] Red Moun- 120.
                  tain & [The] M[erry]
                  Mourners

    "   W. 13 [The] Hunchback & Nature & 260.
Miss V[incent']s   Philosophy
benefit   [Hamblin as Sir Thomas
                    Clifford, Miss Vincent as
                    Julia in *The Hunchback*
                    and as Collin in *Phil-
                    osophy.* USG]

            T. 14 Henri Quatre & [Luke the 100.
                  Labourer]

Kembles   F. 15 Fazio & [The] Purse   820.
                  [Kemble as Giraldi, Miss
                  Kemble as Bianca in
                  Fazio. USG]

    "   S. 16 Much ado [about Nothing] 660.   2180.
                  & [The] Purse
                  [Kemble as Benedick, Miss
                  Kemble as Beatrice.
                  USG]

            M. 18 Venice Preserv'd & Turn Out 780.
Kembles Hamblin   [Kemble as Pierre, Miss
                    Kemble as Belvidera,
                    Hamblin as Jaffier in
                    Venice Preserved. USG]

[547]

" T. 19 [The] Wonder & [The] Day 550.
after [the] Wedding
[Kemble as Don Felix, Miss
Kemble as Donna Viol-
ante in *The Wonder.*
USG]

W. 20 Luke the Lab[u]orer & 65.
C[herry] & fair Star

" T. 21 [The] M[erchant] of Venice & 800.
Mr. K[emble']s Charles the 2d.
benefit [Kemble as Shylock and
Charles, Miss Kemble as
Portia and Mary Copp in
Charles the Second. USG]

F. 22 [The] Stranger & Charles 2d. 920.
Miss F[anny] [Miss Kemble as Mrs. Hal-
Kemble's ben[efi]t ler in *The Stranger* and as
Mary Copp. USG]

S. 23 Pizarro & Clari 140. 3255.
Hamblin [Hamblin as Rolla in *Piz-*
Miss Vincent *arro*, Miss Vincent as
Clari. USG]

Hamblin M. 25 Virginius & Perfection 75.
Miss V[incent] [Hamblin as Virginius, Miss
Vincent as Virginia and
as Kate O'Brian in *Per-*
fection. USG]

T. 26 The S[chool] for Prejudice & 210.
Mr. Wilkinson Amateurs & Actors
[Wilkinson as Ephraim in
The School for Prejudice
and Geoffrey Muffincap
in *Amateurs and Actors.*
USG]

[548]

Walton's ben[efi]t

W. 27 S[weethearts] & Wives, [The] 130.
Purse & Fire & Water
[As Sandford in *Sweethearts and Wives*. USG See preface to this season.]

Booth

T. 28 Richard 3d. & [The] I[rish- 208.
man] in London
[As Richard. USG]

F. 29 [The] Gambler's fate & Deaf 90.
as a post

"

Hamblin
[Miss] Vincent

S. 30 [The] Apostate & Freaks & 331. 1044.
follies
[Hamblin as Hemeya, Booth as Pescara, Miss Vincent as Florinda in *The Apostate*. USG]

April

[Ham]blin Booth
[Miss] Vincent
Wilkinson

M. 1 Othello & Freaks & follies 267.
[Hamblin as Othello, Booth as Iago, Miss Vincent as Desdemona. Wilkinson as Tom Trippet in *Freaks and Follies*. USG]

"

T. 2 Simpson & Co., Freaks & 75.
follies & Family Jars
[Wilkinson as Tom Trippet in *Freaks and Follies* and Delph in *Family Jars*. USG See preface to this season.]

"

W. 3 The Jenkins, Victorine & 65.
[The] Spoil'd Child
[Wilkinson as Mr. Bonassus in *Victorine*. USG]

[549]

T. 4 Hamlet & Deaf as a post   240.
Hamb[lin]   [Hamblin as the ghost,
    Booth as Hamlet, Miss
Booth   Vincent as Ophelia.
[Miss] Vinc[ent]   Wilkinson as Tristram
Wilkinson   Sappy in *Deaf as a Post.*
    USG]

F. 5 [The] Peasant Boy & Rhyme   96.
"   & Reason*
    [Wilkinson as Mr. Pindarus
    pump in *Rhyme and
    Reason.* USG]

" " " S. 6 K[ing] Lear & Rhyme &   260.   1003.
"   Reason
    [Hamblin as Edgar, Booth
    as Lear, Miss Vincent as
    Cordelia. Wilkinson as
    Mr. Pindarus Pump in
    Rhyme and Reason. USG]

M. 8 Julius Caesar & Nat[ure] &   480.
Hamblin's Ben[efi]t   Philosophy
Booth [Miss]   [Hamblin as Brutus, Booth
Vincent   as Cassius, Miss Vincent
    as Collin in *Philosophy.*
    USG]

T. 9 [The] S[chool] for Prejudice &   109.
    Freaks & follies

W. 10 [The] Wheel of Fortune &   232.50
Wood's Ben[efi]t   Rose d'Amour
    [As Penruddock in *The
    Wheel of Fortune.* USG]

T. 11 Jane Shore & Rhyme &   210.
[Hamblin Booth   Reason
Miss Vincent]   [Hamblin as Dumont,

Booth as the Duke of
Gloster, Miss Vincent as
Jane Shore. USG]

F. 12 [The] Spec[tre] Bridegroom &   90.
Victorine

S. 13 [The] Apostate & Cath[erine]   310.   1431.
Miss Vincent's   & Petruchio
Ben[efi]t   [As Florinda in *The Apos-
                      tate*. USG]

Miss Hughes M. 15 Cinderella & [The] P[romis- 340.
Sinclair   sory] Note
Reynoldson   [Miss Hughes as Cinderella,
                    Sinclair as Felix, Rey-
                    noldson as Dandini in
                    Cinderella. USG]

T. 16 S[weethearts] & Wives & Rose   65.
d'Amour

W. 17 No! Masaniello & No Song 275.
No Supper

Hill   T. 18 [The] Green M[ountain] Boy 210.
                   & [A] Roland for [an]
                   Oliver
                   [As Jedediah Homespun in
                   The Green Mountain Boy.
                   USG]

F. 19 Fra Diavolo* & [The] Jenkins 350.

S. 20 Jon[athan] in England &   230.   1470.
Rhyme & Reason

Mon. 22 Fra Diavolo & F[ire] & Water 210.
[See preface to this season.]

[551]

Wilkinson   T. 23 L[overs'] Quarrels, [The] In-   95.
                       quisitive   Yankee,   [A]
                       R[oland] for an Oliver
                       [As Sir Mark in *A Roland
                       for an Oliver*. USG See
                       preface to this season.]

    "   W. 24 St.   Patrick's   day,   [The]   90.
                       G[reen] Moun[tain] Boy
                       & Freaks & follies
                       [Wilkinson as Tom Trippet
                       in *Freaks and Follies*.
                       USG]

    "   T. 25 F[ire] & Water, A[uld] Robin   180.
                       Gray* & [The] Prisoner
                       at large
                       [Wilkinson as Paul Bowbell
                       in *Auld Robin Gray* and
                       Muns in *The Prisoner at
                       Large*. USG]

                   F. 26 2 Acts [of The] Barber of   240.
                       Seville, A[uld] R[obin]
                       Gray & [the] 1st. Act [of]
                       Masaniello.
                       [See preface to this season.]

                   S. 27 Acts of Jon[athan] in Eng-   320.
                       [land, The] G[reen]
                       M[ountain] Boy, [The]
                       Inq[uisitive] Yankee [&]
                       F[amily] Jars
                       [See preface to this season.]

Sin[clair]   M. 29 Fra Diavolo [& The] I[rish-   340.
  Reyn[oldso]n   man] in London
  Miss Hughes   [Sinclair as Fra Diavolo,
                       Reynoldson as Lord Gos-

[552]

lington, Miss Hughes as
Zerlina in *Fra Diavolo*.
USG]

Wilkinson	T. 30	2[nd.], 3[rd.] & 5[th] Acts [of The] Hypocrite & Auld Robin Gray [As Mawworm in *The Hypo crite* and as Paul Bowbell. USG]	65.

May

[Sinclair Reynoldson Miss Hughes Wilkinson]	W. 1	2 Acts [of The] B[arber] of Seville, 2 Acts [of] Paul Pry & N[o] Song No Supper [See preface to this season.]	144.

"	T 2	Victorine & [The] P[risoner] at Large [Wilkinson as Mr. Bonassus in *Victorine* and Muns in *The Prisoner at Large*. USG]	80.

"	F. 3	Speed the plough & Rhyme & Reason [Wilkinson as Mr. Pindarus Pump in *Rhyme and Reason*. USG]	80.

Wilkinson's Ben[efi]t	S. 4	[The] Golden Calf & York & Lancaster* [As Rags in *The Golden Calf* and Master Timothy in *York and Lancaster*. USG]	240.	949.

Mrs. F. A. Drake	M. 6	Fazio, [& The] D[ay] after [the] Wedding [As Bianca in *Fazio*. USG]	140.

[553]

Barton   T. 7 W[illia]m Tell & [The] Prom-   60.
              iss[or]y Note
              [As William Tell. USG]

"   W. 8 [The] Hunchback & [The]   90.
Mr. Hadaway's   Review [Mrs. Drake as
1st. appearance   Julia in *The Hunchback*,
              Hadaway as Caleb Quo-
              tem in *The Review*. USG]

Rice   T. 9 [The] Mountaineers & Jim 210.
              Crow
              [As Jim Crow. USG]

          F. 10 [The] Soldier's Daughter & 140.
              [The] Turnpike Gate

"   S. 11 [The] Golden Calf, J[im] 220.   860.
              Crow & [The] Lottery   ———
              ticket $29207.
              Rice as Jim Crow and as
              Wormwood in *The Lottery
              Ticket*. ADA]

108 Nights av[erage]d 270.

[PHILADELPHIA SEASON, COMMENCING MAY 13, ENDING
JUNE 28, 1833.]

[Maywood & Co.]

PREFACE—**May 17**: Wood has written, to the left of this entry the nota-
tion, "Ben[efi]t [of the] Roberts Children. J. [R.] Scott, Mr. & Mrs.
Jones, Thayer, Sinclair." According to *Durang*, III, Chapter Twenty-
Ninth, "A benefit was . . . announced . . . for the orphan family of Mr.
James Roberts, who died two or three weeks before of consumption; Mrs.
Roberts (his wife) having died only some few months previously to his
decease of the same disease. Mr. Roberts was quite unable, during the

[554]

whole of this season, to appear before the public, save at rare intervals. His physician advised him to try a southern climate during the rigors of our winter . . . Sinclair, J. R. Scott, Jones, Hadaway, Murdoch, Thayer, Howard, &c. volunteered. . . . In the course of the evening Mr. Sinclair sang his favorite song of *Joe Anderson My Joe*. Thayer recited *Bucks, Have at Ye all*." ADA announces J. R. Scott as Philip, with Mrs. Thayer as Jenny in *Luke the Labourer* and Jones as Sir Willoughly, with Mrs. Jones as Lady Worrett, in *Man and Wife*. **May 21:** In this entry Hughes has written a pair of ditto marks under "Sinclair," another under "Hughes" and another under "Reynoldson" of the previous entry. It has been necessary to omit the first two and to substitute "Reynoldson" for the last. USG announces Sinclair as Fra Diavolo and Miss Hughes as Zerlina. **May 29:** USG announces the second and third acts of *The Barber of Seville, Fish Out of Water* and the second act of *Der Freischutz*. Mrs. Austin is to appear as Rosina in *The Barber of Seville* and Linda in *Der Freischutz*, Reynoldson as Figaro in the former and Casper in the latter. **June 3:** In this entry Wood has also written "Scott, Howard, Rice." According to USG, Scott is to appear as William and Howard as Blue Peter in *Black-Eyed Susan*; Rice as Jim Crow. **June 8:** Pratt was a member of the firm of Maywood & Co. **June 10:** To the left of the notation, "Cooper's Benefit," Wood has written "Kembles, Scott." According to USG, Kemble is to appear as Jaffier, Miss Kemble as Belvidera in *Venice Preserved*. J. R. Scott is to appear as William in *Black-Eyed Susan*. **June 11:** *Durang*, III, Chapter Twenty-Ninth, and Fanny Kemble's *Journal*, II, p. 157, tell of this celebrated Indian Chief, who, according to *Durang*, had "arrived in Philadelphia, with his suite under charge of Major Garland, of the United States Army, and [taken] up quarters at the Congress Hall, in Third street." **June 17:** According to USG, Mrs. Rowbotham is to play Winny Jenkins in *Humphrey Clinker*. **June 19:** Dinsmore was the treasurer of the company.

To the left of the entries of May 14 and 15 and obliquely across the page Wood has written the notation, "15 May Edmund Kean died at Richmond, England." It has been advisable, of course, to omit this notation from the printed text. It has been necessary to substitute "Scott" in the entry of June 6 for ditto marks referring to the name of that player in the entry of June 5; and to omit "35 Nights averaged [$]355; after Stars & c[etera], 230," which Wood has written to the left instead of at the end of the final entry of this season.

[Chesnut Street Theatre]

[555]

May

M[onday] 13 [The] S[chool] for Scandal, 330.
Mr. Barton T[urn] Out & Jim Crow
Mrs. Drake Rice [Barton as Charles Surface,
Mrs. Drake as Lady
Teazle in *The School for
Scandal*. Rice as Jim
Crow. USG]

"   T. 14 Macbeth & Raising the Wind 140.
Ben[efi]t   [As Macbeth and as Jeremy
Diddler in *Raising the
Wind*. USG]

" W. 15 Isabella & Fish out of Water 160.
Benefit   [Barton as Biron, Mrs.
Drake as Isabella. USG]

T. 16 [The] Rent day & [The] 100.
Review

F. 17 Man & Wife, Olio & Luke the 816.
Labou[rer]
[See preface to this season.]

S. 18 Fra Diavolo & How to die for 240.   1786.
Love

M. 20 Fra Diavolo & Fish out of 310.
Sinclair   Water
Hughes & Reynoldson [Sinclair as Fra Diavolo,
Miss Hughes as Zerlina,
Reynoldson as Lord Gos-
lington in *Fra Diavolo*.
USG]

Ben[efi]t [of   T. 21 Fra Diavolo & [The] Pris[oner] 260.
Reynoldson]   at Large
[As Lord Goslington. USG
See preface to this
season.]

[556]

W. 22 Cinderella & Fortune's frolic   310.
[Mrs.] Austin   [Mrs. Austin as Cinderella,
  Sinclair   Sinclair as Felix, Rey-
  Reyno[ldso]n   noldson as Dandini. USG]

T. 23 Fra Diavolo & [The] Mid-   240.
Sinclair's ben[efi]t   [night] Hour
                          [As Fra Diavolo. USG]

[Mrs. Austin] F. 24 Der Freyschutz & W[illia]m   265.
                          Thomson
                          [As Linda in *der Freischutz*.
                          USG]

Miss Hughes' S. 25 Fra Diavolo & [The] Rendez-   310.   1695.
  ben[efi]t   vous
                          [As Zerlina in *Frau Diavolo*.
                          USG]

M. 27 [The] Tempest & [The]   330.
[Mrs.] Austin   Hunter of the Alps
  Reyn[oldson]   [Mrs. Austin as Ariel, Rey-
                            noldson as Caliban. USG]

J. R. Scott   T. 28 Napoleon & Deaf as a post   305.
                          [As Napoleon. USG]

[Mrs.] Austin W. 29 2 Acts [of The] B[arber] of   190.
  & Rey[noldson]   Seville, Fish out of
                          Water & 2 Acts [of Der]
                          Freyschutz
                          [See preface to this season.]

Scott   T. 30 Napoleon & [The] T[urnpike   280.
                          Gate
                          [As Napoleon. USG]

Reyn[oldson]   F. 31 [The] Tempest & Music & Prej- 320.
Mrs. Austin's   udice [Reynoldson as Count
Ben[efi]t.   Cremona, Mrs. Austin as
                Alfred in *Music* and *Prej-*
                udice and as Ariel. USG]
         June
J. R. Scott   S. 1 Damon & Pythias & [The] 190.   1615.
              Bold Dragons
              [As Damon. USG]

         M. 3 [The] Man of the World & 675.
Mr. Mayw[oo]d's   B[lack] Ey'd Susan
Benefit   [As Sir Pertinax Mac Syco-
              phant in *The Man of the*
              World. ADA See pref-
              ace to this season.]

[Rice]   T. 4 [The] Golden Calf, Rice & 175.
              [The] 2 Thomsons
              [As Jim Crow. USG]

Scott   W. 5 [The] Rent day, Rice & [The 250.
              Adopted Child
              [As Martin Heywood in *The*
              Rent Day and Michael in
              The Adopted Child. USG]

Miss Riddle   T. 6 [The] Mutiny at the Nore & 285.
[Scott] Murdock's   Therese
Ben[efi]t   [Miss Riddle as Mariette,
              Scott as Carwin in
              Therese and as Jack
              Adams, with Murdock as
              Richard Parker, in *The*
              Mutiny at the Nore. USG]

         F. 7 Town & Country & [The] 245.
Scott's Ben[efi]t   Chil[dren] in the Wood
              [As Reuben Glenroy in

Town and Country and
Walter in *The Children in
the Wood*. USG]

| | S. | 8 | Napoleon & [The] 100 £ Note | 520. | 1850 |

Pratt's ben[efi]t   [Rice as Jim Crow and Billy
Rice.   Black. USG See pref-
ace to this season.]

M. 10 Venice Preserv'd & Bl[ac]k 1665.
Cooper's Benefit   Ey'd Susan
[As Pierre in *Venice Preserved*. USG See pref-
ace to this season.]

Black Hawk T. 11 [The] Flying Dutchman & 510.
& C[eter]a   [The] 100 £ Note
[See preface to this season.]

Kembles W. 12 [The] Stranger & [The] Bold 600.
Dragoons
[Kemble as the Stranger,
Miss Kemble as Mrs.
Haller. USG]

Black Hawk T. 13 Sweethearts & Wives & [The] 190.
& C[eter]a   40 Thieves

Kembles F. 14 [The] Gamester & [The] 470.
A[greeable] Surprize
[Kemble as Beverly, Miss
Kemble as Mrs. Beverly
in *The Gamester*. USG]

S. 15 She W[oul]d be a Soldier & 190. 3525.
Rice's benefit   [The] L[ottery] Ticket
[Rice as Wormwood in *The
Lottery Ticket* and as Jim
Crow. USG]

[559]

M. 17 Richard 3d., J[im] Crow & 220.
Rowbotham's   Hum[phrey] Clinker*
ben[efi]t Rice   [See preface to this season.]

T. 18 [The] Flying Dutchman & 120.
[The] Review

W. 19 [The] Man of the World & 330.
Thayer Dinsmore's   H[igh] life below Stairs
ben[efi]t.   [Mrs. Thayer as Lady Mac-
                     Sycophant in *The Man of
                     the World* and Miss Kitty,
                     with Thayer as Lord
                     Duke, in *High Life below
                     Stairs*. USG See pref-
                     ace to this season.]

T. 20 Fire & Water, [The] Bohemian 130.
Mother & Fish out of
Water

F. 21 [The] Poor Gentleman & [The] 120.
2 Thomsons

S. 22 [The] Bohemian Mother & 135.   1055.
[The] F[lying] Dutchman

M. 24 [The] Rent Day & Humphrey 85.
Clinker

T. 25 [A] Cure for [the] Heartache & 170.
[The] Turnpike Gate

W. 26 [The] Red Rover & [The] 310.
Rendezvous

T. 27 [The] Red Rover & [The] 200.
Spect[re] Bridegroom

[560]

F. 28 [The] Red Rover & [The]   90.   855.
Review
35 Nights averaged 355 after
Stars & [Cetera.]   ———

                                              $41788.

[PHILADELPHIA SEASON, COMMENCING JUNE 29, ENDING
JULY 27, 1833.]

[Maywood & Co.]

PREFACE—**July 22**: In this entry Wood has also written "Scott, Ingersoll & Murdoch." According to USG, Scott is to play Philip in *Luke
The Labourer* and Ingersoll, Luke. Murdoch is to recite, "by popular
request," *The Sailor Boy's Dream*. Mrs. Rowbotham is to appear as
Aladdin. In the entries of July 25 and 27 Wood has written ditto marks
referring to "Ing[ersol]l" in the entry of July 24. It has been necessary,
in the printed version, to substitute for these ditto marks the name of
the player.

[Walnut Street Theatre]

June
S[aturday] 29 [A] Cure for [the] Heartache &   125.
               [The] 40 Thieves
July
Monday   1 [The] H[eart] of Midlothian &   95.
              Fish out of Water

      T.   2 [The] Bohemian Mother &   40.
              Cherry & F[air] Star

      W. 3 [The] Golden Calf & [The]   130.
              A[greeable] Surprize

      T.   4 [The] Pilot & [The] B[old]   315.
              Dragoons

      F.   5 [The] Foundling of [the]   140.
              Forest & H[umphrey
              Clinker

[561]

S. 6 Woodstock & [The] 2 Thom-   150.   870.
sons

M. 8 [The] Soldier's Daughter &   130.
[The] Col[onel's] Come

T. 9 W[illia]m Tell & [The] Review   175.
Mr. [D] Ingersoll   [Ingersoll as William Tell,
Miss Alexina   Miss Fisher as Albert.
Fisher   USG]

W. 10 Victorine & [The] Barber of   130.
Hadaway's ben[efi]t.   Bagdad
                        [As Mr. Bonassus in *Vic-*
                        torine and Hacko in *The*
                        Barber of Bagdad. USG]

T. 11 Pizarro & [The] S[pectre]   110.
Bridegr[oom]

F. 12 Damon & Pythias & [The]   95.
Barber of Bagdad

S. 13 Inkle & Yarico & [The]   110.   750.
P[risoner] at Large

M. 15 Athello, J[im] Crow & L[overs']   125.
D. Ingersoll Rice   Quarrels
                        [Ingersoll as Othello, Rice
                        as Jim Crow. USG]

"   T. 16 John Bull, J[im] Crow &   170.
D[eaf] as a post
[Rice as Jim Crow. USG]

"   " W. 17 [The] Rendezvous, Comrades   130.
& Friends & [The] A[gree-
able] Surprize
[Ingersoll as Charles Val-

[562]

cour in *Comrades and Friends*, Rice as Jim Crow. USG]

" T. 18 F[ortune's] Frolic, I[nkle] & 109.
Yarico & [The] P[risoner] at Large
[Rice as Jim Crow. USG]

"   " F. 19 [The] Mountaineers, & [The] 125.
100 £ Note
[Ingersoll as Octavian in *The Mountaineers*, Rice as Billy Black in *The £ 100 Note*. USG]

"   S. 20 Comrades & Friends, [The 310.   969.
Rice's ben[efit]   Virgin[n]y Cupids & R[aising the] Wind
[Ingersoll as Charles Valcour in *Comrades and Friends*, Rice as Jeremy Diddler in *Raising the Wind* and as Gumba Cuffee in *The Virginny Cupids*. USG]

       M. 22 Luke the Labourer & Aladdin 320.
Mrs. Row[botham's]   [As Aladdin. USG See
ben[efi]t   preface to this season.]

       T. 23 Sweethearts & Wives & 140.
Aladdin

In[gersol]l   W. 24 [The] West Indian & Aladdin 80.
Faulkner's ben[efi]t   [Ingersoll as Charles Dudley, Faulkner as Major O'Flaherty in *The West Indian*. USG]

[563]

[Ingersoll]   T. 25 Ambrose Gwinett & Aladdin 240.
ben[efi]t [of]   [Ingersoll as Ambrose
Rasimi   Gwinett. Rasimi in
                   sailor's hornpipe. USG]

           F. 26 L[overs'] Quarrels, Aladdin 130.
              & [The] S[pectre] Bride-
              groom

[Ingersoll]   S. 27 Ambrose Gwinett & Aladdin 300.   1210.
           [As Ambrose Gwinett. USG]

25 Nights $3919.
159 p[e]r night.
After Stars & Ben[efits] $131.

PHILA[DELPHIA] SEASON[, COMMENCING AUGUST 31, ENDING
SEPTEMBER 21,] 1833.

[Maywood & Co.]

PREFACE—**September 10**: In this entry Wood has also written three pairs of ditto marks referring to "Jones," "Austin" and "Walton" in the entry of September 9. According to USG, Jones is to play Ferdinand John, and Adolphe in *Der Freischutz*; and Walton, Stephano, and Casper in *Der Freischutz*. USG announces the second and third acts of *The Tempest* and the second act of *Der Freischutz*. **September 12**: In this entry Wood has also written three pairs of ditto marks referring to "Jones," "Austin" and "Walton" in the entry of September 9. According to USG, Mrs. Austin is to play Zulima in *Abon Hassan*. *Durang* III, Chapter Thirty-Second, states that she also appeared as Alfred in *Music and Prejudice*. **September 13**: In this entry Wood has also written three pairs of ditto marks referring to "Jones," "Austin" and "Walton" in the entry of September 9. According to USG, Mrs. Austin is to play Polly Peachem in *The Beggar's Opera* and Prince Alphonso in *Masaniello*; and Walton, Mat of the Mint in the former and Pietro in the latter.

It has been necessary to substitute "Jones, Mrs. Austin, Walton" in the entries of September 3, 5 and 6 for three pairs of ditto marks referring to the names of those players in the entry of September 2. *Durang*, III, Chapter Thirty-Second, asserts that, on September 11, Rice also

appeared as Cuffee in *Oh! Hush! or, Gumbo Cuffee*. For a brief account
of Rice's performances, see Wemyss' *Life*, pp. 206–207.

[Walnut Street Theatre]

	August			
	Saty.	31	[The] Mountaineers & Alad-	190.
Mrs. Kent['s]			din	
1st. app[earance]			[As Agnes in *The Moun-* *taineers*. USG]	

	September			
Jones	M.	2	Cinderella & [The] Sp[oil']d	260.
[Mrs.] Austin			Child	
Walton			[Jones as Felix, Mrs. Austin as Cinderella, Walton as Dandini. USG]	

[Jones	T.	3	" & [The] S[pectre]	250.
Mrs. Austin			Bridegroom	
Walton]			[See note, September 2.]	

Rice	W.	4	[The] Foundling of [the] for- est & [The] Virginny Cupids [As Jim Crow. USG]	190.

[Jones	Th.	5	[The] Tempest & [The] Sp[oil']d Child [Jones as Ferdinand, Mrs. Austin as Ariel, Walton as Stephano. USG]	270.
Mrs. Austin				
Walton]				

[Jones	F.	6	[The] Tempest & [The] Bold Dragoons [See note, September 5.]	150.
Mrs. Austin				
Walton]				

	S.	7	Lovers['] Vows & [The] V[ir- ginny] Cupids	280.

[565]

Jones M. 9 Cinderella & [The] V[irginny] 310.
[Mrs.] Austin & Cupids
Walton [See note, September 2.]

Mrs. Austin's T. 10 2 Acts [of The] Tempest, 320.
ben[efi]t J[ohn] of Paris & 3[r]d.
  [Act] of [Der] Freyschutz
  [riel, as Princess of
  Navarre in *John of Paris*
  and as Linda in *Der*
  Freischutz. USG See
  preface to this season.]

  W. 11 Education, [The] V[irginny] 260.
Rice's ben[efit] Cupids & Life in Phila-
  [delphia]
  [As Hector in *Life in Phila-*
  delphia. USG]

  T. 12 Music & Prejudice, Abon 150.
Walton's B[enefi]t Hassan & Aladdin
  [As Count Cremona in
  Music and Prejudice and
  as Abon Hassan. USG
  See preface to this sea-
  son.]

  F. 13 [The] Beggar's Opera & Mas- 250.
Jones' ben[efi]t aniello
  [As Captain Macheath in
  The Beggar's Opera and
  as Masaniello. USG See
  preface to this season.]

Power S. 14 [The] 2 Thomsons, [The] Irish 470. 1760.
  Amb[assado]r & [The]
  Irish Tutor
  [As Sir Patrick in *The Irish*
  Ambassador and Terry
  O'Rourke in *The Irish*
  Tutor. USG]

Power   M. 16 John Bull, T[eddy] the Tiler 440.
                  & L[overs'] Quarrels
                  [As Dennis Brulgruddery
                    in *John Bull* and as
                    Teddy. USG]

"   T. 17 [The] Prom[issor]y Note, 350.
                  [The] I[rish] Ambassador
                  & [The] Irish Tutor
                  [Power as Sir Patrick and
                  Terry. USG]

"   W. 18 [The] Dead Shot, Born to 470.
                  Good luck* & T[eddy] the
                  Tiler
                  [Power as Paudeen O'Raf-
                  ferty in *Born to Good Luck*
                  and as Teddy. USG]

"   T. 19 [The] Rendezvous, [The] 420.
                  I[rish] Ambassador &
                  [The] I[rishman] in Lon-
                  don
                  [Power as Sir Patrick and
                  as Murtoch Delany in
                  The Irishman in London.
                  USG]

"   F. 20 F[ortune's] frolic, B[orn] to 275.
                  Good luck & Teddy the
                  Tiler
                  [Power as Paudeen O'Raf-
                  ferty and Teddy. USG]

" Benefit S. 21 [The] Dead Shot, [The] Nerv- 900.
                  ous Man* & [The] I[rish]
                  Tutor
                  [Power as McShane in *The*

Nervous Man and Terry
O'Rourke in *The Irish
Turor* USG]

———

$6205.

19 nights av[erage]d $325; after Stars, $215.

PHILA[DELPHIA SEASON, COMMENCING SEPTEMBER 23,] 1833, [ENDING
APRIL 5, 1834.]

[Maywood & Co.]

PREFACE—**September 28**: USG also announces *The Spoiled Child.*
According to USG, Mr. Mossie is to give "his celebrated imitations of
Messrs. John Randolph, Dan'l Webster, Robert V. Hayne, Henry Clay,
David Crockett, Tristram Burges, George McDuffie and Thomas D.
Arnold." **October 1**: In this entry Wood has written the notation
"Mr. Mossie." According to USG, a "part" of Mr. Mossie's perform-
ance "will consist of Extemporaneous Speaking, for which purpose Boxes
will be placed in the Lobbies of the Theatre and into them Gentlemen
are respectfully requested to deposit subjects in writing. When Mr.
Mossie's performance begins, they will be brought on the stage, placed
in a wheel and those drawn will form the entertainment." **October 3**:
In this entry Wood has also written ditto marks referring to the notation
"Mossie" of October 1. According to USG, Mossie is to repeat his
performance of that date. **October 4**: In this entry Wood has also
written ditto marks referring, apparently, to the notation "Walton" in
the entry of September 30. According to USG, Walton is to appear as
Ferdinand and as Robin in *No Song No Supper.* **October 15**: In this
entry Wood has also written "Hill." According to USG, he is to appear
as Jedediah Homebred in *The Green Mountain Boy.* **October 21**:
Under the title "G[uy] Mannering" Wood has written "Ch[ange]d from
Cind[erell]a." USG, however, announces Wood as Felix, Mrs. Wood as
Cinderella. **November 2**: Under the title "Jealous Wife" Wood has
written the notation "Ch[ange]d to Hunchback, Mrs. Thayer's Child."
Mrs. Thayer was a member of the company. **November 27**: USG
announces *The Review* in place of *The Irish Tutor.* Power is to play
Larry Hoolagan in *More Blunders than One* and Looney Mactwolter in
The Review. Wood has also written in this entry the notation "George
returned." **November 29**: USG announces *Teddy the Tiler* in place of

[568]

The Irish Tutor, with Power as Teddy and as Dennis Brulgruddery in *John Bull*. **November 30:** In this entry Wood has also written ditto marks referring to "Miss Booth" in the entry November 28. According to USG, Miss Booth is to appear as Cora in *Pizarro*. **December 12:** USG announces the bill of *Etiquette Run Mad*, *Teddy the Tiler* and *Raising the Wind*. Power is also to play the rôle of Teddy. **December 13:** USG announces the bill of *Etiquette Run Mad*, *Paddy Carey* and *Animal Magnetism*. Power is also to play the rôle of Paddy. **December 18:** In this entry Wood has written ditto marks referring to "Master Burke" in the entry of December 16 and also the notations, "Benefit [of the] American Lib[rar]y Institute," "Mr. J. Adams" and "Miss Riddle." USG announces a benefit in aid of a fund for the American Institute of Letters. Burke is to play Sir Callaghan O'Brallaghan in *Love à la Mode*; Adams, Brutus, and Miss Riddle, Tarquinia. **December 27:** To the right of the notation "Kembles" Wood has written "& De Camp." USG announces De Camp as La Fleur in *Animal Magnetism*. *Durang*, III, Chapter Thirty-Fourth, identifies him as a brother-in-law of Vincent De Camp who, on this occasion, appeared "as Rolando" in *The Honey Moon*. **December 28:** In this entry Wood has written ditto marks referring to "Kembles" in the entry of December 23 and the notation, "Volunteered—De Camp, Placide, Taylor." USG announces De Camp as Sir Peter Teazle and T. Placide as Numpo in *'Tis All a Farce*. According to *Durang*, III, Chapter Thirty-Fourth, Mrs. William B. Wood made "her last appearance before" the Philadelphia public on this occasion of her husband's benefit. She played Mrs. Candour. **January 4:** Under "Mr. Howard's benefit" Wood has written "Garrick Thespians played." *Durang*, III, Chapter Thirty-Fourth, records that "the Amateur Garrick Association volunteered their services, and performed for that night only. Previously to the first piece an appropriate address written by J. Augustus Shea, Esq., a member of the association, was delivered by a member." *Durang* identifies Howard as an "invalid vocalist." **January 22:** To the right of the ditto marks referring to Power, Wood has written "volunt[eere]d" and the notation, "Benefit of Mr. Wall, the Blind Harper." According to USG, Harper is to "appear and perform several popular and admired Irish and Scotch Airs." **January 31:** USG announces Paddy Carey in place of *The Irish Tutor*. Power is also to play Paddy.

It has been advisable to omit several financial notations from the printed version and also the following: two pairs of ditto marks in Wood's entry of October 9 referring to "Mr. & Mrs. [Joseph] Wood" in the entry of October 7; ditto marks in Wood's entry of October 10 referring to "Hill" in the entry of October 8; two pairs of ditto marks in Wood's entry of October 11 referring to "Mr. & Mrs. [Joseph Wood]" in the entry of October 7; ditto marks in Wood's entry of October 18 referring to "Mr. & Mrs. Wood" in the entry of October 14; the notations "The Forest dropt down" in the entry of November 22 and "Mr. Clay at Theatre" in the entry of November 25; ditto marks in Wood's entry of December 5 referring to "Ingersoll & Miss Booth" in the entry of December 3; ditto marks in Wood's entry of December 6 referring to "Power" in the entry of December 4; ditto marks in Wood's entry of December 12 referring to "Power" in the entry of December 9; the notation "Harry's 2d. ben[efit,]" in the entry of January 30; ditto marks in Wood's entry of February 20 referring to "Mr. & Mrs. [Joseph] Wood" in the entry of February 17; and the notation "this Even[ing] the 3d. W[illia]m Forrest died" in Wood's entry of March 3. It has also been advisable to omit the notation, "played Rover for Placide at A[rch] S[treet] Theatre," which Wood has written in his entry of December 21. USG announces Wood as Rover in *Wild Oats* for T. Placide's benefit at the Arch Street Theatre on that date.

[Chesnut Street Theatre]

	Sept[ember]	
Power	M. 23	[The] Prom[issory] Note, 640. [The] Nervous Man & Born to Good luck [As McShane in *The Nervous Man* and Paudeen O'Rafferty in *Born to Good Luck*. USG]
"	T. 24	[The] 2 Thomsons, [The] 420. I[rish] Ambassador & [The] Irish Tutor [Power as Sir Patrick in *The Irish Ambassador* and Terry O'Rourke in *The Irish Tutor*. USG]

[570]

"   W. 25 John Bull & Love a la Mode   460.
[Power as Dennis Brulgrud-
dery in *John Bull* and Sir
Callaghan in *Love a la
Mode*. USG]

"   T. 26 [The] Nervous Man, T[eddy]   450.
the Tiler & [The] Bold
dragoons
[Power as McShane and
Teddy. USG]

"   Benefit   F. 27 [The] West Indian & [The]   760.
Irish Ambassador
[Power as Major O'Flaherty
in *The West Indian* and
Sir Patrick in *The Irish
Ambassador*. USG]

Hill   S. 28 [The] Green M[ountain] Boy   240.   2970.
& [Monsieur] Mossie's
imitations
[As Jedediah Homebred in
The Green Mountain Boy.
USG. See preface to this
season.]

Mrs. Austin   M. 30 John of Paris & Abon Hassan   240.
& Walton   [Mrs. Austin as the Princess
of Navarre in *John of
Paris* and Zulina in *Abon
Hassan*. Walton as John
and Abon. USG]

October
           T. 1 East & West & Mr. Mossie   260.
[See preface to this season.]

"   "   W. 2 [The] Man of the World &   190.
Music & Prejudice

[571]

[Mrs. Austin as Alfred,
Walton as Count Cre-
mona in *Music and Pre-
judice.* USG]

[Mrs.] Austin   T.   3   East & West, Mr. Mossie [&   210.
                    The] P[romissory] Note
                    [See preface to this season.]

             F.   4   [The] Tempest & No Song No   430.
Mrs. Austin's benefit   Supper
                    [As Ariel and as Margaretta in
                    No Song No Supper. USG
                    [See preface to this season.]

             S.   5   Napoleon & How to die [for   180.   1510.
                    Love]

Mr. & Mrs.   M.   7   Love in a Village & A[nimal]   700.
[Joseph] Wood   Magnetism
                    [Wood as Hawthorn, Mrs.
                    Wood as Rosetta in *Love
                    in a Village.* USG]

Hill   T.   8   [The] Inquisitive Yankee &   190.
                    Napoleon
                    [As Joe Peep in *The In-
                    quisitive Yankee.* USG]

            W.   9   [The] Barber of Seville & [The]   760.
[Mr. & Mrs. Wood]   Dead Shot
                    [Wood as Count Almaviva,
                    Mrs. Wood as Rosina in
                    The Barber of Seville.
                    USG]

[Hill]   T. 10   Jon[athan] in England & [The]   185.
                    G[reen] Mountain Boy
                    [As Solomon Swap in *Jona-*

than in England and Jede-
diah Homebred in *The
Green Mountain Boy.*
USG]

F. 11 Cinderella & Raising [the] 850.
[Mr. & Mrs. Wood]   Wind
         [Wood as Felix, Mrs. Wood
         as Cinderella. USG]

S. 12 [The] B[arber] of Seville & 420.   3080.
"   [The] 2 Thomsons
         [Wood as Count Almaviva,
         Mrs. Wood as Rosina in
         The Barber of Seville.
         USG]

M. 14 Cinderella & [The] P[risoner] 570.
Mr. & Mrs. Wood   at Large
         [Wood as Felix, Mrs. Wood
         as Cinderella. USG]

"   T. 15 [The] Marriage of Figaro & 550.
         [The] G[reen] Mountain
         Boy
         [Wood as Count Almaviva,
         Mrs. Wood as Susanna in
         The Marriage of Figaro.
         USG See preface to this
         season.]

"   W. 16 G[uy] Mannering & [The] 900.
         Waterman
Mrs. Wood's ben[efi]t [Wood as Henry Bertram in
         Guy Mannering and Tom
         Tug in *The Waterman.*
         Mrs. Wood as Julia Man-
         nering. USG]

[573]

T. 17 [The] Foundling of the Sea*   360.

Hill's benefit   East & West

           [Hill as Zachariah Dicker-
well in *The Foundling of
the Sea* and Joshua Horse-
radish in *East and West*.
USG

F. 18 [The] Slave & A[nimal] Mag-   460.

[Mr. & Mrs. Wood]   netism

           [Wood as Malcolm, Mrs.
Wood as Zelinda in *The
Slave* USG]

"   S. 19 Rob Roy [Macgregor] & [The]   510.   3350.

           Waterman

           [Wood as Francis Osbaldi-
stone, Mrs. Wood as
Diana Vernon in Rob
Roy Macgregor. USG]

Mr. & Mrs.   M. 21 G[uy] Mannering & [The]   350.

[Joseph] Wood   Purse

           [See preface to this season.]

T. 22 Masaniello & [The] Barber of   950.

Mr. Wood's ben[efi]t   Seville

           [Wood as Masaniello and as
Count Almaviva in *The
Barber of Seville.* USG]

W. 23 [The] Stranger & Fish out of   610.

           Water

T. 24 [The] Wonder & [The Dead   375.

           Shot]

F. 25 Fazio & [The Prisoner at   610.

           Large]

S. 26 [The] Hunchback & G[retna]   640.
Green

Kembles   M. 28 [The] Wife & [The] Pris[one]r
at Large
[Kemble as Julian St.
Pierre, Miss Kemble as
Marianna in *The Wife.*
USG]

"   T. 29 [The] Provok'd Husband &
G[retna] Green
[Kemble as Lord Townly,
Miss Kemble as Lady
Townly in *The Provoked
Husband.* USG]

"   W. 30 [The] Wife & [The] Turnpike
Gate
[Kemble as Julian St.
Pierre, Miss Kemble as
Marianna. USG]

"   T. 31 [The] Merchant of Venice &   375.
[The] M[idnight] Hour
[Kemble as Shylock, Miss
Kemble as Portia. USG]

November
"   F. 1 [The Wife & Raising the
Wind]
[Kemble as Julian St.
Pierre, Miss Kemble as
Marianna. USG]

"   S. 2 [The] Jealous Wife & Charles   750.
Miss K[emble's]   the 2d.
Ben[efi]t   [Kemble as Oakly, Miss
Kemble as Mrs. Oakly.
Kemble as Charles, Miss

[575]

Kemble as Mary Copp.
USG See preface to
this season.]

M. 4 [The] Grecian Daughter & Of 710.
Mr. & Miss Kemble   Age Tomorrow
[Kemble as Evander, Miss
Kemble as Euphrasia in
The Grecian Daughter.
USG]

"   T. 5 [The] Red Rover & Turn Out 170.

"   W. 6 [The] Jealous Wife & [The] 800.
Purse
[Kemble as Oakly, Miss
Kemble as Mrs. Oakly in
The Jealous Wife. USG]

"   T. 7 [The] Red Rover & Fish out of 160.
Water

"   F. 8 [The] Point of Honor & 780.
K[atherine] & Petruchio
[Kemble as Durimel, Miss
Kemble as Bertha in *The
Point of Honor.* Kemble
as Petruchio, Miss Kemble
as Katherine. USG]

"   S. 9 Hamlet & [The] Day after 950.
Mr. K[emble's]   [the] Wedding
Benefit   [Kemble as Hamlet, Miss
Kemble as Ophelia.
Kemble as Colonel Free-
love, Miss Kemble as
Lady Elizabeth in *The
Day after the Wedding.*
USG]

[576]

M. 11 [The] Rent Day & Mr. & Mrs.   190.
      Pringle*

T. 12 Mazeppa & [The] M[idnight]   540.
      Hour

W. 13   "   [&] Mr. & Mrs.   310.
      Pringle

T. 14   "   [&]   M[odern]   220.
      Antiques

F. 15   "   [&] Fish out of water

S. 16   "   [&] No Song No
      Supper

Ingersoll Gale's
ben[efi]t

M. 18 Damon & Pythias & [Ma-   275.
      zeppa]
      [Ingersoll as Damon, Gale
      as Mazeppa. USG]

T. 19 [The] Gambler's fate & [Mr.   135.
      &] Mrs. Pringle

Power

W. 20 [The] I[rish] Ambassador, [The]   750.
      I[rish] Tutor & G[retna]
      Green
      [As Sir Patrick in *The Irish
      Ambassador* and Terry
      O'Rourke in *The Irish
      Tutor*. USG]

T. 21 W[illia]m Tell & Fish out of   120.
      Water

F. 22 [The] Nervous Man, T[eddy]   600.
      the Tiller & M[odern]
      Antiques

[577]

S. 23 A[mbrose] Gwinett, My Aunt 140.
& Pringles

Power   M. 25 [The] I[rish] Ambassador, 1010.
Born to Good luck & No
Song [No Supper]
[As Sir Patrick in *The Irish
Ambassador* and Paudeen
O'Rafferty in *Born to
Good Luck*. USG]

"   T. 26 [The] Nervous Man, More 460.
blunders than one &
[Gretna Green]
[Power as McShane in *The
Nervous Man* and Larry
Hoolagan in *More Blund-
ers than One*. USG]

"   W. 27 More Blunders than One, 440.
[The] I[rish] Tutor [&]
2 Strings [to Your Bow]
[See preface to this season.]

          T. 28 Virginius & M[odern] An- 240.
Ingersoll's Benefit   tiques
Miss Booth   [Ingersoll as Virginius, Miss
Booth as Virginia. USG]

Power   F. 29 John Bull & [The] Irish Tutor 600.
[See preface to this season.]

Ingersoll   S. 30 Pizarro & Two Strings [to 220.
your Bow]
[As Rolla in *Pizarro*. USG
See preface to this
season.]

Decem[be]r

Power's Benefit   M. 2 [The] I[rish] Ambassador, 910.
More Blunders [than One
& Mr.] & Mrs. Pringle
[As Sir Patrick in *The Irish
Ambassador* and Hoola-
gan in *More Blunders than
One*. USG]

Ingersoll &   T. 3 Town & Country & A[nimal] 120.
Miss Booth   Magnetism
[Ingersoll as Reuben Glen-
roy, Miss Booth as Rosa-
lie Somers in *Town and
Country*. USG]

Power   W. 4 St. Patrick's Eve* & [The] 575.
I[rish] Tutor
[As Major O'Dogherty in
St. Patrick's Eve and
Terry O'Rourke in *The
Irish Tutor*. USG]

"   T. 5 A[mbrose] Gwinnett & Luke 130.
the labourer
[Ingersoll as Ambrose, Miss
Booth as Lucy Fairlove in
Ambrose Gwinnett. USG]

"   F. 6 St. Patrick's Eve [& The 470.
Irishman in London]
[Power as Major O'Dogherty
in *St. Patrick's Eve* and
Murtoch Delany in *The
Irishman in London* USG]

"   S. 7 St. Patrick's Eve & [Born to 525.
Good Luck]
[Power as Major O'Dogherty

[579]

and as Paudeen O'Rafferty
in *Born to Good Luck*.
USG]

Power M. 9 St. Patrick's Eve, [The Re-   370.
view & The Rendezvous]
[As Major O'Dogherty and
as Looney Mactwolter in
The Review. USG]

"   T. 10 [The] I[rish] Ambass[ador,   550.
The] Nervous Man &
F[ortune's] Frolic
[Power as Sir Patrick in *The
Irish Ambassador* and Mc-
Shane in *The Nervous
Man*. USG]

Ingersolls   W. II Othello & Pringles   125.
ben[efi]t   [As Othello. USG]

"   T. 12 Etiquette Run Mad* & [The]   570.
I[rish] Tutor
[Power as Captain Dennis
O'Moore in *Etiquette Run
Mad*. USG See preface
to this season.]

F. 13 Etiquette [Run Mad & The]   700.
Power's Ben[efi]t   I[rish] Ambass[ador]
[As Captain Dennis O'Moore.
USG See preface to this
season.]

S. 14 [The] Found[ling] of [the]   75.
Forest & [A] Mogul Tale

M. 16 [The] Heir at Law & Whirl-   220.
Master Burke   [igig] Hall

[As Dr. Pangloss in *The Heir at Law* and as six characters in *Whirligig Hall*. USG]

"   T. 17 [The] Poor Gentleman, [& 170.
The] I[rish] Tutor
[Master Burke as Dr. Ollapod in *The Poor Gentle-
man* and Terry O'Rourke
in *The Irish Tutor*. USG]

W. 18 Brutus & L[ove] a la mode   240.
[See preface to this season.]

"   T. 19 Speed the Plough & [The] 280.
Review
[Burke as Sir Abel Handy
in *Speed the Plough* and
Looney Mactwolter in
The Review. USG]

"   F. 20 [The] Weathercock, B[arney] 375.
Burke's farewell   Brallaghan & [The]
Benefit   M[arch] of Intellect
[As Tristram Fickle in *The
Weathercock* and as six
characters in *The March
of Intellect*. USG]

Power   S. 21 Etiquette [Run Mad,] T[eddy] 450.
the Tiler & Pringles
[As Captain Dennis O'-
Moore in *Etiquette Run
Mad* and as Teddy.]

Kembles   M. 23 [The] Wife & [The] M[idnight] 510.
Hour
[Kemble as Julian St.

Pierre, Miss Kemble as
Marianna in *The Wife*.
USG]

"   T. 24 [The] Jealous Wife & Pringles   475.
[Kemble as Oakly, Miss
Kemble as Mrs. Oakly in
The Jealous Wife. USG]

W. 25 Columbus & [A] Mogul tale   610.

"   T. 26 [The] Point of Honor &   410.
Charles 2d.

"   &   F. 27 [The] Honey Moon & Animal   460.
De Camp   Magnetism
[Kemble as Duke Aranza,
Miss Kemble as Juliana
in *The Honey Moon*.
USG   See preface to this
season.]

[Kembles]   S. 28 [The] S[chool] for Scandal &   786.
Wood's Benefit   ['Tis] All a farce
[Kemble as Charles Surface,
Miss Kemble as Lady
Teazle, Wood as Joseph
Surface. USG   See pref-
ace to this season.]

M. 30 Romeo & Juliet & Deaf as a   510.
Kembles De Camp   post
[Kemble as Mercutio, Miss
Kemble as Juliet, De
Camp as Sappy in *Deaf as
a Post*. USG]

T. 31 Much Ado [about Nothing]   400.
"   "   & [The] Lottery Ticket
[Kemble as Benedick, Miss

[582]

Kemble as Beatrice. De
Camp as Wormwood in
The Lottery Ticket. ADA]

1834 January

W. 1 Columbus & [The] Spectre 220.
    " Bridegroom
    [DeCamp as Dickory in *The
    Spectre Bridegroom.* USG]

T. 2 Fazio & Mon[sieur] Tonson 420.
"   "   [Kemble as Fazio, Miss
    Kemble as Bianca. De
    Camp as Monsieur Ton-
    son. USG]

"   F. 3 [The] Honey Moon & Charles 660.
Miss Kembles   the 2d.
ben[efi]t   [Kemble as Duke Aranza,
    Miss Kemble as Juliana
    in *The Honey Moon.*
    Kemble as Charles, Miss
    Kemble as Mary Cappin
    Charles the Second. USG]

S. 4 Paul Pry, Luke [the] Lab- 290.
Mr. Howard's   our[er & 'Tis] All a farce
benefit   [See preface to this season.]

Kembles   M. 6 Jane Shore & 3 & the Deuce 470.
    |Kemble as Lord Hastings,
    Miss Kemble as Jane
    Shore. USG]

"   T. 7 [The] Hunchback & Mons- 340
    s[ieur] Tonson
    [Kemble as Sir Thomas
    Clifford, Miss Kemble as
    Julia in *The Hunchback.*
    USG]

[583]

W. 8 [The] Jealous Wife & Deaf as   350.
"   De Camp's   a post
    ben[efit]   [Kembles as Oakly, Miss
               Kemble as Mrs. Oakly in
               The Jealous Wife. De
               Camp as Lord Trinket in
               The Jealous Wife and
               Sappy in *Deaf as a Post*.
               USG]

"   T. 9 K[ing] John & [The] Pris[oner]   410.
               at large
               [Kemble as Falconbridge,
               Miss Kemble as Con-
               stance. USG]

"   F. 10 Jane Shore & [The] Day after   675.
Miss Kemble's   [the] Wedding
Ben[efit]   [Kemble as Lord Hastings,
               Miss Kemble as Jane.
               Kemble as Colonel Free-
               love, Miss Kemble as
               Lady Elizabeth in *The
               Day after the Wedding*.
               USG]

           S. 11 Columbus & W[illia]m   200.
               Thomson
Mrs. Duff M. 13 Adelgitha & Turning the   240.
               tables
               [As Adelgitha. USG]

"   T. 14 Isabella & [The] A[greeable]   220.
               Surprize
               [Mrs. Duff as Isabella.
               USG]

"   W. 15 [The] F[oundling] of [the]   140.
               Forest & [The] Dead Shot

[584]

[Mrs. Duff as Unknown
Female in *The Foundling
of the Forest.* USG]

"   T. 16 [The] Bride of Lammermoor   290.
       & [The] B[old] Dragoons
       [Mrs. Duff as Lucy Ashton
       in *The Bride of Lammer-
       moor.* USG]

       F. 17 Pizarro, 4th Act [of The]   340.
"   Benefit   Merch[ant of] Venice &
       [The] Boh[emian] Mother
       [Mrs. Duff as Elvira in
       Pizarro, as Portia and as
       Mathilde in *The Bohem-
       ian Mother.* USG]

       S. 18 Mahomet   &   Damon   &   300.
Murdock's ben[efi]t   Pythias*
       [As Zaphna in *Mahomet* and
       as Damon. USG]

Power   M. 20 [The]   I[rish]   Ambassador,   475.
       [The] Omnibus & [Family
       Jars]
       [As Sir Patrick in *The Irish
       Ambassador* and Pat
       Rooney in *The Omnibus.*
       USG]

"   T. 21 [The] Nervous Man & B[orn]   280.
       to Good Luck
       [Power as McShane and
       Paudeen O'Rafferty. USG]

"   W. 22 John Bull, L[overs'] Quarrels, 1054.
       Harp   &   D[amon]   &
       Pythias

[Power as Dennis Brul-
gruddery in *John Bull*.
USG   See preface to this
season.]

Th. 23 [The] B[ride] of Lammermoor, 225.
Harp & [The] Clutter-
bucks

" F. 24 Etiquette [Run Mad], [The] 310.
Omnibus & Pringles
[Power as Captain Dennis
O'Moore in *Etiquette Run
Mad* and Pat Rooney in
The Omnibus. USG]

" S. 25 [The] Robber's Wife, [The] 400.
I[rish] Tutor [&] T[urn-
ing the tables
[Power as Larry O'Gig in
The Robber's Wife and
Terry O'Rourke in *The
Irish Tutor*. USG]

Power M. 27 [The] Robber's Wife, B[orn] 340.
to Good Luck & D[amon]
& Pythias
[As Larry O'Gig and as
Paudeen O'Rafferty in
Born to Good Luck. USG]

" Benefit T. 28 St. Patrick's Eve, [The] Omni- 675.
bus & Family Jars
[Power as Major O'Dogh-
erty in *St. Patrick's Eve*
and Pat Rooney in *The
Omnibus*. USG]

W. 29 Mahomet & [The] Clutter- 106.
bucks

| | T. 30 Columbus & [The] Bold Dragoons | 78. |

| Power | F. 31 More blunders than One, [The] I[rish] Tutor [&] T[urning] the tables [As Larry Hoolagan in *More Blunders than One*. USG See pieface to this season.] | 510. |

February

| " | 1 St. Patrick's Eve, T[eddy] the tiler & [Mr. &] Mrs. Pringle [Power as Major O'Dogherty and as Teddy. USG] | 330. |

| Power | M. 3 [The] I[rish] Ambassador, [The] Invincibles & D[eaf] as a post [As Sir Patrick in *The Irish Ambassador* and Corporal O'Slash in *The Invincibles*. USG] | 375. |

| " | T. 4 [The] Nervous Man, More B[lunders] than One, & ['Tis] all a farce [Power as McShane and Larry Hoolagan. USG] | 350. |

| " | W. 5 Etiquette [Run Mad], [The] Invincibles & [Damon & Pythias [Power as Captain Dennis O'Moore and Corporal Slash. USG] | 350. |

"   Th.   6 [The] Man of the World &   110. L[uke] the Labourer

"   F.   7 Born to Good luck & [The]   450. I[rish] Tutor [Power as Paudeen O'Rafferty in *Born to Good Luck* and Teddy O'Rourke in *The Irish Tutor*.]

" Benefit   S.   8 [The] Rivals & [The] Omnibus   900. [Power as Sir Lucius O' Trigger in *The Rivals* and Pat Rooney in *The Omnibus*. USG]

Mr. & Mrs. [Joseph] Wood   M. 10 [The] M[arriage] of Figaro &   420. [The] Mid[night] Hour [Wood as Count Almaviva, Mrs. Wood as Susanna in *The Marriage of Figaro*. USG]

"   T. 11 Masaniello & Turn[in]g the   470. tables [Wood as Masaniello, Mrs. Wood as the Princess. USG]

"   W. 12 [The] Field of 40 footsteps* [&   210. Mr.] & Mrs. Pringle

"   T. 13 Der Freyschutz & A[nimal]   440. Magnetism [Wood as Rodolph, Mrs. Wood as Agnes in *Der Freischutz*. USG]

	F. 14 Cinderella & ['Tis] All a farce [Wood as Felix, Mrs. Wood as Cinderella. USG]	510.	
"			
	S. 15 [The] Field of 40 footsteps[& The] Pris[oner] at large	240.	
Mr. & Mrs. [Joseph] Wood	M. 17 Fra Diavolo & D[amon] & Pythias [Wood as Fra Diavolo, Mrs. Wood as Zerlina. USG]	650.	
"	T. 18 Fra Diavolo & [The] Spectre Bridegroom [See note, February 17].	420.	
J. Porter's 1st. app[earance]	W. 19 Douglas & [The] B[old] Dragoons [As Young Norval in *Douglas*. USG]	130.	
[Mr. & Mrs. Joseph Wood]	T. 20 Rob Roy [Macgregor] & [Raising the Wind] [Wood as Francis Osbaldistone, Mrs. Wood as Diana Vernon in *Roy Roy Macgregor*. USG]	400.	
" Mrs. Wood's benefit	F. 21 Fra Diavolo & [The] Waterman [Wood as Fra Diavolo, Mrs. Wood as Zerlina. Wood as Tom Tug, Mrs. Wood as Wilhelmina in *The Waterman*. USG]	650.	
	S. 22 [The] Field of 40 footsteps & [The] Purse	140.	2390.

[589]

Mr. & Mrs.   M. 24 [The] Duenna & Turning the 350.
[Joseph] Wood   tables
                     [Wood as Carlos, Mrs.
                     Wood as Clara in *The
                     Duenna.* USG]

              T. 25 Masaniello & [A] Mogul Tale 350.
"   [Wood as Masaniello, Mrs.
                     Wood as the Princess.
                     USG]

             W. 26 [The] Robbers & My Aunt   120.

             T. 27 Fra Diavolo & Fish out of 450.
"   Water
                     [Wood as Fra Diavolo, Mrs.
                     Wood as Zerlina. USG]

Mr. Wood's   F. 28 [The] Devil's Bridge & [The] 650.
benefit   Quaker
                     [Wood as Count Belino,
                     Mrs. Wood as Countess
                     Rosalvina in *The Devil's
                     Bridge.* Wood as Steady,
                     Mrs. Wood as Gillian in
                     The Quaker. USG]

       March
             S. 1 Columbus & High, Low, Jack 130.
                     & [the] Game

Mr. & Mrs.   M. 3 Cinderella & [Mr. &] Mrs. 450.
[Joseph] Wood   Pringle
                     [Wood as Felix, Mrs. Wood
                     as Cinderella. USG]

             T. 4 Guy Mannering & [The] 270.
"   Quaker
                     [Wood as Henry Bertram,

Mrs. Wood as Julia Man-
nering. Wood as Steady,
Mrs. Wood as Gillian.
USG]

W. 5 [The] M[idnight] Hour, High,   150.
Low, Jack & [the] G[ame]
& D[amon] & Pythias

T. 6 [The] Maid of Judah* & High,   700.
"   Low[, Jack] & [the
Game]
[Wood as Ivanhoe, Mrs.
Wood as Rebecca in *The
Maid of Judah.* USG]

F. 7 [The] Maid of Judah & Clari   675.
"   [Wood as Ivanhoe, Mrs.
Benefit   Wood as Rebecca and as
Clari. USG]

S. 8 [The] Rent day, H[igh,] Low,   130.   2375.
Jack & [the] Game

Kembles   M. 10 Isabella & High, Low, [Jack] &   400.
[the Game]
[Kemble as Biron, Miss
Kemble as Isabella. USG]

"   T. 11 Rule a Wife [& Have a Wife]   370.
& Of Age tomorrow
[Kemble as Leon, Miss
Kemble as Stefania in
Rule a Wife. USG]

W. 12 [The] Field of 40 footsteps [&   180.
Mr.] & Mrs. Pringle

[591]

"   T. 13 Macbeth & [Mr. & Mrs.]   350.
Pringle
[Kemble as Macbeth, Miss
Kemble as Lady Mac-
beth. USG]

"   F. 14 Henry 8th & [The] Purse   450.
[Kemble as Wolsey, Miss
Kemble as Queen Kather-
ine. USG]

"   S. 15 [The] Gamester & C[ather- 500.
Miss K[emble's]   ine] & Petruchio
Benefit   [Kemble as Beverly, Miss
Kemble as Mrs. Beverly
in *The Gamester*. Kem-
ble as Petruchio, Miss
Kemble as Katherine.
USG]

Kembles   M. 17 [The] Honey Moon & Turn 460.
Out
[Kemble as Duke Aranza,
Miss Kemble as Juliana in
The Honey Moon. USG]

"   T. 18 [The] Inconstant & [The] Two 310.
Thomsons
[Kemble as Young Mirabel,
Miss Kemble as Bizarre
in *The Inconstant*. USG]

"   W. 19 Henry 8th & [The] Day After 500.
Mr. Kemble's   [the] Wedding
ben[efi]t   [Kemble as Wolsey, Miss
Kemble as Queen Kath-
erine. Kemble as Col-
onel Freelove, Miss Kem-
ble as Lady Elizabeth in
The Day after the Wedding.
USG]

[592]

Kelly's Ben[efit]

T. 20 [A] Cure for the Heartache   270.
[The] Turnpike Gate .
[Kelly as Frank Oatland in
A Cure for the Heart Ache
and Crack in *The Turn-
pike Gate*. USG]

Walton's Benefit
Mr. & Mrs.
[Joseph] Wood

F. 21 [The] Maid of Judah & [No!]   650.
[Walton as Cedric of Roth-
enwood in *The Maid of
Judah* and Frederick in
No! USG NG also an-
nounces Walton as Figaro
in cavatina of *Large
al Factotum*. Wood as
Ivanhoe, Mrs. Wood as
Rebecca. USG]

Mrs. Conduit's
1st app[earance]

S. 22 Pizarro & Rosina   70.
[As Rosina. USG]

Mr. & Mrs.
[Joseph] Wood

M. 24 [The] Maid of Judah & D[am-   350.
on] & Pythias
[Wood as Ivanhoe, Mrs.
Wood as Rebecca. USG]

"

T. 25 Fra Diavolo & [The] Quaker   320.
[Wood as Fra Diavolo, Mrs.
Wood as Zerlina. Wood
as Steady, Mrs. Wood as
Gillian in *The Quaker*.
USG]

Power
Mr. Maywood's
ben[efi]t

W. 26 [The] I[rish] Ambassador, &   910.
Tam O'Shanter*
[Power as Sir Patrick O'
Plenipo, Maywood as
Tam O'Shanter. USG]

T. 27 [The] Mountaineers & Tam 150.
O'Shanter

F. 28 Geo[rge] Barnwell & Tam 130.
O'Shanter

Hackett   S. 29 Rip Van Winkle & [The] 450.
Kentuckian
[As Rip van Winkle and as
Colonel Nimrod Wildfire
in *The Kentuckian*. USG]

Hackett   M. 31 [The First Part of] Henry 4th, 220.
Ist. Act [of The] Ken-
tuckian & [Mr. & Mrs.]
Pringle
[As Falstaff and Colonel
Nimrod Wildfire. USG]

April

"   T. 1 Jon[athan] in England, Mon- 160.
[sieur] Tonson & [The]
B[old] Dragoons
[Hackett as Solomon Swap
in *Jonathan in England*
and as Monsieur Tonson.
USG]

"   W. 2 [Monsieur] Mallet, I[st.] Act 220.
[of The] Kentuckian &
Gretna Green
[Hackett as Monsieur Mal-
let and Colonel Nimrod
Wildfire. USG]

"   T. 3 Rip van Winkle & Jon[athan] 230.
Doubikins
[Hackett as Rip van Winkle
and Jonathan Doubikins.
USG]

"   F. 4 [The] Dead Shot, Monsieur 140.
           Mallet & T[urning] the
           Tables
           [Hackett as Monsieur Mal-
           let. USG]

           S. 5 Rip Van Winkle, Jon[athan] 470.
Hacket[t's] Benefit   Doubikin's [&] 1st. Act
           [of The] Kentuckian
      .   [As Rip van Winkle, Jon[a-
           than] Doubikins and Col-
           onel Nimrod Wildfire.
           USG]

PHILA[DELPHIA] SEASON[, COMMENCING APRIL 7, ENDING
JULY 19,] 1834.

[Maywood & Co.]

PREFACE—**April 18:** Wood has written under "Booth Benefit" the notation "Preston & McDuffie." **April 26:** According to USG, Rice is also to appear "as the Far Famed Jim Crow and sing the celebrated effusions composed by Colonel David Crockett." **May 10:** According to USG, Hatton is to sing the "favorite ballad" of *My Friend and Pitcher* and the "celebrated comic song" of *Paddy's Wedding.* **June 12:** USG announces Signor Giovanni Sciarra "from Marseilles." See June 26. **June 17:** USG announces *The Midnight Hour*; The Ravel family on the tight rope; the laughable pantomime of *Monsieur Molinet; or, A Night of Adventures*; the interlude of *Bouquet d'Amour; or Rose & Colin*, by the infant Ravels; and the tableau of *The Death of Abel.* **June 19:** In this entry Wood has written ditto marks referring to "Ravels" in the entry of June 17. USG announces "a divertisement imitated from the Carnival of Venice, executed by the Ravel family, in which young Gabriel Ravel will dance The Polichinelle." **June 21:** In this entry Wood has also written "played for Placide's ben[efit] at A[rch] S[treet.]" According to USG Wood was to appear as Lieutenant Worthington in *The Poor Gentleman* and Toby Heywood in *The Rent Day.* **June 26:** According to USG, "Signor Giovanni Sciarra will go through his wonderful performances, among which he will swallow an iron bar thirty inches long and an inch and a half in circumference; also the Aerian Dance in which

[595]

he will balance his little daughter on a rope attached to a pole and many other feats too numerous to mention." **July 8:** In this entry Wood has also written the notations, "Mrs. Duff," "Mary Duff," "Jones" and "Mrs. Wood." USG announces W. B. Wood and Sir William Dorillon in *Wives as They Were* and Count Manheim in *The Bohemian Mother*; Mrs. Duff as Mathilde in *The Bohemian Mother*; Mary Duff as Miss Dorillon; and Jones as Lord Priory, with Mrs. Wood as Lady Priory, in *Wives as They Were.* **July 11:** See the entry of April 23, 1823. **July 12:** USG announces *Raymond and Agnes* in place of *The Forest of Rosenwald.* Mrs. Rowbotham is to play Marguerite. According to USG, "A monologue will be spoken by Mr. Rowbotham, written by a gentleman of this city, embracing some of the principal incidents in the life of General Lafayette. In the course of the monologue the following illustrations painted by Mr. [H.] Warren: Likeness of Lafayette. Landing of Lafayette near Charleston in 1777. Battle of Brandywine. Capture of Yorktown, surrender of the British. Prison of Olmutz, where Lafayette was confined for five years. Landing of Lafayette in 1824. To conclude with a grand apotheosis." **July 16:** In this entry Wood has also written the notations, "Mr. Jones," "L. Heyl," "Mrs. Duff" and "Miss M. Duff." Pratt was a member of the firm of Maywood & Co. According to USG, Jones is to appear as Solus in *Every One Has His Fault*; Heyl is to sing the "celebrated song" of *The Swiss Boy* "accompanied by himself on the piano forte" and to appear as Crack in *The Turnpike Gate*; Mrs. Duff is to appear as Lady Eleanor Irwin and Miss Mary Duff as Miss Woodburn in *Every One Has His Fault.* **July 18:** In this entry Wood has also written the notations, "Mrs. Duff," "Jones," "Mrs. Jones," "J. R. Scott," "Miss Duff," and "Mr. & Mrs. Houpt." According to USG, Mrs. Duff is to appear as Elvira in *Pizarro*; Jones as Mr. Primrose, with Mrs. Jones as Mrs. Biffin, in *Popping the Question*; J. R. Scott as Rolla, Miss Duff as Cora, Mr. Houpt as Ataliba in *Pizarro*; and Miss Duff as Lady Elizabeth in *The Day after the Wedding.* Mrs. Houpt is to sing *Love Sounds the Trumpet of Joy.*

It has been necessary to substitute the names of the players, in the entry of April 23, for two pairs of ditto marks in Wood's manuscript, one referring to "C[harles] Mason," in his entry of April 21; the other to "Scott" in Wood's entry of April 22. It has also been necessary to substitute the name of the players, in the entry of April 24, for ditto marks in Wood's manuscript referring to "Hill" in the entry of April 22. In the entry of April 25 it has been necessary to substitute "Charles Mason"

[596]

and "Scott" for two pairs of ditto marks referring respectively to Wood's notations "C. Mason," in his entry of April 21, and "Scott," in his entry of April 22.

It has also been necessary to substitute "Hill" and "Rice" in the entry of April 26 for two pairs of ditto marks referring respectively to the notation "Hill" in Wood's entry of April 22 and the notation "Rice" in his entry of April 25. Under his entry of May 3 Wood has written, "W[alnut] S[treet] Closed & Opened by Italian Opera." In the entries of May 15 and 17 it has been necessary to substitute "Power" for ditto marks in Wood's manuscript referring to the name of that player in the entry of May 12. In the entry of May 29 Wood has written the notation, "Mr. Stone drowned himself." See *Durang*, III, Chapter Twenty-Fifth, for an account of the suicide of the author of *Metamora*.

To the left of the entry of June 7 Wood has written the notations, "7. Miss Kemble married at Christ's Church at 9 A.M. this day." and "W[alnut] Street Opened." It has obviously been advisable to eliminate these notations from the version to be printed. In the entry of June 13 it has been necessary to substitute "Miss Monier" for ditto marks in Wood's manuscript referring to the name of that actress in the entry of June 9. It has also been necessary to substitute "Rice" in the entry of June 14 for ditto marks in Wood's manuscript referring to the name of that actor in the entry of June 12. In the entries of June 19 and 21 it has been necessary to substitute the name of the players for ditto marks referring to the notation "Ravels" in the entry of June 17; and to substitute "Sinclair" in the entries of June 25 and 27 for ditto marks referring to the name of that actor in Wood's entry of June 23.

During the season Maywood & Co. moved from the Walnut to the Chesnut and back to the Walnut.

		April	Walnut St[reet Theat]er	
Booth	M.	7	Richard 3d. & [The] Bold	300.
			Dragoons	
			[As Richard. USG]	

Ingersoll	T.	8	Wacousta*, Sprigs of Laurel &	240
			[The] Review	
			[As Wacousta. USG]	

"   W. 9 [A] New Way to pay old debts   250.
             & [The] A[greeable] Sur-
             prize
             [Booth as Sir Giles Over-
             reach in *A New Way to
             Pay Old Debts.* USG]

"   T. 10 Wacousta & Modern Antiques   230.
             [Ingersoll as   Wacousta.
             USG]

"   F. 11 Hamlet & Gretna Green   250.
             [Booth as Hamlet. USG]

"   S. 12 Wacousta & Ambrose Grin-   220.
             nett
             [Ingersoll as Ambrose and
             Wacousta. USG]

           M. 14 King Lear & The] Colonel's   180.
Booth   Ingersoll   Come
             [Booth as Lear, Ingersoll as
             Edgar. USG]

           T. 15 Pringles, [The] Whistler* &   160.
             [The] Prom[issor]y Note

"   "   W. 16 [The]   Iron   Chest   &   [The]   220.
             Happiest day of my life
             [Booth as Sir Edward Mor-
             timer, Ingersoll as Wil-
             ford in *The Iron Chest.*
             USG]

"   T. 17 W[illia]m Tell & [The] Whist-   170.
             ler
             [Ingersoll as William Tell.
             USG]

Booth Benefit

F. 18 Richard 3d. & [The] Colonel's 450.
Come
[Booth as Richard. USG
See preface to this
season.]

Ingersoll's Benefit

S. 19 [The] Dead Shot, D[amon] & 140.
Pythias [tragedy] &
D[amon] & Pythias [farce]
[As Damon in tragedy.
USG]

C[harles] Mason

M. 21 Macbeth & Animal Mag- 120.
netism
[As Macbeth. USG]

Hill Scott

T. 22 Virginius & Jonathan in Eng- 240.
land
[Scott as Virginius, Hill as
Solomon Swap in *Jona-
than in England*. USG]

[Charles Mason
Scott]

W. 23 Venice Preserv[']d & [The] 90.
Poor Soldier
[Mason as Pierre, Scott as
Jaffier in *Venice Pre-
served*. USG

[Hill]

T. 24 My Aunt, [The] Green M[oun- 180.
t[ain] Boy & [The] In-
quisitive Yankee
[Hill as Jedediah Homebred
in *The Green Mountain
Boy* and Joe Peep in *The
Inquisitive Yankee*. USG]

[Charles Mason
Scott Rice]

F. 25 Othello & [The] 100 £ Note 210.
[Mason as Othello, Scott as
Iago, Rice as Billy Black
in *The £100 Note*. USG]

[599]

S. 26 Jon[athan] in England, Songs 550.
Col[onel] Crockett & O, Hush!
[Hill Rice] [Hill as Solomon Swap, Rice
as Gumba Cuff in *O Hush!*
USG See preface to this
season.]

M. 28 Pizarro, [The] Forest Rose & 190.
Mason Hill Rice J[im] Crow
[Mason as Rolla in *Pizarro*,
Hill as Jonathan in *The
Forest Rose*, Rice as Jim
Crow. USG]

T. 29 Werner, [The] A[dopted] 150.
" Benefit Scott Child & Napoleon
[Mason as Werner and Na-
poleon. Scott as Michael
in *The Adopted Child*.
USG]

W. 30 [The] Foundling of the Sea, 310.
Hill's Benefit [The] 2 Ovids & 2 Acts [of
The] Green M[ountain]
Boy
[As Zachariah Dickerwell in
The Foundling of the Sea,
Ovid Bigelow in *The
Two Ovids* and Jedediah
Homebred in *The Green
Mountain Boy*. USG]

May
T. 1 1st. Act [of] Hamlet, 1st. Act 230.
Scott's ben[efi]t [of] Lear, Imitations, Na-
Mason poleon & [The] L[ady] of
the Lake
[Scott as Hamlet, Lear and
Rhoderick Dhu. Mason
as Napoleon. USG.]

[600]

Murdock's benefit

F. 2 Lovers' Vows & 2 Acts of 160.
Brutus
[As Frederick in *Lovers'*
Vows. USG announces
1st., 3rd. and 5th act of
Brutus.]

S. 3 Pringles, Aladdin & Plot & 250.
Counterplot
Chesnut Street [Theatre]

Power

M. 5 [The] Prom[issor]y Note, 320.
[The] I[rish] Ambassador
& Paddy Carey
[As Sir Patrick in *The Irish*
Ambassador and as Paddy
Carey. USG]

"

T. [6] G[retna] Green, Born to Good 300.
Luck & [The] Omnibus
[Power as Paudeen O'Raf-
ferty in *Born to Good Luck*
and Pat Rooney in *The*
Omnibus. USG]

W. [7 The] Rent day & Inkle &. 90.
Yarico

"

T. [8] T[urning] the tables, [The] 310.
Nervous Man & [The]
I[rish] Tutor
[Power as McShane in *The*
Nervous Man and Terry
O'Rourke in *The Irish*
Tutor. USG]

F. [9 The] D[ead] Shot, Etiquette 300.
run mad & [The] Omni-
bus

[601]

[Power as Captain Dennis
O'Moore in *Etiquette Run
Mad* and Pat Rooney in
The Omnibus. USG]

Hatton	S. 10 Fish out of Water, I[nkle] & Yarico, Songs & Plot & Counterplot [See preface to this season.]	170.
Power	M. 12 [Mr. & Mrs.] Pringle, Married Lovers* & Teddy the tiler [As Colonel O'Dillon in *Married Lovers* and as Teddy. USG]	425.
" Benefit	T. 13 St. Patrick's Eve, Paddy Carey & [The] M[idnight] Hour [Power as Major O'Dogherty in *St. Patrick's Eve* and as Paddy Carey. USG]	460.
	W. 14 [The] Gambler's fate & No Song No Supper	120.
[Power]	T. 15 [The] S[pectre] Brideg[roo]m, M[arried] Lovers & [The] I[rishman] in London [As Colonel O'Dillon in *Married Lovers* and Murtoch Delaney in *The Irishman in London.* USG]	320.
Faulkner's Ben[efi]t	F. 16 D[amon] & Pythias, [The] Recruiting Officer & Com[fortable] Lodgings [As Serjeant Kite in *The*	190.

Recruiting Officer and Sir
Hippington Miff in *Comfortable Lodgings.* USG]

"   S. 17 [The] Rendezvous, Born to   410.
good   Luck   &   M[ore]
Blunders than One
[Power as Paudeen O'Rafferty in *Born to Good Luck*
and Larry Hoolagan in
More Blunders than One.
USG]

Power   M. 19 L[overs] Quarrels, John Bull &   300.
Teddy the tiler
[As Dennis Brulgruddery in
John Bull and as Teddy.
USG]

"   T. 20 W[illiam] Thomson, [The]   240.
Robber's Wife & [The]
Invincibles
[Power as Larry O'Gig in
The Robber's Wife and
Corporal O'Slash in *The
Invincibles.* USG]

"   W. 21 [The] Rivals & [The] 100 £   190.
Note
[Power as Sir Lucius O'-
Trigger in *The Rivals* and
O'Shocknessay in *The £
100 Note.* USG]

"   T. 22 F[ortune's] Frolic, [The]   260.
I[rish] Ambass[ador] &
[The] Review
[Power as Sir Patrick in *The
Irish Ambassador* and
Looney Mactwolter in
The Review. USG]

[603]

"   F. 23 ['Tis] All a farce, St. Patrick's   320.
Eve & M[onsieur] Tonson
[Power as Major O'Dogh-
erty in *St. Patrick's Eve*
and Monsieur Morbleu in
Monsieur Tonson. USG]

"   S. 24 M[onsieur] Tonson & Born to   400.
Good Luck
[Power as Monsieur Morbleu
and as Paudeen O'Rafferty
in *Born to Good Luck.* USG]

Kembles[']   M. 26 Fazio & Com[fortable] Lodg-   375.
farewell   ings
En[gagement]   [Kemble as Fazio, Miss
Kemble as Bianca. USG]

"   T. 27 [The] H[oney]Moon & Plot &   190.
Counterplot
[Kemble as Duke Aranza,
Miss Kemble as Juliana
in *The Honeymoon* USG]

"   W. 28 [The]   Stranger,   L[overs']   280.
Quarrels & D[eaf] as a
post
[Kemble as the Stranger,
Miss Kemble as Mrs.
Haller. USG]

"   T. 29 Much ado [about Nothing, My   275.
Aunt] & [Sprigs of Laurel]
[Kemble as Benedick, Miss
Kemble   as   Beatrice.
USG]

"   F. 30 Pringles, [The] Hunchback &   500.
[A] Mogul tale

[604]

[Kemble as Sir Thomas
Clifford, Miss Kemble as
Julia in *The Hunchback.*
USG]

S. 31 [The] Field of 40 footsteps &   160.
A[nimal] Magnetism

June

| | M. | 2 [The] Point of Honor, C[ather- | 740. |

Miss K[emble's]   ine] & Petruchio, [The]
Benefit   Dead Shot & [A] M[ogul]
Kembles[']   Tale
farewell   [Kemble as Ducimel, Miss
eng[agement]   Kemble as Bertha in *The
                       Point of Honor.* Kemble
                       as Petruchio, Miss Kem-
                       ble as Katherine. USG]

"   T. 3 [The] Rendezvous, Rule a   275.
           Wife [& Have a Wife]
           & W[illia]m Thomson
           [Kemble as Leon, Miss
           Kemble as Estefania in
           Rule a Wife. USG]

"   W. 4 Romeo & Juliet, [The] Secret   400.
           & [Gretna Green]
           [Kemble as Mercutio, Miss
           Kemble as Juliet. USG]

"   T. 5 [The] Provok'd Husband, My   260.
           Aunt & ['Tis All a Farce]
           [Kemble as Lord Townly,
           Miss Kemble as Lady
           Townly in *The Provoked
           Husband.* USG]

[605]

"   F. 6 S[prigs] of Laurel, [The]   950.
                          Wonder & [The] Day
Mr. Kemble's   after [the] Wedding
benefit   [Kemble as Don Felix, Miss
                          Kemble as Donna Vio-
                          lante in *The Wonder*.
                          Kemble as Colonel Free-
                          love, Miss Kemble as
                          Lady Elizabeth in *The
                          Day after the Wedding*.
                          USG]
                          W[alnut] Street [Theatre]

                   S. 7 [A] M[ogul] Tale, Poland &   100.
                          Liberty & [The] H[ap-
                          piest] day of my life

                   M. 9 Evadne & Plot & Counterplot   60.
Miss [Virginia]   [As Evadne. USG]
Monier
                   T. 10 Gabinski, Animal Mag[net-   35.
                          ism] & [The] Rendez-
                          [vou]s

"   W. 11 [The] Castle Spectre & [The]   50.
                          Haunted Inn
                          [Miss Monier as Angela in
                          The Castle Spectre. USG]

Rice   Sciarra   T. 12 [The] Mountaineers, Sign[or]   70.
                          Sciarra, L[overs'] Quar-
                          rels & Jim Crow
                          [Rice as Jim Crow. USG
                          See preface to this
                          season.]

"   F. 13 Town & Country, [The] Romp   80.
[Miss   &   Sciarra's   perf[orm-
Monier]   ance]s

[Miss Monier as Rosalie Sommers in *Town and Country*. USG]

[Rice] "   S. 14 S[prigs] of Laurel, [The] 140.
Whistler, S[ignor] Sciarra & O, Hush [!]
[Rice as Jim Crow and as Gumba Cuff in *O, Hush!* USG]

     M. 16 [A] M[ogul] Tale, Pizarro & Is 160.
Miss Monier's   he Jealous [?]
ben[efi]t   [As Cora in *Pizarro* and Harriet in *Is He Jealous?* USG]

Ravels   T. 17 Ravels   200.
[See preface to this season.]

     W. 18 [The] Haunted Inn, Sign[or] 300.
Rice's benefit   Sciarra, & [The] L[ottery] Ticket
[As Jim Crow and as Worm-wood in *The Lottery Ticket*. USG]

[Ravels]   T. 19 C[omfortable] Lodgings & 180.
Ravels
[See preface to this season.]

     F. 20 St. Patrick's Eve & Gabinski 360.
Benefit of the Poles   [In aid of the Polish Fund.
Power played.   Power as Major O'Dogh-erty in *St. Patrick's Eve*. USG]

[Ravels]   S. 21 Pringles [& The] Ravels 170.
[See preface to this season.]

Sinclair M. 23 T[urning] the tables, Masan- 190.
iello & [The] Rendezvous
[As Masaniello. USG]

T. 24 [The] S[pectre] Bridegroom, 300.
Ravels' Benefit Ravels, Cocomba & F[or-
tune's] Frolic
[Gabriel Ravel as Cocomba,
Jerome Ravel as Zebero
in *Cocomba*. USG]

[Sinclair] W. 25 S[prigs of] Laurel, G[uy] Man- 150.
nering & [The Secret]
[As Henry Bertram in Guy
Mannering. ADA]

T. 26 [The] Dead Shot, S[ignor] 60.
Sig[nor] Sciarra['s] Sciarra & Gabinski
Benefit [See preface to this season.]

[Sinclair] F. 27 [The] 2 Thomsons, [The] 160.
Englishman in India &
Midas
[As Captain Tancred in *The
Englishman in India* and
Apollo in *Midas*. USG]

Mr. Sinclair's S. 28 [The 2nd. & 3rd. acts of The] 220. 1080.
benefit (farewell) Cabinet, G[retna] Green,
Midas & No [!]
[As Prince Orlando in *The
Cabinet*, Apollo in *Midas*
and Frederick in *No!*
USG]

M. 30 [The] Prom[issory] Note, 165.
Hadaway's Benefit F[rank] Foxphipps,* [The]
F[orest] of Rosenwald &
[the] 5[th] Act [of] Richard 3d.

[608]

[As Spicey in *Frank Fox
Phipps*, as Theodore in
The Forest of Rosenwald
and as Richard. USG]

July

	T. 1 R[aising] the Wind, Aladdin & [The Haunted Inn]	110.
Walstein's benefit	W. 2 F[rank] F[ox] Fipps, [The] Bride of Abydos & [The] Board[in]g House [As Giaffar in *The Bride of Abydos* and Peter Fidget in *The Boarding House.* USG]	75.
J. R. Scott	T. 3 Napoleon, [& The] S[pectre] Bridegroom [As Napoleon. USG]	190.
	F. 4 Bunker Hill & Gabinski	280.
"	S. 5 [Frank Fox] Fipps, Black Ey'd Susan & [The] Poor Soldier	150.
J. R. Scott	M. 7 Kair[r]issah* & fish Out of Water [As Kairrissah. USG]	130.
Wood's Ben[efi]t	T. 8 Wives as they Were [& Maids as They Are] & [The] Bohemian Mother [See preface to this season.]	162.50
S. R. Scott's benefit	W. 9 Kairrissah & [The] H[aunte]d Inn [As Kairrissah. USG]	60.

[609]

T. 10 [The] Gambler's fate & [The]   45.
Turnpike Gate

Ticket Night   F. 11 F[rank Fox] Phipps, A[m-   110.
brose] Gwinnett & [Da-
mon and Pythias]
[See preface to this season.]

S. 12 Zembuca, Ode to La Fayette   210.
Mrs. Rowbotham's   & [The] F[orest] of Rosen-
ben[efi]t   wald
[As Ebra in *Zembuca*. USG
See preface to this season]

M. 14 Zembuca, [The]   Secret &   75.
D[eaf] as a post

T. 15 [The] Foundling of [the] for-   60.
est & [A] Mogul Tale

W. 16 Every one has his fault, [The]   195.
Pratt's benefit   Monody on La Fayette,
[& The] T[urnpike] Gate
[See preface to this sason.]

T. 17 G[retna] Green [The] Moun-   40.
taineers & 2 Strings to
Y[ou]r Bow

F. 18 Pizarro, popping the Question   240.
Mr. Rowbotham['s]   & [The] D[ay] after [the]
ben[efi]t   Wedding
[As Orozimbo in *Pizarro*
USG See preface to this
season.]

S. 19 [The] Poor Gentleman & [The]   140.
Hunter of [the] Alps

[PHILADELPHIA] SEASON[, COMMENCING AUGUST 23, ENDING OCTOBER 11,] 1834.

[Maywood & Co.]

PREFACE—**August 26:** USG announces that "Signor Diavolo Antonio will appear and go through his unrivaled exhibition on the Flying Rope." According to *Durang*, III, Chapter Thirty-Fifth, Diavolo Antonio "was admitted to have been the most surprising rope dancer in the world. His extraordinary exertions on the corde volante, in all the principal theatres on the continent, gained for him the title of the 'Little Devil' . . . He had three very small sons—he was a very small man himself, but well proportioned and studded with muscles—who went by the name of three young Diavolos, viz.: Antonio, Lorenzo and Augustus, the eldest of whom was only ten years of age." It has been advisable to delete ditto marks in Wood's entries of August 27, 28, 29 and 30 referring to Diavolo Antonio in his entry of August 26. **September 1:** USG announces, "For the benefit of Il Diavolo Antonio, on which occasion will be presented the miraculous evolutions on the Corde Volante and also the truly elegant performances of his sons, Antonio and Lorenzo, comprised in the most mangificent display of position in the science of gymnastics." **September 3, 8,** and **9:** According to USG, the "three Young Diavolos, Antonio, Lorenzo and Augustus, will go through their truly elegant display of position in the science of gymnastics under the direction of their father, Il Diavolo Antonio." It has been advisable to delete a notation, "Mrs. Francis died," which Wood has written to the left of the entry of September 29. As *Durang*, III, Chapter Thirty-Fifth, points out, "Maywood & Co. had become the lessees of the Chesnut and Arch Streets Theatres. The Walnut was now abandoned by that management and remained closed for a time." See the general introduction, p. 66.

Arch Street [Theatre]

August
    S. 23 Man & Wife & Simpson & Co. 250.

    M. 25 [The] School for Scandal & 225.
Miss Pelham   Fire & Water
               [As Lady Teazle in *The School for Scandal*. USG]

[611]

Miss Elphinstone Diavolo Antonio	T. 26 Romeo & Juliet, D[iavolo] Antonio & Popping the Question [Miss Elphinstone as Juliet. USG See preface to this season.]	275.

W. 27 [The] Stranger, Pringles & 240.

Miss Pelham

D[iavolo] Antonio

[As Mrs. Haller in *The The Stranger*. USG]

T. 28 Jane Shore, D]iavolo] Ant- 220.
[onio] & [A] Mogul Tale

F. 29 [The] Jealous Wife, D[iavolo] 175.
Anto[nio] & F[ortune's]
Frolic

S. 30 [The] P[oint] of Honor, D[ia- 260.
volo] Anto[nio] & [The]
Rendezvous

September

Benefit [of] M. 1 [The] Haunted Inn, [The] 200.
D[iavolo] Antonio H[unter] of [the] Alps,
D[iavolo] Anto[nio &
F[rank] F[ox] Fipps
[See preface to this season.]

T. 2 [The] Hunchback, A[ntonio] 260.
Diav[ol]o & F[rank] F[ox]
Fipps

W. 3 [The] Poor Gent[le]m[an], A[n- 220.
Mr. Burton's tonio] Diav[ol]o & [The]
1st app[ea]r[ance] L[ottery] Ticket
[As Ollapod in *The Poor
Gentleman* and Worm-
wood in *The Lottery
Ticket*. USG See pref-
ace to this season.]

Mr. Hunt's   T. 4 Rob Roy, [Macgregor] D[ia-   180.
1st app[ea]r[ance]   volo] Antonio & Matrimony
[As Francis Osbaldistone in
Rob Roy Macgregor. USG]

F. 5 [The] Hypocrite, D[iavolo]   210.
Anto[nio] & John Jones

S. 6 G[uy] Mannering & Popping   200.
the Question

Diavolos   M. 8 Paul Pry, Diavolos & Jno.   240.
Brown
[See preface to this season.]

T. 9 [The] Rendezvous, [The]   230.
3 Diavolos' Benefit   Housekeeper & F[or-
tune's] Frolic
[See preface to this season.]

W. 10 [The] Rivals & Jno. Brown   280.

T. 11 [The] D[evil's] Bridge & [The]   175.
Housekeeper

F. 12 [The] Soldier's Daughter &   200.
D[eaf] as a post

S. 13 Romeo & Juliet, [the] Y[oung]   210.
Diavolos & F[ortune's]
frolic

M. 15 Born to Good Luck, Simpson   510.
& Co. & [The] H[unter
of the] Alps

[613]

T. 16 M[ore] blunders than One, 470.
[The] I[rish] Tutor [& A]
M[ogul] Tale

W. 17 Much ado [about Nothing] & 110.
[The] Haunted Inn

T. 18 [The] I[rish] Ambassador, 480.
[The] I[rishman] in Lon-
don & [Mr. & Mrs.
Pringle]

F. 19 [She] Stoops to Conquer & 180.
L[ove], Law & Physic

S. 20 [The] Rivals & [The] Omnibus 685.

[Power]   M. 22 [The Nervous Man, Teddy 550.
the Tiler & The Midnight
Hour]
[As McShane in *The Nerv-
ous Man* and as Teddy.
USG]

[Power]   T. 23 John Bull, Jno. [Jones & The 310.
Rendezvous]
[As Dennis Brulgruddery in
John Bull. USG]

[Power]   W. 24 [Etiquette Run Mad, Paddy
Carey & Frank Fox
Phipps]
[As Captain Dennis O'More
in *Etiquette Run Mad* and
as Paddy Carey. USG]

[Power]   T. 25 [The Irish Ambassador, Monsieur Tonson & Fortune's
Frolic]

[As Sir Patrick in *The Irish Ambassador* and Monsieur Morbleu in *Monsieur Tonson*. USG]

[Power] F. 26 [St. Patrick's Eve, The Omnibus & Fire & Water]
[As Major O'Dogherty in *St. Patrick's Eve* and Pat Rooney in *The Omnibus*. USG]

[Power] S. 27 Born to Good Luck, T[eddy] 680. the Tiler & [The Midnight Hour]
[As Paudeen O'Rafferty in *Born to Good Luck* and as Teddy. USG]

Mrs. Austin M. 29 John of Paris, [Lovers' Quar- 340. rels] & [The Master's Rival]
[Mrs. Austin as the Princess of Navarre in *John of Paris*. USG]

T. 30 S[weethearts] & Wives & Po- 130. land & Liberty

October
" W. 1 [The] Tempest & L[ove,] 320. L[aw] & Physic
[Mrs. Austin as Ariel. USG]

" T. 2 [The] Beggar's Opera & D[eaf] 310. as a post
[Mrs. Austin as Polly Peachem in *The Beggar's Opera*. USG]

[615]

F. 3 [The] Busy Body & [The] 125.
    Master's Rival

Mrs. Austin's   S. 4 [The] Lord of the Manor & 470.
Ben[efi]t   Abon Hassan
     [As Annette in *The Lord of*
     the Manor and Zulima in
     Abon Hassan. USG]

J. Wallack   M. 6 Pizarro & Comfortable Lodg= 460.
     ings
     [As Rolla in *Pizarro.* USG]

"   T. 7 Hamlet & [The] Happiest day 310.
     of my life
     [Wallack as Hamlet. USG]

"   W. 8 [The] Wonder & [The] Rent 330.
     Day
     [Wallack as Don Felix in
     The Wonder. USG]

"   T. 9 Richard 3d. [& The] B[old] 280.
     Dragoons
     [Wallack as Richard. USG]

"   F. 10 Spring & Autumn, [The] 340.
     Ad[opted] Child & Po-
     land & Liberty
     [As Rattle in *Spring and*
     Autumn and Michael in
     The Adopted Child. USG]

S. 11 Pizarro & My Aunt
Wallack's Benefit   [As Rolla and as Dick
     Dashall in *My Aunt.*
     USG]

[616]

[PHILADELPHIA SEASON, COMMENCING] OCTOBER 13, 1834, [ENDING FEBRUARY 21, 1835.]

[Maywood & Co.]

PREFACE—October 14, 16, 18: *Durang*, III, Chapter Thirty-Seventh, states that Herr Cline's "astonishing performances on the elastic cord, on his first visit to this city, elicited the most enthusiastic applause." According to *Durang*, "Herr Cline's address and gentlemanly gracefulness on the rope was new to [the Philadelphia] audience, and was ever the theme of eulogy. He had nothing of the usual manner of that class of performers. He was highly polished in style and attitude. His pictorial display of the contending emotions of the human heart, as it was termed, illustrated by a series of pantomime action, combined with the copies of classical statues of ancient masters, was exceedingly well executed." See also November 1. It has been necessary to eliminate ditto marks in the entry of October 16 referring to "Herr Cline" in the entry of October 14 and to replace ditto marks in the entry of October 18 with the name of that player. **October 22:** In this entry Wood has also written "H. Cline" and, under "100£ Note," the notation "Ch[ange]d to [The] M[aster's] Rival." **October 29:** See October 14, 16, 18. **November 1:** In this entry Wood spells the name of the performer "Kline." According to USG, "Herr Kline will make an ascension propelling a wheelbarrow on a single rope from Stage to Gallery, will dance a pas de deux on Elastic Cord with his grandmother! &c. &c." **November 10 and 12:** For an account of Mathews' performances, see the general introduction, p. 43, and *Durang*, III, Chapter Thirty-Seventh. **November 17:** Under the titles in this entry Wood has written the notation, "Ch[ange]d from Mathews ill." USG announces Mathews' *Sketch Book for 1830* and *Before Breakfast*, in which he is to appear as Nicholas Trefoil. **November 21, 28, December 1, 3:** See references of November 10 and 12. **December 11:** It has been necessary to substitute "Miss S. Phillips, Miss Watson, Mr. Latham's" for three pairs of ditto marks in Wood's entry of this date referring to the names of those players in his entry of December 9. To the left of his entry of December 11 Wood has written what appears to be "H's Attempt." The allusion may be to Henry Hunt, the vocalist, who, according to *Durang*, III, Chapter Thirty-Eighth, sang with Miss Phillips, Miss Watson and Mr. Latham in an "intermezzo." **December 12:** It has been necessary to substitute "Miss Watson's" for ditto marks and Wood's entry referring to the notation "Miss

Watson" in his entry of December 9. USG also announces *The Merry Drummer Boy*, which Miss Watson is to sing, accompanied by herself on the drum; and a musical "mélange," in which Miss Watson, Miss Phillips and Latham are to sing. **December 13:** Pratt was a number of the firm of Maywood & Co. In this entry Wood has also written "Miss Jarman" and "Mr. Ternan." According to USG, Miss Jarman is to play Rosalind and Kate O'Brian in *Perfection*; Mr. Ternan, Jacques. **December 20, 22, 23, 24** and **27:** For the performances of Mlle. Celeste see *Durang*, III, Chapter Thirty-Ninth, and the Index to Players. In his entry of December 22, Wood has written, "W[alnut] S[treet] opened by Mr. Wemyss." For an explanation of this notation, see the general introduction, p. 66. **December 29:** USG announces Miss Phillips, "the celebrated tragic actress," as Mrs. Beverly in *The Gamester*. **January 17, 22, 23** and **26:** In the entry of January 12 Wood has also written 'Diav[olo] Anto[ni]o'" and, in the entry of January 13, ditto marks referring to the notation. For an account of Diavolo Antonio's performances consult the preface to the preceding season, August 26, September 1, 3, 8 and 9. **January 31:** It has been advisable to delete ditto marks in Wood's entry referring to the notation "Mrs. Austin" in the entry of January 29 and to replace them with the notation, "Mrs. Austin sick," which Wood has written under the titles of the plays. In this entry Wood has also written "Tempest" but crossed it out. USG announces Mrs. Austin as Ariel. **February 3:** See January 31. **February 4:** In this entry Wood has also written "Miss Jarman & Mr. T[ernan]" and "Mrs. Austin—Walton. Charges [$]250." USG announces Miss Jarman as Letitia Hardy, Ternan as Sir George Touchwood in *The Belle's Stratagem*, Mrs. Austin as the Princess of Navarre and Walton as John of Paris. **February 14:** USG announces the first and part of the second act of *The White Lady*, *Married Life* and the last act of *Luke the Labourer*. **February 19:** USG announces the bill of *Masaniello*, with Mrs. Austin as the Princess, the last act of *Cinderella*, with Mrs. Austin as Cinderella, and *The Master's Rival*. According to *Durang*, III, Chapter Thirty-Eighth, Mrs. Austin's benefit on February 16 "was a failure; and the managers, sympathising in [her] case, appropriated another night for her benefit."

In the entry of October 15 it has been necessary to substitute the names of the players for ditto marks in Wood's manuscript referring to "J. Wallack" and "Miss Phil[l]ips" in his entry of October 13; and to delete a notation "played Jacques," which Wood has written to the right of the ditto marks in his entry of November 5. It has also been necessary to substitute the name of the player for ditto marks in Wood's entries of November 26 and 28 referring to the notation "Mathews" in his entry of November 24; and to substitute the names of the players in Wood's entries of November 27 and 29 for ditto marks referring to "Miss Jarman & Mr. T[ernan]" in his entry of November 25. It has also been necessary to substitute names of players for ditto marks in Wood's entries of December 4, 5, 6, 10, January 30, February 7, 11, 12 and 13.

In Wood's entries of December 16, 17, 18 and 19, it has been advisable to substitute the title of the play for ditto marks referring to "French Spy" in the entry of December 15. It has been advisable also to delete a notation, "Robert Oliver died on Sunday 28 January, 1835," which Wood has written to the left of the entries of December 31 and January 1. *Durang*, III, Chapter Thirty-Eighth, records that the "Chesnut Street closed its season on Saturday, February 21st., 1835. . . . The corps thus evacuated 'Old Drury' and again resumed operations at the Arch Street Theatre."

[Chesnut Street Theatre]

[October]

J. Wallack   M. 13 Romeo & Juliet & [The] H[ap- 700.
  Miss Phil[l]ips   piest] day of my life
                  [Wallack as Romeo, Miss
                  Phillips as Juliet. USG]

Herr Cline   T. 14 F[rank] F[ox] Phipps, R[ay- 190.
               mond] & Agnes & [The]
               Spec[tre] Bridegroom
               [See preface to this season.]

[J. Wallack   W. 15 [The] Stranger & Popping the 660.
  Miss Phillips]   Question
               [Wallack as the Stranger,
               Miss Phillips as Mrs.
               Haller. USG]

          T. 16 [The] Man of the World, 180.
               H[err] Cline & 40 Winks
               [See preface to this season.]

[619]

"   "   F. 17 Venice Preserv'd & Turn Out   700.
            [Wallack as Pierre, Miss
            Phillips as Belvidera in
            Venice Preserved. USG]

[Herr Cline]   S. 18 [The] Gamester & Lock & Key   610.   3040.

            M. 20 Macbeth & 40 Winks   610.
J. Wallack &   [Wallack as Macbeth, Miss
    Miss Phil[l]ips   Phillips as Lady Mac-
                     beth. USG]

            T. 21 [The] S[chool] for Scandal &   740.
" Miss Phil[l]ips'   Cath[erine] & Petruchio
   benefit   [Wallack as Charles Sur-
                     face, Miss Phillips as
                     Lady Teazle in *The School
                     for Scandal.* Wallack as
                     Petruchio, Miss Phillips
                     as Katharine. USG]

            W. 22 [The] Wedding Gown*, H[err]   200.
                  Cline & [The] 100 £ Note
                  [See preface to this season.]

. "   "   T. 23 [The] Honey Moon & Lock &   550.
               Key
               [Wallack as Duke Aranza,
               Miss Phillips as Juliana
               in *The Honey Moon.*
               USG]

    "   F. 24 [The] Gamester, My Aunt &   1040.
Wallack's benefit   [The] Wedd[in]g Day
                     [Wallack as Beverly, Miss
                     Phillips as Mrs. Beverly
                     in *The Gamester.* Wal-
                     lack as Dick Dashall in
                     My Aunt Miss Phillips
                     as Lady Contest in *The
                     Wedding Day.* USG]

[620]

S. 25 [The] Wed[ding] Gown, Tam   260.
O'Shanter, H[err] Cline
[&] 40 Winks

M. 27 Virginius   &   C[omfortable]   510.
[J. Sheridan   Lodgings
Knowles]   [As Virginius. USG]

[Knowles]   T. 28 [The Hunchback & Deaf as a
Post]
[As Master Walter in *The
Hunchback*. USG]

[Herr Cline]   W. 29 [Rob Roy Macgregor & Popping the Question]
[See preface to this season.]

[Knowles]   T. 30 [Macbeth & The Chimney
Piece]
[As Macbeth. USG]

[Knowles]   F. 31 W[illia]m Tell & [The] 100 £   310.
Note
[As William Tell. USG]

November
S. 1 [The] B[ride] of Lammermoor,   630.
H. Kline's ben[efi]t   H. Kline [& The] Chim-
ney piece
[See preface to this season.]

Knowles   M. 3 [The] Hunchback & 40 Winks   290.
[As Master Walter in *The
Hunchback*. USG]

"   T. 4 [The] Wife & [The] Chimney   320.
piece
[Knowles   as   Julia   St.
Pierre in *The Wife*. USG]

[621]

"   W.   5   As you like it & [The] Mummy   670.
                     [Knowles as Jaques. USG]

"   T.   6   W[illia]m Tell & Comf[ortable]   200.
                     Lodgings
                     [Knowles as William Tell.
                     USG]

               F.   7   [The] Wife, [The] Smuggler &   510.
Knowles' ben[efi]t   [The] H[appiest] day of
                     my life
                     [As Julian St. Pierre. Also
                     to recite his tale of *The
                     Smuggler*. USG]

               S.   8   Esmeralda* & [The] Mummy   240.

Mathews   M.   10   Mathews' C[omic] Annual* &   1060.
                     M[onsieur] Tonson
                     [As Monsieur Tonson. USG
                     See   preface   to   this
                     season.]

               T.   11   Esmeralda & 40 Winks   175.

"   W.   12   M[athews']   Sketch   Book,   850.
                     before breakfast & [The]
                     Mummy
                     [Mathews as Nicholas Tre-
                     foil in *Before Breakfast*.
                     USG   See preface to this
                     season.]

               T.   13   [The] Rivals & [The] L[ottery]   110.
                     Ticket

"   F.   14   Mathews' C[omic] Annual [&]   520.
                     M[onsieur] Tonson
                     [Mathews   as   Monsieur
                     Morbleau   in   *Monsieur
                     Tonson*. USG]

Mr. Ternan   S. 15 Richard 3d. & [The] Man &   300.
[the] Tiger
[As Richard. USG]

Mathews ill   M. 17 [The] Rivals & [The] Chimney   90.
piece
[See preface to this season.]

     T. 18 R[omeo] & Juliet & [The] Man   510.
Miss Jarman's 1st.   & [the] Tiger
Mr. Ternan's 2d.   [Miss Jarman as Juliet,
Ternan as Romeo. USG]

"   W. 19 [The] Hunchback & [The]   550.
Mummy
[Ternan as Master Walter,
Miss Jarman as Julia in
The Hunchback. USG]

"   T. 20 [The] Stranger & [The] Bold   420.
dragoons
[Ternan as the Stranger,
Miss Jarman as Mrs.
Haller. USG]

Mathews   F. 21 Sketch Book, Before Break-   670.
fast & [40 Winks]
[As Nicholas Trefoil in
Before Breakfast. USG
See preface to this
season.]

"   S. 22 [The] School for Scandal &   610.
C[omfortable] Lodgings
[Ternan as Joseph Surface,
Miss Jarman as Lady
Teazle in *The School for
Scandal.* USG]

[623]

Mathews M. 24 [The] Poor Gentleman & [The] 425.
May Queen
[As Ollapod in *The Poor
Gentleman* and Caleb
Pipkin in *The May Queen.*
USG]

T. 25 Venice Preserv'd & [The] 460.
Miss Jarman & Happi[est] day of my life
Mr. T[ernan] [Miss Jarman as Belvidera,
Ternan as Jaffier in
Venice Preserved. USG]

[Mathews] W. 26 [The] Heir at Law & Mon- 380.
[sieur] Tonson
[Mathews as Dr. Pangloss
in *The Heir at Law* and
Monsieur Morbleau in
Monsieur Tonson. USG]

T. 27 [The] Wife & [The] Man & 560.
[Miss Jarman & [the] Tiger
Mr. Ternan.] [Miss Jarman as Mariana,
Ternan as Julian St. Pierre
in *The Wife.* USG]

[Mathews] F. 28 2 Vol[ume] of Comic Annual 350.
& [The] Lone House
[See preface to this season.]

S. 29 [The] Belle's Stratagem & 950. 3125.
[Miss Jarman & [The] Rent day
Mr. Ternan.] [Ternan as Sir George
Touchwood, Miss Jar-
man as Letitia Hardy in
The Belle's Stratagem.
Ternan as Martin Hey-
wood, Miss Jarman as
Rachel Heywood in *The
Rent Day.* USG]

[624]

December

Mathews	M.	1 [The] Sketch Book* & [The] May Queen [As Caleb Pipkin in *The May Queen*. USG See preface to this season.]	420.
Miss Phil[l]ips Mr. Latham	T.	2 Cinderella & [The Chimney Piece] [Miss Phillips as Cinderella, Latham as Dandini. USG]	450.
Mathews' Benefit	W.	3 [The] Youthful Days [of Mr. Mathews, The] Lone House & W[ays] & Means [As five characters in *The Lone House* and Sir David Dunder in *Ways and Means*. USG See preface to this season.]	920.
[Miss Phillips Mr. Latham] Miss Watson	T.	4 [The] Barber of Seville & Old & Young [Miss Phillips as Rosina, Latham as Figaro in *The Barber of Seville*. Miss Watson as the four Mowbrays in *Old and Young*. USG]	500.
[Miss Phillips Mr. Latham Miss Watson]	F.	5 [The] Marriage of Figaro & [The] Spoil'd Child [Miss Phillips as Susanna, Latham as Figaro, Miss Watson as Cherubino in *The Marriage of Figaro* and Little Pickle in *The Spoiled Child*. ADA]	460.

[625]

S. 6 Guy Mannering & Old & 480.
[Miss Phillips   Young
Mr. Latham   [Miss Phillips as Lucy Bert-
Miss Watson]   ram, Latham as Dandie
                           Dinmont, Miss Watson
                           as Julia Mannering and
                           as the four Mowbrays.
                           USG]

M. 8 [The] B[ride] of Lammermoor, 1150.
Mr. Maywood's   [The] W[edding] Day &
Ben[efit] Miss   John Jones
Jarman &   [Maywood as Caleb Balder-
Mr T[ern]an   stone, Miss Jarman as
                           Lucy Ashton, Ternan as
                           Edgar Ravenswood in
                           *The Bride of Lammer-
                           moor.* Miss Jarman as
                           Lady Contest in *The
                           Wedding Day.* USG]

T. 9 [The] M[arriage] of Figaro & 475.
Miss S. Phil[l]ips   Rosina
Miss Watson   [Miss Phillips as Susannah,
Mr. Latham   Miss Watson as Cherubin
                           and Latham as Figaro.
                           Miss Phillips as Rosina,
                           Miss Watson as William.
                           USG]

W. 10 Love in a Village & Charles 420.
[Miss S. Phillips']   Twelfth
Benefit   [Miss Phillips as Rosetta,
[Miss Watson   Miss Watson as Lucinda,
Mr. Latham]   Latham as Hawthorn in
                           Love in a Village. Latham
                           as Adam Brock in *Charles
                           the Twelfth.* USG]

[626]

T. 11 G[uy] Mannering, Concert & 325.
[Miss S. Phillips   [Old & Young]
Miss Watson   [Miss Phillips as Lucy Bert-
Mr. Latham's]   tram, Miss Watson as
Benefit   Julia Mannering, Latham
      as Dandie Dinmont in
      Guy Mannering. USG
      See preface to this
      season.]

W. 12 Charles 2d., [The] Sp[oil']d 610.
[Miss Watson's]   Child & J[ohn] Jones
Benefit   [As Mary Copp in *Charles
      the Second* and Little
      Pickle in *The Spoiled
      Child.* USG See preface
      to this season.]

Pratt's Benefit S. 13 As you Like it [&] Perfection 800.
      [See preface to this season.]

M. 15 [The] French Spy [&] 2 farces 610.
[Mademoiselle]   [As Mathilde de Meric in
Celeste   *The French Spy.* USG
      also announces *The Chim-
      ney Piece* and *Fire and
      Water.*]

"   T. 16 [The French Spy,] Matrimony 475.
      & [Popping the Question]
      [As Mathilde de Meric.
      Celeste also to dance.
      USG]

"   W. 17 [The French Spy, A] M[ogul] 400.
      Tale [&] J[ohn] Jones
      [See note, December 16.]

"   T. 18 [The French Spy,] A[nimal] 360.
      Magnetism & [The] Secret
      [See note, December 16.]

[627]

"   F. 19 [The French Spy, The Hap-   300.
                 piest Day of My Life &
                 Animal Magnetism]
                 [See note, December 16.]

            S. 20 [The] Wizard Skiff,* [The]   1320.   3465.
Celeste's Benefit   W[edding] Day, Dance &
                 [The] Mummy
                 [See preface to this season.]

Celeste   M. 22 [The] Wizard Skiff, 40 Winks 370.
                 [&] C[omfortable] Lodgings
                 [See preface to this season.]

"   T. 23 [The Wizard Skiff,] 25 John   350.
                 St[reet,] & D[eaf] as a post
                 [See preface to this season.]

"   W. 24 [The Wizard Shiff, The] Secret 300.
                 & [The] Man & [the] Tiger
                 [See preface to this season.]

        Xmas
"   T. 25 [The] Wept of Wish-ton-Wish, 600.
                 Dances, [23] John Street
                 & Turn Out
                 [Celeste as Hope Gough
                 and Maramattah in *The
                 Wept* and in Danse des
                 Folies. USG]

"   F. 26 [The Wept of Wish-ton-Wish,   340.
                 The] Secret & Love, Law
                 & Physic
                 [Celeste as Hope Gough and
                 Maramattah. USG]

            S. 27 [The Wept of Wish-ton-Wish,] 560.   2520.
"   Mad[ame]   John Jones & [The] Wiz-
Celeste's Benefit   ard Skiff
                 [See note, December 26 and
                 preface to this season.]

Miss P[hillips] not arrived.	M. 29 [The] Wonder & [The] Master's Rival [See preface to this season.]	50.

Miss Phil[l]ips	T. 30 [The] Gamester & [The] Mummy [As Mrs. Beverly in *The Gamester.* USG]	100.

Wood's benefit	W. 31 [The] Jealous Wife, Jno. Jones [&] 23 John St[reet] [Wood as Oakly, Miss Phillips as Mrs. Oakly in *The Jealous Wife.* USG]	714.50

1835. January

Miss Phil[l]ips	T. 1 Venice Preserved & [Esmeralda] [As Belvidera in *Venice Preserved.* USG]	110.

"	F. 2 [The] Stranger, & Comf[ortable] Lodgings [Miss Phillips as Mrs. Haller in *The Stranger.* USG]	115.

"	S. 3 [The] Wife & 40 Winks [Miss Phillips as Marianna in *The Wife.* USG]	100.	1199.50

Miss Phil[l]ips	M. 5 [The] Hunchback & [The] Wrong Box [As Julia in *The Hunchback.* USG]	110.

"	T. 6 Jane Shore & [The] Mummy [Miss Phillips as Jane Shore. USG]	80.

[629]

W. 7 Gustavus 3d. [& The] 90.
Haunted Inn

" T. 8 [The] Jealous Wife & [The] 80.
Sleeping Draught
[Miss Phillips as Mrs. Oakly
in *The Jealous Wife*.
USG]

F. 9 [The] Provok'd Husband, 250.
Miss Phi[l]lips' Matrimony & M[odern
Benefit Antiques
[As Lady Townly in *The
Provoked Husband* and
Clara in *Matrimony*.
USG]

S. 10 Gustavus 3d., [The] Secret & 180. 790.
John Jones

M. 12 Fazio, D[iavolo] Antonio & 140.
Miss E. Wheatley [The] Ladies' Man
[As Bianca in *Fazio*. USG]

T. 13 Gustavus 3d., D[iavolo] An- 240.
to[nio] & [My] Uncle John

" W. 14 Virginius, Diavolos & [The] 110.
Mr. Knowles Ladies' Man
[Miss Wheatley as Virginia,
Knowles as Virginius.
USG]

" " T. 15 [The] Hunchback [& My] 160.
Uncle John
[Miss Wheatley as Julia,
Knowles as Master
Walter in *The Hunch-
back*. USG]

[630]

" " F. 16 [The] Stranger, Diavolo [An- 90.
tonio] & [The] L[adies]
Man
[Miss Wheatley as Mrs.
Haller, Knowles as the
Stranger. USG]

D. Antonio's S. 17 Gustavus 3d. [&] Diavolos 320. 1060.
benefit [See preface to this season.]

M. 19 [The] Wife, Diavolo [Antonio] 220.
Miss Wheatley's & Cath[erine] & Petru-
benefit chio
[As Marianna in *The Wife*
and as Katherine. USG]

T. 20 [The] Blind Beggar of Beth- 250.
Miss Wheatley nal Green, Diavolos &
Mr. Knowles' [My Uncle John]
Benefit [Miss Wheatley as Bess and
Knowles as Lord Wilford
in *The Blind Beggar*.
USG]

W. 21 Wild Oats, Diavolos & Gus- 470.
Mr. Murdock's tavus [3d.]
Benefit [As Jack Rover in *Wild
Oats*. USG]

T. 22 [The] Blind Beggar [of Bethnal 120.
[Miss Wheatley] Green,] Diavo[los] & Uncle
Thomas
[As Bess in *The Blind Beg-
gar*. USG] See preface
to this season.]

F. 23 [The] Blind Beggar [of Bethnal 200.
" Mr. Green,] Diav[olos] & [The
Knowles' benefit Review]

[631]

[Miss Wheatley as Bess,
Mr. Knowles as Lord
Wilford in *The Blind Beggar* and Looney Mact-
wolter in *The Review.*
USG] See preface to this
season.]

Mr. Knowles	S. 24	W[illia]m Tell, Diavolos & Gustavus [3d.] [As William Tell. USG]	140.	1400.
Young Diavolos' benefit	M. 26	Wild Oats, Diavolos & Kill or Cure [See preface to this season.]	120.	
	T. 27	[The] Point of Honor & Gustavus [3d.]	100.	
Miss Jarman Mr. Ternan	W. 28	As You Like it & Kill or Cure [Miss Jarman as Rosalind, Ternan as Jaques. USG]	270.	
Mrs. Austin	T. 29	Cinderella & John Jones [As Cinderella. USG]	250.	
[Miss Jarman Mr. Ternan]	F. 30	Wives as they Were [& Maids as They Are] & No Song No Supper [Miss Jarman as Miss Dorillon in *Wives as They Were.* USG]	200.	
Mrs. Austin sick.	S. 31	Gustavus 3d. & Luke the Labourer [See preface to this season.]	140.	1080.

February

Miss Jarman Mr. Ternan	M. 2	[A] Bold Stroke for a husband [&] Modern Antiques	250.	

[Miss Jarman as Donna
Olivia, Ternan as Don
Carlos in *A Bold Stroke
for a Husband*. USG]

Mrs. Austin sick   T. 3 [The] Wedding Gown & Gus-   120.
tavus 3d.
[See preface to this season.]

Benefit of   W. 4 [The] Belle's Stratagem, Dia-   942.
disabled firemen   volos & John of Paris
[See preface to this season.]

Mrs. Austin   T. 5 [The] White Lady* & [The   230.
Walton   Lady's Man]
[Mrs. Austin as Louise,
Walton as Gaveston in
The White Lady. USG]

Miss J[arman] F. 6 Fazio & Perfection   220.
& Mr. T[ernan]   [Miss Jarman as Bianca in
Fazio and Kate O'Brien
in *Perfection*. Ternan as
Fazio. USG]

[Mrs Austin   S. 7 [The] White Lady & [The]   240.   2002.
Walton]   Mummy
[Mrs. Austin as Louise,
Walton as Gaveston in
The White Lady. USG]

Miss J[arman] M. 9 [The] Winter's Tale & Kill or   170.
& Mr. T[ernan]   Cure
[Miss Jarman as Hermione,
Mr. Ternan as Leontes.
USG]

Mrs. Austin Walton   T. 10 [The] White Lady & [John   200.
Jones]

[633]

[Mrs. Austin as Louise,
Walton as Gaveston in
The White Lady. USG]

[Miss Jarman W. 11 All in the Wrong & [The] 230.
Mr. Ternan] Sleeping Draught
[Miss Jarman as Lady Rest-
less, Ternan as Sir John
Restless in *All in the
Wrong*. USG]

[Mrs. Austin T. 12 Married Life & [The] White 220.
Walton] Lady
[Mrs. Austin as Louise,
Walton as Gaveston in
The White Lady. USG]

[Miss Jarman F. 13 [The] Soldier's Daughter & 190.
Mr. Ternan] Clari
[Miss Jarman as the Widow
Cheerly in *The Soldier's
Daughter* and as Clari.
Ternan as Rolamo in
Clari. USG]

S. 14 2 Acts [of The] White Lady, 200. 1210.
Walton's Benefit Married Life & 1st. Act
[of] Luke the Labourer
[As George Brown in *The
White Lady* and Phillip
in *Luke the Labourer*.
USG   See preface to this
season.]

M. 16 [The] Tempest & Abon 250.
Mrs. Austin's Hassan
Benefit [Mrs. Austin as Ariel and
as Zulima in *Abon Has-
san*. USG]

T. 17 Married Life & Gustavus 3d.　60.

Miss Jarman's
benefit

W. 18 All in the Wrong & Turn Out　780.
　　　 [As Lady Restless in *All in
　　　　the Wrong* and Marian
　　　　Ramsey in *Turn Out.*
　　　　USG]

Mrs. Austin's
2d. Ben[efit]

T. 19 3[rd.] Act [of] Cinderella, 2[nd.　250.
　　　 &] 3[rd. Act of The]
　　　 Tempest & [The] M[ast-
　　　 er's] Rival
　　　 [See preface to this season.]

Miss J[arman] &
Mr. T[ernan]

F. 20 [The] Soldier's Daughter &　240.
　　　 [The] Rent day
　　　 [Miss Jarman as the Widow
　　　 Cheerly in *The Soldier's
　　　 Daughter* and Rachel
　　　 Heywood, with Ternan
　　　 as Martin Heywood, in
　　　 The Rent Day. USG

Mr. Ternan's
Benefit

S. 21 Fazio & [The] Young Widow　670.　　2250.
　　　 [As Fazio and as Mande-
　　　 ville in *The Young
　　　 Widow.* USG]

INDEX TO PLAYS

The letters used as symbols, which indicate classifications of the period, are as follows: *B* for Ballet, *Bur.* for Burletta, *C* for Comedy, *CO* for Comic Opera, *E* for Entertainment, *F* for Farce, *H* for Historical Play, *M* for Melodrama, *MD* for Musical Drama, *MF* for Musical Farce, *O* for Opera, *P* for Pantomime, *R* for Recitation and *T* for Tragedy. Special identifications are made in the cases of plays for which no classifications are available. In the advertisements of the period, the "dramas," evidently serious plays with happy endings, include the following: *Esmeralda, Eugene Aram* (a dramatization of a novel), *The Field of Forty Footsteps, Gabinski, Humphrey Clinker* (another dramatization of a novel), *The Hunchback* (by Knowles), *Jack Robinson, The May Queen, The Miller's Maid, The Mutiny at the Nore, The North American, The Pirate, The Point of Honor, The Press Gang, Rip Van Winkle, The Wanderer, The Water Witch, The Whistler, The Wife,* and *Wreck Ashore.* Asterisks are used, as they are in the text of Wood's diary, to signify first performances in the city.

ALEXANDRIA

Adelgitha (*T*): 1816, Sept. 2.

Africans, The (*MD*): 1810, Aug. 6.

Agreeable Surprize, The (*CO*): 1810, Sept. 22.

Battle of Hexham, The (*H*): 1816, Sept. 12.*

Beehive, The (*CO*): 1815, Sept. 7.*

Blind Boy, The (*M*): 1810, Aug. 28.*

Blue Beard (*M*): 1810, Sept. 4.

Bold Stroke for a Husband, A (*C*): 1815, Sept. 23.*

Budget of Blunders, A (*F*): 1815, Aug. 29.

Caravan, The (*M*): 1810, Sept. 6.*

Columbus (*H*): 1810, Sept. 6.

Day after the Wedding, The (*C*): 1816, Sept. 5.

Deaf Lover, The (*F*): 1810, Sept. 1.

Don Juan (*P*): 1810, Sept. 15.

Ella Rosenberg (*M*): 1810, Aug. 23.*

Every One Has His Fault (*C*): 1815, Sept. 21.

Exile, The (*M*): 1815, Aug. 26, Sept. 12.

Forest of Bondy, The (*M*): 1816, Sept. 3,* 10.

Fortune of War, The (*F*): 1816, Sept. 14.

Fortune's Frolic (*F*): 1810, Aug. 11.

Forty Thieves, The (*M*): 1810, Aug. 28, Sept. 11.

Foundling of the Forest, The (*M*): 1810, Aug. 25,* 30; 1816, Sept. 24.

George Barnwell (*T*): 1810, Sept. 20.

Half an Hour after Supper (*F*): 1810, Aug. 30.*

[637]

BALTIMORE

June 30; 1821, May 21; 1822, Sept. 28; 1823, May 7, June 2.

Dead Alive, The (*MF*): 1821, May 9, June 8; 1822, June 17, Nov. 1; 1823, May 31, Oct. 14.

Deaf and Dumb (*H*): 1819, May 31.

Deaf Lover, The (*F*): 1812, April 11; 1821, May 2, June 9.

Death of Life in London, The ("operatic parody"): 1823, Oct. 14,* 18.

Debtor and Creditor (*C*): 1815, Nov. 10,* 13.

De Montfort (*T*): 1810, Nov. 12.*

Deserted Daughter, The (*C*): 1810, Nov. 7; 1812, May 15.

Deuce Is in Him, The (*F*): 1817, Oct. 6.*

Devil's Bridge, The (*O*): 1818, May 29,* 30, June 8, 19; 1822, May 8; 1823, Nov. 14.

Devil to Pay, The (*MF*): 1812, May 18; 1813, Nov. 13; 1815, Nov. 18; 1816, May 29, Nov. 13; 1817, June 18, Nov. 15; 1820, June 26; 1821, May 18, Nov. 2; 1822, June 5; 1823, Nov. 3.

Distressed Mother, The (*T*): 1810, Oct. 10; 1823, May 12, Oct. 6.

Don Juan (*P*): 1810, Oct. 13; 1811, May 20; 1813, Oct. 13.

Doubtful Son, The ("melodramatic comedy"): 1811, May 25,* 29.

Douglas, (*T*): 1812, April 20; 1815, Oct. 23; 1822, Oct. 18; 1823, Oct. 25.

Dramatist, The (*C*): 1810, Oct. 31; 1813, June 8; 1815, June 9; 1816, Nov. 15; 1823, May 5.

Duenna, The (*CO*): 1818, June 15.

Education (*C*): 1814, April 20,* 25, May 6.

Ella Rosenberg (*M*): 1810, Nov. 3; 1811, May 15; 1812, June 6; 1813, June 4; 1815, May 17, Nov. 11; 1816, June 12; 1817, Nov. 24; 1819, May 26; 1820, Sept. 22; 1821, June 11; 1822, May 30; 1823, Oct. 23.

Elopement, The (*P*): 1812, May 11.

Enterprize, The (*MD*): 1822, May 27,* June 14.

Ethiop, The (*M*): 1814, Nov. 18, 19, 21; 1815, May 1; 1817, Oct. 8.

Every One Has His Fault (*C*): 1812, May 25; 1813, June 2; 1815, April 29; 1820, April 28; 1823, Oct. 30.

Exchange No Robbery (*C*, adaptation of He Would be a Soldier?): 1821, June 15.*

Exile, The (*M*): 1814, May 18,* 20, 23, 25, June 10, Nov. 14, 16; 1815, May 13, Oct. 7, 21, Nov. 8; 1816, May 4; 1818, Sept. 18, Oct. 12; 1819, May 17.

Fair American, The (*C*): 1817, Nov. 26;* 1818, May 4, 18, Sept. 21; 1820, May 8; 1821, Oct. 13; 1823, Sept. 29.

Faithful Slave, The (*O?*): 1818, May 11.

Falls of Clyde, The (*M*): 1820, April 8,* 14, 22, Sept. 27; 1822, May 6.

Family Legend, The (*H*): 1816, June 7.*

Farmer, The (*CO*): 1816, July 1; 1817, Nov. 24.

Farmer's Wife, The (*MD*): 1816, June 10.*

Fazio (*T*): 1819, June 14;* 1820, April 19.

Fire and Water (*F*): 1823, May 10,* 19, Sept. 24.

Follies of a Day, The (*C*): 1816, June 1; 1820, June 28; 1821, Oct. 19.

Fontainbleau (*CO*): 1822, May 29.

Forest of Bondy, The (*M*): 1816, May 29,* 31, June 1; 1818, May 11; 1819, May 7.

Forest of Hermanstadt, The (*M*): 1814, May 9,* 1815, June 3.

Fortress, The (*M*): 1814, May 27, Oct. 12; 1815, Oct. 27; 1816, May 22.

Fortune of War, The (*F*): 1816, May 8,* 11; 1820, May 1.

Fortune's Frolic (*F*): 1811, June 8; 1813, Nov. 16; 1814, Oct. 14; 1815, May 5; 1816, Nov. 6; 1821, May 4; 1822, May 4.

PHILADELPHIA

[655]

1815, March 11; 1817, April 12; 1818, March 19; 1820, Feb. 14, Nov. 15; 1821, July 6; 1823, Feb. 24, March 19; 1828, April 19; 1831, April 21, June 21.

Robber of Genoa, The (P): 1813, Dec. 11;* 1814, April 6.

Robbers, The (T): 1811, Feb. 15, April 24; 1812, Jan. 4; 1813, Jan. 23, Feb. 3, Dec. 18; 1814, Dec. 3; 1815, Dec. 11; 1817, Feb. 8; 1818, Feb. 28, Nov. 16; 1819, Oct. 9; 1821, Jan. 3, Dec. 24; 1822, April 3; 1823, Jan. 4; 1828, Oct. 23, 28, Nov. 20; 1831, Oct. 14, Nov. 5, Dec. 8; 1833, Jan. 12, Feb. 5; 1834, Feb. 26.

Robbers Tableau, The: 1832, Oct. 13.

Robber's Wife, The (M): 1834, Jan. 26, 27, May 20.

Robin Hood (CO): 1817, April 7; 1822, April 10.

Robinson Crusoe (M): 1820, Feb. 22,* 23, March 17.

Rob Roy Macgregor (MD): 1819, Jan. 1,* 2, 6, Oct. 2, Nov. 6, Dec. 6; 1820, March 8 (postponed), 22, Nov. 25, Dec. 9; 1821, July 13, Nov. 17, Dec. 1, 11; 1822, Feb. 20, April 22, Dec. 24; 1823, Feb. 15, March 5; 1827, Nov. 15, Dec. 20; 1828, Nov. 12; 1831, July 12, Sept. 3, Oct. 17, 26, Dec. 2, 28; 1832, May 11, July 14, Oct. 3; 1833, Feb. 23, Oct. 19; 1834, Feb. 20, Sept. 4, Oct. 29.

Rock of Charbonnière, The (as announced by ADA): 1828, July 9, 10, 11.

Rokeby (M): 1816, Dec. 21.*

Roland for an Oliver, A (C): 1819, Dec. 3;* 1820, Feb. 23, March 15; 1823, April 14; 1827, Nov. 8; 1830, Dec. 13; 1833, April 18, 23.

Roman Actor, The (T): 1831, April 16.

Roman Father, The (T): 1811, Jan. 16.

Romeo and Juliet (T): 1810, Dec. 15; 1811, Oct. 23, 30; 1812, Jan. 24, Nov. 25; 1813, Nov. 27; 1815, Jan. 9, Feb.

18, Nov. 4; 1816, March 16, Dec. 6; 1818, Feb. 21, Dec. 14; 1819, Jan. 25; 1821, Feb. 21, Dec. 31; 1827, Oct. 29, Dec. 15; 1828, May 27, Nov. 17; 1831, Sept. 21, Oct. 5; 1832, Oct. 1, 15, Nov. 3, Dec. 5; 1833, March 7, Dec. 30; 1834, June 4, Aug. 26, Sept. 13, Oct. 13, Nov. 18.

Romp, The (F): 1813, Feb. 24; 1815, Dec. 1; 1816, Feb. 16; 1818, April 25; 1819, April 3, Oct. 15; 1821, Feb. 12, Dec. 7; 1823, April 2; 1827, Nov. 2, Dec. 4; 1828, Jan. 5, Feb. 29, March 31, April 28, June 5, 13; 1830, Dec. 22; 1831, May 20, 31; 1834, June 13.

Rose d' Amour (B): 1832, Dec. 31; 1833, Jan. 1, April 10, 16.

Roses and Thorns (C): 1831, June 7.*

Rosina (MF): 1816, March 11, April 15, Nov. 25; 1817, Dec. 8, 19; 1820, Nov. 13; 1827, Oct. 30, Dec. 14, 24; 1828, March 25; 1830, Oct. 20; 1832, Jan. 2; 1834, March 22, Dec. 9.

Ruffian Boy, The (M): 1820, March 8 (postponed), 22,* 27, Dec. 2, 6, 27; 1821, Nov. 23.

Rugantino (M): 1822, April 12.

Rule a Wife and Have a Wife (C): 1811, Oct. 12; 1812, Jan. 10, Oct. 12; 1813, Jan. 27; 1814, Jan. 14; 1815, Feb. 1; 1816, Feb. 2; 1817, Jan. 31; 1821, Jan. 24; 1823, Feb. 14; 1830, Oct. 26; 1831, April 27; 1834, March 11, June 3.

Rumfustian (?): 1831, July 13.

Rural Grace (B): 1813, Feb. 15.

Russian Imposter, The (O): 1822, March 25,* 27, 30.

Sailor's Daughter, The (C): 1813, March 19.

St. Patrick's Day (see The Scheming Lieutenant.)

St. Patrick's Eve (T): 1833, Dec. 4,* 6, 7, 9; 1834, Jan. 28, Feb. 1, May 13, 23, June 20, Sept. 26.

Sleepwalker, The (F): 1813, March 10,*
12, April 21, Nov. 29, Dec. 10; 1814,
Jan. 17, March 4, Dec. 9; 1815, Feb.
10; 1817, April 5; 1818, Jan. 19; 1823,
Feb. 26; 1828, Feb. 19, March 29, Nov.
14, Dec. 1; 1830, Nov. 18, 24; 1831,
Jan. 5, Feb. 3, 21, July 7, Aug. 29,
Oct. 7, 15, Dec. 5; 1832, Jan. 3, July
25.

Smuggler, The (R): 1834, Nov. 7.

Snakes in the Grass (C): 1831, Oct. 27;
1833, Feb. 8.

Snowstorm, The (M): 1818, March 23,*
27, April 1, 4, Nov. 9, Dec. 4; 1819,
Oct. 8; 1822, April 8.

Soldier's Daughter, The (C): 1811, Sept.
11; 1812, Jan. 6, March 13, Sept. 28;
1814, Feb. 22; 1816, Feb. 9, Dec. 23;
1819, Oct. 23; 1820, March 27; 1822,
Dec. 9; 1828, March 12, Oct. 7, 27;
1831, Feb. 5; 1833, May 10, July 8;
1834, Sept. 12; 1835, Feb. 13, 20.

Soldier's Return, The (O): 1814, April 9.

Songs: 1828, May 27, June 4; 1832,
Sept. 29; 1834, April 26, May 10.

Sons of Erin, The (C): 1812, Nov. 9,*
13, Dec. 14; 1814, March 18.

Spanish Barber, The (CO): 1811, March
1, 15; 1814, Feb. 8, March 16; 1816,
Jan. 17; 1818, March 23.

Spectre Bridegroom, The (F): 1831,
June 25, July 5, Sept. 15; 1832, Jan.
14, 16, 21, March 3, May 5,
16, 24, 31, June 9, Sept. 10, Oct. 4,
18, Dec. 21; 1833, Jan. 15, Feb. 20,
April, 12, June 27, July 11, Sept. 3;
1834, Jan. 1, Feb. 18, May 15, June 24,
July 3, Oct. 14.

Speed the Plough (C): 1810, Dec. 8;
1811, Sept. 14, Dec. 24; 1813, Jan. 30;
1814, Dec. 28; 1815, March 27, Dec.
29; 1816, April 13, Dec. 30; 1817,
April 19; 1818, March 7, Dec. 29;
1819, Dec. 31 (postponed); 1820,
Feb. 5; 1821, March 10; 1822, Jan.
19; 1823, April 23; 1828, Dec. 17;

1831, Jan. 4, Nov. 11, 17; 1832, Jan.
24; 1833, Jan. 11, May 3, Dec. 19.

Spoiled Child, The (F); 1811, Jan. 28,
April 10; 1815, April 11; 1816, Feb.
9, 19, March 9, Dec. 2, 20; 1818,
Jan. 24, Dec. 9; 1820, March 3; 1821,
March 30, July 9, Nov. 15; 1822, Dec.
6, 20; 1823, Jan. 16, Feb. 3, 17; 1827,
Nov. 1; 1828, Jan. 7, Feb. 27, June
11, July 18; 1831, April 12, June 23,
Sept. 21; 1832, Jan. 9, Feb. 24, March
16, 28, April 27, June 27; 1833, April
3, Sept. 2, 5; 1834, Dec. 5, 12.

Sprigs of Laurel (see The Rival Soldiers).

Spring and Autumn (C): 1832, Nov. 3,
Dec. 1; 1834, Oct. 10.

Spy, The (H): 1822, April 23,* 26, Dec.
26; 1828, Dec. 13; 1833, Jan. 8.

State Secrets (?): 1831, July 14.

Steward, The (C): 1820, Dec. 8;* 1821,
March 17.

Stories: 1828, Jan. 2.

Stranger, The (C): 1811, Jan. 4,* Feb.
23, Sept. 30, Dec. 7; 1812, Oct. 2, Dec.
28; 1814, Feb. 2; 1815, March 17,
Dec. 20; 1817, March 24; 1818, March
4, Nov. 26; 1819, Feb. 25, Oct. 8; 1821,
March 3; 1827, Dec. 8; 1828, Jan. 3,
Feb. 7; 1830, Nov. 2; 1831, March 1,
April 12, May 24; 1832, Oct. 22, Dec.
8, 22; 1833, Jan. 26, March 22, June
12, Oct. 23; 1834, May 28, Aug. 27,
Oct. 15, Nov. 20; 1835, Jan. 2, 16.

Students of Salamanca, The (C): 1815,
Jan. 16,* 18.

Such Things Are (C): 1813, Jan. 8; 1823,
March 27.

Sultan, The (F): 1810, Dec. 5, 17; 1812,
Dec. 9; 1815, March 22; 1816, March
16; 1818, Feb. 11; 1819, Jan. 20.

Surrender of Calais, The (H): 1811,
March 2; 1817, April 7; 1818, Feb. 23.

Suspicious Husband, The (C): 1817,
Feb. 24, March 5; 1831, Jan. 10,
March 4.

Sweethearts and Wives (C): 1828, Oct.
2, 8, Nov. 18; 1831, Jan. 5, Feb. 8,

Wept of Wish-ton-Wish, The (*T*): 1831, April 18, 29, 20, Miantonimoh, May 23; The Wept, 1834, Dec. 25, 26, 27.

Werner (*T*): 1831, April 4, 6; 1834, April 29.

West Indian, The (*C*): 1811, Oct. 14; 1813, Feb. 26; 1815, Jan. 11, Nov. 27; 1817, March 29, Dec. 29; 1819, March 31; 1820, Feb. 11; 1821, Nov. 13; 1833, July 24, Sept. 27.

What Next? (*F*): 1817, March 26.*

Wheel of Fortune, The (*C*): 1811, Feb. 25, Oct. 25, Nov. 15; 1813, Feb. 1, April 23; 1814, Jan. 29; 1816, April 16; 1817, Feb. 17; 1819, Feb. 5; 1833, April 10.

Where Shall I Dine? (*F*): 1820, Jan. 1,* 3, 8, 22, Feb. 7, Nov. 17, Dec. 15; 1821, Jan. 10, Nov. 26; 1822, Dec. 4; 1827, Nov. 13; 1828, March 25, May 6; 1831, Jan. 14, April 1.

Where to Find a Friend (*C*): 1818, Nov. 18,* Dec. 5; 1820, Feb. 16.

Which is the Man? (*C*): 1816, March 23.

Whims of a Comedian, The (*E*): 1828, Oct. 9, 11.

Whirligig Hall (*E*): 1831, Nov. 8, 17; 1832, July 28; 1833, Jan. 14, Dec. 16.

Whistler, The (drama): 1834, April 15,* 17, June 14.

White Lady, The (*O*): 1835, Feb. 5,* 7, 10, 12, 14.

Who's the Dupe? (*F*): 1811, Jan. 12, Nov. 29; 1814, March 12; 1815, March 1; 1821, March 28; 1822, Dec. 27; 1823, Jan. 18.

Who Wants a Guinea? (*C*): 1815, Jan. 25, 28, March 6; 1818, April 17, Nov. 14; 1823, March 1; 1828, Dec. 19, 20.

Who's Who? (*F*): 1819, March 31,* April 5, 12, Oct. 6, 20; 1820, March 10; 1828, April 11, 29, May 5, June 19.

Who Wins? (*CO*): 1810, Dec. 14.

Widow's Vow, The (*F*): 1814, March 28; 1815, Jan. 9, 27; 1816, Jan. 29.

Wife, The (drama): 1833, Oct. 28, 30,

Nov. 1, Dec. 23; 1834, Nov. 4, 7, 27; 1835, Jan. 3, 19.

Wild Oats (*C*): 1813, March 12,* 17, April 5, Dec. 29; 1814, Dec. 7; 1816, Feb. 26, Dec. 27; 1817, Dec. 31; 1818, Dec. 8 (no performance), 30; 1820, March 11, Nov. 10; 1821, Nov. 21; 1822, Dec. 18; 1823, March 7, 24; 1835, Jan. 21, 26.

Will, The (*C*): 1810, Dec. 19; 1816, Feb. 16; 1817, Jan. 10; 1821, Feb. 19; 1828, Feb. 20, Nov. 24; 1831, Jan. 27, Sept. 23; 1832, June 8.

William Tell (*H*): 1812, Dec. 26;* 1813, Dec. 31; 1823, Feb. 22; 1827, Nov. 7, 10, 28; 1828, Jan. 8, March 4; 1830, Dec. 13; 1831, March 31, July 11; 1832, Feb. 28, May 31; 1833, May 7, July 9, Nov. 21; 1834, April 17, Oct. 31, Nov. 6; 1835, Jan. 24.

William Thomson (*F*): 1832, May 7, 11, 30; 1833, Feb. 11, May 24; 1834, Jan. 11, May 20, June 3, 27.

Winning a Husband (*F*): 1828, March 10, 14, 21, Nov. 24; 1830, Oct. 21, Seven's the Main, 26; Winning a Husband, 1832, June 12.

Winter's Tale, The (tragicomedy): 1835, Feb. 9.

Wives as They Were and Maids as They Are (*C*): 1812, Jan. 17; 1813, Nov. 26; 1828, Feb. 8, March 21, Oct. 17, Nov. 15; 1830, Oct. 22; 1831, Jan. 20, Feb. 17; 1832, Jan. 9, June 14; 1834, July 8; 1835, Jan. 30.

Wizard Skiff, The (*M*): 1834, Dec. 20,* 22, 23, 24, 27.

Wolf and the Lamb, The (*C*): 1833, Dec. 3.

Wonder, The (*C*): 1811, Dec. 6; 1812, Nov. 21; 1813, Dec. 1; 1816, Feb. 10; 1817, Jan. 6; 1819, Jan. 23; 1820, Nov. 22; 1821, Feb. 5; 1827, Nov. 8; 1828, Feb. 2, Oct. 18, Dec. 8; 1830, Nov. 1; 1831, Feb. 18, 21; 1832, Dec. 19, 29; 1833, March 19, Oct. 24; 1834, June 6, Oct. 8, Dec. 29.

Wood Demon, The (*M*): 1823, Jan. 1, 6, 13.

Woodsman's Hut, The (*M*): 1816, Dec. 26,* 27, 28, 30; 1817, March 14.

Woodstock (dramatization of Scott's): 1833, July 6.

Wreck Ashore (drama): 1831, Sept. 1, 9.

Wrong Box, The (*E?*): 1835, Jan. 5.

Wyandot Indians (E by): 1818, Dec. 12.

XYZ (*F*): 1831, Jan. 3, 12.

Yankee in England, The (*C*): 1830, Dec. 22.

Yankee Story (*E*): 1833, Feb. 27.

York and Lancaster (*F*): 1833, May 4.*

Young Hussar (*MD*): 1832, Oct. 5; 1833, Feb. 23.

Young Widow, The (*F*): 1827, Oct. 31, Nov. 7, 14; 1828, March 5, Nov. 25, 28; 1830, Oct. 18, Dec. 3; 1831, July 28, Sept. 14; 1832, Jan. 14, Feb. 17, May 4; 1835, Feb. 21.

Youthful Days of Mr. Mathews, The (*E*): 1823, March 21,* 26; 1834, Dec. 3.

Youth, Love and Folly (*MD*): 1830, Nov. 8, 10.

Youth's Errors (*C*): 1811, Dec. 13.*

Yusef Caramalli (see Usef Caramalli).

Zembuca (*M*): 1816, Jan. 1,* 3, 5, 6, 8, 10, 12, 15, Feb. 23, March 18, Nov. 30; 1817, Feb. 22, Dec. 24; 1818, Dec. 23; 1819, Jan. 1, Oct. 23; 1831, June 11, 17; 1834, July 12, 14.

Zorinski (*MD*): 1815, March 31.

WASHINGTON

Abaellino (*T*): 1810, June 21; 1812, Aug. 4; 1815, July 20; 1817, July 15; 1821, Sept. 29.

Adelgitha (*T*): 1813, Aug. 28;* 1816, Aug. 13; 1818, March 6.

Adeline (*M*): 1823, July 29.*

Adelmorn (*M*): 1815, July 25.

Adopted Child, The (*MD*): 1812, June 28; 1813, Sept. 13; 1821, Sept. 15, 20.

Adrian and Orrilla ("sentimental"): 1814, June 16.

Africans, The (*MD*): 1810, July 30.

Agreeable Surprize, The (*CO*): 1810, July 9; 1813, July 5; 1814, Aug. 4; 1817, Aug. 15; 1818, Aug. 18; 1821, Sept. 18; 1824, Sept. 1, 15.

Aladdin (*M*): 1817, Aug. 19, 21, 24.

Alexander the Great (*T*): 1813, July 10;* 1814, July 23; 1822, Aug. 31.

All the World's a Stage (*CO*): 1813, June 22.

American Captive, The (*F*): 1818, Feb. 23.

Anatomist, The (*F*): 1818, Aug. 8.*

Animal Magnetism (*F*): 1814, Aug. 9.

Apostate, The (*T*): 1818, Jan. 30; 1823, June 28.

As You Like It (*C*): 1815, Aug. 12

Barbarossa (*T*): 1815, June 20.

Battle of Hexham, The (*H*): 1816, Aug. 8.*

Bee Hive, The (*CO*): 1813, June 19,* July 10; 1814, July 30.

Bellamira (*T*): 1818, Aug. 20.*

Belle's Stratagem, The (*C*): 1818, Feb. 19.

Belles Without Beaux (*F*): 1821, Aug. 11.*

Bertram (*T*): 1817, July 24, 29; 1818, Jan. 27; 1822, Aug. 27.

Birthday, The (*C*): 1813, June 15; 1817, July 12; 1822, July 20; 1824, Sept. 1.

Blind Boy, The (*M*): 1810, July 4;* 1813, June 19; 1817, Sept. 23; 1823, Sept. 13.

Blue Beard (*M*): 1810, July 12, 26; 1813, Sept. 2; 1815, Aug. 12; 1817, Sept. 2.

Blue Devils, The (*F*): 1818, Aug. 29;* 1823, Aug. 21; 1824, Sept. 10, Oct. 5.

[679]

School of Reform, The (C): 1813, Sept. 6; 1815, June 22; 1818, Feb. 12.

Scotch Ghost, The (B): 1821, Aug. 14; 1824, Sept. 20.

Sea-Side Story, The ("musical"): 1810, July 23.

She Stoops to Conquer (C): 1812, Aug. 10; 1816, Aug. 1; 1817, Sept. 4; 1818, Feb. 16; 1821, Aug. 8; 1822, Sept. 14.

She Would be a Soldier (H): 1821, Aug. 16;* 1822, Aug. 17; The Plains of Chippewa, 1824, Sept. 22.

Shipwreck, The (CO): 1810, June 23; 1815, July 6; 1816, Aug. 13.

Short Reign and a Merry One, A (C): 1821, Aug. 14.*

Sleepwalker, The (F): 1813, June 24;* 1818, Feb. 6.

Snow Storm, The (M): 1818, July 28,* Aug. 1.

Soldier's Daughter, The (C): 1812, July 2; 1813, Aug. 21; 1818, Jan. 31; 1822, Sept. 19.

Sons of Erin, The (C): 1814, Aug. 6.*

Spanish Barber, The (CO): 1821, Oct. 2.

Speed the Plough (C): 1812, July 23; 1813, June 24; 1815, Aug. 1; 1817, Sept. 16; 1818, March 3; 1821, Sept. 10; 1824, Sept. 3.

Spoiled Child, The (F): 1810, July 21; 1814, July 12; 1816, July 16; 1817, July 15; 1821, Aug. 8; 1822, Aug. 3.

Spy, The (H): 1823, July 4,* 15.

Stranger, The (C): 1812, June 21; 1813, July 8; 1814, June 18; 1818, Aug. 11.

Sultan, The (F): 1812, July 23; 1813, Aug. 14; 1814, July 16.

Surrender of Calais, The (H): 1812, July 21; 1818, July 18.

Sylvester Daggerwood (F): 1810, June 30; 1812, July 21; 1821, Oct. 4; 1823, July 12.

Tale of Mystery, A (M): 1812, July 2; 1818, July 14.

Tancred and Sigismunda (T): 1810, Aug. 27.*

Tekeli (M): 1810, June 25,* July 14; 1812, July 30; 1818, March 14.

Tennessee Hunter, The (H): 1815, Aug. 3,* 5.

Thérèse (M): 1822, July 25,* Aug. 22; 1823, July 31; 1824, Sept. 27.

Three and the Deuce (MD): 1812, June 22;* 1815, July 15; Aug. 8; 1818, Jan. 30; 1823, Aug. 28; 1824, Sept. 11.

Three Weeks after Marriage (C): 1812, June 24; 1813, Aug. 3; 1816, July 27.

Timour the Tartar (M): 1813, Aug. 3,* 7, 31; 1814, June 21; 1818, March 12, 13, 14.

'Tis All a Farce (F): 1814, June 30;* 1818, Feb. 9, March 5.

Tom and Jerry (Bur.): 1823, Aug. 7,* 21, 23, 26.

Tom Thumb the Great (Bur.): 1818, Aug. 22.

Too Late for Dinner (C): 1821, Aug. 23.*

Too Many Cooks (MF): 1810, July 4.

Toothache, The (F): 1814, Aug. 9;* 1815, Aug. 5; 1818, July 14.

Town and Country (C): 1813, June 29; 1814, Aug. 13; 1817, Sept. 13; 1818, Feb. 17; 1821, Aug. 25; 1822, Aug. 8; 1823, July 22.

Transformation (F): 1815, Aug. 17.*

Turn Out (CO): 1815, July 20,* 25, Aug. 3; 1816, July 20; 1817, Aug. 11; 1818, Jan. 29, Feb. 16, Aug. 1; 1822, Aug. 15; 1824, Oct. 4.

Turnpike Gate, The (CO): 1815, June 27;* 1816, Aug. 3; 1818, Feb. 2, 26.

Two Pages of Frederick the Great, The (C): 1823, Sept. 2,* 9.

Two Strings to Your Bow (F): 1813, Sept. 4;* 1818, Aug. 20.

Valentine and Orson (M): 1812, Aug. 7; 1813, July 3; 1814, June 25; 1815, Aug. 15; 1817, Sept. 13.

Vampire, The (M): 1821, Sept. 1.*

Venice Preserved (T): 1818, March 5; 1821, Aug. 10; 1823, July 10.

[681]

INDEX TO PLAYERS

Some of the following names, like some of the titles in the Index to Plays, have variant spellings. Barbere, for instance, is sometimes Barbiere; Feron, Fearon; Green, Greene; and Wheatley, Wheatly. In using this index, it should be borne in mind that the Abercrombies include the father and the two daughters, Charlotte and Sophia; the Barretts, mother and son; the Chapmans, the brothers Samuel and William; the Forrests, the brothers Edwin and William; the Hathwells, the father and the three daughters, Matilda, Henrietta and Louisa; the Holmans, father and daughter; the Jeffersons, the elder Jeffersons, the daughters Euphemia and Elizabeth and the sons, Thomas, John and Joseph; the Keans, Edmund and his son Charles; and the Kembles, the father, Charles, and his famous daughter Fanny. As for the Durangs, it would be advisable, if detailed information about the family is desired, to consult *Durang*, in which there are excellent biographies of many players of the period.

ALEXANDRIA

BALTIMORE

PHILADELPHIA

24, 26, 28, 31, Feb. 1, 2, 3, 5, 7, 8, 9, 10, 11, 12, June 1, 2, 3, 4, 6, 7, 8, 9, 10, 11, 13, 14, 15, 16, Oct. 18, 20, 22, 25, 27; 1833, Feb. 6, 7, 8, 9, 11, 12, 13, 15.

Fisher, Alexina: 1833, July 9.

Fisher, Clara: 1828, Feb. 20, 23, 25, 27, 29, March 3, 4, 5, 6, 7, 8, June 6, 9, 11, 13, 16; 1831, Sept. 19, 21, 22, 23, 26, 28.

Flynn: 1830, Dec. 23.

Flynn, Mrs.: 1830, Dec. 3, 23.

Forrest, Edwin: 1820, Nov. 27, Dec. 2, 29; 1821, Jan. 6; 1828, Jan. 5, 7, 8, 9, April 30, May 2, 5; 1830, Dec. 8, 10, 15, 20.

Forrest, William: 1822, Feb. 2.

Francis: 1811, Feb. 23; 1812, Feb. 26; 1813, March 17, 26; 1814, March 21; 1815, March 25; 1816, March 27; 1817, April 3; 1818, April 13; 1819, March 29; 1821, April 6.

Francis, Mrs.: 1811, March 4; 1812, Feb. 26; 1814, April 1; 1817, April 23; 1818, April 13; 1819, March 29; 1821, April 6.

Gale: 1833, Nov. 18.

Gallot: 1831, May 21.

Gamble: 1831, March 12.

George, Miss: 1828, Jan. 10, 12, 14, 16, 18, 21, 23, 25 (ill), 28.

Gilfert, Mrs.: 1831, Feb. 28, March 1, 2, 3, 7, April 1, 2, 11, 14.

Gilman, Mr. (?): 1831, July 23.

Giraud, Mons.: 1818, Feb. 18, 21.

Green: 1831, April 15, July 13.

Green, Mrs.: 1812, Oct. 5; 1813, March 20; 1814, March 25; 1815, March 29.

Hackett: 1828, Jan. 2; 1830, Dec. 6, 22, 24, 27, 29, 31; 1831, March 24, 26, 28, 29, June 9, Oct. 29, Nov. 1, 2, 3, 4; 1834, March 29, 31, April 1, 2, 3, 4, 5.

Hackett, Mrs.: 1830, Dec. 22, 24, 29.

Hadaway: 1833, May 8, July 10; 1834, June 30.

Hamblin: 1831, Dec. 7, 10, 13, 15, 17; 1833, March 7, 9, 11, 13, 18, 23, 25, 30, April 1, 4, 6, 8, 11.

Hamilton, Miss: 1831, July 28.

Hardinge: 1811, March 2; 1812, Feb. 29; 1813, April 2; 1814, April 9; 1815, April 5.

Harris, Mrs.: 1816, April 11; 1817, April 19; 1818, April 18; 1819, April 9.

Hatton (singer): 1834, May 10.

Hawthorn, Miss: 1828, April 22.

Herbert: 1818, Nov. 10; 1820, March 10; 1821, April 2.

Hess (rope dancer): 1831, July 14, 16.

Heyl: 1828, Jan. 25, April 15.

Hill: 1833, Feb. 22, 25, 27, March 1, April 18, Sept. 28, Oct. 8, 10, 17; 1834, April 22, 24, 26, 28, 30.

Holland: 1828, Oct. 11.

Holman: 1812, Nov. 16, 18, 20, 21, 23, 25, 27, 28, 30, Dec. 2, 4, 5, 7, 9, 11, 12.

Holman, Miss: 1812, Nov. 16, 18, 20, 21, 23, 25, 27, 28, 30, Dec. 2, 4, 5, 7, 9, 11, 12.

Horn: 1827, Nov. 14, 15, Dec. 3, 5; 1828, May 7, 12, 16, 19, 21, Nov. 12; 1832, Nov. 5, 7, 8, 9, 10, 12, 13, 15.

Howard: 1834, Jan. 4.

Hughes: 1831, Dec. 26, 28, 30; 1832, Nov. 5, 7, 8, 9, 10, 12, 13, 15; 1833, April 15, 29, May 1, 20, 25.

Hughes: 1818, Nov. 6; 1819, April 5, Dec. (ill) 13, 15, 17, 18; 1820, March 13.

Hunt: 1834, Sept. 4.

Hutin, Mme.: 1831, Feb. 17, 19, 21, 22, 23.

Incledon: 1817, Dec. 8, 10, 12, 13, 15, 17, 19, 20.

Ingersoll: 1833, July 9, 15, 17, 19, 20, 24, 25, 27, Nov. 18, 28, 30, Dec. 3, 5, 11; 1834, April 8, 10, 12, 14, 16, 17, 19.

INDEX TO PLAYERS

McCahen: 1828, Jan. 29, April 12.

McDougall: 1831, June 29.

McFarland: 1816, April 6; 1817, April 14; 1818, April 17.

McKenzie: 1811, Feb. 25.

McKenzie, Mrs.: 1810, Nov. 30.

Mercer: 1828, April 21; 1831, Oct. 1.

Mercer, Master: 1828, April 21.

Monier, Miss.: 1834, June 9, 11, 13, 16.

Mossie, Mons.: 1833, Sept. 28, Oct. 1, 3.

Moreland, Mrs.: 1831, April 21, May 12.

Murdoch: 1831, June 22; 1833, June 6; 1834, Jan. 18, May 2; 1835, Jan. 21.

Murstack (?): 1831, July 23.

Norton (musician): 1827, Nov. 20; 1831, Oct. 8, 10, 11.

Page, Mrs.: 1831, May 5.

Palmer: 1831, May 17, July 1.

Payne: 1811, Dec. 9, 23.

Pearman: 1828, May 7, 12, 16, 21, 23.

Pearson: 1831, July 11.

Pelby: 1821, Nov. 26, Dec. 10, 12.

Pelham, Miss: 1834, Aug. 25, 27.

Philipps: 1818, Jan. 5, 7, 9, 10, 12, 14, 16, 17, Feb. 4, 7, 9, 11, 13, 14, 16; 1822, Feb. 4, 6, 8, 9 (no performance), 11, 13, 15, 18, 25, 27, March 1, 4, 6, 8, 11, 18, 20, 23, 25, 27, 29, 30, April 1.

Phillips, Miss: 1834, Oct. 13, 15, 17, 20, 21, 23, 24, Dec. 2, 4, 5, 6, 9, 10, 11, 29 (not arrived), 30, 31; 1835, Jan. 1, 2, 3, 5, 6, 8, 9.

Pindar, Mrs.: 1831, Oct. 3, 4, 5, 6, 7.

Plantou: 1828, May 6.

Plumer: 1830, Oct. 19, Nov. 4.

Plumer, Mrs.: 1830, Oct. 19, Nov. 8.

Porter: 1831, June 27; 1834, Feb. 19.

Potter (juggler): 1831, July 14, 16.

Power: 1833, Sept. 14, 16, 17, 18, 19, 20, 21, 23, 24, 25, 26, 27, Nov. 20, 25, 26, 27, 29, Dec. 2, 4, 6, 7, 9, 10, 12, 13, 21; 1834, Jan. 20, 21, 22, 24, 25, 27, 28, 31, Feb. 1, 3, 4, 5, 6, 7, 8, March 26, May 5, 6, 8, 9, 12, 13, 15,

17, 19, 20, 21, 22, 23, 24, June 20, Sept. 22, 23, 24, 25, 26, 27.

Pratt (producer): 1833, Jan. 1, June 8; 1834, July 16, Dec. 13.

Pullen (treasurer): 1811, April 22; 1812, March 9; 1813, April 24; 1814, April 16; 1815, April 16; 1816, April 16; 1817, April 24; 1818, April 25; 1819, April 10, 21; 1820, March 27.

Rasimi: 1833, July 25.

Ravel Family: 1832, Sept. 13, 15, 18, 20, 21, 22, 24, 25, 27, Oct. 2, 4, 6, 9, 11, 13; 1833, Jan. 7, 9, 10, 12, 15, 17, 19, 22, 24; 1834, June 17, 19, 21, 24.

Reinagle, T. (scene painter): 1820, March 20.

Reynoldson: 1833, April 15, 29, May 1, 20, 21, 22, 27, 29, 31.

Rice: 1831, July 1; 1832, Sept. 29; 1833, Feb. 20, 22, 23, 25, 27, May 9, 11, 13, June 4, 5, 8, 15, 17, July 15, 16, 17, 18, 19, 20, Sept. 4, 11; 1834, April 25, 26, 28, June 12, 14, 18.

Riddle, Miss: 1833, June 6.

Riddle, Mrs.: 1813, Feb. 26.

Riley: 1831, July 11.

Roberts: 1828, March 29; 1830, Dec. 2; 1831, March 9, July 7, 8, 9, 14; 1833, Jan. 2, March 4.

Robertson: 1817, April 9; 1818, April 15.

Robins (scene painter): 1811, March 6; 1813, March 19; 1814, March 23; 1815, March 27; 1816, March 30.

Rock, Miss: 1828, March 10, 12, 14, 15, 17, 19, 21, 24, Nov. 24.

Rosalie, Mme.: 1828, July 7, 9, 10, 11.

Rowbotham: 1828, May 13, 22; 1833, June 17; 1834, July 18.

Rowbotham, Mrs.: 1832, Dec. 31; 1833, July 22; 1834, July 12.

Sciarria, Signor: 1834, June 12, 13, 14, 18, 26.

Scott: 1833, Jan. 1, May 28, 30, June 1, 5, 6, 7; 1834, April 22, 23, 25, 29, May 1, July 3, 5, 7, 9.

INDEX TO PLAYERS

White, Miss: 1811, March 15; 1813, April 5; 1814, April 13; 1815, April 11; 1816, April 15.

Whitlock, Mrs.: 1812, Oct. 19, 21, 23, 26, 28, 29, Nov. 2; 1814, March 26.

Wilkinson: 1833, March 26, April 1, 2, 3, 4, 5, 6, 23, 24, 25, 30, May 1, 2, 3, 4.

Williams: 1820, Nov. 11; 1821, April 4.

Williams, Mrs.: 1816, Feb. 9, 10, 12, 19; 1820, Nov. 13; 1821, April 4.

Wills, Master: 1831, June 24.

Willis, Mrs.: 1830, Dec. 30.

Wilmot, Mrs.: 1811, March 1.

Wilson: 1823, April 21.

Wood, J.: 1833, Oct. 7, 9, 11, 12, 14, 15, 16, 18, 19, 21, 22; 1834, Feb. 10, 11, 13, 14, 17, 18, 20, 21, 24, 25, 27, 28, March 3, 4, 6, 7, 21, 24, 25.

Wood, Mrs. J.: 1833, Oct. 7, 9, 11, 12, 14, 15, 16, 18, 19, 21; 1834, Feb. 10, 11, 13, 14, 17, 18, 20, 21, 24, 25, 27, 28, March 3, 4, 6, 7, 21, 24, 25.

Wood, Wm.: 1811, Feb. 8, Nov. 30; 1813, Jan. 18; 1814, Feb. 5; 1815, March 10; 1816, Jan. 17; 1817, Feb. 24 (postponed), March 5; 1818, March 4; 1819, April 30; 1820, Feb. 11, Dec. 19 (ill); 1822, Jan. 14; 1823, March 31; 1828, April 14, Oct. 1; 1831, Jan. 3, April 4, Oct. 14; 1832, Nov. 29; 1833, April 10, Dec. 28; 1834, July 8, Dec. 31.

Wood, Mrs. Wm.: 1812, Feb. 19; 1813, March 12; 1814, March 16; 1816, March 22; 1820, March 1.

Woodhull: 1817, Dec. 2; 1831, April 7.

Workman, Miss: 1828, April 22.

Young, Mrs.: 1831, Jan. 7, March 31.

WASHINGTON

Abercrombie: 1813, Aug. 14; 1817, Sept. 13; 1818, Aug. 15.

Abercrombie, Sophia: 1813, Aug. 14; 1814, Aug. 6.

Anderson: 1815, Aug. 15.

Anderson, Mrs.: 1817, Sept. 11; 1818, Aug. 6; 1824, Oct. 4.

Baker, Mrs.: 1821, Sept. 29.

Barrett: 1810, July 23 (dismissed); 1812, July 25; 1813, Aug. 24; 1814, Aug. 11; 1816, Aug. 17; 1817, Sept. 9.

Barrett, Mrs.: 1810, July 23 (dismissed); 1812, July 25; 1813, Aug. 24.

Blissett: 1818, Aug. 8.

Booth: 1822, Aug. 1, 3, 6, 8.

Bray: 1812, July 30; 1813, Aug. 26.

Bray, Mrs.: 1812, July 30.

Brown: 1818, Feb. 13, 16, 17.

Burke: 1817, Sept. 2; 1821, Sept. 27.

Burke, Mrs.: 1817, Sept. 2; 1821, Sept. 27.

Caldwell: 1824, Sept. 7, 10, 11, 13.

Cooper: 1823, Aug. 9.

Darley: 1818, Aug. 13; 1821, Oct. 6.

Darley, Mrs.: 1818, Aug. 13; 1821, Oct. 6.

Doyle: 1813, Aug. 28.

Duff: 1812, July 28; 1815, Aug. 8.

Duff, Mrs.: 1812, July 28; 1815, Aug. 8.

Entwisle: 1815, Aug. 12; 1816, Aug. 13.

Entwisle, Mrs.: 1815, Aug. 12; 1816, Aug. 13.

Finn: 1818, Aug. 8.

Francis: 1810, July 28; 1812, Aug. 4; 1813, Aug. 26; 1814, Aug. 9; 1815, Aug. 10; 1816, Aug. 15; 1817, Sept. 25; 1818, Aug. 11.

Francis, Mrs.: 1812, Aug. 4; 1814, Aug. 9; 1815, Aug. 10; 1816, Aug. 15; 1817, Sept. 25; 1818, Aug. 11.